The McGraw-Hill Companies

McGraw-Hill Ryerson
Connect. Learn. Succeed.

SOC
Canadian Edition

VICE-PRESIDENT AND EDITOR-IN-CHIEF: **Joanna Cotton**

PUBLISHER: **Cara Yarzab**

SPONSORING EDITOR: **Marcia Siekowski**

MARKETING MANAGER: **Michele Peach**

SENIOR DEVELOPMENTAL EDITOR: **My Editor Inc.**

PHOTO/PERMISSIONS RESEARCH: **My Editor Inc.**

SUPERVISING EDITOR: **Kara Stahl**

EDITORIAL ASSOCIATE: **Stephanie Hess**

COPY EDITOR: **Erin Moore**

TEAM LEAD, PRODUCTION: **Paula Brown**

COVER AND INTERIOR DESIGN: **Kyle Gell**

COVER IMAGE CREDIT: **© Brand X Pictures/Getty Images**

PAGE LAYOUT: **Valid Design & Layout/Valerie Bateman**

PRINTER: **Worldcolor**

Statistics Canada information is used with the permission of Statistics Canada. Users are forbidden to copy the data and redisseminate them, in an original or modified form, for commercial purposes, without permission from Statistics Canada. Information on the availability of the wide range of data from Statistics Canada can be obtained from Statistics Canada's Regional Offices, its World Wide Web site at www.statcan.gc.ca, and its toll-free access number: 1-800-263-1136.

ISBN-13: 978-0-07-026433-5
ISBN-10: 0-07-026433-3

1 2 3 4 5 6 7 8 9 0 WCD 1 9 8 7 6 5 4 3 2 1 0

Printed and bound in the United States.

Care has been taken to trace ownership of copyright material contained in this text; however, the publisher will welcome any information that enables them to rectify any reference or credit for subsequent editions.

Library and Archives Canada Cataloguing in Publication

Witt, Jon
Soc / Jon Witt, Alana Hermiston. — Canadian ed.

Includes bibliographical references and index.
ISBN 978-0-07-026433-5

1. Sociology—Textbooks. I. Hermiston, Alana J. (Alana Jean), 1970– II. Title.

HM586.W58 2010   301   C2009-906968-7

>> About the Authors

Jon Witt was born and raised in Sheboygan, Wisconsin. He attended college and graduate school in the Chicago area and received his Ph.D. in Sociology from Loyola University Chicago. Jon has been teaching at Central College in Pella, Iowa, since 1993. His first book, *The Big Picture: A Sociology Primer* (McGraw-Hill), provides an accessible and interesting introduction to what it means to look at the world sociologically. The website at www.soc101.com accompanies *SOC* and *The Big Picture,* and is dedicated to providing links to sociological stories, research, ideas, data, and more.

Alana J. Hermiston discovered Sociology in her first year of undergraduate studies at Trent University and graduated from Trent with an Honours B.A. She went on to earn her M.A. from Queen's University, and her Ph.D. from Carleton University. Alana is currently an Assistant Professor back where it all started: in the Sociology department at Trent University, where she teaches a variety of courses.

>> Acknowledgements

Thanks first of all to Jon Witt, the author of *SOC,* First Edition, which was published in the U.S. My sincere thanks to McGraw-Hill Ryerson in Canada for asking me to consider the possibility of working on this Canadian edition and encouraging me to join a terrific development and production team. Their enthusiasm and support are truly appreciated.

I am very grateful to senior developmental editor Katherine Goodes at My Editor Inc., for her guidance, patience, and support. Many thanks to Tammie Hyde, whose excellent research assistance aided enormously in the completion of this project.

Thanks also to copy editor Erin Moore for the careful editing of the final manuscript and her good humour throughout the process.

I am grateful to the students whose survey responses initiated the creative design of *SOC;* we publish this book for them. Finally, I would like to thank the reviewers, whose honest feedback and willingness to share ideas and resources have greatly enhanced this Canadian edition. They are:

Francis Adu-Febiri, *Camosun College*
Salvatore Albanese, *Langara College*

Michael Del Balso, *Dawson College*
Jill Esmonde, *Georgian College*
Renee Justine Ferguson, *Georgian College*
Laurie Forbes, *Lakehead University*
Noga A. Gayle, *Capilano University*
Gail Hunter, *George Brown College*
Lori Lockey, *Durham College*
Kim Luton, *University of Western Ontario*
Fred Neale, *Lethbridge College*
Mary Louise Noce, *Sheridan College*
Siân Reid, *Carleton University*
Sheldon Ungar, *University of Toronto, Scarborough*

SOC Canadian Edition

BRIEF CONTENTS

Ch. 14
GLOBAL WARMING
AFFECTS US ALL

Ch. 10
THE CLASS
DIVIDE

Ch. 12 >
"DOING"
GENDER

< Ch. 6
WHO IS
DEVIANT?

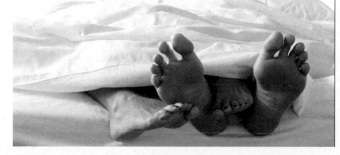

SOC (SŌSH)

What makes

SOC offers instructors **scholarly** engages students. SOC consistently encourages them to **get involved**

What's Inside

Engaging pedagogy designed to be eye-catching and visually appealing can be found throughout the text. SOC shows students how they can apply sociological concepts to their everyday lives.

>

^

Therory: A Matter of Perspective
boxes connect content to the theoretical views of the various schools of sociological thought.

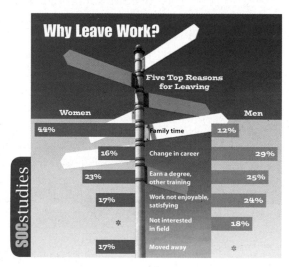

Why Leave Work?

SOCstudies

Five Top Reasons for Leaving

	Women		Men
Family time	44%		12%
Change in career		16%	29%
Earn a degree, other training		23%	25%
Work not enjoyable, satisfying		17%	24%
Not interested in field		*	18%
Moved away		17%	*

^

SOC Studies boxes include up-to-date sociological research brought to life through graphs, tables, and maps.

Canadian examples throughout the text provide a Canadian perspective and bring sociology closer to students' day-to-day experiences.

Hot or Not?
Do private medical clinics represent a threat to Canada's public health care system?

Hot or Not >>
features ask students to consider their opinions on topical issues.

<< Get Involved
sections push students to actively participate in sociological issues that are relevant to their lives.

SOCthink

> > > What norms are you abiding by right now, as you read this book?

^

SOC Think sections include stimulating questions that prompt students to use their sociological imagination and think deeper about the topics being discussed.

SOC special?

content and *unmatched currency* in a succinct magazine format that encourages students to **foster their sociological imagination** and and MAKE A DIFFERENCE in the world around them.

Going **GLOBAL**

Percentage of People Ages 20–24 Ever Married, Selected Countries

<< **Going Global** boxes give insight into sociological facts and figures from around the world.

POPSOC

<< **POP SOC** features illustrate sociological concepts through popular culture.

Did You Know?

. . . Federal government agencies regularly release reports with information on social trends and emergent social policy issues of interest to Canadians. One example is the General Social Survey, which has been conducted annually since 1985, with each year dedicated to a particular topic. Recent surveys have focused upon social engagement, technology use, and social support and aging. For more information about the GSS and other research, check out Statistics Canada at www.statcan.gc.ca.

∧

Did You Know? boxes offer tidbits of sociological insight from the past and present.

For REVIEW

<< **For Review** sections answers questions from the "As You Read" sections at the beginning of each chapter, refreshing students' memories of the important aspects of each chapter's content.

∧

At the Movies lists highlight movies that relate to various sociological concepts.

Thinking Critically >> questions challenge students to think beyond the text.

Thinking CRITICALLY...

Pop Quiz

1. A social position we inherit and about which we can do little to change, such as age, race, or sex, is known as
   a. an ascribed status.
   b. role strain.

6. Canada Post, Def Jam Records, and the college or university in which you are currently enrolled as a student are all examples of
   a. primary groups.
   b. reference groups.

<< POP QUIZZES ensure students understand what they've learned before moving on to the next chapter.

Resources

McGraw-Hill Connect™

www.mcgrawhillconnect.ca

FOR STUDENTS:

Developed in partnership with Youthography, a Canadian youth research company, and hundreds of students from across Canada, McGraw-Hill Connect™ embraces diverse study behaviours and preferences to maximize active learning and engagement.

With McGraw-Hill Connect™, students complete pre- and post-diagnostic assessments that identify knowledge gaps and point them to concepts they need to learn. McGraw-Hill Connect™ provides students the option to work through recommended learning exercises and create their own personalized study plan using multiple sources of content, including a searchable e-book, multiple-choice and true/false quizzes, chapter-by-chapter learning goals, interactivities, personal notes, and more. Using the copy, paste, highlight, and sticky note features, students collect, organize, and customize their study plan content to optimize learning outcomes.

FOR INSTRUCTORS:

McGraw-Hill Connect™ assessment activities don't stop with students! There is material for instructors to leverage as well, including a personalized teaching plan where instructors can choose from a variety of quizzes to use in class, assign as homework, or add to exams. They can edit existing questions and add new ones; track individual student performance—by question, assignment, or in relation to the class overall—with detailed grade reports; integrate grade reports easily with Learning Management Systems such as WebCT and Blackboard; and much more. Instructors can also browse or search teaching resources and text-specific supplements and organize them into customizable categories. All the teaching resources are now located in one convenient place.

McGraw-Hill Connect™—helping instructors and students *Connect, Learn, Succeed!*

Instructor Resources:

- Instructor's Manual. The Instructor's Manual contains a chapter outline, learning objectives, chapter summary, lecture outline, key terms, additional lecture ideas, classroom discussion topics, topics for student research, essay questions, critical thinking questions, sources for student research, video resources, additional readings, and journals.

- Test Bank in Rich Text Format. The Test Bank features multiple-choice, true/false, and essay questions. Each question is accompanied by an answer, a learning objective, and a page reference in the text.

- Computerized Test Bank. This flexible and easy-to-use electronic testing program allows instructors to create tests from book-specific items. It accommodates a wide range of question types, and instructors may add their own questions. Multiple versions of the test can be created and printed.

- Microsoft® PowerPoint® Slides. These presentations offer high quality visuals to bring key concepts to life. Additional examples are included for instructors to use in their lectures.

SUPERIOR SERVICE

Your Integrated Learning Sales Specialist is a McGraw-Hill Ryerson representative who has the experience, product knowledge, training, and support to help you assess and integrate any of the below-noted products, technology, and services into your course for optimum teaching and learning performance. Whether it's using our test bank software, helping your students improve their grades, or putting your entire course online, your iLearning Sales Specialist is there to help you do it. Contact your local iLearning Sales Specialist today to learn how to maximize all of McGraw-Hill Ryerson's resources!

TEACHING & LEARNING CONFERENCE SERIES

The educational environment has changed tremendously in recent years and McGraw-Hill Ryerson continues to be committed to helping you acquire the skills you need to succeed in this new milieu. Our innovative Teaching & Learning Conference Series brings faculty together from across Canada with 3M Teaching Excellence award winners to share teaching and learning best practices in a collaborative and stimulating environment. Pre-conference workshops on general topics, such as teaching large classes and technology integration, are also offered. We will also work with you at your own institution to customize workshops that best suit the needs of the faculty at your institution.

COURSESMART

Coursesmart brings together thousands of textbooks from across hundreds of courses in an eTextbook format providing unique benefits to students and faculty. By purchasing an eTextbook, students can save up to 50 per cent off the cost of a print textbook, reduce their impact on the environment, and gain access to powerful Web tools for learning, including full text search, notes and highlighting, and e-mail tools for sharing notes between classmates. For faculty, CourseSmart

provides instant access to review and compare textbooks and course materials in their discipline area without the time, cost, and environmental impact of mailing print examination copies. For further details, contact our iLearning Sales Specialist or go to www.coursesmart.com.

COURSE MANAGEMENT

Content cartridges are available for the course management systems such as WebCT and Blackboard. These platforms provide instructors with user-friendly, flexible teaching tools. Please contact your iLearning Sales Specialist for details.

CREATE ONLINE

McGraw-Hill's Create Online gives you access to the most abundant resource at your fingertips—literally. With a few mouse clicks, you can create customized learning tools simply and affordably. McGraw-Hill Ryerson has included many of our market-leading textbooks within Create Online for e-book and print customization, as well as many licensed readings and cases. For more information, go to www.mcgrawhillcreate.com.

1

THE SOCIOLO

GICAL
IMAGINATION

In this chapter you will...

- learn what sociology is, its foundations, and its importance today

- understand the different theoretical perspectives

- develop your own "sociological imagination"

THE INDIVIDUAL AND SOCIETY

Jack Campbell is a successful businessman in New York City. As he drives around Manhattan in his Ferrari, sporting one of his many designer suits, he relishes his life as a wealthy bachelor. Even intervening in a grocery store robbery doesn't interrupt his charmed life. As he tells the would-be holdup man, "he has everything."

Unlike Jack, George Bailey never got the chance to live the kind of life he wanted to live. He desperately wanted to escape small-town life, go to college, travel the world, and achieve even more, but obligations and a sense of duty conspired against him. Now, feeling like a failure, he stands on a snowy bridge ready to commit suicide.

Jack Campbell is *The Family Man*; George Bailey is the main character in *It's a Wonderful Life*. These films, released over 50 years apart, share a common theme: both men are granted the opportunity to see how their lives and the lives of others would have been different had they chosen another path, or indeed, had never existed at all. In his alternate suburban existence, complete with a wife, children, a cluttered house, and minivan, Jack discovers that his "charmed" life was in fact an empty one. As for George, escorted by angel Clarence, he learns he has had a major impact on family, friends, and community. As Clarence says: "One [person's] life touches so many others, when he [or she]'s not there, it leaves an awfully big hole."

In their focus on the relationship between the individual and society, these films are fundamentally sociological. On the one hand, we see that our individual actions matter and it is through our actions that "society" is made. On the other hand, we are reminded of the power of community, of family, and of social context. The paths taken or not taken and the options available to us are limited by position and circumstance.

We create society by the choices we make and the things we do. At the same time, we are products of society, shaped by the people around us. For each of us, just as for the fictional characters above, many endings are possible—that is the nature of individual choice—but not all endings are equally probable—that is the nature of social position and the unequal distribution of resources. Throughout its history, sociology has sought to describe and explain this relationship between the individual and society.

As You READ

>>

- What is sociology?
- How do sociologists look at the world?
- How might someone practise sociology?

>> What Is Sociology?

We need each other. We may like to think that we can make it on our own, but our individualism is made possible by our interdependence. We praise the Olympic gold medallist for her impressive skill, dedicated training, and single-minded determination. Yet, if it weren't for her mom driving her to the pool every day, for the building manager waking up at 4:00 A.M. to make sure the pool is open, for the women working overnight to make sure the locker room is clean and safe, and so many others who fade into the background in such moments of glory, she would never have had that chance to stand on the podium.

Sociology as a discipline is committed to investigating and understanding the full scope of our interdependence. **Sociology** is the systematic study of the relationship between the individual and society and of the consequences of difference. It focuses on social relationships, looking at how others influence our behaviour; how major social institutions like the government, religion, and the economy affect us; and how we ourselves affect other individuals, groups, and even organizations. In doing this analysis, sociologists focus less on what one individual does or does not do than on what people do as members of a group or in interaction with one another, and on what that means for individuals and for society as a whole.

Sociology at its heart seeks to understand and explain our interdependence. With whom do we connect? How do we organize those connections? What gets in the way? Who benefits? Whether sitting in a classroom, working in an office or a factory, or exercising in a health club, we rely on others who shape how we think and act. As individuals, we make choices, but we cannot divorce our individual preferences from the influence of parents, teachers, friends, enemies, the media, and more, or from our access to resources such as money, social networks, and knowledge. We influence and are influenced by the world around us. Sociology studies those influences.

THE SOCIOLOGICAL IMAGINATION

Sociology is a way of seeing the world. A leading sociologist, C. Wright Mills, described this perspective as the **sociological imagination**—an awareness of the relationship between an individual and the wider society. This awareness allows us to look at how we as individuals connect with the larger social and historical forces that shape our lives, to comprehend the links between our immediate, personal social settings and the remote, impersonal social world that surrounds and helps to shape us. Mills wrote that "neither the life of an individual nor the history of society can be understood without understanding both" (1959:3). Practising the sociological imagination involves grasping the intersection between biography and history, between self and society.

A key element in the sociological imagination is the ability to view our society as an outsider might, rather than relying only on our individual perspective, which is shaped by our cultural biases. Consider something as simple as sporting events. In arenas all over Canada, thousands of people cheer well-trained hockey players. In Bali, Indonesia, dozens of spectators gather around a ring to cheer on well-trained roosters engaged in cockfights. In both instances, the spectators root for their favourites and might bet on the outcome. Yet what is considered a normal sporting event in one part of the world is considered unusual or even illegal in another part.

In applying the sociological imagination, Mills (1959) suggested that we distinguish between obstacles that individuals face as individuals, which he called **private troubles,** and obstacles that individuals in similar positions face, which he called **public issues**—or what sociologists

---

sociology The systematic study of the relationship between the individual and society and of the consequences of difference.

sociological imagination An awareness of the relationship between an individual and the wider society.

private troubles Obstacles that individuals face as individuals rather than as a consequence of their social position.

public issues Obstacles that individuals in similar positions face; also referred to by sociologists as "social problems."

often call "social problems." Consider unemployment. An individual might lose his or her job because of some inappropriate action or personal incompetence. In such

an instance, it might be enough to explain what happened only on an individual level—we might say that the person got what he or she deserved. In applying the sociological imagination, however, we know that unemployment rates vary based on shifts in the larger economy. At such times, to blame unemployment only on individuals is an insufficient diagnosis of the problem. For example, a rise in gas prices leads to an increase in transportation prices, which leads to a rise in product costs, which leads to a decrease in demand, which leads to fewer production workers, which leads to layoffs and unemployment. Even in the above instance, the individual's inappropriate action or personal incompetence may be tied to social position, which shaped his or her access to resources, knowledge, and training.

The sociological imagination is an empowering tool. It allows us to go beyond a limited understanding of human behaviour, to see the world and its people in a new way and through a broader lens than we might otherwise use. As Mills notes, by recognizing our individual *milieu*—the social settings that influence us—we can gain a greater appreciation of differences in tastes, decisions, opportunities, and actions. It may be as simple as understanding why a roommate prefers country music to hip-hop, or it may open up a whole new way

of understanding other populations in the world. It was Mills' hope that we would use the sociological imagination to understand the impact that society has on our lives. Sociologists understand the relationship of the individual to society to be a reciprocal one; that is, we collectively make up society, and it in turn has an effect upon us. Our shared meanings and concepts become so embedded in society that they are perceived as objective "reality" rather than as emerging out of human interaction. Peter Berger and Thomas Luckmann (1966), in their influential work, refer to this as *the social construction of reality.*

THE HAMBURGER AS MIRACLE

Many people take for granted that it would be easy to provide for their needs if they had to, and they are eager to strike out on their own and prove themselves. As an example of using the sociological imagination, however, suppose you had to do something as seemingly simple as making a hamburger but had to do so without relying on any knowledge, skills, tools, or resources obtained from someone else. Without an interdependent network of people performing myriad small tasks that we take for granted, we would be hard-pressed to provide for ourselves. As we will see, like anything we might produce, a hamburger is a miracle because it is a symbol of our society's shared knowledge and skills.

How hard can it be to make a hamburger from scratch? Considering the ingredients, which seem fairly simple, there are any number of ways to proceed. Let's begin with the burger itself. First, you need to find a cow. How hard can that be? Well, you can't buy one from a farmer, as doing so means relying on resources from others. For the same reason, you can't go out to the country (getting there itself might present something of a challenge) and steal one from a farm (which implies a farmer, which means dependence on another person). So you need to find a wild cow.

Assuming you do find a wild cow, you then have to kill it. Perhaps you might bash it with a large rock or stampede it off a cliff. Next, you need to butcher it, but cow hide is tough. Imagine what it takes to produce a metal knife (finding ore, smelting, forging, tempering, and so on). Perhaps

a sharp rock will do. Assuming you came up with a cutting tool, you now have a chunk of raw cow meat. Given that it's hamburger we're after (though you might want to settle for steak at this point), next you need to grind the meat. You might use a couple of those rocks to pulverize the meat into something of a meat mash, although a meat grinder would work better if it weren't so hard to make one. In any event, at last you have a raw hamburger patty.

Now you need to cook it. How will you do that? Where will you get the fire? Perhaps you could strike two rocks together in hopes of creating a spark, or maybe rub two sticks together. If you were allowed to get help from an outside source, you might check how Tom Hanks' character did it in the film *Cast Away*—but you aren't. Perhaps it would be easiest to wait around for lightning to strike a nearby tree. In any case, after you get fire, you still have to cook the meat. No frying pans are available, so either you make one or perhaps cook it on that handy rock you used to kill the cow. Or you could just put the meat on a stick that you cut down and whittled with the knife you made (or was that a "sharp" stone?) and roast it over the fire.

Assuming you are successful, you now have a cooked hamburger patty. But that's not enough. There are still many other steps that need to be completed. You need a bun, which involves figuring out how to come up with flour, water, salt, shortening, sugar, and yeast. What about condiments such as ketchup, mustard, pickles, and onions? What if at the end of all that you decide to make it a cheeseburger?

Making something that seems so simple, that we take for granted, that we can get for a dollar at a fast-food restaurant like Harvey's or McDonald's, turns out to be quite complicated. The knowledge and skill to acquire all the ingredients in a hamburger is beyond the capacity of most individuals. Yet when we eat a burger, we think nothing of it. When you think about it—when you apply the sociological imagination—the hamburger seems miraculous; not in a supernatural sense, but as a symbol pointing to the astonishing complexity and taken-for-grantedness of our human interdependence, and to the knowledge we share collectively without even realizing it. Of course, this is true not just for hamburgers but for virtually any product we use.

> ## The function of sociology, as of every science, is to reveal that which is hidden.
>
> Pierre Bourdieu

It could be a veggieburger, a book, a desk, a shirt, a car, a house, or a computer. Look around you and try to imagine making, by yourself, all the things that we as humans have produced. The knowledge and skill that these things represent is overwhelming. Thankfully, our interdependence means that we do not have to rely on our own knowledge and skill alone for our survival.

KEY COMPONENTS OF SOCIOLOGY

To better understand what sociology involves, we will look at each of the four key components of the definition in turn.

Systematic Study Sociologists are engaged with the world, gathering empirical data through systematic research. Relying on empirical data means that sociologists draw their conclusions about society based on experiences or observations rather than beliefs or the authority of others. If they want to understand the impact of television on community or the phenomenon of binge drinking on college and university campuses, they must gather data from those involved in these activities and base their conclusions upon that information.

Sociological research historically has been divided between quantitative and qualitative approaches to data collection. Quantitative approaches emphasize counting things and analyzing them mathematically or statistically. The most common way to collect this type of data is through surveys. In contrast, qualitative approaches focus on listening to and observing people and allowing them to interpret what is happening in their own lives. The most common way to collect this type of data is through participant observation, in which the researcher interacts with those she or he studies. In practice, sociologists often draw on both techniques in conducting their research. We will investigate these research techniques, along with others, in more detail in Chapter 2.

The Individual Although sociology is most commonly associated with the study of groups, there is no such thing as a group apart from the individuals who compose it. As

SOCthink

> > > Imagine spending the afternoon people watching at the mall. What differences might you observe in how people present themselves? What factors might shape how they dress and talk, whether they are alone or in a group, and how much they buy? How might C. Wright Mills have explained such differences?

individuals we are constantly choosing what to do next. Most of the time, we follow guidelines for behaviour we have learned from others, but we have the ability to reject those guidelines at any time. A term sociologists sometimes use to describe this capacity is **agency,** meaning the freedom individuals have to choose and to act. In professional sports, for example, we use the term "free agent" to describe a player who has the power to negotiate with whatever team he or she wishes. We, too, have such freedom. We could choose not to go to class, not to go to work, not to get out of bed in the morning, not to obey traffic signals, not to respond when spoken to, not to read the next sentence in this book, and on and on.

"*Actually, Lou, I think it was more than just my being in the right place at the right time. I think it was my being the right race, the right religion, the right sex, the right socioeconomic group, having the right accent, the right clothes, going to the right schools . . .*"

Our self exists in an interactive relationship with its environment, and we act within the context of our relationships. The same is true for that free agent athlete. While he or she can choose any team, in order to get a big payday, he or she is limited to choosing within the confines of the league. Our choices, too, are constrained by our positions. Having access to varieties of resources, we choose among an array of options with knowledge of various possible outcomes. We usually follow "paths of least resistance"—the accepted and expected actions and beliefs—but the choice of whether to continue to follow them is ours each and every second of our lives (Johnson 1997).

Society The study of society is at the core of sociology. While we will spend most of this book describing various aspects of society, we can begin by thinking of it as our social environment. Society consists of persistent patterns of relationships and social networks within which we operate. The social structure it provides is analogous to a building: the structure of a building both encourages and discourages different activities in different rooms (such as kitchens, bedrooms, and bathrooms), and many of the most essential operations of a building (such as heating and air conditioning) are mostly invisible to us. In the same way, the structure of our *institutions*—a term sociologists use to describe some of the key components of social structure, including economy, family, education, government, and religion—shapes what is expected of us. Nested within institutions are the groups, subgroups, and statuses that we occupy. Within the context of society, we construct culture and engage in social interaction. We will address the topics of structure, culture, and interaction in detail in coming chapters.

> **agency** The freedom individuals have to choose and to act.

The Consequences of Difference The final part of the definition of sociology involves the consequences of difference. Sociology does more than just describe our structure, culture, and interaction; it also looks at how economic, social, and cultural resources are distributed and at the consequences of these patterns in terms of the opportunities and obstacles they create for individuals and groups. Since the founding of sociology, sociologists have

been concerned with the impact our social positions have on our opportunities or lack thereof.

Sociologists have noted, for example, that the 2004 Indian Ocean tsunami affected Indonesian men and women differently. When the waves hit, following traditional cultural patterns, mothers and grandmothers were at home with the children; men were outside working, where they were more likely to become aware of the impending disaster. Moreover, most of the men knew how to swim, a survival skill that women in these traditional societies usually do not learn. As a result, many more men than women survived the catastrophe—about 10 men for every 1 woman. In one typical Indonesian village, 97 of 1300 people survived; only 4 were women. The impact of this gender imbalance will be felt for some time, given women's primary role as caregivers for children and the elderly (BBC 2005a).

The analysis of social power deserves particular attention because it shapes how and why we think and act as we do. The simple fact is that those who have access to and control over valued material, social, and cultural resources have different options available to them than do those without such access. One of the main tasks of sociology is to reveal and report the degree of **social inequality**—a condition in which members of society have differing amounts of wealth, prestige, or power. That is why the definition of sociology draws particular attention to the consequences of difference.

In combination, these four aspects of sociology help us to understand the things that influence our beliefs and actions and, in so doing, can help us to make choices that are more free. Failure to appreciate the relationship between the individual and society, for example, leads us to misdiagnose our individual and social problems, and so to develop inadequate cures for those things that ail us. French sociologist Pierre Bourdieu (1998a) put it this way: "Sociology teaches how groups function and how to make use of the laws governing the way they function so as to try to circumvent them" (p. 57). Only by appreciating the degree to which our thoughts and actions are determined by our social position and our lack of freedom are we able to make more realistic choices to change ourselves and our worlds.

social inequality A condition in which members of society have differing amounts of wealth, prestige, or power.

science The body of knowledge obtained by methods based on systematic observation.

natural science The study of the physical features of nature and the ways in which they interact and change.

social science The study of the social features of humans and the ways in which they interact and change.

SOCIOLOGY AND THE SOCIAL SCIENCES

Is sociology a science? The term **science** refers to the body of knowledge obtained by methods based on systematic observation. Just like other scientific disciplines, sociology involves the organized, systematic study of phenomena (in this case, human behaviour) in order to enhance understanding. All scientists, whether studying mushrooms or murderers, attempt to collect precise information through methods of study that are as objective as possible. They rely on the careful recording of observations and the accumulation of data.

Of course, there is a great difference between, say, sociology and physics, or between psychology and astronomy. For this reason, the sciences are commonly divided into natural and social sciences. **Natural science** is the study of the physical features of nature and the ways in which they interact and change. Astronomy, biology, chemistry, geology, and physics are all natural sciences. **Social science** is the study of the social features of humans and the ways in which they interact and change. The social sciences include sociology, anthropology, economics, history, psychology, and political science.

These social science disciplines have a common focus on the social behaviour of people, yet each has a particular

Poverty Rates in Hurricane Katrina Disaster Area

orientation. Anthropologists usually study past cultures and preindustrial societies that continue today, as well as the origins of humans. Economists explore the ways in which people produce and exchange goods and services, along with money and other resources. Historians are concerned with the peoples and events of the past and their significance for us today. Psychologists investigate personality and individual behaviour. Political scientists study international relations, the workings of government, and the exercise of power and authority. Sociologists, as we have already seen, study the influence that society has on people's attitudes and behaviour and the ways in which people interact and shape society.

Let's consider how different social sciences would study the impact of the 2009 Manitoba flood. Historians would compare the damage done by natural disasters in the 20th century to that caused by the flooding in Manitoba, including considering it alongside previous floods in the province. Economists would conduct research on the economic impact of the damage, such as crops destroyed due to submerged farmland. Psychologists would study individual cases to assess the emotional trauma of the event. And political scientists would study the stances taken by different elected officials, along with their implications for the provincial and federal governments' response to the disaster.

What approach would sociologists take? They might look at the flood's impact on different communities and on different social classes. For instance, First Nations communities were significantly affected by the flood. Of the approximately 2000 people forced to flee their homes, nearly 65 percent were from native communities, and more than 100 homes on the Peguis First Nations reserve were destroyed. Such consequences raise questions about which neighbourhoods are best served by government flood-prevention initiatives.

An example of a larger scale is that of Hurricane Katrina, which ravaged the coast of the United States in 2005. Some sociologists have undertaken neighbourhood and community studies to determine how to maintain the integrity of storm-struck neighbourhoods during the rebuilding phase. Researchers have focused in particular on Katrina's impact on marginalized groups; they found that issues of race, class, and disability were key. The disaster area was among the poorest in the United States. In terms of family income, for example, New Orleans ranked 63rd (7th lowest) among the nation's 70 largest cities. With Katrina bearing down on the Gulf Coast, thousands of poor inner-city residents had no automobiles or other available means by which to escape the storm. Added to that difficulty was the high incidence of disability in the area. New Orleans ranked second among the nation's 70 largest cities in the proportion of people over age 65 who are disabled—56 percent. Moving wheelchair-bound residents to safety requires specially equipped vehicles, to say nothing of accessible accommodations in public shelters. Clearly, officials must consider such factors in developing evacuation plans (Bureau of the Census 2005f).

Sociologists would take a similar approach in studying episodes of extreme violence. On September 13, 2006, a lone male went on a shooting spree at Montreal's Dawson College, killing one student and injuring 16 other students and staff. As school shootings are relatively rare occurrences in Canada, observers struggled to describe the events and place them in some social context. For sociologists in particular, this tragedy raised numerous issues and topics for study, including the role of the media and the right to privacy for victims' families, the politics of gun control and individual freedoms, the inadequacy of the mental health system, and the stereotyping and stigmatization of those who suffer from mental illness.

SOCIOLOGY AND COMMON SENSE

At times all of us practise some form of the sociological imagination, weighing the balance between individual and society. So what's the difference between sociology and common sense—the knowledge we get from our experiences and conversations, from what we read, from what we see on television, and so forth? Commonsense knowledge, while sometimes accurate, is not always reliable, because it rests on commonly held beliefs rather than on systematic analysis of facts.

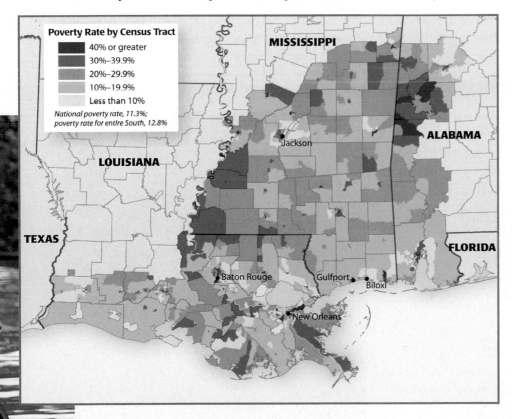

Poverty Rate by Census Tract
- 40% or greater
- 30%–39.9%
- 20%–29.9%
- 10%–19.9%
- Less than 10%

National poverty rate, 11.3%; poverty rate for entire South, 12.8%

MISSISSIPPI

ALABAMA

LOUISIANA

Jackson

TEXAS

FLORIDA

Baton Rouge   Gulfport
         Biloxi

New Orleans

Sociological research shows that the choice of a marriage partner is heavily influenced by societal expectations.

Contrary to the common notion that women tend to be chatty compared to men, for instance, researchers have found little difference between the sexes in terms of their talkativeness. One study, conducted over a five-year period, found that both women and men speak approximately 16,000 words per day (Mehl et al. 2007).

Similarly, "common sense" tells us that military marriages are more likely to end in separation or divorce than in the past due to the strain of long deployments in Afghanistan. Yet in recent examinations of family life among members of the Canadian Forces, most respondents described themselves as happy and satisfied in their relationships (Dowden 2001; Dunn 2004). Interestingly, this is not the first study to disprove the widely held notion that military service strains the marital bond. Two generations earlier, during the Vietnam era, researchers came to the same conclusion (Call and Teachman 1991; Karney and Crown 2007).

theory In sociology a set of statements that seeks to explain problems, actions, or behaviour.

Like other social scientists, sociologists do not accept something as fact just because "everyone knows it." At times, the findings of sociologists may seem like common sense because they deal with familiar facets of everyday life. The difference is that such findings have been tested by researchers, analyzed in relation to other data, and evaluated in light of what is known by sociologists in the form of sociological theory.

>> What Is Sociological Theory?

Sociology, like all sciences, involves a conversation between theory and research. We gather data through systematic research, and we seek to describe and explain what we find using theories. Theories represent our attempts to tell the stories of our lives but they do so in a particular way. Initially, theories might be general and vague. However, over time, as they become more fully informed by research, they are modified and refined into fuller, more accurate accounts of why we think and act as we do. In the following sections, we will use Émile Durkheim's classic research on suicide to demonstrate this process.

FORMULATING SOCIOLOGICAL THEORIES

Why do people commit suicide? Durkheim's answer to this question over a hundred years ago helped to establish sociology as a discipline. Among the traditional "commonsense" answers that Durkheim rejected were the notions that people inherit the desire to kill themselves or that sunspots drive people to take their own lives. He even suspected that psychological or biological explanations that pointed toward depression or chemical imbalance as causal factors were insufficient. He sought to prove that *social forces* existed that influenced an individual's likelihood of committing suicide.

In order to undertake this research, Durkheim developed a theory that offered a general explanation of suicidal behaviour. We can think of theories as attempts to explain events, forces, materials, ideas, or behaviour in a comprehensive manner. In sociology a **theory** is a set of statements that seeks to explain problems, actions, or behaviour. An effective theory may have both explanatory and predictive power. That is, it can help us to see the relationships among seemingly isolated phenomena, as well as to understand how one type of change in an environment leads to other changes.

Durkheim theorized that people commit suicide because they lack the social integration to prevent them from taking this most final and individualistic of all acts. His hypothesis (see Chapter 2 for further explanation of hypotheses) was this: "Suicide varies inversely with the degree of integration of the social groups of which the individual forms a part" ([1897] 1951:209). He chose religious affiliation as an indicator of social integration, arguing that Protestants are less socially integrated than are Roman Catholics. He felt that Catholicism's emphasis on hierarchical authority and promotion of tradition leaves individuals with little freedom to deviate from Church teachings on such topics as contraception, abortion, and gender and marital status of priests. Protestantism, in contrast, puts the Bible into the believers' hands to interpret. The many schisms found among Protestants occurred as a consequence of individuals choosing to interpret matters of faith based on their own understanding of God's word. Whereas there is only one Roman Catholic Church, Protestantism includes Anglican, United, Presbyterian, and many other denominational and nondenominational

churches. These contrasting contexts shaped the degree to which individuals felt integrated into the religious community, leading Durkheim to predict that Protestants would be more likely to commit suicide than Catholics.

TESTING SOCIOLOGICAL THEORIES

In order to test his theory, Durkhiem gathered data from different countries to see whether suicide rates varied. Looking at France, England, and Denmark, he found that whereas England had only 67 reported suicides per million inhabitants, France had 135 per million and Denmark had 277 per million. The question then became: "Why did Denmark have a comparatively high rate of reported suicide?" Durkheim concluded that it was due to the fact that Denmark was a more Protestant nation than either France or England. In other words, it was the social makeup of these nations that shaped their suicide rates. More recent research focusing on individuals rather than national rates continues to find this same relationship.

In extending his analysis to look at other indicators of social integration, Durkheim continued to obtain results that confirmed his underlying theory: for example, in comparing suicide rates and marital status, unmarried people were found to have higher rates of suicide than married people. There also appeared to be higher rates of suicide in times of peace than in times of war or revolution, suggesting that citizens band together during politically unstable times. Durkheim concluded that the suicide rates of a society reflect the extent to which people are or are not integrated into the group life of the society. Durkheim presented his results in his landmark work *Suicide,* published in 1897.

APPLYING SOCIOLOGICAL THEORIES

Built into Durkheim's theory is the presupposition that we find meaning in life through our interconnections with others. The more interconnected and interdependent we feel, the less likely we are to kill ourselves. Attempting to summarize the significance of our attachment to society, Durkheim put it this way: "The individual alone is not a sufficient end for

SOCthink

> > > Following Durkheim's assertion that the level of social integration influences the likelihood of suicide, how would you explain the following variations? Why are there more suicides among men than women? Why is the rate of suicide higher among Aboriginal peoples, especially youths? Why are the suicide rates of immigrants to Canada lower than those of the native-born population? Why is there a midlife suicide peak? What might these patterns suggest about the social integration of people in these categories?

Suicides in Canada

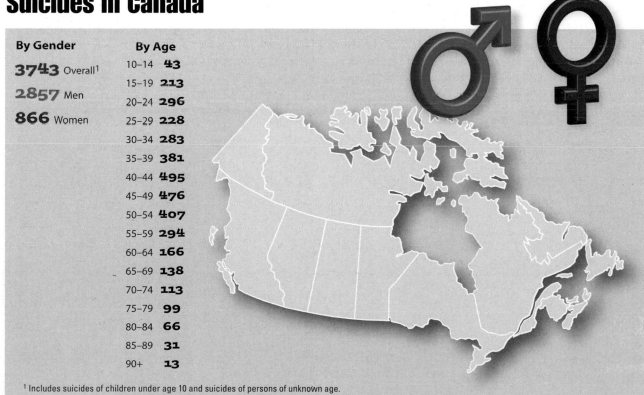

By Gender	By Age	
3743 Overall[1]	10–14	**43**
	15–19	**213**
2857 Men	20–24	**296**
866 Women	25–29	**228**
	30–34	**283**
	35–39	**381**
	40–44	**495**
	45–49	**476**
	50–54	**407**
	55–59	**294**
	60–64	**166**
	65–69	**138**
	70–74	**113**
	75–79	**99**
	80–84	**66**
	85–89	**31**
	90+	**13**

[1] Includes suicides of children under age 10 and suicides of persons of unknown age.

Source: Statistics Canada, CANSIM, table 102-0551 and Catalogue no. 84F0209X. Last modified: 2009-07-06, www.40.statcan.gc.ca/l01/cst01/hlth66-eng.htm.

What Makes a Country Happy?

Looking on the bright side of life, happiness rates also vary from country to country. The nations that score highest on the "Happiness Index" (rating subjective well-being and satisfaction with life) are Denmark and Switzerland, while Zimbabwe and Burundi have the lowest scores. Canada ranks 10th out of over 100 nations, with strong correlations of well-being and health, wealth, and access to education (White 2007). Researcher Stefan Klein (2006) suggests that societies that are characterized by a strong sense of social solidarity, active civic engagement, a commitment to social equality, and sufficient individual autonomy tend to be happier.

his activity. He is too little. . . . When, therefore, we have no other object than ourselves we cannot avoid the thought that our efforts will finally end in nothingness. . . . Under these conditions one would lose the courage to live, that is, to act and struggle" ([1897] 1951:210). Human beings are, at their very foundation, social beings. According to Durkheim, we cannot consider what it means to be an individual apart from our position in society. This social dimension of individual behaviour is what Durkheim wants sociology to explore, elaborate, and explain.

Durkheim's work on suicide provides a classic case of sociological theory at work. He theorized that social forces shape individual actions. He tested this theory by investigating suicide as one such individual choice—perhaps the most individual of all choices—and demonstrated that the likelihood of committing suicide varied based on group membership. Analysis of more recent data shows that suicide rates continue to vary based on social position. Durkheim maintained that if social forces are at work in such an extreme example of individual choice, probably most of our choices are similarly shaped. He argued that if social forces have such power in our lives, there must be a discipline dedicated to their study. As a result, Durkheim established Europe's first department of sociology at the University of Bordeaux in 1895.

>> The Development of Sociology

Given the complexity of human life, not surprisingly, sociologists have developed a wide range of theories in which they describe and explain the diversity of social behaviour. Sometimes their theories can be grand in scope, seeking to encompass the "big picture"; other times they can be more personal, intimate, and immediate. While we will spend most of the rest of this book investigating the insights sociological theories provide, here we will briefly address just five questions sociologists have asked, questions that represent significant doors sociologists have opened as they have elaborated on what is meant by the sociological perspective. The questions are these: How is social order maintained? How do power and inequality shape outcomes? How do we construct our worlds and ourselves through everyday interaction? How does group membership (especially class, race, and gender) shape opportunity? What responsibility do sociologists bear to bring about positive social change? The answers to these questions may differ depending upon which theoretical perspective one employs. These approaches will be explored in greater detail throughout the text, but we introduce some of them in the following discussions.

By investigating who participates in public protests and the issues being raised, sociologists learn which issues unite or divide society. Here, order is maintained during a protest rally in Toronto on the International Day of Protest Against the Canadian Seal Hunt.

SOCIAL ORDER

The discipline of sociology grew up in the midst of significant social upheaval. The advent of the Industrial Revolution and urbanization in the early 19th century led to changes in patterns of government, thought, work, and everyday life. Aristocracy was on the decline while democracy was spreading; people were moving from a primary reliance on religious explanations to more scientific ones; and the world of the village and farm was rapidly giving way to the world of the city and factory. It was in this context that Auguste Comte (1798–1857), in hopes of emulating what natural scientists did for nature, sought to establish a science of society that would reveal the basic "laws of society." Comte believed that knowing these laws would help us to understand what he referred to as "social statics"—the principles by which societies hold together and order is maintained—and social dynamics—the factors that bring about change and that shape the nature and direction of that change. Sociologists would then use their knowledge of these laws to help lead us toward the good society, balancing the needs for social order and positive social change. Comte coined the term *sociology* which literally means "the study of the processes of companionship"—to describe this new science (Abercrombie, Hill, and Turner 2000:333).

Scholars learned of Comte's works largely through translations by the English sociologist Harriet Martineau (1802–1876). Seeking to systematize the research essential to conducting a science of society, Martineau ([1838] 1989) wrote the first book on sociological methods. But she was a pathbreaking theorist in her own right, introducing the significance of inequality and power into the discipline. Martineau's book *Society in America* ([1837] 1962) examined religion, politics, child rearing, and immigration in the young nation. It gave special attention to social class distinctions and to such factors as gender and race. In Martineau's ([1837] 1962) view, intellectuals and scholars should not simply offer observations of social conditions; they should act on their convictions in a manner that will benefit society. She spoke out in favour of the rights of women, the emancipation of slaves, and religious tolerance.

These two themes—analysis of social order and analysis of social inequality—have shaped the theoretical paths sociologists have pursued since this beginning. In early sociological theory, they find their fullest development in the works of Émile Durkheim and Karl Marx, respectively. As we will see throughout this book, they continue to be primary concerns for sociologists.

Émile Durkheim
....

Harriet Martineau ([1838] 1989) argued that we could learn a lot about a culture by analyzing the ideas, images, and themes reflected in their popular songs. She wrote, "The Songs of every nation must always be the most familiar and truly popular part of its poetry. ...They present also the most prevalent feelings on subjects of the highest popular interest. If it were not so, they would not have been popular songs." What might we learn about Canadian culture based on analysis of the lyrics of the current top-10 songs? (Canadian lists are compiled by Nielsen Soundscan at www.soundscan.com.)

Émile Durkheim (1858–1917) emphasized the significance of social order. As we saw in his analysis of suicide, he saw society as a real, external force existing above the level of the individual and exerting its influence on individual behaviour. In modern societies, Durkheim saw the traditional bases of solidarity (those elements that keep people together) being eroded. He observed that individuals had fewer common experiences, ideas, and values, and noted that communities increasingly lacked the moral regulation characteristic of earlier societies. People were thus at greater risk of experiencing what Durkheim called **anomie**—the loss of direction felt in a society when social control of individual behaviour has become ineffective. Anomie increases the likelihood of

> **anomie** The loss of direction felt in a society when social control of individual behaviour has become ineffective.

alienation, loneliness, and isolation (you can read more on solidarity in Chapter 5). Inspired by Comte's vision, Durkheim sought to establish sociology as a science to study these processes, but moreover, he advocated the usefulness of sociology as a means of fixing the problems of modern societies.

POWER AND INEQUALITY

While Karl Marx (1818–1883), like all sociologists, was concerned about social order and integration, his work emphasized the significance of power and control over resources. Marx viewed our creative capacity to transform raw materials into products—for example, to take clay and make a pot, or a tree and make a desk—as the key factor distinguishing humans from other animals (whose behaviour is ruled by their instincts). For Marx, human history is the progressive unfolding of human creativity in the form of new technology through which we establish our relationship to the natural world and with each other. Unfortunately, for most of human history, certain members of society have been denied access to the technology necessary to meet their needs. Those who own and control the means of production—the tools and resources necessary for that transformation to happen—rule the world. Members of the working class, in contrast, own only their capacity to transform raw materials into products, something they cannot do without access to the means of production, which is controlled by the ruling class. While Durkheim was concerned with anomie, Marx was concerned with *alienation*, by which he meant loss of control over our creative human capacity to produce, separation from the products we make, and isolation from our fellow workers. We will consider Marx's work as it relates to capitalism in more detail in a later chapter. His influence on sociological theory,

Karl Marx

macrosociology Sociological investigation that concentrates on large-scale phenomena or entire civilizations.

microsociology Sociological investigation that stresses the study of small groups and the analysis of our everyday experiences and interactions.

however, extends beyond social class to an analysis of group identification and association, such as how class, gender, race, ethnicity, nationality, and age influence individual opportunity.

Seeking to expand sociological theory further, Max Weber (1864–1920; pronounced "VAY-ber") outlined a multidimensional explanation of power. While Weber agreed with Marx that social class (and its associated control over material resources) is a significant determinant of power, it is not the *only* basis for power. Others he identified include social status, in which people defer to others out of respect for their social position or prestige, and organizational resources, in which members of a group gain power through their ability to organize to accomplish some specific goal by maximizing their available resources. Weber argued that these social resources draw their power from people's willingness to obey the authority of another person, which in turn is based on their perception of the legitimacy of that person's right to rule.

INTERACTION

Much of the work of Durkheim, Marx, and Weber involves **macrosociology,** which concentrates on large-scale phenomena or entire civilizations. A later school of sociologists turned away from this approach in favour of **microsociology,** which stresses the study of small groups and the analysis of our everyday experiences and interactions. Microsociology emphasizes the significance of perception, of how we see others and how they see us. Canadian sociologist Erving Goffman (1922–1982) popularized a method known as the *dramaturgical approach* (see Chapter 4), which compares everyday life to the setting of the theatre and

Max Weber

stage and sees people as theatrical performers. Just as actors project certain images to an audience, all of us seek to present particular features of our personalities to others even as we hide certain qualities. Thus, in a class, we may feel the need to project a serious image; at a party, we want to look relaxed and friendly. In this approach, sociologists must analyze our lived experience at the everyday level where our actions create, sustain, and modify our understanding of reality itself.

A BRIEF NOTE ON CANADIAN SOCIOLOGY

Though Canadian by birth, Goffman's notable academic and professional accomplishments took place in the United States, and his work was not particularly Canadian in focus. In contrast, other sociologists, such as Léon Gérin, S.D. Clark, and John Porter have contributed to our understanding of this country and its regional differences.

Léon Gérin (1863–1951) worked primarily outside the formal university setting, conducting empirical studies of changing work and family life in rural Quebec society. His work demonstrated an awareness of the social problems brought about by social change, and concern for how these might be addressed. Gérin's contributions set the stage for further explorations of the transition from rural to urban life, a fundamental aspect of modern society.

In contrast to francophone sociology's historical tendency toward political engagement, early sociological work in English Canada was more politically neutral, focusing instead upon establishing sociology as distinct from other disciplines. The work of Samuel D. Clark (1910–2003) on the social development of Canada is an important example of this approach.

But it is John Porter (1921–1979) who is most often credited with putting Canadian sociology "on the map." *The Vertical Mosaic*, Porter's study of social inequality in Canada, has received international recognition for its analysis of differential opportunities and for its objective to encourage social reform through policy change.

Canadian sociology has a unique history, reflecting both English and French Canada, demonstrating an evident sensibility to issues of diversity and tolerance, and incorporating both academic and activist influences.

GROUPS AND OPPORTUNITY

Over time, sociologists came to more fully understand and appreciate the consequences that group membership, especially class, race, and gender, has for opportunity. African-American sociologist W. E. B. Du Bois (1868–1963; pronounced "dew BOYS") combined an emphasis on the analysis of the everyday lived experience with a commitment to investigating power and inequality based on race. He was critical of those who relied on common sense or on all-too-brief investigations, arguing that a researcher has to be more than just a "car-window sociologist" because true understanding demands more than "the few leisure hours of a holiday trip to unravel the snarl of centuries" (Du Bois [1903] 1994:94). Through engaged and sustained research on the lives of African Americans, he documented their relatively low status in

Philadelphia and Atlanta. Through this research he revealed the social processes that contributed to the maintenance of racial separation, which extended beyond material differences to include social separation, which he referred to as the "color line."

Similarly, feminist scholarship has broadened our understanding of social behaviour by extending the analysis beyond the male point of view that dominates classical sociology. An early example of such work is that of Nellie McClung (1873–1951). Though not a trained sociologist, as an advocate for women's suffrage McClung critiqued the social and political structures that created and perpetuated inequality. A well-published author, McClung brought attention to issues largely ignored by male social critics of the era; an approach that continues to inform feminist work today.

THEORETICAL PERSPECTIVES

The questions asked and the insights offered by sociologists are categorized by dividing them into four approaches: functionalist, conflict, feminist, and interactionist.

Durkheim's work is considered an example of the **functionalist perspective,** which views society as akin to a living organism in which each part of the organism contributes to its survival. The various parts of a society, including institutions such as the family and government, are structured to maintain its stability. Where the functionalist approach focuses more on stability and consensus, the **conflict perspective**

> **functionalist perspective** A sociological approach that emphasizes the way in which the parts of a society are structured to maintain its stability.
>
> **conflict perspective** A sociological approach that assumes that social behaviour is best understood in terms of tension between groups over power or the allocation of resources, including housing, money, access to services, and political representation.

Did You Know?

. . . Stéphane Dion, former leader of the federal Liberal Party, has a Ph.D. in sociology.

feminist perspective Actually comprised of many perspectives, this approach focuses upon the differential treatment of women and men, alongside other forms of inequality.

interactionist perspective A sociological approach that generalizes about everyday forms of social interaction in order to explain society as a whole.

emphasizes the distribution of power and the allocation of resources in society. According to the conflict perspective, social order cannot be fully understood apart from a consideration of how the status quo is established and maintained and who benefits and who suffers from the existing system. Marx's work fits best within the conflict perspective.

Four Perspectives on Sports

Functionalist: Social Order

- Sports socialize young people into such values as competition and patriotism.

- Sports bring together members of a community (supporting local athletes and teams) or even a nation (as seen during World Cup soccer matches and the Olympics) and promote an overall feeling of unity and social solidarity.

Conflict: Inequality & Power

- Sports are a form of big business in which profits are more important than the health and safety of the workers (athletes).

- Sports serve as an "opiate" that encourages people to seek a "fix" or temporary "high" rather than focus on personal problems and social issues.

Feminist: Gendered Differences

- Sports reflect the gendered patterns of the larger society, with women's sports receiving less funding, media attention, and status than men's sports.

- Women and men who participate in "gender inappropriate" sports may experience criticism and stigma due to cultural ideals of masculinity and femininity.

Interactionist: Perception & Interaction

- Despite class, racial, and religious differences, teammates may work together harmoniously and may even abandon previous stereotypes and prejudices.

- Relationships in the sports world are defined by people's social positions as players, coaches, and referees—as well as by the high or low status that individuals hold as a result of their performances and reputations.

Sources: Acosta and Carpenter 2001; H. Edwards 1973; Eitzen 2003; Fine 1987.

SOCthink

> > > In many occupational fields, women earn less than their male counterparts. Why do you think this is the case? How might looking at the issue from the functionalist, conflict, feminist, and interactionist perspectives shape how we frame an answer?

The **feminist "perspective"** is actually comprised of many perspectives, each with its own emphasis and theoretical foundations. The feminist perspective shares the conflict perspective's attention to inequality, but goes beyond its focus on social class to address the role of gender in creating and sustaining inequality. While there is variation among feminist theories, they all begin from the standpoint of women. Whereas functionalist and conflict theorists analyze large-scale, society-wide patterns of behaviour, many feminist theorists consider the smaller day-to-day events that affect us. In this, they have something in common with the **interactionist perspective**, in which theorists such as Goffman (and to some extent, Weber) draw generalizations from everyday forms of social interaction in order to explain society as a whole. The key elements of each perspective are presented to the left, and we will be returning to these perspectives throughout the text. Look for the "A Matter of Perspective" feature in each chapter.

The four-perspectives model has the advantage of providing us with conceptual hooks that allow us to recall some of the key concerns and issues sociologists have raised. A key disadvantage, however, is that it gives the illusion that these four are discrete categories with fundamentally different and incompatible ways of looking at the world. In practice, research rooted in one perspective almost inevitably should draw on or address insights from the others.

PURSUING SOCIAL CHANGE

Throughout sociology's history, a recurring theme common to all perspectives has been the idea that sociological theory and research should contribute to positive social change. In the early 1900s, many leading sociologists in the United States saw themselves as social reformers dedicated to systematically studying and then improving a corrupt society. They were genuinely concerned about the lives of immigrants in the nation's growing cities, whether those immigrants came from Europe or from the rural American South. Early female sociologists, in particular, often took active roles in poor urban areas as leaders of community centres known as settlement houses. For example, Jane Addams (1860–1935), an early member of the American Sociological Society, cofounded the famous Chicago settlement, Hull House. Addams and other pioneering female sociologists commonly combined intellectual inquiry, social service work, and political activism—all with the goal

Jane Addams

of assisting the under-privileged and creating a more egalitarian society. Working with journalist and educator Ida Wells-Barnett, Addams successfully prevented racial segregation in the Chicago public schools, and her efforts to establish a juvenile court system and a women's trade union reflect the practical focus of her work (Addams 1910, 1930; Deegan 1991; Lengermann and Niebrugge-Brantley 1998).

This commitment to positive social change was not unique to Addams and her colleagues. From the very beginning through to the present, sociologists have recognized an obligation to go beyond explaining how the world works and become actively engaged in making the world a better place. In the words of French sociologist Pierre Bourdieu, "I have come to believe that those who have the good fortune to be able to devote their lives to the study of the social world cannot stand aside, neutral and indifferent, from the struggles in which the future of that world is at stake" (1998a:11). For some this has meant releasing the results of their research to the public so that we might make more informed decisions; for others it has meant active engagement in establishing social policy or assisting in the lives of others. For example, Durkheim, who considered an educated citizenry essential to democratic success, used his appointment to the Department of Science of Education and Sociology at the Sorbonne in Paris, along with his political connections and appointments, to shape French educational policy and practice. Du Bois cofounded the National Association for the Advancement of Colored People, better known as the NAACP. In fact, one of the dominant reasons students choose to major in sociology is because they want to make a difference, and sociology provides a pathway to do just that.

>> Practising Sociology

For those who would like to pursue a career in sociology, a variety of paths are available. In recent decades, the number of students who have graduated with a degree in sociology has risen steadily. While few occupations specifically require an undergraduate degree in sociology, sociological skills such as the ability to observe, interpret, and report on both macro- and micropatterns; to analyze and interpret data; and to work to bring about positive change are important assets in a wide range of occupations. Employment options for sociology majors include entry-level positions in business, social services, community organizations, not-for-profit groups, law enforcement, social work, and more. The figure on page 17 summarizes the occupational placement of those with degrees in sociology. One way to investigate a possible future in sociology is through an internship. Studies show that students who choose an internship have less trouble finding jobs, obtain better jobs, and enjoy greater job satisfaction than students without internship placements (American Sociological Association 2006a; Salem and Grabarek 1986).

APPLIED SOCIOLOGY

Applied sociology is the use of the discipline of sociology with the specific intent of yielding practical applications for human behaviour and organizations. Often, the goal of such work is to assist in resolving a social problem. For example, sociologists are often involved in governmental research into major societal concerns facing the country, including Royal Commissions that produce policy recommendations. Sociologists are often asked to apply their expertise to studying such issues as violence, pornography, crime, immigration, and population. In Europe both academic and governmental research departments are offering increasing financial support for applied studies.

One example of applied sociology involves the growing interest in the ways in which nationally recognized

> **applied sociology** The use of the discipline of sociology with the specific intent of yielding practical applications for human behaviour and organizations.

Hot or Not?

Is it your responsibility to get involved to make things better for society?

Did You Know?

...NBA star Steve Nash graduated with a B.A. in sociology from Santa Clara University in 1996. In a 2006 interview, he credited sociology with opening his eyes to people, society, and the world: "The impact of sociology was definitely one of the foundations for me in building a need and a want to get involved and help people."

Theory

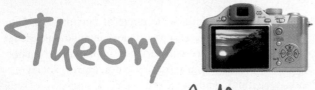

A Matter of Perspective

MAJOR SOCIOLOGICAL PERSPECTIVES

	Functionalist	Conflict	Feminist	Interactionist
View of Society	Stable, well integrated	Characterized by tension and struggle between groups	Characterized by gender and inequality; causes and solutions vary	Active in influencing and affecting everyday social interaction
Levels of Analysis Emphasized	Macro	Macro	Both macro and micro levels of analysis	Micro, as a way of understanding the larger macro phenomena
Key Concepts	Manifest functions Latent functions Dysfunctions	Inequality Capitalism Stratification	Gender as social construct Standpoint of women Political action Gender inequality	Symbols Nonverbal communication Face–to-face interaction
View of the Individual	People are socialized to perform societal functions	People are shaped by power, coercion, and authority	Differs according to social class, race, ethnicity, age, sexual orientation, and physical ability	People manipulate symbols and create their social worlds through interaction
View of the Social Order	Maintained through cooperation and consensus	Maintained through force and coercion	Maintained through standpoints that do not include those of women	Maintained by shared understanding of everyday behaviour
View of Social Change	Predictable, reinforcing	Change takes place all the time and may have positive consequences	Essential in order to bring about equality	Reflected in people's social positions and their communications with others
Example	Public punishments reinforce the social order	Laws reinforce the positions of those in power	Economic inequality needs to be eliminated	People respect laws or disobey them based on their own past experience
Proponents	Émile Durkheim Talcott Parsons Robert Merton	Karl Marx W. E. B. Du Bois Ida Wells-Barnett	Dorothy Smith Margrit Eichler Nellie McClung	George Herbert Mead Charles Horton Cooley Erving Goffman

Source: Schaefer, Smith, Grekul, *Sociology*, Second Canadian Edition, McGraw-Hill Ryerson, 2009.

social problems manifest themselves locally. Since 2003, sociologist Greg Scott and his colleagues have been seeking to better understand the connection between illicit drug use and the spread of HIV/AIDS. In 2009, the study had to date employed 14 researchers from colleges, universities, and public health agencies, assisted by 15 graduate and 16 undergraduate students. By combining a variety of methods, including interviews and observation, with photo and video documentation, these researchers have found that across all drug users, HIV/AIDS transmission is highest among users of crystal methamphetamine. Meth users are also most likely to engage in risky sexual behaviour and

Occupational Fields of Sociology B.A./M.A. Graduates

- Education **12%**
- Government and law enforcement **17%**
- Social services **23%**
- Professions **7%**
- Research **4%**
- Business and commerce **37%**

Source: Schaefer, Smith, Grekul, *Sociology*, Second Canadian Edition, McGraw-Hill Ryerson, 2009.

to have partners who do so. Fortunately, of all drug users, meth users are the ones most closely connected to treatment programs, which allows them to receive substance abuse education and treatment from their health care providers. However, their cases, brought to the forefront by Scott and his team, highlight the need for public health officials to identify other individuals who engage in high risk sexual behaviour and to get them into appropriate treatment programs (G. Scott 2005).

Applied sociology has led to such specializations as medical sociology and environmental sociology. The former includes research on how health care professionals and patients deal with disease. For example, medical sociologists have studied the social impact of the AIDS crisis on families, friends, and communities. Environmental sociologists examine the relationship between human societies and the physical environment. One focus of their work is the issue of "environmental justice," raised when researchers and community activists found that hazardous waste dumps are especially likely to be situated in poor and minority neighbourhoods (M. Martin 1996).

Practising sociology can lead to a variety of career paths, and the skills one learns in sociology—critical thinking, analysis, problem solving—are highly sought in many occupations.

For sociology graduates interested in academic careers, the road to a Ph.D. (or doctorate) can be long and difficult. This degree symbolizes competence in original research; each candidate must prepare a book-length study known as a dissertation. Typically, a doctoral student in sociology will engage in four to seven years of intensive work, including the time required to complete the dissertation. Yet even this effort is no guarantee of a job as a sociology professor.

Most people who take an introductory course in sociology will never take another sociology course, so what does sociology have to offer them? Practising sociology is about so much more than a career; it is a way of looking at the world around us and understanding its complexity and interconnections in a new way. It is about understanding others from their perspective and even understanding ourselves through their eyes. It is a way of assessing the accuracy of claims and refining our knowledge about why we think the way we think and act the way we act. Sociology is something you do; it's a way of life.

>> Developing a Sociological Imagination

Learning to apply the sociological imagination may be more important now than ever. Through **globalization**—the worldwide integration of government policies, cultures, social movements, and financial markets through trade and the exchange of ideas—our lives are more connected with and dependent upon diverse groups of people around the world whose beliefs and practices may be quite different from our own. University campuses often provide a microcosm of this trend, drawing together people from around the world with radically different values, political views, customs, and more into a relatively confined social space and providing opportunities for them to interact. If such interactions are to be meaningful, positive, and respectful, we must learn to use the sociological imagination to better understand ourselves and our culture.

> **globalization** The worldwide integration of government policies, cultures, social movements, and financial markets through trade and the exchange of ideas.

Sociologists expect the next quarter century to be perhaps the most exciting and critical period in the history of the discipline. That is because of a growing recognition—both in Canada and around the world—that current social problems must be addressed before their magnitude overwhelms human societies. Sociologists plan to play an increasing role through theory, research, and action.

SOCthink

> > > Consider the obstacles to cross-cultural interaction on college and university campuses. What function might such group homogeneity serve? How might it perpetuate inequality? Why might people be unwilling to interact with others who have different cultural practices?

Investigate! Descriptions of the major sociological theorists in this chapter only begin to scratch the surface of these fascinating and creative people. Learn more at Sociology Professor (www.sociologyprofessor.com), a website where you can find biographical information on a variety of historical figures in the discipline.

get involved!

>> Summary

Developing the sociological imagination is a rewarding experience, enabling us to better understand the social world. From its early foundations, sociology has been concerned with how we might improve the lives of individuals and the communities in which they live. Four key perspectives—functionalist, conflict, feminist, and interactionist—offer insights into the individual–social connection. Sociology is not just an academic subject we study; sociology is something we *do*.

For REVIEW

I. What is sociology?
- Sociology is a way of seeing that joins theory and research to investigate the relationship between the individual and society and the impact unequal distribution of resources has on opportunity.

II. How do sociologists look at the world?
- Sociologists develop theories that provide windows into our lives, allowing us to better understand social order, inequality, and interaction.

III. How might someone practise sociology?
- Sociology can provide a pathway to a career in a related applied or academic context. But more than that, we can practise sociology in our everyday lives by utilizing the sociological imagination to better understand ourselves and others.

Thinking CRITICALLY...

1. How does a sociological explanation differ from other kinds of explanations?
2. What points of overlap do you see among the various theoretical perspectives?
3. In what ways is reality "constructed"?

Pop Quiz

1. Sociology is
   a. the analysis of individual motivations and internal struggles.
   b. concerned with predicting what particular individuals do or do not do.
   c. the systematic study of the relationship between the individual and society and of the consequences of difference.
   d. the integration of government policies, cultures, social movements, and financial markets through trade and the exchange of ideas.

2. Which of the following thinkers introduced the concept of the sociological imagination?
   a. Émile Durkheim
   b. Max Weber
   c. Karl Marx
   d. C. Wright Mills

3. Émile Durkheim's research on suicide found that
   a. Catholics had much higher suicide rates than Protestants.
   b. there seemed to be higher rates of suicide in times of peace than in times of war and revolution.
   c. social position has little to do with suicide rates.
   d. suicide is a solitary act, unrelated to group life.

4. Karl Marx argued that in order to understand social order we must include analysis of
   a. anomie.
   b. ownership of the means of production.
   c. the sociological imagination.
   d. microsociology.

5. According to Erving Goffman's dramaturgical theory
   a. analysis of inequality and power must be front and centre.
   b. social order is a critical problem for sociologists to investigate due to the threats to social order presented by the Industrial Revolution.
   c. early sociological research failed to see the significant impact that group membership (especially gender, race, and social class) played in shaping individual action and opportunity.
   d. we can analyze social interaction as if we were actors in a play.

6. Which sociologist made a major contribution to society through his in-depth studies of urban life, including both Blacks and Whites?
   a. W. E. B. Du Bois
   b. Robert Merton
   c. Auguste Comte
   d. Charles Horton Cooley

7. Though not a trained sociologist, Nellie McClung's efforts to bring attention to the social issues affecting women may be considered early contributions to
   a. the feminist perspective.
   b. the conflict perspective.
   c. dramaturgy.
   d. globalization.

8. Thinking of society as a living organism in which each part of the organism contributes to its survival is a reflection of which theoretical perspective?
   a. the functionalist perspective
   b. the conflict perspective
   c. the feminist perspective
   d. the interactionist perspective

9. Karl Marx's view of the struggle between social classes inspired the contemporary
   a. functionalist perspective.
   b. conflict perspective.
   c. interactionist perspective.
   d. dramaturgical approach.

10. Which of the following statements is an accurate assessment of Canadian sociology?
    a. Research is primarily conducted at the request of the federal and provincial governments.
    b. Canada's reputation for tolerance and fairness has meant that examples of inequality are rare, and thus are not considered worthwhile subjects for study.
    c. It has a unique history, reflecting both English and French Canada, demonstrating an evident sensibility to issues of diversity and tolerance, and incorporating both academic and activist influences.
    d. Canada has not produced any sociological work of significance.

1 (c); 2 (d); 3 (b); 4 (b); 5 (d); 6 (a); 7 (a); 8 (a); 9 (b); 10 (c)

Mc Graw Hill connect™

2

SOCIOLOG

In this chapter you will...

- learn to identify the different steps in the research process

- gain an understanding of the different kinds of research sociologists conduct and the designs used to do so

- assess the ethics of social research

ASKING QUESTIONS AND FINDING ANSWERS

Part of the fun of sociology is asking questions and finding answers, and sociologists Patricia and Peter Adler seem to have had more fun than most. Their search to understand our social lives has led them to spend extended periods of time with college athletes, drug dealers, school kids, Hawaiian resort workers, graduate students, self-injurers, and others. In each such study their underlying sociological commitment has remained the same: to answer the questions "Why do we think the way we think?" and "Why do we act the way we act?"

To better understand the tourism industry, for example, the Adlers spent eight years gathering information at five Hawaiian hotels, studying the staff and operations in minute detail (Adler and Adler 2004). This allowed them to better understand how tourist experiences are scripted (including the ceremonial lei provided upon arrival) and the significance of race, ethnicity, and social class when it comes to access to resources (including the kinds of jobs available to new immigrants such as Filipinos, Samoans, and Vietnamese).

Similarly, in their effort to better understand self-injury—including self-cutting, burning, branding, biting, and bone-breaking—the Adlers conducted lengthy, emotionally intense interviews with self-injurers over a six-year period, becoming friends with many. "Rather than remaining strictly detached from our subjects," they write, "we became involved in their lives, helping them and giving voice to their experiences and beliefs" (2007:542).

In other studies they found that student athletes go to big-time sports schools with the best of intentions to be good students but get worn down by the obligations of being an athlete, and resign themselves to inferior academic performance (Adler and Adler 1985).

As is the case with all good sociological research, such studies seek to tell our stories and help us to understand ourselves in light of our interdependence. Sociologists such as the Adlers systematically gather our stories together through research and make sense of them with theory.

ICAL RESEARCH

As You READ

- What steps do sociologists take when seeking to answer why people think and act the way they do?
- What techniques do sociologists use to collect data?
- What ethical concerns must sociologists consider while conducting research?

>> Steps in the Research Process

scientific method A systematic, organized series of steps that ensures maximum objectivity and consistency in researching a problem.

Sociology at its core represents a conversation between theory and research. Sociologists seek to describe and explain the patterns and practices of our lives through systematic investigation of what we do and why. If we want to

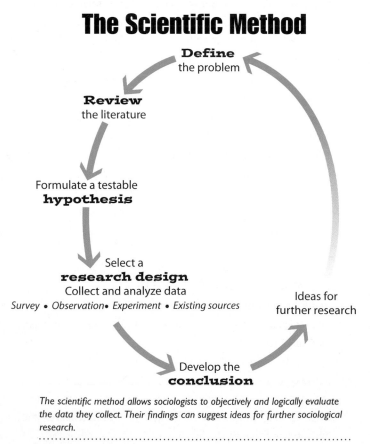

The Scientific Method

Define the problem

Review the literature

Formulate a testable **hypothesis**

Select a **research design**
Collect and analyze data
Survey • Observation• Experiment • Existing sources

Develop the **conclusion**

Ideas for further research

The scientific method allows sociologists to objectively and logically evaluate the data they collect. Their findings can suggest ideas for further sociological research.

know why people think and act the way they do, we need to know more about what they actually think and do. We need to observe them, ask them questions, participate in their lives, or in other ways come to understand their experiences from their perspective. We cannot sit back and guess.

Sociology inherits this commitment in part from early attempts by some sociologists to emulate the scientific method. The **scientific method** is a systematic, organized series of steps that ensures maximum objectivity and consistency in researching a problem. While not all sociologists today would tie the task of sociology as strongly to the natural science model, the commitment to making sense of the world through engagement with the world remains.

Conducting sociological research in the spirit of the scientific method requires adherence to a series of steps designed to ensure the accuracy of the results. Sociologists and other researchers follow five basic steps in the scientific method: (1) defining the problem, (2) reviewing the literature, (3) formulating the hypothesis, (4) selecting the research design and then collecting and analyzing data, and (5) developing the conclusion (see the figure to the left). Although research does not always proceed in such an orderly way (and other methods challenge the sequential approach), to better understand the steps in this process, we will follow an example about the relationship between education and income from start to finish.

DEFINING THE PROBLEM

Does it "pay" to go to college or university? Many people make great sacrifices and work hard to get a post-secondary degree or diploma. Parents borrow money for their children's tuition. Students work part-time or even take full-time jobs while attending evening or weekend classes. Does it pay off? Are there sufficient monetary returns for that effort?

The first step in any research project is to state as clearly as possible what you hope to investigate—that is, to define the problem. Typically, this means explicitly identifying both the concepts we are interested in learning more about and the nature of the relationship we suspect might exist between those concepts. In our example, we are interested in knowing if increased education influences economic position.

In defining the problem, we draw on theories about why people think and act the way they do. These theories might be fairly simple and tentative guesses about the relationships, or they might be more elaborate and fully formed, such as we saw in the works of Karl Marx, Max Weber, and Émile Durkheim. For example, Durkheim developed a prediction regarding suicide based on his theory that social integra-

How do we know things?

Through...
- Personal experience—discovering things for ourselves
- Tradition—how things have "always been" done or understood
- Religion—following the teachings and rules of particular faiths

And through...
- Science—using controlled, systematic research, we come to know and understand in a different way

tion influences individual action, and he set about to test this theory using social research. Through research we seek to assess and refine our theories so that the explanations and descriptions of the world we get through sociology are fuller and more complete, more accurately reflecting both the simplicity and the complexity of human behaviour.

Several competing theories exist concerning the relationship between education and income. One theory states that society needs people to develop their skills in order for society to realize its full potential, so it rewards those who make the sacrifices necessary to develop those skills through education. Another theory states that education does not so much provide opportunity as reinforce the existing system of inequality by providing the illusion of opportunity. In this theory, people more or less end up in the same economic position in which they began their educational journey. Which theory we start with will shape the kind of data we collect. We will look into both of these theories about education in a later chapter, but for the purpose of our example, we will focus on the first.

Often the concepts in our theories are too general or abstract to study in a systematic fashion. In order to investigate those concepts, we need to move from the abstract to the concrete. To do so, social science researchers develop an operational definition of each concept being studied. An **operational definition** transforms an abstract concept into indicators that are observable and measurable, allowing researchers to assess the concept. For example, a sociologist interested in status might use membership in exclusive social clubs as an operational definition of status. Someone studying religiosity might consider the frequency of a person's participation in religious services or the amount of time spent in prayer or meditation as an operational definition of how religious the person is. In our example, we need operational definitions for both education and earnings. Although we could argue that education involves more than just years of schooling completed, it is

conventional to operationalize it that way. Similarly, income is conventionally operationalized as the total income an individual reports having received in the last year.

REVIEWING THE LITERATURE

The next phase of research involves a review of the literature: investigating previous research conducted by sociologists and others regarding the concepts we wish to study. Analyzing how others have studied these concepts allows researchers to refine the problem under study, clarify possible techniques for collecting data, and eliminate or reduce avoidable mistakes. An excellent place to start such research is the many sociological journals that regularly publish articles in which sociologists carefully document their findings. (See the "Finding Information" table on page 24 for more useful tips.)

In our example, we would need to seek out existing research about the relationship between education and income. In that literature we would find significant evidence that the two are linked. We would also learn that other factors besides years of schooling influence earning potential. For example, a person's occupational category (such as plumber, tool-and-die worker, secretary, or professor) might shape her or his income in a way different than just educational level alone. We would also find that background factors such as class, gender, and race affect income. For example, the children of wealthy parents are more likely to pursue a post-secondary education than those from modest backgrounds, so we might consider the possibility that the same parents may later help their children secure better-paying jobs. This might lead us to consider adding additional concepts to our definition of the problem.

> **operational definition**
> Transformation of an abstract concept into indicators that are observable and measurable.

Begin with material you already have, including this text and others.

Search using computerized periodical indexes to find related academic journal articles.

Use the library catalogue.

Examine government documents (including Statistics Canada resources).

Contact people, organizations, and agencies related to your topic.

Use newspapers.

When using the Internet, consider the source; always double-check claims with a reputable source or organization.

Consult with your instructor, teaching assistant, or reference librarian.

---

hypothesis A testable statement about the relationship between two or more variables.
variable A measurable trait or characteristic that is subject to change under different conditions.
independent variable The variable in a causal relationship that causes or influences a change in a second variable.
dependent variable The variable in a causal relationship that is subject to the influence of another variable.

FORMULATING THE HYPOTHESIS

After reviewing earlier studies and drawing on the contributions of sociological theorists, we would next formulate our hypothesis. A **hypothesis** is more than just an educated guess; it is a testable statement about the relationship between two or more factors known as variables.

Income, religion, occupation, and gender can all serve as variables in a study. We can define a **variable** as a measurable trait or characteristic that is subject to change under different conditions.

Where theories are more general statements of explanation, hypotheses are built on a presupposition of cause-and-effect relationships, and researchers who formulate a hypothesis generally must suggest how one variable influences or affects another. The variable hypothesized to cause or influence another is called the **independent variable.** The variable that is affected is known as the **dependent variable** because change in it depends on the influence of the independent variable. In other words, the researcher believes that the independent variable predicts or causes change in the dependent variable. For example, a researcher in sociology might anticipate that the availability of affordable housing (the independent variable; often referred to in equations as x) affects the level of homelessness in a

Did You Know?

. . . Federal government agencies regularly release reports with information on social trends and emergent social policy issues of interest to Canadians. One example is the General Social Survey, which has been conducted annually since 1985, with each year dedicated to a particular topic. Recent surveys have focused upon social engagement, technology use, and social support and aging. For more information about the GSS and other research, check out Statistics Canada at www.statcan.gc.ca.

community (the dependent variable; typically represented in equations as y).

We can put these pieces together to generate a generic hypothesis statement: knowledge of the independent variable (x) allows us to better explain or predict the value or position of the dependent variable (y). We could then place variables we are interested in studying, such as those in the figure to the right, into this statement in order to clearly present the nature of the relationships we expect to find between variables we wish to study.

In our example, our hypothesis suggests that knowing how many years of schooling a person has completed will allow us to better predict how much money he or she will earn. Further, we expect that this relationship will be positive, meaning the higher a person's educational

SOCthink

> > > What independent variables do you think would have the greatest effect on the academic performance of college and university students? To what extent do you think each of the independent variables listed in the "Causal Logic" figure would contribute to this explanation?

attainment, the more money she or he will make. The independent variable we are measuring is the level of education, and income is the dependent variable.

Identifying independent and dependent variables is a critical step in clarifying cause-and-effect relationships. **Causal logic** involves the relationship between a condition or variable and a particular consequence, with one event leading to the other. For instance, as Durkheim hypothesized, being less integrated into society produces a greater likelihood of suicide. Similarly, the time students spend reviewing material for a quiz may bring about a greater likelihood of getting a high score on the quiz. In our example, we are suggesting that increased education results in higher income.

Sometimes a change in one variable coincides with a change in the other but is not necessarily caused by it. Such a relationship between two variables is called a **correlation.** For example, data indicate that people who prefer to watch televised news programs are less knowledgeable than those who read newspapers and newsmagazines. This correlation between people's relative knowledge and their choice of news media seems to make sense because it agrees with the common belief that television "dumbs down" information. But the correlation between the two variables is actually caused by a third variable, people's training in processing large amounts of information. People with poor reading skills are much more likely than others to get their news from television, while those who are more educated or skilled turn more often to the

Causal Logic

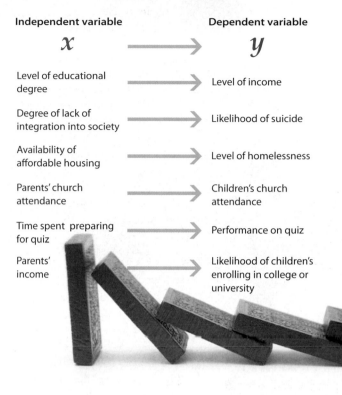

Independent variable x		Dependent variable y
Level of educational degree	→	Level of income
Degree of lack of integration into society	→	Likelihood of suicide
Availability of affordable housing	→	Level of homelessness
Parents' church attendance	→	Children's church attendance
Time spent preparing for quiz	→	Performance on quiz
Parents' income	→	Likelihood of children's enrolling in college or university

In causal logic, an independent variable (usually designated by the symbol x) influences a dependent variable (usually designated by the symbol y).

print media. Thus, although television viewing is correlated with lower news comprehension, it does not *cause* it. Correlation does not equal causation. Not all correlations are spurious; some are valuable in their own right, and may lead us to other research questions. However, sociologists seek to identify the *causal* link between variables; the suspected causal link is generally described in the hypothesis (Neuman 2000:139).

> **causal logic** The relationship between a condition or variable and a particular consequence, with one event leading to the other.
> **correlation** A relationship between two variables in which a change in one coincides with a change in the other.

COLLECTING AND ANALYZING DATA

How do you test a hypothesis in order to support or refute it? You must collect data. There are a variety of ways, known as research designs, that sociologists go about doing this, including surveys, observation, experiments, and use of existing data. Because the design selected is so critical to the research process, we will go into greater depth about each of those research designs later in this chapter. For now we will focus on some key issues that you must address regardless of which research design you select.

Selecting the Sample Sociologists cannot study everybody, so they seek ways to select individuals and groups that are representative of the population that is the subject of the research. In most large-scale studies, social scientists carefully choose what is known as a **sample**—a selection from a larger population that is statistically representative of that population. There are many kinds of samples, but the one social scientists use most frequently is the random sample. In a **random sample**, every member of the entire population being studied has the same chance of being selected. Thus, if researchers want to examine the opinions of people listed in a city directory (a book that, unlike the telephone directory, lists all households), they might use a computer to randomly select names from the directory. The results would constitute a random sample. The advantage of using specialized sampling techniques is that sociologists can be confident that the results they obtain will be representative of the larger population, freeing them from having to question everyone in the population (Igo 2007).

It is all too easy to confuse the careful scientific techniques used in representative sampling with the many nonscientific polls that receive so much more media attention. For example, television viewers are often encouraged to "visit our website and express your views" in an online poll about headline news or political contests. Such polls reflect nothing more than the views of those who happened to see the television program and took the time to register their opinions. These data do not necessarily reflect (and indeed may distort) the views of the broader population. Not everyone has access to a television or radio, time to watch or listen to a program, or the means and/or inclination to vote in this way. Even when these techniques include answers from tens of thousands of people, they will be far less accurate than a carefully selected representative sample of 1500 respondents.

For the purposes of our research example on the relationship between higher education and income levels, we will use information collected in the census of Canada. Conducted every five years (most recently in 2006), the census collects data pertaining to all aspects of Canadians' lives.

Ensuring Validity and Reliability In order to have confidence in their findings, and in keeping with the scientific method, sociologists pursue research results that are both valid and reliable. **Validity** refers to the degree to which a measure or scale truly reflects the phenomenon under study. In our example, a valid measure of income would accurately represent how much money a person earned in a given year. Although income can be a touchy subject, various studies show that people are reasonably accurate in reporting how much money they earned in the most recent year. If a question is written unclearly, however, the resulting data might not be accurate. For example, respondents to an unclear question about income might report partial-year earnings or total household income (perhaps including their parents' or spouse's income as well as their own).

Reliability refers to the extent to which a measure produces consistent results. The General Social Survey, conducted by telephone, has a response rate of approximately 80 percent, with respondents sometimes refusing to answer some or all of the questions. However by law, all questions included in the census must be answered, and thus we may assume the data pertaining to education and income is reasonably accurate.

> **sample** A selection from a larger population that is statistically representative of that population.
> **random sample** A sample for which every member of an entire population has the same chance of being selected.
> **validity** The degree to which a measure or scale truly reflects the phenomenon under study.
> **reliability** The extent to which a measure produces consistent results.

Did You Know?

...A classic case of sampling error occurred when pollsters for *Literary Digest* declared that Alf Landon would defeat President Franklin Roosevelt in 1936. They predicted Landon would win 55 percent of the vote; he received only 37 percent. Although the *Digest* polled 2 million people, they selected names from telephone books and auto registration records. With the country in the midst of the Great Depression, phones and cars were luxuries many people could not afford. As a result, the poll underrepresented poorer people, who were more likely to support Roosevelt.

DEVELOPING THE CONCLUSION

Sociological research, like all scientific studies, does not aim to answer all the questions that can be raised about a particular subject. Therefore, the conclusion of a research study represents both an end and a beginning. It terminates one specific phase of the investigation but should also generate ideas for future study.

Supporting Hypotheses In our example, we find that the data support our hypothesis: People with more formal schooling do earn more money than those with less schooling. Data consistently show that those with a high school diploma earn more than those who failed to complete high school, that those with some post-secondary education earn more than do those with just a high school diploma, that those with a university degree earn still more, and on up the line so that those with graduate degrees earn the most. The figure below demonstrates this relationship. Those with a high school diploma or less have a very small portion of the high-income slice of the pie compared to those who have more education.

The relationship is not perfect, however. There are people who have a high school degree or less who end up with high incomes, and there are those with advanced degrees who earn modest incomes. A successful entrepreneur, for example, might not have much formal schooling, while a holder of a doctorate may choose to work for a low-paying, not-for-profit institution. Sociologically speaking, both these findings—that education shapes income and that the relationship is not perfect—are interesting and would likely

SOCthink

> > > While education plays a significant role in explaining income, some people with minimal education earn high incomes, and some with advanced degrees earn relatively little. What additional social factors do you think might help to explain a person's income? What impact might a person's gender, race, ethnicity, religion, age, or social background have on income?

lead to more questions about how and why such variation occurs.

Sociological studies do not always generate data that support the original hypothesis. In many instances, the results refute the hypothesis, and researchers must reformulate their conclusions. This often leads to additional research in which sociologists reexamine their theory and methods, making appropriate changes in their research design.

> **control variable** A factor that is held constant to test the relative impact of an independent variable.

Controlling for Other Factors Given the complexity of human behaviour, it is seldom sufficient to study only the independent and dependent variables. While such analyses can provide us with insight, we also need to consider other causal factors that might influence the dependent variable. One way to do this is to introduce a **control variable,** which is a factor that the researcher holds constant to test the relative impact of an independent variable.

In our example, as we have already implied, we might want to control for the effect of additional variables that shape income. Not everyone enjoys equal educational opportunities, a disparity linked to income inequality. What impact does a person's race or gender have? Is a woman with a post-secondary degree likely to earn as much as a man with similar schooling? In later chapters, we will consider such additional factors and variables. That is, we will examine the impact that education has on income while controlling for variables such as gender and race.

IN SUMMARY: THE RESEARCH PROCESS

We began with a general question about the relationship between education and income. By following the steps in the research process—defining the problem, reviewing the literature, formulating a hypothesis, collecting and analyzing data, and developing a conclusion—we were

Impact of a Post-Secondary Education on Income

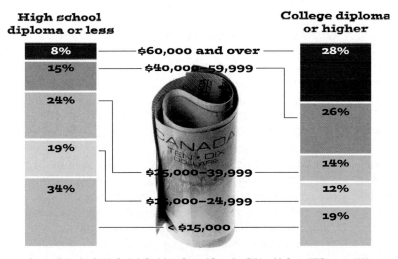

High school diploma or less

8%	$60,000 and over	28%
15%	$40,000–59,999	
24%		26%
19%	$25,000–39,999	14%
34%	$15,000–24,999	12%
	< $15,000	19%

College diploma or higher

Source: Schaefer, Smith, Grekul, *Sociology,* Second Canadian Edition, McGraw-Hill Ryerson, 2009.

Fifty-three percent of people with a high school diploma or less (left) earn under $25,000 a year, while only 23 percent earn $40,000 or more. In contrast, 54 percent of those with a college diploma or higher (right) earn $40,000 or more, while only 31 percent earn less than $25,000.

able to show that education does pay. One of the ways we can check the validity of our findings is to share them with sociologists, policy makers, and others in a public forum in the form of a paper at a professional conference or an article in a refereed academic journal. By exposing what we did, how we did it, and what we found, others can serve as a useful check to make sure we did not miss anything and that we proceeded in an appropriate manner.

Research is cyclical in nature. At the end of the process, researchers almost always find that they have more questions they would like to pursue, and most research papers include a specific section addressing how they might define the problem and carry out the research next time. Along the way, researchers may have discovered new concepts they should consider, better ways to ask questions to get the information they need, individuals or groups they should include in the study, or a whole host of other possibilities. In the end, the studies researchers produce become part of the literature review for the next project, whether theirs or someone else's.

>> Major Research Designs

As we have seen, sociologists go about gathering and making sense of the stories of our lives in a variety of ways. Sometimes sociologists want to tell our larger collective story; other times they want to tell the stories of individuals and groups who are often left out of such large-scale accounts. Different research designs are available to tell these different types of stories. For example, large national surveys allow us to get a sense of the national mood about issues such as politics or religion, and statistics can provide insight into where we stand in relationship to each other on such issues. To explore the stories of individuals, researchers may employ methods such as observation, that emphasize more direct and personal interaction with their subjects.

Sociologists draw on a variety of research designs when considering how to collect their data. A **research design** is a detailed plan or method for obtaining data scientifically.

research design A detailed plan or method for obtaining data scientifically.

survey A study, generally in the form of an interview or questionnaire, that provides researchers with information about how people think and act.

Often a research design is based on the theories and hypotheses with which the researcher begins (Merton 1948). The choice requires creativity and ingenuity because it directly influences both the cost of the project and the time needed to collect the data. As noted previously, research designs that sociologists regularly use to generate data include surveys, observation, experiments, and existing sources.

SURVEYS

Almost all of us have responded to surveys of one kind or another. We may have been asked what kind of detergent we use, which political candidate we intend to vote for, or what our favourite television program is. A **survey** is a study, generally in the form of an interview or questionnaire, that provides researchers with information about how people think and act. Two of Canada's most widely consulted polling firms are Ipsos-Reid and Harris Decima. Allan Gregg is a successful and well-known pollster, particularly with respect to Canadian voter trends. As anyone who watches the news during election campaigns knows, these polls have become a staple of political life.

Issues in Designing Surveys As indicated earlier, a survey must be based on precise, representative sampling if it is to genuinely reflect a broad range of the population. We might be sceptical that feedback from just a few hundred people can provide an accurate picture of how 30 million people think, but correctly run surveys can do just that. When it comes to voter polling, for example, we can compare the results of such polls against actual election results. We can also get a sense of the accuracy of polls by looking at "polls of polls" that combine various results into a single report or graph to see closeness of discrepancies among predictions. Polling is not without controversy. Some critics argue that pre-election polls influence voter behaviour, swaying them towards the leader or the underdog, and thus compromising the objectivity of the process. And sometimes the pollsters fail to get it right—such as the now infamous proclamations that Dewey would defeat Truman in the 1948 United States presidential election—but most often their predictions are accurate to an impressive degree.

In preparing to conduct a survey, sociologists need not only to develop representative samples but also to exercise great care in the wording of questions. An effective survey

Theory

A Matter of Perspective

THEORETICAL–METHODOLOGICAL CONNECTIONS

Methodological Orientation	Emphasis of Research	Corresponding Theoretical Perspective
Scientific	Objective understanding of the social order	Functionalist
Critical	Encouraging social change	Conflict, Feminist
Interpretive	Understanding how people make sense of the world	Interactionist, Feminist

question must be simple and clear enough for people to understand. It must also be specific enough that researchers have no problems interpreting the results. Open-ended questions ("What do you think of the programming on educational television?") must be carefully phrased to solicit the type of information desired. Surveys can be indispensable sources of information, but only if the sampling is done properly and the questions are worded accurately and without bias.

Studies have also shown that the characteristics of the interviewer have an impact on survey data. For example, female interviewers tend to receive more feminist responses from female subjects than do male researchers, and interviewers tend to receive more detailed responses about race-related issues when they are of the same racial or ethnic background as the person being interviewed. The possible impact of gender and race indicates again how much care social research requires (D.W. Davis 1997; Huddy et al. 1997).

Types of Surveys There are two main forms of the survey: the **interview,** in which a researcher obtains information through face-to-face or telephone questioning, and the **questionnaire,** in which a researcher uses a printed or written form to obtain information from a respondent. Each of these has its advantages. An interviewer can obtain a higher response rate because people find it more difficult to turn down a personal request for an interview than to throw away a written questionnaire. In addition, a skillful interviewer can go beyond written questions and probe for a subject's underlying feelings and reasons. For their part, questionnaires have the advantage of being cheaper, especially in large samples. Either way, what we can learn from surveys can be amazing.

Why do people have sex? A seemingly straightforward question, but until recently one that rarely was investigated scientifically, despite its significance to public health, marital counselling, and criminology. In an exploratory study published in 2007, researchers surveyed nearly 2000 undergraduates at the University of Texas at Austin. They began phase one of the research by asking approximately

> **interview** A face-to-face or telephone questioning of a respondent to obtain desired information.
> **questionnaire** A printed or written form used to obtain information from a respondent.

Hot or Not?

Should results of pre-election polls be kept from the public? Do you think they influence how people vote?

Chicago Daily Tribune

DEWEY DEFEATS TRUMAN

G.O.P. Sweep Indicated in State; Boyle Leads in City

400 students in a variety of psychology courses to answer this question: "Please list all the reasons you can think of why you, or someone you have known, has engaged in sexual intercourse in the past." The explanations were highly diverse, ranging from "I was drunk" to "I wanted to feel closer to God."

In phase two of the research, the team asked another sample of 1500 students to rate the importance of each of the 287 reasons given by the first group. Nearly every one of the reasons was rated most important by at least some respondents. Although there were some gender differences in the replies, there was significant consensus between men and women on the top 12 reasons (see the table below). Based on their overall results, the researchers identified four major categories of reasons why people have sex: Physical (pleasure, stress reduction), Goal Attainment (social status, revenge), Emotional (love, commitment), and Insecurity (self-esteem boost, duty/pressure) (Meston and Buss 2007). After reviewing the study results, critics argued that the researchers' sample was not sufficiently representative to permit generalizing their findings to the population as a whole. The researchers acknowledged as much from the beginning, having undertaken the project as exploratory research. They have since conducted research using a more representative sample, and their findings were largely the same (Melby 2007).

quantitative research Research that collects and reports data primarily in numerical form.

mean A number calculated by adding a series of values and then dividing by the number of values.

median The midpoint, or number that divides a series of values into two groups of equal numbers of values.

mode The single most common value in a series of scores.

qualitative research Research that relies on what is seen in field or naturalistic settings more than on statistical data.

observation A research technique in which an investigator collects information through direct participation and/or by closely watching a group or community.

Top 12 Reasons Why Men and Women Have Sex

Men	Reason	Women
1	I was attracted to the person	1
2	It feels good	3
3	I wanted to experience the physical pleasure	2
4	It's fun	8
5	I wanted to show my affection to the person	4
6	I was sexually aroused and wanted the release	6
7	I was "horny"	7
8	I wanted to express my love for the person	5
9	I wanted to achieve an orgasm	14
10	I wanted to please my partner	11
17	I realized I was in love	9
13	I was "in the heat of the moment"	10

Source: Meston and Buss 2007:506.

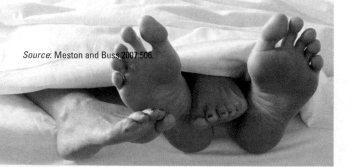

Quantitative and Qualitative Research Surveys most often represent an example of **quantitative research,** which collects and reports data primarily in numerical form. Analysis of these data depends upon statistics, from the simple to the complex, which provide basic summaries describing what variables look like and how they are related. Basic descriptive statistics, such as percentages, are likely familiar. The **mean,** or average, is a number calculated by adding a series of values and then dividing by the number of values. The **median** is the midpoint in a series of values. The median is most often used when there are extreme scores (called "outliers") that would distort the mean. The **mode** is the single most common value in a series of scores and is seldom used in sociological research. The mean, median, and mode all seek to provide a single score that is representative of or provides a summary for the whole distribution of scores. Though today researchers often rely on computer programs to deal with more complex analysis of quantitative data, they still must have the knowledge to interpret that data. Technology can facilitate research, but humans are still fundamental to the process.

While quantitative research can make use of large samples, it can't offer great depth and detail on a topic. That is why researchers also make use of **qualitative research,** which relies on what they see in field and naturalistic settings, often focusing on small groups and communities rather than on large groups or whole nations. Max Weber was an early proponent of going beyond observation to understanding *why* people do what they do. His concept of *verstehen* (German for "understanding") encourages us to put ourselves in the shoes of those we study and try to see things as they do. Unlike the impersonal numerical presentation of data, qualitative research enables sociologists to present greater contextual details of their work. In feminist methodology, the qualitative method is particularly valued for its potential to facilitate connections between researchers and those they are investigating, and to allow the voices of those subjects to be heard. We will return to this idea later in this chapter. The most common form of qualitative research is observation.

OBSERVATION

Investigators who collect information by participating directly and/or by closely watching a group or community are engaged in **observation.** This method allows

> **Research is formalized curiosity. It is poking and prying with a purpose.**
>
> Zora Neale Hurston

sociologists to examine certain behaviours and communities that they could not investigate through other research techniques. Though observation may seem a relatively informal method compared to surveys, researchers are careful to take detailed notes while observing their subjects.

An increasingly popular form of qualitative research in sociology today is **ethnography**—the study of an entire social setting through extended systematic observation. Typically, the emphasis is on how the subjects themselves view their social life in some setting. In some cases, the sociologist actually joins the group for a period to get an accurate sense of how it operates. This approach is called *participant observation.*

During the late 1930s, in a classic example of participant observation research, William F. Whyte moved into a low-income Italian neighborhood in Boston. For nearly four years, he was a member of the social circle of "corner boys" whom he described in *Street Corner Society.* Whyte revealed his identity to these men and joined in their conversations, bowling, and other leisure-time activities. His goal was to gain greater insight into the community that these men had established. As Whyte (1981:303) listened to Doc, the leader of the group, he "learned the answers to questions I would not even have had the sense to ask if I had been getting my information solely on an interviewing basis." Whyte's work was especially valuable since,

at the time, the academic world had little direct knowledge of the poor and tended to rely for information on the records of social service agencies, hospitals, and courts (P. Adler et al. 1992).

> **ethnography** The study of an entire social setting through extended systematic observation.

The initial challenge that Whyte faced—and that every participant observer encounters—was to gain acceptance into an unfamiliar group. It is no simple matter for an academically trained sociologist to win the trust of a religious group, a youth gang, a traditional maritime community, or a group of homeless people. It requires a great deal of patience and an accepting, nonthreatening type of personality on the part of the observer.

SOCthink

> > > What social group or context (such as a religious group, political organization, campus club, or workplace) might you want to learn more about through in-depth participant observation? How would you go about making contact? How would you gain members' trust?

Observation research poses other complex challenges for investigators. Sociologists must be able to fully understand what they are observing. In a sense, then, researchers must learn to see the world as the group sees it in order to fully comprehend the events taking place around them.

This raises a delicate issue. If the research is to be successful, the observer cannot allow the close associations or even friendships that inevitably develop to influence the subjects' behaviour or the conclusions of the study. Anson Shupe and David Bromley (1980), two sociologists who have used participant observation, have likened this challenge to that of walking a tightrope. Even while working hard to gain acceptance from the group being studied, the participant observer *must* maintain some degree of detachment.

Recently, the issue of detachment became a controversial one for social scientists embedded with the U.S. military in Afghanistan and Iraq. Among other studies, the researchers participated in the creation of the Army's Human Terrain System, a US$4-million effort to identify the customs, kinship structures, and internal social conflicts in the two countries. The intention was to provide military leaders with information that would help them make better decisions. Although the idea of scholars cooperating in any way with soldiers struck many social science researchers as inappropriate, others countered that the information they developed would help the military to avoid needless violence and might even facilitate the withdrawal of troops from the region (Glenn 2007).

experiment An artificially created situation that allows a researcher to manipulate variables.

experimental group The subjects in an experiment who are exposed to an independent variable introduced by a researcher.

control group The subjects in an experiment who are not introduced to the independent variable by the researcher.

EXPERIMENTS

When scientists want to study a possible cause-and-effect relationship, they conduct an **experiment**—an artificially created situation that allows a researcher to manipulate variables. Researchers carefully control the experimental context in order to measure the degree to which the independent variable causes change in the dependent variable.

The classic experimental design selects two groups of people and

SOCthink

> > > Imagine you are a researcher interested in the effect TV watching has on schoolchildren's grades. How might you go about setting up an experiment to measure this effect?

matches them on similar characteristics, such as age or education. The researchers then assign the subjects to one of two groups: the experimental or the control group. The **experimental group** is exposed to an independent variable; the **control group** is not. Thus, if medical researchers were testing a new type of antibiotic, they would administer the drug to an experimental group but not to a control group. As sociology focuses upon humans in their social context, experimentation is generally not as feasible as the other research designs.

One of the disadvantages of experiments, just as in observation research, is that the presence of a social scientist or other observer may affect the behaviour of the people being studied. The recognition of this phenomenon grew out of an experiment conducted during the 1920s and 1930s at the Hawthorne plant of the Western Electric Company. A group of researchers set out to determine how to improve the productivity of workers at the plant. The investigators manipulated such variables as lighting and working hours to see what impact the changes would have on productivity. To their surprise, they found that every step they took seemed to increase productivity. Even measures that seemed likely to have the opposite effect, such as reducing the amount of lighting in the plant, led to higher productivity.

Why did the plant's employees work harder even under less favourable conditions? The researchers concluded that the workers modified their behaviour because they knew they were being studied. They responded positively to the novelty of being subjects in an experiment and to the fact that researchers were interested in them. Since that

These workers at the Hawthorne plant modified their behaviour in response to being observed; this phenomenon has since been termed the Hawthorne effect.

Major Research Designs

Method	Examples	Advantages	Limitations
Survey	Questionnaires Interviews	Yields information about specific issues	Can be expensive and time-consuming
Observation	Ethnography	Yields detailed information about specific groups or organizations	Involves months if not years of labour-intensive data collection
Experiment	Deliberate manipulation of people's social behaviour	Yields direct measures of people's behaviour	Has ethical limitations on the degree to which subjects' behaviour can be manipulated
Existing sources/ Secondary analysis	Analysis of census or health data Analysis of films or TV commercials	Cost-efficiency	Limited to data collected for some other purpose

Source: Schaefer, Smith, Grekul, *Sociology*, Second Canadian Edition, McGraw-Hill Ryerson, 2009.

time, sociologists have used the term **Hawthorne effect** to describe the unintended influence that observers of experiments can have on their subjects (S. Jones 1992; Lang 1992; Pelton 1994). It highlights the difficulties experiments present in seeking to understand how people behave in their real-world environments.

Sociologists do sometimes try to approximate experimental conditions in the field. Sociologist Devah Pager (2003) devised an experiment to assess the impact of a criminal background on individuals' employment opportunities. She sent four polite, well-dressed young men out to look for an entry-level job in Milwaukee, Wisconsin. All four were 23-year-old college students, but they presented themselves as high school graduates with similar job histories. Two of the men were Black and two were White. One Black applicant and one White applicant claimed to have served 18 months in jail for a felony conviction—possession of cocaine with intent to distribute.

The experiences of the four men with 350 potential employers were vastly different. The White applicant with a purported prison record received only half as many callbacks as the other White applicant—17 percent compared to 34 percent (see the graphic to the right). But as dramatic as the effect of his criminal record was, the effect of his race was more significant. Despite his prison record, he received slightly more callbacks than the Black applicant with no criminal record (17 percent compared to 14 percent). Race, it seems, was more of a concern to potential employers than a criminal background.

USE OF EXISTING SOURCES

Sociologists do not necessarily need to collect new data in order to conduct research and test hypotheses. The term **secondary analysis** refers to a variety of research techniques that make use of previously collected and publicly accessible information and data. Often, in conducting secondary analysis, researchers use data in ways that were unintended by the initial collectors of the information. For example, the federal government compiles census data for its own specific uses, but marketing specialists also find the data valuable for determining the demand for everything from bicycle stores to nursing homes.

> **Hawthorne effect** The unintended influence that observers of experiments can have on their subjects.
> **secondary analysis** A variety of research techniques that make use of previously collected and publicly accessible information and data.

White Privilege in Job Seeking

Percent chance of getting a call back

White
No criminal record **34%**
17% Criminal record

Black
14% No criminal record
5% Criminal record

Source: Pager 2003:958.

Top 25 Baby Names in Canada and Quebec

	Girls		Boys	
	Canada	Quebec	Canada	Quebec
1.	Emma	Lea	Ethan/Ethen	Samuel
2.	Emily/Emilie	Jade	Matthew	William
3.	Sarah/Sara	Sarah	Joshua	Alexis
4.	Madison/Madisyn	Noemie	Jacob/Jakob	Gabriel
5.	Hannah/Hanna	Rosalie	Nicholas/Nickolas	Felix
6.	Olivia	Laurence	Aidan/Aiden	Nathan
7.	Hailey/Hayley	Camille	Ryan	Antoine
8.	Maya/Mia	Florence	Alexander	Olivier
9.	Kaitlyn/Katelyn	Megane	Nathan	Thomas
10.	Abigail/Abigayle	Coralie	Benjamin	Xavier
11.	Grace	Megan	Owen	Justin
12.	Jessica	Oceane	Michael/Micheal	Jeremy
13.	Megan/Meghan	Ariane	Noah	Mathis
14.	Julia	Gabrielle	Daniel	Anthony
15.	Sophia/Sofia	Audrey	Liam	Raphael
16.	Lauren/Lauryn	Laurie	Tyler	Alexandre
17.	Isabella	Juliette	William	Zachary
18.	Samantha	Justine	Dylan/Dillon	Jacob
19.	Chloe/Chloë	Emilie	Connor/Conner	Vincent
20.	Rachel/Rachael	Elodie	Andrew	Nicolas
21.	Brianna/Breanna	Marianne	Lucas/Lukas	Emile
22.	Ava	Chloe	Evan	Benjamin
23.	Paige	Emy	Zachary/Zachery	Maxime
24.	Taylor	Charlotte	James	Mathieu
25.	Alyssa	Emma	Samuel	Simon

The 25 most popular girls' and boys' names in Canada and Quebec, ranked by popularity, reveal differences between the province and the rest of the country.

Sociologists can learn a great deal using available information. For example, every year provincial Vital Statistics agencies receive thousands of registrations for newborns. Using these data, we can identify some regional trends in Canada when it comes to naming children. Reviewing the "Top 25 Baby Names in Canada," there is no evident "ethnicity" associated with them, whereas the top names in Quebec suggest a preference for cultural distinctiveness.

Surnames in Canada are more reflective of the growth of our ethnically diverse population. Although Statistics Canada does not release this information, an unofficial (and unscientific) study of surnames in searchable telephone directories suggests considerable variation, with the five most common surnames being Li, Smith, Lam,

SOCthink

> > > "NameVoyager" at www.babynamewizard.com is a very cool application that allows you to type in any name to trace its popularity over time. Go there and enter several names to see how they have changed over time. Considering some of the specific names you tried, what factors might have contributed to their rise and fall? How popular is your first name? How and why has its popularity changed over time?

34 • *SOC*

portray women. The ads he studied typically showed women as subordinate to or dependent on others, or as taking instruction from men. Women engaged in caressing and touching gestures more than men. Even when presented in leadership roles, women were likely to be shown striking seductive poses or gazing out into space.

Today researchers who analyze film content are finding an increase in smoking in motion pictures, despite heightened public health concerns. Research studying television programs demonstrates that sexual content on TV continues to rise (see the figure below).

You can observe a lot by just watching.

Yogi Berra

Martin, and Brown (*infoUSA*; www.cbc.ca). Such name changes reflect an overall shift in the Canadian population from a nation comprised primarily of European descendants to one that is more globally diverse, a trend sociologists expect will continue (Baby Name Wizard 2008; Levitt and Dubner 2005; Lieberson 2000; Word et al. 2007).

Part of the appeal of secondary analysis to sociologists is that it is nonreactive—that is, doing this type of study does not influence what you find. For example, Émile Durkheim's statistical analysis of existing suicide data neither increased nor decreased human self-destruction. Researchers, then, can avoid the Hawthorne effect by using secondary analysis. However, there is one inherent problem: The researcher who relies on data collected by someone else may not find exactly what he or she needs. Social scientists who are studying family violence can use statistics from police and social service agencies on reported cases of spouse abuse and child abuse, but how many cases are not reported? Government bodies have no precise data on all cases of abuse.

Secondary analysis also allows us to study social contexts, both present and past, through careful analysis of cultural, economic, and political documents, including newspapers, periodicals, radio and television recordings, the Internet, scripts, diaries, songs, folklore, and legal papers. In examining these sources, researchers employ a technique known as **content analysis**—the systematic coding and objective recording of data, guided by a given rationale.

Using content analysis, Erving Goffman (1979) conducted a pioneering exploration of how advertisements

Other researchers have found a growing difference in the way men and women use sexually explicit language. For example,

> **content analysis** The systematic coding and objective recording of data, guided by some rationale.

Percentage of Television Shows That Contain Sexual Content

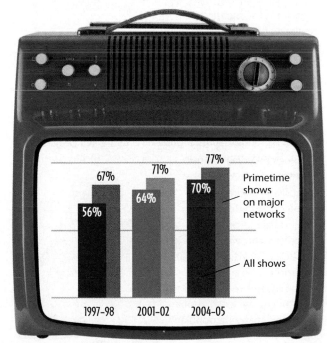

56%	67%	64% 71%	70% 77%
1997–98	2001–02	2004–05	

Primetime shows on major networks

All shows

Source: Kaiser Family Foundation 2005:4.

an analysis of the lyrics of *Billboard* magazine's top 100 hits indicates that, since 1958, male artists have increased their use of such language while female artists have decreased theirs (Dukes et al. 2003). In all such cases, content analysis allows us a better understanding of our cultural practices.

>> Research Ethics

A biochemist cannot inject a drug into a human being unless the drug has been thoroughly tested and the subject agrees to the shot. To do otherwise would be both unethical and illegal. Sociologists, too, must abide by certain specific standards in conducting research, called a **code of ethics.**

code of ethics The standards of acceptable behaviour developed by and for members of a profession.

The professional society of the discipline, the Canadian Sociology and Anthropology Association (recently renamed the Canadian Sociological Association), adopted a code of ethics in 1994, the complete statement of which is available at www.csaa.ca. Among its principles:

- Respect the rights, and be concerned with the welfare of all vulnerable and subordinate populations affected by the research.
- Protect the integrity of the research process.
- Respect citizens' rights to privacy, confidentiality, and anonymity.
- Obtain informed consent.
- Refuse grants, contracts, or research assignments that may require violation of the principles.
- Disclose all sources of financial support and any other sponsorship.

Content analysis of popular song lyrics shows that over the last 50 years, top female artists such as Beyoncé Knowles have used fewer sexually explicit words, while male artists like Jay-Z have used more.

Because most sociological research uses people as sources of information—as respondents to survey questions, subjects of observation, or participants in experiments—these principles are important. In all cases, sociologists need to be certain they are not invading their subjects' privacy. Generally, they do so by assuring subjects of anonymity or by guaranteeing the confidentiality of personal information. In addition, research proposals involving human subjects must gain approval from a review board (for example, colleges and universities have committees for this purpose). Board members seek to ensure that the research does not place subjects at an unreasonable level of risk. If necessary, the board may ask researchers to revise their research designs to conform to the code of ethics.

One example of research that would not be approved today is that conducted by sociologist Laud Humphreys in the mid-1960s. For his Ph.D. dissertation, Humphreys studied "tearooms," public restrooms frequented by men who engage in brief, impersonal sexual acts with other men. Interested in understanding what kinds of men belong to the "tearoom trade," Humphreys secretly followed some of the subjects he observed, recording their licence plates, and obtained their addresses through the help of a friend in the police department. A year later, in disguise, he visited these men at their homes, conducting interviews for an alleged "medical study" but in fact gathering significant information about their personal lives. Although Humphreys' work has been praised for debunking stereotypes of men who engage in this behaviour (most were married men, and seemingly exemplary citizens), the ethical violations committed in obtaining this information generated considerable criticism. (For another example of questionable ethics, see the work of Stanley Milgram in Chapter 6.)

These basic principles and procedures may seem clear-cut in the abstract but can be difficult to adhere to in practice. For example, should a sociologist who is engaged in participant observation research always protect the confidentiality of subjects? What if the subjects are members of a group involved in unethical or illegal activities? What if the sociologist is interviewing political activists and is questioned by government authorities about the research?

Hot or Not?

Should researchers sometimes deceive subjects, even if it might result in their emotional harm, in order to get more genuine responses?

CONFIDENTIALITY

Like journalists, sociologists occasionally find themselves facing the ethical dilemma of whether to reveal their sources to law enforcement authorities. In 1994, Russel Ogden, a graduate student at Simon Fraser University (SFU), conducted interviews with people who had been involved in assisted suicides of people with AIDS. Due to the sensitive nature of his research, Ogden assured his participants of "absolute confidentiality." Upon hearing of Ogden's work, the Vancouver coroner subpoenaed him to testify at an inquest into the death of an "unknown female," but Ogden refused to reveal his sources, arguing that his promise of confidentiality had been authorized by the research ethics board of SFU.

Initially Ogden was found to be in contempt of court, but it was later accepted that communications between Ogden and his participants were privileged. But while Ogden's promise of confidentiality was upheld, he received no support from the university during the ordeal, and his attempt to sue SFU for legal costs was thrown out by the courts. Only after their actions were condemned by the judge did SFU respond with a written apology, compensation for legal costs and lost wages, and a guarantee that in future, the university would provide assistance for researchers who found themselves in a similar conflict. This case serves to demonstrate the challenges of maintaining the integrity and neutrality of social research.

RESEARCH FUNDING

The CSA's statement of professional ethics cautions researchers to the possibility of funding having "strings attached." Disclosure of all sources of funding does not

necessarily guarantee ethical conduct, as evidenced by the Exxon Corporation's support for research on jury verdicts.

On March 24, 1989, the Exxon oil tanker *Valdez* hit a reef off the coast of Alaska, spilling over 41 million litres of oil into Prince William Sound. Two decades later, the *Valdez* disaster is still regarded as the world's worst oil

they interpret their results. Max Weber ([1904] 1949) recognized that personal values would influence the topics that sociologists select for research. In his view, that was perfectly acceptable, but he argued that researchers should not allow their personal feelings to influence the interpretation of data. In Weber's phrase, sociologists must practise **value neutrality** in their research.

> ## If we knew what it was we were doing, it would not be called research, would it?
>
> Albert Einstein

spill in terms of its environmental impact. In 1994, a federal court ordered Exxon to pay US$5.3 billion in damages for the accident. Exxon appealed the verdict and began approaching legal scholars, sociologists, and psychologists who might be willing to study jury deliberations. The corporation's objective was to develop academic support for its lawyers' contention that the punitive judgments in such cases result from faulty deliberations and do not have a deterrent effect.

value neutrality Max Weber's term for objectivity of sociologists in the interpretation of data.

Some scholars have questioned the propriety of accepting funds under these circumstances, even if the source is disclosed. The scholars who accepted Exxon's support deny that it influenced their work or changed their conclusions. To date, Exxon has spent roughly US$1 million on the research, and at least one compilation of studies supporting the corporation's point of view has been published. As ethical considerations require, the academics who conducted the studies disclosed Exxon's role in funding the research. In 2006, drawing on these studies, Exxon's lawyers succeeded in persuading an appeals court to reduce the corporation's legal damages from US$5.3 to US$2.5 billion (Associated Press 2007; Freudenburg 2005). Then, in 2008, the amount was reduced to a mere US$500 million.

VALUE NEUTRALITY

The ethical considerations of sociologists lie not only in the methods they use and the funding they accept but in the way

SOCthink

> > > Is it possible to maintain value neutrality when studying a social group with which you might disagree (such as White supremacists or convicted child molesters)? Why might sociologists choose to study such groups?

As part of this neutrality, investigators have an ethical obligation to accept research findings even when the data run counter to their own personal views, to theoretically based explanations, or to widely accepted beliefs. For example, Émile Durkheim challenged popular conceptions when he reported that social forces were an important factor in suicide.

Some sociologists believe that neutrality is impossible. They worry that Weber's insistence on value-free sociology may lead the public to accept sociological conclusions without exploring researchers' biases. Others have suggested that sociologists may use objectivity as a justification for remaining uncritical of existing institutions and centres of power (Gouldner 1970). Despite the work of conflict and feminist theorists, along with social reformers, sociologists still need to be reminded that the discipline often fails to adequately consider all people's social behaviour.

Sociologists should not focus only on those in the majority but must also seek out the stories of those who are often invisible due to their relative lack of power and resources. In her book *The Death of White Sociology* (1973), Joyce

5 Movies on RESEARCH

Kinsey
The father of modern sexual research employs individual case studies.

Awakenings
Scholars conduct a medical trial and gather data from a man trapped in a schizophrenic coma.

Twister
Storm chasers amass large amounts of data via field research.

Phenomenon
A man with supernatural powers is put under extreme and intensive testing to determine the source.

Medicine Man
A tenacious woman and an eccentric man learn to work together in the Amazon jungle while they search for a cure for cancer.

Ladner called attention to the tendency of mainstream sociologists to investigate the lives of members of visible minority groups solely in the context of social problems. More recently, feminist sociologist Shulamit Reinharz (1992) has argued that sociological research should be not only inclusive but open to drawing on relevant research by nonsociologists who might provide additional depth and understanding of social life. Both Reinharz and Ladner maintain that researchers should always analyze whether women's unequal social status has affected their studies in any way. For example, we might broaden the study of the impact of education on income to consider the implications of the unequal pay status of women and men. The issue of value neutrality does not mean that sociologists can't have opinions, but it does mean that they must work to overcome any biases, however unintentional, that they may bring to their analysis of research.

FEMINIST METHODOLOGY: LEARNING FROM OUR OVERSIGHTS

Although researchers must be objective, their theoretical orientation necessarily influences the questions they ask—or just as important, the questions they fail to ask. Because their contributions have opened up so many new lines of inquiry, sociologists using the feminist perspective have had perhaps the greatest impact on the current generation of social researchers. Until recently, for example, researchers frequently studied work and family separately, as though they were two discrete institutions. Feminist theorists, however, reject the notion that these are separate spheres. They were the first sociologists to look at housework as real work and to investigate the struggles people face in balancing the demands of work and family (Hochschild 1989; Lopata 1971).

Feminist theorists have drawn attention to the tendency for researchers to overlook women in sociological studies. For much of the history of sociology, researchers conducted studies of male subjects and generalized the findings to all people. Feminist methodology seeks to redress the exclusionary character of this work, extending its focus not only to women, but other marginalized groups as well.

Feminist scholars have also contributed to a greater global awareness within sociology. To feminist theorists, the traditional distinction between industrial nations and developing countries overlooks the close relationship between these two supposedly separate worlds. Feminist theorists have called for more research on the special role that immigrant women play in maintaining their households, on the use of domestic workers from less developed nations by households in industrial countries, and on the global trafficking of sex workers (Cheng 2003; Cooper et al. 2007; Sprague 2005).

Finally, feminist researchers tend to involve and consult their subjects more than other researchers, contributing to a significant increase in more qualitative and participatory research. They are also more oriented toward seeking

get involved!

Investigate! Learn more about what sociologists are discovering. Take a look at recent sociology journals, visit the CSA and ASA websites, ask your professors about their research projects, look into internships and community-based learning opportunities.

change, raising the public consciousness, and influencing policy, which represents a return to sociology's roots (Baker 1999; Lofland 1975; Reinharz 1992).

Sociologists must be engaged with the world. While there are numerous ways in which they accomplish this, first and foremost this involvement comes through research. As we have seen throughout this chapter, it is not enough for sociologists to stand back and theorize or even hypothesize about why we think and act the way we do. We must go out, collect data, and use it to inform our interpretations and explanations of human behaviour. Having done so, we bear a responsibility for that knowledge, whether that means simply sharing it with other sociologists through conference presentations and journal articles or actively working for positive social change.

>> Summary

To find the answers to our questions, we conduct research, and we must determine the most appropriate methods of gathering information (such as surveys or observation) as well as our preferred approach (quantitative or qualitative). While our personal interests influence what we choose to study, we must recognize our biases and strive for objectivity. The breadth of sociology means there are many, many possible topics, at both the micro and macro levels. As a result, sociological research is very diverse!

For REVIEW

I. What steps do sociologists take when seeking to answer why people think and act the way they do?
   • They need to define the problem, review existing literature, formulate a hypothesis, collect and analyze data, and develop a conclusion.

II. What techniques do they use to collect data?
   • Research designs used to collect data include surveys, observation, experiments, and use of existing sources.

III. What ethical concerns must they consider while conducting research?
   • They have a responsibility to follow the CSA's Statement of Professional Ethics, particularly respecting confidentiality, revealing research funding, maintaining value neutrality, and overall, treating their subjects with respect.

Thinking CRITICALLY...

1. Should sociologists study groups they personally find offensive? Do you think they can maintain value neutrality?
2. If your research requires asking questions that people might find embarrassing, what research methods would be most useful to ensure you get truthful responses?
3. Based on what you've learned about the types of research conducted and the methods employed by sociologists, what do you think would not be a suitable subject for sociological study?

Pop Quiz

1. The first step in any sociological research project is to
   a. collect data.
   b. define the problem.
   c. review previous research.
   d. formulate a hypothesis.

2. An explanation of an abstract concept that is specific enough to allow a researcher to measure the concept is a(n)
   a. hypothesis.
   b. correlation.
   c. operational definition.
   d. variable.

3. The variable hypothesized to cause or influence another is called the
   a. dependent variable.
   b. hypothetical variable.
   c. correlation variable.
   d. independent variable.

4. A correlation exists when
   a. one variable causes something to occur in another variable.
   b. two or more variables are causally related.
   c. a change in one variable coincides with a change in another variable.
   d. a negative relationship exists between two variables.

5. Through which type of research technique does a sociologist ensure that data are statistically representative of the population being studied?
   a. sampling
   b. experiments
   c. validity
   d. control variables

6. In order to obtain a random sample, a researcher might
   a. administer a questionnaire to every fifth woman who enters a business office.
   b. examine the attitudes of residents of a city by interviewing every 20th name in the city's telephone book.
   c. study the attitudes of registered Conservative voters by having a computer randomly select names from a city's list of registered members of the Conservative Party.
   d. circulate a survey at the college or university where they are employed.

7. A researcher can obtain a higher response rate by using which type of survey?
   a. an interview
   b. a questionnaire
   c. representative samples
   d. observation techniques

8. In the 1930s, William F. Whyte moved into a low-income Italian neighbourhood in Boston. For nearly four years, he was a member of the social circle of "corner boys" whom he describes in *Street Corner Society*. His goal was to gain greater insight into the community established by these men. What type of research technique did Whyte use?
   a. experiment
   b. survey
   c. secondary analysis
   d. participant observation

9. Feminist methodology has made significant contributions to how sociologists conduct research in reminding researchers
   a. that the private and public spheres are equally worthy of study.
   b. that research subjects deserve to be consulted and apprised of the findings.
   c. that sociological research has the potential to influence social policy and bring about social change.
   d. all of the above.

10. Émile Durkheim's statistical analysis of suicide was an example of what kind of research technique?
    a. ethnography
    b. observation research
    c. secondary analysis
    d. experimental research

1 (b); 2 (c); 3 (d); 4 (c); 5 (a); 6 (c); 7 (a); 8 (d); 9 (d); 10 (c)

McGraw-Hill **connect**™

3

CULTURE

WHAT'S TO COME

In this chapter you will...

- gain an understanding of the role of culture in society
- learn how knowledge is constructed and controlled
- learn about cultural variation among societies

BREAKING RULES AND LOWERING BARRIERS

Juan Mann was depressed. His fiancée had left him. His parents had just divorced. He had dropped out of college, and his friends had scattered. He felt all alone in the world. So on Wednesday, June 30, 2004, he decided to do something different. He took a homemade sign to the Pitt Street Mall In Sydney, Australia, that said "Free Hugs." Someone at a party had given him his first hug in a long time, and it had brightened his day. He figured that if he needed a hug like that more than he even knew, there were probably many other people out there feeling similarly isolated who might want one too. Every Thursday he would head back to the mall to offer more. Before long, with the help of a viral video on the Internet, Juan's "Free Hugs Campaign" went global with over 25 million views on You-Tube alone. People were not just watching the video; in many countries and in many languages, they were making their own signs and heading out to a public place to offer hugs. (A YouTube or Google image search on "free hugs" will turn up the original video along with many other videos and images of people from around the world who were inspired by it.)

One of the interesting things about this movement is that it calls for us to go outside our comfort zones and act in ways that are not "normal." As children we are told not to talk to strangers, much less hug them. If we see a stranger offering a hug, we will be suspicious, and question their motives. We have rules about such things—laws, even—and when people do things differently, we get nervous. It disrupts our sense of order. We want and need the actions of others to be predictable, so we create both formal and informal rules to guide our behaviours. Such rules are part of culture.

But culture is not set in stone. We create it, and we therefore have the power to change it. People doing new things, stepping outside the lines of expected behaviour, is precisely how change happens. So, when confronted with the offer "Free Hugs," we face a choice: Act like the majority of people who pass free huggers by, thus reaffirming expected behaviours, or seize the opportunity to do the unexpected, thereby creating new pathways for us to follow. It is in such moments that new culture is born.

>>
- Why do humans create culture?
- What does culture consist of?
- How does culture both enable and constrain?

>> Culture and Society

We need culture. As humans, we lack the complex instincts other species are born with that enable them to survive. Unlike birds, for example, our genes do not provide us with the knowledge of how to build nests (or homes) for ourselves, and we lack the good sense to fly to warmer climates for the winter. In place of such instincts, we construct culture through which we establish relationships both to the natural world and with each other. **Culture** consists of the totality of our shared language, knowledge, material objects, and behaviour.

culture The totality of our shared language, knowledge, material objects, and behaviour.

Culture shapes our perception, knowledge, and understanding of the external world. While our senses experience the external world in a physical way, we must interpret the meaning and significance of those sensations. We do not perceive nature directly; we perceive the world around us through the lens of culture. Our retinas may send visual images to our brains, but recognition comes only through culture. We see this at work with optical illusions: We can look at the same thing over and over, but it is not until someone says to us, "No, look at it this way" that we recognize it. To see this for yourself, ask your friends what they see in the picture to the right.

SOCthink

> > > Something as seemingly simple as reading these words relies on taken-for-granted cultural knowledge. What cultural knowledge does reading this chapter take for granted?

Culture thus provides us with a kind of tool kit of habits, skills, and styles (Swidler 1986). It allows us to take for granted that others will understand what we mean, and it helps make it possible for us to get what we want. Shared culture simplifies day-to-day interactions. For example, if we buy a big-ticket item such as an airline ticket, a plasma television, or a computer, we take for granted that we do not have to bring along hundreds or thousands of dollars in cash; we can pay with a credit card. In a similar vein, we assume that theatres will provide seats for the audience, physicians will not disclose confidential information, and parents will be careful when crossing the street with young children. All these assumptions reflect basic values, beliefs, and customs of our culture.

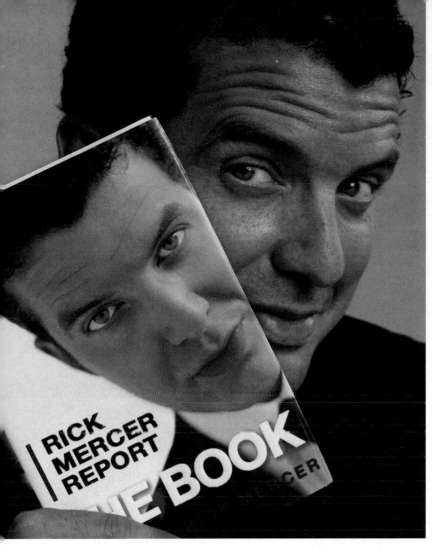

Because our culture represents the core of who we are, including our knowledge, values, beliefs, rules for behaviour, and more, we seek both to preserve it and to pass it along to others. We preserve it through literature, art, video recordings, and other means of expression. We pass it along in families, through mass media, among peers, and, more formally, at school, investing substantial amounts of resources to do so. Were it not for the social transmission of culture, each generation would have to start from scratch, reinventing not just the wheel but all other forms of culture as well.

While it is through culture that we establish a relationship to the external world, society provides the context within which those relationships develop. **Society** consists of the structure of relationships within which culture is created and shared through regularized patterns of social interaction. How

SOCthink

> > > How does social context influence how we relate to others? If you were talking about how school is going, how might you respond differently at home with your parents as compared to in a campus pub with friends or at work with colleagues?

we structure society constrains the kind of culture we construct. Some ways of thinking, acting, and simply "being" are more acceptable, while others may not even be recognized as possible. People often confront this reality when they travel abroad and find their taken-for-granted ideas and actions to be out of place and inappropriate.

Cultural preferences vary across societies. Educational methods, marriage ceremonies, religious doctrines, and other aspects of culture are learned and transmitted through human interaction within specific societies. Most parents in India are accustomed to arranging marriages for their children; in Canada, most parents leave marital decisions up to their children. Lifelong residents of Cairo consider it natural to speak Arabic; lifelong residents of Buenos Aires feel the same way about Spanish.

>> The Development of Culture Around the World

Through our creation of culture, we have come a long way from our prehistoric heritage. The human species has managed to produce such achievements as stories by Alice Munro, paintings by Picasso, music by Scott Joplin, and films such as *Schindler's List*. We now take for granted what once seemed impossible, from air travel, to the cloning of cells, to organ transplants. We can peer into the outermost reaches of the universe or analyze our innermost feelings. In all these ways, our cultural creativity sets us apart as remarkably different from other species of the animal kingdom.

CULTURAL UNIVERSALS

Given that we have a certain amount of freedom to construct culture in a multitude of ways, one of the early sociological questions was whether there are any aspects of culture shared by all people. Some sociologists sought to discover whether there are fundamental laws of society, equivalent to long-known laws of nature. Such patterns were referred to as **cultural universals**—common practices and beliefs shared by all societies. What this search revealed was that components of culture can be called universal only if they are expressed in the most general terms. Many cultural universals are, in fact, adaptations to meet essential human needs, such as the need for food, shelter, and clothing. Anthropologist George Murdock's (1945:124) list of cultural universals included sports, cooking, funeral ceremonies, medicine, marriage, and sexual restrictions.

> **society** The structure of relationships within which culture is created and shared through regularized patterns of social interaction.
>
> **cultural universal** A common practice or belief shared by all societies.

The ways in which different groups address these human needs vary significantly. One group may not allow marriage

The foods people eat, and the customs around eating and preparation of food, reflect their culture as well as their economic circumstances.

between first cousins while another encourages it. Not only does the expression of cultural universals vary from one society to another, but it can change dramatically over time.

Sociobiology is a discipline committed to the systematic study of how biology affects human social behaviour; it looks at cultural universals from a biological perspective. Sociobiologists argue that our thoughts and actions as a species can ultimately be explained through our genes and our biological makeup. While most sociologists would agree that our biology can certainly influence our social behaviour, the degree of variability within and between societies suggests that sociobiological theories are limited as a means to explain complex human behaviour.

Part of the reason sociologists are suspicious of biological explanations for human behaviour is the fact that such claims have been used in the past to justify inequality—claims that were later revealed to be scientifically untrue. For example, it was once thought that women were not capable of success in college or university because their brains were too small and their wombs made them too emotional. Over time we learned that such presuppositions are false—women now comprise over 60 percent of undergraduate students in Canadian universities—but at one time they were accepted as "natural" and therefore resistant to change. One of the lessons we learn about culture throughout human history is that variety and change are the norm.

sociobiology The systematic study of how biology affects human social behaviour.

innovation The process of introducing a new idea or object to a culture through discovery or invention.

discovery The process of making known or sharing the existence of an aspect of reality.

invention The combination of existing cultural items into a form that did not exist before.

INNOVATION

Humans have the ability to create new things. A robin's nest in the year 2010 looks very much like one in 1910 or 910 because robins act on a nest-building instinct. Human abodes, however, vary widely—we can live in a cave, a castle, a sod house, a pueblo, a high-rise apartment, a mansion, or a residence room. Such variation is possible because we are free to innovate. **Innovation**—the process of introducing a new idea or object to a culture—interests sociologists because it can have ripple effects across a society.

SOCthink

> > > How has the invention of the microscope changed our lives (including our lifespan) and therefore our communities? How has the personal computer changed the way we interact?

There are two main forms of innovation: discovery and invention. **Discovery** involves making known or sharing the existence of an aspect of reality. The finding of the DNA molecule and the identification of a new moon of Saturn are both acts of discovery. A significant factor in the process of discovery is the sharing of newfound knowledge with others. By contrast, an **invention** results when existing cultural items are combined into a form that did not exist before. The bow and arrow, the automobile, and the television are all examples of inventions, as are abstract concepts such as Protestantism and democracy.

Going GLOBAL

Communication, Corporations, and Consumerism

Communication, corporations, and consumerism combine to spread particular cultural preferences around the globe. What are the consequences of such diffusion for local cultures around the world?

GLOBALIZATION AND DIFFUSION

Cultural innovation can be highly globalized in today's world. Imagine walking into Starbucks with its familiar green logo and ordering a decaf latte and a cinnamon ring—only this Starbucks happens to be located in the heart of Beijing's Forbidden City, just outside the Palace of Heavenly Purity, former residence of Chinese emperors. The first Starbucks in mainland China opened in 1999, and by 2008 there were more than 300, with 65 stores in Beijing alone. The success of Starbucks in a country in which coffee drinking is still a novelty (most Chinese are tea drinkers) has been striking (*China Daily* 2004).

> **diffusion** The process by which a cultural item spreads from group to group or society to society.

The emergence of Starbucks in China demonstrates the cultural impact of globalization. Starbucks' expansion affects not only coffee consumption patterns but also the international trade in coffee beans, which are harvested mainly in developing countries. Our consumption-oriented culture supports a retail price of two to three dollars for a single cup of premium coffee. At the same time, the price of coffee beans on the world market has fallen so low that millions of farmers around the world can barely eke out a living. Worldwide, the growing demand for coffee, tea, chocolate, fruit, and other natural resources is straining the environment, as poor farmers in developing countries clear more and more forestland to enlarge their fields.

Even as people in Asia have begun to drink coffee, people in North America have discovered the Japanese cuisine known as sushi. More and more cultural expressions and practices are crossing national borders and influencing the traditions and customs of the societies exposed to them. Sociologists use the term **diffusion** to refer to the process by which some aspect of culture spreads from group to group

Canadian military personnel at the Kandahar air base in Afghanistan enjoy a taste of home.

or society to society. Historically, diffusion typically occurred through a variety of means, including exploration, war, military conquest, and missionary work. Today, societal boundaries that were once relatively closed due to the constraints of transportation and communication have become more permeable, with cross-cultural exchange occurring more quickly. Through the mass media, the Internet, immigration, and tourism, we regularly confront the people, beliefs, practices, and artifacts of other cultures.

Diffusion often comes at a cost. In practice, globalization has led to the cultural domination of developing nations by more affluent nations. In these encounters, people in developed nations often pick and choose the cultural practices they find intriguing or exotic, while people in developing nations often lose their traditional values and begin to identify with the culture of the dominant nations. They may discard or neglect their native language and dress, attempting to imitate the icons of mass-market entertainment and fashion. In this way Western popular culture represents a threat to native cultures. As Sembene Ousmane, one of Africa's most prominent writers and filmmakers, noted,

material culture The physical or technological aspects of our daily lives.

nonmaterial culture Ways of using material objects, as well as customs, ideas, expressions, beliefs, knowledge, philosophies, governments, and patterns of communication.

Hot or Not?

Social networking service "Twitter" enables its users to send and receive short text-based updates (known as "tweets"). Do you think such technology improves communication among people?

"[Today] we are more familiar with European fairy tales than with our own traditional stories" (World Development Forum 1990:4). So something is gained and something is lost through diffusion, and often it is the poorer societies that sacrifice more of their culture.

>> Elements of Culture

To better understand how culture operates, it is helpful to distinguish among its different forms. A simple twofold model of culture was proposed by sociologist William F. Ogburn (1922). He drew a line between material and nonmaterial culture. **Material culture** refers to the physical or technological aspects of our daily lives, including food, houses, factories, and raw materials. **Nonmaterial culture** refers to ways of using material objects and to customs, ideas, expressions, beliefs, knowledge, philosophies, governments, and patterns of communication. While this simple division is helpful, the concept of nonmaterial culture is so inclusive that we break it down into four key components: language, values, norms, and sanctions.

Theory

A Matter of Perspective

THEORETICAL PERSPECTIVES ON CULTURE

	Functionalist	Conflict	Feminist	Interactionist
Norms	Reinforce societal standards	Reinforce patterns of dominance	Reinforce gender roles for men and women	Are maintained through face-to-face interaction
Values	Are collective conceptions of what is good	May perpetuate social inequality	May perpetuate men's dominance	Are defined and redefined through social interaction
Culture and Society	Culture reflects a society's strong central values	Culture reflects a society's dominant ideology	Culture reflects society's view of men and women	A society's core culture is perpetuated through daily social interactions
Cultural Variation	Subcultures serve the interests of subgroups; ethnocentrism reinforces group solidarity	Countercultures question the dominant social order; ethnocentrism devalues groups	Cultural relativism respects variations in the way men and women are viewed in different societies	Customs and traditions are transmitted through intergroup contact and through the media

Source: Schaefer, Smith, Grekul, *Sociology*, Second Canadian Edition, McGraw-Hill Ryerson, 2009.

MATERIAL CULTURE AND TECHNOLOGY

It is easy to underestimate the degree to which we live in a humanly constructed world. Even for those of us who live close to nature, material culture is everywhere. It includes the clothes we wear, the books we read, the chairs we sit in, the carpets we walk on, the lights we use, the buildings we live in, the cars we drive, the roads we drive on, and so much more. Even those things that seem natural, like yards or parks, are human constructs.

What is sociologically important about material culture is the role it plays, like all forms of culture, in connecting individuals with one another and to the external environment. Advances in technology, especially when it comes to the revolutions in communication and transportation, have linked more individuals in a global network than was ever possible in the past. Cell phones, for example, enable us to stay in touch with friends and family from almost anywhere, and laptop computers allow us to bring the workplace with us wherever we go.

However, while the objects we create open up new possibilities, they also constrain us. The material objects we construct direct us toward certain ends but have the unintended consequence of limiting our awareness of possible alternatives. The invention of cars, for example, led to changes in the layout of cities, altering the makeup of neighbourhoods, possibilities for face-to-face interaction, and the nature of local community.

Technology is a form of material culture. We tend to think of it only as the physical object itself, but sociologist Gerhard Lenski suggests that it represents a way of knowing. He defined **technology** as "cultural

> **technology** "Cultural information about how to use the material resources of the environment to satisfy human needs and desires."

SOCthink

> > > Canadians send over 63 million text messages per day. How does frequent "texting" and less talking affect the nature of our relationships, both positively and negatively?

Culture, Technology, and Superhero Powers

What makes characters such as Ironman, Batman, and even the villain Syndrome so impressive is that, unlike mutants who are born with superhuman powers, they come by their powers the old-fashioned way: they invent them. In the same way, technology, starting at least with the steam engine, gave us the strength and stamina to exert great physical force over and over again.

information about how to use the material resources of the environment to satisfy human needs and desires" (Nolan and Lenski 2006:37). Technology enhances our human abilities, giving us power, speed, and even flight.

Sometimes technological change outstrips our capacity to interpret and understand the impact of such changes. Because it goes to the core of our perception of reality, nonmaterial culture is often more resistant to change than is the material culture. Ogburn introduced the term **culture lag** to refer to the period of adjustment when the nonmaterial culture is struggling to adapt to new conditions of the material culture. For example, the ethics of the Internet—particularly issues concerning privacy and censorship—have not yet caught up with the explosion in Internet use and technology.

culture lag A period of adjustment when the nonmaterial culture is still struggling to adapt to new material conditions.

language A system of shared symbols; it includes speech, written characters, numerals, symbols, and nonverbal gestures and expressions.

Did You Know

. . . The first Canadian patent was issued in 1869. Since then, more than 2.5 million patents have been registered with CIPO (Canadian Intellectual Property Office). Check out the federal government's "Cool Canada" website for examples of Canadian innovation!

LANGUAGE

Turning to nonmaterial culture, we begin with language, its most basic building block. **Language** is a system of shared symbols; it includes speech, written characters, numerals, symbols, and nonverbal gestures and expressions. It provides the foundation of a common culture because it facilitates day-to-day exchanges with others, making collective action possible.

Even as we learn the meanings of existing words through interactions with others, we create new words and modify old meanings—especially in our modern culture, where innovation is never ending. Dictionaries are regularly modified to include new words. Not so long ago, words such as *ginormous, spamming, feng shui, crunk, IED, caffe latte, hoodie, frankenfood,* and *longneck* did not appear in English-language dictionaries. Whether something is recognized as a word can be a contested process. McDonald's Corporation, for example is seeking to get the word *McJob,* a term coined by sociologist Amitai Etzioni, removed from the Oxford English Dictionary for fear that people might see their products and jobs as something less than prestigious.

Analysis of language gives us insight into cultures. The English language, for example, makes extensive use of words related to war. We speak of "conquering" space, "fighting the battle" of the budget, "waging war" on drugs, making a "killing" in the stock market, and "bombing" an examination; something monumental or great is "the bomb." An observer from another culture could gauge the importance of warfare and the military in Western cultures simply by recognizing the prominence of militaristic terms in our language. As another example, in the Old West, words such as *gelding, stallion, mare, piebald,* and *sorrel* were all used to describe one animal—the horse. Even if we knew little about that period in history, we could conclude from the list of terms that horses were important to the culture. Similarly, the Slave Indians of northern Canada, who live in a frigid climate, have 14 terms to describe ice, including eight for different kinds of "solid ice" and others for "seamed ice," "cracked ice," and "floating ice." Clearly, language reflects the values and priorities of a culture (Basso 1972; Haviland 2002).

Different languages express reality in different ways, and crossing one language with another can lead to embarrassment. To lend authenticity to his 1990 film *Dances with Wolves,* actor-director Kevin Costner hired a Lakota woman to teach the Lakota language to the cast. Lakota is a gendered language in which women and men speak slightly different dialects. The cast members found the language so difficult to learn that the teacher decided to dispense with the complexities of gendered speech. When members of the Lakota Sioux tribe saw the film, they could not help laughing at the men sounding like women (Haviland et al. 2005:109).

Because different groups share different languages, the ability to speak other languages is crucial to intercultural relations. Canadian Parliament adopted the first Official Languages Act in 1969, recognizing and granting equal federal status to both French and English languages. In the United States, following the terrorist attacks of September 11, 2001, the American government recognized its lack of skilled translators for Arabic and other languages spoken in Muslim countries. Language quickly became a key not only to tracking potential terrorists but also to building diplomatic bridges with Muslim countries willing to help in the war against terrorism.

Sapir-Whorf Hypothesis Language does more than simply describe reality; it also shapes the reality of a culture. For example, most people in Canada cannot easily make the verbal distinctions concerning ice that are possible in the Slave Indian culture. As a result, they are less likely to notice differences in types of ice.

According to the **Sapir-Whorf hypothesis,** named for two linguists, the language a person uses shapes his or her perception of reality and therefore his or her thoughts and actions. Edward Sapir and Benjamin Whorf argued that since people can conceptualize the world only through language, language *precedes* thought. Thus, the word symbols and grammar of our language organize the world for us. The Sapir-Whorf hypothesis also holds that language is not a given. Rather, it is culturally determined and encourages a distinctive interpretation of reality by focusing our attention on certain phenomena. While the influence and importance of language is undeniable, the Sapir-Whorf hypothesis has come under criticism for being overly deterministic. Words do not only *construct* new phenomena, but they also *reflect* them and are created in order to depict them.

In a literal sense, language may colour how we see the world. Berlin and Kay (1991) noted that humans possess the physical ability to make millions of colour distinctions, yet languages differ in the number of colours they recognize. For example, the English language distinguishes between yellow and orange, but some other languages do not. In the Dugum Dani language of New Guinea's West Highlands, there are only two basic colour terms—*modla* for "white" and *mili* for "black." By contrast, there are 11

SOCthink

> > > What are some slang terms we use to refer to men and to women? What images do such terms convey for what it means to be male or female?

basic terms in English. Russian and Hungarian, though, have 12 colour terms. Russians have terms for light blue and dark blue, while Hungarians have terms for two different shades of red (Roberson et al. 2000).

Feminists have noted that gender-related language can reflect—although in itself it does not determine—the traditional acceptance of men and women in certain occupations. Each time we use a term such as *mailman, policeman,* or *fireman,* we are implying (especially to young children) that these occupations can be filled only by males. Yet many women work as *letter carriers, police officers,* and *firefighters*—a fact that is being increasingly recognized and legitimized through the use of such nonsexist language.

> **Sapir-Whorf hypothesis** The idea that the language a person uses shapes his or her perception of reality and therefore his or her thoughts and actions.

Did You Know?

...There are approximately 7000 languages spoken in the world today. However, over 500 of them are considered nearly extinct because they have fewer than 100 living speakers. Another 3000 are endangered, with fewer than 10,000 speakers.

after closing a business deal. The gesture, which would shock many North Americans, is considered a compliment in that culture. The meaning of hand signals is another form of nonverbal communication that can differ from one culture to the next. For instance, in Australia the thumbs-up sign is considered rude (Passero 2002).

VALUES

Although each of us has our own personal set of standards—which may include caring or fitness or entrepreneurship—we also share a general set of objectives as members of a society. **Values** are these collective conceptions of what is considered good, desirable, and proper—or bad, undesirable, and improper—in a culture. Values may be specific, such as honouring one's parents and owning a home, or they may be more general, such as health, love, and democracy. Even individualism represents a collective value. As Richard Rodriguez points out, "American individualism is a communally derived value, not truly an expression of individuality. The teenager persists in rebelling against her parents, against tradition or custom, because she is shielded . . . by American culture from the knowledge that she inherited her rebellion from dead ancestors and living parents" (2002:130). Of course, all members of a society do not uniformly share its values. Angry political debates and billboards promoting conflicting causes tell us that much.

The values of a culture may change, but most remain relatively stable during any one person's lifetime. Socially shared, intensely felt values are a fundamental part of our lives in Canada.

In recent decades, scholars have made extensive efforts to compare values in different nations, even while recognizing the challenges in interpreting value concepts in a similar manner across cultures. Psychologist Shalom Schwartz has measured values in more than 60 countries. Around the world,

Language can also transmit stereotypes related to race. Look up the meanings of the adjective *black* in dictionaries published in the United States, and you will find "dismal, gloomy or forbidding, destitute of moral light or goodness, atrocious, evil, threatening, clouded with anger." By contrast, dictionaries list "pure" and "innocent" among the meanings of the adjective *white*. Through such patterns of language, our culture reinforces positive associations with the term (and skin colour) *white* and negative associations with *black*. Is it surprising, then, that a list meant to prevent people from working in a profession is called a "blacklist," while a fib that we think of as somewhat acceptable is called a "white lie"?

nonverbal communication The use of gestures, facial expressions, and other visual images to communicate.

value A collective conception of what is considered good, desirable, and proper—or bad, undesirable, and improper—in a culture.

As you can see from these examples, language can shape how we see, taste, smell, feel, and hear. It also influences the way we think about the people, ideas, and objects around us.

Nonverbal Communication

Of course, we communicate using more than just words. If you do not like the way a meeting is going, you might suddenly sit back, fold your arms, and turn down the corners of your mouth. When you see a friend in tears, you may give her a quick hug. After winning a big game, you may high-five your teammates. These are all examples of **nonverbal communication**—the use of gestures, facial expressions, and other visual images to communicate. We are not born with these expressions. We learn them, just as we learn other forms of language, from people who share our culture. We learn how to show—and to recognize—happiness, sadness, pleasure, shame, distress, and other emotional states (Fridlund et al. 1987).

Like other forms of language, nonverbal communication is not the same in all cultures. For example, people from various cultures differ in the degree to which they touch others during the course of normal social interactions. Even experienced travellers are sometimes caught off guard by these differences. In Saudi Arabia a middle-aged man may want to hold hands with a male partner

In Arab cultures, men may hold hands as a sign of affection and friendship.

certain values are widely shared, including benevolence, which is defined as "forgiveness and loyalty." In contrast, power, defined as "control or dominance over people and resources," is a value that is endorsed much less often (Hitlin and Piliavin 2004; S. Schwartz and Bardi 2001).

In 1991, Citizens' Forum on Canada's Future asked over 400,000 Canadians which values they considered "Canadian" values. From this study, the largest to date initiated by the federal government, a number of values emerged as defining our national character:

1. Equality and fairness in a democratic society
2. Consultation and dialogue
3. Accommodation and tolerance
4. Support for diversity

SOCthink

> > > What does being Canadian mean to you? How do you think Canadians are perceived by people from other cultures? Do these overlap?

5. Compassion and generosity
6. Respect for Canada's national beauty
7. Commitment to freedom, peace, and non-violent change

These values to which we attach great importance are also the source of much humour and generally good-natured stereotypes about Canadians. In fact, adherence to several of these values is captured in the well-known joke: "How do you get a group of Canadians out of a swimming pool? —You ask them."

Canadians also have great fondness for our national symbols. In a recent poll conducted by Ipsos Reid and The Dominion Institute, the maple leaf was the unanimous choice as "the" symbol of Canada. Others on the list included hockey, the Canadian flag, the beaver, the RCMP, wilderness, the Stanley Cup, and maple syrup. And indeed, when Canada is portrayed in television or film, there will most likely be reference to at least one of these!

But in every society, there are discrepancies between principles and practice; that is, what we claim to value and what we actually do. For instance, despite Canadians' espoused commitment to fairness and democracy, cheating has become a serious concern in our society, particularly at universities and colleges.

Professors who take advantage of computerized services that can identify plagiarism, such as the search engine Google or TurnItIn.com, have found that many of the papers their students hand in are plagiarized, in whole or in part. When high school students were asked how many times they had copied an Internet document for a classroom assignment in the past year, 32.9 percent said that they had done so at least once. When asked how many times they had cheated during a test at school in the past year, 60.2 percent said that they had done so at least once (Josephson Institute of Ethics 2006). In a study conducted by researchers from the University of Guelph and Rutgers University, more than 50 percent of undergraduate students admitted to cheating on written work. Moreover, the results of this study revealed a climate in which there is little social stigma or perceived repercussions associated with academic dishonesty (Christensen Hughes and McCabe 2006). Perhaps cheating has become a normal part of student culture even if it is at odds with the dominant school values.

Another value that has begun to change recently, not just among students but among the public in general, is the right to privacy. Canadians and Americans have always valued their privacy and resented government intrusions into their personal lives. In the aftermath of the terrorist attacks of September 11, 2001, however, many citizens called for greater protection against the threat of terrorism. In response, the U.S. federal government broadened its surveillance powers and increased its ability to monitor people's behaviour without court approval. In 2001, shortly after the attacks, Congress passed the USA Patriot Act, which empowers the FBI to access individuals' medical, library, student, and phone records without informing them or obtaining a search warrant. In December of the same year, the Canadian Anti-Terrorism Act (Bill C-36) came into effect. Like its American counterpart, Bill C-36 expanded the powers of the federal government. Some provisions in the act were considered incompatible with the Charter of Rights and Freedoms. While most Canadians agreed that the threat of terrorism must be addressed, many were concerned about the potential violation of individual rights.

Hot or Not?

If you could cheat on your next sociology test and get away with it, would you? Why or why not?

norm An established standard of behaviour maintained by a society.

formal norm A norm that generally has been written down and that specifies strict punishments for violators.

laws Formal norms enforced by the state.

informal norm A norm that is generally understood but not precisely recorded.

NORMS

While values express our core beliefs, norms provide guidance for how to act: "Wash your hands before dinner." "Thou shalt not kill." "Respect your elders." All societies have ways of encouraging and enforcing what they view as appropriate behaviour while discouraging and sanctioning what they consider to be improper behaviour. **Norms** are the established standards of behaviour maintained by a society. However, they are more than just the rules we think about and know—we come to embody them as part of our everyday actions.

For a norm to become significant, it must be widely shared and understood. For example, in movie theatres in Canada, we typically expect that people will be quiet while the film is shown. Of course, context matters, and the application of this norm can vary, depending on the particular film and type of audience. People who are viewing a serious artistic film will be more likely to insist on the norm of silence than those who are watching a slapstick comedy or a horror movie.

Types of Norms Sociologists distinguish between norms in two ways. First, norms are classified as either formal or informal. **Formal norms** generally have been written down and specify strict punishments for violators. In Canada we often formalize norms into laws, which are very precise in defining proper and improper behaviour. Sociologist Donald Black (1995) defined *law* as "governmental social control"; that is, **laws** are formal norms enforced by the state. But laws are just one example of formal norms. The requirements for a college or university major and the rules of a card game are also considered formal norms.

By contrast, **informal norms** are generally understood but not precisely recorded. Standards of proper dress are a common example of informal norms. Our society has no specific punishment or sanction for a person who comes to school wearing, say, a gorilla suit. Making fun of the nonconforming student is the most likely response. Sometimes we deliberately fail to conform just to see what happens. Sociologist Harold Garfinkel (1967) conducted "breaching" experiments in which people were directed to act in violation of everyday norms. For example, responding in great

detail to simple questions, or treating family members as though they were strangers. His research led him to develop *ethnomethodology*, the study of the ways in which people make sense of their everyday lives. By breaching (or violating) norms, we become aware of the often taken for granted shared understandings and expectations that make social interaction possible.

SOCthink

> > > What norms are you abiding by right now, as you read this book?

Norms are also classified by their relative importance to society. When classified in this way, they are known as *mores* and *folkways*. **Mores** (pronounced "MOR-ays") are norms deemed highly necessary to the welfare of a society, often because they embody the most cherished principles of a people. Each society demands obedience to its mores; violation can lead to severe penalties. Thus, Canada has strong mores against murder, treason, and child abuse, which have been institutionalized into formal norms.

Folkways are norms governing everyday behaviour. They play an important role in shaping the daily behaviour of members of a culture. Society is less likely to formalize folkways than mores, and their violation raises comparatively little concern. For example, fashion is a folkway, and there is wide latitude in what we might wear. But what about not wearing *any* clothes in public? For most of us, most of the time, that would be crossing the line into the territory of mores, and we might expect a strong and swift response. However,

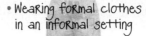

Break-a-Norm Day

- Wearing formal clothes in an informal setting
- Eating with the wrong utensil or none at all
- Responding to friends or family the same as to a boss or teacher
- Having long gaps in speech when talking with someone
- Standing just a little too close to or far from someone when talking with him or her
- Facing the back of an elevator instead of getting in and turning around

Norms provide us with rules that guide our everyday behaviour. All we need to do is step outside the lines even a little bit to see the influence they have over our lives. These are some examples of how people violate norms. How would you feel about violating any of these norms? How might others respond to you?

this too may be undergoing a change: in April 2008, *The New York Times* reported that the nude vacation business is booming (Higgins 2008).

In many societies around the world, folkways exist to reinforce patterns of male dominance. For example, various folkways reveal men's hierarchical position above women within the traditional Buddhist areas of Southeast Asia. In the sleeping cars of trains, women do not sleep in upper berths, above men. Hospitals that house men on the first floor do not place female patients on the second floor. Even on clotheslines, folkways in Southeast Asia dictate male dominance: women's attire is hung lower than that of men (Bulle 1987).

Acceptance of Norms People do not follow norms, whether mores or folkways, in all situations. In some cases they can evade a norm because they know it is weakly enforced. For instance, it is illegal for Canadian teenagers to drink alcoholic beverages, yet drinking by minors is common throughout the nation. In fact, teenage alcoholism is a serious social problem.

In some instances behaviour that appears to violate society's norms may actually represent adherence to the norms of a particular group. Teenage drinkers are

mores Norms deemed highly necessary to the welfare of a society.

folkways Norms governing everyday behaviour, whose violation raise comparatively little concern.

Canadian attributes
as seen on TV

Little Mosque on the Prairie
Respect for cultural and religious diversity.

The Rick Mercer Report
Canadians are not just polite, but funny and clever.

APTN
Appreciation of tradition and talent.

The Molson "I Am Canadian!" commercial
We are a unique people!

Hockey Night in Canada
Determination, loyalty, and pride.

often conforming to the standards of their peer group when they violate norms that condemn underage drinking. Similarly, business executives who use shady accounting techniques may be responding to a corporate culture that demands the maximization of profits at any cost, including the deception of investors and government regulatory agencies.

Acceptance of norms is subject to change as the political, economic, and social conditions of a culture are transformed. Until the 1960s, for example, formal norms throughout much of the United States prohibited the marriage of people from different racial groups. Over the past half century, however, such legal prohibitions have been cast aside. In 2005, Canada became

Strangers in a new culture see only what they know.

Anonymous

Norms are violated in some instances because one norm conflicts with another. For example, suppose you live in an apartment building and one night hear the screams of the woman next door, who is being beaten by her partner. If you decide to intervene by knocking on their door or calling the police, you are violating the norm of minding your own business while at the same time following the norm of assisting a victim of domestic violence.

Even if norms do not conflict, there are exceptions to any norm. The same action, under different circumstances, can cause one to be viewed as either a hero or a villain. For instance, secretly taping telephone conversations is normally considered not just illegal but abhorrent. However, it can be done with a court order to obtain valid evidence for a criminal trial. We would heap praise on a government agent who used such methods to convict an organized crime figure. In our culture we tolerate killing another human being in self-defence, and we actually reward killing in warfare.

only the third country (after The Netherlands in 2000, and Belgium in 2003) to grant national legal recognition to same-sex marriages. In both of these cases, popular support and acceptance led to changes in norms, though there is still resistance to these changes among some segments of the population.

When circumstances require the sudden violation of longstanding cultural norms, the change can upset an entire population. In Iraq, where Muslim custom strictly forbids touching by strangers for men and especially for women, the war that began in 2003 has brought numerous daily violations of the norm. Outside mosques, government offices, and other facilities likely to be targeted by terrorists, visitors must now be patted down and have their bags searched by Iraqi security forces. To reduce the discomfort caused by the procedure, women are searched by female guards and men by male guards. Despite that concession, and the fact that many Iraqis admit to or even insist on the need for such measures, people still wince at the invasion of their personal privacy. In reaction to the searches, Iraqi women have

A female soldier searches Iraqi women.

begun to limit the contents of the bags they carry or simply to leave them at home (Rubin 2003).

SANCTIONS

Suppose your basketball coach sends you into the game as the sixth player on your team. Or imagine you have graduated from university and show up in shorts for a job interview at a large bank. Or, on the way to that interview, suppose you park your car on the street but neglect to put any money into the parking meter. In each case you have violated widely shared and understood norms. So what happens? In each of these situations, you would receive some form of negative repercussion if your behaviour was detected.

5 Movies on CULTURES OUTSIDE CANADA

Rabbit-Proof Fence
Aborigines in Australia.

Tsotsi
A harsh tale from Africa.

Eat Drink Man Woman
Romance and cooking in Taiwan.

Children of Heaven
Iranian schoolchildren.

Satin Rouge
A Tunisian widow studying belly dancing.

Sanctions are penalties and rewards for conduct concerning a social norm. They include both negative and positive responses to behaviour; their purpose is to influence future behaviour. Adhering to norms can lead to positive sanctions such as a pay raise, a medal, a word of gratitude, or a pat on the back. Negative sanctions might include fines, threats, imprisonment, and stares of contempt. In this way sanctions work to enforce the order that the norms represent. Most of the time we do not even need others to sanction our acts. Having internalized society's norms, we police ourselves, using such internal motivations as guilt or self-satisfaction to regulate our own behaviour.

As we saw with the "Free Hugs" campaign, norms provide order, but norms change, and change represents potential chaos.

As social scientist Gustave Le Bon said in 1895, "Civilization is impossible without traditions, and progress impossible without the destruction of those traditions. The difficulty, and it is an immense difficulty, is to find a proper equilibrium between stability and variability." In a world of norms, we constantly face this tension: to obey or not to obey.

>> Culture and the Dominant Ideology

Together the elements of culture provide us with social coherence and order. Culture clarifies for us what we think is good and bad, and right and wrong, giving us a sense of direction. That is not to say, however, that there is universal agreement on values and norms or that culture works on behalf of all for the greater good. While culture helps to unify and provide meaning, it also serves the interests of some individuals and groups to the detriment of others. Some people benefit from existing norms and values, while others are denied opportunities or access to resources simply due to the positions they occupy—positions we have culturally defined as inferior.

> **sanction** A penalty or reward for conduct concerning a social norm.
>
> **dominant ideology** A set of cultural beliefs and practices that legitimates existing powerful social, economic, and political interests

One of the ways culture can function to maintain the privileges of certain groups is through the establishment of a **dominant ideology**—the set of cultural beliefs and practices that legitimate existing powerful social, economic, and political interests. The dominant ideology helps to explain and justify who gets what and why in a way that supports and maintains the status quo. Dominant ideas can even squelch alternative expressions of what might be, casting such alternatives as threats to the existing order. In Karl Marx's view, a capitalist society has a dominant ideology that serves the interests of the ruling class.

As conflict theorists such as Marx have long argued, a society's most powerful groups and institutions control wealth and property. Armed with a dominant ideology, they can also control the means of producing beliefs about reality

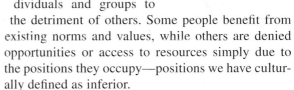

through religion, education, and the media, and in so doing, they can shape what we come to accept as true. For instance, the feminist perspective has been instrumental in pointing out how the dominant ideology of many cultures has served to perpetuate hierarchical gender relations, with women being constructed as "less than" men and thus historically restricted from participating fully in society. However, functionalists argue that culture is fundamental to the operation of society, helping to fulfill our human needs, and symbolic interactionists remind us how shared culture facilitates communication and interaction within and between societies.

subculture A segment of society that shares a distinctive pattern of mores, folkways, and values that differs from the pattern of the larger society.

argot Specialized language used by members of a group or subculture.

But the functionalist perspective assumes there is a consensus about what our culture *is*, and this is problematic. One of the limitations of the dominant ideology thesis is that, in Canada, it is not easy to identify a singular, all-inclusive "core culture." Studies report a lack of consensus on national values and a wide range of cultural traits from a variety of cultural traditions. In addition, significant intergenerational shifts in cultural values can occur.

Yet there is no denying that certain expressions of values have greater influence than others, even in so complex a society as Canada. For example, the value of competition in the marketplace—a cornerstone of any capitalist economy—remains powerful, and we often look down on those who we suspect might be lazy.

>> Cultural Variation

While societies can be defined in part by the culture their inhabitants share, culture varies both among and within societies. Cultures adapt to meet specific sets of circumstances, such as climate, level of technology, population, and geography. This adaptation to different conditions shows up in differences in all elements of culture, including language, values, norms, and sanctions. Thus, despite the presence of cultural universals such as courtship and religion, great diversity exists among the world's many cultures. Moreover, even within a single nation, certain segments of the populace develop cultural patterns that differ from the patterns of the dominant society.

ASPECTS OF CULTURAL VARIATION

Subcultures Skateboarders, residents of a retirement community, biker gangs, rodeo riders—all are examples of what sociologists refer to as *subcultures*. A **subculture** is a segment of society that shares a distinctive pattern of mores, folkways, and values that differs from the pattern of the larger society. In a sense, a subculture can be thought of as a culture existing within a larger, dominant culture. The existence of many subcultures is characteristic of complex societies such as Canada.

Members of a subculture participate in the dominant culture while at the same time engaging in unique and distinc-

SOCthink

> > > Are people who participate in *World of Warcraft* or *Second Life* part of subcultures? What are some characteristics of these groups that typify subcultures?

tive forms of behaviour. Frequently, a subculture will develop its own slang known as **argot**—specialized language that distinguishes it from the wider society. For example, back in the 1940s and 1950s, New York City's sanitation workers developed a humorous argot used to this day to describe the dirty and smelly aspects of their job. They call themselves *g-men* (a term more typically applied to

government agents); a garbage scow or barge is known as a *honey boat;* and trash thrown from an upper-storey window is called *airmail.* More recent coinages include *disco rice* (maggots) and *urban whitefish* (used condoms). Administrators at the Sanitation Department practise a more reserved humour than those who work on the trucks. When they send a *honey boat* to New Jersey, they are not dumping the city's garbage; they're *exporting* it. Policy makers at the department have also invented some novel acronyms to describe New Yorkers' attitude toward the construction of new sanitation facilities: *banana* (build absolutely nothing anywhere near anyone) and *nope* (not on planet earth) (Urbina 2004).

Such argot allows insiders—the members of the subculture—to understand words with special meanings and establishes patterns of communication that outsiders cannot understand. In so doing, it clarifies the boundary between "us" and "them" and reinforces a shared identity. We see something like this in the taken-for-granted words and acronyms in the instant-messaging and text-messaging world. There, abbreviations come fast and furious, from the well-known, such as *lol* (laughing out loud), *brb* (be right back), and *g2g* (got to go), to the more obscure, such as *1337* (meaning "elite" and referring to symbolic language or "leetspeak") or *pwned* (leet term meaning "defeated").

In India a new subculture has developed among employees at the international call centres established by multinational corporations. To serve customers in North America and Europe, the young men and women who work there must be fluent speakers of English. But the corporations that employ them demand more than proficiency in a foreign language; they expect their Indian employees to adopt Western values and work habits, including demanding work schedules. In return, the corporations offer perks such as Western-style dinners and dances and coveted consumer goods. Ironically, they allow employees to take the day off only on Western holidays like Labour Day and Thanksgiving—not on Indian holidays like Diwali, the Hindu festival of lights. While most Indian families are home celebrating, call centre employees see only each other; when they have the day off, no one else is free to socialize with them. As a result, these employees have formed a tight-knit subculture based on hard work and a taste for Western luxury goods and leisure time pursuits. Increasingly, they are the object of criticism from Indians who live a more conventional Indian lifestyle centred on family and holiday traditions (Kalita 2006).

Countercultures Sometimes a subculture can develop that seeks to set itself up as an alternative to the dominant culture. When a subculture conspicuously and deliberately opposes certain aspects of the larger culture, it is known as a **counterculture.** Countercultures typically thrive among the young, who have the least investment in the existing culture.

Subculture Slang

Anime and Manga Fans
Chibi eyes: the characteristic, big childlike eyes used in anime

Majoko: a girl anime character with magical powers who must save the world

Carnival Workers
86'ed: banned from carnival grounds

Blade glommer: a sword swallower

Flat store: a carnival game rigged so that it can't be won

Graffiti Writers
Bite: to copy another graffiti writer's work

Burner: a stylistically impressive, brilliantly coloured piece of graffiti, usually written in a complex pattern of interlocking letters and other visual elements

Toy: an inexperienced or unskilled graffiti writer

Kill: to saturate an area with one's graffiti

Bikers (Motorcyclists)
Brain bucket: a helmet

Ink slinger: a tattoo artist

Pucker factor: the degree of panic felt during a near-accident

Yard shark: a dog that races out to attack passing motorcyclists

Skateboarders
Deck: a skateboard platform

Face plant: a face-first crash

Sketchy: in reference to a trick, poorly done

Subcultures often produce their own unique jargon. The words may be appropriate in those subcultures, but they have the effect of drawing a line between insiders and the rest of us.

Source: Luc Reid. 2006. *Talk the Talk: The Slang of 65 American Subcultures.* Cincinnati, OH: Writer's Digest Books.

The 1960s, now often characterized by the phrase "turn on, tune in, drop out" provide a classic case of an extensive counterculture. Largely composed of young people, members of this counterculture were turned off by a society they believed was too materialistic and technological. It included many political radicals and "hippies" who had "dropped out" of mainstream social institutions, but its membership was extensive and diverse. The young people expressed in their writings, speeches, and songs their visions, hopes, and dreams for a new society. These young women and men rejected the pressure to accumulate more expensive cars, larger homes, and an endless array of material goods. Instead, they expressed a desire to live in a culture based on more humanistic values, such as sharing, love, and coexistence with the environment. As a political force, they worked for peace—opposing U.S.

> **counterculture** A subculture that deliberately opposes certain aspects of the larger culture.

involvement in the war in Vietnam and encouraging draft resistance—as well as racial and gender equality (Flacks 1971; Roszak 1969). Though many members of this counterculture ended up living the very lifestyle they had once rejected, it was nonetheless an important social, political, and ideological movement in its time.

In the wake of the attacks of September 11, 2001, people around the United States learned of the existence of terrorist groups operating as a counterculture within their own country. In Northern Ireland, Israel, the Palestinian territory, and other parts of the world, many generations have lived in such circumstances. But terrorist cells are not

necessarily fuelled only by outsiders. Frequently, people become disenchanted with the policies of their own country, and a few take very violent steps (Juergensmeyer 2003). However, it is important to remember that most countercultures, while challenging the dominant norms, do not pose a threat to the larger society.

Culture Shock Today we are more and more likely to come into contact with and even immerse ourselves in cultures unlike our own. For example, it has become increasingly common for students to study abroad. Though they may well have predeparture orientation sessions, when they get in-country, they often have a difficult time adjusting because so many of the little things that they took for granted, things they barely noticed before, no longer apply. Anyone who feels disoriented, uncertain, out of place, or even fearful when they encounter unfamiliar cultural practices may be experiencing **culture shock.** For example, a resident of Canada who visits certain areas in China and wants meat for dinner may be stunned to learn that the local specialty is dog meat. Similarly, someone from a strict Islamic culture may be shocked upon first seeing the comparatively provocative dress styles and open displays of affection that are common in Western cultures.

culture shock The feelings of disorientation, uncertainty, and even fear that people experience when they encounter unfamiliar cultural practices.

Interestingly, once students who study abroad return home, they may experience a kind of reverse culture shock. Their time away has changed them, often in ways they were unaware of, and they find that they cannot so easily slip back into the old routines that those who remained at home expect of them. Culture shock reveals to us both the power and the taken-for-granted nature of culture. The rules we follow are so ingrained that we barely notice that we were following them until they are no longer there to provide the structure and order we assume as a given.

All of us, to some extent, take for granted the cultural practices of our society. As a result, it can be surprising and even disturbing to realize that other cultures do not follow our way of life. The fact is, customs that seem strange to us are considered normal and proper in other cultures, which may view our own mores and folkways as odd.

ATTITUDES TOWARD CULTURAL VARIATION

Ethnocentrism Because we are now more likely to encounter people from a whole range of cultural backgrounds than we were in the past, we are also more likely to struggle with what we think about the beliefs, values, and practices of others. When we hear people talking about "our" culture versus "their" culture, we are often confronted with statements that reflect the attitude that "our" culture is best. Terms such as *underdeveloped, backward,* and *primitive* may be used to refer to other societies. What "we" believe is a religion; what "they" believe is superstition and mythology.

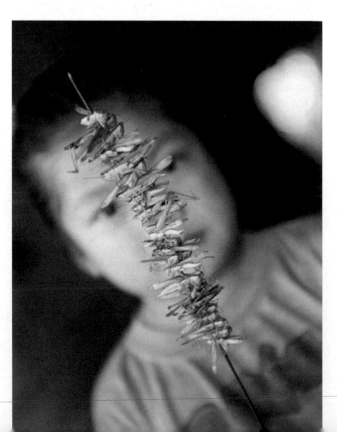

It is tempting to evaluate the practices of other cultures on the basis of our own perspectives. Sociologist William Graham Sumner (1906) coined the term **ethnocentrism** to refer to the tendency to assume that one's own culture and way of life represent the norm or are superior to all others. The ethnocentric person sees his or her own group as the centre or defining point of culture and views all other cul-

Japanese cultures, loyalty to the family and the extended clan comes before patriotism and the common good. In a country in which almost half of all people, even those in the cities, marry a first or second cousin, citizens are predisposed to favour their own kin in government and business dealings. Why trust a stranger from outside the family? What Westerners would criticize as nepotism, then, is

You don't have to burn books to destroy a culture. Just get people to stop reading them.

Ray Bradbury

tures as deviations from what is "normal." Thus, Westerners who see cattle as a food source might look down on the Hindu religion and culture, which view the cow as sacred. People in one culture may dismiss as unthinkable the mate selection or child-rearing practices of another culture.

Ethnocentric value judgments have complicated U.S. efforts at democratic reform of the Iraqi government. Prior to the 2003 war in Iraq, U.S. planners had assumed that Iraqis would adapt to a new form of government in the same way the Germans and Japanese did following World War II. But in the Iraqi culture, unlike the German and

Learn about another culture. One of the most effective ways is to immerse yourself in one. Seek out opportunities for deep and prolonged interaction with a group of people from a culture unlike your own. Contact your school's service learning program or study-abroad office to find out what possibilities exist.

get involved!

actually an acceptable, even admirable, practice to Iraqis (J. Tierney 2003).

One of the reasons ethnocentrism develops is because it contributes to a sense of solidarity by promoting group pride. Denigrating other nations and cultures can enhance our own patriotic feelings and belief in our way of life. Yet this type of social stability is established at the expense of other peoples. For example, Canadian television personality Rick Mercer's feature, "Talking to Americans,"

> **ethnocentrism** The tendency to assume that one's own culture and way of life represent the norm or are superior to all others.
>
> **cultural relativism** The viewing of people's behaviour from the perspective of their own culture.

enjoyed immense popularity for its portrayal of our southern neighbours as embarrassingly ignorant of Canadian culture. But while this was considered harmless fun, one of the negative consequences of ethnocentric value judgments is that they serve to devalue groups and to deny equal opportunities.

Of course, ethnocentrism is hardly limited to citizens of Canada. Visitors from many African cultures are surprised at the disrespect that children in Western societies show their parents. People from India may be repelled by our practice of living in the same household with dogs and cats. Many Islamic fundamentalists in the Arab world and Asia view the United States as corrupt, decadent, and doomed to destruction. All these people may feel comforted by membership in cultures that in their view are superior to ours.

Cultural Relativism Whereas ethnocentrism means evaluating foreign cultures using the familiar culture of the observer as a standard of correct behaviour, **cultural relativism** means viewing people's behaviour from the perspective of their own culture. It places a priority on understanding other cultures, rather than dismissing them as "strange" or "exotic." Unlike ethnocentrists, cultural relativists employ the kind of value neutrality in scientific study that Max Weber saw as so important.

Cultural relativism stresses that different social contexts give rise to different norms and values. Thus, we must examine practices such as polygamy, bullfighting, and monarchy within the particular contexts of the cultures in which they are found. Cultural relativism is not the same as moral relativism and thus does not suggest that we must unquestionably accept every cultural variation. But it does require a serious and unbiased effort to evaluate norms, values, and customs in light of their distinctive culture.

Practising the sociological imagination calls for us to be more fully aware of the culture we as humans have created for ourselves and to be better attuned to the varieties of culture other people have established for themselves. Culture shapes our everyday behaviours all the time, and for the most part, we are not aware of the degree to which we are immersed in a world of our own making. Whether that includes the capacity to read a book, make a meal, or hug a stranger on the street, it is through culture that we establish our relationship to the external world and with each other.

>> Summary

Culture is the totality of our shared language, knowledge, material objects, and behaviour. In this chapter we have considered the basic elements of culture, explored some cultural universals, and noted variations among cultures. Life would be boring if we all saw things the same way; differences in culture reflect social, political, and ideological diversity among the earth's people.

For REVIEW

I.   Why do humans create culture?
   • Humans lack the complex instincts present in other animals, and as such they must construct a relationship to nature and with each other. We do this through the construction of shared culture.

II. What does culture consist of?
   • Culture can be broken down into two categories. The first is material culture, which consists of our modification of the physical environment and includes technology. The second is nonmaterial culture, which consists of a number of components including language, values, norms, and sanctions.

III. How does culture both enable and constrain?
   • While culture provides us with the knowledge, rules, and artifacts we need to survive, it also limits our options. Words enable us to see, and tools enable us to make things, but both are designed for particular purposes and shield us from alternative possibilities. Further, with ethnocentrism, we cut ourselves off to new possibilities from different cultures.

Thinking CRITICALLY...

1. To what subcultures do you belong? In what ways do they complement or conflict with one another?
2. Does Canada have an identifiable "core culture"? Why is it so difficult to come to a consensus on Canadian values?
3. What challenges to adopting a culturally relativist position would you anticipate when confronted with a cultural practice that you have been socialized to consider unacceptable? Is it appropriate to critique or condemn it? What criteria would you use to decide this?

Pop Quiz

1. Which of the following is an aspect of culture?
   a. a comic book
   b. the patriotic attachment to the Canadian flag
   c. slang
   d. all of the above

2. People's need for food, shelter, and clothing are examples of what George Murdock referred to as
   a. norms.
   b. folkways.
   c. cultural universals.
   d. cultural practices.

3. The appearance of Starbucks coffeehouses in China is a sign of which aspect of culture?
   a. innovation
   b. globalization
   c. discovery
   d. cultural relativism

4. What term do sociologists use to refer to the process by which a cultural item spreads from group to group or society to society?
   a. diffusion
   b. globalization
   c. innovation
   d. cultural relativism

5. Which of the following statements is true according to the Sapir-Whorf hypothesis?
   a. Language simply describes reality.
   b. Language does not transmit stereotypes related to race.
   c. Language shapes our perception of reality.
   d. Language is not an example of a cultural universal.

6. Which of the following statements about values is correct?
   a. Values never change.
   b. The values of a culture may change, but most remain relatively stable during any one person's lifetime.
   c. Values are constantly changing; sociologists view them as being very unstable.
   d. all of the above

7. Which of the following statements about norms is correct?
   a. People do not follow norms in all situations. In some cases, they evade a norm because they know it is weakly enforced.
   b. In some instances, behaviour that appears to violate society's norms may actually reflect adherence to the norms of a particular group.
   c. Norms are violated in some instances because one norm conflicts with another.
   d. all of the above

8. Which of the following terms describes the set of cultural beliefs and practices that help to maintain powerful social, economic, and political interests?
   a. mores
   b. dominant ideology
   c. consensus
   d. values

9. Rodeo riders, surfers, and bodybuilders are all examples of
   a. cultural universals.
   b. countercultures.
   c. subcultures.
   d. dominant ideologies.

10. According to the conflict perspective, culture
    a. is an important means of representing all views in society.
    b. has little to do with language.
    c. reflects the dominant ideology of the society.
    d. helps to create solidarity in society.

1 (d); 2 (c); 3 (b); 4 (a); 5 (c); 6 (b); 7 (d); 8 (b); 9 (c); 10 (c)

4

SOCIALIZ

ISOLATION AND SOCIALIZATION

For the first six years of her life, Isabelle lived in almost total seclusion in a darkened room. She had little contact with other people, with the exception of her mother, who could neither speak nor hear. Isabelle's grandparents had been so deeply ashamed of Isabelle's illegitimate birth that they kept her hidden away from the world. Ohio authorities finally discovered Isabelle in 1938, when her mother escaped from her parents' home, taking Isabelle with her.

Six years old at the time of her rescue, Isabelle could not speak. While she could make various croaking sounds, her only communication with her mother involved simple gestures. Isabelle had been largely deprived of the typical interactions and socialization experiences of childhood. Since she had seen few people, she initially showed a strong fear of strangers and reacted almost like a wild animal when confronted with an unfamiliar person. As she became accustomed to seeing certain individuals, her reaction changed to one of extreme apathy. At first, observers believed that Isabelle was deaf, but she soon began to react to nearby sounds. On tests of her educational development, she scored at the level of an infant rather than a six-year-old.

Specialists developed a systematic training program to help Isabelle adapt to human relationships and socialization. After a few days of training, she made her first attempt to verbalize. Although she started slowly, Isabelle quickly passed through six years of development. In a little over two months, she was speaking in complete sentences. Nine months later, she could identify both words and sentences. Before Isabelle reached the age of nine, she was ready to attend school with other children. By her 14th year she was in grade 6, doing well in school, and emotionally well adjusted.

Yet without an opportunity to experience socialization in her first six years, Isabelle initially lacked what we often take for granted as natural human abilities. While we may be born with the propensity toward language and other social skills, Isabelle's inability to communicate at the time of her discovery—despite her physical and cognitive potential to learn—and her remarkable progress over the next few years underscore the importance of socialization in human development (K. Davis 1940, 1947).

As You READ >>

- How do we become ourselves?
- Who shapes our socialization?
- How does our development change over time?

>> The Role of Socialization

What makes us who we are? Is it the genes we are born with, or the environment in which we grow up? Researchers have traditionally clashed over the relative importance of biological inheritance and environmental factors in human development—a conflict called the nature versus nurture (or heredity versus environment) debate. While most social scientists today acknowledge the significance of the interaction between these variables in shaping human development, sociologists tend to come down more strongly on the side of nurture. They argue that the rules we follow, the language we speak, and the values we believe in have less to do with our DNA than with the cultural context into which we emerge. Parents, teachers, friends, co-workers, and even television personalities provide us with the cultural tools we require to survive and thrive. We need to internalize the culture that has been constructed by others who came before us, and we do this through **socialization**—the lifelong process through

> **socialization** The lifelong process through which people learn the attitudes, values, and behaviours appropriate for members of a particular culture.

SOCthink

> > > List the skills you had to learn by the age of two. Why do we tend to think of such skills as "natural"?

which people learn the attitudes, values, and behaviours appropriate for members of a particular culture.

SOCIAL ENVIRONMENT: THE IMPACT OF ISOLATION

We can better appreciate how heredity and environment interact and influence the socialization process by examining situations in which one factor operates almost entirely without the other (Homans 1979). As we saw above, Isabelle was able to proceed through the typical stages of socialization with the help of experts. Unfortunately, others raised in even more extreme isolation have not been so fortunate. Similarly, as we will see below, experiments with primates point toward our desire for intimacy and interaction. We want and need the influence of others.

Extreme Childhood Isolation

Children who have been isolated or severely neglected typically have a difficult time recovering from the loss of early childhood socialization. For example, in 1970, California authorities discovered a 14-year-old girl named Genie locked in a room where she had been confined since she was 20 months old. During her years of isolation, no family member had spoken to her, nor could she hear anything other than swearing. Since there was no television or radio in her home, she had never heard the sounds of normal human speech. One year after beginning extensive therapy, Genie's grammar resembled that of a typical 18-month-old. Though she made further advances with continued therapy, she never achieved full language ability. Today Genie, now in her early fifties, lives in a home for developmentally disabled adults (Curtiss 1977, 1985; Rymer 1993).

While researchers know of only a few cases of children reared in near total isolation, they are aware of many cases of children raised in extremely neglectful social circumstances. Infants and young children in orphanages in the formerly communist countries of Eastern Europe often suffer from profound neglect. In many Romanian orphanages, babies once lay in their cribs for 18–20 hours a day, curled against their feeding bottles and receiving little adult care. Such minimal attention continued for the first five years of

10 Cases of Feral Children

Shamdeo, the Sultanpur Wolf Boy	He was about 4 years old when discovered playing with wolves in 1974.
Memmie LeBlanc, the Wild Girl of Champagne	About 18 to 20 years old when found, she had learned language before having been abandoned.
John Ssebunya, the Ugandan Monkey Boy	Found living with a pack of monkeys in 1991 at age 6, he now gives talks about his experience.
The Syrian Gazelle Boy	An agile runner, he was found among gazelles at about the age of 10 in 1946.
Oxana Malaya, the Ukrainian Dog Girl	She was found living in the dog pen in her family's back yard in 1991 at the age of 8.
The Russian Bird Boy	Found in February 2008, he was cared for by his mother but never spoken to and chirps like a bird.
The Leopard Boy of Dihungi	He was found among leopards at age 5 in 1915 after having been in the wild three years.
Kamala and Amala, the Wolf Girls of Midnapore. These two girls were found living among wolves at about the ages of 8 and 2 in 1920.	
The Turkish Bear Girl	This 9-year-old girl was found living with bears in 1937.
Wild Peter	One of the earliest famous cases, he was found in the wild in Germany at age 12 in 1724.

Kamala

of the earliest socialization experiences for children. We now know that it is not enough to attend to an infant's physical needs; parents must also concern themselves with children's social development. If parents discourage their children from having friends—even as toddlers—those children will miss out on social interactions with peers that are critical for emotional growth.

Primate Studies Studies of animals raised in isolation also support the importance of socialization in development. Harry Harlow (1971), a researcher at the primate laboratory of the University of Wisconsin, conducted tests with rhesus monkeys that had been raised away from their mothers and away from contact with other monkeys. As was the case with Isabelle, the rhesus monkeys raised in isolation were fearful and easily frightened. They did not mate, and the females who were artificially inseminated became abusive mothers. Apparently, isolation had a damaging effect on the monkeys.

A creative aspect of Harlow's experimentation was his use of "artificial mothers." In one such experiment, Harlow presented monkeys raised in isolation with two substitute mothers—one a cloth-covered replica and one a wire-covered model that had the capacity to offer milk. Monkey after monkey went to the wire mother for the life-giving milk, yet spent much more time clinging to the more motherlike cloth model. Apparently, the infant monkeys developed greater social attachments based on their need for warmth, comfort, and intimacy than their need for milk.

THE INFLUENCE OF HEREDITY

Researchers who argue for a stronger role for biological explanations of our behaviour point to different research to support their position—studies of twins, especially identical twins raised apart from each other. Oskar Stohr and Jack Yufe, identical twins who were separated soon after their birth, were raised on different continents and in very different cultural settings. Oskar was reared as a strict Catholic by his maternal grandmother in the Sudetenland of Czechoslovakia. As a member of the Hitler Youth movement in Nazi Germany, he learned to hate Jews. By contrast, his brother Jack was reared in Trinidad by the twins' Jewish father. Jack joined an Israeli kibbutz (a collective settlement) at age 17 and later served in the Israeli army. When the twins were reunited in middle age, however, some startling similarities emerged. They both wore wire-rimmed glasses and mustaches. They both liked spicy foods and

A cloth-covered "artificial mother" of the type used by Harry Harlow.

their lives. Many of them were fearful of human contact and prone to unpredictable antisocial behaviour.

This situation came to light only when families in North America and Europe began adopting thousands of these children in the 1990s. The adjustment problems were often so dramatic that about 20 percent of the adopting families concluded that they were ill-suited to be adoptive parents. Many of them have asked for assistance in dealing with the children. Since these conditions were brought to light by international aid workers, the Romanian government has made efforts to introduce the deprived youngsters to social interaction and its consequent feelings of attachment, which they have never experienced before (Groza et al. 1999; Craig Smith 2006).

Cases of extreme isolation demonstrate the importance

sweet liqueurs, were absent-minded, flushed the toilet before using it, stored rubber bands on their wrists, and dipped buttered toast in their coffee (Holden 1980).

It is tempting in such cases to focus almost exclusively on such quirky similarities, but the twins also differed in many important respects. For example, Jack was a workaholic, while Oskar enjoyed leisure-time activities. Whereas Oskar was a traditionalist who was domineering toward

Researchers have also been impressed with the similar scores on intelligence tests of twins reared apart in *roughly similar* social settings. Most of the identical twins register scores even closer than those that would be expected if the same person took a test twice. However, identical twins brought up in *dramatically different* social environments score quite differently on intelligence tests—a finding that supports the importance of socialization in human devel-

> ## It matters not what someone is born,
> ## but what they grow to be.
>
> J. K. Rowling

women, Jack was a political liberal much more accepting of feminism. Finally, Jack was extremely proud of being Jewish, while Oskar never mentioned his Jewish heritage. Oskar and Jack are prime examples of the interplay of heredity and environment (Holden 1987).

For a number of years, the Minnesota Twin Family Study has been following pairs of identical twins reared apart to determine what similarities, if any, they show in personality traits, behaviour, and intelligence. Preliminary results from the available twin studies indicate that both genetic factors and socialization experiences are influential in human development. Certain characteristics—such as temperament, voice patterns, nervous habits, and leadership or dominance tendencies—appear to be strikingly similar even in twins reared apart, suggesting that these qualities may be linked to heredity. However, identical twins reared apart differ far more in their attitudes; values; chosen mates; need for intimacy, comfort and assistance; and even drinking habits. These qualities, it would seem, are influenced by environmental factors.

Did You Know?

. . . Each year close to 10,000 twin babies and 400 higher order multiple birth children (three or more) are born in Canada. Between 1994 and 2003, Canada's multiple birth rate increased 35 percent, while the single crude birth rate dropped 25 percent. Increased maternal age, the use of fertility drugs, and procedures such as in vitro fertilization are major contributing factors to this trend.

Source: www.multiplebirthscanada.org.

opment (Joseph 2004; McGue and Bouchard 1998; Minnesota Center for Twin and Family Research 2008).

Results from twin studies suggest that the nature–nurture debate is likely to continue. As sociologists we cannot dismiss the significance of biology in shaping human behaviour. It does appear, however, that while some general behavioural propensities may be shaped by our genes, their manifestation is dependent upon socialization and cultural context. For example, while we may inherit tendencies toward temperament, the ways we express anger (or other emotions) depends upon our environment.

>> The Self and Socialization

At the heart of this debate about nature versus nurture is the question "Who am I?" In both approaches the implicit assumption is that we are shaped by factors beyond our control. Sociologically speaking, however, we are not simply passive recipients of external forces. As individuals we are engaged in an ongoing dance with the world. We choose what to think and how to act, but we do so within the confines of the cultural resources to which we have access.

SOCIOLOGICAL APPROACHES TO THE SELF

Our concept of who we are, our self, emerges as we interact with others. The **self** is a distinct identity that sets us apart from others. It is not a static phenomenon but continues to develop and change throughout our lives. Sociologists and psychologists alike have expressed interest in how the individual develops and modifies his or her sense of self as a result of social interaction.

> **self** A distinct identity that sets us apart from others.

Cooley: The Looking-Glass Self In the early 1900s, American sociologist Charles Horton Cooley (1864–1929) proposed that we learn who we are by interacting with others. Our view of ourselves, then, comes not only from direct contemplation of our personal qualities but also from the use of others as a mirror through which we develop our impressions of our self. Cooley used the phrase **looking-glass self** to emphasize that the self is the product of our social interactions.

The process of developing a self-identity, or self-concept, has three phases. First, we imagine how others see us—relatives, friends, even strangers on the street. Then we imagine how others evaluate what we think they see—as intelligent, attractive, shy, or strange. Finally, we define our self as a result of these impressions—"I am smart" or "I am beautiful" (Cooley 1902; M. Howard 1989). This process is ongoing; it happens during each and every one of our interactions. Our understanding of our self, then, involves a complex calculation in which we come to be who we are based not simply on how others see us or how they will judge us but also on how we *think* they will see us and how we *think* they will judge us based on what we think they see.

According to Cooley, then, our self results from our "imagination" of how others view us. As a result, we can develop self-identities based on *incorrect* perceptions of how others see us. We can develop a sense of confidence or a sense of doubt based on how we think others react to our performance, but we might be completely wrong. Imagine you are on a first date. All the cues you receive throughout the evening are positive—your companion smiles, laughs, and seems to be having a genuinely good time. You go home feeling happy, confident that the evening went really well. But your date never returns your calls, and there is no second date. You go from a feeling of elation and confidence to a sense of disappointment and doubt, perhaps even asking, "What's wrong with me?"

Mead: Stages of the Self George Herbert Mead (1863–1931), another American sociologist, sought to expand upon Cooley's theory that we become our self through interaction with others. He argued that there are two core components of the self: the "I" and the "Me." The **I** is our acting self. It is the part of us that walks, reads, sings, smiles, speaks, or performs any other action we might undertake. The **Me** is our socialized self. Based on the

"I"
impulsive, spontaneous self

makes each of us unique (what makes you "you")

"Me"
socialized self, has internalized society's norms and expectations

places limits on the impulsive "I"

looking-glass self A concept that emphasizes the self as the product of our social interactions.

I The acting self that exists in relation to the Me.

Me The socialized self that plans actions and judges performances based on the standards we have learned from others.

significant other An individual who is most important in the development of the self, such as a parent, friend, or teacher.

standards we have learned from others, the Me plans action and then judges our performance afterward.

For Mead the self represents an ongoing interaction between our socialized self and our acting self. The Me plans. The I acts. The Me judges. Take participating in classroom discussions as an example. Our Me may have something to say but fears that the words won't come out quite right, which could lead to embarrassment, so our I stays silent. Our Me then kicks our self afterwards when someone else says exactly what we planned to say and receives praise from the professor for having said it.

It is through our interactions with others that we get the social expectations of the Me into our heads. According to Mead (1964b), when we are young, we see ourselves as the centre of the universe and find it difficult to consider the perspectives of others. For example, when shown a mountain scene and asked to describe what an observer on the opposite side of the mountain might see, young children describe only objects visible from their own vantage point. Although we always retain a certain level of self-centredness, as we mature, the self changes and begins to reflect greater concern with the reactions of others.

Parents, friends, co-workers, coaches, and teachers are often among those who play a major role in shaping a person's self. The term **significant others** refers to individuals who are most important in the development of the self. Many young people, for example, choose the same occupational field as their parents or adopt the same pop culture preferences as their friends (Sullivan [1953] 1968).

As we grow up, we develop a sense of who people are, how

they fit together, and where we might fit into that map. We take the cues we learn from our significant others and learn how to jump through the necessary hoops to get to where and who we want to be. Mead (1934, 1964a) described that transformation as a three-stage process of self-development: the preparatory stage, the play stage, and the game stage.

The Preparatory Stage During the *preparatory stage,* which lasts until about age three, children merely imitate the people around them, especially family members with whom they continually interact. Thus, a small child will bang on a piece of wood while a parent is engaged in carpentry work or will try to throw a ball if an older sibling is doing so nearby. This imitation is largely mindless— simple parroting of the actions of others.

As they grow older, children begin to realize that we attach meanings to our actions, and they become more adept at using symbols to communicate with others. **Symbols** are the gestures, objects, and words that form the basis of human communication. By interacting with family and friends, as well as by watching cartoons on television and looking at picture books, children in the preparatory stage begin to develop interaction skills they will use throughout their lives. They learn that they can use symbols to get their way, such as saying please and thank you, or perhaps throwing a tantrum in the candy aisle of the local grocery store.

The Play Stage As children develop skill in communicating through symbols, they gradually become more aware of social relationships out of which those symbols grow. During the *play stage*, from about ages three through five, they begin to pretend to be other people: a doctor, parent, superhero, or teacher. Such play need not make a lot of sense or be particularly coherent to adults, and young children are able to move in and out of various characters with ease. For Mead, playing make-believe is more than just fun; it is a critical part of our self-development.

Mead, in fact, noted that an important aspect of the play stage is role playing. **Role taking** is the process of mentally assuming the perspective of another and responding from that imagined viewpoint. Through this process a young child internalizes the performances of other people and gradually learns, for example, when it is best to ask a parent for favours. If the parent usually comes home from work in a bad mood, the child will wait until after dinner, when the parent is more relaxed and approachable.

The Game Stage In Mead's third stage, the *game stage,* the child of about six to nine years of age no longer merely plays roles but now begins to consider several tasks and relationships simultaneously. At this point in development, children grasp not only their own social positions but also those of others around them. The transition from play to game is evident when teaching kids to play team sports such as t-ball or soccer. When they are little, you will often see a clump of kids chasing after a ball or moving up the field together. They have yet to learn that different people play different positions and that they will be more successful as a team if everyone plays the position to which they are assigned. When they do, they can take for granted that someone will be covering a base so they can throw a runner out or that a goalie will be there to make a save if the ball gets behind them. This map of who should be where and who should do what serves as a kind of blueprint for society, and internalizing it represents the final stage of development in Mead's model; the child can now respond to numerous members of the social environment.

> **symbol** A gesture, object, or word that forms the basis of human communication.
>
> **role taking** The process of mentally assuming the perspective of another and responding from that imagined viewpoint.
>
> **generalized other** The attitudes, viewpoints, and expectations of society as a whole that we take into account in our behaviour.

Mead uses the term **generalized other** to refer to the attitudes, viewpoints, and expectations of society as a whole that we take into account in our behaviour. Simply put, this concept suggests that when an individual acts, he or she takes into account an entire group of people. For example, a child will not act courteously merely to please a particular parent. Rather, the child comes to understand that courtesy is a widespread social value endorsed by parents, teachers, and other authority figures.

At the game stage, children can take a more sophisticated view of people and the social environment. They now understand what specific occupations and social positions are and no longer equate Mr. Williams only with the role of "librarian" or Ms. Chen only with "principal." It has become clear to the child that Mr. Williams can be a librarian, a parent, and a marathon runner at the same time and that Ms. Chen is one of many principals in our society. Thus, the child

dramaturgical approach
A view of social interaction in which people are seen as theatrical performers.

has reached a new level of sophistication in observations of individuals and institutions.

Goffman: Presentation of the Self

Given that others play such a powerful role in shaping who we are and how we think about ourselves, the way we represent our self to others becomes a major concern for us and a significant interest to sociologists. Erving Goffman, a Canadian sociologist, provided a helpful model for better understanding how we go about constructing and maintaining our self through interactions with others. He suggested that each of us seeks to convey impressions of who we are to others even as those others are doing the same, creating a kind of performance that we can analyze and understand.

To analyze our everyday social interactions, Goffman offers the **dramaturgical approach,** which studies interaction as if we were all

POPSOC

Momsense

From June Cleaver in the 1950s to Marge Simpson today, TV moms have played with the idea that there are common scripts that mothers use as they perform their role. Comedian Anita Renfroe has taken this a step further. She condensed the things a mom would say in a 24-hour period down to 2 minutes and 35 seconds and set it to the William Tell Overture. A YouTube search on "Momsense" will take you there.

actors on a stage. Our interactions can be better understood, according to Goffman, when viewed as attempts to carry out successful performances, equivalent to putting on a play. As actors, we prepare ourselves *back stage* to perform *front stage*. For instance, we choose appropriate props, including costumes, to make our performance convincing. We practise lines, plan our entrance, get "into character"— all the things we need to do to ensure we put on "a good show." Once front stage, while some improvisation is permissible, too much threatens the credibility of the character we are trying to play, so we largely follow *scripts*. In order to give a successful performance, we also may need other cast members with whom we work as a team. Finally, our performance is carried out before an audience that judges how well we do. Whether in our role as students, restaurant servers, or even lovers, we all know that we have a part to play and that if we don't say the right lines or use the correct

props our performance will be unconvincing, the show will collapse, and our sense of self will be undermined.

Early in life, the individual learns to slant his or her presentation of the self in order to create distinctive appearances and satisfy particular audiences. Goffman (1959) referred to this altering of the presentation of the self as **impression management.** We want others to see us in a positive light, and in order to maximize the possibility of this outcome, we engage in **face-work.** How often do you initiate some kind of face-saving behaviour when you feel embarrassed or rejected? In response to a rejection at a singles' bar, a person may engage in face-work by saying, "There really isn't an interesting person in this entire crowd." Or, if we do poorly on an exam, we may say to a friend who did likewise, "This professor is incompetent." We feel the need to maintain a proper image of the self if we are to continue social interaction.

In some cultures, people engage in elaborate deceptions to avoid losing face. In Japan, for example, where lifetime employment has until recently been the norm, "company men" thrown out of work during a severe economic recession may feign employment, rising as usual in the morning, donning suit and tie, and heading for the business district. But instead of going to the office, they

congregate at places such as Tokyo's Hibiya Library, where they pass the time by reading before returning home at the usual hour. Many of these men are trying to protect family members, who would be shamed if neighbours discovered that the family breadwinner was unemployed. Others are deceiving their wives and families as well (French 2000).

Goffman's work on the self represents a logical progression of sociological studies begun by Cooley and Mead on how personality is acquired through socialization and how we manage the presentation of our self to others. Cooley stressed the process by which we create a self; Mead focused on how the self develops as we learn to interact with others; Goffman emphasized the ways in which we consciously create images of ourselves for others.

PSYCHOLOGICAL APPROACHES TO THE SELF

Psychologists have shared the interest of Cooley, Mead, and other sociologists in the development of the self. Early work in psychology, such as that of Sigmund Freud (1856–1939), stressed the role of inborn drives—among them the drive for sexual gratification—in channelling human behaviour. Later psychologists such as Jean Piaget emphasized the stages through which human beings progress as the self develops.

Like Cooley and Mead, Freud believed that the self is a social product and that aspects of one's personality are influenced by other people (especially one's parents). However, unlike Cooley and Mead, Freud suggested that the self has components that work in opposition to each other. According to Freud, we have a natural instinct that seeks limitless pleasure, but this is at odds with our societal needs for order and constraint. By interacting with others, we learn the expectations

> **impression management** The altering of the presentation of the self in order to create distinctive appearances and satisfy particular audiences.
>
> **face-work** The efforts people make to maintain a proper image and avoid public embarrassment.

of society and then select behaviour most appropriate to our own culture. (Of course, as Freud was well aware, we sometimes distort reality and behave irrationally.)

Through his research on children, including newborns, the Swiss child psychologist Jean Piaget (1896–1980) underscored the importance of social interactions in developing a sense of self. In his well-known **cognitive theory of development,** Piaget (1954) identified four stages in the development of children's thought processes. In the first, or *sensorimotor,* stage, young children use their senses to make discoveries. For example, through touching they discover that their hands are actually a part of themselves. During the second, or *preoperational,* stage, children begin to use words and symbols to distinguish objects and ideas. The milestone in the third, or *concrete operational,* stage is that children engage in more logical thinking. For example, they learn that even when a formless lump of clay is shaped into a snake, it is still the same clay. Finally, in the fourth, or *formal operational,* stage, adolescents become capable of sophisticated abstract thought and can deal with ideas and values in a logical manner.

cognitive theory of development The theory that children's thought progresses through four stages of development.

Piaget suggested that moral development becomes an important part of socialization as children develop the ability to think more abstractly. When children learn the rules of a game such as checkers or jacks, they are learning to obey societal norms. Those under eight years of age display a rather basic level of morality: rules are rules, and there is no concept of "extenuating circumstances." As they mature, children become capable of greater autonomy, and they begin to experience moral dilemmas and doubts as to what constitutes proper behaviour.

According to Piaget, social interaction is the key to development. As children grow older, they pay increasing attention to how other people think and why they act in particular ways. In order to develop a distinct personality, each of us needs opportunities to interact with others. As we saw earlier, Isabelle was deprived of the chance for normal social interactions, and the consequences were severe (Kitchener 1991).

Theory
A Matter of Perspective

THEORETICAL PERSPECTIVES ON THE SELF AND SOCIALIZATION

Functionalist:
- social institutions work together to shape us into competent members of society
- family is key agent of socialization

Conflict:
- social institutions work to produce certain kinds of people; factors such as class, race, and ethnicity affect sense of self and responses from others
- reproduction of status quo power relations through socialization
- not all families are functional, and thus socialization that occurs within may be negative

Feminist:
- socialization promotes behaviours, attitudes, and activities as appropriate along gender lines
- gendered socialization reflects and reinforces social expectations of girls and boys, and women and men

Interactionist:
- sense of self develops through interaction with others
- rest of society—especially significant others—serves as "mirror" for the emergent self

>> Agents of Socialization

The people with whom we interact influence how we think about ourselves and how we represent ourselves to others, and the positions they occupy determine the kind of influence they have. Family, friends, schools, peers, the mass media, the workplace, religion, and the state are among the agents of socialization that play the most powerful roles in shaping the self.

FAMILY

The family is the most important agent of socialization, especially for children. We can see the power of family socialization among the Hutterites. While the Hutterites of western Canada do embrace some modern agricultural and manufacturing technology, they maintain the simple lifestyle of their ancestors. Thus, children in Hutterite communities are raised in a highly structured and disciplined manner, but they are not immune to the temptations posed by their peers in the non-Hutterite world, such as drinking, going to movies, and wearing makeup. Hutterite parents do not become too concerned, as they know the strong influence they exert and indeed, the small number of youth who leave the community usually return.

While the Hutterites provide what seems like an extreme case, the truth is that all families play a powerful role in shaping their children. Although peer groups and the media do influence us, almost all available research shows that the role of the family in socializing a child cannot be overestimated (W. Williams 1998; for a different view see J. Harris 1998). The lifelong process of learning begins shortly after birth. Since newborns can hear, see, smell, and taste, and can feel heat, cold, and pain, they are constantly orienting themselves to the surrounding world. Human beings, especially family members, constitute an important part of their social environment. People minister to the baby's needs by feeding, cleaning, carrying, and comforting her or him. It is in the context of families that we learn to talk, walk, feed ourselves, go to the bathroom, and so on—basic skills that we take for granted as natural but that we learned thanks to our families.

Cultural Influences
As both Cooley and Mead noted, the development of the self is a critical aspect of the early years of one's life. How children develop this sense of self, however, can vary from one society to another.

For example, most parents in Canada do not send six-year-olds to school unsupervised. However, that is the norm in Japan, where parents push their children to commute to school on their own from an early age. In cities like Tokyo, first-graders must learn to negotiate buses, subways, and long walks. To ensure their safety, parents carefully lay out rules: never talk to strangers; check with a station attendant if you get off at the wrong stop; stay on to the end of the line, then call, if you miss your stop; take stairs, not escalators; don't fall asleep. Some parents equip the children with cell phones or pagers. One parent acknowledges that she worries, "but after they are 6, children are supposed to start being independent from the mother. If you're still taking your child to school after the first month, everyone looks at you funny" (Tolbert 2000:17).

Family structures also reproduce themselves through socialization. In the contexts of families, children learn expectations regarding relationships (including marriage) and parenthood. Children observe their parents expressing affection, dealing with finances, quarrelling, complaining about in-laws, and so forth. Their learning represents an informal process of anticipatory socialization in which they develop a tentative model of what being in a domestic relationship and being a parent are like.

While we consider the family's role in socialization, we need to remember, however, that children are not simply robots that we can program as we wish. They do not play a passive role in their socialization. As Mead's "I" implies, they choose, sometimes to the consternation of their parents, and in so doing are active participants in their self-creation. Through the choices they make, they influence and alter the families, schools, and communities of which they are a part.

The Impact of Race and Gender
In Canada, social development includes exposure to cultural assumptions regarding gender and race. From a very young age, children are exposed to images and messages promoted by the dominant culture, images that portray certain groups favourably and others in less positive ways, or not at all. Books, toys, and television shows have been criticized for their lack of cultural and social diversity and for perpetuating stereotypical images of gender, race, and ethnicity.

The term **gender roles** refers to expectations regarding the proper behaviour, attitudes, and activities of males and females. For example, we traditionally think of "toughness" as masculine—and desirable only in men—while we view "tenderness" as feminine. As the primary agents of childhood socialization, parents play a critical role in guiding children into those gender roles deemed appropriate in a society.

Other adults, older siblings, the mass media, and religious and educational institutions also have a noticeable impact on a child's socialization into feminine and masculine norms. A culture or subculture may require that one sex or the other take primary responsibility for the socialization of children, economic support of the family, or religious or intellectual leadership. In some societies girls are socialized mainly by their mothers and boys by their fathers—an arrangement that may prevent girls from learning critical survival skills. In South Asia, for example, fathers teach their sons to swim to prepare them for a life as fishermen; girls typically do not learn to swim. When the deadly tsunami hit the coast of South Asia in 2004, many more men than women survived. The impact of race and gender varies among families, social settings, cultures, and countries. As we will see in Chapter 12, not all cultures embrace the restrictive understandings of gender common to North America. The effects of race

gender role Expectations regarding the proper behaviour, attitudes, and activities of males and females.

and ethnicity are also differentially experienced, as will be discussed in Chapter 13.

SCHOOL

In school we typically move beyond the more sheltered confines of our family and learn to become members of the larger social groups to which we belong. Schools teach us the taken-for-granted knowledge of the broader society—not only basic skills such as reading, writing, and arithmetic, but also shared *cultural* knowledge such as the national anthem, our first Prime Minister, and principles of good character. Like the family, schools have an explicit mandate to socialize people in Canada—especially children—into the norms and values of Canadian culture.

Schools teach children the values and customs of the larger society because that shared culture provides the glue that holds us together as a society. If we did not transmit our knowledge and skills from one generation to the next, society would collapse. The knowledge we gain there, however, goes beyond just the official curriculum to include the more informal lessons we learn on the playground. We do learn the facts and figures of history, science, reading, math, and more, but we also learn how to stand up for ourselves when our parents or teachers are not there to hover over us or to bail us out. In other words, we are socialized to become competent citizens.

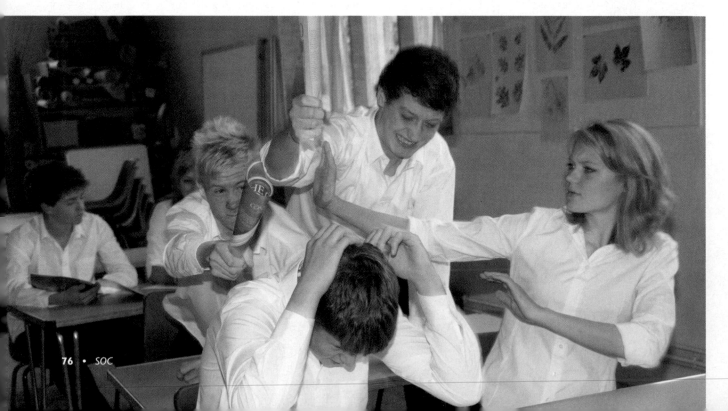

In addition to providing social order, schools open doors for us as individuals. We are exposed to new ways of thinking and acting that allow us to make new choices about our future. While this can include training for careers that allow us to "get ahead," it also involves exposure to new cultures, ideas, practices, and possibilities. It might even lead us to an unexpected future such as a career in sociology!

While schools provide both social order and individual opportunity, they can also reinforce existing inequality through the ways students are socialized. As economists Samuel Bowles and Herbert Gintis (1976) have observed, schools produce teachable students who become manageable workers. They argue that schools have less to do with transmitting academic content than with socializing students into the proper attitudes and behaviours of the workplace. Schools teach students how to work for rewards, how to work in teams, how to meet deadlines, how to take responsibility for a task or work product, how to comply with instructions, and so on. The students who internalize these skills best are rewarded with opportunities in the workplace while others are left behind.

These differential outcomes are compounded by the fact that your position when you enter school shapes where you end up. For example, higher education is expensive in Canada, despite the existence of bursaries, financial aid programs, and government loans. Students from affluent backgrounds therefore have an advantage in gaining access to universities and professional training. At the same time, less affluent young people may never receive the preparation that would qualify them for the best-paying and most prestigious jobs.

PEER GROUPS

While families and schools do shape us, if you ask any 13-year-old who matters most in his or her life, the likely answer is "friends." As children grow older, the family becomes somewhat less important in social development. Instead, peer groups increasingly assume the role of Mead's significant other. Within the peer group, young people associate with others who are approximately their own age and who often enjoy a similar social status (Giordano 2003).

In the context of peer groups, a hierarchy often develops. Sociologists Patricia and Peter Adler conducted participant observation at elementary schools to investigate how popularity works amongst students in grades 4 to 6. They found that, even this early, a pecking order is established ranging from the "popular clique" at the top that includes the "cool kids" on down to what they call the "social isolates" at the bottom, whom other kids sometimes call "dweebs" or "nerds" (Adler and Adler, 1996). Children get the message about where they fit and how they should behave. Sociologist Murray Milner, Jr. found similar status patterns in his examination of teenage culture in high schools, clearly delineated in the title of his book: *Freaks, Geeks, and Cool Kids* (2006).

In other research the Adlers also found that popularity reinforces gender stereotypes. To be popular as a boy is to be athletic, tough, and not too academic. To be popular as a girl is to be attractive, to be able to manipulate others using social skills, and to come from a family wealthy enough to permit shopping for the latest cool stuff (Adler, Kless, and Adler 1992). In similar research, college students were asked to reflect back on what made people popular in high school. Researchers found that male and female students named many of the same paths to popularity—such as physical attractiveness, participation in sports, and grades/intelligence—but gave them different orders of importance. While neither men nor women named sexual activity, drug use, or alcohol use as one of the top five paths, college

High School Popularity

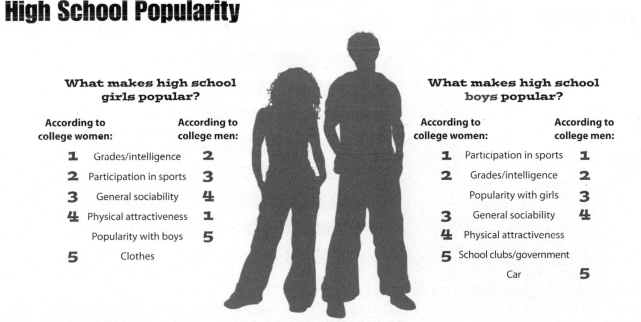

What makes high school girls popular?

According to college women:		According to college men:
1	Grades/intelligence	**2**
2	Participation in sports	**3**
3	General sociability	**4**
4	Physical attractiveness	**1**
	Popularity with boys	**5**
5	Clothes	

What makes high school boys popular?

According to college women:		According to college men:
1	Participation in sports	**1**
2	Grades/intelligence	**2**
	Popularity with girls	**3**
3	General sociability	**4**
4	Physical attractiveness	
5	School clubs/government	
	Car	**5**

Source: Suitor et al. 2001:445.

men were much more likely than women to mention those behaviours as a means to becoming popular, for both boys and girls (Suitor et al. 2001).

Though we value the importance of kids establishing themselves as individuals, the irony is that peer culture is not very individualistic. Children, and especially adolescents, run in packs and look, talk, and act alike (often in the name of individualism). Of course, although parents often lecture their kids about not giving in to peer pressure, they don't really mean it. What they mean is to not give in to the *wrong kinds* of peer pressure. They love peer pressure if it makes their children more like the "good kids" or, even better, if the form of social pressure they give in to is parental pressure.

MASS MEDIA AND TECHNOLOGY

In the past 80 or so years, media innovations—radio, motion pictures, recorded music, television, and the Internet—have become important agents of socialization of North Americans. One U.S. survey indicates that 68 percent of children have a television in their bedroom, and nearly half of all youths ages 8–18 use the Internet every day (see "How Young People Use the Media" below). While television watching among Canadian teenagers has declined in recent years, Internet use in households with children under the age of 18 has risen to over 80 percent (Statistics Canada 2006b). We are spending more and more of our time interacting with technology, which has an inevitable impact on our interactions with each other.

Did You Know?

. . . Canadians watch an average of just over 21 hours of television per week.

Television programs and even commercials can introduce young people to unfamiliar lifestyles and cultures, not only in regards to other nations, but differences within our own country as well. For instance, children who live in

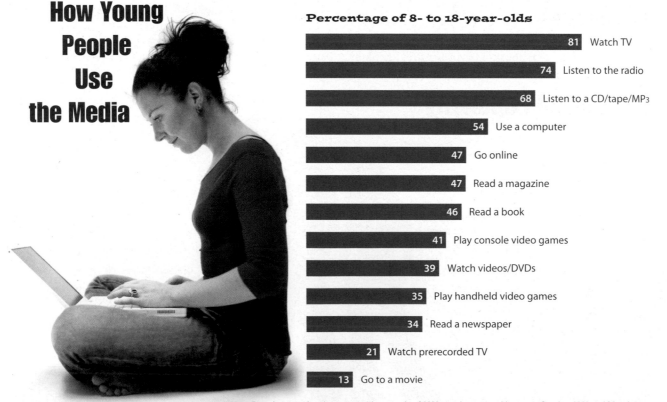

How Young People Use the Media

Percentage of 8- to 18-year-olds

81	Watch TV
74	Listen to the radio
68	Listen to a CD/tape/MP3
54	Use a computer
47	Go online
47	Read a magazine
46	Read a book
41	Play console video games
39	Watch videos/DVDs
35	Play handheld video games
34	Read a newspaper
21	Watch prerecorded TV
13	Go to a movie

Note: Based on a national representative sample of 2032 people surveyed between October 2003 and March 2004.
Source: Rideout et al. 2005:7.

cities learn about the rural life in Canada, and farm children are exposed to the urban experience.

New technologies are changing how we interact with family, friends, and even strangers. Through email, cell phones, texting, and instant messaging, we can maintain close, almost constant, connections with family and friends both near and far. Through Facebook and MySpace, we can establish and extend networks with "friends" both known and unknown. But new technologies can also lead to *narrowcasting*, in which we interact mainly with people who are most like ourselves. This can limit the number of significant relationships we have with people with whom we might share fundamental differences, thus weakening our conflict resolution skills. Other skills, however, may be strengthened. Researchers studying technology use among families in northern California's Silicon Valley (a technology corridor) found that families are socialized into multitasking (doing more than one task at a time) as the social norm; devoting one's full attention to one task—even eating or driving—is less and less common on a typical day (Silicon Valley Cultures Project 2004).

Not just in Silicon Valley but in Africa and other developing areas people have been socialized into relying on new communications technologies. For instance, not long ago, if Zadhe Iyombe wanted to talk to his mother, he had to make an eight-day trip from the capital city of Kinshasa (in the Democratic Republic of the Congo) up the Congo River by boat to the rural town where he was born. Now both he and his mother have access to a cell phone, and they send text messages to each other daily. And Iyombe and his mother are not atypical.

Although cell phones are not inexpensive, 1.4 billion owners in developing countries have come to consider them a necessity. Today, there are more cell phones in developing countries than in industrial nations—the first time in history that developing countries have outpaced the developed world in the adoption of a telecommunications technology (K. Sullivan 2006).

Access to media can increase social cohesion by presenting a common, more or less standardized view of culture through mass communication. Sociologist Robert Park (1922) studied how newspapers helped immigrants to the United States adjust to their environment by changing their customary habits and teaching them the values and views of people in their new home country. Unquestionably, the mass media play a significant role in providing a collective experience for members of society. Think about how the mass media bring together members of a community or even a nation by broadcasting important events and ceremonics (such as elections, press conferences, parades, state funerals, and the Olympics) and by covering disasters.

SOCthink

> > > To what extent does multitasking have a negative impact on our interpersonal skills? How do you feel when people do this to you? Why might you have done it to others?

Radio, television, and telephone have been important means by which people have stayed connected and bonded over events—for instance, many Canadians can remember watching or listening to the "shot heard around the world," Paul Henderson's goal in the 1972 Canada-Russia hockey series. Today, the Internet plays an increasingly prominent role in the communication of   news, as well as communication among people.

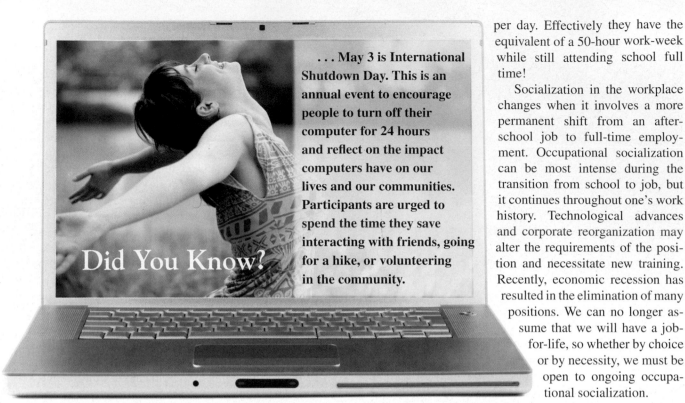

... May 3 is International Shutdown Day. This is an annual event to encourage people to turn off their computer for 24 hours and reflect on the impact computers have on our lives and our communities. Participants are urged to spend the time they save interacting with friends, going for a hike, or volunteering in the community.

per day. Effectively they have the equivalent of a 50-hour work-week while still attending school full time!

Socialization in the workplace changes when it involves a more permanent shift from an after-school job to full-time employment. Occupational socialization can be most intense during the transition from school to job, but it continues throughout one's work history. Technological advances and corporate reorganization may alter the requirements of the position and necessitate new training. Recently, economic recession has resulted in the elimination of many positions. We can no longer assume that we will have a job-for-life, so whether by choice or by necessity, we must be open to ongoing occupational socialization.

As a library director noted, "The Internet has become for many the public commons, a place where they can come together and talk" (D. L. Miller and Darlington 2002; Mirapaul 2001:E2; Rainie 2001).

THE WORKPLACE

Learning to behave appropriately in an occupation is a fundamental aspect of human socialization. In Canada, working full time confirms adult status; it indicates that one has passed out of adolescence. In a sense, socialization into an occupation can represent both a harsh reality ("I have to work in order to buy food and pay the rent") and the realization of an ambition ("I've always wanted to be an airline pilot") (W. Moore 1968:862).

It used to be that our work life began with the end of our formal schooling, but that is no longer necessarily the case, at least not in Canada. More and more young people work today, and not just for a parent or relative.

Some observers feel that the increasing number of teenagers who are working earlier in life and for longer hours are finding the workplace to be almost as important an agent of socialization as school. In fact, a number of educators complain that time spent at work is adversely affecting students' schoolwork. Time-use data from the 2005 General Social Survey revealed that on average over a week, Canadian teenagers perform 7.1 hours of unpaid and paid labour

RELIGION AND THE STATE

Increasingly, social scientists are recognizing the growing importance of government ("the state") and the continued significance of religion as agents of socialization. Traditionally, family members served as the primary caregivers in Canada, but in the 20th century, with the expansion of the welfare state, the family's protective function was

Child Care Arrangements for Preschoolers

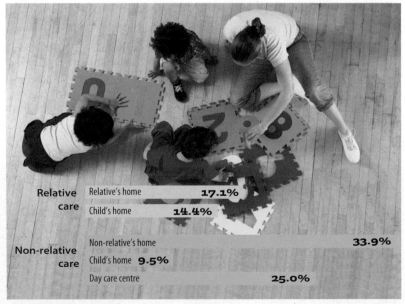

Relative care	Relative's home	17.1%
	Child's home	14.4%
Non-relative care	Non-relative's home	33.9%
	Child's home	9.5%
	Day care centre	25.0%

Source: Statistics Canada 2006g.

steadily transferred to outside agencies such as public schools, hospitals, mental health clinics, and child care centres, many of which receive at least some federal or provincial funding, and are regulated by the state. Historically, religious groups also provided such care and protection. Despite early sociological predictions that religion would cease to play a substantial role in modern society, these groups continue to provide private schools, hospitals, day care facilities, nursing homes, and more. The importance of religion to contemporary society will be discussed further in Chapter 8.

Preschool children in particular are often cared for by someone other than a parent. Eighty-five percent of children aged six months to five years living with a single parent who is working or in school are in some form of child care. In the years 2002 and 2003, more than half (54 percent) of Canadian children in this age group were in some form of child care. As illustrated in the "Child Care Arrangements for Preschoolers" figure on the previous page, a significant proportion of children are in home-based care (Statistics Canada 2006g).

Both government and organized religion act to provide markers representing significant life course transitions. For example, religious organizations continue to celebrate

Muslim men at prayer.

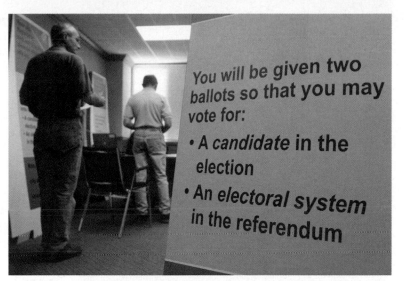

You will be given two ballots so that you may vote for:
• A *candidate* in the election
• An *electoral system* in the referendum

Canadians aged 19–25 have the lowest voter turnout in the country, with less than 25 percent of eligible voters having done so in recent elections (Elections Canada 2007).

meaningful ritual events—such as baptism, bismillah, or bar/bat mitzvah—that often bring together all the members of an extended family, even if they never meet for any other reason. Government regulations stipulate the ages at which a person may drive a car, drink alcohol, vote in elections, marry without parental permission, work overtime, and retire. While these regulations do not constitute strict rites of passage—many 19-year-olds choose not to vote, and most people choose their age of retirement without reference to government dictates—they do symbolize the fact that we have moved on to a different stage of our life, with different expectations regarding our behaviour.

>> Socialization Throughout the Life Course

Adolescents among the Kota people of the Congo in Africa paint themselves blue. Cuban American girls go on a daylong religious retreat before dancing the night away. These are all **rites of passage**— symbolic representations of significant transitions that serve as a means of dramatizing and validating changes in a person's status.

> **rite of passage** A ritual marking the symbolic transition from one social position to another.

In the Kota rite the colour blue—the colour of death—symbolizes the death of childhood and the passage to adulthood. For adolescent girls in Miami's Cuban American community, the *quinceañera* ceremony celebrating the attainment of womanhood at age 15 supports a network of party planners, caterers, dress designers, and the Miss Quinceañera Latina pageant. For thousands of years, Egyptian mothers have welcomed their newborns to the world in the Soboa ceremony by stepping over the seven-

Body painting is a ritual marking the passage to puberty in some cultures.

or four years later. Interestingly, the significance of these markers has declined, with only about one-third of survey respondents identifying marriage and less than one-third identifying parenthood as important markers representing adulthood (S. Furstenberg et al. 2004; Smith 2003).

One result of these staggered steps to independence is that in Canada and the United States, unlike some other societies, there is no clear dividing line between adolescence and adulthood. Nowadays, the number of years between childhood and adulthood has grown, and few young people finish school, get married, and leave home at about the same age, clearly establishing their transition to adulthood. The term *youthhood* has been coined to describe the prolonged ambiguous status that young people in their twenties experience (Côté 2000).

ANTICIPATORY SOCIALIZATION AND RESOCIALIZATION

In our journey through our lives, we seek to prepare ourselves for what is coming and to adapt to change as necessary. To prepare, we undergo **anticipatory socialization,**

day-old infant seven times. And some North American students celebrate their graduation from university by tossing their hats in the air.

THE LIFE COURSE

Such specific ceremonies mark stages of development in the life course. They indicate that the process of socialization continues through all stages of the life cycle. In fact, some researchers have chosen to concentrate on socialization as a lifelong process. Sociologists and other social scientists who take such a **life course approach** look closely at the social factors, including gender and income, that influence people throughout their lives, from birth to death. They recognize that biological changes help shape but do not dictate human behaviour.

In the transition from childhood to adulthood, we can identify certain markers that signify the passage from one life stage to the next. These markers vary from one society and even one generation to the next. According to one U.S. survey, completion of formal schooling has risen to the top, with 90 percent of people identifying it as an important rite of passage. On average, Americans expect this marker to be attained by a person's 23rd birthday. Other major events in the life course, such as getting married or becoming a parent, are expected to follow three

life course approach A research orientation in which sociologists and other social scientists look closely at the social factors that influence people throughout their lives, from birth to death.

anticipatory socialization Processes of socialization in which a person "rehearses" for future positions, occupations, and social relationships.

Milestones in the Transition to Adulthood

Expected Age	Life Event	Percentage who view event as extremely/quite important
20.9	Financial independence from parents/gaurdians	80.9%
21.1	Separate residence from parents	57.2%
21.2	Full-time employment	83.8%
22.3	Completion of formal schooling	90.2%
24.5	Capability of supporting family	82.3%
25.7	Marriage	33.2%
26.2	Parenthood	29.0%

Note: Based on the 2002 U.S. General Social Survey of 1398 people.
Source: Smith 2003.

which refers to processes of socialization in which a person "rehearses" for future positions, occupations, and social relationships. A culture can function more efficiently and smoothly if members become acquainted with the norms, values, and behaviour associated with a social position before actually assuming that status. Preparation for many aspects of adult life begins with anticipatory socialization during childhood and adolescence and continues throughout our lives as we prepare for new responsibilities.

High school students experience a bit of anticipatory socialization when they prepare for college or university. They begin to imagine what post-secondary life will be like and what kind of person they will be when they get there. They may seek out information from friends and family in order

SOCthink

> > > What are some of the markers of youth-hood? When does it begin? When does it end? To what extent do you feel like an adult? What characteristics of our society contribute to ambiguity in our passage into adulthood?

to get a better sense of what to expect, but increasingly, they also rely on campus websites and Facebook entries. To assist in this process and to attract more students, colleges and universities are investing more time and money in websites through which students can take "virtual" campus tours, listen to podcasts, and stream videos of everything from campus events to a sample biology lecture.

Occasionally, assuming a new social or occupational position requires that we *unlearn* an established orientation. **Resocialization** refers to the process of discarding old behaviour patterns and accepting new ones as part of a life transition. Often resocialization results from explicit efforts to transform an individual, as happens in reform schools, therapy groups, prisons, religious conversion settings, and political indoctrination camps. The process of resocialization typically involves considerable stress for the individual—much more so than socialization in general, or even anticipatory socialization (Gecas 1992).

Resocialization is particularly effective when it occurs within a total institution. Erving Goffman (1961) coined the term **total institution** to refer to an institution that regulates all aspects of a person's life under a single authority. Examples can be more or less extreme, from summer camp or

Life in prison is highly regulated—even at recreation time.

boarding school to prison, the military, a mental hospital, or a convent. Because the total institution is generally cut off from the rest of society, it provides for all the needs of its members. In its extreme form, so elaborate are its requirements, and so all-encompassing its activities, that the total institution represents a miniature society.

Goffman (1961) identified several common traits of total institutions:

- All aspects of life are conducted in the same place under the control of a single authority.
- Any activities within the institution are conducted in the company of others in the same circumstances—for example, army recruits or novices in a convent.
- The authorities devise rules and schedule activities without consulting the participants.
- All aspects of life within a total institution are designed to fulfill the purpose of the organization. Thus, all activities in a monastery might be centred on prayer and communion with God (Davies 1989; P. Rose et al. 1979).

People often lose their individuality within total institutions. For example, a person entering prison may experience the humiliation of a **degradation ceremony** as he or she is stripped of clothing, jewellery, and other personal possessions. From that point on, scheduled daily routines allow for little or no personal initiative. The individual becomes secondary and rather invisible in the overbearing social environment (Garfinkel 1956).

resocialization The process of discarding former behaviour patterns and accepting new ones as part of a transition in one's life.

total institution An institution that regulates all aspects of a person's life under a single authority, such as a prison, the military, a mental hospital, or a convent.

degradation ceremony An aspect of the socialization process within some total institutions, in which people are subjected to humiliating rituals.

ROLE TRANSITIONS DURING THE LIFE COURSE

As we have seen, one of the key transitional stages we pass through occurs as we enter the adult world, perhaps by moving out of the parental home, beginning a career, or entering a marriage. As we age, we move into the midlife

transition, which typically begins at about age 40. Men and women often experience a stressful period of self-evaluation, commonly known as the **midlife crisis,** in which they realize that they have not achieved basic goals and ambitions and may feel they have little time left to do so. Psychologist Daniel Levinson (1978, 1996) found that most adults surveyed experienced tumultuous midlife conflicts within the self and with the external world. Compounding such stresses that are often associated with one's career or partner is the growing responsibility for caring for two generations at once.

5 Movies on SOCIALIZATION

Nell
A woman who grew up in isolation is brought into civilization by a sociologist.

Great Expectations
A poor, lower-class boy is introduced to high society.

Witness
A man is introduced and integrated into Amish culture while trying to protect a young witness to a murder.

Hannibal
A sociopathic cannibal lacks social skills.

The Last King of Scotland
A Scottish man is introduced to the horrors of authoritarian-ruled Uganda.

During the late 1990s, social scientists focused on the **sandwich generation**—adults who simultaneously try to meet the competing needs of their parents and their children. Their caregiving goes in two directions: to children, who even as young adults may still require significant support and direction, and to aging parents, whose health and economic problems may demand intervention by their adult children.

midlife crisis A stressful period of self-evaluation that begins at about age 40.

sandwich generation The generation of adults who simultaneously try to meet the competing needs of their parents and their children.

Like the role of caring for children, that of caring for aging parents falls disproportionately on women. Overall, women provide 60 percent of the care their parents receive, and even more as the demands of the role grow more intense

and time consuming. Increasingly, middle-aged women and younger are finding themselves on the "daughter track," as their time and attention are diverted by the needs of their aging mothers and fathers (Gross 2005).

ADJUSTING TO RETIREMENT

The last major transition identified by Levinson occurs after age 60—sometimes well after that age, due to advances in health care, greater longevity, and gradual acceptance by society of older people. In fact, yesterday's 60 may be today's 70 or even 75. Nonetheless, at some point, people transition to a different lifestyle.

Retirement is a rite of passage that marks a critical transition from one phase of a person's life to another. Typically, symbolic events are associated with this rite of passage, such as retirement gifts, a retirement party, and special moments on the last day on the job. The preretirement period itself can be emotionally charged, especially if the retiree is expected to train his or her successor (Atchley 1976).

Recent research has revealed that Canadians in their late 40s and early 50s are pushing back their retirement plans, anticipating staying in the workforce longer than they initially expected. People approaching retirement age are expressing uncertainty about their retirement plans, a trend particularly evident among immigrants to Canada (Schellenberg and Ostrovsky 2007). A variety of factors may explain these patterns, including downturns in the economy, the elimination of mandatory retirement, and workers' concerns with maintaining their benefits.

Gerontologist Robert Atchley (1976) has identified several phases of the retirement experience:

- *Preretirement,* a period of anticipatory socialization as the person prepares for retirement.
- *The near phase,* when the person establishes a specific departure date from his or her job.
- *The honeymoon phase,* an often euphoric period in which the person pursues activities that he or she never had time for before.
- *The disenchantment phase,* in which retirees feel a sense of letdown or even depression as they cope with their new lives, which may include illness or poverty.
- *The reorientation phase,* which involves the development of a more realistic view of retirement alternatives.
- *The stability phase,* in which the person has learned to deal with life after retirement in a reasonable and comfortable fashion.
- *The termination phase,* which begins when the person can no longer engage in basic, day-to-day activities such as self-care and housework.

Retirement is not a single transition, then, but a series of adjustments that varies from one person to another. The length and timing of each phase will differ for each

Average Effective Age of Retirement vs the Official Age, 2002–2007[a, b]

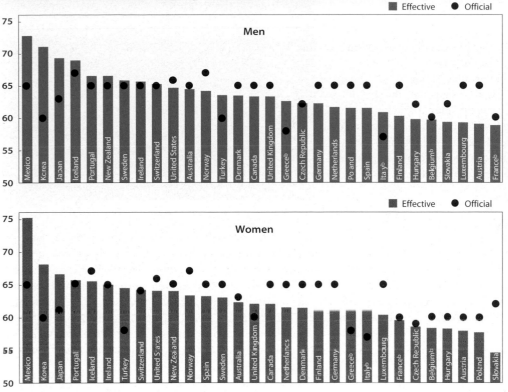

■ Effective ● Official

Men

(bar chart, vertical axis 50–75)
Mexico, Korea, Japan, Iceland, Portugal, New Zealand, Sweden, Ireland, Switzerland, United States, Australia, Norway, Turkey, Denmark, Canada, United Kingdom, Greece[b], Czech Republic, Germany, Netherlands, Po and, Spain, Italy[b], Finland, Hungary, Belgium[b], Slovakia, Luxembourg, Austria, France[b]

■ Effective ● Official

Women

(bar chart, vertical axis 50–75)
Mexico, Korea, Japan, Portugal, Iceland, Ireland, Turkey, Switzerland, United States, New Zea and, Norway, Spain, Sweden, Australia, United Kingdom, Carada, Netherlancs, Denmark, Finland, Germany, Greece[b], Italy[b], Luxembourg, France[b], Czech Republic, Belgium[b], Hungary, Austria, Poland, Slovakia

a) The average effective age of retirement is defined as the average age of exit from the labour force during a five-year period. Labour force (net) exits are estimated by taking the difference in the participation rate for each five-year age group (40 and over) at the beginning of the period and the rate for the corresponding age group aged five-years older at the end of the period. The official age corresponds to the age at which a pension can be received irrespective of whether a worker has a long insurance record of years of contributions.

b) For Belgium and France, workers can retire at age 60 with 40 years of contributions; for Greece, at age 58 with 35 years of contributions; and for Italy, at 57 (56 for manual workers) with 35 years of contributions

Source: OECD estimates derived from the European and national labour force surveys.

Retirement Expectations

Other/don't know **4%**

Retire from your current job but work full-time doing something else **7%**

Not work at all **20%**

Start your own business/go into business for yourself **15%**

Work part-time mainly for interest or enjoyment **30%**

Work part-time mainly for needed income it provides **25%**

Note: Survey of the baby boom generation (people born from 1946 to 1964) conducted in 2003.

Source: Baby Boomers Envision Retirement II: Survey of Baby Boomers' Expectations for Retirement. AARP 2004.

individual, depending on such factors as financial and health status. In fact, a person will not necessarily go through all the phases identified by Atchley. For example, people who are forced to retire or who face financial difficulties may never experience a honeymoon phase. And many retirees continue to be part of the paid labour force of Canada, often taking part-time jobs to supplement their pensions. That is certainly the expectation of baby boomers, as fully 79 percent expect to work in some capacity after they retire (see "Retirement Expectations" to the left).

Like other aspects of life in Canada, the experience of retirement varies according to gender, race, ethnicity, and socioeconomic class. White males are most likely to benefit from retirement wages, as well as to have participated in a formal retirement preparation program. In contrast, members of visible minority groups are more likely to exit the paid labour force through disability or unemployment than through retirement. The nature of one's work, the income earned, and the occupational status reached all impact retirement pensions and thus one's ability to leave the workforce. (These issues are explored further in Chapter 10.) It must also be remembered that throughout their lives, women have primary responsibility for *unpaid* domestic work, so for many, "retirement" is only an analytical distinction.

We encounter some of the most difficult socialization challenges (and rites of passage) in these later years of life. Retirement undermines the sense of self we had that was based in our occupation, a particularly significant source of identity in Canada. Similarly, taking stock of our accomplishments and disappointments, coping with declining physical abilities, and recognizing the inevitability of death may lead to painful adjustments. Part of the difficulty is that potential answers to the "Now what?" question that we might have asked in previous life stages are dwindling, and we begin to face the end of our days.

And yet, as we reflect on the story of our lives, we can look back to see all the people who shaped us into becoming who we are. Such relationships play a crucial role in our overall self-concept and self-satisfaction. As we have already seen, we are interdependent. And, though the influences of others on our life can be both a blessing and a curse, we wouldn't be who we are without them.

>> Summary

We tend to take for granted "who we are," that is, we assume the self to be inherent, but in fact we *become* ourselves through socialization. Socialization is an ongoing process; the self is developed and changed throughout the life course. Our families, our friends, our schools, and our jobs all contribute to our social identity, and help us to become competent members of society. Although we may be subject to many of the same influences, socialization is not the same for everyone. Girls and boys (and subsequently women and men) have very different expectations placed upon them. As well, tensions may arise between the norms and values of members of particular ethnic groups and those of the larger society. While we may identify agents of socialization and steps through the life course, this is not a straightforward path; we must navigate many twists and turns and new directions.

For REVIEW

I. How do we become our self?
  • While we are born with innate tendencies, we depend upon the socializing influences of others with whom we interact to provide us with the cultural tools necessary for our survival.

II. Who shapes our socialization?
  • While almost anyone with whom we interact can have a significant influence on us, particularly important to our development are the family, school, peer group, mass media, religion, and the state.

III. How does our development change over time?
  • We learn new things at various stages of our life course, experiencing significant transitions as we pass from childhood to adulthood and again from adulthood into retirement. At each stage, the kinds of things expected of us by others shift significantly.

Thinking CRITICALLY...

1. To what extent does body image play a role in your sense of self? What agents of socialization (the media, your peers, your parents?) have the greatest influence upon how you feel about yourself?
2. Why have gendered stereotypes remained intact, despite the gains women have made in Canadian society?
3. Imagine you have a job interview. Explain your preparation and performance using Goffman's dramaturgical approach.

Pop Quiz

1. Which of the following social scientists used the phrase *looking-glass self* to emphasize that the self is the product of our social interactions with other people?
   a. George Herbert Mead
   b. Charles Horton Cooley
   c. Erving Goffman
   d. Jean Piaget

2. In what he called the *play stage* of socialization, George Herbert Mead asserted that people mentally assume the perspectives of others, thereby enabling them to respond from that imagined viewpoint. This process is referred to as
   a. role taking.
   b. the generalized other.
   c. the significant other.
   d. impression management.

3. George Herbert Mead is best known for his theory of what?
   a. presentation of the self
   b. cognitive development
   c. the self
   d. impression management

4. Suppose a clerk tries to appear busier than he or she actually is when a supervisor happens to be watching. Erving Goffman would say this is a form of what?
   a. degradation ceremony
   b. impression management
   c. resocialization
   d. looking-glass self

5. Which sociological perspective takes a critical view of socialization, arguing that it reproduces existing power relations?
   a. feminist
   b. conflict
   c. interactionist
   d. functionalist

6. Upon arriving at the federal penitentiary, an inmate is showered, subjected to a body cavity search, given prison-issue clothing, and assigned a shared cell that affords him no privacy from the other prisoners or the guards. All these humiliating procedures are part of
   a. impression management
   b. face-work
   c. a degradation ceremony
   d. the life course

7. Which social institution is considered to be the most important agent of socialization in Canada, especially for children?
   a. the family
   b. the school
   c. the peer group
   d. the mass media

8. The term *gender role* refers to
   a. the biological fact that we are male or female.
   b. a role that is given to us by a teacher.
   c. a role that is given to us in a play.
   d. expectations regarding the proper behaviour, attitudes, and activities of males and females.

9. Which of the following statements about peer groups is *not* true?
   a. Peer groups have become less significant in Canadian culture.
   b. Peers can be the source of harassment as well as support.
   c. Peer groups increasingly assume the role of Mead's generalized other.
   d. Boys and girls are socialized differently.

10. The process of discarding former behaviour patterns and taking on new ones is known as what?
    a. resocialization
    b. impression management
    c. anticipatory socialization
    d. the I

1. (b); 2. (a); 3. (c); 4. (b); 5. (b); 6. (c); 7. (a); 8. (d); 9. (a); 10. (a)

5

SOCIAL

BECOMING AN INDIVIDUAL IN SOCIETY

"Tattooing had really never entered my awareness very much. When it did, the associations were always with sailors first, ex-convicts second, and various toughs and gangsters last. . . . I had read in some obscure novel about the three signs of 'badness'—socks rolled down to the ankle, long sideburns, and a tattoo showing on the wrist. Robert Mitchum's demented killer had *Love* and *Hate* tattooed on the fingers of each hand." So writes Samuel M. Steward (1990:8) of his perception of tattoos back in the 1950s, a perception widely shared by others at the time. Steward had been a college professor for 20 years, but he decided to walk away from that to become a tattoo artist. You might say he was ahead of his time.

Times change, and so do we. Nowadays almost 40 percent of people 18–40 years old have at least one tattoo. So many people have them—including society's trendsetters and major sports figures—that mainstream culture accepts tattoos. Yet, for those who grew up in an earlier era, perhaps the stigma remains: Only 10 percent of people aged 41–64 have tattoos.

In fact, knowing a person's age allows us to predict a variety of things about how they think and what they do. Research on what has been called "Generation Next," which includes people born between 1981 and 1988, finds them less cynical about government and political leaders, less critical of business, and more tolerant on issues of immigration, race, and homosexuality than those from earlier generations. When it comes to technology, they were actually less likely to have sent or received an email within the past 24 hours than those ages 26–40. However, just over half had sent or received a text message making them twice as likely to have done so (Kohut 2007a).

While we like to think of our preferences as a matter of our own individual choice, the age into which we are born shapes our tastes. Like age, our gender, race, class, ethnicity, nationality, education, religious affiliation, occupation, and income all shape how we think, what we do, and even how we feel. Sociology investigates how those positions combine to form our social structure.

STRUCTURE &INTERACTION

>>
- What makes up society?
- How does social structure shape individual action?
- How do sociologists describe traditional versus modern societies?

>> Social Interaction

When we create culture, we establish a relationship with each other and to the external world. The more we share culture with others, the more resistant it becomes to change, because change would involve getting all the people who now share that culture to think and act in new ways. Because shared culture tends to remain stable, over time we come to take certain cultural expectations for granted. In so doing, we construct the context or social environment within which we live. The result is society—the structure of relationships within which culture is created and shared through regularized patterns of social interaction.

social interaction The ways in which people respond to one another.

Sociologists use the term **social interaction** to refer to the ways in which people respond to one another, whether face-to-face, over the telephone, or on the computer. It is through interaction that society comes alive. To use an analogy, think of society as a board game. The various components of the game—the board, game pieces, dice, rules, and so on—provide the structure of the game, but it is not truly a game until someone plays it. Society, too, must be enacted, embodied, and brought to life by individuals interacting.

How we interact with other people is shaped by our perception of their position relative to our own. According to sociologist Herbert Blumer (1969:79), the distinctive characteristic of social interaction is that "human beings interpret or 'define' each other's actions instead of merely reacting to each other's actions." In other words, our response to someone's behaviour is based on the meaning we attach to his or her actions. Our perceptions, evaluations, and definitions shape our reality. The meanings we ascribe to others' actions typically reflect the norms and values of the dominant culture and our socialization experiences within that culture. Our understanding of social reality is literally constructed from our social interactions (Berger and Luckmann 1966).

The ability to define social reality reflects a group's power within a society. In fact, one of the crucial aspects of the relationship between dominant and subordinate groups is the ability of the former to define a society's values. Sociologist William I. Thomas (1923), an early critic of theories of racial and gender differences, recognized that the "definition of the situation" could mould the thinking and personality of the individual. Thomas observed that people respond not only to the objective features of a person or situation but also to the meaning that person or situation has for them.

Changing the meanings we attach to the positions people occupy often involves a struggle because those who wield power and influence in a society are reluctant to relinquish their positions of control. Beginning with the struggle of women in the early 20th century to be recognized as persons under the law, and their ongoing fight for fair treatment in society, through the civil rights movement of the 1950s and 1960s, to more recent advocacy by the elderly, people with disabilities, and gay, lesbian, and transgendered people, an important aspect of the process of social change has involved redefining or reconstructing social reality. When

... According to the Thomas theorem, established by sociologists W. I. Thomas and Dorothy Swaine Thomas, "If men define situations as real, they are real in their consequences" (Thomas and Thomas 1928:571–572). In other words, our perceptions of what is real determine how we act more so than does reality itself.

Did You Know?

members of subordinate groups challenge traditional social assumptions, they can raise our consciousness about the consequences of group membership or social position and help us perceive and experience reality in a new way. For example, when Olympic gold medallist Muhammad Ali began his professional boxing career in the early 1960s, he was much like any other young Black fighter. He was managed and sponsored by a White syndicate and went by his given name, Cassius Clay. Soon, however, the young boxer rebelled against the old stereotypes of the self-effacing Black athlete and began to define his own social role. He joined the Nation of Islam and took the name Muhammad Ali. He insisted on expressing his own political views, including refusing to fight in the Vietnam War. Ali not only changed the world of sports but also helped to alter the world of race relations. Viewed from a sociological perspective, Ali was redefining social reality by rebelling against the racist thinking and terminology that restricted him.

>> Elements of Social Structure

All social interaction takes place within a **social structure** —a series of predictable relationships composed of various positions that people occupy. Occupying those positions shapes how we think and act and what resources we have access to. For example, our position as parent, employee, or student exists in relation to other positions, such as child, boss, or professor. Further, each of these positions implies certain expectations and obligations on our part, such as discipline, labour, and studying. In short, how we interact with others is shaped by the positions we occupy.

For purposes of study, we can break down any social structure into six elements: statuses, social roles, groups, social networks, virtual worlds, and social institutions. These elements make up the social structure just as a foundation, walls, and ceilings make up a building's structure. The elements of social structure are developed through the lifelong process of socialization described in Chapter 4.

STATUSES

We normally think of a person's "status" as having to do with influence, wealth, and fame. However, sociologists use the term **status** to refer to any of the full range of socially defined positions within a large group or society, from the lowest to the highest. Within our society, a person can occupy the status of Prime Minister of Canada, farmer, son or daughter, violinist, teenager, resident of Peterborough, dental technician, or neighbour. A person can hold a number of statuses at the same time.

Ascribed and Achieved Statuses Sociologists categorize statuses as either ascribed or achieved (see the "Social Statuses" figure above). An **ascribed status** is assigned to a

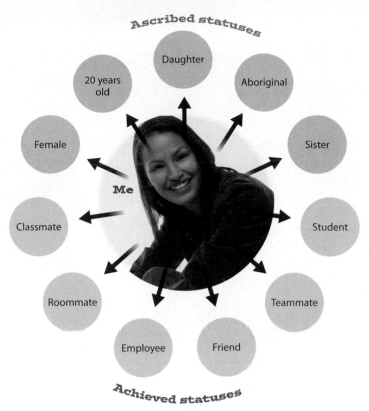

Social Statuses

Ascribed statuses

- Daughter
- 20 years old
- Aboriginal
- Female
- Sister
- Me
- Classmate
- Student
- Roommate
- Teammate
- Employee
- Friend

Achieved statuses

person by society without regard for the person's unique talents or characteristics. Generally, the assignment takes place at birth; thus, a person's age, race/ethnicity, and sex (and by extension, gender) are all considered ascribed statuses. Though such characteristics (with the exception of gender) are biological or physiological in origin, the key is the *social* meaning we attach to such categories. Ascribed statuses are often used to justify privileges or reflect a person's membership in a subordinate group. We will analyze the social significance and implications of race, ethnicity, sex, and gender more fully in Chapters 12 and 13.

In most cases, we can do little to change an ascribed status. We can, however, attempt to change the traditional constraints associated with it. For example, since its founding in 1971, the activist political group Gray Panthers has worked for the rights of older people and tried to modify society's negative and confining stereotypes of the elderly. As a result of their work and that of other groups supporting older citizens, the ascribed status of "senior citizen" is no longer as difficult for millions of older people.

An ascribed status does not necessarily have the same social meaning in every society. In a cross-cultural study, sociologist Gary Huang (1988) confirmed the long-held view that respect for the elderly is an important cultural norm in

> **social structure** The way in which a society is organized into predictable relationships.
> **status** A term used by sociologists to refer to any of the full range of socially defined positions within a large group or society.
> **ascribed status** A social position assigned to a person by society without regard for the person's unique talents or characteristics.

position. How, then, do others view our overall social position? According to sociologist Everett Hughes (1945), societies deal with inconsistencies by agreeing that certain statuses are more important than others. A **master status** is a status that dominates others and thereby determines a person's general position in society. For example, Arthur Ashe, who died of AIDS in 1993, had a remarkable career in tennis, but at the end of his life, his status as a well-known personality with AIDS may have outweighed his statuses as a retired athlete, author, and political activist. Due to the significance our society assigns to ascribed statuses, they frequently influence our achieved status, affecting our professional and social opportunities.

China. There, in many cases, the prefix "old" is used respectfully: calling someone "old teacher" or "old person" is like calling a judge in Canada "your honour." Huang points out that such positive old-age-related language distinctions are uncommon in North America; consequently, we view the term "old man" as more of an insult than a celebration of seniority and wisdom.

> **achieved status** A social position that is within our power to change.
> **master status** A status that dominates others and thereby determines a person's general position in society.

Unlike ascribed statuses, an **achieved status** is a social position that is within our power to change. Both bank president and prison guard are achieved statuses, as are lawyer, pianist, student, convict, and social worker. We must do something to acquire an achieved status—go to school, learn a skill, establish a friendship, invent a new product, and so on. But as we will see in the next section, our ascribed status heavily influences our achieved status. Being male in Canada, for example, still decreases the likelihood that a person will consider child care as a career.

Master Status Each of us holds many different and sometimes conflicting statuses; some may connote a higher social position, and others a lower

People with disabilities often observe that the nondisabled see them only as blind, or only as wheelchair users, and so on, rather than as complex human beings with individual strengths and weaknesses whose disability is merely one aspect of their lives. Often people with disabilities find that their status as "disabled" receives undue weight, overshadowing their actual ability to hold meaningful employment and contributing to widespread prejudice, discrimination, and segregation. Activists argue that unnecessary and discriminatory barriers present in the environment—both physical and attitudinal—restrict people with disabilities more than do any biological limitations.

The Honourable David Onley, Lieutenant Governor of Ontario, who lives with the effects of polio and post-polio syndrome, is a high profile champion of accessibility.

SOCIAL ROLES

Throughout our lives, we acquire what sociologists call social roles. A **social role** is a set of expectations for people who occupy a given social position or status. While we occupy a status, we play a role. Thus, in Canada, we expect that cab drivers will know how to get around a city, that receptionists will handle phone messages, and that police officers will take action if they see a citizen being threatened. With each distinctive social status—whether ascribed or achieved—come particular role expectations. However, actual performance varies from individual to individual. One secretary may assume extensive administrative responsibilities, while another may focus on clerical duties.

Roles are a significant component of social structure. Roles can contribute to a society's stability by enabling members to anticipate the behaviour of others and to pattern their own actions accordingly. Yet social roles can also restrict people's interactions and relationships. If we view a person *only* as a police officer or a supervisor, it will be difficult to relate to him or her as a friend or neighbour.

Role Conflict Sometimes the positions we occupy can clash. **Role conflict** occurs when incompatible expectations arise from two or more social positions held by the same person. Fulfillment of the roles associated with one status may directly violate the roles linked to a second status.

Hot or Not?

Is there is no such thing as our true self? Are we only actors performing roles based on the positions we occupy?

Imagine the delicate situation of a woman who has worked for a decade on an assembly line in an electrical plant and has recently been named supervisor of her unit. How is this woman expected to relate to her longtime friends and co-workers? Should she still have lunch with them, as she has done almost daily for years? Should she recommend the firing of an old friend who cannot keep up with the demands of the assembly line? She will most likely experience a sharp conflict between her social and occupational roles. Such role conflicts involve difficult ethical choices. The new supervisor will have to make a difficult decision about how much allegiance she owes her friend and how much she owes her employers, who have given her supervisory responsibilities.

Another type of role conflict occurs when individuals move into occupations that are not common among people with their ascribed status. Male preschool teachers and female police officers often experience this type of role conflict. In the latter case, the women must strive to reconcile their workplace role in law enforcement with the societal view of a woman's role, which historically has not embraced many skills associated with police work. And even as female police officers encounter sexual harassment, as women do throughout the labour force, they must also deal with the "code of silence," an informal norm that precludes their implicating fellow officers in wrongdoing (Fletcher 1995; S. Martin 1994).

> **social role** A set of expectations for people who occupy a given social position or status.
> **role conflict** The situation that occurs when incompatible expectations arise from two or more social positions held by the same person.

SOCthink

> > > List the social statuses you occupy. Which ones are ascribed, and which are achieved? What roles are you expected to play as a consequence of the positions you occupy? How do you resolve possible role conflicts?

Role Strain

Role conflict describes the situation of a person dealing with the challenge of occupying two social positions simultaneously. However, even a single position can cause problems. Sociologists use the term **role strain** to describe the difficulty that arises when the same social position imposes conflicting demands and expectations.

People who belong to minority subcultures may experience role strain while working in the mainstream culture. Criminologist Larry Gould (2002) interviewed officers of the Navajo Nation Police Department about their relations with conventional law enforcement officials, such as sheriffs and FBI agents. Besides enforcing the law, Navajo Nation officers practise an alternative form of justice known as Peacemaking, in which they seek reconciliation between the parties to a crime or grievance. The officers expressed great confidence in Peacemaking but worried that if they did not make arrests, other law enforcement officials would think they were too soft or were "just taking care of their own." Regardless of the strength of their ties to traditional Navajo ways, all felt the strain of being considered "too Navajo" or "not Navajo enough."

role strain The difficulty that arises when the same social position imposes conflicting demands and expectations.

role exit The process of disengagement from a role that is central to one's self-identity in order to establish a new role and identity.

Role Exit Often, when we think of assuming a social role, we focus on the preparation and anticipatory socialization a person undergoes for that role. Such is true if a person is about to become an attorney, a chef, a spouse, or a parent. Yet, social scientists have paid less attention to the adjustments involved in leaving social roles.

Sociologist Helen Rose Fuchs Ebaugh (1988) used the term **role exit** to describe the process of disengagement from a role that is central to one's self-identity in order to establish a new role and identity. Drawing on interviews—with, among others, ex-convicts, divorced men and women, recovering alcoholics, ex-nuns, former doctors, retirees, and transsexuals—Ebaugh (herself a former nun) studied the process of voluntarily exiting from significant social roles.

Ebaugh has offered a four-stage model of role exit. The first stage begins with doubt. The person experiences frustration, burnout, or simply unhappiness with an accustomed status and the roles associated with that social position. The second stage involves a search for alternatives. An individual who is unhappy with his or her career may take a leave of absence; an unhappily married couple may begin what they see as a trial separation.

The third stage of role exit is the action stage, or departure. Ebaugh found that the vast majority of her respondents could identify a clear turning point when it became essential to take final action and leave their jobs, end their marriages, or engage in some other type of role exit. Only 20 percent of respondents saw their role exit as a gradual, evolutionary process that had no single turning point.

The last stage of role exit involves the creation of a new identity. Traditionally, students experience a form of role exit when they make the transition from high school to college or university. They may leave behind the role of a child living at home and take on the role of a somewhat independent student living with peers in residence. Sociologist Ira Silver (1996) has studied the central role that material objects play in this transition. The objects students choose to leave at home (like stuffed animals and dolls) are associated with their prior identities. They may remain deeply attached to those objects but not want them to be seen as part of their new identities at college or university. The objects they bring with them symbolize how they now see themselves and how they wish to be perceived. iPods and wall posters, for example, are calculated to say, "This is me."

SOCthink

> > > Whether from a sports team, a religious group, the military, or some other close-knit group, what experience, if any, have you had with role exiting? To what extent does your experience match the four stages Ebaugh describes?

Sociologist Helen Rose Fuchs Ebaugh interviewed transsexuals (as pictured here) and others exiting from significant social roles in order to develop her four-stage model of role exit.

GROUPS

Statuses combine in various ways to form social groups. In sociological terms, a **group** is any number of people with similar norms, values, and expectations who interact with one another on a regular basis. The members of a women's basketball team, a hospital's business office, a synagogue, or a symphony orchestra constitute a group. However, the residents of a suburb would not be considered a group, since they rarely interact with one another at one time.

Groups play a vital part in a society's social structure. Much of our social interaction takes place within groups and is influenced by their norms and sanctions. Being a teenager or a retired person, for example, takes on special meaning when we interact within groups designed for people with that particular status. The expectations associated with many social roles, including those accompanying the statuses of sibling and student, become more clearly defined in the context of a group.

Primary and Secondary Groups Charles Horton Cooley (1902) coined the term **primary group** to refer to a small group characterized by intimate, face-to-face association and cooperation. Such groups often entail long-term commitment and involve more of what we think of as our whole self. The members of a street gang can constitute a primary group; so can members of a family occupying the same household, or a group of "sisters" living in a college or university sorority.

Primary groups shape who we are and what we think about ourselves, thus playing a pivotal role both in the socialization process and in the development of our statuses and roles. Indeed, whether with family, friends, or

Comparison of Primary and Secondary Groups

Primary group	Secondary group
Generally small	Usually large
Relatively long period of interaction	Relatively short duration, often temporary
Intimate, face-to-face association	Little social intimacy or mutual understanding
Some emotional depth to relationships	Relationships generally superficial
Cooperative, friendly	More formal and impersonal

teammates, primary groups can be instrumental in our day-to-day existence. When we find ourselves identifying closely with a group, it is probably a primary group.

We also participate in many groups that are not characterized by close bonds of friendship, such as large college and university classes and business associations. The term **secondary group** refers to a formal, impersonal group in which there is little social intimacy or mutual understanding. Participation in such groups is often more instrumental or goal-directed, often involving only what we think of as one part of our self. Given these characteristics, we are more likely to move into and out of such groups as suits our needs. The distinction between primary and secondary groups is not always clear-cut, however. Some social clubs may become so large and impersonal that they no longer function as primary groups; similarly, some work groups can become so close-knit that they are experienced as primary groups (Hochschild 1989). The accompanying table demonstrates some significant differences between primary and secondary groups.

> **group** Any number of people with similar norms, values, and expectations who interact with one another on a regular basis.
>
> **primary group** A small group characterized by intimate, face-to-face association and cooperation.
>
> **secondary group** A formal, impersonal group in which there is little social intimacy or mutual understanding

In-Groups and Out-Groups In addition to degree of intimacy, groups can hold special meaning for members because of their relationship to other groups. For example, people in one group sometimes feel antagonistic toward or threatened by another group, especially if that group is perceived as being different either culturally or racially. To identify these "we" and "they" feelings, sociologists

use two terms first employed by William Graham Sumner (1906): in-group and out-group.

An **in-group** can be defined as any group or category to which people feel they belong. Simply put, it comprises everyone who is regarded as "we" or "us." The in-group may be as narrow as a teenage clique or as broad as an entire society. The very existence of an in-group implies the

existence of an out-group that is viewed as "they" or "them." An **out-group** is a group or category to which people feel they do not belong. These groups are perhaps most evident in high school; belonging to the "right" group or clique is important for social status. As sociologist Martin Milner, Jr. discovered, being a "freak," a "geek," or a "cool kid" has a significant impact on one's social opportunities (2006).

In-group members typically feel distinct and superior, seeing themselves as better than people in the out-group. Proper behaviour for the in-group is simultaneously viewed as unacceptable behaviour for the out-group. This double standard enhances the sense of superiority. Sociologist Robert Merton (1968) described this process as the conversion of "in-group virtues" into "out-group vices." We can see this differential standard operating in the context of terrorism. When a group or a nation takes aggressive actions, it usually justifies them as necessary even if civilians are hurt or killed. Opponents are quick to assign the emotion-laden label of *terrorist* to such actions and to appeal to the world community for condemnation. Yet these same people may themselves retaliate with actions that hurt civilians, which the first group will then condemn.

Conflict between in-groups and out-groups can turn violent on a personal as well as a political level. In 1999 two disaffected students at Columbine High School in Littleton, Colorado, launched an attack in the school that left 15 students and teachers dead, including themselves. The following week, W.R. Myers High School in Taber, Alberta, was the scene of a similar incident. One student was killed and another seriously wounded when a 14-year-old former student walked into the school and began shooting. In both of these cases, the assailants were described as social outcasts who were shunned or bullied. Sadly, similar episodes have occurred where rejected adolescents, overwhelmed by personal and family problems, peer group pressure, academic responsibilities, or media images of violence, have lashed out against more popular classmates.

Reference Groups Both in-groups and primary groups can dramatically influence the way an individual thinks and behaves. Sociologists call any group that individuals use as a standard for evaluating themselves and their own behaviour a **reference group.** For example, a high school student who aspires to join a social circle of hip-hop music devotees will pattern his or her behaviour after that of the group. The student will begin dressing like these peers, listening to the same downloads and DVDs, and hanging out at the same stores and clubs.

We're getting closer to our nature.

Clifford Geertz

SOCthink

> > > How do in-groups and out-groups function in a typical Canadian high school? What groups are common? How are boundaries separating insiders and outsiders maintained?

Reference groups have two basic purposes. They serve a normative function by setting and enforcing standards of conduct and belief. The high school student who wants the approval of the hip-hop crowd will have to follow the group's dictates, at least to some extent. Reference groups also perform a comparison function by serving as a standard against which people can measure themselves and others. For example, an actor will evaluate him- or herself against a reference group composed of others in the acting profession (Merton and Kitt 1950).

Often, two or more reference groups influence us at the same time. Our family members, neighbours, and co-workers all shape different aspects of our self-evaluation. In addition, reference group attachments change during the life cycle. A corporate executive who quits the rat race at age 45 to become a social worker will find new reference groups to use as standards for evaluation. We shift reference groups as we take on different statuses during our lives.

> **coalition** A temporary or permanent alliance geared toward a common goal.

Coalitions As groups grow larger, coalitions begin to develop. A **coalition** is an alliance, whether temporary or permanent, geared toward a common goal. Coalitions can be broad-based or narrow and can take on many different objectives. Sociologist William Julius Wilson (1999) has reported on community-based organizations in which Whites and visible minorities, both working-class and affluent, have banded together to work for improved sidewalks, better drainage systems, and comprehensive street paving. Out of this type of coalition building, Wilson hopes, will emerge better interracial understanding.

Some coalitions are intentionally short-lived. Short-term coalition building is a key to success in popular TV programs like *Survivor* in which players gain a strategic advantage by banding together to vote others off the island.

The political world is also the scene of many temporary coalitions. For example, in 2008, in an attempt to force the sitting Conservative government into an early election, the leaders of the other federal parties announced their intention to form a coalition government. However, when the Governor General chose to prorogue Parliament, the parties quickly lost interest in working together.

SOCIAL NETWORKS

Groups do not merely serve to define other elements of the social structure, such as roles and statuses; they also link the individual with the larger society. We all belong to a number of groups, and through our acquaintances, we connect with people in different social circles. These connections are known as a **social network**—a series of social relationships that links individuals directly to others, and through them indirectly to still more people. Social networks can centre on virtually any activity, from sharing job information to exchanging news and gossip. Some networks may constrain people by limiting the range of their

social network A series of social relationships that links individuals directly to others, and through them indirectly to still more people.

interactions, yet networks can also empower people by making vast resources available to them (Watts 2004).

Sometimes the connections are intentional and public; other times networks can develop that link us together in ways that are not intentional or apparent. Sociologists Peter Bearman, James Moody, and Katherine Stovel (2004) investigated one such network, asking themselves this question: If you drew a chart of the romantic relationship network at a typical high school, what would it look like? Using careful data collection techniques to enhance the validity of their findings, they found that 573 of the 832 students they surveyed had been either romantically or sexually involved in the past 18 months. Of these, 63 couples connected only with each other as pairs with no other partners. Other students connected directly or indirectly with a handful of partners. One larger group, however, connected 288 students directly or indirectly into a single extended network (see the figure below). Such an example points to the fact that the choices we make often link us with others both known and unknown.

Networks can also serve as a social resource that is every bit as valuable to us as economic resources when it comes to shaping our opportunities. Involvement in social networks—commonly known

Adolescent Sexual Networks

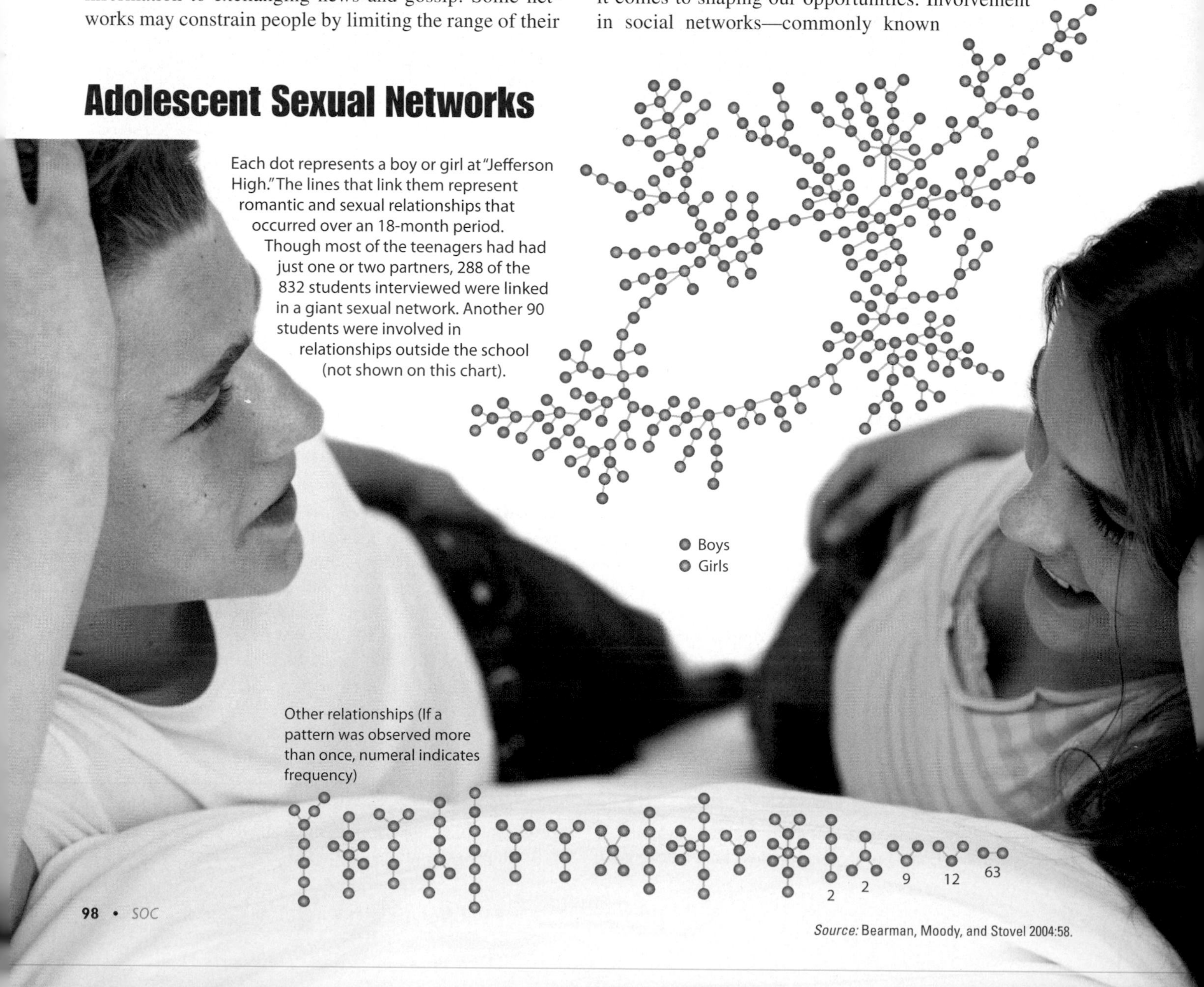

Each dot represents a boy or girl at "Jefferson High." The lines that link them represent romantic and sexual relationships that occurred over an 18-month period.
Though most of the teenagers had had just one or two partners, 288 of the 832 students interviewed were linked in a giant sexual network. Another 90 students were involved in relationships outside the school (not shown on this chart).

● Boys
● Girls

Other relationships (If a pattern was observed more than once, numeral indicates frequency)

2   2   9   12   63

Source: Bearman, Moody, and Stovel 2004:58.

as "networking"—can be especially valuable in finding employment. Albert Einstein was successful in finding a job only when a classmate's father put him in touch with his future employer. These kinds of contacts—even those that are weak and distant—can be crucial in establishing social networks and facilitating the transmission of information.

As feminists have pointed out, in the workplace, networking pays off more for men than for women because of the traditional presence of men in leadership positions. One survey of executives found that 63 percent of the men used networking to find new jobs, compared to 41 percent of the women. Thirty-one percent of the women used classified ads to find jobs, compared to only 13 percent of the men. Still, women at all levels of the paid labour force are beginning to make effective use of social networks. A study of women who were leaving social assistance to enter the paid workforce found that networking was an effective tool in their search for employment. Informal networking also helped them to locate child care and better housing—keys to successful employment (Carey and McLean 1997; Henly 1999).

VIRTUAL WORLDS

Today, with recent advances in technology, people can maintain their social networks electronically; they don't need face-to-face contacts. Whether through text messaging, Blackberry devices, or social networking sites like Facebook, a significant amount of networking occurs online. Adolescents can now interact freely with distant friends, even under close scrutiny by parents or teachers. And employees with a taste for adventure can escape their work environments without leaving their cubicles.

The future of virtual networking and the effects it will have are difficult to imagine. Consider Second Life (SL), a virtual world that included about 15 million networked "players" as of September 2008. Nearly 500,000 of those players were active over a seven-day period. Participants in such virtual worlds typically create an *avatar* that is their online representation as a character, whether in the form of a 2-D or 3-D image or simply through text. The avatar that a player assumes may represent a very different looking-glass self from his or her actual identity. Once equipped with an avatar, the player goes about his or her life in the virtual world, establishing a business and even buying and decorating a home (Bainbridge 2007; Second Life 2008).

Just like real worlds, virtual worlds have become politicized and consumer-oriented. MySpace has been purchased by the global media giant News Corp, which has added targeted advertising to the site. If a MySpace user confesses to liking, say, tacos, a banner ad for Taco Bell may appear at the top of the page. And SL is now open to real-world corporations that want to "build" their stores in SL. The commercialization of these spaces has been met with a good deal of antagonism: Reebok has

weathered a virtual nuclear bomb attack, and "customers" have been "shot" outside the American Apparel store. Elsewhere in SL, virtual protesters have marched on behalf of a far-right French group in a confrontation with anti-Nazi protesters. In 2007, Sweden became the first real-world country to place an "embassy" in SL (Burkeman 2007; A. Hamilton 2007; Semuels 2007).

Virtual life can and does migrate into real life. In 2007, college and university housing officials became worried when freshmen and their parents began checking out the Facebook profiles of prospective roommates. Soon, colleges and universities were fielding requests for new roommates before students even arrived on campus. Concerns went far beyond tastes in music; the reservations expressed most often by parents included a potential roommate's race, religion, and sexual orientation (Collura 2007).

Sociologist Manuel Castells (1997, 1998, 2000) views these emerging electronic social networks as fundamental to

social institution An organized pattern of beliefs and behaviour centred on basic social needs.

As something of a spoof, CNET's online game review site, GameSpot, offered a tongue-in-cheek review of "Real Life." They gave it a 9.6 out of 10, saying that it features "believable characters, plenty of lasting appeal, and a lot of challenge and variety," and they described the game play as "extremely open-ended." They concluded that "if you take a step back and look at the big picture, you'll see that real life is an impressive and exciting experience, despite its occasional and sometimes noticeable problems." Part of what makes such a post amusing is that there is a sense that the boundary between the "real world" and virtual reality continues to blur. What, for example, are the consequences for a real-life marriage when one of the partners marries someone else's virtual-world character (Alter 2007; Kasavin 2003)?

new organizations and the growth of existing businesses and associations. With other scholars, sociologists are now scrambling to understand these environments and their social processes. Internet consultant and analyst Clay Shirky (2008) suggests that what makes the Internet unique relative to previous media revolutions is that it combines both two-way communication (like the telephone) and group formation (such as newspaper readers or television viewers). He summarizes its significance this way: "group action just got easier." This is clearly evident in the massive popularity of Twitter, which allows people to share important (and not so important) news quickly. In political hotspots, it has become an effective way of letting people around the world know what is happening. Shirky suggests that we are seeing only the beginnings of the collective action made possible through the social networking potential that the Internet represents (see the accompanying table).

Finally, virtual networks can help to preserve real-world networks interrupted by war and other dislocations. For the families of Canadian Forces personnel serving in Afghanistan, email has become an important means of keeping in contact. Digital photos and sound files allow for greater sharing of events, and soldiers can even view family celebrations live via webcam. And through online journals or blogs, both soldiers and citizens can express their feelings about Canada's presence in Afghanistan.

Shirky's Four Steps Toward Increased Internet Interaction

Step	Site
Sharing	Flikr; Bit Torrent; Del.icio.us
Conversation	Forums; MAKE; How To
Collaboration	Linux; Aegisub
Collective action	Flash Mob activism; NetRoots activisism

Source: Based on Shirky 2008.

SOCIAL INSTITUTIONS

Combinations of statuses, groups, and networks can coalesce to address the needs of a particular sector of society, forming what sociologists refer to as institutions. A **social institution** is an organized pattern of beliefs and behaviour centred on basic social needs. The family, education,

POPSOC

government, religion, and the economy are all examples of social institutions found in our society. For example, in the context of families, we reproduce members of the society, and in the context of government, we work to preserve order. Though these institutions frequently overlap and interact, the concept is helpful in thinking about the various aspects of society that we need to take into account as we seek to better understand why we think and act the way we do.

One way to understand social institutions is to see how they fulfill essential functions. The functionalist approach emphasizes the importance of social order. It identifies five major needs or tasks that all societies must address, and it connects these tasks to five major institutions (Aberle et al. 1950; Mack and Bradford 1979). First, if they are to continue to exist, all societies must reproduce their membership. The primary means is biological reproduction, which takes place in the context of families. Societies also often gain members through immigration, which tends to be regulated by the government. A second task involves reproducing the culture by teaching it to those new members. This, too, is carried out primarily in the context of families, but education serves to teach people the knowledge and skills they need to be members of the wider society. A third task involves producing and distributing goods and services so that people's needs are fulfilled; the economy is the primary institution for this function. A fourth task is preserving order, a function carried out through the policing and diplomatic responsibilities of government. Finally, societies must provide and maintain a sense of meaning and purpose, a role historically filled by religion, although patriotism often plays a critical role as well.

This list of functional prerequisites does not specify how a society and its corresponding social institutions will perform each task. For example, one society may protect itself from external attack by amassing a large arsenal of weaponry, while another may make determined efforts to remain neutral in world politics and to promote cooperative relationships with its neighbours. No matter what its particular strategy, any society or relatively permanent group must address all these functional prerequisites for survival.

While this functionalist approach does a good job of laying out some of the issues we must address as we seek to understand and establish social order, it often implies that the way things are is the way they ought to be. Sociologists who focus more on power, the consequences of difference, and resource distribution (such as conflict and feminist theorists) suggest that we must also look at the ways our construction of these institutions reinforces inequality. We can meet these needs in a variety of ways, so we must address the interest some groups have in maintaining the status quo.

The educational structure has also been critiqued by feminist theorists, who highlight the unequal gendered representation in many school materials and the differential

SOCthink

> > > How is it possible for education to provide both a path for opportunity and an instrument for maintaining inequality? Where in your experience have you seen both at work?

Theory

A Matter of Perspective

THEORETICAL PERSPECTIVES ON SOCIAL STRUCTURE AND INTERACTION

Functionalist:

- emphasizes the importance of social order; sees institutions as carrying out the key tasks in this regard

Conflict:

- emphasizes power differentials among groups; sees institutions as reinforcing inequality and maintaining the status quo

Feminist:

- emphasizes how social structure and interaction are gendered, how women and men receive differential treatment

Interactionist:

- focuses upon everyday interactions as basis for the construction of social reality; our institutions reflect and reinforce that constructed reality

informal social norms that emerged in this work environment and the rich social network these female employees created.

Duneier learned that, despite working in a large office, these women found private moments to talk (often in the halls or outside the washroom) and shared a critical view of the firm's attorneys and day-shift secretaries. Expressing their frustration about their relative lack of power and respect, the word processors routinely suggested that their assignments represented work that the "lazy" secretaries should have completed during the normal workday. One word processor, seeking to reclaim a sense of personal power, reacted against the lawyers' superior attitude and pointedly refused to recognize or speak with any attorney who would not address her by name (Duneier 1994b). Through such analysis, sociologists can better explain both how social order is attained and how social inequality is produced in the context of the workplace.

Such approaches to viewing life in the contexts of social institutions allow us to better understand what it means to live in the world as it is structured today. Looking at society through the lens of social institutions gives us a sense of what is going on with regard to both the "big picture" and the intimate details of our daily interactions. One of the ways that sociologists have characterized the structure of our modern world is in terms of bureaucracy, which not only describes the social structure but also shapes our everyday experiences.

treatment of girls and boys in the classroom. This perspective notes similar trends occur in all of our major social institutions.

Symbolic interactionists suggest that examining everyday interactions within the contexts of these institutions can help us to further understand why we think and act the way we do. As conflict theorists point out, major institutions, such as education, help to maintain the privileges of the most powerful individuals and groups within a society while contributing to the powerlessness of others. To give one example, schools in Native communities are frequently poorly equipped, with outdated texts and equipment, as well as materials that fail to reflect the students' culture. Due to widespread poverty, these communities are unable to engage in fundraising activities characteristic of schools located in more affluent areas. As a result, these children are less prepared to compete academically than children from prosperous communities. These disadvantages will be further examined in Chapter 8.

Focusing on the economy, sociologist Mitchell Duneier (1994a, 1994b) studied the social behaviour of the word processors, all women, who worked in the service centre of a large Chicago law firm. Duneier was interested in the

> **bureaucracy** A component of formal organization that uses rules and hierarchical ranking to achieve efficiency.

"Frankly, at this point in the flow chart, we don't know what happens to these people..."

>> Bureaucracy

A **bureaucracy** is a component of a formal organization that uses rules and hierarchical ranking to achieve efficiency. Rows of desks staffed by seemingly faceless people, endless lines and forms, impossibly complex language, and frustrating encounters with red tape—all these unpleasant images have combined to make "bureaucracy" a dirty word and an easy target in political campaigns. As a result, few people want to identify their occupation as "bureaucrat," despite the fact that all of us perform various bureaucratic tasks. In an industrial society, elements of bureaucracy enter into almost every occupation.

CHARACTERISTICS OF A BUREAUCRACY

Max Weber ([1913–1922] 1947) first directed researchers to the significance of bureaucratic structure. In an important sociological advance, Weber emphasized the basic similarity of structure and process found in the otherwise dissimilar enterprises of religion, government, education, and business. Weber saw bureaucracy as a form of organization quite different from the family-run business. For analytical purposes, he developed an ideal type of bureaucracy that would reflect the most characteristic aspects of all human organizations. By **ideal type**, Weber meant a construct or model for evaluating specific cases. In actuality, perfect bureaucracies do not exist; no real-world organization corresponds exactly to Weber's ideal type.

Weber proposed that whether the purpose is to run a church, a corporation, or an army, the ideal bureaucracy displays five basic characteristics: division of labour, hierarchy of authority, written rules and regulations, impersonality, and employment based on technical qualifications. Let's look at each in turn; the accompanying table provides a summary.

Division of Labour Specialized experts perform specific tasks. In a hospital, for example, doctors do not see to the maintenance of the building; cafeteria workers do not diagnose illnesses. By working at a specific task, people are more likely to become highly skilled and carry out a job

with maximum efficiency. This emphasis on specialization is so basic a part of our lives that we may not realize it is a fairly recent development in Western culture.

Division of labour has freed people up to specialize, enhancing their knowledge and skill and leading to significant advances and innovation. However, fragmenting work into smaller and smaller tasks can isolate workers from one another and weaken any connection they might feel to the overall objective of the bureaucracy. In *The Communist Manifesto* (1848), Karl Marx and Friedrich Engels charged that capitalism's inherent drive toward increased efficiency and productivity reduces workers to a mere "appendage of the machine" (L. Feuer 1989). Such a work arrangement, they wrote, produces extreme **alienation**—loss of control over our creative human capacity to produce, separation from the products we make, and isolation from our fellow producers. Restricting workers to very small tasks also can lessen their job security, since new employees can easily be trained to replace them.

Another potential downside of the division of labour is that, even though it makes us more interdependent, our relative isolation can result in our failing to recognize our links with others. As we saw with the "hamburger as miracle" example in Chapter 1, we take other people's skills for granted and assume they will do their jobs, even though we are unaware of what most of those jobs are. In some cases this can lead to **trained incapacity**—a situation in which workers become so specialized that they develop blind spots and fail to notice potential problems. Even worse, workers can become so isolated that they may not care about what is happening in the next department. Some observers believe that such

> **ideal type** A construct or model for evaluating specific cases.
> **alienation** Loss of control over our creative human capacity to produce, separation from the products we make, and isolation from our fellow producers.
> **trained incapacity** The tendency of workers in a bureaucracy to become so specialized that they develop blind spots and fail to notice potential problems.

Characteristics of a Bureaucracy

	Positive consequences	Negative consequences	
		For the individual	**For the organization**
Division of labour	Produces efficiency in a large-scale corporation	Produces trained incapacity	Produces a narrow perspective
Hierarchy of authority	Clarifies who is in command	Deprives employees of a voice in decision making	Permits concealment of mistakes
Written rules and regulations	Let workers know what is expected of them	Stifle initiative and imagination	Lead to goal displacement
Impersonality	Reduces bias	Contributes to feelings of alienation	Discourages loyalty to company
Employment based on technical qualifications	Discourages favouritism and reduces petty rivalries	Discourages ambition to improve oneself elsewhere	Fosters "Peter principle"

developments have caused workers in Canada and the United States to become less productive on the job.

Sometimes the bureaucratic division of labour can have tragic results. In May 2000, the people of Walkerton, in southwestern Ontario, were exposed to the E. coli bacteria through the town's contaminated water supply. In the following weeks, seven people would die, and over 2300 became ill, many of whom have experienced ongoing health problems. The finger-pointing that ensued demonstrates one of the weaknesses of bureaucracy: where ideally everyone has a specific duty and performs it competently, what too often happens is the denial of responsibility for the task at hand. In the case of Walkerton, the provincial government dismissed criticisms that funding cuts were a factor. The Public Utilities Commission denied knowledge of contamination, despite lab reports indicating there was a problem. Water manager Stan Koebel was found to be aware of the lab results, yet he failed to notify either the Ministry of the Environment or the Public Health Office. Testifying at the inquiry, Koebel admitted his ignorance of the seriousness of E. coli, and deflected blame onto other parties. Further evidence revealed routine falsification of safety tests by Koebel and his brother, who was the water foreman at that time. And despite their respective roles in this preventable tragedy, both Koebels were awarded generous settlements upon being removed from their positions. In this case, the division of labour helped to obfuscate the chain of command, and complicate assignation of responsibility, thus illustrating the disjuncture between Weber's ideal type of bureaucracy and how things may actually work.

goal displacement Overzealous conformity to official regulations of a bureaucracy.

The organizations of major corporations are often complex, but most typically have a single CEO (chief executive officer). Jean LaRose, pictured here, is CEO of Aboriginal Peoples Television Network (APTN).

corporations there are various levels of authority. To track relationships, such companies map those connections using organizational charts that identify all the links of who answers to whom, ultimately leading to the president or CEO at the top. Another example of hierarchical organization is found in the Roman Catholic Church, in which the Pope is the supreme authority; under him are Cardinals, Bishops, and so forth. An expanded discussion of authority, including Weber's typology, is found in Chapter 9.

Written Rules and Regulations

Through written rules and regulations, bureaucracies generally offer employees clear standards for an adequate (or exceptional) performance. If situations arise that are not covered by the rules, bureaucracies are self-correcting. They have rules in place to ensure that new rules are established that make work expectations as clear and comprehensive as possible. Because bureaucracies are hierarchical systems of interrelated positions, such procedures provide a valuable sense of continuity for the organization. Individual workers may come and go, but the structure and past records of the organization give it a life of its own that outlives the services of any one particular person.

Of course, rules and regulations can overshadow the larger goals of an organization to the point that they become dysfunctional. If blindly applied, rules no longer serve as a means to achieving an objective but instead become important (perhaps too important) in their own right. Robert Merton (1968) used the term **goal displacement** to refer to overzealous conformity to official regulations.

Hierarchy of Authority Bureaucracies follow the principle of hierarchy; that is, each position is under the supervision of a higher authority. In business, the most basic relationship is between boss and worker, but in large

SOCthink

> > > Why do we tend to associate bureaucracies with red tape and inefficiency when they are explicitly organized to be the opposite? To what extent is our desire to be treated as an individual at odds with the principles of bureaucracies?

Impersonality Max Weber wrote that, in a bureaucracy, work is carried out *sine ira et studio*—"without hatred or passion." Bureaucratic norms dictate that officials perform their duties without giving personal consideration to people as individuals. Although this norm is intended to guarantee equal treatment for each person, it also contributes to the cold, uncaring feeling often associated with modern organizations.

We typically think of big government and big business when we think of impersonal bureaucracies, and bureaucratic impersonality often produces frustration and dis-

always follow that ideal pattern. Dysfunctions within bureaucracies have become well publicized, particularly because of the work of Laurence J. Peter. According to the **Peter principle,** every employee within a hierarchy tends to rise to his or her level of incompetence (Peter and Hull 1969). This hypothesis, which has not been directly or

> ## We all know we are unique individuals, but we tend to see others as representatives of groups.
>
> Deborah Tannen

affection. Whether it involves registering for classes or getting tech support for a malfunctioning computer, most people have had some experience of feeling like a number and longing for some personal attention. The larger the organization or society, however, the less possible such personal care becomes, because attending to individual wants and needs is inefficient.

Employment Based on Technical Qualifications

Within the ideal bureaucracy, hiring is based on technical qualifications rather than on favouritism, and performance is measured against specific standards. Written personnel policies dictate who gets promoted, and people often have a right to appeal if they believe that particular rules have been violated. In combination with the principle of impersonality, the driving personnel principle is supposed to be that it is "what you know, not who you know" that counts. Such procedures protect bureaucrats against arbitrary dismissal, provide a measure of security, and encourage loyalty to the organization.

Although any bureaucracy ideally will value technical and professional competence, personnel decisions do not

systematically tested, reflects a possible dysfunctional ultimate outcome of advancement on the basis of merit. Talented people receive promotion after promotion until, sadly, some of them finally achieve positions that they cannot handle with their usual competence (Blau and Meyer 1987).

Weber developed his five indicators of bureaucracy almost 100 years ago, and they describe an ideal type rather than bureaucracy in practice. Not every formal organization will fully realize all of Weber's characteristics. The underlying logic they represent, however, points toward a way of doing things that is typical of life in modern societies.

Peter principle A principle of organizational life according to which every employee within a hierarchy tends to rise to his or her level of incompetence.
bureaucratization The process by which a group, organization, or social movement increasingly relies on technical-rational decision making in the pursuit of efficiency.
McDonaldization The process by which the principles of efficiency, calculability, predictability, and control shape organization and decision making,

BUREAUCRATIZATION AS A WAY OF LIFE

Bureaucracy for Weber was an indicator of a larger trend in modern society toward rational calculation of all decision making using efficiency and productivity as the primary standards of success. We recognize this pattern first at the level of businesses and organizations. More companies seek greater efficiency through **bureaucratization**—the process by which a group, organization, or social movement increasingly relies on technical-rational decision making in the pursuit of efficiency. Over time, however, the technical-rational approach pervades more and more areas of our lives.

The Spread of Bureaucratization

One example of the expansion of bureaucratization is found in the spread of what sociologist George Ritzer (2008) calls **McDonaldization**—the process by which the principles of efficiency, calculability, predictability, and control shape organization and decision making, in North America and around the world. Ritzer argues that these principles, which are at the heart of the success of the

... In Canada, there are over 30,000 job titles, organized into 520 occupational group definitions by the National Occupation Classification (NOC). Check them out at www.hrsdc.gc.ca/noc.

Did You Know?

McDonald's fast-food chain, have been emulated by many organizations, ranging from medical care to wedding planning to education. Even sporting events reflect the influence of McDonaldization. Around the world, stadiums are becoming increasingly similar, both physically and in the way they present the sport to spectators. Swipe cards, "sports city" garages and parking lots, and automated ticket sales maximize efficiency. All seats offer spectators an unrestricted view, and a big screen guarantees them access to instant replays. Scores, player statistics, and attendance figures are updated by computer and displayed on an automated scoreboard. Spectator enthusiasm is manufactured through video displays urging applause or rhythmic chanting. At food counters, refreshments include well-known brands whose customer loyalty has been nourished by advertisers for decades. And, of course, the merchandising of teams' and even players' names and images is highly controlled.

Normally, we think of bureaucratization in terms of large organizations, but bureaucratization also takes place within small-group settings. Sociologist Jennifer Bickman Mendez (1998) studied domestic houseworkers employed in central California by a nationwide franchise. She found that housekeeping tasks were minutely defined, to the point that employees had to follow 22 written steps for cleaning a bathroom. Complaints and special requests went not to the workers but to an office-based manager.

Weber predicted that eventually even the private sphere would become rationalized. That is, we would turn to rational techniques in an effort to manage our self in order to handle the many challenges of modern life. A trip to any bookstore would seem to prove his point: we find countless self-help books, each with its own system of steps to help us solve life's problems and reach our goals.

Weber was concerned about the depersonalizing consequences of such rationalization, and he was pessimistic about our chances of escaping them. Because it is guided by the principle of maximum efficiency, the only way to beat bureaucratization, he thought, was to be more bureaucratic. He added that,

As hilariously demonstrated in the cult classic Office Space, *bureaucracies are rarely as efficient as Weber's ideal type suggests.*

unfortunately, something human was lost in the process. Weber described the effects of rationalization as *the iron cage*, in which we become trapped by our quest for efficiency, predictability, and order, losing our sense of mys-

> # Civilization degrades the many to exalt the few.
>
> Amos Bronson Alcot

tery, individuality, and creativity in the process. Culture critic Mike Daisey describes something like this through his experience working at Amazon.com. His job performance was measured based on five factors: time spent on each call, number of phone contacts per hour, time spent on each customer email, number of email contacts per hour, and the sum total of phone and email contacts per hour. Of these calculations, he writes, "Those five numbers are who you are. They are, in fact, all you are. . . . Metrics will do exactly what it claims to do: it will track everything your employees do, say, and breathe, and consequently create a measurable increase in their productivity" (Daisey 2002:114). Metrics do work, but they do so by dehumanizing the worker. "The sad thing," Daisey continues, "is that metrics work so well precisely because it strips away dignity—it's that absence that makes it possible to see precisely who is pulling his weight and who is not" (p. 114). In addition to placing pressure on workers, clients also suffer under metrics, as it is in workers' interests to deal with clients quickly, to avoid "wasting time" on their concerns. When workers' performance is measured only

in numbers, the only part of the self that counts is that part that produces those numbers. Weber predicted that those parts of the self deemed not necessary to the job, such as emotional needs and family responsibilities, would be dismissed as irrelevant.

From Bureaucracy to Oligarchy One of the dangers, then, is that bureaucratization overwhelms other values and principles, that how we organize to accomplish our goals overwhelms and alters the goals themselves. Sociologist Robert Michels (1915) studied socialist parties and labour unions in Europe prior to World War I and found that such organizations were becoming increasingly bureaucratic. The emerging leaders of the organizations—even some of the most radical—had a vested interest in clinging to power. If they lost their leadership posts, they would have to return to full-time work as manual labourers.

Through his research, Michels originated the idea of the **iron law of oligarchy,** which describes how even a democratic organization will eventually develop into a bureaucracy ruled by a few (called an oligarchy). Why do oligarchies emerge? People who achieve leadership roles usually have the skills, knowledge, or charisma to direct, if not control, others. Michels argued that the rank and file of a movement or organization look to leaders for direction and thereby reinforce the process of rule by a few. In addition, members of an oligarchy are strongly motivated to maintain their leadership roles, privileges, and power.

In such instances, actions that violate the core principles of bureaucracy can seep in. Ascribed statuses such as gender, race, and ethnicity can influence how people are treated in formal organizations. For example, a study of women lawyers in large law firms found significant differences in the women's self-images, depending on the relative presence or absence of women in positions of power. In firms in which fewer than 15 percent of partners were women, the female lawyers were likely to believe that "feminine" traits were strongly devalued and that masculinity was equated with success. As one female attorney put it, "Let's face it: this is a man's environment, and it's sort of Jock City, especially at my firm." Women in firms where female lawyers were better represented in positions of power had a stronger desire for and higher expectations of promotion (Ely 1995:619).

BUREAUCRACY AND ORGANIZATIONAL CULTURE

Weber's model also predicted that organizations would take steps to remedy worker concerns. Faced with sabotage and decreasingly productive workers, for example, early bureaucratic managers realized that they could not totally dismiss workers' emotional needs as irrelevant. Various schools of management arose in an attempt to establish meaningful relationships within the context of the workplace in order to enhance productivity.

According to the classical theory of formal organizations, known as the **scientific management approach,** workers are motivated almost entirely by economic rewards. This theory stresses that only the physical constraints on workers limit their productivity. Therefore, workers may be treated as a resource, much like the machines that began to replace them in the 20th century. Under the scientific management approach, management attempts to achieve maximum work efficiency through scientific planning, established performance standards, and careful supervision of workers and production. Planning involves efficiency studies but not studies of workers' attitudes or job satisfaction.

Not until workers organized unions—and forced management to recognize that they were not objects—did theorists of formal organizations begin to revise this approach. Along with management and administrators, social scientists became aware that informal groups of workers have an important impact on organizations (Perrow 1986). An alternative way of considering bureaucratic dynamics, the **human relations approach,** emphasizes the role of people, communication, and participation in a bureaucracy. This type of

> **iron law of oligarchy** A principle of organizational life under which even a democratic organization will eventually develop into a bureaucracy ruled by a few individuals.
> **scientific management approach** An approach to the study of formal organizations that emphasizes maximum work efficiency and productivity through scientific planning of the labour process.
> **human relations approach** An approach to the study of formal organizations that emphasizes the role of people, communication, and participation in a bureaucracy and tends to focus on the informal structure of the organization.

Gemeinschaft A close-knit community, often found in rural areas, in which strong personal bonds unite members.

Gesellschaft A community, often urban, that is large and impersonal, with little commitment to the group or consensus on values.

mechanical solidarity Social cohesion based on shared experiences, knowledge, and skills in which things function more or less the way they always have, with minimal change.

analysis reflects the significance of interaction and small-group behaviour. Unlike planning under the scientific management approach, planning based on the human relations perspective focuses on workers' feelings, frustrations, and emotional need for job satisfaction. Today, many workplaces—primarily for those in higher-status occupations—have been transformed to more family-friendly environments. To the extent that managers are convinced that helping workers meet all their needs increases productivity, care and concern are instituted as a result of rational calculation.

>> Social Structure in Global Perspective

Principles of bureaucratization may influence more and more spheres of our lives today, but it has not always been thus. In fact, sociology arose as a discipline in order to better understand and direct the transition from traditional to modern society. Early sociologists sought to develop models that described the basic differences between the two. They hoped that by better understanding how traditional societies operate, we might more effectively identify the underlying factors that shape core concerns in modern society, such as social order, inequality, and interaction.

GEMEINSCHAFT AND GESELLSCHAFT

Ferdinand Tönnies (1855–1936) was appalled by the rise of industrial cities in his native Germany during the late 1800s. In his view, the city marked a dramatic change from the ideal of a close-knit community, which Tönnies termed a *Gemeinschaft,* to that of an impersonal mass society, or *Gesellschaft* (Tönnies [1887] 1988).

The *Gemeinschaft* (pronounced "guh-MINE-shoft") is typical of rural life. It is a small community in which people have similar backgrounds and life experiences. Virtually everyone knows one another, and social interactions are intimate and familiar, almost like an extended family. In this community there is a sense of commitment to the larger social group and a sense of togetherness among members. People relate to others in a personal way, not just as, say, clerk or manager. However, with such personal interaction comes little privacy: Community members have few secrets from one another.

Social control in the *Gemeinschaft* is largely, though not exclusively, maintained through informal means such as moral persuasion, gossip, and even gestures. These techniques work effectively because people genuinely care how others feel about them. Social change is relatively limited in the *Gemeinschaft;* the lives of members of one generation may be quite similar to those of their parents, grandparents, and so on.

In contrast, the *Gesellschaft* (pronounced "guh-ZELL-shoft") is characteristic of modern urban life. In modern societies most people are strangers who feel little in common with other residents. Relationships are governed by social roles that grow out of immediate tasks, such as purchasing a product or arranging a business meeting. Self-interest dominates, and there is little consensus concerning values or commitment to the group. As a result, social control must rest on more formal techniques, such as laws and legally defined sanctions. Social change is a normal part of life in the *Gesellschaft,* with substantial shifts evident even within a single generation.

Sociologists have used these two terms to compare social structures that stress close relationships with those that feature less personal ties. It is easy to view the *Gemeinschaft* with nostalgia, as a far better way of life than the rat race of contemporary existence. However, the more intimate relationships of the *Gemeinschaft* come at a price. The prejudice and discrimination found there can be quite confining; ascribed statuses such as family background often outweigh a person's unique talents and achievements. In addition, the *Gemeinschaft* tends to distrust individuals who are creative or simply different.

SOCthink

> > > How would you classify the communities with which you are familiar? Are they more *Gemeinschaft* or *Gesellschaft?*

MECHANICAL AND ORGANIC SOLIDARITY

While Tönnies looked nostalgically back on the *Gemeinschaft,* Émile Durkheim was more interested in the transition to modern society, which he felt represented the birth of a new form of social order. Durkheim hoped to use sociology as a science to better understand this transition. In his book *The Division of Labor in Society* ([1893] 1933), Durkheim, not unlike Weber, highlighted the significance of the degree to which jobs are specialized in society. For Durkheim, however, the extent of division of labour that exists in a society shapes the degree to which people feel connected with each other.

In societies in which there is minimal division of labour,

a shared way of thinking develops that emphasizes group solidarity. Durkheim termed this collective frame of mind **mechanical solidarity.** It involves a sense of social cohesion based on shared experiences, knowledge, and skill, in which things function more or less the way they always have, with minimal change. Most individuals perform the same basic tasks, and they do so together. In this type of society, no one needs to ask, "What do your parents do?" since all are engaged in similar work. Each person hunts, prepares food, makes clothing, builds homes, and so forth. Because people have few options regarding what to do with their lives, there is little concern for individual needs. Instead, the group is the dominant force in society. Both social interaction and negotiation are based on close, intimate, face-to-face social contacts. Since there is little specialization, there are few social roles.

As societies become more advanced technologically, they rely on greater division of labour. The person who cuts down timber is not the same person who puts up your roof. With increasing specialization, many different tasks must be performed by many different individuals—even in manufacturing a single item, such as a radio or stove. In general, social interactions become less personal than in societies characterized by mechanical solidarity. People begin relating to others on the basis of their social positions (butcher, nurse, and so on) rather than their distinctive human qualities. Because the overall social structure of the society continues to change, statuses and social roles are in perpetual flux.

As we saw in the "hamburger as miracle" example in Chapter 1, once society has become more complex and division of labour is greater, no individual can go it alone. Dependence on others becomes essential for group survival. In Durkheim's terms, mechanical solidarity is replaced by **organic solidarity**—a collective consciousness resting on the need a society's members have for one another. Durkheim chose the term organic solidarity because he believed that role specialization forces individuals to become interdependent in much the same way as the various organs of the human body: Each performs a vital function, but none can exist alone. Also, like a living organism, society can grow and adapt to change.

TECHNOLOGY AND SOCIETY

Some sociologists focus more explicitly on technology than on social organization, expressed as division of labour, to understand distinctions between traditional and modern societies. In sociologist Gerhard

Lenski's view, a society's level of technology is critical to the way it is organized. As we saw in Chapter 3, Lenski defines technology as "cultural information about the ways in which the material resources of the environment may be used to satisfy human needs and desires" (Nolan and Lenski 2006:361). As technology changes, new social forms arise, from pre-industrial, to industrial, to post-industrial. The available technology does not completely define the form that a particular society and its social structure will take. Nevertheless, a low level of technology may limit the degree to which a society can depend on such things as irrigation or complex machinery.

organic solidarity A collective consciousness that rests on mutual interdependence, characteristic of societies with a complex division of labour.
hunting-and-gathering society A pre-industrial society in which people rely on whatever foods and fibres are readily available in order to survive.
horticultural society A pre-industrial society in which people plant seeds and crops rather than merely subsist on available foods.
agrarian society The most technologically advanced form of pre-industrial society. Members are engaged primarily in the production of food, but they increase their crop yields through technological innovations such as the plough.

Pre-industrial Societies Perhaps the earliest form of pre-industrial society to emerge in human history was the **hunting-and-gathering society,** in which people simply rely on whatever foods and fibres are readily available. Such groups are typically small and widely dispersed, and technology in such societies is minimal. Organized into groups, people move constantly in search of food. There is little division of labour into specialized tasks because everyone is engaged in the same basic activities. Since resources are scarce, there is relatively little inequality in terms of material goods.

In **horticultural societies,** people plant seeds and crops rather than merely subsist on available foods. Members of horticultural societies are much less nomadic than hunter-gatherers. They place greater emphasis on the production of tools and household objects. Yet technology remains rather limited in these societies, whose members cultivate crops with the aid of digging sticks or hoes (Wilford 1997).

The third type of pre-industrial development is the **agrarian society.** As in horticultural societies, members of agrarian societies are engaged primarily in the production of food, but technological innovations such as the plough allow farmers to dramatically increase their crop yields and cultivate the same fields over generations. As a result it becomes possible for larger, more permanent settlements to develop.

Agrarian societies continue to rely on the physical power of humans and animals (as opposed to mechanical power). Division of labour increases because technological advances free some people up from food production to focus on specialized tasks, such as the repair of fishing nets or blacksmithing. As human settlements become more stable and established, social institutions become more elaborate and property rights more important. The comparative permanence and greater surpluses of an agrarian society allow members to specialize in creating artifacts such as statues, public monuments, and art objects and to pass them on from one generation to the next.

Industrial Societies

The Industrial Revolution transformed social life in England during the late 1700s, and within a century its impact had extended around the world. By applying nonanimal (mechanical) sources of power to most labour tasks, industrialization significantly altered the way people lived and worked, and it undercut taken-for-granted norms and values. An **industrial society** is one that depends on mechanization to produce its goods and services. Industrial societies rely on new inventions that facilitate agricultural and industrial production, and on new sources of energy, such as steam.

> **industrial society** A society that depends on mechanization to produce its goods and services.
>
> **post-industrial society** A society whose economic system is engaged primarily in the processing and control of information.
>
> **postmodern society** A technologically sophisticated, pluralistic, interconnected, globalized society.

During the Industrial Revolution, many societies underwent an irrevocable shift from an agrarian-oriented economy to an industrial base. Specialization of tasks and manufacture of goods increasingly replaced the practice of individuals or families making an entire product in a home workshop. Workers, generally men but also women and even children, left their family homesteads to work in central locations such as urban factories.

The process of industrialization had distinctive social consequences. Families and communities could not continue to function as self-sufficient units. Individuals, villages, and regions began to exchange goods and services and to become interdependent. As people came to rely on the labour of members of other communities, the family lost its unique position as the main source of power and authority. The need for specialized knowledge led to more formalized schooling, and education emerged as a social institution distinct from the family.

Post-industrial Societies

Mechanized production continues to play a substantial role in shaping social order, relationships, and opportunities, but technological innovation once again has reshaped social structure by freeing up some people from the demands of material production. This has led to the rise of the service sector of the economy in many technologically advanced countries. In the 1970s, sociologist Daniel Bell wrote about the technologically advanced **post-industrial society,** whose economic system is engaged primarily in the processing and control of information. The main output of a post-industrial society is services rather than manufactured goods. Large numbers of people become involved in occupations devoted to the teaching, generation, or dissemination of ideas. Jobs in fields such as advertising, public relations, human resources, and computer information systems are typical of a post-industrial society (D. Bell 1999).

Bell views this transition from industrial to post-industrial society as a largely positive development, assuming the functionalist position that it is a consensual shift, and as such, conflict among diverse groups will diminish. However, conflict theorists point to the often hidden consequences that result from differential access to resources in post-industrial society. For example, Michael Harrington (1980), who brought attention to the problems of the poor in his book *The Other America*, questions the significance that Bell attaches to the growing class of white-collar workers. Harrington concedes that scientists, engineers, and economists are involved in important political and economic decisions, but he disagrees with Bell's claim that they have a free hand in decision making, independent of the interests of the rich. Harrington follows in the tradition of Marx by arguing that conflict between social classes will continue in the post-industrial society.

POSTMODERN LIFE

Sociologists recently have gone beyond discussion of the post-industrial society to contemplate the emergence of postmodern society. A **postmodern society** is a technologically sophisticated, pluralistic, interconnected, globalized society. While it is difficult to summarize what a whole range of thinkers have said about postmodern life, four elements provide a sense of the key characteristics of such societies today: stories, images, choices, and networks.

Did You Know?

...TV talk-show host Regis Philbin was a sociology major. He graduated from the University of Notre Dame with a B.A. in sociology in 1953. Sociology, he says, "gave me a great insight into human nature."

Best and Worst Places to Live

Highest HDI:	Lowest HDI:
1. Iceland	1. Sierra Leone
2. Norway	2. Central African Republic
3. Canada	3. Congo, Dem. Rep.
4. Australia	4. Liberia
5. Ireland	5. Mozambique

Note: The 2008 HDI is based on statistical data from 2006.

Source: United Nations Development Reports 2008.

The UN assigns each nation a ranking in the Human Development Index based upon three main criteria: that persons living within the nation enjoy a long and healthy life, access to knowledge, and a decent standard of living. Although not a comprehensive measure of human development, the HDI does help illustrate global patterns of advantage and disadvantage.

Stories Because postmodern societies are pluralistic and individualistic, people hold many different, often competing, sets of norms and values. Fewer people assume that a single, all-inclusive story—whether a particular religious tradition, or an all-encompassing scientific theory of everything, or even the faith many early sociologists had in the inevitability of modern progress—can unite us all under a common umbrella. Instead, we embrace the various individual and group stories that help us to make sense of the world and our place in it. We do so in the full knowledge that others out there are doing exactly the same thing and often coming to dramatically different conclusions. This multiplicity of stories undercuts the authority that singular accounts of reality have had in the past.

Images Postmodern society is also characterized by the explosion of the mass media, which emphasizes the importance of images. We are bombarded by images everywhere we turn, but in postmodern theory, the significance of the image goes much deeper than television and advertisements; it impacts our taken-for-granted notion of material reality itself. Theorists argue that we do not confront or interact with the material world directly. Just as language shapes our perception of reality according to the Sapir-Whorf hypothesis, our experience of "reality" is always mediated through representations of reality in the form of signs, symbols, and words. According to postmodernists, our images or models of reality come before reality itself. Postmodern theorists use a geography metaphor to illuminate this concept: "the map precedes the territory" (Baudrillard [1981] 1994). In other words, the images we construct draw our attention to certain features that we might not otherwise single out. A road map, for example, highlights different features, and for different purposes, than does a topographical map or political map. In so doing, it shapes what we see. We cannot step around or look through such cultural constructs to approach the thing itself, and so our knowledge of what is real is always constrained by the images we construct.

Choices In a postmodern world, reality is not simply given; it is negotiated. We pick and choose our reality from the buffet of images and experiences presented to us. In fact, we *must* choose. In contrast to societies characterized by mechanical solidarity, where one's life path is virtually set at birth, members of postmodern societies must make life choices all the time. Assuming we have access to sufficient resources, we choose what to eat, what to wear, and what to drive. Shopping, which in the past would have been viewed primarily as an instrumental necessity to provide for our basic needs, becomes an act of self-creation. As James B. Twitchell (2000) put it, "We don't buy things, we buy meanings" (p. 47). An iPhone, a Coach purse, and a hybrid vehicle are more than just a phone, a handbag, and a car. They are statements about the kind of person we are or want to be. The significance of choice goes much deeper than just consumer products. We also choose our partners, our schools, our jobs, our faith, and even our identities. As individuals, we may choose to affirm traditions, language, diet, and values we inherited from our family through socialization, but we can also choose to pursue our own path.

Networks Members of postmodern societies live in a globally interconnected world. The food we eat, the clothes we wear, the books we read, and the products we choose often come to us from the other side of the world. The computer technician we talk to for assistance in Canada may be located in India. McDonald's has even experimented with centralized drive-through attendants—who might even be located in another province—who take your order and transmit it to the restaurant you are ordering from. Increasingly, all corners of the globe are linked into a vast, interrelated social, cultural, political, and economic system. A rural Saskatchewan farmer, for example, must be concerned with more than just the local weather and community concerns; he or she must know about international innovations in farming technology, including biotech, as well as the current and future state of international markets.

Whether in the form of traditional, modern, or postmodern society, social structure provides order, shaping the options that are available to us. It provides the context within which we interact with others. The statuses we occupy shape the roles we perform. What we think and do is influenced by the relationships we have with others in the contexts of groups, networks, and institutions. Sociology as a discipline is committed to making sense of our structural context and the impact it has on our lives.

Still, society and social structure are not singular things—as the turn toward the micro, bottom-up perspective in sociology has helped us to appreciate. Though we are, in many respects, products of society, socialized to think and act in appropriate ways, we always have the option to think and act in new ways and to construct new culture. The possibility for such change may be more apparent in our pluralistic world. Ours is a world not of "the" structure, "the" family, and "the" religion, but of structures, families, and religions. We have the possibility for more contact with more people who have more ways of thinking and acting than at any time in the past. As such, we can become aware of more alternatives for how we might think and act that might lead us to change our worlds.

>> Summary

The elements of social structure shape who we are and what we do. The statuses we achieve and are ascribed, the roles we juggle, the groups to which we belong, the social institutions with which we must engage, the opportunities we find through social networks, and the possibilities envisioned within the virtual world all affect our interactions with the self and others. Social structure brings order to our lives, but as with the example of bureaucracy, it can also create frustration. Neither societies nor individuals remain the same; we are constantly changing.

For REVIEW

I. **What makes up society?**
- Society provides a structure that is built up out of the statuses we occupy, the roles we perform, and the groups, networks, and institutions that connect us.

II. **How does social structure shape individual action?**
- The positions we occupy shape our perceptions, the resources to which we have access, and the options that are available. For example, in the context of bureaucracies, our social position, connections, and performance expectations are clearly defined.

III. **How do sociologists describe traditional versus modern societies?**
- Sociologists highlight the impact that division of labour and technological development have on the organization of community, work, and social interaction in traditional and modern societies.

Thinking CRITICALLY...

1. What is your master status? Is it an ascribed or achieved status?
2. In the current economic climate, would you agree with Durkheim that division of labour helps to promote solidarity?
3. Are virtual worlds increasing human interaction or limiting it?

Pop Quiz

1. A social position we inherit and about which we can do little to change, such as age, race, or sex, is known as
    a. an ascribed status.
    b. role strain.
    c. goal displacement.
    d. a master status.

2. In Canada, we expect that judges know and understand the many laws of this country. This expectation is an example of which of the following?
    a. role conflict
    b. role strain
    c. social role
    d. master status

3. What occurs when incompatible expectations arise from two or more social positions held by the same person?
    a. role conflict
    b. role strain
    c. role exit
    d. both a and b

4. In sociological terms, what do we call any number of people with similar norms, values, and expectations who interact with one another on a regular basis?
    a. a category
    b. a group
    c. an aggregate
    d. a society

5. Primary groups are characterized by
    a. a series of relationships that link individuals directly to others and through them indirectly to still more people.
    b. formal, impersonal relationships with minimal social intimacy or mutual understanding.
    c. a sense of belonging.
    d. intimate, face-to-face association and cooperation.

6. Canada Post, Def Jam Records, and the college or university in which you are currently enrolled as a student are all examples of
    a. primary groups.
    b. reference groups.
    c. formal organizations.
    d. triads.

7. The principle of bureaucracy that establishes that work should be carried out "without hatred or passion" is known as
    a. impersonality.
    b. hierarchy of authority.
    c. written rules and regulations.
    d. employment based on technical qualifications.

8. According to the Peter principle,
    a. all bureaucracies are notoriously inefficient.
    b. if something *can* go wrong, it *will*.
    c. every employee within a hierarchy tends to rise to his or her level of incompetence.
    d. all line workers get burned in the end.

9. Social control in *Gemeinschaft* communities relies most heavily upon
    a. formal laws and legislation.
    b. a coordinated police force.
    c. informal means, such as gossip and public shaming.
    d. an elaborate moral code.

10. Sociologist Daniel Bell uses which of the following terms to refer to a society whose economic system is engaged primarily in the processing and control of information?
    a. postmodern
    b. horticultural
    c. industrial
    d. post-industrial

1. (a); 2. (c); 3. (a); 4. (b); 5. (d); 6. (c); 7. (a); 8. (c); 9. (c); 10. (d)

6

DEVIANC

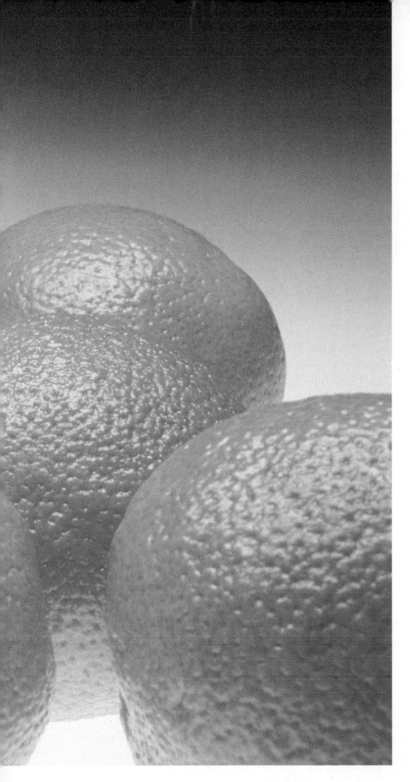

In this chapter you will...

- **learn how deviance is socially constructed**

- **gain an understanding of formal and informal methods of social control**

- **compare and contrast various sociological perspectives on deviance and crime**

LIVING THE GANG LIFE

Sociology student Sudhir Venkatesh (2008), wanting to better understand the lives of poor African Americans, ventured into the housing projects in inner-city Chicago. After a rocky beginning, his naïveté and genuine curiosity helped to open the door to what became a seven-year, in-depth participation research project about gangs, drugs, crime, public housing, and more.

Venkatesh's commitment to going beyond what W.E.B. DuBois dismissed as "car window sociology" ultimately provided him access to information about crime and deviance that he could never have found through a survey. In his work, he found gang members do not necessarily resemble the popular cultural portrayals.

And this is a timely study: While many Canadians think gang activity is restricted to large American cities such as Los Angeles, Chicago, or Miami, gang activity is on the rise in this country. In British Columbia, for example, there are at least 129 known gangs operating; a decade ago, there were 10 (Kirby et al. 2008). While some of these gangs have connections to wealthy overseas syndicates, other gangs—most notably Aboriginal gangs—are fuelled by poverty. Researcher and consultant Mark Totten identifies substance abuse, poverty, and racism as contributing to the exponential growth of Aboriginal youth gangs in Canada: "Within the next five to 10 years, we're going to again see a very, very different face in gang members in the western provinces and B.C." (CBC News 2007).

But gangs are not simply groups of deviants who join together to break the law. As Venkatesh discovered, gangs have a highly organized structure. He also found that some gangs seek to support their community, require young members to stay in school, and prohibit members from using hard drugs—in part because it affects their ability to do business, and in part because it is bad for the image of the gang.

Through research like Venkatesh's, sociologists can better understand crime and deviance. A gang may attempt to contribute to their neighbourhood, but they rely on crime and violence as tools of their trade. What social factors lead to such outcomes, and can those factors or outcomes be changed? In this chapter, we will consider these questions and more.

- How do groups maintain social control?
- What is the difference between deviance and crime?
- How do sociologists explain deviance and crime?

>> Social Control

The tension between the individual and society, between our freedom to do whatever we want and our need for so-

social control The techniques and strategies for preventing deviant human behaviour in any society.
sanction A penalty or reward for conduct concerning a social norm.

cial order, is at the heart of the definition of sociology. Sociologists study social control, deviance, and crime to more fully understand and explain this balance. In this chapter we will address all three.

We seek to enforce the norms we create whether in the form of laws, dress codes, organizational bylaws, course requirements, or the rules of sports and games. We do so through **social control**—the techniques and strategies for preventing deviant human behaviour in any society. Social control occurs on all levels of society. In the family, we are socialized to obey our parents simply because they are our parents. Peer groups introduce us to informal norms, such as dress codes, that govern the behaviour of their members. Schools establish the standards they expect of students. In bureaucratic organizations, workers encounter a formal system of rules and regulations. Finally, the government of every society legislates and enforces social norms.

Most of us respect and accept basic social norms and assume that others will do the same. Even without thinking, we usually obey the instructions of police officers, follow the day-to-day rules at our jobs, and move to the rear of

elevators when people enter. Such behaviour reflects an effective process of socialization to the dominant standards of a culture. At the same time, we are well aware that individuals, groups, and institutions expect us to act "properly." This expectation is enforced through **sanctions**—penalties and rewards for conduct concerning a social norm. If we fail to live up to the norm, we may face punishment through informal sanctions such as fear and ridicule or formal sanctions such as jail sentences or fines.

Sanctions point to the reality that all societies, institutions, and groups rely on the use of power. On the one hand, we want people to respect social norms so that the group or society can survive. Society is defined in part by people's willingness to accept shared beliefs and practices, even if doing so sometimes constrains their selfish pursuits. On the other hand, society can be oppressive, limiting individual freedom and advancing the interests of some at the expense of others. Entrenched interests seek to maintain the status quo and use their power over sanctions to do so. In fact, positive social change often comes through resistance to the status quo, with individuals and groups rejecting existing norms and following new paths. Such attempts may meet with significant opposition, as was evident in

the civil rights movement. Similar struggles were necessary in Canada to secure women's right to vote, for Quebec to be granted status as a distinct society, and to gain expanded rights for Aboriginal peoples.

CONFORMITY AND OBEDIENCE

Techniques for social control operate on both the group and the societal level. People we think of as peers or equals influence us to act in particular ways; the same is true of people who hold authority over us or whose positions we respect. Social psychologist Stanley Milgram (1975) made a useful distinction between these two levels of social control.

Milgram used the term **conformity** to mean going along with peers—individuals of our own status who have no special right to direct our behaviour. In contrast, **obedience** is compliance with higher authorities in a hierarchical structure. Thus, a recruit entering military service will typically conform to the habits and language of other recruits and obey the orders of superiors. Students will conform to the drinking behaviour of their peers and obey the requests of campus security officers.

In a classic experiment, Milgram (1963, 1975) sought to answer this question: Would you comply with a scientific researcher's instruction to administer increasingly painful electric shocks to a subject? He found that, contrary to what we might believe about ourselves, most of us would obey such orders. In his words (1975:xi), "Behavior that is unthinkable in an individual . . . acting on his own may be executed without hesitation when carried out under orders."

Milgram placed advertisements in New Haven, Connecticut, newspapers to recruit subjects for a learning experiment at Yale University. Participants included postal clerks, engineers, high school teachers, and labourers. They were told that the purpose of the research was to investigate the effects of punishment on learning. The experimenter, dressed in a grey technician's coat, explained that in each test, one subject would be randomly selected as the "learner" and another would function as the "teacher." However, the experiment was rigged so that the "real" subject would always be the teacher while an associate of Milgram's served as the learner.

> **conformity** The act of going along with peers—individuals of our own status who have no special right to direct our behaviour.
>
> **obedience** Compliance with higher authorities in a hierarchical structure.

A participant in the Milgram experiment.

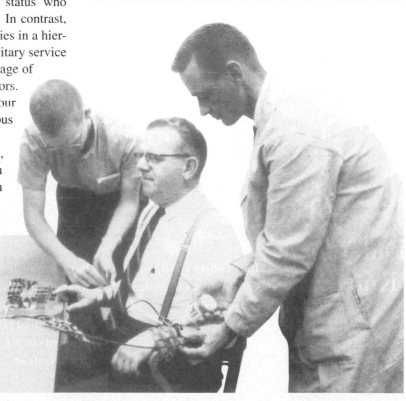

Durkheim concluded that deviance and crime serve important functions in society. For example, identifying acts as deviant clarifies our shared beliefs and values and thus brings us closer together. We say, in effect, "This is who we are, and if you want to be one of us you cannot cross this line. Some things we might let go, but if you push the limits too far you will face sanctions." Punishment, too, can draw a group together, uniting members in their opposition to the offender. Sanctions also discourage others from similar violations, thus increasing conformity. When we see a driver receiving a speeding ticket, a department store cashier being fired for yelling at a customer, or a student getting a failing grade for plagiarizing a term paper, we are reminded of our collective norms and values and of the consequences of their violation. Finally, Durkheim also recognized that deviant acts can force us to recognize the limits of our existing beliefs and practices, opening up new doors and leading to cultural innovation.

anomie Durkheim's term for the loss of direction felt in a society when social control of individual behaviour has become ineffective.

anomie theory of deviance Merton's theory of deviance as an adaptation of socially prescribed goals or of the means governing their attainment, or both.

Based on Durkheim's analysis, it is possible to conclude that societies identify criminals for the sake of social order. No matter how much unity a society might appear to have, there will always be some who push the limits. Regardless of how "good" such people may appear to be to outsiders, they may face sanction within the group for the good of the whole.

SOCthink

> > > Think of a situation where an act of deviance brought you closer to those around you. For example, perhaps you were part of a group of students protesting the suspension of a "disruptive" classmate, or maybe you took part in committing the "deviant" act.

typically occurs during a period of profound social change and disorder, such as a time of economic collapse, political or social revolution, or even sudden prosperity. The power of society to constrain deviant action at such times is limited because there is no clear consensus on shared norms and values. Just as we saw with Durkheim's analysis of suicide, at times when social integration and regulation are weak, people are freer to pursue their own deviant paths.

Merton's Theory of Deviance Sociologist Robert Merton (1968) took Durkheim's theory a step further. He realized that sometimes members of a society share collective values or goals and other times they do not. He also realized that some people accept the means to attain those goals and others don't. To understand deviance and crime, he felt it was necessary to go beyond the general state of society to look more closely at where people fit in relationship to both goals and means.

Merton maintained that one important cultural goal in North America is success, measured largely in terms of money. In addition to providing this goal for people, our society offers specific instructions on how to pursue success—go to school, work hard, do not quit, take advantage of opportunities, and so forth. A mugger and a merchant may share the common goal of economic success, but their means of attaining it are radically different. What happens to individuals in a society with a heavy emphasis on wealth as a basic symbol of success? Merton reasoned that people adapt in certain ways, either by conforming to or by deviating from such cultural expectations. His **anomie theory of deviance** posits five basic forms of adaptation.

Conformity to social norms, the most common adaptation in Merton's typology, is the opposite of deviance. It involves *acceptance* of both the overall societal goal (for example, to become wealthy) and the approved means (hard work). In Merton's view, there must be some consensus regarding accepted cultural goals and the legitimate means for attaining them. Without such a consensus, societies could exist only as collectives of people rather than as unified cultures, and they might experience continual chaos.

Law and justice are not always the same.

Gloria Steinem

Durkheim did, however, also recognize that some social circumstances increase the likelihood of turning toward deviance and crime. As we have already seen, Durkheim ([1897] 1951) introduced the term **anomie** into the sociological literature to describe the loss of direction felt in a society when social control of individual behaviour has become ineffective. Anomie is a state of normlessness that

The other four types of behaviour all involve some departure from conformity. The *innovator* accepts the goals of society but pursues them with means that are regarded as improper. For instance, a safecracker may steal money to buy consumer goods and expensive vacations.

In Merton's typology, the *ritualist* has abandoned the goal of material success and become compulsively committed

Theory

A Matter of Perspective

THEORETICAL PERSPECTIVES ON DEVIANCE

Functionalist:

- all societies contain deviance; deviance helps to reaffirm societal norms and values

Conflict:

- deviance may result from social inequality; differential justice for different members of society

Feminist:

- gendered expectations of behaviour may result in differential definitions of, and responses to, deviance

Interactionist:

- deviance is constructed through societal response, including labelling

---

to the institutional means. Work becomes simply a way of life rather than a means to the goal of success. An example would be the bureaucratic official who blindly applies rules and regulations without remembering the larger goals of the organization. Certainly, that would be true of a social worker who refuses to assist a homeless family because their last apartment was in another district.

The *retreatist*, as described by Merton, has basically withdrawn (or retreated) from both the goals and the means of society. In Canada, drug addicts and vagrants are typically portrayed as retreatists. Concern has been growing that adolescents who are addicted to alcohol will become retreatists at an early age.

The final adaptation identified by Merton reflects people's attempts to create a *new* social structure. The *rebel* feels alienated from the dominant means and goals and may seek a dramatically different social order. Members of a revolutionary political organization, such as a militia group, can be categorized as rebels according to Merton's model.

Merton's theory, though popular, does not fully account for patterns of deviance and crime. While it is useful in explaining certain types of behaviour, such as illegal gambling by disadvantaged "innovators," it fails to explain key differences in crime rates. Why, for example, do some disadvantaged groups have lower rates of reported crime than others? Why do many people in adverse circumstances reject criminal activity as a viable alternative? Merton's theory does not easily answer such questions (Clinard and Miller 1998). In order to more fully appreciate such

nuances, we must add to what we can learn from Merton by turning to theories that seek to better understand deviance and crime at an interpersonal level.

INTERPERSONAL INTERACTION AND LOCAL CONTEXT

Perhaps the likelihood of committing deviant acts is not solely shaped by social integration or the acceptance of society's larger goals and means to attain them. Maybe mothers around the world were right all along that it really does depend on who your friends are. If we are to understand and explain such acts, we must also consider the local context and the importance of social interaction.

> **cultural transmission** A school of criminology that argues that criminal behaviour is learned through social interactions.
> **differential association** A theory of deviance that holds that violation of rules results from exposure to attitudes favourable to criminal acts.

Cultural Transmission As humans, we learn how to behave in social situations, whether properly or improperly. Sociologist Edwin Sutherland (1883–1950) proposed that, just as individuals are socialized to conform to society's basic norms and values, they are also socialized to learn deviant acts. It's not that we are born to be wild; we learn to be wild.

Sutherland drew on the **cultural transmission** school, which emphasizes that individuals learn criminal behaviour by interacting with others. Such learning includes not only the techniques of lawbreaking (for example, how to break into a car quickly and quietly) but also the motives, drives, and rationalizations of the criminal. The cultural transmission approach can also be used to explain the behaviour of those who habitually abuse alcohol or drugs.

Sutherland maintained that through interactions with a primary group and significant others, people acquire definitions of proper and improper behaviour. He used the term **differential association** to describe the process through which exposure to attitudes favourable to criminal acts leads to the violation of rules. Research suggests that this view of differential association also applies to non-criminal deviant acts, such as smoking, truancy, and early sexual behaviour (E. Jackson et al. 1986).

To what extent will a given person engage in activity that is regarded as proper or improper? For each individual, it will depend on the frequency, duration, and importance of two types of social interaction—those experiences that endorse deviant behaviour and those that promote acceptance of social norms. People are more likely to engage in norm-defying behaviour if they are part of a group or subculture that stresses deviant values, such as a street gang.

Sutherland offers the example of a boy who is sociable, outgoing, and athletic and who lives in an area with a high rate of delinquency. The youth is very likely to come into contact with peers who commit acts of vandalism, fail to attend school, and so forth, and he may come to adopt such behaviour. However, an introverted boy who lives in the same neighbourhood may stay away from his peers and avoid delinquency. In another community, an outgoing and athletic boy may join a minor league baseball team or a scout troop because of his interactions with peers. Thus, Sutherland views improper behaviour as the result of the types of groups to which one belongs and the kinds of friendships one has (Sutherland et al. 1992).

While the cultural transmission approach may not explain the conduct of the first-time, impulsive shoplifter or the impoverished person who steals out of necessity, it does help to explain the deviant behaviour of juvenile delinquents or graffiti artists. It directs our attention to the paramount role of social interaction and context in increasing a person's motivation to engage in deviant behaviour (Morselli et al. 2006; Sutherland et al. 1992).

Social Disorganization Theory

The social relationships that exist in a community or neighbourhood affect people's behaviour. Psychologist Philip Zimbardo (2007:24–25) conducted an experiment that demonstrated the power of communal relationships. He abandoned a car in each of two different neighbourhoods, leaving its hood up and removing its hub caps. In one neighbourhood, people started to strip the car for parts even before Zimbardo had finished setting up a remote video camera to record their behaviour. In the other neighbourhood, weeks passed without the car being touched, except for a pedestrian who stopped to close the hood during a rainstorm.

social disorganization theory The theory that attributes increases in crime and deviance to the absence or breakdown of communal relationships and social institutions, such as the family, school, church, and local government.

Social disorganization theory attributes increases in crime and deviance to the absence or breakdown of communal relationships and social institutions, such as the family, school, church, and local government. The lack of such local community connections, with their associated cross-age relationships, makes it difficult to exert informal control within the community, especially of children. Without community supervision and controls, playing outside becomes an opportunity for deviance, and older violators socialize children into inappropriate paths. Crime becomes a normal response to a local context.

This theory was developed at the University of Chicago in the early 1900s to describe the apparent disorganization that occurred as cities expanded with immigrants from abroad and migrants from rural areas. Using the latest survey techniques, Clifford Shaw and Henry McKay literally mapped the distribution of social problems in Chicago. They found high rates of social problems in neighbourhoods where buildings had deteriorated and the population had declined. Interestingly, the patterns persisted over time, despite changes in the neighbourhoods' ethnic and racial composition.

Did You Know?

... In a 2006 survey of over 5000 students at 32 graduate schools, 56 percent of master of business administration (MBA) students admitted to cheating within the past academic year. This contrasted with 47 percent of nonbusiness students. Considering goals and means, into which category of Merton's model might those MBA students belong?

Labelling Theory

Sometimes when it comes to deviance, what you see is what you get. The Saints and Roughnecks were two groups of high school males who were continually engaged in excessive drinking, reckless driving, truancy, petty theft, and vandalism. There the similarity ended. None of the Saints was ever arrested, but every Roughneck was frequently in trouble with police and townspeople. Why the disparity in their treatment? On the basis of observation research in their high school, sociologist William Chambliss (1973) concluded that how they were seen, as rooted in their social class positions, played an important role in the varying fortunes of the two groups.

The Saints hid behind a facade of respectability. They came from "good families," were active in school organizations, planned on attending college, and received good grades. People generally viewed their delinquent acts as a few isolated cases of sowing wild oats. The Roughnecks had no such aura of respectability. They drove around town in beat-up cars, were generally unsuccessful in school, and aroused suspicion no matter what they did.

We can understand such discrepancies by

using an approach to deviance known as **labelling theory,** which emphasizes how a person comes to be labelled as deviant or to accept that label. Unlike Sutherland's work, labelling theory does not focus on why some individuals come to commit deviant acts. Instead, it attempts to explain why society views certain people (such as the Roughnecks) as deviants, delinquents, bad kids, losers, and criminals, while it sees others whose behaviour is similar (such as the Saints) in less harsh terms. Sociologist Howard Becker (1963:9; 1964), who popularized this approach, summed up labelling theory with this statement: "Deviant behavior is behavior that people so label." Most of us will occasionally engage in behaviour that violates the norm—we might drink too much, tell lies, or skip school. Such actions, although deviant, usually generate only a slight response from others and have no lasting effect on our self-image. Edwin Lemert (1951) calls this *primary deviance*. But when our behaviour provokes a more intense reaction, causing us to be labelled, Lemert argues this response can trigger *secondary deviance*, in which we assume the deviant identity and act in accordance with it.

Labelling theory is also called the **societal-reaction approach,** reminding us that it is the response to an act, not the act itself, that determines deviance. Traditionally, research on deviance has focused on people who violate social norms. In contrast, labelling theory focuses on police, probation officers, psychiatrists, judges, teachers, employers, school officials, and other regulators of social control. These agents, it is argued, play a significant role in creating the deviant identity by designating certain people (and not others) as deviant. An important aspect of labelling theory is the recognition that some individuals or groups have the power to define labels and apply them to others. This view ties into the conflict perspective's emphasis on the social significance of power.

In recent years, the practice of racial profiling, in which people are identified as criminal suspects purely on the basis of their race, has come under public scrutiny. Studies confirm the public's suspicion that in some jurisdictions, police officers are much more likely to stop members of visible minorities than other drivers for routine traffic violations, in the expectation of finding drugs or guns in their cars. It is thus unsurprising that perceptions of the local police are less positive among Aboriginal and visible minority persons compared to the overall population (Gannon 2005).

While the labelling approach does not fully explain why certain people accept a label and others manage to reject it, labelling theorists do suggest that the power an individual has relative to others is important in determining his or her ability to resist an undesirable label. It opens the door to additional emphasis on the undeniably important actions of people with power who can shape what counts as deviance (N. Davis 1975; compare with Cullen and Cullen 1978).

POWER AND INEQUALITY

In addition to its significance for labelling theory, the story of the Saints and Roughnecks points toward the role that power and control over valued resources can play in defining deviance. Sociologist Richard Quinney (1974, 1979, 1980) is a leading proponent of the view that the criminal justice system serves the interests of the powerful; people with power protect their own interests and define deviance to suit their own needs. Crime, according to Quinney (1970) and other conflict theorists, is defined as such by legislators who may be influenced by the economic elites to advance their interests.

> **labelling theory** An approach to deviance that attempts to explain why certain people are viewed as deviants while others engaged in the same behaviour are not.
> **societal-reaction approach** Another name for labelling theory.
> **differential justice** Differences in the way social control is exercised over different groups.

Race and Class Looking at crime from this perspective draws our attention to the effects that power and position might have throughout the criminal justice system. Researchers have found that the system treats suspects differently based on their racial, ethnic, or social class background. In many cases, officials using their own discretion make biased decisions about whether to press charges or drop them, whether to set bail and how much, and whether to offer parole or deny it. Researchers have found that this kind of **differential justice**—differences in the way social control is exercised over different groups—places certain populations at a disadvantage in the justice system, both as juveniles and as adults. On average, White offenders receive shorter sentences than comparable offenders of other races or ethnicities, even when prior arrest records and the relative severity of the crime are taken into consideration (Brewer and Heitzeg 2008; Quinney 1974).

The discrimination against certain groups is evident throughout the correctional system. Aboriginal offenders are significantly overrepresented in the Canadian justice system. While Aboriginal people represent less than 4 percent of

Executions by State Since 1976

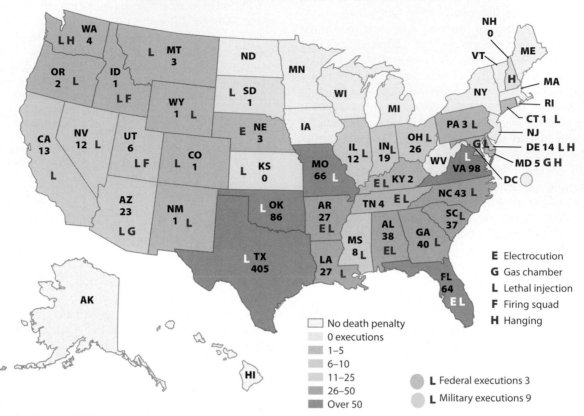

E Electrocution
G Gas chamber
L Lethal injection
F Firing squad
H Hanging

- No death penalty
- 0 executions
- 1–5
- 6–10
- 11–25
- 26–50
- Over 50

L Federal executions 3
L Military executions 9

Note: As of January 2, 2008.

Source: Based on Death Penalty Information Center 2008 and NAACP Legal Defense and Education Fund 2007.

the Canadian population, they account for 18 percent of the federally incarcerated population and 16 percent of people sentenced (Treasury Board of Canada Secretariat 2005). In 2006, the report of the Office of the Correctional Investigator revealed that the Correctional Service of Canada classifies Aboriginal offenders at higher security levels than other inmates, places them in segregation more often, and identifies them as having lower potential for reintegration than non-Aboriginal offenders (Office of the Correctional Investigator 2006). These outcomes are even more pronounced in the

and instead must rely on court-appointed attorneys, who are typically overworked and underpaid.

Various studies show that defendants are more likely to be sentenced to death if their victims were White rather than Black. About 79 percent of the victims in death penalty cases are White, even though only 50 percent of *all* murder victims are White. There is some evidence that Black defendants, who constituted 42 percent of all death row inmates in 2007, are more likely to face execution than Whites in the same legal circumstances. About 70 percent of those who

> ## Whenever you find yourself on the side of the majority, it is time to pause and reflect.
>
> Mark Twain

case of female Aboriginal offenders. The overall incarceration rate for Aboriginal people in Canada is nine times higher than that of non-Aboriginal people.

Sentencing practices often reveal evidence of differential justice. Although the death penalty has been abolished in Canada, cases in the United States demonstrate disturbing patterns. The poor cannot afford to hire top lawyers,

have been exonerated by DNA testing were members of minority groups. Evidence exists, too, that capital defendants receive poor legal services because of the racist attitudes of their own defence counsel. Apparently, discrimination and racism do not end even when the stakes are life and death (Death Penalty Information Center 2008; Innocence Project 2008; D. Jacobs et al. 2007).

In the mid-1990s, police in Vancouver came under public criticism for their slow response to the disappearance of more than 50 women from the city's downtown. Critics charge that because the missing women were poor, and many were Aboriginal, police did not accord the disappearances the attention they deserved, despite the evidence that these crimes were connected, suggesting a serial killer was responsible.

5 Movies on ORGANIZED CRIME/CORPORATE CRIME

The Godfather
An organized crime family makes offers you can't refuse.

Michael Clayton
A law firm has a dark secret.

Traffic
Organized drug trafficking.

The Constant Gardener
A pharmaceutical company puts profit above human life.

Goodfellas
Not so "good"…

The intersection of race, gender, and class appear to have influenced both the public and police response. It would be over 10 years before Robert Pickton would be charged and convicted in the case.

Differential justice is not limited to the United States. In 2007, the people of India were alarmed to learn that police had never investigated a series of killings in the slums of New Delhi. Only after residents found 17 bodies of recently murdered children in a sewer drain on the edge of a slum were police moved to act. For many onlookers, it was just the latest example of the two-tier justice system found in India and many other countries (Gentleman 2007).

Such dramatic differences in social treatment may lead to heightened violence and crime. People who view themselves as the victims of unfair treatment may lash out, not against the powerful so much as against fellow victims. In studying crime in rural Mexico, Andrés Villarreal (2004) found that crime rates were high in the areas where land distribution was most inequitable. In areas where land was distributed more equally, communities appeared to suffer less violence and to enjoy greater social cohesion.

Gender Feminist criminologists such as Freda Adler and Meda Chesney-Lind have suggested that many of the existing approaches to deviance and crime were developed with only men in mind. For example, prior to reforms introduced only within the last few decades, rape within marriage was not a prosecutable offence; sexual history of victims could be introduced in sexual assault cases; and corroboration requirements meant many charges of sexual violence were dropped. Extensive lobbying by women's groups in Canada created awareness of these injustices and ultimately contributed to legislative changes.

When it comes to crime and to deviance in general, society tends to treat women in a stereotypical fashion. For example, consider how women who have many and frequent sexual partners are more likely to be viewed with scorn than men who are promiscuous. Cultural views and attitudes toward women influence how they are perceived and labelled. The feminist perspective also emphasizes that deviance, including crime, tends to flow from economic relationships. Traditionally, men have had greater earning power than their wives. As a result, wives may be reluctant to report acts of abuse to the authorities and thereby lose what may be their primary or even sole source of income. In the workplace, men have exercised greater power than women in pricing, accounting, and product control, giving them greater opportunity to engage in such crimes as embezzlement and fraud. But as women have taken more active and powerful roles both in the household and in business, these gender differences in deviance and crime have narrowed (F. Adler 1975; F. Adler et al. 2004; Chesney-Lind 1989).

Together these perspectives on deviance and crime direct our attention to multiple factors that we should consider when seeking to explain such acts. Based only on the theories we looked at—sociologists of crime have more to offer—we need, at the very least, to take into account the following: the extent to which deviance exists for the sake of social order, the degree of opportunity to attain both means and ends, the role of socialization into deviance, the strength of local community networks, the power to administer labels and make them stick, and differential access to valuable resources based on class, race, and gender. As Sudhir Venkatesh found in his research on gangs, if we are to fully understand something, we need to dig deep enough

and consider what is going on from enough angles and with sufficient care, concern, and curiosity.

>> Summary

Deviance and crime, while most often associated with unacceptable activities and negative consequences, also serve to bring people together. Durkheim suggested that as a society, we collectively determine what we will and will not tolerate, what values we will uphold, and thus we punish those who deviate from those expectations and norms. But one's position and status in society influences the degree of punishment or stigma those labelled as deviant will receive. There are two dimensions to deviance: the objective—the behaviour or action—and the subjective—the collective meanings assigned to that behaviour. Sociology seeks to understand both dimensions; in so doing, we can begin to understand not only why some people act in certain ways, but why other people punish them for doing so.

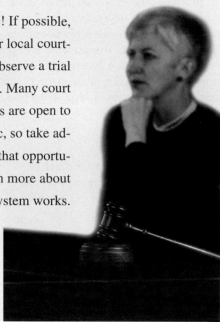

get involved!

Observe! If possible, visit your local courthouse to observe a trial in action. Many court proceedings are open to the public, so take advantage of that opportunity to learn more about how our system works.

For REVIEW

I. How do groups maintain social control?
   • They use positive and negative sanctions in both formal and informal ways to bring about conformity and obedience.

II. What is the difference between deviance and crime?
   • Deviance involves violating a group's expected norms, which may lead the offender to be stigmatized. Crime is a form of deviance that involves violating the formal norms administered by the state for which the offender may receive formal sanctions.

III. How do sociologists explain deviance and crime?
   • Sociologists offer up a number of theories of crime, each of which provides additional factors to be considered—such as the need for social order, the significance of interpersonal relationships and local context, and the importance of power and access to resources—that help us to better understand why deviance and crime occur.

Thinking CRITICALLY...

1. What do you think would be more effective in stopping binge drinking on campus—formal or informal social control?
2. Do you think alternative forms of justice—such as dispute resolution or healing circles—are appropriate responses to deviance? Are they appropriate responses to crime? If so, which kinds of offences?
3. Why do students cheat on assignments? How might the various theoretical perspectives on deviance explain this phenomenon?

Pop Quiz

1. Society brings about acceptance of basic norms through techniques and strategies for preventing deviant human behaviour. This process is termed
   a. stigmatization.
   b. labelling.
   c. law.
   d. social control.

2. The penalties and rewards we face for conduct concerning a social norm are known as
   a. informal social controls.
   b. stigmas.
   c. sanctions.
   d. conformities.

3. Stanley Milgram used the word *conformity* to mean
   a. going along with peers.
   b. compliance with higher authorities in a hierarchical structure.
   c. techniques and strategies for preventing deviant behaviour in any society.
   d. penalties and rewards for conduct concerning a social norm.

4. According to Hirschi's control theory,
   a. deviance involves acceptance and/or rejection of society's goals and means.
   b. our connection to members of society leads us to systematically conform to society's norms.
   c. we come to view ourselves as deviant based on how others view us.
   d. power and access to resources shape whose norms and values determine individual action.

5. Which of the following statements is true of deviance?
   a. Deviance is always criminal behaviour.
   b. Deviance is behaviour that violates the standards of conduct or expectations of a group or society.
   c. Deviance is perverse behaviour.
   d. Deviance is inappropriate behaviour that cuts across all cultures and social orders.

6. If an Aboriginal person is given a harsher sentence than a non-Aboriginal person who commits the same offence, this is an example of
   a. differential justice.
   b. labelling.
   c. conformity.
   d. anomie.

7. Which of the following is *not* one of the basic forms of adaptation specified in Robert Merton's anomie theory of deviance?
   a. conformity
   b. innovation
   c. ritualism
   d. hostility

8. Which sociologist first advanced the idea that an individual undergoes the same basic socialization process whether learning conforming or deviant acts?
   a. Robert Merton
   b. Edwin Sutherland
   c. Travis Hirschi
   d. William Chambliss

9. Which of the following theories contends that criminal victimization increases when communal relationships and social institutions break down?
   a. labelling theory
   b. conflict theory
   c. social disorganization theory
   d. differential association theory

10. Who of the following conducted observation research on two groups of high school males (the Saints and the Roughnecks) and concluded that social class played an important role in the varying fortunes of the two groups?
    a. Richard Quinney
    b. Edwin Sutherland
    c. Émile Durkheim
    d. William Chambliss

1. (d); 2. (c); 3. (a); 4. (b); 5. (b); 6. (a); 7. (d); 8. (b); 9. (c); 10. (d)

7

FAMILIES

LOVING, MARRYING, AND RAISING FAMILIES

"Do you love me?" This is the question that Tevye asks Golde, his wife, in the musical *The Fiddler on the Roof* (Jewison 1971). They had married 25 years ago in the old-fashioned way—a matchmaker had set them up—and they were not "in love" when they got married. They did not necessarily expect to ever love each other, but times were changing in their small Russian village in the early 1900s, and now Tevye wants to know.

Tevye and Golde's questions about love and marriage arise because their three daughters all reject the matchmaker tradition, believing that their own hearts should drive their matches. Their oldest turns down the matchmaker's choice of an older, wealthy butcher, opting instead for a poor tailor her own age. Their next daughter falls in love with a revolutionary university student from the big city and she seeks Tevye's blessing but not his permission. Finally, their youngest daughter seeks neither blessing nor permission in marrying a Russian who is outside their Jewish faith. Along the way, Tevye asks himself if he can accept such violations of "tradition."

In the story, the daughters' breaks with tradition are tied to the larger social, economic, and historical upheavals in Russia at the time. Tradition has always ruled in the community, and these changes in tradition challenge Tevye and Golde's ability to accept their daughters' relationships and even their ability to understand their own. Tevye and Golde decide that they do, in fact, love each other. But their affirmation of love emerges only with the decline of traditions that have guided village life for generations.

Such forces continue to shape our understanding of marriage and of families. We often think that the way things are is the way that things have always been, but when it comes to love, marriage, and families, there is significant variation over time and across cultures. Understanding our beliefs and actions from within the context of an institution such as the family allows us to better see and understand both the "big picture" of our interconnections and the intimate realities of our everyday interactions.

- What is the family?
- How do people pick partners?
- How do families vary?

>> Global View of the Family

Among Tibetans, a woman may be married simultaneously to more than one man, usually brothers. This system allows sons to share the limited amount of good land. Among the Betsileo of Madagascar, a man has multiple wives, each one living in a different village where he cultivates rice. Wherever he has the best rice field, that woman is considered his first or senior wife. Among the Yanomami of Brazil and Venezuela, it is considered proper to have sexual relations with one's opposite-sex cousins if they are the children of one's mother's brother or father's sister. But if one's opposite-sex cousins are the children of one's mother's sister or father's brother, the same practice is considered to be incest (Haviland et al. 2005; Kottak 2004).

In Canada, the family of today is not what it was a century or even a generation ago. New roles, new gender distinctions, and new child-rearing patterns have all combined to create new forms of family life. Today, for example, more and more women are taking the breadwinner's role, whether as a spouse or as a single parent. Blended families—the result of divorce and remarriage—are common. And many people are electing to cohabit, instead of marry.

Did You Know?

. . . Niagara Falls, Ontario bills itself as the "Honeymoon Capital of the World." Every honeymoon couple receives an official honeymoon certificate signed by the mayor. In 2006, over 10,000 certificates were issued.

We see such changes reflected in popular culture representations of families. The 1950s Western family was epitomized on television by shows such as *Leave It to Beaver* and *Father Knows Best* with a stay-at-home mom, working dad, and assorted kids. Times have changed. *Two and a Half Men* features a father, son, and uncle; *Hannah Montana* depicts a single father with his daughter and son; and shows such as *The New Adventures of Old Christine* portray blended families with divorced parents, new partners, and adult siblings sharing household responsibilities. Perhaps the closest you get these days to the 1950s family is *The Simpsons* with Homer, Marge, Lisa, Bart, and Maggie. This shift in how families are portrayed

is consistent with changes we have seen both in practice and in our understanding of what constitutes a family.

Because families as we experience them are varied in structure and style, we need a sociological approach that is sufficiently broad to encompass all those things we experience as family. We will look at two different definitional approaches. The first is a substantive definition that focuses on what a family is, and the second is a functional definition that focuses on what families do.

SUBSTANCE: WHAT A FAMILY IS

Perhaps the most conventional approach to defining family is the **substantive definition,** which focuses on blood and law. Blood, in this case, means that people are related because they share a biological heritage passed on directly from parent to child, linking people indirectly to grandparents, aunts and uncles, and other biological relatives. By law, we mean the formal social recognition and affirmation of a shared bond among members. Marriage and adoption are examples of this.

The primary advantage of this definitional approach is that boundaries are clear; we can tell who is in and who is out. This makes it easier to count such families. In Canada, the **census family** is "composed of a married or common-law couple, with or without children, or a lone parent living with at least one child, in the same dwelling." A couple can be of the opposite sex or the same sex (Statistics Canada).

Kinship Patterns Many of us can trace our roots by looking at a family tree or by listening to elderly family members talk about their lives—and about the lives of ancestors who died long before we were born. Yet a person's lineage is more than simply a personal history; it also reflects

societal traditions that govern descent. In every culture, children encounter relatives to whom they are expected to show an emotional attachment. The state of being related to others is called **kinship.** Kinship is culturally learned, however, and is not totally determined by biological or marital ties. For example, adoption creates a kinship tie that is legally acknowledged and socially accepted.

The family and the kin group are not necessarily one and the same. Whereas the family is a household unit, kin do not always live together or function as a collective body on a daily basis. Kin groups include aunts, uncles, cousins, in-laws, and so forth. In a society such as Canada, the kinship group may come together only rarely, for a wedding or funeral. However, kinship ties frequently involve obligations and responsibilities. We may feel compelled to assist our kin, and we feel free to call upon them for many types of aid, including loans and babysitting.

How do we identify kinship groups? The principle of descent assigns people to kinship groups according to their

> **substantive definition of the family** A definition of the family based on blood, meaning shared genetic heritage; and law, meaning formal social recognition and affirmation of a shared bond among members.
> **census family** A married or common-law couple, with or without children, or a lone parent living with at least one child, in the same dwelling.
> **kinship** The state of being related to others.

SOCthink

> > > How important are intergenerational kinship networks and extended family members in your family? How has this changed since your parents' and grandparents' generations?

extent of polygamy in North America, the legal, religious, and ethical debates are sure to grow more heated.

Once we begin to look at the varieties of family types around the world, we see the main limitation of the substantive definition implies. People in Canada seem to agree that traditional definitions of family are too restrictive. In one survey, only 22 percent of the respondents defined family as per the substantive definition. Instead, 74 percent con-

> ## Family isn't about whose blood you have. It's about who you care about.
>
> Trey Parker and
> Matt Stone

definition: There are people who seem to be family but who do not fit neatly into blood or law. For example, the biological parent-to-child tie was expanded by including adoption as part of law. We accept stepparents and stepsiblings as family members even when the children have not been formally adopted by the stepparent. But what about pushing the definition of family still further? Is dad's university friend "Uncle" Bob part of the family? New forms of reproductive technology, involving donated sperm and eggs and surrogate parents, also challenge conventional thinking. Any substantive definition we might come up with runs the risk of excluding those whom we think of as family members. In response sociologists turn toward the more inclusive functionalist definition of families to address such limitations.

functionalist definition of families A definition of families that focuses on what families do for society and for their members.

FUNCTIONS: WHAT FAMILIES DO

When we ask people how they would define family, their conception is much more inclusive than the substantive sidered a family to be "any group whose members love and care for one another" (Coontz 1992:21).

We need a definition of families that is inclusive enough to encompass the broad range of intimate groups that people form, such as extended families, nuclear families, single-parent families, blended or reconstituted or step families, gay and lesbian families, child-free families, racially and ethnically mixed families, commuter marriage families, surrogate or chosen families, and more. One way to avoid getting trapped into overly narrow conceptions of families, and to embrace their diversity is to shift focus from a substantive definition of what families *are* to a **functionalist definition** of what families *do* for society and for their members.

Sociologist William F. Ogburn (Ogburn and Tibbits 1934) identified six primary functions that families perform for us:

- *Reproduction.* For a society to maintain itself, it must replace dying members. Families provide the context within which biological reproduction takes place.

- *Socialization.* Parents and other family members monitor a child's behaviour and transmit the norms, values, and language of their culture to the child.

- *Protection.* Unlike the young of other animal species, human infants need constant care and economic security. In all cultures, the family assumes the ultimate responsibility for the protection and upbringing of children.

- *Regulation of sexual behaviour.* Sexual norms are subject to change both over time (for instance, in the customs for dating) and across cultures (compare strict Saudi Arabia to the more permissive Denmark). However, whatever the time period or cultural values of a society, standards of sexual behaviour are most clearly defined within the family circle.

- *Affection and companionship.* Ideally, families provide members with warm and intimate relationships, helping them to feel satisfied and secure. Of course, a family member may find such rewards outside the family—from peers, in school, at work—and may even perceive the home as an unpleasant or abusive setting. Nevertheless, we expect our relatives to understand us, to care for us, and to be there for us when we need them.

- *Provision of social status.* We inherit a social position because of the family background and reputation of our parents and siblings. For example, the race, ethnicity, social class, education level, occupation, and religion of our parents all shape the material, social, and cultural resources to which we have access and therefore the options we might have.

No matter how it is composed, any group that fulfills these functions is family to us. We might count teammates, close schoolmates, or a long-term circle of friends as family. We look to such groups in moments of need for all kinds of support, including care and affection, guidance in how to think and act, dating advice, and sometimes even material support, whether borrowing a car or just some money for pizza. We may use the expression that they are "like family" to convey that sense, or we may even refer to such significant people in our lives as our sister, brother, mom, or dad. In fact, given the survey results above, people may already be defining as family any group that provides sufficient love and care for each other. According to this functionalist definition, a family *is* what a family *does.*

As discussed above, many of us apply a broad definition of "family," and to some degree, who we consider family is based on individual perception and experience. However, whether family is *officially* understood in terms of form or function has significant implications from a social policy perspective. For instance, you may consider

Hot or Not?

Should pets, including dogs, cats, birds, or others, count as family?

SOCthink

> > > Matchmaker services still exist, some charging as much as $20,000 for a membership with additional annual fees. Why might people turn to matchmaking services today? What are the limitations of relying on our own contacts and judgment when it comes to finding a romantic partner?

your best friend to be "family," but unless you had written provision to that effect, it is unlikely that they would be permitted to make decisions about your medical care; instead, a "family member," i.e., a relative or partner, would need to be consulted. Decisions involving child custody, parental leave, spousal benefits, and other important family issues are very much affected by legal definitions of what constitutes "family."

AUTHORITY PATTERNS: WHO RULES?

Regardless of what a family looks like, within the context of any group we define as family, we will inevitably have to address issues of power. Imagine, for example, that you have recently married and must begin to make decisions about the future of your new family. You and your partner face many questions: Where will you live? How will you furnish your home? Who will do the cooking, shopping, and cleaning? Whose friends will be invited to dinner? Each time a decision must be made, an issue is raised: Who has the power to make the decision? In simple terms, who rules the family?

Societies vary in the way that power is distributed within the family; historically, however, the answer to that question has largely been shaped by gender. A society that expects males to dominate in all family decision making is termed a **patriarchy.** In patriarchal societies, such as Iran, the eldest male often wields the greatest power, although wives are expected to be treated with respect and kindness. An Iranian woman's status is typically defined by her relationship to a male relative, usually as a wife or daughter. In many patriarchal societies, women find it more difficult to obtain a divorce than a man does. In contrast, in a **matriarchy,** women have greater authority than men. Formal matriarchies, which are uncommon, emerged among Native American tribal societies and in nations in which men were absent for long periods because of warfare or food-gathering expeditions (Farr 1999).

Over a century ago, Friedrich Engels ([1884] 1959), a colleague of Karl Marx, went so far as to say that the

> **patriarchy** A society in which men dominate in family decision making.
> **matriarchy** A society in which women dominate in family decision making.

family is the ultimate source of social inequality because of its role in the transfer of power, property, and privilege. Historically, the family has legitimized and perpetuated male dominance. It has contributed to societal injustice, denied women opportunities that are extended to men, and limited freedom in sexual expression and mate selection. In Canada, it was not until the first wave of contemporary feminism that there was a substantial challenge to the historical status of wives and children as the legal property of husbands and fathers.

Due in part to the efforts of women and men in similar movements over the years, we have seen the rise of a third type of authority pattern. In the **egalitarian family,** spouses are regarded as equals. This shift has been driven at least in part by occupational and financial opportunities for women that previously had been denied them (Wills and Risman 2006). That does not mean, however, that all decisions are shared in such families. Wives may hold authority in some spheres, and husbands in others. For example, sociologists have found that, in terms of paid and unpaid labour in two-parent families, the total hours worked by mothers and fathers is roughly equal at about 65 hours per week, though the distribution of tasks varies (Bianchi, Robinson, and Milkie 2006).

egalitarian family An authority pattern in which spouses are regarded as equals.

Historian Stephanie Coontz (2008) suggests that, when it works, marriage today is better than ever. She writes that it "delivers more benefits to its members—adults and children—than ever before. A good marriage is fairer and more fulfilling for both men and women than couples of the past could ever have imagined." She points to shared decision making and housework, increases in time spent with children, and declines in violence and sexual coercion and in the likelihood of adultery. These positive aspects of marriage may help us understand the continued popularity of the *idea* of getting married, despite the recent decline in marriage rates in Canada. As sociologist Reginald Bibby (2004) discovered, the vast majority of Canadians express traditional hopes and aspirations regarding marriage and family, even though the reality often fails to match those dreams.

While the egalitarian family has become somewhat more common in Canada in recent decades, male dominance over the family has hardly disappeared. Sociologists have found that although married men are increasing

their involvement in child care, their wives still perform a disproportionate amount of it. Furthermore, for every stay-at-home dad there are 38 stay-at-home moms (Fields 2004:11–12; Garcia-Moreno et al. 2004; Sayer et al. 2004). And unfortunately, many husbands reinforce their power and control over wives and children through acts of domestic violence.

In addition to the issue of authority within relationships, families also continue to provide a foundation for power within the larger society. Family serves as the basis for transferring power, property, and privilege from one generation to the next. Although Canada is widely viewed as a land of opportunity, social mobility is restricted in important ways. Children inherit the privileged or less-than-privileged social and economic status of their parents (and in some cases, of earlier generations as well). The social class of parents significantly influences children's socialization experiences and the degree of protection they receive. Thus,

Did You Know?

...In 2006, 51.5 percent of the population aged 15 and over was unmarried, the first time in history that married people were the minority in Canada. "Unmarried" includes those who are widowed, divorced, separated, or have never been legally married (Statistics Canada 2009).

Ten Questions Couples Should Ask (or Wish They Had) Before Marrying

- Do you want to have children?
- Who will do what when it comes to housework?
- What are your expectations regarding sex?
- What do you think about having a television in the bedroom?
- What do you expect regarding religious training for our children?
- How much money do you owe?
- Do you like and respect my friends?
- What do you really think about my parents?
- What does my family do that annoys you?
- Are there some things you are not willing to give up in the marriage?

Source: New York Times 2006.

the socioeconomic status of a child's family will have a marked influence on his or her nutrition, health care, housing, educational opportunities, and in many respects, life chances as an adult. In many ways the family helps to maintain inequality.

>> Marriage and Family

Historically, the most consistent aspect of family life in this country has been the high rate of marriage. Although the 2006 Census revealed marriage rates are declining in Canada, most Canadians do live with other people, as indicated by the increase in common-law unions. When it comes to picking partners, most of us—unlike *Fiddler*

Going GLOBAL

Percentage of People Ages 20–24 Ever Married, Selected Countries

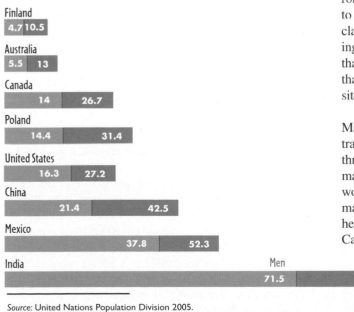

Country	Men	Women
Finland	4.7	10.5
Australia	5.5	13
Canada	14	26.7
Poland	14.4	31.4
United States	16.3	27.2
China	21.4	42.5
Mexico	37.8	52.3
India	71.5	94.3

Source: United Nations Population Division 2005.

on the Roof's Tevye and Golde—assume that romantic love alone will guide our choice. But as sociology demonstrates, our "realities" are socially constructed; what it means to be "in love," appropriate expressions of love, and how love is portrayed in popular culture all reflect prevailing ideologies, and in many instances, effective marketing strategies. This is not to dismiss the wonderful feeling we call "love," but the symbols we use to express it are culturally specific, and not completely natural. So as we now consider the bases for courtship and mate selection, it is important to remember that our social positions shape our choices and our freedom to express our desires and preferences.

COURTSHIP AND MATE SELECTION

"My rugby mates would roll over in their graves," says Tom Buckley of his online courtship of and subsequent marriage to Terri Muir. But Tom and Terri are hardly alone these days in turning to the Internet for matchmaking services. A generation or two ago, most couples met in high school, college or university, but now that people are marrying later in life, the Internet has become the new meeting place for the romantically inclined. Today, thousands of websites offer to help people find mates. For example, eHarmony, which claims to be the first to use a "scientific approach" to matching people based on a variety of abilities and interests, says that it "facilitates" 46 marriages a day. A 2005 survey found that 12 percent of couples who visited an online wedding site had met online (Kapos 2005; B. Morris 1999:D1).

Internet romance is only the latest courtship practice. Many other traditional cultures, including those of the central Asian nation of Uzbekistan, define courtship largely through the interaction of two sets of parents, who arrange marriages for their children. Typically, a young Uzbekistani woman is socialized to eagerly anticipate her marriage to a man whom she has met only once, when he is presented to her family at the time of the final inspection of her dowry. In Canada, by contrast, courtship occurs primarily by individuals who have a romantic interest in each other. In Canadian culture, courtship often requires these individuals to rely heavily on intricate games, gestures, and signals. Despite such differences, the norms and values of the larger society—whether in Canada, Uzbekistan, or elsewhere—influence courtship (C. J. Williams 1995).

One unmistakable trend in mate selection is that the process appears to be taking longer today than in the past. A variety of factors, including concerns about financial security and personal independence, has contributed to this delay in marriage. Most people are now well into their 20s before they marry, both in Canada and in other countries.

Many societies have explicit or unstated rules that define potential mates as acceptable or unacceptable. These norms can be distinguished in terms of endogamy and exogamy. **Endogamy** (from the Greek *endon,* "within") specifies the groups within which a spouse must be found and prohibits marriage with others. For example, in Canada, many people are expected to marry within their own racial, ethnic, or religious group and are strongly discouraged or even prohibited from marrying outside the group. Endogamy is intended to reinforce the cohesiveness of the group by suggesting to the young that they should marry someone "of their own kind."

In contrast, **exogamy** (from the Greek *exo,* "outside") requires mate selection outside certain groups, usually one's own family or certain kinfolk. The **incest taboo,** a social norm common to virtually all societies, prohibits sexual relationships between certain culturally specified relatives. In Canada, this taboo means that we must marry outside the nuclear family. We cannot marry our siblings, and marriage between first cousins is culturally discouraged.

Endogamous restrictions may be seen as preferences for one group over another. In North America, marrying outside of one's own racial, ethnic, or religious group is gaining social acceptance. The most common type of mixed race/ethnic relationship in Canada is between a Caucasian and a member of a visible minority, accounting for 2.8 percent of all couples. More common are interreligious relationships, constituting 19 percent of Canadian couples (Clark 2006). Even though these examples of exogamy are noteworthy, endogamy remains the social norm in Canada.

Another factor that influences the selection of marriage partner is **homogamy**—the conscious or unconscious tendency to select a mate with personal characteristics similar to one's own. The "like marries

5 Movies on MARRIAGE

Green Card
The business arrangement of marriage.

Arranged
Arranged marriages lead to unexpected friendship.

The Squid and the Whale
How divorce affects children.

The Story of Us
The ups and downs of marriage.

Kramer vs. Kramer
A custody battle.

like" rule can be seen in couples with similar personalities and interests. Internet dating services depend upon this principle to help find matches. Sociologist Pepper Schwartz, who works as a consultant for PerfectMatch.com, has developed a 48-question survey that covers everything from prospective mates' decision-making style to their degree of impulsivity (Gottlieb 2006). While it is certainly possible that "opposites attract," when it comes to romance, we tend to gravitate toward people more like ourselves.

VARIATIONS IN FAMILY LIFE AND INTIMATE RELATIONSHIPS

Within Canada, social class, race, ethnicity, and sexual orientation create variations in family life. Studying these variations will give us a more sophisticated understanding of contemporary family styles in our country. The desire to avoid having to negotiate such differences also helps to explain why people often practise homogamy.

Social Class Differences Social class differences in family life are less striking today than they once were. In the past, family specialists agreed that the contrasts in child-rearing practices were pronounced. Poor and working-class families were found to be more authoritarian in rearing children and more inclined to use physical punishment. Middle-class families were more permissive and more restrained in punishing their children. Compared to poor and working-class families, middle-class families tended to schedule more of their children's time, or even to overstructure it. However, these differences may have narrowed as more and more families from all social classes turned to the same books, magazines,

endogamy The restriction of mate selection to people within the same group.
exogamy The requirement that people select a mate outside certain groups.
incest taboo The prohibition of sexual relationships between certain culturally specified relatives.
homogamy The conscious or unconscious tendency to select a mate with personal characteristics similar to one's own.

SOCthink

> > > How important are factors such as age, education, race, ethnicity, social class, gender, and religion in whom you might choose for a serious relationship? To what extent are you conscious of such influences when you pick someone to date?

and even television talk shows for advice on rearing children (Kronstadt and Favreault 2008; Luster et al. 1989).

Among the poor, women often play a significant role in the economic support of the family. Men may earn low wages, may be unemployed, or may be entirely absent from the family. In 2005, 29 percent of all families headed by women with no husband present were living below the low income cut-off. The rate for married couples was only 7.4 percent (Statistics Canada 2007c). Many racial and ethnic groups appear to have distinctive family characteristics. However, racial and class factors are often closely related. In examining family life among racial and ethnic minorities, keep in mind that certain patterns may result from class as well as cultural factors.

men have been described as exhibiting a sense of virility, personal worth, and pride in their maleness that is called **machismo.** Mexican Americans are also described as being more familistic than many other subcultures. **Familism** refers to pride in the extended family, expressed through the maintenance of close ties and strong obligations to kinfolk outside the immediate family. Traditionally, Mexican Americans have placed proximity to their extended families above other needs and desires.

> ## The goal in marriage is not to think alike, but to think together.
>
> Robert C. Dodds

Racial and Ethnic Differences The subordinate status of Canada's Aboriginal peoples and other visible minorities has profound effects on their family life. For Aboriginal peoples, for whom kinship and community are so central to their culture, years of European domination has had a dramatic and detrimental impact. Among the indignities endured: families (and entire bands) were uprooted and forced onto reservations, children were removed from their homes and placed in residential schools, and also put up for adoption into non-Aboriginal families. In 2006, Phil Fontaine, (then) National Chief of the Assembly of First Nations noted that the key reason for Aboriginal children being taken into care is physical neglect due to poverty. The life expectancy of First Nations people is approximately five years shorter than that of the total Canadian population, due in large part to poor living conditions and a high suicide rate (Campaign 2000).

Like the First Nations people of Canada, Native Americans draw on family ties to cushion many of the hardships they face. On the Navajo reservation, for example, teenage parenthood is not regarded as the crisis that it is elsewhere in the United States. The Navajo trace their descent matrilineally. Traditionally, couples reside with the wife's family after marriage, allowing the grandparents to help with the child rearing. While the Navajo do not approve of teenage parenthood, the deep emotional commitment of their extended families provides a warm home environment for fatherless children (Dalla and Gamble 2001).

Sociologists also have taken note of differences in family patterns among other racial and ethnic groups. For example, Mexican American

Research on Black families in Nova Scotia and Toronto reveals significantly more families headed by women, compared to non-Black families. These families earn approximately half the income of Black families headed by a married couple, who in turn earn less than their equivalent non-Black counterparts (Calliste 2001). This study concludes that high rates of teenage pregnancy and the feminization of poverty are serious issues among the Black community, and suggests a range of educational and community initiatives are required to address these factors contributing to inequality.

Members of ethnic minority groups—particularly new immigrants to Canada—may face challenges in sustaining their family traditions as they adapt to their new country. As discussed earlier in this chapter, official family definitions can be quite restrictive, especially if one is accustomed to living in a society that embraces less rigid understandings of kinship and practises greater cooperation in such tasks

machismo A sense of virility, personal worth, and pride in one's maleness.
familism Pride in the extended family, expressed through the maintenance of close ties and strong obligations to kinfolk outside the immediate family.

as domestic chores and child care. In addition to cultural and ideological differences, Canadian housing is generally not designed to accommodate extended family forms.

Sexual Orientation Sexual orientation is another significant factor contributing to variations in family life. At one time, homosexuality was considered to be a mental illness by the medical community; a sin in many religious traditions; and considered by many segments of society as something that should be "hidden." In some countries, homosexuality remains illegal and subject to severe sanctions, including the death penalty. While Canada's social structure, like that of most nations, is premised upon and organized according to a heterosexual model, in recent years legislative changes and cultural awareness have made it relatively easier for gay, lesbian, bisexual, and transgendered persons to express their preferences and establish relationships accordingly. Today Canada is one of a handful of countries to legally recognize same-sex marriage. The popularity of and support for Toronto's annual Pride Parade (one of the largest in the world) is indicative of changing attitudes among Canadians. See page 151 for survey findings about such changing opinions.

As immigration and exogamy continue to bring together people of diverse racial and ethnic backgrounds, family patterns will likely change. And with greater social acceptance of diverse sexualities, we shall likely continue to see new compositions of families. Yet regardless of how families are organized, in North American culture, there is a common assumption: families are supposed to be responsible for raising children.

CHILD-REARING PATTERNS

Caring for children is a universal function of the family, yet the ways in which different societies assign this function to family members can vary significantly. The Nayars of southern India acknowledge the biological role of fathers, but the mother's eldest brother is responsible for her children. In contrast, uncles play only a peripheral role in child care in Canada. Even within Canada, child-rearing patterns are varied. Just as our conception of families has changed, so also has our practice of child rearing.

Parenthood and Grandparenthood The socialization of children is essential to the maintenance of any culture. Consequently, parenthood is one of the most important (and most demanding) social roles in Canada. Sociologist Alice Rossi (1968, 1984) has identified four factors that complicate the transition to parenthood and the role of socialization. First, there is little anticipatory socialization for the social

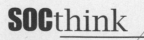

SOCthink

> > > What are the advantages and disadvantages of the dual-income model for women, for men, for children, and for society as a whole?

role of caregiver. The normal school curriculum gives scant attention to the subjects most relevant to successful family life, such as child care and home maintenance. Second, only limited learning occurs during the period of pregnancy itself. Third, the transition to parenthood is quite abrupt. Unlike adolescence, it is not prolonged; unlike the transition to work, the duties of caregiving cannot be taken on gradually. Finally, in Rossi's view, our society lacks clear and helpful guidelines for successful parenthood. There is little consensus on how parents can produce happy and well-adjusted offspring—or even on what it means to be well adjusted. For these reasons, socialization for parenthood involves difficult challenges for most men and women.

One recent development in family life in Canada has been the extension of parenthood, as adult children continue to live at home or return home after college or university. In 2006, 43.5 percent of young adults aged 20 to 29 lived with their parents. Some of these adult children were still pursuing an education, but in many instances, these living arrangements were prompted by financial difficulties. While rents and real estate prices have skyrocketed, salaries for

POPSOC

Parenthood has been a frequent source of entertainment in the movies. Examples of such films include *Mr. Mom, Parenthood, Finding Nemo, Freaky Friday, Cheaper by the Dozen, Daddy's Little Girls, Juno, Baby Mama,* and even *Alvin and the Chipmunks.* They all convey messages of what it means to be a parent. What lessons might we learn from an analysis of how mothers and fathers are portrayed in such films? What recurring images and themes occur? How common is the bungling dad or the career mom who wonders if she is making the right choices? What are the consequences of such films for how we practise parenting?

younger workers have not kept pace, and many find themselves unable to afford their own homes. Moreover, with many marriages now ending in divorce, divorced sons and daughters often return to live with their parents, sometimes with their own children (Statistics Canada 2007o).

Given that the dominant cultural expectation in Canada remains some form of the nuclear family, in which children are expected to set up households on their own once they reach adulthood, such arrangements present challenges for everybody involved. Social scientists have just begun to examine the phenomenon, sometimes called the "boomerang generation" or the "full-nest syndrome." One survey in the U.S. showed that neither the parents nor their adult children were happy about continuing to live together. The children often felt resentful and isolated, but the parents suffered too. Learning to live without children in the home is an essential stage of adult life and may even be a significant turning point for a marriage (*Berkeley Wellness Letter* 1990; Mogelonsky 1996).

In some homes, the full nest holds grandchildren. In 2006, more than 2 million children in Canada lived in a household with a grandparent. In many of these homes, no parent was present to assume responsibility for the youngsters. Special difficulties are inherent in such relationships, including legal custodial concerns, financial issues, and emotional problems for adults and youths alike. Perhaps not surprisingly, support groups such as Grandparents as Parents and CanGrands have emerged to provide assistance (Kreider 2008; Statistics Canada 2007k).

Adoption In a legal sense, **adoption** is a "process that allows for the transfer of the legal rights, responsibilities, and privileges of parenthood" to a new legal parent or parents (E. Cole 1985:638). In many cases, these rights are transferred from a biological parent or parents (often called birth parents) to an adoptive parent or parents.

From a functionalist perspective, adoption is beneficial not only in that children are ideally placed in stable family environments, but also for the consequent reduction to the government's social welfare expenses. But many children who need homes are passed over due to societal preference to adopt infants. For every child who is adopted, many more remain in foster care or other child protective services. In Canada, infants are rarely available, due to improved contraception methods and social supports that enable people to parent children who might otherwise have been given up for adoption. As

Hot or Not?

Should adoption records be open or closed?

Hollywood stars Angelina Jolie and Brad Pitt and several of their children, many from overseas adoptions.

a result, many people turn to international adoption. This practice is not without controversy: Interactionists acknowledge the potential challenges of adjustment when children are adopted into families with dramatically different backgrounds and experiences. Furthermore, international adoption agencies charge exorbitant "administration" fees to prospective parents, thus barring many potentially excellent parents from pursuing the option. On a global scale, the "purchasing" of children reinforces the image of wealthy citizens (and by extension, countries) exploiting poorer people (and nations). China, the source for a significant number of overseas adoptions, recently began to tighten the rules for foreigners. Applicants who are single, obese, or older than 50 may now be disqualified automatically (Carr 2007; Gross 2007).

> **adoption** In a legal sense, a process that allows for the transfer of the legal rights, responsibilities, and privileges of parenthood to a new legal parent or parents.

Dual-Income Families The idea of a family consisting of a wage-earning husband and a stay-at-home wife has largely given way to the dual-income household. Among married people, 94 percent of men and 74 percent of women were in the paid labour force in 2005 (Luffman 2006).

Both opportunity and need have driven the rise in the number of dual-income couples. Women now have the opportunity to pursue careers in a way that previously had been closed due to cultural expectations regarding gender. This has resulted in increased education levels for women and increased participation in occupational fields that had been largely closed. As well, many couples find it increasingly difficult to make ends meet with a single income.

Single-Parent Families The 2004 *American Idol* winner Fantasia Barrino's song "Baby Mama" offers a tribute to young single mothers—a subject she knows about. Barrino was 17 when she became pregnant with her daughter. Though critics charged that the song sends the wrong message to teenage girls, Barrino says it is not about encouraging teens to have sex. Rather, she sees the song as an anthem for young mothers courageously trying to raise their children alone (Cherlin 2006).

In recent decades, the stigma attached to unwed mothers and other single parents has significantly diminished. **Single-parent families,** in which only one parent is present to care for the children, can hardly be viewed as a rarity in Canada. In 2006, a single parent headed approximately 16 percent of families with children, and increasing numbers of these parents have never been married (as demonstrated in the figure below).

> **single-parent family** A family in which only one parent is present to care for the children.

The life of single parents and their children is not inevitably more difficult than that of a traditional nuclear family. It is as inaccurate to assume that a single-parent family is necessarily deprived as it is to assume that a two-parent family is always secure and happy. Nevertheless, to the extent that such families have to rely on a single income or a sole caregiver, life in the single-parent family can be extremely stressful. A

Comedians Tina Fey and Amy Poehler starred in the 2008 film Baby Mama, in which Fey played a would-be single mother.

many young women face because of their gender, race, ethnicity, and class, many teenagers may believe they have little to lose and much to gain by having a child.

Although 80 percent of single parents in Canada are mothers, the number of households headed by single fathers more than doubled between 2001 and 2006, to

> What greater thing is there for human souls than to feel that they are joined for life—to be with each other in silent unspeakable memories.
>
> George Eliot

family headed by a single mother faces especially difficult problems when the mother is a teenager, as she is more likely to lack access to significant social and economic resources.

Why might low-income teenage women wish to have children and face the obvious financial difficulties of motherhood? Some theorists argue that these women tend to have low self-esteem and limited options; a child may provide a sense of motivation and purpose for the teenager whose economic worth in our society is limited at best. Given the barriers that

19.9 percent. While single mothers often develop social networks, single fathers are typically more isolated. In addition, they must deal with schools and social service agencies that are more accustomed to women as custodial parents (Kreider 2008; Statistics Canada 2007k).

Stepfamilies Approximately 64 percent of all divorced people in Canada will remarry at some point in their lives. The patterns of divorce and remarriage have led to

Single-Parent Families in Canada, 1951–2006

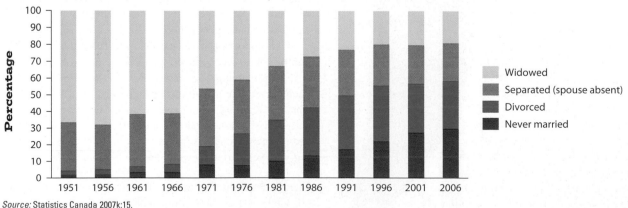

Legend: Widowed; Separated (spouse absent); Divorced; Never married

Source: Statistics Canada 2007k:15.

a noticeable increase in stepfamily relationships. The exact nature of blended families has social significance for adults and children alike.

Family members in stepfamilies must deal with resocialization issues when an adult becomes a stepparent or a child becomes a stepchild and stepsibling. In evaluating these stepfamilies, some observers have assumed that children would benefit from remarriage because they would be gaining a second custodial parent and would potentially enjoy greater economic security. However, after reviewing many studies of stepfamilies, sociologist Andrew J. Cherlin (2008:800) concluded that "the well-being of children in stepfamilies is no better, on average, than the well-being of children in divorced, single-parent households."

Same-Sex Families

In July 2005, same-sex couples were granted the legal right to marry in Canada. While there hasn't been as dramatic an increase in same-sex marriages as many anticipated, perhaps the extension of that right has made it easier for gay and lesbian people to be open about their relationships: according to Statistics Canada (2007k), the number of same-sex couples has increased at five times the rate of opposite-sex couples.

Same-sex couples account for 0.6 percent of all couples in Canada, which is comparable to both Australia (0.6 percent) and New Zealand (0.7 percent). Of Canada's more than 45,000 same-sex couples, 16.5 percent are married. Same-sex married couples are twice as likely to be raising children as same-sex cohabiting couples, and more lesbian couples than gay male couples have children in their families (Statistics Canada 2007k).

Some gays and lesbians live in long-term, monogamous relationships; others live alone or with roommates. Some remain in heterosexual marriages for "appearances" and do not publicly acknowledge their homosexuality. Same-sex families take many forms, as do heterosexual families, and they fulfill the same important functions.

>> Divorce

"Do you promise to love, honour, and cherish . . . until death do you part?" Every year, people of all social classes and

Attitudes Toward Gay Rights Depend on Who You Know

	Doesn't know someone gay or lesbian	Knows someone gay or lesbian
Gay couples should be able to adopt	28%	50%
Gay partners should have social welfare benefits	43%	60%
Gay and lesbian people should serve openly in the military	48%	63%
Hate-crime laws should include violence committed against gay and lesbian people	54%	69%
Gay partners should have inheritance rights	50%	73%
Gay and lesbian people should have equal rights in employment	77%	90%

Source: www/hrc.org.

racial and ethnic groups make this legally binding agreement. Yet a significant number of these promises shatter prior to divorce.

STATISTICAL TRENDS IN DIVORCE

Just how common is divorce? Surprisingly, this is not a simple question to answer; divorce statistics are difficult to interpret. The media frequently report that one out of every three marriages ends in divorce. But that figure is misleading in that many marriages last for decades. It is based on a comparison of all divorces that occur in a single year (regardless of when the couples were married) with the number of new marriages in that same year. We get a somewhat more complete picture by looking at marital milestones people reach based on the year they first married (as shown in the table on page 152). These data include marriages that end due to the death of the partner; given that life expectancy has increased, it does provide a sense of shifting patterns. Following either the rows or the columns provides insight into both the generational effect and the impact of changing attitudes and practices over time.

In Canada and many other countries, overall divorce rates began to increase in the late 1960s It peaked in the late 1980s, then declined and has levelled off at 38 percent (see "Trends in Marriage and Divorce in Canada, 1967–2006" on page 153). This trend is due partly to the aging of the baby boomer generation and the corresponding decline in the proportion of people of marriageable age.

Percentage of Marriages to Reach Milestones*

Men, year of first marriage	Anniversary (percentage still married)*							
	5th	10th	15th	20th	25th	30th	35th	40th
1955–59	96.4	88.3	80.3	73.8	70.4	67.3	64.7	61.4
1960–64	95.1	85.0	75.2	69.7	65.0	62.4	59.7	52.5
1965–69	90.5	76.9	67.4	62.3	58.6	55.5	48.2	
1970–74	88.5	74.4	64.6	58.1	53.8	46.2		
1975–79	88.1	73.0	65.2	59.6	49.5			
1980–84	88.7	73.7	65.3	53.8				
1985–89	89.3	76.4	60.6					
1990–94	89.4	70.0						

Women, year of first marriage	Anniversary (percentage still married)*							
	5th	10th	15th	20th	25th	30th	35th	40th
1955–59	94.0	86.8	79.4	72.4	67.2	63.5	58.9	54.7
1960–64	92.8	82.3	72.7	66.5	60.4	56.1	52.7	44.9
1965–69	89.5	74.9	65.7	60.0	55.1	51.3	43.8	
1970–74	87.1	71.6	61.4	55.4	50.6	42.1		
1975–79	85.3	70.0	61.4	55.7	46.4			
1980–84	86.5	70.7	63.1	52.4				
1985–89	85.7	73.0	56.9					
1990–94	87.2	69.2						

*Counts marriages ended by divorce, separation, and death

Source: U.S. Census Bureau 2004:Table 2.

Getting divorced obviously does not sour people on marriage. About 70 percent of divorced men and 58 percent of divorced women in Canada have remarried. Women are less likely than men to remarry because many retain custody of their children after a divorce, which complicates a new adult relationship (Bianchi and Spain 1996; Saad 2004; Statistics Canada 2007h).

Some people regard the nation's high rate of remarriage as an endorsement of the institution of marriage, but it does lead to the new challenges of a kin network characterized by both current and prior marital relationships. Such networks can be particularly complex if children are involved or if an ex-spouse remarries.

FACTORS ASSOCIATED WITH DIVORCE

One of the major factors shaping the increase in divorce over the past 100 years has been the greater social acceptance of divorce. It is no longer considered necessary to endure an unhappy marriage. Even major religious groups have relaxed what were often negative attitudes toward divorce, commonly having treated it as a sin.

The growing acceptance of divorce is a worldwide phenomenon. Only a decade ago, Sunoo, South Korea's foremost matchmaking service, had no divorced clients. Few Koreans divorced, and those who did felt social pressure to resign themselves to the single life. But in recent years, South Korea's divorce rate has doubled, and thus now 15 percent of Sunoo's membership is divorced (Onishi 2003).

In Canada, a number of factors have contributed to the growing social acceptance of divorce. No-fault divorce laws, which allow a couple to end their marriage without assigning blame (by specifying adultery, for instance), accounted for an initial surge in the divorce rate after they were introduced in 1985, though these laws appear to have had little effect beyond that. Additionally, a general increase in family incomes, coupled with the availability of free legal aid to some poor people, has meant that more couples can afford costly divorce proceedings. Also, as society provides greater opportunities for women, more and more wives are becoming less dependent on their husbands, both economically and emotionally. They may feel more able to leave a marriage if it seems hopeless. The trend toward having fewer or no children may also contribute to a sense of being "allowed" to end a marriage.

IMPACT OF DIVORCE ON CHILDREN

Divorce is traumatic for all involved, but it has special meaning for the many children whose parents divorce each year. Of course, for some of these children, divorce signals the welcome end to a highly dysfunctional relationship. A national sample conducted by sociologists Paul R. Amato and Alan Booth (1997) showed that in about a third of divorces, the children actually benefitted

Did You Know?

... For women, the likelihood of getting a divorce decreases for each year she waits to get married. Women who got married at age 35 or older have the lowest chance of getting divorced.

Trends in Marriage and Divorce in Canada, 1967–2006

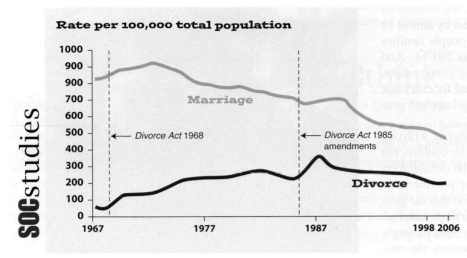

Rate per 100,000 total population

Marriage

← Divorce Act 1968

Divorce Act 1985
amendments →

Divorce

1967   1977   1987   1998 2006

Source: Baker 2001a; calculations from Statistics Canada 2007k.

SOCstudies

from parental separation because it lessened their exposure to conflict. But in about 70 percent of divorces, the parents engaged in a low level of conflict; in those cases, the realities of divorce appeared to be harder for the children to bear than living with the marital unhappiness.

Other researchers, using differing definitions of conflict, have found greater unhappiness for children living in homes with marital differences. Still, it would be simplistic to assume that children are automatically better off following the breakup of their parents' marriage. The interests of the parents do not necessarily serve children well.

FAMILY VIOLENCE

The functionalist view of the family emphasizes its importance to reproduction and socialization, and the protection and affection extended to those considered family members. This view is mirrored by common media portrayals of the family as the source of comfort, safety, and security—what Christopher Lasch (1977) called the "haven in a heartless world." But such characterizations ignore the reality that for many, family is a source of conflict, and possibly danger.

Indeed, research on crime has revealed one is most likely to be physically assaulted or killed in one's own home, by someone they know—usually an intimate partner. Family violence (also known as domestic violence) includes, but is not limited to, spousal or partner violence, violence against women, violence against children, and elder abuse. In Canada, Aboriginal women are at particular risk of domestic violence, with reported rates more than three times those of non-Aboriginal women (CCJS 2007). Feminist and conflict theorists note the limitations of a functionalist view of the family; clearly there are many *dysfunctions* within families, and as sociologists, we must be critical of unrealistic portrayals that ignore these.

>> Diverse Lifestyles

Marriage is no longer the presumed route from adolescence to adulthood. In fact, it has lost much of its social significance as a rite of passage. Now, establishing oneself through education and a career has taken precedence (Cherlin 2004). The nation's marriage rate has declined since the 1960s because people are postponing marriage until later in life and because more couples, including same-sex couples, are deciding to form partnerships without marriage.

COHABITATION

In Canada, testing the marital waters by living together before making a commitment is a common practice among marriage-wary 20- and 30-somethings. The tremendous increase in the number of couples who choose to live together without marrying, a practice called **cohabitation,** is one of the most dramatic social trends of recent years.

> **cohabitation** The practice of living together as a couple without marrying.

Theory

A Matter of Perspective

THEORETICAL PERSPECTIVES ON FAMILY

Functionalist:
- emphasizes the contribution of family to social stability

Conflict:
- views family as perpetuator of inequality along class, racial, and ethnic lines; transmission of poverty or wealth across generations

Feminist:
- sees families as diverse and changeable; however, may serve to reinforce gendered expectations of members

Interactionist:
- emphasizes relationships among family members in constructing "family" life

In
more
ily s
the r
of th
com
perc
incre
whil
rates
grou
(Sta

I
of th
wor
rate
muc
eral
In Ic
moth
port
cour
unm
2006
grea
peop
thos

RE

Mor
into

Sourc

8

EDUCATION&R

FAITH AND LEARNING

Patrick Henry College, located near Washington, D.C., was founded in 2000 with the explicit intention of competing with Ivy League schools. The elite students it pursues, however, come from a particular niche: Approximately 80 percent of them were home-schooled, and they all share a strong commitment to evangelical Christian faith.

In keeping with the school's expectation of a high level of religious commitment, students must sign a "Statement of Faith" that sets out a series of Christian beliefs, including the virgin birth of Jesus Christ, the existence of Satan, and eternal punishment in hell for non-Christians. Students are required to abide by a strict dress code, attend daily chapel, and abstain from alcohol, smoking, and premarital sex.

The students by and large take these commitments quite seriously. As journalist Hannah Rosin (2007) recounts in her book on Patrick Henry College entitled *God's Harvard,* "To them, a 'Christian' keeps a running conversation with God in his or her head . . . and believes that at any moment God might in some palpable way step in and show He either cares or disapproves" (p. 5).

Student Elisa Muench was something of a trailblazer at Patrick Henry College. She was the first woman to run for a leadership position in student government, in the face of disapproval by students who thought it inappropriate that a woman should serve in such an office. As a junior, she had an internship in the White House. Yet she found herself fearing that what counted as success in the eyes of the dominant society, including a professional career, might conflict with success in the eyes of God (Rosin 2007:85). Elisa struggled to be true to both her educational and religious teachings.

It is within such educational and religious communities that we learn what to believe and how to act. All of us are, in some respects, like Elisa, seeking to balance the sometimes conflicting demands of the various spheres of our lives, including family, education, religion, work, and politics. In this chapter, we focus on the roles education and religion play both for individuals and for society as a whole.

ELIGION

- How does education help to maintain social order?
- How does education support the existing system of inequality?
- How do sociologists define religion?

>> Education in Society

Historically, we counted on families to be significant agents of socialization, teaching us the basic knowledge, values, and norms we needed to survive. As societies became more diverse and the division of labour increased, however, our educational needs expanded, and we placed a greater emphasis on more formal socialization. When learning is explicit and formalized—when some people consciously teach, while others adopt the role of learner—the process of socialization is called **education.**

> **education** A formal process of learning in which some people consciously teach, while others adopt the social role of learner.

We invest a significant amount of time and money in education. Why? The simple answer is that we believe the individual and collective benefits are worth it. In schools we investigate the deeper mysteries of life so that we might have a better understanding of ourselves and our world. As sociologist W. E. B. Du Bois ([1903] 1994) put it, "The true college will ever have one goal,—not to earn meat, but to know the end and aim of that life which meat nourishes" (p. 51). As individuals we also acquire skills and credentials that we need to find a good job. In terms of both how we think and what we are capable of doing, education provides pathways for social change.

The history of education in Canada is one of expansion and institutionalization. Expansion is reflected in the growing percentage of Canadians going to school for more

SOCthink

> > > Who most influenced you to pursue higher education? Considering people you know who did not go to college or university, what influenced them to make that choice? How powerful are socialization and social networks in making such decisions?

Did You Know?

...According to the Canadian Federation of Students, on January 21, 2009, Canadian student loan debt surpassed the $13-billion mark. This figure does not include debt from provincial loans or personal debt.

years and for higher degrees. For example, from 1990 to 2006, the proportion of people aged 25 to 64 with a high school diploma increased from 74 percent to more than 85 percent. In the same period, the proportion of those with a post-secondary degree increased from 42 percent to approximately 60 percent (Statistics Canada 2008i). Institutionalization has occurred as education has become more formalized—a distinct part of the public sphere. Educational organizations have become more professional and bureaucratic in their attempt to more efficiently provide services to the whole population.

Early Canadian education advocates believed public education to be an essential component of democratic societies. They argued that public education provides individuals with essential knowledge and skills for development and advancement and that it provides society with informed citizens who can serve as social, economic, and political leaders.

Public education was seen as a means to opportunity. Egerton Ryerson, widely considered the "father of public education" in Canada, envisioned a system in which all children, regardless of religious faith or social status, would receive the skills and knowledge necessary to be productive citizens. As superintendent of education for Upper Canada, Ryerson introduced the first Schools Act, the principles of which continue to inform public education today: standardized texts, formal teacher training, and compulsory taxation to fund the system and thus make it truly open to all,

Going GLOBAL

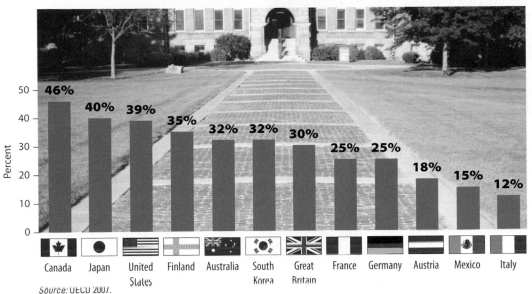

Percentage of Adults Ages 25–64 Who Have Completed Post-Secondary Education, 2005

Country	Percent
Canada	46%
Japan	40%
United States	39%
Finland	35%
Australia	32%
South Korea	32%
Great Britain	30%
France	25%
Germany	25%
Austria	18%
Mexico	15%
Italy	12%

Source: OECD 2007.

regardless of means. Horace Mann, an American contemporary of Egerton and a public education advocate in his country, wrote in 1848: "Education, beyond all other devices of human origin, is the great equalizer of the conditions of men,—the balance-wheel of the social machinery" ([1848] 1957). Initially, schools were open only to those from elite White families and stratified along religious lines. But thanks to the efforts of advocates such as Ryerson, the work of the feminist movement, and the contributions of sociologists—including Durkheim and DuBois—public education expanded to include everyone regardless of race, ethnicity, sex, religion, or national origin. As we will see, however, the principle of equal educational opportunity does not necessarily result in the practice of educational equality.

>> Sociological Perspectives on Education

Sociologists have closely examined the degree to which education actually succeeds in providing social order and individual opportunity. They have found that while it does offer opportunity and help to establish social order, it also perpetuates inequality. Fulfilling the hopes of its visionaries, it has produced an educated citizenry equipped to take on the challenges of modern life. At the same time, however, it reinforces existing beliefs, values, and norms that justify the status quo and its inequalities. The dominant sociological perspectives on education focus on the role education plays in society.

EDUCATION AND SOCIAL ORDER

As functionalists assert, society needs people with the knowledge and skills to perform the tasks necessary for its continued existence, and individuals need this know-how to survive and prosper. Schools teach students how to read, speak foreign languages, repair automobiles, and much more. In this section, we will look at some of the collective and individual benefits of education that sociologists have identified.

Transmitting Culture

As a social institution, education preserves and transmits the dominant culture. Schooling exposes each generation of young people to the existing beliefs, norms, and values of their culture. In Canada, we learn respect for existing values and norms and reverence for established institutions, such as the economy, the family, and the government. Of course, this is true of many other cultures as well. While schoolchildren in Canada are hearing about the accomplishments of Sir John A. Macdonald and Laura Secord, American children are hearing about the distinctive contributions of George Washington and Abraham Lincoln.

In Great Britain, the transmission of the dominant culture through schools goes beyond traditional content such as learning about monarchs, prime ministers, and generals. In 1996 the government's chief curriculum advisor—noting the need to fill a void left by the diminishing authority of the Church of England—proposed that British schools socialize students into a set of core values. The set included honesty, respect for others, politeness, a sense of fair play, forgiveness, punctuality, non-violent behaviour, patience, faithfulness, and self-discipline (Charter

and Sherman 1996). Similar programs have been established in Canada, such as the emphasis on "character education," which highlights such qualities as responsibility, respect, fairness, and citizenship.

Sometimes nations reassess the ways in which they transmit culture to students. Recently, the Chinese government revised the nation's history curriculum. Students are now taught that the Chinese Communist Party, not the United States, played a central role in defeating Japan in World War II. No mention is made of the estimated 30 million Chinese who died from famine because of party founder Mao Zedong's disastrous Great Leap Forward (1958–1962), a failed effort to transform China's agrarian economy into an industrial powerhouse. In urban, Western-oriented areas such as Shanghai, textbooks acknowledge the technological advances made in Western industrial countries but avoid any criticism of past policies of the Chinese government (French 2004b; Kahn 2006b).

SOCthink

> > > Why do you think there has been a move toward character education in schools? What changes in society might contribute to that perceived need?

Hot or Not?

Who should get to decide what is taught in schools?

the dominant culture. The common identity and social integration fostered by education contributes to societal stability and consensus (Touraine 1974). At the same time, in keeping with the country's multicultural demographics, Canadian educators are expected to encourage cultural diversity and acknowledge different backgrounds and experiences in the classroom.

In the past, the integrative function of education was most obvious in its emphasis on promoting a common language. In Canada, this has meant that immigrant and Aboriginal children have historically been expected to learn French or English (depending upon the region) and discouraged from speaking their native languages in the school setting. In addition to linguistic restrictions, public education in this country has long maintained separate systems, with provisions for distinct Catholic and Protestant systems enshrined in the British North America Act of 1867. Today, the "Protestant" system is a secular, public one, while the Catholic board is commonly known as the "separate" system. Individual provinces set their own guidelines regarding funding of this separate system as well as other faith-based schooling.

Recent decades have brought greater acceptance and appreciation of diversity. French immersion learning has become a popular choice for many parents who recognize their children may benefit from fluency in both of Canada's official languages. And schools with large numbers of Aboriginal students are introducing them to their original languages, thus encouraging these students to reclaim their history and identity, and also work toward preserving these dialects. More controversially, Alberta has allowed the establishment of Charter schools with particular curricular emphases, and the fall of 2009 saw the opening of Toronto's first Africentric Alternative School, offering instruction from junior kindergarten to grade 5.

Promoting Social Integration

Schools seek to bring students together to provide a sense of community. Many colleges and universities encourage first- and second-year students to live on campus for just this reason. Such programs become even more important when students come from diverse backgrounds with different cultural expectations. The goal is to provide experiences that will unify a population composed of diverse racial, ethnic, and religious groups into a community whose members share—to some extent—a common identity. Historically, schools at all levels in Canada have played an important role in socializing the children of immigrants into the norms, values, and beliefs of

Did You Know?

. . . In 2007, two Nova Scotia high school students started an international anti-bullying movement. After a younger student was harassed and called a homosexual for wearing a pink shirt to school, David Shepherd and Travis Price responded by organizing a "sea of pink" campaign. Hundreds of students joined their cause, donning pink shirts in a statement against bullying. Their message has spread around the world, and "pink days" have become an annual event.

Training and Social Control

Schools teach students how to behave.

In the early grades in particular, significant time and effort is spent getting students to do what the teacher wants them to do, when and how the teacher wants them to do it. Through the exercise of social control, schools teach students various skills and values essential to their future positions in the labour force. Students learn punctuality, discipline, scheduling, and responsible work habits, as well as how to negotiate the complexities of a bureaucratic organization. Schools train students for whatever lies ahead, whether it be the assembly line or a physician's office. In effect, then, schools serve as a transitional agent of social control, bridging the gap between parents and employers in the life cycle of most individuals (Bowles and Gintis 1976; M. Cole 1988).

In a society with a complex division of labour, schools help in the essential process of selecting and training individuals for specialized jobs. We expect schools to choose those with the most ability to pursue degrees in fields that demand the greatest skill. For example, we want students with aptitude in math and science to become engineers. We use grades as an indicator of such ability and provide degrees to certify that the graduate has sufficient training to perform the job well. We hold out the promise of higher pay to reward those who make the sacrifices that higher education calls for in terms of time and money. In these ways, schools are very much functionalist in their organization and approach. As we will see below, however, many people are concerned about the degree to which this is accomplished fairly.

Stimulating Social Change and Cultural Innovation While schools do preserve and transmit existing culture, education can also stimulate social change. For example, public schools began to offer sex education classes in response to the soaring pregnancy rate among teenagers. The spread of sexually transmitted diseases prompted expanded education on sexual health. In an attempt to address the low participation of females in maths and sciences, initiatives such as "girls only" classes and "camps" were introduced. Anti-racism programs have been established in elementary and high schools. As a means of countering discrimination, many colleges and universities especially encourage applications from women, visible minorities, Aboriginal persons, and the disabled.

In the 1990s, the federal government established the Aboriginal Head Start program, designed to help prepare young First Nations children for school. The program is aimed at children living in urban centres and Northern communities, and there is also a "Head Start on Reserve" initiative.

The history of residential schools in Canada is one of the most extreme examples of forced assimilation. Aboriginal children were taught that their own culture was inferior; they were stripped of their language, knowledge, and identity. Many years later, the federal government formally apologized for the abuse these children endured, and financial compensation was offered. Today, many adults remain traumatized from this attempt at "social integration."

In keeping with First Nations beliefs, parents and communities are included in the program, which includes elements such as culture and language, nutrition, social support, and instilling a sense of pride in learning.

Colleges and universities are particularly committed to cultural innovation. Faculty members, especially at large universities, must pursue research and publish articles and books. In so doing, they produce new technology, techniques, knowledge, and practices. Cultural innovation on campuses goes beyond such concrete results, however, because higher education provides a context within which we can challenge existing ideas and try out new practices. Such experimentation sometimes leads people to accuse professors, especially those with innovative or unpopular ideas, of being out of touch or out of line, but we need people to experiment with new ideas so that our culture does not stagnate.

Campuses also provide an environment in which students from around the world with widely divergent ideas and experiences can interact. In 2007, Canada was host to over 63,000 international students. Such exposure provides opportunities for cultural innovation as people from various cultures are exposed to and experiment with new and different cultural norms and values.

Did You Know?

... Of the 1700 private schools in Canada, approximately half are faith-based.

Source: www.globecampus.ca.

EDUCATION AND INEQUALITY

Although education does promote social order and provide individual opportunity, conflict theorists note there are significant inequalities in the educational opportunities available to different groups. Wide disparities exist in funding and facilities among urban and rural schools, particularly those in Northern communities and on Aboriginal reserves. For example, some on-reserve schools lack running water and other basic necessities, let alone qualified teachers and up-to-date curricular materials. Recent reports have estimated roughly $200 million is needed to bring the conditions of on-reserve schools in Canada to acceptable levels. Jonathan Kozol (2005:321), who has studied educational inequality in the United States for decades, reports that in a given year, Chicago public schools spent $8482 per student while the wealthy northern suburban Highland Park and Deerfield school district spent $17,291. Schools in well-off areas have the funding to offer programs and facilities that poor districts cannot hope to match, including high-tech labs, athletic facilities, and elective classes in art, music, and languages. As a former principal, in an interview with Kozol, puts it, "I'll believe money doesn't count the day the rich stop spending so much on their own children" (Kozol 2005:59). In this section, we will look at a number of such ways that the experience of and outcomes from education are not equal for everyone.

hidden curriculum Standards of behaviour that are deemed proper by society and are taught subtly in schools.

teacher-expectancy effect The impact that a teacher's expectations about a student's performance may have on the student's actual achievements.

SOCthink

> > > In most provinces, the majority of funding comes from local property taxes. What are the consequences of this model for equitable funding of education?

The Hidden Curriculum One of the ways that schools reinforce the existing system of inequality is through the teaching of what Philip Jackson (1968) has called the **hidden curriculum**—standards of behaviour that society deems proper and that teachers subtly communicate to students. It prepares students to submit to authority. For example, children learn not to speak until the teacher calls on them, and they learn to regulate their activities according to the clock or bells. A classroom environment that is overly focused on obedience rewards students for pleasing the teacher and remaining compliant, rather than for creative thought and academic learning. In this way, schools socialize students to submit to authority

Theory
A Matter of Perspective

THEORETICAL PERSPECTIVES ON EDUCATION

Functionalist:
- emphasis on the role of the education system in transmitting the dominant culture and promoting social norms and values
- social integration and production of competent members of society

Conflict:
- highlights inequalities of access to, and treatment within, the education system
- notes the effects of the *hidden curriculum* and tracking practices supporting the *correspondence principle*

Feminist:
- focuses on the treatment of female students within the education system,
- notes the overrepresentation of women in certain disciplines, and the absence of women in curricular materials

Interactionist:
- highlights the *teacher-expectancy effect*
- also notes the effects of parent and peer expectations on student performance

figures, including bosses and political leaders. In conveying to students what kinds of behaviours—and by extension, people—are acceptable, the hidden curriculum may include elements of racism, sexism, and homophobia.

Teacher Expectancy Interactionists suggest student outcomes can also become a self-fulfilling prophecy based on how teachers perceive students. Psychologist Robert Rosenthal and school principal Lenore Jacobson (1968) documented what they referred to as a **teacher-expectancy effect**—the impact that a teacher's expectations about a student's performance may have on the student's actual achievements. They conducted experiments to document this effect.

Rosenthal and Jacobson informed teachers that they were administering a verbal and reasoning pretest to children in a San Francisco elementary school. After administering the tests, the researchers told the teachers that some of the students were "spurters"—children who showed

The Influence of Parents' Education on Test Performance

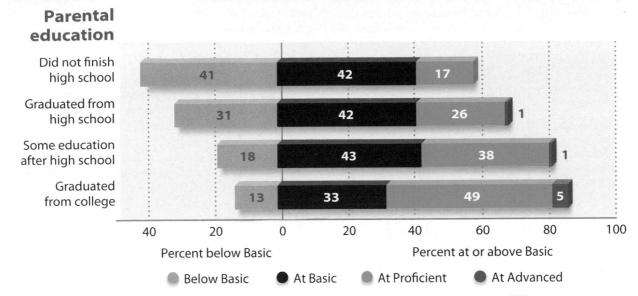

Parental education

	Percent below Basic		Percent at or above Basic	
Did not finish high school	41	42	17	
Graduated from high school	31	42	26	1
Some education after high school	18	43	38	1
Graduated from college	13	33	49	5

40   20   0   20   40   60   80   100

Percent below Basic   Percent at or above Basic

● Below Basic   ● At Basic   ● At Proficient   ● At Advanced

Note: Percentage distribution of grade 12 students across NAEP economics achievement levels, by highest level of parental education, 2006.

Source: Planty et al. 2008:25.

particular academic potential. However, rather than using the actual test scores to make this determination, the researchers randomly selected the 20 percent of the students they identified as spurters. When the students were later retested, the spurters scored not only significantly higher than they had in previous tests but also significantly higher than their peers. Moreover, teachers evaluated the spurters as more interesting, more curious, and better adjusted than their classmates. These results were striking. Apparently, teachers' perceptions that the students were exceptional led to noticeable improvements in the students' performances. Such effects are of particular concern if factors such as race, ethnicity, class, or gender shape teachers' perceptions.

Bestowal of Status As we saw above, part of the public school ideal was that education would contribute to the creation of opportunity and the establishment of a more open society. According to functionalist sociologists Kingsley Davis and Wilbert E. Moore (1945), all societies have positions that are more important for the society's survival or that require greater skill or knowledge to perform. Ideally, the institution of education selects those with ability and trains them for such positions. We reward people in such positions with social prestige and high pay, Davis and Moore claim, because we value such skills and respect the fact that these individuals sacrificed the time and energy necessary to acquire those skills. For example, not everyone has the skill necessary to become a medical doctor, and in order to encourage people who do have the potential to pursue that path, we promise them sufficient social and economic compensation.

Conflict theorists point out that the problem with this model is that, in practice, people apparently are picked for success based not on potential and ability, but on factors such as social class, race, ethnicity, and gender. Although the educational system helps certain poor children to move into middle-class professional positions, it denies most disadvantaged children the same educational opportunities afforded to children of the affluent. In this way, schools tend to preserve social class inequalities in each new generation (Giroux 1988; Pinkerton 2003).

Even a single school can reinforce class differences by putting students in tracks. The term **tracking** (also known as streaming) refers to the practice of placing students in specific curriculum groups on the basis of their test scores and other criteria. Tracking begins very early, often in grade 1 reading groups. The practice can reinforce the disadvantages that children from less affluent families may face if they haven't been exposed to reading materials, computers, and other forms of educational stimulation during their early-childhood years. To ignore this connection between tracking and students' race and social class is to fundamentally misunderstand how schools perpetuate the existing social structure.

tracking The practice of placing students in specific curriculum groups on the basis of their test scores and other criteria.

correspondence principle The tendency of schools to promote the values expected of individuals in each social class and to prepare students for the types of jobs typically held by members of their class.

credentialism An increase in the lowest level of education required to enter a field.

SOCthink

> > > What experiences have you had with tracking? To what extent do you believe it was effective both for high-track and low-track students? What are its limitations in terms of equal opportunity?

Most recent research on tracking raises questions about its effectiveness, especially for low-ability students. In one study of low-income schools in California, researchers discovered a staggering difference between students who were tracked and those who were not. At one school, all interested students were allowed to enroll in advanced placement (AP) courses, not just those who were selected by the administration. Half the open-enrollment students scored high enough to qualify for college credit—a much higher proportion than in selective programs, in which only 17 percent of students qualified for college credit. Tracking programs do not necessarily identify those students with the potential to succeed (B. Ellison 2008; Sacks 2007).

Sociologists Samuel Bowles and Herbert Gintis (1976) have argued that the educational inequalities produced by tracking are designed to meet the needs of modern capitalist societies. They claim that capitalism requires a skilled, disciplined labour force and that North American education systems are structured with that objective in mind. Citing numerous studies, they offer support for what they call the **correspondence principle.** According to this approach, schools promote the values expected of individuals in each social class and perpetuate social class divisions from one generation to the next. Thus, working-class children, assumed to be destined for subordinate positions, are likely to be placed in high school vocational and general tracks, which emphasize close supervision and compliance with authority. In contrast, young people from more affluent families are likely to be directed to post-secondary preparatory tracks, which stress leadership and decision making—the skills they are expected to need as adults.

Credentialism Students today also face elevated expectations. When it comes to educational attainment, they now have to go farther just to stay in the same place. Fifty years ago, a high school diploma was considered quite acceptable for entry into many areas of the paid labour force. Today, a college diploma or undergraduate degree is expected at minimum, and in many cases, offers no guarantee of employment. This change reflects the process of **credentialism**—a term used to describe an increase in the lowest level of education needed to enter a field.

In recent decades, the number of occupations considered professions has risen. Credentialism is one symptom of this trend. Employers and occupational associations typically contend that such changes are a logical response to the increasing complexity of many jobs. However, in many cases, employers raise the degree requirements for a position simply because all applicants have achieved the existing minimum credential (D. Brown 2001; Hurn 1985).

One potential effect of credentialism is to reinforce social inequality. Applicants from poor and minority backgrounds are especially likely to suffer from the escalation of qualifications, since they lack the financial resources needed to obtain degree after degree. In addition, upgrading of credentials serves the self-interest of the two groups most responsible for this trend. First, educational institutions profit from prolonging the investment of time and money that people make by staying in school. Moreover, as C. J. Hurn (1985) has suggested, current jobholders have a stake in raising occupational requirements, since credentialism can increase the status of an occupation and lead to demands for higher pay.

Max Weber anticipated this possibility as early as 1916, concluding that the "universal clamor for the creation of educational certificates in all fields makes for the formation of a privileged stratum in businesses and in offices" (Gerth and Mills 1958:240–41).

Did You Know?

The effects of credentialism are evident in education trends in Canada. According to Statistics Canada, in 1971, three-quarters of young adults had left school by age 22; in 2001, only half had left school by that age.

Gender The educational system of Canada, like many other social institutions, has long been characterized by discriminatory treatment of women. Some of the more creative arguments advanced to justify excluding women from higher education included women's physical, emotional, and intellectual unsuitability for the rigours of study; the disruption they would cause and the necessity of chaperones to be assigned to them; and the cost of building separate washroom facilities. Women persevered, and in 1862, New Brunswick's Mount Allison University became the first Canadian university to admit female students. Admission to higher education did not mean equality of treatment: some schools would only allow women to listen from corridors, not to actually be present at classes! Women were subjected to pranks from their male classmates, and deliberate attempts at embarrassment and humiliation from their male professors.

Throughout the 20th century, sexism in education showed up in many ways—in textbooks with negative stereotypes of women, in pressure on female students to prepare for "women's work," and in unequal funding for women's and men's athletic programs. Gendered differences were especially evident in the traditional distribution of teaching and administrative positions, with women overrepresented in elementary teaching, and most principal and superintendent positions being held by men. In higher education, similar patterns were prevalent, and in some institutions, continue to exist.

to better understand how these seemingly contradictory goals can be accomplished through education. As women's educational success demonstrates, positive social change is possible. Having a better appreciation of how education functions enables us to more effectively work toward realizing the initial goal of education: to provide opportunity and a more open society.

5 Movies on EDUCATION

Dangerous Minds
An ex-marine teacher changes an inner-city school.

Dead Poets Society
An English professor teaches his students to "seize the day."

The History Boys
An unruly class of gifted boys in search of sex, sports, and higher education.

Good Will Hunting
A janitor at MIT has a gift for mathematics greater than that of the school's students.

Finding Forrester
An author mentors a teen writing prodigy.

> ## Good schools, like good societies and good families, celebrate and cherish diversity.
>
> Deborah Meier

Today, women have greater educational and occupational opportunities, largely as a result of the efforts of the women's movement and feminists within the academy. The proportion of women who continue their schooling has risen dramatically. Today, women outnumber men in many undergraduate programs. Moreover, women's access to graduate education and to medical, dental, and law schools has increased significantly in recent decades. In fact, women now regularly outperform men academically.

Education does establish social order and provide opportunities for individuals to get ahead. At the same time, in preserving the existing order, it reproduces practices of inequality. Sociology allows us

Drop-out Rate in Urban and Non-Urban Areas, by Region, 2002–2003 to 2005–2006 (Percent)

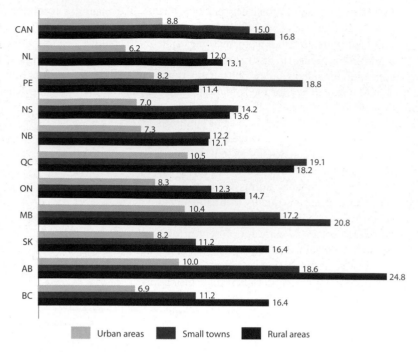

Urban areas ■ Small towns ■ Rural areas

	Urban	Small towns	Rural
CAN	8.8	15.0	16.8
NL	6.2	12.0	13.1
PE	8.2	11.4	18.8
NS	7.0	14.2 / 13.6	
NB	7.3	12.2 / 12.1	
QC	10.5	19.1	18.2
ON	8.3	12.3	14.7
MB	10.4	17.2	20.8
SK	8.2	11.2	16.4
AB	10.0	18.6	24.8
BC	6.9	11.2	16.4

Note: Data are based on a four-year average for the academic years 2002–2003 to 2005–2006.

Source: Calculations of HRSDC based on special data request from Statistics Canada, *Labour Force Survey* 2006. Ottawa, Statistics Canada 2006.

>> Schools as Formal Organizations

The early advocates of public education would be amazed at the scale of the education system in Canada in the 21st century. In many respects, today's schools, when viewed as an example of a formal organization, are similar to factories, hospitals, and business firms. Like those organizations, schools do not operate autonomously; they are influenced by the market of potential students. This is especially true of private schools, but it could have broader application if adoption of voucher plans and other school choice programs continues to increase. The parallels between schools and other types of formal organizations will become more apparent as we examine the bureaucratic nature of schools, teaching as an occupation, and the student subculture (K. Dougherty and Hammack 1992).

THE BUREAUCRATIZATION OF SCHOOLS

It simply is not possible for a single teacher to transmit all the necessary culture and skills to children who will enter many diverse occupations. The growing number of students being served by school systems and the greater degree of specialization required within a technologically complex society have combined to bureaucratize schools.

In many respects, schools put into practice all of Max Weber's principles of bureaucracy that we considered in Chapter 5. When it comes to the division of labour, teachers specialize in particular age levels and specific subjects. Schools are hierarchically organized, with teachers reporting to principals, who are themselves answerable to the superintendent of schools and the board of education. In terms of written rules and regulations, teachers must submit written lesson plans, and students, teachers, and administrators must all adhere to established policies and procedures or face sanctions for not doing so. As schools grow, they become increasingly impersonal, and teachers are expected to treat all students in the same way, regardless of their distinctive personalities and learning needs. Finally, hiring and promotion—and even grading—are based on technical qualifications alone, and standards are established and rubrics created in an effort to ensure this practice.

The trend toward more centralized education particularly affects disadvantaged people, for whom education promises to be a path to opportunity. The standardization of educational curricula, including textbooks, generally reflects the values, interests, and lifestyles of the most powerful groups in our society, and may ignore those of racial and ethnic minorities. In addition, in comparison to the affluent, the disadvantaged often lack the time, financial resources, and knowledge necessary to sort through complex educational bureaucracies and to organize effective lobbying groups. As a result, low-income and minority parents will have even less influence over provincial educational administrators than they have over local school officials (Bowles and Gintis 1976; M. Katz 1971).

SOCthink

> > > Do you think the powerful teachers' unions have brought credibility to the occupation or have they undermined the perceptions of teachers as professionals?

TEACHING AS A PROFESSION

As schools become more bureaucratic, teachers increasingly encounter the conflicts inherent in serving as a professional within the context of a bureaucracy. The organization follows the principles of hierarchy and expects adherence to its rules, but professionalism demands the individual responsibility of the practitioner. While teachers want to practise their craft as professionals, the demands on their time remain diverse and contradictory. Conflicts arise from having to serve simultaneously as instructor, disciplinarian, administrator, and employee of a school district.

As professionals, teachers feel pressure from a number of directions. First, the level of formal schooling required for teaching remains high, and in recent years, ongoing training and competency requirements have been enacted. Second, while by many standards well-paid, many teachers feel they are not sufficiently compensated for the hours worked and the range of tasks they are expected to perform. Finally, the overall prestige of the teaching profession has declined in the last decade, perhaps in part due to the large numbers of people graduating with degrees in education.

STUDENT SUBCULTURES

Schools also provide for students' social and recreational needs. Education helps toddlers and young children develop interpersonal skills that are essential during adolescence and adulthood. In their high school, college, and university years, students may meet future spouses and establish lifelong friendships.

School leaders often seek to develop a sense of school spirit and collective identity, but student subcultures are actually complex and diverse. High school cliques and social groups may crop up according to race, social class, physical attractiveness, academic placement, athletic ability, and leadership roles in the school and community. In his classic community study of "Elmtown," August B. Hollingshead (1975) found some 259 distinct cliques in a single high school. The cliques, whose average size was five, were centred on the school itself, on recreational activities, and on religious and community groups.

Amid these close-knit and often rigidly segregated cliques, some students get left out. Historically, gay and lesbian students have been particularly vulnerable to such exclusion. Many have organized to establish their own stronger sense of collective identity, including through the establishment of gay–straight alliances (GSAs)—school-sponsored support groups that bring gay teens together with sympathetic straight peers.

We can find a similar diversity of student groups at the post-secondary level. Burton Clark and Martin Trow (1966) and, more recently, Helen Lefkowitz Horowitz (1987) have identified four distinctive subcultures among students:

- The *collegiate* subculture focuses on having fun and socializing. These students define what constitutes a "reasonable" amount of academic work (and what amount of work is "excessive" and leads to being labelled as a "grind"). Members of the collegiate subculture have little commitment to academic pursuits.

- The *academic* subculture identifies with the intellectual concerns of the faculty and values knowledge for its own sake.

- The *vocational* subculture is interested primarily in career prospects and views higher education as a means of obtaining degrees that are essential for advancement.

- The *nonconformist* subculture is hostile to the school environment and seeks out ideas that may or may not relate to academic studies. This group may find outlets through campus publications or issue-oriented groups.

Each student is eventually exposed to these competing subcultures and must determine which (if any) seems most in line with his or her feelings and interests.

The typology used by the researchers reminds us that the school is a complex social organization—almost like a community with different neighbourhoods. Of course,

In the classic movie The Breakfast Club, *various student subcultures are brought to light during detention.*

these four subcultures are not the only ones evident on campuses in Canada. For example, one might find subcultures of mature students and part-time students. And as more and more students from minority groups decide to continue their formal education beyond high school, subcultures based on race and ethnicity will continue to grow. Future graduating classes are projected to be more diverse.

Sociologist Joe R. Feagin has studied a distinctive collegiate subculture: Black students at predominantly White

Educational Portrait: Aboriginal Peoples in Canada, Aged 25 to 64, 2006

- 20 percent of adults had a high school diploma as their highest level of educational attainment

- 38 percent had less than high school

- 42 percent of adults had a post-secondary qualification

- Among those with a post-secondary qualification, 17 percent had a college diploma, 13 percent had a trades certificate, and 7 percent had a university degree

- Most common college diploma: Business, Management, Marketing and Related Support Services

- Most common trades certificate: Construction trades

- Most common university degree: Education

- At all levels, educational attainment is higher among peoples living off-reserve

Source: Statistics Canada 2008c; Canadian Council on Learning 2009.

universities. These students must function academically and socially within universities where there are few Black faculty members or Black administrators, where harassment of Blacks by campus police is common, and where the curricula place little emphasis on Black contributions. Feagin (1989:11) suggests that "for minority students life at a predominantly White college or university means long-term encounters with pervasive whiteness." In Feagin's view, visible minority students at such institutions experience both blatant and subtle racial discrimination, which has a cumulative impact that can seriously damage the students' confidence (see also Feagin et al. 1996). The experience of being outside the institutional mainstream—due to race, ethnicity, sexual identity, ability, or gender—can be a very cold one indeed. In education, feminists have referred to this as "the chilly climate."

HOMESCHOOLING

Some people have decided to opt out of the formal organization of schools altogether. They look at the state of schools described above and, in conjunction with additional concerns, decide to educate their children themselves. Exact figures are unavailable, but estimates suggest approximately 60,000 children are homeschooled in Canada (www.ontariohomeschool.org). Many home schools are not registered, despite provincial requirements.

After the establishment of formal public schools in the late 19th century, most families that taught their children at home lived in isolated environments or held strict religious views. Religion continues to play a significant role in the decision to homeschool, but increasing numbers of people now are opting to do so for other reasons. Poor academic quality, peer pressure, and school violence are motivating many parents to teach their children at home. Many parents express concern that the public system contravenes their values on issues such as homosexuality, gay rights, sexual behaviour, abortion, and origins of the world. In addition, some immigrants choose homeschooling as a way to ease their children's transition to a new society.

Critics argue that homeschooled children are isolated from the larger community, which causes them to lose the opportunity to improve their socialization skills. Supporters of homeschooling counter that children can do just as well or better in home schools as in public schools. They claim that homeschooled children benefit from contact with others besides their own age group. They also see homeschooling as a good alternative for children who suffer from attention-deficit/hyperactivity disorder (ADHD) and learning disorders (LDs). Such children often do better in smaller classes, which present fewer distractions to disturb their concentration. A study by the Home School Legal Defense Association (2005), a home school advocacy organization, reported that homeschooled students score higher than others on standardized tests, in every subject and every grade.

The rise in homeschooling points to concerns people have about the institutionalized practice of education. In a sense, this movement represents a rejection of the larger society and its norms and values as institutionalized in education and is part of the trend toward greater individualism. In a survey of families that homeschooled their children, 72.3 percent cited providing religious or moral instruction as a factor in their decision to homeschool (Princiotta and Bielick 2006). In such cases, parents are often concerned that the instruction their children receive at school will contradict or undermine the faith they learn at home. Although such new forms of schooling may better meet the individual needs of diverse groups in today's society, they also tend to undermine the historical commitment to education as a means of fostering unity among society as a whole.

>> Defining Religion

Religion historically has played a powerful role in people's lives, and it continues to shape individual behaviour, national policy, and international actions. It has been a central part of social life but, just as we saw with families, religion is not a singular thing. It takes a variety of forms among different peoples and over time. Sociologists have sought to better understand both what it is and what it does.

As with families, sociologists have taken two main approaches to defining religion. The first focuses on the substance of religion, or what it is. The second emphasizes the functions religion performs, or what it does.

SUBSTANCE: WHAT RELIGION IS

According to a **substantive definition of religion,** religion has a unique content or substance that separates it from other forms of knowledge and belief. Most commonly, this unique focus involves some conception of a supernatural

realm, such as heaven, but it does not have to be outside the physical world. The key is that religion centres around something that goes above and beyond the mundane realities of our everyday existence, that points to something larger, and that calls for some response from us in terms of how we think and act. Sociologist Peter Berger (1969) provided a substantive definition of religion as "the human enterprise by which a sacred cosmos is established" (p. 25). The sacred here refers to that extraordinary realm that becomes the focus of religious faith and practice. It provides believers with meaning, order, and coherence. In describing that sacred realm, people might touch on concepts such as gods and goddesses, angels and demons, heaven and hell, nirvana, or other beings or realms. A society with broad agreement about the nature and importance of this sacred realm is, by definition, more religious.

> **substantive definition of religion** The idea that religion has a unique content or substance relating to the sacred that separates it from other forms of knowledge and belief.
> **sacred** Elements beyond everyday life that inspire respect, awe, and even fear.

Following a substantive approach, sociologists focus on the ways in which religious groups rally around what they define to be sacred. The **sacred** encompasses elements beyond everyday life that inspire respect, awe, and even fear. People interact with the sacred realm through ritual practices, such as prayer or sacrifice. Because believers have faith in the sacred, they accept what they cannot understand. The sacred realm exists in contrast to the **profane,** which includes the ordinary and commonplace.

Different religious groups define their understanding of the sacred or profane in different ways. For example, who or what constitutes "god" varies between Muslims, Christians, and Hindus. Even within a group, different believers may treat the same object as sacred or profane, depending on whether it connects them to the sacred realm. Ordinarily, a piece of bread is profane, but it becomes sacred during the Christian practice of communion because through it believers enter into connection with God.

Similarly, a candelabrum becomes sacred to Jews if it is a menorah. For Confucians and Taoists, incense sticks are not mere decorative items, but highly valued offerings to the gods in religious ceremonies that mark the new and full moons.

FUNCTION: WHAT RELIGIONS DO

A functionalist approach focuses less on what religion is than on what religions do, with a particular emphasis on how religions contribute to social order. According to a **functionalist definition of religion,** religion unifies believers into a community through shared practices and a common set of beliefs relative to sacred things. The emphasis here is on the unifying dimension of religion rather than on the substance of that which unifies. For functionalists, the supernatural or something like it is not an essential part of religion. Religion need not have gods or goddesses, an afterlife, or other such conventional elements. In fact, many social practices, such as being a sports fan, can function like religion for the individual and for society.

Hot or Not?

Is it appropriate for religious leaders, such as pastors, priests, rabbis, or imams, to discuss political issues during religious services?

The functional approach to defining religion has roots in the work of Émile Durkheim. He defined religion as "a unified system of beliefs and practices relative to sacred things, that is to say things set apart and forbidden—beliefs and practices which unite into a single moral community, called a 'church,' all those who adhere to them" ([1887] 1972:224). This definition points to three aspects sociologists should focus on when studying religion: a unified system of beliefs and practices, relative to sacred things, and in the context of community.

The first element of Durkheim's functional approach is the unified system of beliefs and practices. What those beliefs and practices are matters less than the fact that they are shared. Terms historically used to describe religious beliefs include *doctrine, dogma, creeds,* and *scripture,* all representing principles believers share through faith. Practices refer to shared rituals such as attendance at services, prayer, meditation, and fasting. Because beliefs and practices are central to religion, regardless of which definitional approach you take, we will look at them in more detail below.

Unlike the substantive approach, Durkheim's emphasis on sacred things focuses less on the objects themselves than on the believers' attitude toward those objects. Sacred objects and sacred places convey a sense of awe, and religion calls upon believers to treat them with reverence and care. Roman Catholics, for example, treat the bread and wine of communion with respect because they believe that the sacrament transforms those elements into the body and blood of Christ. For Muslims, the Qur'an is a sacred object, and the Kaaba in Mecca is a sacred place. In the functional approach to religion, however, sacredness is in the eyes of the beholders. Any object can be sacred so long as people define it as such and treat it accordingly.

The most important component of Durkheim's definition is this third part: community. It is not the church, mosque, or temple as a building that matters, but the

Theory

A Matter of Perspective

THEORETICAL PERSPECTIVES ON RELIGION

Functionalist:

- emphasis on religion as a source of social integration, bringing meaning and purpose to people's lives
- Durkheim studied religion's integrative and regulatory effects

Conflict:

- views religion as supporting status quo and social inequalities
- Marx argued that religion is used to distract people from the unfairness in the world

Feminist:

- views religion as historically contributing to women's subordinate position in society
- the majority of religions accord women only marginal roles

Interactionist:

- emphasis on individual religious expression
- Weber suggested religion could be an impetus for social change

SOCthink

> > > What other things function like religion for us? How about followers of bands, TV shows, or politics? To what extent might consumerism or even work function like religion?

unification of a body of believers into a shared community. What they believe, what they practise, or what they view as sacred is less important than that they have these beliefs, practices, and shared sacred things in common.

As suggested above, according to this approach, religion need not look like what we conventionally think of as religion. Anything that does what Durkheim's three elements do can function as religion. Just as our understanding of what families are has expanded to include people who are "like family" to us, so also has the definition of religion expanded to include things that function like religion. Sports

provides a classic example. When it comes to beliefs and practices, sports fans—short for *fanatics,* a term that historically had religious connotations—share beliefs about the superiority of their team and regularly practise rituals in hopes that it will help their team win. They may wear the same jersey to watch the game, sit in the same chair, or do a touchdown dance after their team scores, all out of superstitious fear that failure to do so will lead to a negative outcome for the game. In terms of sacred things, there are autographs, jerseys, balls, and so on. In terms of a sacred place, there is the stadium where the team plays, often referred to by fans as a shrine. Finally, fans are united into a community with other fans of the team. Being a fan of the team becomes part of their identity. It provides them with joy, satisfaction, and even a sense of purpose. In a personal essay recounting his obsession with soccer, Michael Elliott (2005) put it this way: "What does being a fan mean? It means you will never walk alone" (p. 76).

>> Components of Religion

In studying religion, regardless of which definitional approach they take, sociologists investigate components of religion that are common to most groups. Their goal is to gain a more complete picture of the role religion plays for both individuals and groups. Sociologists using both approaches focus on how religious groups organize beliefs, rituals, experience, and community. We will look at some examples of what they learn about religion by focusing on each in turn.

BELIEFS

Some people believe in life after death, in supreme beings with unlimited powers, or in supernatural forces. **Religious beliefs** are statements to which members of a particular religion adhere. These views can vary dramatically from religion to religion.

In the late 1960s, a significant shift occurred in the nature of religious belief in North America, though particularly pronounced in the United States. Denominations that held to relatively liberal interpretations of religious scripture (such as the Presbyterians, Methodists, and Lutherans) declined in membership, while those that held to more conservative interpretations and sought a return to the fundamentals of the faith grew in numbers. The term **fundamentalism** refers to a rigid adherence to core religious doctrines. Often, fundamentalism is accompanied by a literal application of scripture or historical beliefs to today's world. Fundamentalism grows out of a sense that the world is falling apart due to a decline in true religious

> **religious belief** A statement to which members of a particular religion adhere.
> **fundamentalism** Rigid adherence to core religious doctrines, often accompanied by a literal application of scripture or historical beliefs to today's world.

belief and practice. Fundamentalists see themselves as presenting a positive vision for the future through a return to the purity of the original religious message.

The phrase "religious fundamentalism" was first applied to Protestant believers who took a literal interpretation of the Bible, but fundamentalism is found worldwide among most major religious groups, including Roman Catholicism, Islam, and Judaism. Fundamentalists vary immensely in their beliefs and behaviour. Some stress the need to be strict in their own personal faith but take little interest in broad social issues. Others are watchful of societal actions, such as government policies, that they see as conflicting with fundamentalist doctrine.

Christian fundamentalists have fought against the teaching of evolution in public schools because they believe not only that it represents a threat to their beliefs but also that it is itself a type of religious faith in naturalism (as opposed to the supernaturalism of God). The first, and most famous, court case over the teaching of evolution in public schools occurred in 1925 and is often referred to as the "Scopes Monkey Trial." In that trial, high school biology teacher John T. Scopes was convicted of violating a Tennessee law that made it a crime to teach the scientific theory of evolution in public schools. Since that time there have been numerous other court challenges. The most recent major case, known as the "Dover Case," occurred in Pennsylvania in 2005. Those opposed to the teaching of evolution sought to force schools to teach the "science" of intelligent design—the idea that life is so complex that there had to be some form of intelligence behind its creation. The judge ruled that intelligent design was a variation on creationism, the teaching of which in a public school would violate the separation of church and state.

RITUALS

Religious rituals are practices required or expected of members of a faith. Rituals usually honour the divine power (or powers) worshipped by believers; they also remind adherents of their religious duties and responsibilities. Rituals and beliefs can be interdependent; rituals generally affirm beliefs, as in a public or private statement confessing a sin. Like any social institution, religion develops distinctive norms to structure people's behaviour. Moreover, sanctions are attached to religious rituals, in the form of either rewards (such as bar mitzvah gifts) or penalties (such as expulsion from a religious institution for violation of norms).

religious ritual A practice required or expected of members of a faith.

Rituals may be very simple, such as saying grace at a meal or observing a moment of silence to commemorate someone's death. Other rituals, such as the process of canonizing a saint, are quite elaborate. Most religious rituals in Canada focus on services conducted at houses of worship. Attendance at a service, silent and spoken prayers, communion, and the singing of hymns and chants are common forms of ritual behaviour that generally take place in group

Going **GLOBAL**

Religious Participation in Selected Countries, 1981 and 2001

Percentage attending religious services other than weddings, funerals, and christenings once a week or more

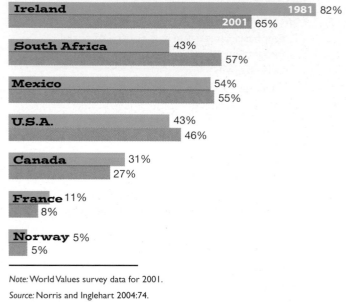

Country	1981	2001
Ireland	82%	65%
South Africa	43%	57%
Mexico	54%	55%
U.S.A.	43%	46%
Canada	31%	27%
France	11%	8%
Norway	5%	5%

Note: World Values survey data for 2001.

Source: Norris and Inglehart 2004:74.

settings. These rituals serve as important face-to-face encounters in which people reinforce their religious beliefs and their commitment to their faith. Religious participation varies widely from country to country.

For Muslims, a very important ritual is the *hajj*—a pilgrimage to the Grand Mosque in Mecca, Saudi Arabia. Every Muslim who is physically and financially able is expected to make this trip at least once. Each year 2 million

Did You Know?

... The number of Canadians expressing no religious affiliation has recently doubled. Between 1985 and 2005, the proportion of people aged 15 and over who self-identified as agnostic, atheist, humanist, or having no religion climbed from 11 percent to 22 percent (Lindsay 2008). However, esteemed social researcher Reginald Bibby (2002) points out that this does not spell the demise of religion in Canada, as people still have spiritual needs.

The collective nature of religion, as emphasized by Durkheim, is evident in these statistics. The beliefs and rituals of a particular faith can create an atmosphere either friendly toward or less conducive to this type of religious experience. Thus, a Baptist would be encouraged to "come forward" to make such a commitment and then to share her or his experience with others. An Episcopalian who claimed to have been born again, on the other hand, would receive much less attention within his or her church (Gallup 2008c; Gallup Opinion Index 1978).

COMMUNITY

Religious communities organize themselves in varieties of ways. Specific structures such as churches and synagogues have been constructed for religious worship; individuals have been trained for occupational roles within various fields. These developments make it possible to distinguish clearly between the sacred and secular parts of one's life—a distinction that could not be made easily in earlier times, when religion was largely a family activity carried out in the home.

Sociologists find it useful to distinguish between four basic forms of organization: the ecclesia, the denomination, the sect, and the new religious movement, or cult. We can see differences among these four forms of organization in their size, power, degree of commitment expected from members, and historical ties to other faiths.

pilgrims go to Mecca during the one-week period indicated by the Islamic lunar calendar. Muslims from all over the world make the *hajj,* including those in Canada, where many tours are arranged to facilitate the trip.

EXPERIENCE

In the sociological study of religion, the term **religious experience** refers to the feeling or perception of being in direct contact with the ultimate reality, such as a divine being, or of being overcome with religious emotion. A religious experience may be rather slight, such as the feeling of exaltation a person might receive from hearing a choir sing Handel's "Hallelujah Chorus." Many religious experiences, however, are more profound, such as a Muslim's experience on a *hajj.* In his autobiography, the late African American activist Malcolm X (1964:338) wrote of his *hajj* and how deeply moved he was by the way that Muslims in Mecca came together across racial and colour lines. For Malcolm X, the colour blindness of the Muslim world "proved to me the power of the One God."

Another profound religious experience for many Christians is being "born again," which involves making a personal commitment to Jesus Christ, marking a major turning point in one's life. According to a 2006 national survey, 43 percent of people in the United States claim they have had a born-again Christian experience at some time in their lives. An earlier survey found that Southern Baptists (75 percent) were the most likely to report such experiences; in contrast, only 21 percent of Catholics and 24 percent of Episcopalians stated that they had been born again.

Ecclesiae When studying how groups organize their communities, sociologists have used the term **ecclesia** (plural, *ecclesiae*) to describe a religious organization that claims to include most or all members of a society and is recognized as the national or official religion. Since virtually everyone belongs to the faith, membership is by birth rather than conscious decision. The classic example in sociology was the Roman Catholic Church in medieval Europe. Contemporary examples of ecclesiae include Islam in Saudi Arabia and Buddhism in Thailand. However, significant differences exist within this category. In Saudi Arabia's Islamic regime, leaders of the ecclesia hold vast power over actions of the state. In contrast, the historical state church in Sweden, Lutheranism, holds no such power over the Riksdag (Parliament) or the Prime Minister.

> **religious experience** The feeling or perception of being in direct contact with the ultimate reality, such as a divine being, or of being overcome with religious emotion.
>
> **ecclesia** A religious organization that claims to include most or all members of a society and is recognized as the national or official religion.

Generally, ecclesiae are conservative, in that they do not challenge the leaders of a secular government. In a society with an ecclesia, the political and religious institutions often act in harmony and reinforce each other's power in their relative spheres of influence. In the modern world, ecclesiae are declining in power.

Immigrants by Major Religious Denominations and Period of Immigration, Canada, 2001

	Period of Immigration (%)				
	Before 1961	1961–1970	1971–1980	1981–1990	1991–2001
Total immigrants	100.0	100.0	100.0	100.0	100.0
Roman Catholic	39.2	43.4	33.9	32.9	23.0
Protestant	39.2	26.9	21.0	14.5	10.7
Christian Orthodox	3.8	6.3	3.8	3.0	6.3
Christian, not included elsewhere	1.3	2.2	3.8	4.9	5.3
Jewish	2.7	2.0	2.2	1.9	1.2
Muslim	0.2	1.3	5.4	7.5	15.0
Hindu	0.0	1.4	3.6	4.9	6.5
Buddhist	0.4	0.9	4.8	7.5	4.6
Sikh	0.1	1.1	3.9	4.3	4.7
No religion	11.0	13.5	16.5	17.3	21.3
Other religions	2.1	1.0	1.1	1.3	1.4

Source: Statistics Canada 2003b.

Denominations A **denomination** is a large, organized religion that is not officially linked to the state or government. Like an ecclesia, it tends to have an explicit set of beliefs, a defined system of authority, and a generally respected position in society. Denominations often claim large segments of a population as members. Generally, children accept the denomination of their parents and give little thought to membership in other faiths. Although considered respectable and not viewed as a challenge to the secular government, unlike ecclesia, denominations lack the official recognition and power held by an ecclesia (Doress and Porter 1977).

Canada is home to a large number of denominations. This diversity is largely the result of the nation's immigrant heritage. Many settlers brought with them the religious commitments native to their homelands. Some Christian denominations in Canada, such as the Roman Catholics, Episcopalians, and Lutherans, are the outgrowth of ecclesiae established in Europe. New Christian denominations also emerged, including the Mormons and Christian Scientists.

The majority of Canadians currently claim affiliation with either Protestant or Catholic denominations. However, as demonstrated by the table above, within the last generation immigrants have increased the number of Muslim, Sikh, and Hindu adherents living in Canada.

Sects A **sect** can be defined as a relatively small religious group that has broken away from some other

denomination A large, organized religion that is not officially linked to the state or government.

sect A relatively small religious group that has broken away from some other religious organization to renew what it considers the original vision of the faith.

established sect A religious group that is the outgrowth of a sect, yet remains isolated from society.

religious organization to renew what it considers the original vision of the faith. Many sects, such as that led by Martin Luther during the Reformation in the 1500s, claim to be the "true church" because they seek to cleanse the established faith of what they regard as extraneous beliefs and rituals (Stark and Bainbridge 1985). Max Weber ([1916] 1958b:114) termed the sect a "believer's church" because affiliation is based on conscious acceptance of a specific religious dogma.

Sects are at odds with the dominant society and do not seek to become established national religions. Unlike ecclesiae and denominations, they require intensive commitments and demonstrations of belief by members. Partly owing to their outsider status, sects frequently exhibit a higher degree of religious fervour and loyalty than more established religious groups. They actively recruit adults as new members, and acceptance comes through conversion.

Sects are often short-lived. Those that are able to survive may become less antagonistic to society over time and begin to resemble denominations. In a few instances, sects have been able to endure over several generations while remaining fairly separate from society. Sociologist J. Milton Yinger (1970:226–73) uses the term **established sect** to describe a religious group that is the outgrowth of a sect, yet remains isolated from society. The Hutterites, Jehovah's Witnesses, Seventh-Day Adventists, and Amish are contemporary examples of established sects in Canada. (Some controversial sects are also discussed in Chapter 7.)

Throughout the world, including North America, Muslims are divided into a variety of sects, such as Sunni and Shia (or Shiite). The great majority of Muslims in North America are Sunni Muslims—literally, those who follow the *Sunnah,* or way of the Prophet. Compared to other Muslims, Sunnis tend

to be more moderate in their religious orthodoxy. The Shia, who come primarily from Iraq and Iran, are the second-largest group. Shia Muslims are more attentive to guidance from accepted Islamic scholars than are Sunnis. About two-thirds of Muslims in North America are native-born citizens.

Cults or New Religious Movements

Historically, sociologists have used the term *cult* to describe alternative religious groups with unconventional religious beliefs. Partly as a result of the notoriety generated by some of these more extreme groups—such as the Heaven's Gate cult members who committed mass suicide in 1997 so that their spirits might be freed to catch a ride on the spaceship hidden behind the Hale-Bopp comet—many sociologists have abandoned the use of the term. In its place they have adopted the expression "new religious movement."

A **new religious movement (NRM)** or **cult** is generally a small, alternative religious group that represents either a new faith community or a major innovation in an existing faith. NRMs are similar to sects in that they tend to be small and are often viewed as less respectable than more established faiths. Unlike sects, however, NRMs normally do not result from schisms or breaks with established ecclesiae or denominations. Some cults, such as those focused on UFO sightings, may be totally unrelated to existing faiths. Even when a cult does accept certain fundamental tenets of a dominant faith—such as a belief in Jesus as divine or in Muhammad as a messenger of God—it will offer new revelations or insights to justify its claim to being a more advanced religion (Stark and Bainbridge 1979, 1985).

Like sects, NRMs may be transformed over time into other types of religious organization. An example is the Christian Science Church, which began as a new religious movement under the leadership of Mary Baker Eddy. Today, this church exhibits the characteristics of a denomination. In fact, most major religions, including Christianity, began as cults. NRMs may be in the early stages of developing into a denomination or new religion, or they may just as easily fade away through the loss of members or weak leadership (Schaefer and Zellner 2007). Weber's work on charismatic authority offers an explanation of why only some NRMs survive.

> **new religious movement (NRM)** or **cult** A small, alternative faith community that represents either a new religion or a major innovation in an existing faith.

Comparing Forms of Religious Organization

How can we determine whether a particular religious group falls into the sociological category of ecclesia, denomination, sect, or NRM? As we have seen, these types of religious organization have somewhat different relationships to society. Ecclesiae are recognized as national churches; denominations, although not officially approved by the state, are generally widely respected. In contrast, sects and NRMs are much more likely to be at odds with the larger culture.

Still, ecclesiae, denominations, and sects are best viewed as types along a continuum in terms of their level of accommodation with the larger society. With ecclesiae, church and state merge together as one. On the other end, however, sects find themselves at odds with the dominant society. Denominations fall between the two. Because they offer an alternative to the mainstream, NRMs might fall close to sects. But NRMs could be said to lie outside the continuum because they define themselves in terms of a new view of life rather than in terms of existing religious faiths. Since Canada has no ecclesiae, sociologists studying this country's religions have focused on denominations, sects, and NRMs.

secularization Religion's diminishing influence in the public sphere, especially in politics and the economy.

Consequently, in countries that are predominantly Muslim, the separation of religion and the state is not considered necessary or even desirable. In fact, Muslim governments often reinforce Islamic practices through their laws. Muslims do vary sharply in their interpretation of several traditions, some of which—such as the wearing of veils by women—are more cultural than religious in origin.

Like Christianity and Islam, Judaism is monotheistic. Jews believe that God's true nature is revealed in the Torah, which Christians know as the first five books of the Old Testament. According to these scriptures, God formed a covenant, or pact, with Abraham and Sarah,

>> World Religions

Early sociologists predicted that modern societies would experience widespread **secularization,** which involves religion's diminishing influence in the public sphere, especially in politics and the economy. Nevertheless, religion continues to play a significant role. Worldwide, tremendous diversity exists in religious beliefs and practices.

Overall, about 85 percent of the world's population adheres to some religion; only about 15 percent is nonreligious. This level of adherence changes over time and also varies by country and age group. In Canada today, those who consider themselves nonreligious account for 22 percent of the population, significantly higher than in the United States, where the nonreligious account for only 10–14 percent (Lindsay 2008).

Christianity is the largest single faith in the world; the second largest is Islam (see the table on page 180). Although global news events often suggest an inherent conflict between Christians and Muslims, the two faiths are similar in many ways. Both are monotheistic (that is, based on a single deity), and both include a belief in prophets, an afterlife, and a judgment day. In fact, Islam recognizes Jesus as a prophet, though not as the son of God. Both faiths impose a moral code on believers, which varies from fairly rigid proscriptions for fundamentalists to relatively relaxed guidelines for liberals.

The followers of Islam, called Muslims, believe that the prophet Muhammad received Islam's holy scriptures from Allah (God) nearly 1400 years ago. They see Muhammad as the last in a long line of prophets, preceded by Adam, Abraham, Moses, and Jesus. Islam is more communal in its expression than Christianity, particularly the more individualistic Protestant denominations.

Going GLOBAL

Religions of the World

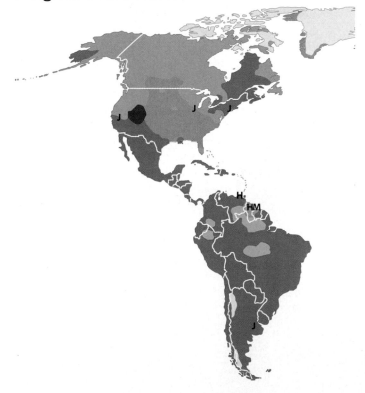

Religious adherence is one of the defining social characteristics of a culture.

Source: J. Allen 2008.

the ancestors of the 12 tribes of Israel. Even today, Jews believe, this covenant holds them accountable to God's will. If they follow both the letter and the spirit of the Torah, a long-awaited Messiah will one day bring paradise to earth. Although today Judaism has a relatively small following compared to other major faiths, it forms the historical foundation for both Christianity and Islam. That is why Jews revere many of the same sacred Middle Eastern sites as Christians and Muslims.

Two other major faiths developed in a different part of the world—India. The earliest, Hinduism, originated around 1500 B.C. Hinduism differs from Judaism, Christianity, and Islam in that it embraces a number of gods and minor gods, although most worshippers are devoted primarily to a single deity, such as Shiva or Vishnu. Hinduism is also distinguished by a belief in reincarnation, or the perpetual rebirth of the soul after death. Unlike Judaism, Christianity, and Islam, which are based largely on sacred texts, Hindu beliefs have been preserved mostly through oral tradition.

Buddhism developed in the 6th century B.C. as a reaction against Hinduism. This faith is founded on the teachings of Siddhartha (later called Buddha, or "The Enlightened One"). Through meditation, followers of Buddhism strive to overcome selfish cravings for physical or material pleasures, with the goal of reaching a state of enlightenment, or nirvana. Buddhists created the first monastic orders, which are thought to be the models for monastic orders in other religions, including Christianity. Though Buddhism emerged in India, its followers were eventually driven out of that country by the Hindus. It is now found primarily in other parts of Asia.

Although the differences among religions are striking, they are exceeded by variations within faiths. Consider the differences within Christianity, from relatively liberal denominations such as Presbyterians or Episcopalians to the more conservative Mormons and Greek Orthodox Catholics. Similar divisions exist within Hinduism, Islam, and other world religions (Barrett et al. 2006; Swatos 1998).

Predominant Religions

Christianity (C)*
Roman Catholic
Protestant
Mormon (LDS)
Eastern Churches
Mixed Sects

Islam (M)
Sunni
Shi'a

Buddhism (B)
Hinayanistic
Lamaistic

Hinduism (H)
Judaism (J)
Sikhism
Animism (Tribal)
Chinese Complex
(Confucianism, Taoism, and Buddhism)

Korean Complex
(Buddhism, Confucianism, Christianity, and Chondogyo)

Japanese Complex
(Shinto and Buddhism)

Vietnamese Complex
(Buddhism, Taoism, Confucianism, and Cao Dai)

Unpopulated Regions

* Capital letters indicate the presence of locally important minority adherents of nonpredominant faiths.

>> Sociological Perspectives on Religion

Sociology emerged as a discipline in the 19th century in the context of significant intellectual, political, and economic upheaval. Intellectuals at the time felt that the religious teachings that had guided society in times of crisis in the past were failing. Auguste Comte and other early sociologists sought to provide a science of society that would tap the ways of knowing built into the scientific method and apply them to the study of society. They recognized the significant role that religion had played in maintaining social order in the past and believed it essential to understand how it had accomplished this, so the study of religion became a significant topic in early

Major World Religions

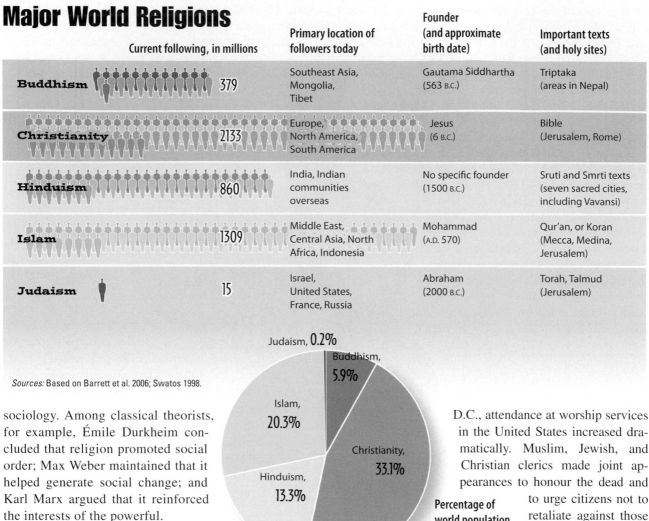

	Current following, in millions	Primary location of followers today	Founder (and approximate birth date)	Important texts (and holy sites)
Buddhism	379	Southeast Asia, Mongolia, Tibet	Gautama Siddhartha (563 B.C.)	Triptaka (areas in Nepal)
Christianity	2133	Europe, North America, South America	Jesus (6 B.C.)	Bible (Jerusalem, Rome)
Hinduism	860	India, Indian communities overseas	No specific founder (1500 B.C.)	Sruti and Smrti texts (seven sacred cities, including Vavansi)
Islam	1309	Middle East, Central Asia, North Africa, Indonesia	Mohammad (A.D. 570)	Qur'an, or Koran (Mecca, Medina, Jerusalem)
Judaism	15	Israel, United States, France, Russia	Abraham (2000 B.C.)	Torah, Talmud (Jerusalem)

Judaism, 0.2%
Buddhism, 5.9%
Islam, 20.3%
Christianity, 33.1%
Hinduism, 13.3%

Percentage of world population

Sources: Based on Barrett et al. 2006; Swatos 1998.

sociology. Among classical theorists, for example, Émile Durkheim concluded that religion promoted social order; Max Weber maintained that it helped generate social change; and Karl Marx argued that it reinforced the interests of the powerful.

INTEGRATION

Durkheim viewed religion as an integrative force in human society. He sought to answer a perplexing question: "How can human societies be held together when they are generally composed of individuals and social groups with diverse interests and aspirations?" In his view, religious bonds often transcend these personal and divisive forces.

How does religion provide this "societal glue"? Religion, whether it be Buddhism, Islam, Christianity, or Judaism, gives meaning and purpose to people's lives. It offers certain ultimate values and ends to hold in common. Although they are subjective and not always fully accepted, these values and ends help society to function as an integrated social system. For example, funerals, weddings, bar and bat mitzvahs, and confirmations serve to integrate people into larger communities by reaffirming shared beliefs and values related to the ultimate questions of life.

Religion also serves to bind people together in times of crisis and confusion. Immediately after the terrorist attacks of September 11, 2001, on New York City and Washington,

D.C., attendance at worship services in the United States increased dramatically. Muslim, Jewish, and Christian clerics made joint appearances to honour the dead and to urge citizens not to retaliate against those who looked, dressed, or sounded different from others. A year later, however, attendance levels had returned to normal (D. Moore 2002).

The integrative power of religion can be seen, too, in the role that churches, synagogues, and mosques have traditionally played and continue to play for immigrant groups in Canada. For example, Roman Catholic immigrants may settle near a parish church that offers services in their native language, such as Polish or Spanish. Similarly, Korean immigrants may join a Presbyterian church that has many Korean Canadian members and follows religious practices similar to those of churches in Korea. Like other religious organizations, these Roman Catholic and Presbyterian churches help to integrate immigrants into their new homeland.

Religion also strengthens feelings of social integration within specific faiths and denominations. In many faiths, members share certain characteristics that help to bind them together, including their race, ethnicity, and social class.

Such integration, while unifying believers, can come at the expense of outsiders. In this sense, religion can contribute to tension and even conflict between groups or nations.

In late 2008, the British Humanist Association raised funds to have posters placed on London buses with the slogan: "There's probably no God. Now stop worrying and enjoy your life."

As expected, the message generated backlash from many Christian groups, but some mainstream churches praised the campaign for prompting people to engage with deeper questions.

By 2009, the campaign had gone international. The Freethought Association of Canada sponsored ads on public transit in major cities including Toronto and Calgary. In response, pro-religion forces raised money for rebuttal ads.

Clearly, religion evokes strong emotion—that's why it's both unifying and divisive.

During World War II, Nazi Germany attempted to exterminate the Jewish people; approximately 6 million European Jews were killed. In modern times, nations such as Lebanon (Muslims versus Christians), Israel (Jews versus Muslims, as well as Orthodox versus secular Jews), Northern Ireland (Roman Catholics versus Protestants), and India (Hindus versus Muslims and, more recently, Sikhs) have been torn by clashes that are in large part based on religion. Such conflicts often do, however, have the effect of drawing the believers closer together.

SOCIAL CHANGE

Max Weber sought to understand how religion, which so often seems conservative in that it works to maintain order, might also contribute to social change. To do so, he focused on the relationship between religious faith and the rise of capitalism. Weber's findings appeared in his sociology classic, *The Protestant Ethic and the Spirit of Capitalism* ([1904] 2009).

The Weberian Thesis Weber noted that in European nations with both Protestant and Catholic citizens, an overwhelming number of business leaders, owners of capital, and skilled workers were Protestant. In his view, this was no mere coincidence. Weber explained it as a consequence of what he called the **Protestant ethic**—a disciplined commitment to worldly labour driven by a desire to bring glory to God that was shared by followers of Martin Luther and John Calvin. Weber argued that this emphasis on hard work and self-denial provided capitalism with an approach toward labour that was essential to capitalism's development.

To explain the impact of the Protestant ethic on the rise of capitalism, Weber looked to Luther's concept of a calling, Calvin's concept of predestination, and Protestant believers' resulting experience of "salvation anxiety." According to Protestant reformer Martin Luther (1483–1546), God called believers to their position in life, and they had to work hard in that calling so as to bring glory to God, regardless of whether they were rich or poor. Protestant Reformer John Calvin (1509–1564) added to this the concept of predestination, according to which God, before the beginning of time, picked who would go to heaven and who would go to hell, and there was nothing anyone could do to change their fate. It was impossible to earn salvation through good works; salvation was totally dependent upon the grace of God. Complicating this was the fact that no individual could ever know for sure that he or she was saved because none could presume to know the mind of God. Weber concluded that this created a sense of salvation anxiety among believers who wanted to know if they were going to heaven or not.

> **Protestant ethic** Max Weber's term for the disciplined commitment to worldly labour driven by a desire to bring glory to God, shared by followers of Martin Luther and John Calvin.

SOCthink

> > > To what extent do you think religion can be a force for social change? What examples have you seen in your lifetime?

Weber theorized that believers would seek to resolve this uncertainty by leading the kinds of lives they thought God would expect godly people to lead. This meant hard work, humility, and self-denial, not for the sake of salvation or individual gain, but for the sake of God. Although doing so would not earn them salvation, it could earn them signs that they were among the chosen, and thus alleviate some of the anxiety. Thus they worked hard not because they had to (either for subsistence or because they were forced), but because they wanted to in response to the call they hoped would come from God. It was precisely this kind of worker—internally motivated to work hard—that capitalism needed if it was to engage in rationally planned production. This "spirit of capitalism," to use Weber's phrase, was a motivational precondition for rational modern capitalism. Weber does not argue that it *caused* capitalism as we know it, but it did significantly influence its development.

> **liberation theology** Use of a church, primarily Roman Catholicism, in a political effort to eliminate poverty, discrimination, and other forms of injustice from a secular society.

In this way, religion contributed, through the Protestant Reformation, to one of the most significant examples of social change, in the form of the rise of capitalism and its effects, in human history. Weber's argument has been hailed as one of the most important theoretical works in the field and as an excellent example of macrolevel analysis. Like Durkheim, Weber demonstrated that religion is not solely a matter of intimate personal beliefs. He stressed that the collective nature of religion has consequences for society as a whole.

associated with liberation theology believe that organized religion has a moral responsibility to take a strong public stand against the oppression of the poor, racial and ethnic minorities, and women (C. Smith 1991).

The *term liberation theology* dates back to the publication in 1973 of the English translation of *A Theology of Liberation*. The book was written by a Peruvian priest, Gustavo Gutiérrez, who lived

5 Movies on RELIGION

Little Buddah
The story of the Buddah interwoven with a tale of reincarnation.

The Chosen
Two Jewish boys with very different ways of life become friends.

The Passion of the Christ
The story of Jesus Christ.

Monsoon Wedding
A traditional Hindu wedding ceremony.

Malcolm X
A biography of Malcolm X and his conversion to Islam.

in a slum area of Lima in the early 1960s. After years of exposure to the vast poverty around him, Gutiérrez concluded that "in order to serve the poor, one had to move into political action" (R. M. Brown 1980:23; Gutiérrez 1990). Eventually, politically committed Latin American

> **But the poor person does not exist as an inescapable fact of destiny. . . . The poor are a by-product of the system in which we live and for which we are responsible.**
>
> Liberation Theologian
> Gustavo Gutierrez

Liberation Theology A more contemporary example of religion serving as a force for social change came through liberation theology, in which the clergy were at the forefront. Many religious activists, especially in the Roman Catholic Church in Latin America, support **liberation theology**—the use of a church in a political effort to eliminate poverty, discrimination, and other forms of injustice from a secular society. Advocates of this religious movement sometimes sympathize with Marxism. Many believe that radical change, rather than economic development in itself, is the only acceptable solution to the desperation of the masses in impoverished developing countries. Activists

theologians came under the influence of social scientists who viewed the domination of capitalist multinational corporations as central to the hemisphere's problems. One result was a new approach to theology that built on the cultural and religious traditions of Latin America rather than on models developed in Europe and North America.

SOCIAL CONTROL

Liberation theology is a relatively recent phenomenon that marks a break with the traditional role of churches. It was this traditional role that Karl Marx opposed. In his view,

religion inhibited social change by encouraging oppressed people to focus on otherworldly concerns rather than on their immediate poverty or exploitation.

Marx on Religion Marx described religion as an "opiate" that was particularly harmful to oppressed peoples. He felt that religion often, in essence, drugged the masses into submission by offering a consolation for their harsh lives on earth: the hope of salvation in an ideal afterlife. For example, during the period of slavery in the United States, White masters forbade Blacks to practise native African religions. Instead, they encouraged slaves to adopt Christianity, which taught that obedience would lead to salvation and eternal happiness in the hereafter. Indigenous peoples in Canada also had Christianity forced upon them, first by missionaries, then early settlers, and most directly through residential schools. Viewed from this perspective, Christianity may have pacified oppressed peoples and blunted the rage that often fuels rebellion.

Marx acknowledged that religion plays an important role in propping up the existing social structure. The values of religion, as already noted, tend to reinforce other social institutions and the social order as a whole. From Marx's perspective, however, religion's promotion of social stability only helps to perpetuate patterns of social inequality.

According to Marx, the dominant religion reinforces the interests of those in power.

From a Marxist perspective, religion keeps people from seeing their lives and societal conditions in political terms—for example, by obscuring the overriding significance of conflicting economic interests. Marxists suggest that by inducing a "false consciousness" among the disadvantaged, religion lessens the possibility of collective political action that could end capitalist oppression and transform society. Sociological analysis in this tradition seeks to reveal the ways in which religion serves the interests of the powerful at the expense of others.

Gender and Religion Drawing on the feminist approach, researchers and theorists point to the fundamental role women play in religious socialization. Most people develop their allegiance to a particular faith in their childhood, with their mothers playing a critical role in the process. Yet when it comes to positions of leadership, women generally take a subordinate role in religious governance. Indeed, most faiths have a long tradition of exclusively male spiritual leadership. Furthermore, because most religions are patriarchal, they tend to reinforce men's dominance in secular as well as spiritual matters. Women do play a vital role as volunteers, staff, and religious educators, but even today, religious decision making and leadership typically fall to the men. An exception to this rule is the United Church in Canada, which has permitted the ordination of women since 1936. Among Canada's First Nations peoples, women are traditionally viewed as spiritual leaders and healers. Other exceptions include the Shakers, Christian Scientists, and the goddess heritage of Hinduism, but it is otherwise rare for women to have a central role in religion.

provides opportunity and reinforces the status quo, including its system of inequality. Sociologists believe that by having a better appreciation for both the opportunities and constraints such institutions present, we can better act both individually and collectively to bring about positive social change.

>> Summary

In this chapter, we have looked at both education and religion. In both cases we find institutions that play a powerful role in shaping how we think and act. Each

get involved!

Visit! Attend at least two religious services for a group that is significantly different from what you might have experienced in the past. Interview the religious leader of the group to gain a better understanding of their beliefs and practices and their reasons for faith.

For REVIEW

I.   How does education help to maintain social order?
   • Education transmits culture, promotes social integration, provides training and social control, and contributes to cultural innovation.

II. How does education support the existing system of inequality?
   • Education reinforces the status quo, and therefore its existing inequalities, through the hidden curriculum, teacher expectancy, bestowal of status, and credentialism.

III. How do sociologists define religion?
   • One approach focuses on the substance of what religion is, defining religion as knowledge and beliefs relating to the sacred realm. The other approach looks at what religions do for society in terms of social order and integration. Both approaches analyze common components including belief, ritual, experience, and community.

Thinking CRITICALLY...

1. Should colleges and universities grant space to religious groups whose beliefs and practices may be seen as contributing to the subordination of women?
2. Compare and contrast the social institutions of religion and education. In what ways are they similar and different from one another?
3. Should the separate school system or other faith-based schools be eligible for public (provincial) funding?

Pop Quiz

1. The term given to describe the impact that teacher expectations have on student performance is the
   a. teacher-expectancy effect.
   b. chilly climate.
   c. correspondence principle.
   d. hidden curriculum.

2. One of the ways education contributes to social order is by providing an environment within which we can challenge existing ideas and experiment with new norms and values. This is known as
   a. transmitting culture.
   b. promoting social integration.
   c. training and social control.
   d. cultural innovation.

3. Samuel Bowles and Herbert Gintis have argued that capitalism requires a skilled, disciplined labour force and that the North American educational system is structured with that objective in mind. Citing numerous studies, they offer support for what they call
   a. tracking.
   b. credentialism.
   c. the correspondence principle.
   d. the teacher-expectancy effect.

4. Fifty years ago, a high school diploma was the minimum requirement for entry into the paid labour force. Today, a college diploma is virtually the bare minimum. This change reflects the process of
   a. tracking.
   b. credentialism.
   c. the hidden curriculum.
   d. the correspondence principle.

5. The college and university student subculture that focuses on having fun and socializing and not taking studies too seriously is the
   a. collegiate subculture.
   b. academic subculture.
   c. vocational subculture.
   d. nonconformist subculture.

6. The approach to defining religion that emphasizes the significance of the sacred, most often supernatural, realm is known as the
   a. functionalist approach.
   b. component approach.
   c. substantive approach.
   d. ecclesiae approach.

7. Religious rituals are
   a. statements to which members of a particular religion adhere.
   b. the feelings or perceptions of being in direct contact with the ultimate reality, such as a divine being.
   c. the religious structures through which faith communities organize themselves.
   d. practices required or expected of members of a faith.

8. Looking at world religions, the religion with the most followers around the world is
   a. Buddhism.
   b. Islam.
   c. Judaism.
   d. Christianity.

9. Sociologist Max Weber pointed out that the followers of John Calvin emphasized a disciplined work ethic, worldly concerns, and a rational orientation to life. Collectively, this point of view has been referred to as
   a. capitalism.
   b. the Protestant ethic.
   c. the sacred.
   d. the profane.

10. The use of a church, primarily Roman Catholic, in a political effort to eliminate poverty, discrimination, and other forms of injustice evident in a secular society is referred to as
    a. creationism.
    b. ritualism.
    c. religious experience.
    d. liberation theology.

1. (a); 2. (d), 3. (c); 4. (b); 5. (a); 6. (c); 7. (d); 8. (d); 9. (b); 10. (d)

Mc Graw Hill connect™

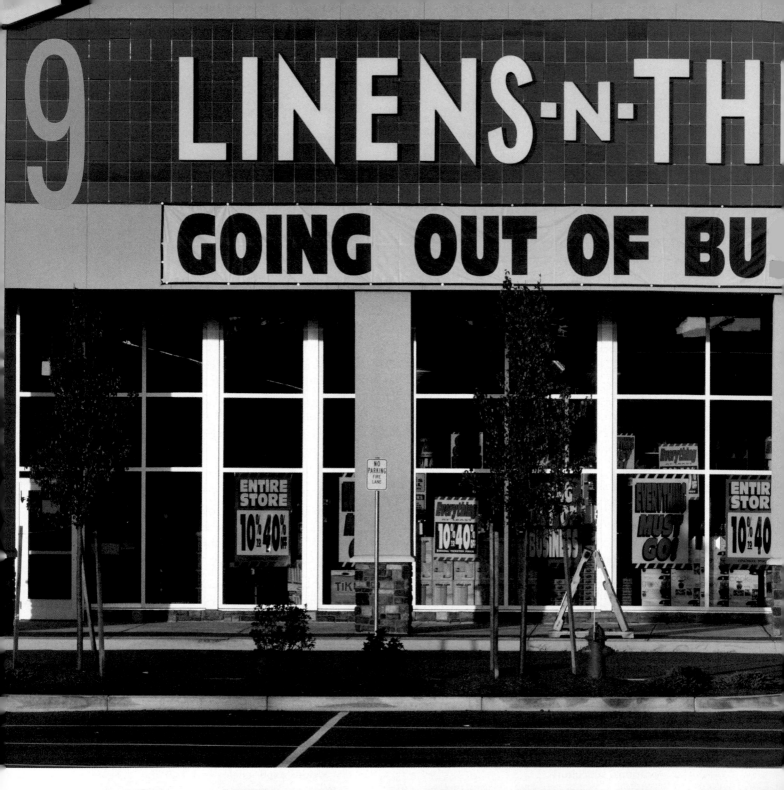

In this chapter you will...

- gain an understanding of how power and authority are distributed and exercised

- identify and explain different economic systems and forms of government

- learn about changing economic trends

ADAPTING AND SURVIVING IN A MULTINATIONAL WORLD

In 2002, Jim Wier headed to Wal-Mart's corporate headquarters in Bentonville, Arkansas, to tell their executives that he would no longer be selling his company's Snapper lawn mowers in Wal-Mart stores. This was highly unusual for a Wal-Mart supplier. Most would go to great lengths to get their products on Wal-Mart shelves because, with many millions of customers per week, the possibilities for high-volume sales are immense. In fact, when they pulled their mowers from Wal-Mart, Snapper's sales dropped 20 percent (Fishman 2006).

Wal-Mart began as a single American store in 1962, and has grown to over 4000 stores in the United States, and 2800 in other countries. It is the world's largest private employer: in 2009, almost 80,000 people were employed in Canadian Wal-Mart stores, part of the 1.9 million "associates" worldwide.

Wier understood the appeal of gaining access to all those Wal-Mart customers, but as he put it, "Once you get hooked on the volume, it's like getting hooked on cocaine" (Fishman 2006:117). The need to maintain volume, he argued, would change the character of the company, requiring it to cut corners and change operating procedures. He opted instead to sell to a different kind of customer, one who wants quality, durability, and service more than up-front savings.

Snapper faces an uphill battle, but continues to thrive. Other businesses have not been as successful. Although Wal-Mart promotes the positive economic impact it has on communities, many independent retailers have suffered when the giant company has come to their towns. And those who work for Wal-Mart have also felt its power: attempts to unionize at Canadian stores have been successfully squashed by the corporation.

Companies and workers have no choice but to adapt to compete with huge multinational corporations such as Wal-Mart and with firms and workers globally. When a company's revenues are greater than the gross national income for the majority of the world's nations—Wal-Mart would rank 21st out of 209 nations—it cannot help but have economic and political consequences (World Bank 2008). In this chapter we will look at both the economy and politics to better understand how both shape our lives.

- How is economic and political power organized?
- How does power operate?
- How has the economy changed over time?

>> Power and Authority

Sociologists have been concerned about the exercise of power since the birth of the discipline in the 1800s. In the context of those times, traditional forms of power were changing even as economic and political contexts were shifting. The movement away from agricultural to industrial economies, and from the rule of

power The ability to exercise one's will over others even if they resist.
force The actual or threatened use of coercion to impose one's will on others.
influence The exercise of power through a process of persuasion.
authority Institutionalized power that is recognized by the people over whom it is exercised.

monarchs to more democratic forms of government, meant that the taken-for-granted processes of power were shifting. Early sociologists sought to develop theories of power that were sufficiently broad to explain the success of companies such as Wal-Mart or the outcomes of international conflicts, yet sufficiently narrow to explain who gets their way within interpersonal relationships.

POWER

According to Max Weber, **power** is the ability to exercise

one's will over others, even if they resist. To put it another way, if you can make people do what you want them to do—whether that is to go to war, coordinate a business meeting, clean their room, or even take an exam—you have power. Power relations can involve large organizations, small groups, or even people in an intimate association.

There are three basic sources of power within any political system: force, influence, and authority. **Force** is the actual or threatened use of coercion to impose one's will on others. When leaders imprison or even execute political dissidents, they are applying force; so, too, are terrorists when they seize or bomb an embassy or assassinate a political leader. **Influence,** on the other hand, refers to the exercise of power through a process of persuasion. A citizen may change his or her view of a political candidate because of a newspaper editorial, or in response to a stirring speech by an activist at a rally. In each case, sociologists would view such efforts to persuade people as examples of influence. Now let's take a look at the third source of power—authority.

TYPES OF AUTHORITY

Authority refers to institutionalized power that is recognized by the people over whom it is exercised. Sociologists commonly use the term in connection with those who hold legitimate power through elected or publicly acknowledged positions. A person's authority is often limited by her or his position. Thus, a referee has the authority to decide whether a penalty should be called during a football game but has no authority over the price of tickets to the game.

Max Weber ([1913] 1947) developed a classification system for authority that has become one of the most useful and frequently cited contributions of early sociology. He identified three ideal types of authority: traditional, rational-legal, and charismatic. Weber did not insist that only one type applies to a given society or organization. All can be present, but their relative importance will vary. Sociologists have found Weber's typology valuable in understanding different manifestations of legitimate power within a society.

SOCthink

> > > Which of these three forms of power do parents, bosses, or professors most rely on? Are there times when each of those groups use each of the three types of power?

Traditional Authority Until the middle of the 20th century, Japan was ruled by a revered emperor whose absolute power was passed down from generation to generation. In a political system based on **traditional authority,** legitimate power is conferred by custom and accepted practice. The past is a justification of the present. A king or queen is accepted as ruler of a nation simply by virtue of inheriting the crown; a tribal chief rules because that is the accepted practice. The ruler may be loved or hated, competent or destructive; in terms of legitimacy, that does not matter. For the traditional leader, authority rests in custom, not in personal characteristics, technical competence, or even written law. People accept the ruler's authority because that is how things have always been done. Traditional authority is absolute when the ruler has the ability to determine laws and policies.

Rational-Legal Authority The Confederation Act of 1867 gave the Canadian Parliament and its elected members the authority to make and enforce laws and policies. Power made legitimate by law is a form of rational-legal authority. **Rational-legal authority** involves formally agreed-upon and accepted rules, principles, and procedures of conduct that are established in order to accomplish goals in the most efficient manner possible. Such authority extends beyond governments to include any organization. Bureaucracies are the purest form of rational-legal authority. Generally, in societies based on rational-legal authority, leaders are thought to have specific areas of competence and authority, but are not thought to be endowed with divine inspiration, as in certain societies with traditional forms of authority.

> **traditional authority**
> Legitimate power conferred by custom and accepted practice.
> **rational-legal authority**
> Authority based on formally agreed-upon and accepted rules, principles, and procedures of conduct that are established in order to accomplish goals in the most efficient manner possible.
> **charismatic authority**
> Power made legitimate by a leader's exceptional personal or emotional appeal to his or her followers.

Charismatic Authority Joan of Arc was a simple peasant girl in medieval France, yet she was able to rally the French people and lead them into major battles against English invaders despite having no formally recognized position of power. How was this possible? As Weber observed, power can be legitimized by the charisma of an individual. **Charismatic authority** refers to power made legitimate by a leader's exceptional personal or emotional appeal to his or her followers.

Charisma lets a person such as Joan of Arc lead or inspire without relying on set rules or traditions. In fact, charismatic authority is derived more from the beliefs of followers than from the actual qualities of leaders. So long as people perceive a charismatic leader such as Jesus, Joan of Arc, Gandhi, Pierre Elliott Trudeau, or Martin Luther King, Jr., as having qualities that set him or her apart from ordinary citizens, that leader's authority will remain secure and often unquestioned. That unfortunately is also the case with malevolent figures such as Adolf Hitler, whose charismatic appeal turned people toward violent and destructive ends in Nazi Germany.

The expansion of the electronic media facilitated the development of charismatic authority (Couch 1996). During the 1930s and 1940s, the heads of state of Canada, the United States, Great Britain, and Germany all used radio to issue direct appeals to citizens. Now, television and the Internet allow leaders to "visit" people's homes and communicate with them via broadcasts, email, blogposts, and YouTube videos. In both Taiwan and South Korea in 1996, troubled political leaders facing reelection campaigns spoke frequently to national audiences and exaggerated military threats from neighbouring China and North Korea, respectively. In 2008, facing political upset, Prime

Minister Stephen Harper appeared on television to convince the Canadian public of the dangers a coalition government would pose.

>> Economic Systems

Out of the Industrial Revolution grew a new kind of political and economic structure known as the **industrial society,** a society that depends on mechanization to produce its goods and services. People left their rural agricultural communities and migrated to the cities to work in factories. In 1850, Montreal was home to approximately 50,000 people. As a result of the rapid growth in manufacturing industries, within 50 years its population had grown to over 300,000. Such changes, driven by economic transformations and opportunities, had radical impacts on the lives of urban residents. In fact, we cannot fully understand what happens in the context of families or education without taking into account such economic change.

This new, more global economy of the industrial age called for large-scale systems of power and authority. The term **economic system** refers to the social institution through which goods and services are produced, distributed, and consumed. Two basic types of economic system distinguish contemporary industrial societies: capitalism and socialism. As described in the following sections, capitalism and socialism serve as ideal types of economic systems. In practice, no nation fully embodies either model. Instead, the economy of each individual state represents a mixture of capitalism and socialism, although one type or the other is generally more useful in describing a society's economic structure.

CAPITALISM

In pre-industrial societies based on an agricultural economy, land functioned as the source of virtually all wealth. The Industrial Revolution changed all that. It required that certain individuals and

institutions be willing to take substantial monetary risks in order to finance new inventions, machinery, and business enterprises. Eventually, bankers, industrialists, and other holders of large sums of money replaced landowners as the most powerful economic force. These people invested their funds in the hope of realizing even greater profits and thereby became owners of property and business firms.

The transition to private ownership of business was accompanied by the emergence of **capitalism**—an economic system in which the means of production are held largely in private hands and the main incentive for economic activity is the accumulation of profits. In practice, capitalist systems vary in the degree to which the government regulates private ownership and economic activity (D. Rosenberg 1991).

Immediately following the Industrial Revolution, the prevailing form of capitalism was what is termed **laissez-faire** ("let them do [as they choose]"). Under the principle of laissez-faire, as expounded and endorsed by British economist Adam Smith (1723–1790), people could compete freely, with minimal government intervention in the economy. Business retained the right to regulate itself and operated essentially without fear of government interference (Smelser 1963).

In principle, through competition in the free market, capitalist economies should reach a natural balance between what consumers demand and what producers supply. In practice, capitalism produces monopolistic conditions. A **monopoly** exists when a single business firm controls the market. Domination of an industry allows the firm to effectively control a commodity by dictating pricing, quality standards, and availability. Buyers have little choice but to yield to the firm's decisions; there is no other place to purchase the product or service. Monopolistic practices violate the ideal of free competition cherished by Adam Smith and other supporters of laissez-faire capitalism.

SOCthink

> > > Why is competition essential to capitalism? Why might capitalists seek to establish monopolies?

Some capitalistic nations, such as Canada, outlaw monopolies through antitrust legislation. Such laws prevent any business from taking over so much of the competition in an industry that it controls the market. The federal government allows monopolies to exist only in certain exceptional cases, such as the utility and transportation industries. Even then, regulatory agencies scrutinize these officially approved monopolies to protect the public. In Canada, there are also *Crown corporations*, which are monopolistic in that they are owned by the government, but they operate as independent financial entities. Some of these companies earn a profit for the government; others (such as the CBC) survive only due to government subsidies.

Globalization and the rise of multinational corporations have spread the capitalistic pursuit of profits around the world. Especially in developing countries, governments are not always prepared to deal with the sudden influx of foreign capital and its effects on their economies. One particularly striking example of how unfettered capitalism can harm developing nations is found in the Democratic Republic of Congo (formerly Zaire). The Congo has significant deposits of the metal columbite-tantalite—coltan, for short—which is used in the production of electronic circuit boards. Until the market for cell phones, pagers, and laptop computers heated up recently, North American manufacturers obtained most of their coltan from Australia. But at the height of consumer demand, they turned to miners in the Congo to increase their supply.

Predictably, the escalating price of the metal—as much as $400 per kilogram at one point, or more than three times the average Congolese worker's yearly wages—attracted undesirable attention. Soon the neighbouring countries of Rwanda, Uganda, and Burundi, at war with one another and desperate for resources to finance the conflict, were raiding the Congo's national parks, slashing and burning to expose the coltan underneath the forest floor. Indirectly, the sudden increase in the demand for coltan was financing war and the rape of the environment. Many manufacturers have since cut off their sources in the Congo in an effort to avoid abetting the destruction. However, their action has only penalized legitimate miners in the impoverished country (Austin 2002; Delawala 2002).

> **monopoly** Control of a market by a single business firm.
> **socialism** An economic system under which the means of production and distribution are collectively owned.

SOCIALISM

In their writings, Karl Marx and Friedrich Engels developed and refined socialist theory. They were disturbed by the exploitation of the working class during the Industrial Revolution. In their view, capitalism forced large numbers of people to exchange their labour for low wages. Marx and Engels argued that the owners of industry profit from the labour of workers primarily by paying workers less than the value of the goods produced.

In principle, a socialist economic system attempts to eliminate such economic exploitation. Under **socialism,** the means of production and distribution in a society are collectively rather than privately owned. Marx predicted that technological advances would make it possible for society to produce enough for everyone, and a socialist system would ensure that everyone got enough. Socialists reject the laissez-faire philosophy that free competition benefits the general public. Instead, they believe that the central government, acting as the representative of the people, should make basic economic decisions. Therefore, government ownership of all major industries—including steel production, automobile manufacturing, and agriculture—is a primary feature of socialism as an ideal type.

Marx believed further that socialist states would eventually "wither away" and evolve into communist societies. In principle, **communism** is an economic system under

> **communism** As an ideal type, an economic system under which all property is communally owned and no social distinctions are made on the basis of people's ability to produce.
>
> **mixed economy** An economic system that combines elements of both capitalism and socialism.

which all property is communally owned and no social distinctions are made on the basis of people's ability to produce. In recent decades, the former Soviet Union, the People's Republic of China, Vietnam, Cuba, and the nations of Eastern Europe were popularly thought of as examples of communist economic systems. However, this usage represents an incorrect application of a term with sensitive political connotations. All nations known as communist in the 20th century actually fell far short of the ideal type.

By the early 1990s, Communist parties were no longer ruling the nations of Eastern Europe. As of 2007, however, China, Cuba, Laos, and Vietnam remained socialist societies ruled by Communist parties. Even in those countries, however, capitalism has begun to make inroads. By 2000, fully 25 percent of China's production originated in the private business sector.

THE MIXED ECONOMY

In practice, national economic systems combine elements of both capitalism and socialism. A **mixed economy** features elements of more than one economic system. Moving from a capitalist ideal toward a mixed economy typically involves removing some goods and services from the competitive free market and providing them for all or subsidizing them to assure broader access. In Canada, we do this with goods and services such as police and fire protection, roads, and public schools. We argue that all people should have access to such public goods without regard for their ability to pay. Perhaps the most defining example is Canada's universal health care system—see Chapter 14 for details.

Also in contrast to the laissez-faire ideal, capitalism today features government regulation of economic relations. Without regulation, business firms would be more likely to mislead consumers, endanger workers' safety, and even defraud the companies' investors—all in the pursuit of greater profits. That is why governments in capitalist nations often monitor prices, set safety and environmental standards for industries, protect the rights of consumers, and regulate collective bargaining between labour unions and management. Yet, under capitalism, government rarely takes over ownership of an entire industry.

Starting from a socialist ideal and moving toward a mixed economy means opening up some aspects of the economy to competition and the free market. When communists assumed leadership of China in 1949, they cast themselves as the champions of workers and peasants and the enemies of those who exploited workers, namely landlords and capitalists. Profit making was outlawed, and those who engaged in it were arrested. By the 1960s,

Fifty Years of Growth, 1970–2020

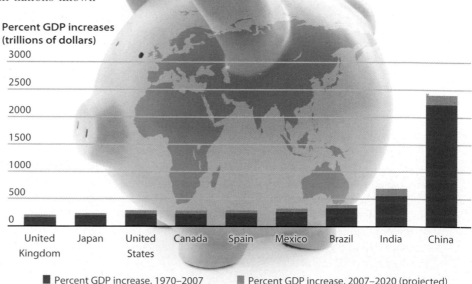

Percent GDP increases (trillions of dollars)

Chart categories (left to right): United Kingdom, Japan, United States, Canada, Spain, Mexico, Brazil, India, China

Y-axis values: 0, 500, 1000, 1500, 2000, 2500, 3000

■ Percent GDP increase, 1970–2007   ■ Percent GDP increase, 2007–2020 (projected)

Source: U.S. Department of Agriculture 2007.

China's economy was dominated by huge state-controlled enterprises, such as factories. Peasants essentially worked for the government, receiving payment in goods based on their contribution to the collective good. It did not work well economically.

In the 1980s, party leaders in China began to make market-oriented reforms, revising the nation's legal structure to promote private business. For the first time, private entrepreneurs were allowed to compete with some state-controlled businesses. By the mid-1990s, party officials had begun to hand some ailing state-controlled businesses over to private entrepreneurs, in hopes that the firms could be turned around. Today, those entrepreneurs are among the nation's wealthiest citizens, and some even hold positions on government advisory boards. For Chinese workers, the loosening of state control over the economy has opened up opportunities for occupational mobility.

However, critics in China point to the negative consequences of taking this path. For one thing, the accumulation of wealth by a few violates a core socialist principle. Further, workers often receive minimal pay and face poor working conditions; wages average $120–$200 for a six-day week. They also suffer from high injury rates, and harsh working conditions contribute to rapid turnover in the labour force. In addition, there is no pension system in China, so retirees must struggle to find other ways to support themselves. Further, pollution is common in urban areas, and environmental problems are extensive (Barboza 2008; French 2008). Finally, Chinese women traditionally have been relegated to subservient roles in the patriarchal family structure, and despite recent economic changes, women receive lower wages than men who work in the same job sectors, not unlike what we see in North America (Wang and Cai 2006).

Hot or Not?

Should governments be expected to bail out struggling companies?

transfers of money, goods, or services take place but are not reported to the government. Examples of the informal economy include bartering in which people trade goods and services with someone (say, exchanging a haircut for a computer lesson), selling goods on the street, and engaging in illegal transactions, such as drug deals. Participants in this type of economy avoid taxes and government regulations.

In the developing world, governments often create burdensome business regulations that overworked bureaucrats must administer. When requests for licences and permits pile up, delaying business projects, legitimate entrepreneurs find that they need to "go underground" to get anything done. Despite its apparent efficiency, this type of informal economy is dysfunctional for a country's overall political and economic well-being. Since informal firms typically operate in remote locales to avoid detection, they cannot easily expand when they become profitable. And given the limited protection for their property and contractual rights, participants in the informal economy are less likely than others to save and invest their income.

Informal economies can also be dysfunctional for workers. Working conditions in these businesses are often unsafe or dangerous, and the jobs rarely provide any benefits to those who become ill or cannot continue to work. Perhaps more significant, the longer a worker remains in the informal economy, the less likely he or she is to make the transition to the regular economy. No matter how efficient or productive a worker may be, employers expect to see experience in the formal economy on a job application. Experience as a successful street vendor or self-employed cleaning person does not carry much weight with interviewers (Venkatesh 2006).

SOCthink

> > > When doing jobs in the informal economy such as babysitting, lawn mowing, house cleaning, or construction, it can be nice to get cash under the table without having to pay taxes. What are the long-term disadvantages of doing so for the individual? What about for society? Why might someone opt to do so anyway?

>> Changing Economies

Economies are not static. Just as they changed due to the impact of the Industrial Revolution, economies continue to adapt to new contexts. Increased opportunity for workers, regardless of race, ethnicity, or gender—made possible in part by various social movements—has made the workforce more diverse. Technological innovation and globalization have reduced the number of traditional blue-collar jobs through deindustrialization. Microfinancing has opened up opportunities for poor people, especially women, around the world.

informal economy Transfers of money, goods, or services that are not reported to the government.

THE INFORMAL ECONOMY

An informal economy operates within the confines of the dominant macroeconomic system in many countries, whether capitalist or socialist. In this **informal economy,**

THE CHANGING FACE OF THE WORKFORCE

The workforce in Canada is constantly changing. During World War II, when men were mobilized to fight abroad, women entered the workforce in large numbers. Legislation such as the Charter of Rights and Freedoms and policies such as employment equity have increased workplace opportunities for women and members of visible minorities. While predictions are not always reliable, sociologists and labour specialists foresee an increasingly diverse workforce in Canada.

More and more, then, the workforce reflects the diversity of the population, as ethnic minorities enter the labour force and immigrants and their children move from marginal jobs or employment in the informal economy to positions of greater visibility and responsibility. The impact of this changing labour force is not merely statistical. A more diverse workforce means that relationships between workers are more likely to cross gender, racial, and ethnic lines. People will soon find themselves supervising and being supervised by people very different from themselves. In response to these changes, many businesses have instituted some type of cultural diversity training program (Melia 2000).

DEINDUSTRIALIZATION

In recent decades, the North American economy has moved away from its industrial base through the process of **deindustrialization,** which refers to the systematic, widespread withdrawal of investment in basic aspects of productivity, such as factories and plants. Giant corporations that deindustrialize are not necessarily refusing to invest in new economic opportunities. Rather, the targets and locations of investment change, and the need for labour decreases as advances in technology continue to automate production. First, companies may move their plants from the nation's central cities to the suburbs. The next step may be relocation from suburban areas to other countries, such as the United States or Mexico, or perhaps international relocation. Or—as has been the case far too frequently in the current economy—facilities are forced to close (Lynn 2003).

Although deindustrialization often involves relocation, it can also take the form of corporate restructuring known as **downsizing,** which involves reducing the size of a company's workforce. The goal is to increase efficiency and reduce costs in the face of growing worldwide competition. When such restructuring occurs, the impact on the bureaucratic hierarchy of formal organizations can be significant. A large corporation may choose to sell off or entirely abandon less productive divisions and to eliminate layers of management it views as unnecessary. Wages and salaries may be frozen and fringe benefits cut—all in the name of restructuring. Increasing reliance on automation also spells the end of work as we have known it.

North American firms have been outsourcing certain types of work for generations. For example, moderate-sized businesses such as furniture stores and commercial laundries have long relied on outside trucking firms to make deliveries to their customers. The new trend toward **offshoring** carries this practice one step further by transferring other types of work to foreign contractors. Now,

deindustrialization The systematic, widespread withdrawal of investment in basic aspects of productivity, such as factories and plants.
downsizing Reductions in a company's workforce as part of deindustrialization.
offshoring The transfer of work to foreign contractors.

even large companies are turning to overseas firms, many of them located in developing countries. Offshoring has become the latest tactic in the time-worn business strategy of raising profits by reducing costs.

Offshoring began when North American companies started transferring manufacturing jobs to foreign factories, where wage rates were much lower. But the transfer of work from one country to another is no longer limited to manufacturing. Office and professional jobs are being exported, too, thanks to advanced telecommunications and the growth of skilled, English-speaking labour forces in developing nations with relatively low wage scales. The trend includes even those jobs that require considerable training, such as accounting and financial analysis, computer programming, claims adjustment, telemarketing, and hotel and airline reservations. Today, when you call a toll-free number to reach a customer service representative, chances are that the person who answers the phone will not be speaking from Canada.

The social costs of deindustrialization and downsizing cannot be overemphasized. Plant closings lead to substantial unemployment in a community, which can have a devastating impact on both the micro and macro levels. On the micro level, the unemployed person and his or her family must adjust to a loss of spending power. Painting or re-siding the house, saving for retirement, even thinking about having another child—all must be put aside. Both marital happiness and family cohesion may suffer as a result. Although many dismissed workers eventually reenter the paid labour force, they often must accept less desirable positions with lower salaries and fewer benefits. Unemployment and underemployment are tied to many of the social problems discussed throughout this

> **The gap in our economy is between what we have and what we think we ought to have—and that is a moral problem, not an economic one.**
>
> Paul Heyne

Due to the financial woes of the North American auto industry, the GM truck manufacturing plant in Oshawa, Ontario, was forced to stop production In May 2009. This is but one example of massive job losses recently in Canada. In March 2009, the unemployment rate hit 8 percent, the highest rate in seven years.

textbook, among them the need for child care and the controversy over social assistance.

Alan S. Blinder (2006), former vice chair of the U.S. Federal Reserve, predicts that offshoring will become the "third Industrial Revolution"—a life-altering shift in the way goods and services are produced and consumed. Blinder says we have barely seen the "tip of the offshoring iceberg." While offshoring may not lead to large-scale unemployment, it will likely produce a shift in Western labour markets. Jobs that are easily outsourced, like accounting and computer programming, will migrate to developing countries, leaving those that must be done on site, like nursing and construction, at home. In Canada, offshoring is occurring most of all in business services, followed by financial services and insurance services (Baldwin and Gu 2008).

While this shift has brought jobs and technology to nations such as India, there is a downside to offshoring for foreign workers as well. Although outsourcing is a significant source of employment for India's upper middle class, hundreds of millions of other Indians have benefitted little if at all from the trend. Instead of improving these people's lives, the new business centres have siphoned water and electricity away from those who are most in need. Even the high-tech workers are experiencing negative consequences. Many suffer from stress disorders such as stomach problems and difficulty sleeping; more than half quit their jobs before the end of a year (Waldman 2004a, 2004b, 2004c).

MICROFINANCING

Economic development can, however, have a positive impact on people's lives around the globe. Microfinancing, for example, involves lending small sums of money to the poor so that they can work their way out of poverty. Borrowers use the money to get small businesses off the ground—to buy the tools, equipment, and bamboo to make stools, the yarn to weave into cloth, or cows to produce milk. They then sell the products they produce in local shops. The typical microloan is less than $100, and often as little as $12. The recipients are people who ordinarily would not be able to qualify for banking services.

Theory
A Matter of Perspective

THEORETICAL PERSPECTIVES ON POLITICS AND THE ECONOMY

Functionalist:
- Durkheim asserts that the modern division of labour can create interdependence and thus foster solidarity
- the economy and political spheres require people to work at all levels so as to ensure smooth functioning of society
- sees power as democratically distributed

Conflict:
- power is concentrated in society's elites
- Marx and Engels condemn capitalism's inherent exploitation
- argue that the economic and political structure will develop into socialism—in which the means of production are collectively owned
- in turn, the state will "wither away" and evolve into communist society

Feminist:
- power is concentrated among men, particularly White men of privilege
- critiques the restricted participation of women in political life and the economy
- highlights women's gains while acknowledging the need to continue fighting for greater representation

Interactionist:
- power and authority must be recognized by members of society
- considers individual motivations for economic and political participation
- examines interpersonal understandings of power, conflict, and peace

Sometimes referred to as "banking the unbanked," microfinancing was the brainchild of Bangladeshi economist Muhammad Yunus. In 1976, in the midst of a devastating famine in Bangladesh, Yunus founded the Grameen (meaning "village") Bank. The idea came to him when he reached into his pocket to lend $27 to a group of villagers who had asked him for help. Working through local halls or meeting places, the Grameen Bank has now extended credit to nearly 7 million people. The idea has spread, and microloans have even been underwritten by multinational organizations such as the International Monetary Fund and for-profit banks like Citigroup. Estimates suggest that by 2007 microfinancing had reached 60 million people.

Microfinancing works well in countries that have experienced economic devastation. For example, in 2002, after decades of conflict and military occupation, Afghanistan did not have a single functioning bank. Five years later, with the help of the World Bank and other donors, Afghans could get microloans and other financial services in 22 of the country's 34 provinces. The new microlenders are the first evidence of a formal financial sector that Afghanistan has seen in years. Their funds have helped to start businesses and allowed farmers to convert from opium growing to other crops.

Because an estimated 90 percent of the recipients of microcredit are women, feminist theorists are especially interested in the growth of microfinancing. Women's economic status has been found to be critical to the well-being of their children, and the key to a healthy household environment. In developing countries, where women often are not treated as well as men, being entrusted with credit is particularly empowering to them. In recognition of these social and economic benefits of microfinancing, the United Nations proclaimed 2005 the International Year of Microcredit (Dugger 2006; Flynn 2007; World Bank 2006c).

>> Types of Government

Just as new economic systems developed in response to broader historical changes, political systems also adapted. In all societies, someone or some group—whether it be a tribal chief, a dictator, a council, or a parliament—makes important decisions about how to use resources and allocate goods. Inevitably, the struggle for power and authority involves **politics,** which political scientist Harold Lasswell (1936) tersely defined as "who gets what, when, and how." Politics takes place within the context of a **political system,** which is the social institution that is founded on a recognized set of procedures for implementing and achieving society's goals, such as the allocation of valued resources.

Government represents an institutionalized form of authority. Given the scope of international relations and the globalization of national economies, these formal systems of authority make a significant number of critical political decisions. Such systems take a variety of forms, including monarchy, oligarchy, dictatorship, totalitarianism, and democracy.

MONARCHY

A **monarchy** is a form of government headed by a single member of a royal family, usually a king, queen, or some other hereditary ruler. In earlier times, many monarchs claimed that God had granted them a divine right to rule. Typically, they governed on the basis of traditional forms of authority, sometimes accompanied by the use of force. By the beginning of the 21st century, however, monarchs held genuine governmental power in only a few nations, such as Monaco. Most monarchs, such as Queen Elizabeth II in England, now have little practical power; they serve primarily ceremonial purposes. This is the case in Canada, which is a constitutional monarchy. The Governor General acts as the Queen's representative, primarily performing ceremonial functions.

> **politics** In Harold Lasswell's words, "who gets what, when, and how."
> **political system** The social institution that is founded on a recognized set of procedures for implementing and achieving society's goals.
> **monarchy** A form of government headed by a single member of a royal family, usually a king, queen, or some other hereditary ruler.
> **oligarchy** A form of government in which a few individuals rule.

OLIGARCHY

An **oligarchy** is a form of government in which a few individuals rule. A venerable method of governing that flourished in ancient Greece and Egypt, oligarchy now often takes

Did You Know?

...One of Queen Elizabeth's official duties is to appoint England's Prime Minister. Given that political power rests with Parliament, however, this too has become largely a ceremonial duty.

the form of military rule. In developing nations in Africa, Asia, and Latin America, small factions of military officers may forcibly seize power, either from legally elected regimes or from other military cliques.

Strictly speaking, the term *oligarchy* is reserved for governments that are run by a few selected individuals. However, the People's Republic of China can be classified as an oligarchy if we stretch the meaning of the term. In China, power rests in the hands of a large but exclusive ruling *group,* the Communist Party. In a similar vein, we might argue that many industrialized nations of the West should be considered oligarchies (rather than democracies), since only a powerful few—leaders of big business, government, and the military—actually rule. Later in this chapter, we will examine the "elite model" of the Canadian political system in greater detail.

dictatorship A government in which one person has nearly total power to make and enforce laws.

totalitarianism Virtually complete government control and surveillance over all aspects of a society's social and political life.

democracy In a literal sense, government by the people.

representative democracy A form of government in which certain individuals are selected to speak for the people.

DICTATORSHIP AND TOTALITARIANISM

A **dictatorship** is a government in which one person has nearly total power to make and enforce laws. Dictators rule primarily through the use of coercion, which often includes imprisonment, torture and executions. Typically, they *seize* power rather than being freely elected (as in a democracy) or inheriting power (as in a monarchy). Some dictators are quite charismatic and manage to achieve a certain popularity, although their supporters' enthusiasm is almost certainly tinged with fear. Other dictators are bitterly hated by the people over whom they rule.

Frequently, dictators develop such overwhelming control over people's lives that their governments are called totalitarian. (Monarchies and oligarchies may also achieve this type of dominance.) **Totalitarianism** involves virtually complete government control and surveillance over all aspects of a society's social and political life. Germany during Hitler's reign, the Soviet Union under Stalin in the 1930s, and North Korea today are classified as totalitarian states.

DEMOCRACY

In a literal sense, **democracy** means government by the people. The word comes from two Greek roots—*demos,* meaning "the populace" or "the common people," and *kratia,* meaning "rule." Of course, in large, populous nations such as Canada, government by the people is impractical at the national level. Canadians cannot vote on every important issue that comes before Parliament. Consequently, popular rule is generally maintained through **representative democracy,** a form of government in which certain individuals are selected to speak for the people.

A longstanding dispute in Canada involves the power of First Nations peoples to govern themselves. In a 1995 policy statement, the federal government recognized the inherent right of Aboriginal self-government, and outlined an approach for negotiating self-government agreements. Many agreements have been reached or are in negotiations; however, the provision of land, money, and authority to Aboriginal groups has also met with opposition. The identification of Quebec as a distinct nation has met with similar resistance. The idea of granting individual groups their own "nationhood" within (what many think of as) a single nation has proven divisive.

>> Political Behaviour in Canada

Canadian citizens take for granted many aspects of their political system. They are accustomed to living in a nation with a Charter of Rights and Freedoms, a variety of political parties, and the right to vote by secret ballot. They

Hot or Not?

Should members of Parliament be obligated to toe the party line when it comes to voting on major issues?

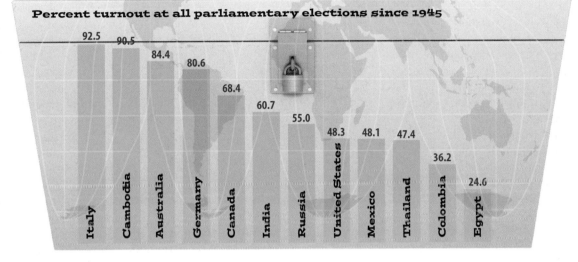

Percent turnout at all parliamentary elections since 1945

Country	Percent
Italy	92.5
Cambodia	90.5
Australia	84.4
Germany	80.6
Canada	68.4
India	60.7
Russia	55.0
United States	48.3
Mexico	48.1
Thailand	47.4
Colombia	36.2
Egypt	24.6

Source: International Institute for Democracy and Electoral Assistance 2006.

SOCthink

> > > Canada is commonly classified as a representative democracy, since the elected members of Parliament and appointed members of the Senate make our laws. However, critics have questioned how representative our democracy really is. Does Parliament genuinely represent the masses? Are the people of Canada legitimately self-governing, or has our government become a forum for powerful elites?

are responsible for electing the governing political party (the leader of which becomes Prime Minister), and provincial and local governments that are distinct from the federal government. Because it is, in principle, a representative democracy, the system depends upon all individuals having equal access to and input into the political process in order to be fully responsive. In practice, two particular concerns—voter participation and race and gender representation—raise questions about the degree to which this is happening.

PARTICIPATION AND APATHY

In Canada, virtually all citizens are familiar with the basics of the political process, and most tend to identify to some extent with a political party. However, only a small minority of citizens, often members of the higher social classes, actually participate in political organizations at the local, provincial, or federal level. Studies reveal that "political participation" in Canada means searching for political information, volunteering at a political event, or writing to politicians to express views on relevant issues (Keown 2007). Approximately 13 percent of Canadians are "card-carrying" members of a political party, but less than 5 percent are actually actively involved.

By the 1980s, it had become clear that many people in Canada were beginning to be turned off by political parties, politicians, and big government. The most dramatic indication of this growing alienation came from voting statistics. Today, voters appear to be less enthusiastic than ever about elections, even at the federal level. Participation of eligible voters in federal elections declined from 75 percent in 1998 to 59 percent in 2008. Obviously, even modestly higher voter turnout could dramatically change election outcomes.

While a few nations still command high voter turnout, it is increasingly common to hear national leaders of other countries complain of voter apathy. Political participation makes government accountable to the voters. If participation declines, government operates with less of a sense of accountability to society. This issue is most serious for the least powerful individuals and groups in Canada. Voter turnout is especially low among Aboriginal peoples and recent immigrants (defined

Did You Know?

... The Green Party of Canada won 6.8 percent of the vote in the 2008 federal election. While this does not translate to seats, it does indicate voter interest in an alternative to the long-established parties.

by Statistics Canada as those who have been in the country for less than five years). And many more potential voters fail to register to vote. The poor—whose focus understandably is on survival—are traditionally underrepresented among voters as well. The low turnout found among these groups is due at least in part to their common feeling of powerlessness. By the same token, by declining to vote, they encourage political power brokers to continue to ignore the interests of the less affluent and the nation's minorities. The segment of the voting population that has shown the most voter apathy is the young (Holder 2006). However, as new parties offer alternative visions to the established political regime, more Canadians may feel motivated to exercise their right to vote.

Reasons for Not Voting, 18- to 24-Year Olds

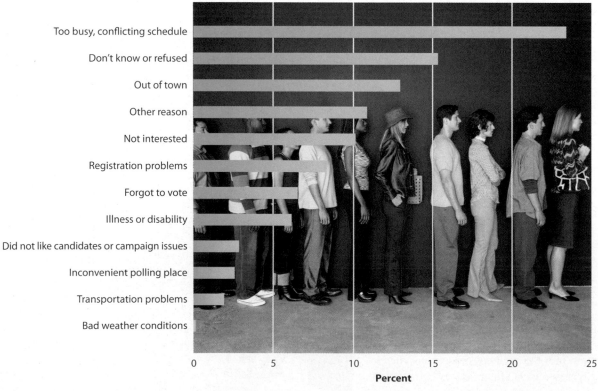

Too busy, conflicting schedule
Don't know or refused
Out of town
Other reason
Not interested
Registration problems
Forgot to vote
Illness or disability
Did not like candidates or campaign issues
Inconvenient polling place
Transportation problems
Bad weather conditions

0   5   10   15   20   25
Percent

Source: U.S. Census Bureau, Current Population Survey, May 25, 2005.

RACE AND GENDER IN POLITICS

Because politics is synonymous with power and authority, we should not be surprised that marginalized groups, such as women and racial and ethnic minorities, lack political strength. In Canada, women gained the right to vote in federal elections in 1918, but provincially, that milestone varied between 1916 (Manitoba) to 1940 (Quebec). Canadians of Asian descent were not allowed to vote until 1948. First Nations peoples received unconditional voting rights in 1961; previously, they had to give up their First Nations status in order to vote. Predictably, it has taken these groups some time to develop their political power and begin to exercise it effectively.

Progress toward the inclusion of minority groups in government has been slow as well. As of 2008, with 68 seats, women comprised only 22 percent of Parliament. Members of visible minorities comprised approximately 8 percent of the government (and these categories overlap in some instances).

Female politicians may be enjoying more electoral success now than in the past, but there is evidence that the media cover them differently than male politicians. A content analysis of newspaper coverage of recent U.S. gubernatorial races showed that reporters wrote more often about a female candidate's personal life, appearance, or personality than a male candidate's, and less often about

SOCthink

> > > Canada has a "first past the post" system, in which the party that wins the most seats forms the government. Critics point out that these results often do not reflect the popular vote. Proportional representation distributes seats based on the number of votes received by a party. Which system do you prefer, and why?

her political viewpoints and voting record. Furthermore, when political issues were raised in newspaper articles, reporters were more likely to illustrate them with statements made by male candidates than by female candidates (Devitt 1999; Jost 2008).

Going GLOBAL

Women in National Legislatures, Selected Countries, 2007

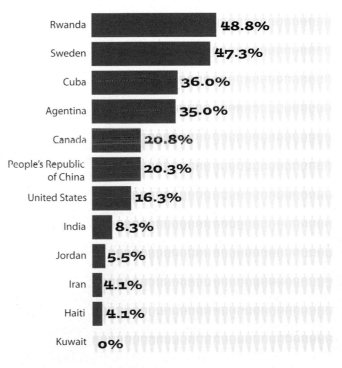

Country	Percentage
Rwanda	48.8%
Sweden	47.3%
Cuba	36.0%
Agentina	35.0%
Canada	20.8%
People's Republic of China	20.3%
United States	16.3%
India	8.3%
Jordan	5.5%
Iran	4.1%
Haiti	4.1%
Kuwait	0%

Note: Data are for lower legislative houses only, as of March 31, 2007; data on upper houses, such as the U.S. Senate or the U.K. House of Lords, are not included. In 2005, the all-male Kuwati Parliament granted women the right to vote and serve in elected offices, which could allow women to run for office as soon as 2007.

Source: Inter-Parliamentary Union 2007.

While the proportion of women in national legislatures has increased in Canada and many other nations, women still do not account for even half the members of the national legislature in any country. The African Republic of Rwanda ranks the highest, with 48.8 percent of its lower legislative seats held by women, reflecting a significant restructuring of the country.

To address this imbalance, many countries have adopted quotas for female representatives. In some, the government sets aside a certain percentage of seats for women, usually 10–30 percent. In others, political parties have decided that 20–40 percent of their candidates should be women. In Canada, the federal NDP and Liberal parties have both established quota targets for female candidates and elected seats, though these have yet to be met. Thirty-two countries now have some kind of quota system (Vasagar 2005).

elite model A view of society as being ruled by a small group of individuals who share a common set of political and economic interests.

power elite A small group of military, industrial, and government leaders who control the fate of the United States.

>> The Power Structure in Canada

The issue of power extends beyond just politics and the people who occupy formally recognized offices. Over the years, sociologists repeatedly have sought to discover who really holds power in complex societies. Do the citizens of Canada genuinely run the country through our elected representatives? Or does a small elite behind the scenes control both the government and the economic system? It is difficult to determine the location of power in a society as complex as Canada. In exploring this critical question, social scientists have developed two basic views of our nation's power structure: the power elite and the pluralist models.

POWER ELITE MODELS

Karl Marx believed that 19th-century representative democracy was essentially a sham. He argued that industrial societies were dominated by relatively small numbers of people who owned the factories and controlled natural resources. In Marx's view, government officials and military leaders were essentially servants of this capitalist class and followed their wishes. Therefore, any key decisions made by politicians inevitably reflected the interests of the dominant business owners. Like others who hold an **elite model** of power relations, Marx believed that society is ruled by a small group of individuals who share political and economic interests.

Mills' Model Sociologist C. Wright Mills, who developed the concept of the sociological imagination that we looked at in Chapter 1, put forth a model similar to Marx's in his pioneering work *The Power Elite* ([1956] 2000b). Mills described a small group of military, industrial, and government leaders who controlled the fate of the United States—the **power elite.** This analysis has been extended to other capitalist nations as well, including Canada. Power

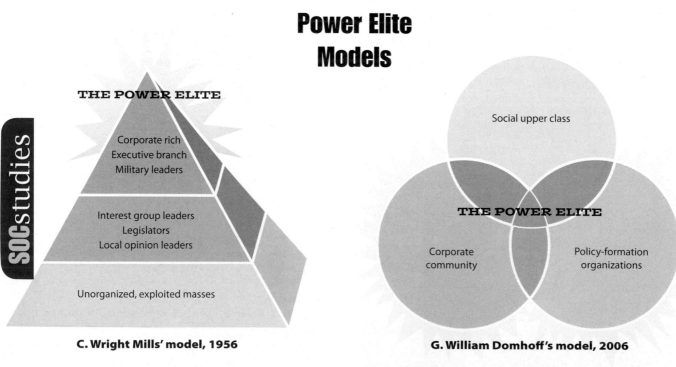

Power Elite Models

SOCstudies

THE POWER ELITE

Corporate rich
Executive branch
Military leaders

Interest group leaders
Legislators
Local opinion leaders

Unorganized, exploited masses

C. Wright Mills' model, 1956

Social upper class

THE POWER ELITE

Corporate community

Policy-formation organizations

G. William Domhoff's model, 2006

Source: Left, based on C. W. Mills (1956) 2000b; right, Domhoff 2006:105.

is seen to rest in the hands of a few, both inside and outside government.

A pyramid illustrates the power structure in Mills' model. The power elite rests at the top and includes the corporate rich, leaders of the executive branch of government, and heads of the military (whom Mills called the "warlords"). Directly below are local opinion leaders, members of the legislative branch of government, and leaders of special-interest groups. Mills contended that these individuals and groups basically follow the wishes of the dominant power elite. At the bottom of the pyramid are the unorganized, exploited masses.

A fundamental element in Mills' thesis is that the power elite not only includes relatively few members but also operates as a self-conscious, cohesive unit. Although not necessarily diabolical or ruthless, the elite comprises similar types of people who interact regularly with one another and have essentially the same political and economic interests. Mills' power elite represents not a conspiracy, but rather a community of interest and sentiment among a small number of influential people (A. Hacker 1964).

Critics claim that Mills failed to clarify when the elite opposes protests and when it tolerates them, making it difficult to test his model. Furthermore, they say, he failed to provide detailed case studies that would substantiate the interrelationships among members of the power elite. Nevertheless, his challenging theories forced scholars to look more critically at democratic political systems.

In commenting on the scandals that have rocked major corporations such as Enron and Hollinger International over the past decade, observers have noted that members of the business elite are closely interrelated. In a study of the members of the boards of directors of Fortune 1000 corporations, researchers found that each director can reach *every* other board of directors in just 3.7 steps. That is, by consulting acquaintances of acquaintances, each director can quickly reach someone who sits on each of the other 999 boards. Furthermore, the face-to-face contact directors regularly have in their board meetings makes them a highly cohesive elite. Finally, the corporate elite not only is wealthy, powerful, and cohesive but also is overwhelmingly White and male (G. Davis 2003, 2004; Kentor and Jang 2004; Mizruchi 1996; Strauss 2002).

Domhoff's Model Sociologist G. William Domhoff (2006) agrees with Mills that a powerful elite runs the industrialized capitalist nations of the developed world. Domhoff stresses the role played by elites from within networks of organizations including the corporate community; policy formation organizations such as think tanks, chambers of commerce, and labour unions; and the social upper class. Membership in these groups overlaps, and members with connections in more than one of these spheres have more power and influence. Domhoff finds that those in this latter group are still largely White, male, and upper class, but he notes the presence of a small number of women and minority men in key positions—groups that were excluded from Mills' top echelon and are still underrepresented today (Zweigenhaft and Domhoff 2006).

Although the three groups in Domhoff's power elite model do overlap, they do not necessarily agree on specific policies.

Domhoff notes that in politics, two different coalitions have exercised influence. A corporate-conservative coalition has played a large role in politics, generating support for particular candidates through direct-mail appeals. A liberal-labour coalition is based in unions, local environmental organizations, a segment of the minority group community, liberal churches, and the university and arts communities (Zweigenhaft and Domhoff 2006). This suggests that the interests of members of the power elite are not always singular or uniform but that overall they do work together to advance their larger interests.

THE PLURALIST MODEL

Other theorists argue that power in Western democratic nations is shared more widely, that there is no core group at the top who are able to advance their common interests. In their view, a pluralist model more accurately describes the power structure of these nations. According to the **pluralist model,** many competing groups within the community have access to government, so that no single group is dominant.

The pluralist model suggests that a variety of groups play a significant role in decision making. Typically, pluralists make use of intensive case studies or community studies based on observation research. One of the most famous—an investigation of decision making in New Haven, Connecticut—was reported by Robert Dahl (1961). Dahl found that, although the number of people involved in any important decision was rather small, community power was nonetheless diffuse. Few political actors exercised decision-making power on all issues, and no one group got its way all the time. One individual or group might be influential in a battle over urban renewal but have little impact on educational policy.

The pluralist model, too, has its critics. Domhoff (1978, 2006) reexamined Dahl's study of decision making in New Haven and argued that Dahl and other pluralists had failed to trace how local elites who were prominent in decision making belonged to a larger national ruling class. In addition, studies of community power, such as Dahl's work in New Haven, can examine decision making only on issues that become part of the political agenda. They

pluralist model A view of society in which many competing groups within the community have access to government, so that no single group is dominant. **war** Conflict between organizations that possess trained combat forces equipped with deadly weapons.

fail to address the potential power of elites to keep certain matters entirely out of the realm of political debate. Furthermore, the pluralist model fails to consider the gap between principle and reality when it comes to representation. For instance, Canada has an official commitment to multiculturalism, yet large segments of the population are relatively powerless to make their voices heard.

Historically, pluralists have stressed ways in which large numbers of people can participate in or influence governmental decision making. New communications technologies like the Internet are increasing the opportunity to be heard, not just in countries like Canada but in developing countries the world over. The ability to communicate with political leaders via email, for example, increases the opportunity for the average citizen to have a voice in politics.

>> War and Peace

When it comes to political power, perhaps no decision is as weighty as the decision to go to war. Conflict is a central aspect of social relations. Sociologists Theodore Caplow and Louis Hicks (2002:3) have defined **war** as conflict between organizations that possess trained combat forces equipped with deadly weapons. This meaning is broader than the legal definition, which typically requires a formal declaration of hostilities.

WAR

Sociologists approach war in three different ways. Those who take a global view study how and why two or more nations become engaged in military conflict. Those who take a nation-state view stress the interaction of internal political, socioeconomic, and cultural forces. And those who take a micro view focus on the social impact of war on individuals and the groups to which they belong (Kiser 1992).

Analysis at the global level focuses on macro issues such as the distribution of resources, struggles over political philosophies, and debates about boundaries. Often it involves nations with competing political and economic systems, as was the case in World War I, World War II, and the Cold War. Some have argued that the conflict in Iraq is about bringing freedom and democracy to the Middle East, while others argue it was motivated by oil and profits. Sociologists have devoted much effort to studying the internal decision-making process that leads to war. Even though government leaders make the decision to go to war, public opinion plays a significant role in its execution. By 1971, the number of U.S. soldiers killed in Vietnam had surpassed 50,000, and antiwar sentiment was strong. Surveys done at that time showed that the public was split roughly equally on the question of whether war was an appropriate way to settle differences between nations. This division in public opinion continued until the United States led the charge in the Gulf War following Iraq's invasion of Kuwait in 1990. Since then, U.S. sentiment has been more supportive of war as a means of resolving disputes. Polls conducted in Canada indicate that this sentiment is not shared by the majority of Canadians, perhaps because of Canada's traditional peacekeeping role. For further discussion on opinion polls, see the SOC studies box below.

A major change relating to the conduct of war involves the composition of the Canadian military. Women represent a growing presence among the troops. In 2006, women made up 15 percent of the Canadian military; about 2 percent of the regular combat force is female. In May, 2006, Canada experienced its first loss of an active combat female soldier—Captain Nichola Goddard died in battle in Afghanistan. First Nations, Inuit, and Métis Canadians make up approximately 4 percent of the Canadian military. In an attempt to increase their participation, the Canadian Forces now offer religious and cultural accommodations, such as permission to wear their hair long or braided (National Defence 2009).

At the level of interpersonal interaction, war can bring out the worst as well as the best in people. In 2004, graphic images of the abuse of Iraqi prisoners by U.S. soldiers at Iraq's Abu Ghraib prison shocked the world. For social scientists, the deterioration of the guards' behaviour brought to mind Philip Zimbardo's mock prison experiment, conducted in 1971. Though the results of the experiment have been applied primarily to civilian correctional facilities, Zimbardo's study was actually funded by the Office of Naval Research. In July 2004, the U.S. military began using a documentary film about the experiment to train military

POPSOC

During World War II, the U.S. government sponsored films to garner support for the war effort, boost people's morale, and even demonize the enemy. From cartoons featuring Mickey Mouse and Donald Duck to films including *This Is the Army* (which starred Ronald Reagan), Hollywood cooperated in getting the message out in the 1940s. In more recent years, antiwar films have also raised difficult questions that governments would sometimes rather not be aired. During the Cold War, *Dr. Strangelove* called into question the insanity of the nuclear standoff; in 1970, the film version of *M*A*S*H*, though set in Korea, raised questions about the conflict in Vietnam. More recently, there have been numerous films about the war in Iraq, including Michael Moore's *Fahrenheit 9/11*, *No End in Sight*, *Stop-Loss*, and *War, Inc.*

SOCstudies

Public Support for Canadian Military Action in Afghanistan

Polls suggest declining support for Canada's participation in the Afghanistan mission. For example, a 2008 Environics survey found only 14 percent of respondents strongly approved and 27 percent somewhat approved, in contrast to 22 percent who somewhat disapproved and 34 percent who strongly disapproved (3 percent did not answer/did not know). An Ipsos Reid poll conducted the same year found 37 percent of respondents supporting withdrawal of Canadian troops.

But Brian MacDonald, Senior Defence Analyst with the Conference of Defence Associations notes that responses differ dramatically depending on how the survey questions are worded. For instance, if the question asks about support or opposition to participation "to secure the environment for the civilian population through activities that include combat," support for the mission rises by over 10 percent (MacDonald 2007).

This example reminds us that we must look carefully at statistics.

Aftermath of a terrorist attack.

interrogators to avoid mistreatment of prisoners (Zarembo 2004; Zimbardo 2004).

TERRORISM

As North Americans learned on September 11, 2001, the ability to instill fear through large-scale violent acts is not limited to recognized political states, and it can involve political groups that operate outside the bounds of legitimate authority. Acts of terror, whether perpetrated by a few or by many people, can be a powerful force. Formally defined, **terrorism** is the use or threat of violence against random or symbolic targets in pursuit of political aims. For terrorists, the end justifies the means. They believe that the status quo is oppressive and that desperate measures are essential to end the suffering of the deprived.

An essential aspect of contemporary terrorism involves use of the media. Terrorists may wish to keep secret their individual identities, but they want their political messages and goals to receive as much publicity as possible. The purpose of many acts of terrorist violence is more symbolic than strategic or tactical. These attacks represent a statement made by people who feel that the world has gone awry, that accepted political paths to problem resolution are ineffective or blocked, and that there is a larger or cosmic struggle going on, raising the stakes and so justifying the means (Juergensmeyer 2003). Whether through calls to the media, anonymous manifestos, or other means, terrorists typically admit responsibility for and defend their violent acts.

terrorism The use or threat of violence against random or symbolic targets in pursuit of political aims.
peace The absence of war, or more broadly, a proactive effort to develop cooperative relations among nations.

Terrorism is a global concern. Since September 11, 2001, governments around the world have renewed their efforts to fight terrorism. Even though the public generally regards increased surveillance and social control as a necessary evil, these measures have nonetheless raised governance issues. For example, some citizens in the United States and elsewhere have expressed concern that measures such as the USA Patriot Act of 2001 threaten civil liberties. Citizens also complain about the heightened anxiety created by the vague "terror alerts" their federal government issues from time to time. Relations between Canada and the United States have changed, as the U.S. tightens regulations on border crossings, such as requiring travellers to carry a valid passport. Worldwide, including Canada, immigration and the processing of refugees have slowed to a crawl, separating families and preventing employers from filling job openings. As these efforts to combat political violence illustrate, the term *terrorism* is an apt one (R. Howard and Sawyer 2003; Lee 1983; R. Miller 1988).

PEACE

Sociologists have considered **peace** both as the absence of war and as a proactive effort to develop cooperative relations among nations. While we often focus on international relations, we should note that in the 1990s, 90 percent of the world's armed conflicts occurred *within* rather than between states. Often, outside powers became involved in these internal conflicts, either as supporters of particular factions or as brokers of a potential peace accord. In at least 28 countries where such conflicts occurred—none of which would be considered core nations in world systems analysis—at least 10,000 people died (Kriesberg 1992; Dan Smith 1999).

Sociologists and other social scientists who draw on sociological theory and research have tried to identify conditions that deter war. One of their findings is that international trade may act as a deterrent to armed conflict. As countries exchange goods, people, and then cultures, they become more integrated and less likely to threaten each other's security. Viewed from this perspective, not just trade but also immigration and foreign exchange programs have a beneficial effect on international relations.

Another means of fostering peace is the activity of international charities and activist groups, or nongovernmental organizations (NGOs). The Red Cross and Red Crescent, Doctors Without Borders, and Amnesty International donate their services wherever they are needed, without regard to nationality. In the past decade or so, these NGOs have been expanding in number, size, and scope. By sharing news of local conditions and clarifying local issues, they often prevent conflicts from escalating into violence and war. Some NGOs have initiated cease-fires, reached settlements, and even ended warfare between former adversaries.

Finally, many analysts stress that nations cannot maintain their security by threatening violence. Peace, they contend, can best be maintained by developing strong mutual security agreements among potential adversaries (Etzioni 1965; Shostak 2002). Following this path involves active diplomacy and, to the extent that it involves negotiations with countries viewed as enemies, can be controversial.

Going GLOBAL

The Global Reach of Terrorism

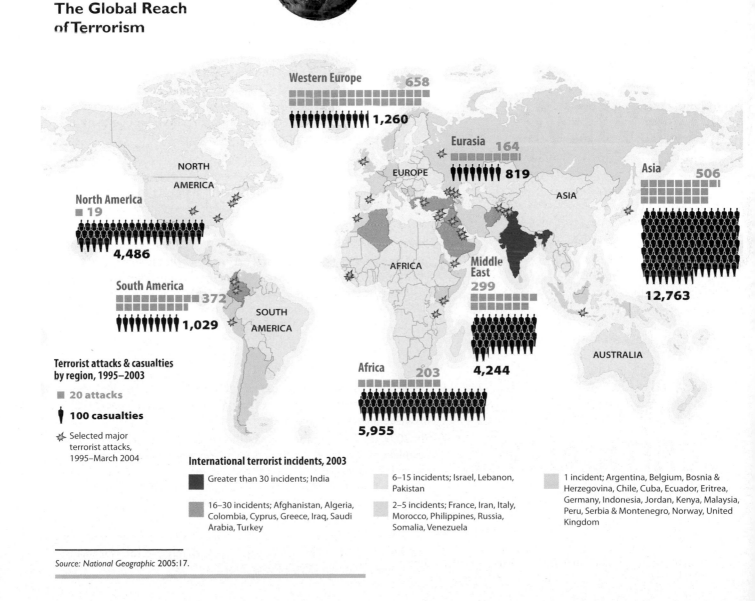

Terrorist attacks & casualties by region, 1995–2003

■ **20 attacks**

▮ **100 casualties**

✧ Selected major terrorist attacks, 1995–March 2004

Western Europe 658 / 1,260
Eurasia 164 / 819
Asia 506 / 12,763
North America 19 / 4,486
South America 372 / 1,029
Middle East 299 / 4,244
Africa 203 / 5,955

International terrorist incidents, 2003

■ Greater than 30 incidents; India

■ 16–30 incidents; Afghanistan, Algeria, Colombia, Cyprus, Greece, Iraq, Saudi Arabia, Turkey

■ 6–15 incidents; Israel, Lebanon, Pakistan

■ 2–5 incidents; France, Iran, Italy, Morocco, Philippines, Russia, Somalia, Venezuela

■ 1 incident; Argentina, Belgium, Bosnia & Herzegovina, Chile, Cuba, Ecuador, Eritrea, Germany, Indonesia, Jordan, Kenya, Malaysia, Peru, Serbia & Montenegro, Norway, United Kingdom

Source: National Geographic 2005:17.

get involved!

Learn about the various kinds of political systems in the world. Hold mock elections and experiment with different electoral systems of representation. Discuss and debate the issues that concern you, and take action to change things.

>> Summary

From Snapper mowers to microloans to peace movements, stories such as these provide hope. Even though large-scale economic trends can have negative impacts on companies, communities, and individuals and can shape political outcomes, positive social change is possible. Sociological analysis helps us to see the underlying processes at work in the economy and politics, and in so doing can assist us in recognizing places in those systems where opportunities for bringing about such change exist.

For REVIEW

I. How is economic and political power organized?

- The two major economic systems are capitalism and socialism, though in practice most economies are some mix of the two. Political systems of government include monarchy, oligarchy, dictatorship, totalitarianism, and democracy. A debate exists when looking at formal power in Canada about the degree to which there is a small, cohesive group of power elites who effectively rule or if leadership is more diverse and pluralistic, operating through democratic processes.

II. How does power operate?

- Power involves the capacity to get others to do what you want, which can involve force, influence, and authority. In the case of authority, followers accept your power as legitimate, whether based on a traditional, rational-legal, or charismatic foundation.

III. How has the economy changed over time?

- The rise of a global economy has brought with it a changing composition of the national and international workforce, deindustrialization, and in the form of microfinancing, economic opportunities for people who are poor.

Thinking CRITICALLY...

1. Consider the three ideal types of authority described by Max Weber. Which is the predominant type in Canadian government? Do you see elements of the others?

2. In 2009, the Democratic Party of the United States had two strong candidates seeking the party's nomination: Hillary Clinton and Barack Obama. Obama won the party's nomination and went on to become President. How do you think gender and race affect Canadian politics? Could a woman, an Aboriginal person, or a member of a visible minority become Prime Minister?

3. How have you or members of your family been affected by changing economic trends? If you were appointed to improve the Canadian economy, what would you focus upon?

Pop Quiz

1. What are the three basic sources of power within any political system?
   a. force, influence, and authority
   b. force, influence, and democracy
   c. force, legitimacy, and charisma
   d. influence, charisma, and bureaucracy

2. Which of the following is *not* part of the classification system of authority developed by Max Weber?
   a. traditional authority
   b. pluralist authority
   c. legal-rational authority
   d. charismatic authority

3. Under capitalism, laissez-faire means that
   a. the means of production and distribution in a society are collectively held.
   b. people should compete freely, with minimal government intervention in the economy.
   c. a single business firm controls the market.
   d. society depends on mechanization to produce its goods and services.

4. Transfers of money, goods, and services that take place but are not reported to the government are best described as
   a. globalization.
   b. the mixed economy.
   c. laissez-faire capitalism.
   d. the informal economy.

5. The systematic, widespread withdrawal of investment in basic aspects of productivity such as factories and plants is called
   a. deindustrialization.
   b. downsizing.
   c. post-industrialization.
   d. gentrification.

6. Political scientist Harold Lasswell defined *politics* as
   a. the struggle for power and authority.
   b. the allocation of valued resources.
   c. who gets what, when, and how.
   d. a cultural universal.

7. The type of government in which a few individuals rule is known as
   a. a monarchy.
   b. a democracy.
   c. a dictatorship.
   d. an oligarchy.

8. Women make up what proportion of Canadian Parliament?
   a. more than 50 percent
   b. more than 40 percent
   c. 0 percent
   d. less than 25 percent

9. According to C. Wright Mills, power rests in the hands of the
   a. people.
   b. power elite.
   c. aristocracy.
   d. representative democracy.

10. The use or threat of violence against random or symbolic targets in pursuit of political aims is referred to as
    a. politics.
    b. power.
    c. terrorism.
    d. authority.

1. (a); 2. (b); 3. (b); 4. (d); 5. (a); 6. (c); 7. (d); 8. (d); 9. (b); 10. (c)

SOCIAL C

LIVING THE GOOD LIFE— OR NOT

Grayer is four years old. He takes lessons in French, Latin, music, swimming, ice skating, karate, and physical education—in addition to attending preschool. When he failed to get into the elite kindergarten of her choice, his mother hired a grief counsellor for him. He lives on Park Avenue in Manhattan with his mother and father, but the person with whom he spends most of his time is his nanny.

Grayer's fictional character was drawn from the real-life experiences of Emma McLaughlin and Nicola Kraus (2002), who worked as nannies to help pay their way through college. They told their stories in the book *The Nanny Diaries*, which later became a film (2007). They depict a world in which, like ours, social class matters.

Sima, one of the nannies in the novel, was an engineer in her home country of El Salvador. She came to the United States with her husband and children, but when he was unable to obtain a green card her husband went back to El Salvador with the kids. Nan, the main nanny character in the book, refers to Sima as "a woman who has a higher degree than I will ever receive, in a subject I couldn't get a passing grade in, and who has been home [to see her husband and children] less than one month in the last twenty-four" (p. 173).

According to a recent *Toronto Star* investigation, the number of foreign nannies granted permits to work in Canada tripled between 2002 and 2007, from 3458 to 11,878. The majority are women from the Philippines (Brazao and Cribb 2009). Sadly, the story of women leaving behind their own children to raise the children of others, effectively "on the clock" 24 hours a day with minimum pay and benefits, going for months or years without seeing their own children, is hardly unique (Ehrenreich and Hochschild 2003). Yet in Canada, we often act as though social class does not matter. Stories like *The Nanny Diaries*, films such as *Brown Women, Blond Babies*, and the accounts we gather through sociological studies tell a very different tale. As we will see in this chapter, one of the most significant structural determinants shaping our individual lives grows out of our economic position and involves the distribution of economic resources. However, we will see that social class involves more than just unequal economic resources; it also reflects significant social and cultural differences.

LASS

As You READ >>

- What is social class?
- How does social class operate?
- What are the consequences of social class?

>> Understanding Stratification

Social class was among the earliest interests of sociologists and remains so to this day. Marx, Weber, and Durkheim all highlighted the significance of class differences and sought to understand both their causes and consequences. Du Bois and Addams carried this a step further, actually working to ameliorate the excesses of social stratification.

In Canada, however, social class has long been a touchy subject (DeMott 1990). When the topic of social class does come up here, many people's first response is to deny that it exists. Some even angrily argue that opportunity is open to everyone and that individual effort alone determines one's life outcome. From a sociological perspective, however, we must understand the consequences of social class differences if we are to understand why we think and act the way we do. This is especially true in capitalist societies, in which the significance of economic position is heightened. To provide context, we begin by considering the varieties of ways in which societies are stratified.

social inequality A condition in which members of society have different amounts of wealth, prestige, or power.

stratification A structured ranking of entire groups of people that perpetuates unequal economic rewards and power in a society.

ascribed status A social position assigned to a person by society without regard for the person's unique talents or characteristics.

achieved status A social position that a person attains largely through his or her own efforts.

SYSTEMS OF STRATIFICATION

Ever since people first began to speculate about the nature of human society, they have focused on the differences between individuals and groups within society. The term **social inequality** describes a condition in which members of society have different amounts of wealth, prestige, or power. Some degree of social inequality characterizes every society. Sociologists refer to social inequality that is built into the structure of society as **stratification**—the structured ranking of entire groups of people that perpetuates unequal economic rewards and power in a society.

Stratification shapes individual opportunity based on the position that one occupies in the system. Certain groups of people stand higher in social rankings, control scarce resources, wield power, and receive special treatment. Unequal rewards include income and wealth, but they are also related to the power conveyed by social networks (who you know) and knowledge (what you know). Control over such resources enables one generation to pass on social advantages to the next, producing groups of people arranged in rank order, from low to high.

Sociologists focus on four major systems of stratification: slavery, caste, estate, and class. To understand these systems better, it is helpful to recall the distinction between achieved status and ascribed status from Chapter 5. **Ascribed status** is a social position assigned to a person by society without regard for his or her unique talents or characteristics. In contrast, **achieved status** is a social position that a person attains largely through his or her own efforts. Members of the two are closely linked. The nation's most affluent families generally inherit wealth and status, while many members of racial and ethnic minorities inherit disadvantaged status. Age and gender are additional ascribed statuses that influence a person's wealth and social position.

Slavery The most extreme form of legalized social inequality for

Did You Know?

...There are approximately 12 million people worldwide who are enslaved today. About 80 percent of them are women, and half are children, according to the International Labour Organization.

individuals and groups is **slavery.** Enslaved individuals are the property of other people, who have the right to treat them as they please, as if they were tools or draft animals.

The practice of slavery has varied over different times and places. Most of the slaves in ancient Greece were prisoners of war or individuals captured and sold by pirates. Although succeeding generations could inherit slave status, it was not necessarily permanent. A person's status might change, depending on which city-state happened to triumph in a military conflict. In effect, all citizens had the potential to become slaves or gain freedom, depending on the historical circumstances. By contrast, slavery in North America and Latin America was an ascribed status, and slaves faced racial and legal barriers to freedom.

Today, the Universal Declaration of Human Rights, which is binding on all members of the United Nations, prohibits slavery in all its forms. Yet around the world, millions of people still live as slaves. In many developing countries, bonded labourers are imprisoned in virtual lifetime employment; in some countries, human beings are owned outright. Though slavery is outlawed in North America and Europe, guest workers and illegal immigrants have been forced to labour for years under terrible conditions, either to pay off debts or to avoid being turned over to immigration authorities. In 2007 a wealthy couple from New York was convicted of holding two Indonesian women as slaves in their home for four years (Eltman 2007; S. Greenhouse 2007). In 2009, an investigation conducted by *Toronto Star* reporters found widespread abuse of the live-in caregiver program, including workers arriving in Canada to bogus jobs, long hours of work in poor living conditions, and having their passports and other documents taken from them by employers. This practice received national attention in May 2009 when two caregivers publicly accused Liberal MP Ruby Dhalla of mistreatment.

Castes Castes are hereditary ranks, usually dictated by religion, that tend to be fixed and immobile. The caste system is generally associated with Hinduism in India and other countries. In India there are four major castes, or *varnas*: priests (*Brahman*), warriors (*Kshatriya*), merchants (*Vaishya*), and artisans/farmers (*Shudra*). A

> **slavery** A system of enforced servitude in which some people are owned by others as property.
> **caste** A hereditary rank, usually religiously dictated, that tends to be fixed and immobile.

fifth category of outcastes, referred to as the *dalit,* or untouchables, is considered to be so lowly and unclean as to have no place within this system of stratification. There are also many minor castes. Caste membership is an ascribed status (at birth, children automatically assume the same position as their parents). Each caste is quite sharply defined, and members are expected to marry within that caste.

In 1950, after gaining independence from Great Britain, India adopted a new constitution that formally outlawed the caste system. Over the past two decades, however,

urbanization and technological advances have brought more change to India's caste system than the government has in more than half a century. The anonymity of city life tends to blur caste boundaries, allowing the *dalit* to pass unrecognized in temples, schools, and workplaces. The globalization of high technology also has opened up India's social order, bringing new opportunities to those who possess the skills and ability to capitalize on them, regardless of caste.

Estates A third type of stratification system developed within the feudal societies of medieval Europe. Under the **estate system,** or feudalism, nobles owned the land, which they leased to peasants who worked it and lived on it. The peasants turned over a portion of what they produced to the landowner, who in return offered the peasants military protection against bandits and rival nobles. The basis for the system was the nobles' ownership of land, which was critical to their superior and privileged status. As in systems based on slavery and caste, inheritance of one's position largely defined the estate system. The nobles inherited their titles and property; the peasants were born into a subservient position within an agrarian society.

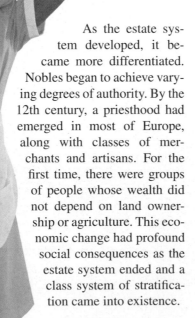

As the estate system developed, it became more differentiated. Nobles began to achieve varying degrees of authority. By the 12th century, a priesthood had emerged in most of Europe, along with classes of merchants and artisans. For the first time, there were groups of people whose wealth did not depend on land ownership or agriculture. This economic change had profound social consequences as the estate system ended and a class system of stratification came into existence.

Social Classes A **class system** is a social ranking based primarily on economic position in which achieved characteristics can influence social mobility. In contrast to slavery and caste systems, in a class system the boundaries between classes are imprecisely defined, and one can move from one stratum, or level, of society to another. Even so, class systems maintain stable stratification hierarchies and patterns of class divisions, and they, too, are marked by an unequal distribution of wealth and power. Class standing, though it can be achieved, is heavily dependent on family and on ascribed factors such as race and ethnicity.

Sociologist Daniel Rossides (1997) uses a five-class model to describe the class system of capitalist societies such as the United States and Canada: the upper class, the upper-middle class, the lower-middle class, the working class, and the lower class. Although the lines separating social classes in his model are not as sharp as the divisions between castes, members of the five classes differ significantly in ways other than just income level.

The upper class is an elite group, limited to the very wealthy. These people associate in exclusive clubs and social circles. In Canada, the majority of the upper class is White. In

SOCthink

> > > People with incomes well above average often prefer to identify themselves as middle class. Why might they do this? How might this tendency be an outgrowth of the dominant Canadian values of equality and democracy?

contrast, the lower class consists of people who cannot find regular work or must make do with low-paying jobs. There is a disproportionate representation of visible minorities and Aboriginal peoples in this class. The lower class lacks both wealth and income and is too politically weak to exercise significant power. This class lacks both wealth and income and is too weak politically to exercise significant power.

Sandwiched between the upper and lower classes in this model are the upper-middle class, the lower-middle class, and the working class. The upper-middle class is composed of professionals such as doctors, lawyers, and architects. They participate extensively in politics and take leadership roles in voluntary associations. The lower-middle class, includes less affluent professionals, owners of small businesses, and a sizable number of clerical workers. While not all members of this varied class hold a post-secondary degree, they share the goal of sending their children to college or university.

Rossides describes the working class as people who hold regular manual or blue-collar jobs. Certain members of this class, such as electricians and auto industry workers, may have higher incomes than people in the lower-middle class. Yet even if they have achieved some degree of economic security, they tend to identify with manual workers and their long history of involvement in the labour movement of North America. Of the five classes, the working class is declining noticeably in size. In the current economy, service and technical jobs are replacing those involved in the actual manufacturing or transportation of goods.

SOCIAL MOBILITY

A key component of each of these systems of stratification is **social mobility**—the degree to which one can change the social stratum into which one is born. The ascent of a person from a poor background to a position of prestige, power, or financial reward—such as in the movie *Maid in Manhattan*—is an example of social mobility. In the film, Jennifer Lopez plays a chambermaid in a big-city hotel who rises to become a company supervisor and the girlfriend of a well-to-do politician. While stories in which the commoner marries the prince truly were fairy tales in the era of the estate system, today they are metaphors for the seeming permeability of modern class boundaries.

social mobility Movement of individuals or groups from one position in a society's stratification system to another.
open system A social system in which the position of each individual is influenced by his or her achieved status.
closed system A social system in which there is little or no possibility of individual social mobility.

Open Versus Closed Stratification Systems Sociologists distinguish between stratification systems that are open versus closed to indicate the degree of social mobility in a society. An **open system** implies that a person's achieved status influences his or her social position. Such a system encourages competition among members of society. Canada has sought to move toward this ideal by removing once-legal barriers faced by women, racial and ethnic minorities, and people born in lower social classes.

At the other extreme is the **closed system,** which allows little or no possibility of individual social mobility. Slavery and caste systems are examples of closed systems.

SOCthink

> > > Into which class would you place most of the people in your community? Are there relatively clear boundaries between class neighbourhoods there?

SAVE JOBS!
Flaherty, Carrie and the rest of Harper's team could
But they choose not to!
Let them know that manufacturing Jobs Matter To Canadians!

horizontal mobility The movement of an individual from one social position to another of the same rank.

vertical mobility The movement of an individual from one social position to another of a different rank.

intergenerational mobility Changes in the social position of children relative to their parents.

intragenerational mobility Changes in social position within a person's adult life.

In such societies, social placement is based on ascribed statuses, such as race or family background, which cannot be changed.

Types of Social Mobility

Sociologists also distinguish between mobility within a social class versus movement between social classes. For example, a bus driver who becomes a hotel clerk moves from one social position to another of approximately the same rank. Sociologists call this kind of movement **horizontal mobility.** However, if the bus driver were to become a lawyer, he or she would experience **vertical mobility**—the movement of an individual from one social position to another of a different rank (Sorokin [1927] 1959). Vertical mobility can also involve moving downward in a society's stratification system, as would be the case if the lawyer became a bus driver.

Sociologists also consider the differences between intergenerational and intragenerational mobility when evaluating mobility. **Intergenerational mobility** involves changes in the social position of children relative to their parents. Thus, a plumber whose father was a physician provides an example of downward intergenerational mobility. A film star whose parents were both factory workers illustrates upward intergenerational mobility. Because education contributes significantly to upward mobility, any barrier to the pursuit of advanced degrees can definitely limit intergenerational mobility (Isaacs et al. 2008).

Intragenerational mobility, on the other hand, involves changes in social position within a person's adult life. Thus, a woman who enters the paid labour force as a teacher's aide and eventually becomes superintendent of the school district experiences upward intragenerational mobility. A man who becomes a cab driver after his accounting firm goes bankrupt undergoes downward intragenerational mobility.

In Canadian society, upward mobility is highly valued and promoted within this "land of opportunity." It is believed that an individual could experience a significant shift in social class position over the course of her or his career, from a relatively low-level position to one of significant wealth and power. While this does happen, as we will see below, the reality is that we tend to end up in positions relatively close to where we began.

SOCIOLOGICAL PERSPECTIVES ON STRATIFICATION

Sociologists have examined the relative significance of key resources that shape social stratification. Early in the development of sociology, Karl Marx argued that material resources were most important, especially ownership of the means of production. Max Weber, who sought to extend Marx's model and make it more broadly applicable, argued that three primary resources shape social position: class, status, and party. More recently, Pierre Bourdieu has highlighted the significance of culture as an additional resource. We will look at each of their models in turn.

Marx on Class Karl Marx has been aptly described as both a revolutionary and a social scientist. Marx was concerned with stratification in all types of human societies, beginning with primitive agricultural tribes and continuing into feudalism. But his main focus was on the effects of economic inequality on all aspects of his own society— 19th-century Europe. The plight of the work-

5 Movies on SOCIAL CLASS

Water
An Indian widow attempts to escape the social restrictions of her position.

The Departed
A man from a family of crooks wants to become a cop.

Save the Last Dance
An upper-class White girl at an inner city Chicago school.

Atonement
Two people from two classes fall in love and face the consequences.

Titanic
A first-class and third-class love affair.

ing class made him feel that it was imperative to strive for changes in the class structure of society (Beeghley 1978:1).

In Marx's view, social relations during any period of history depend on who controls the primary mode of economic production, such as land or factories. Differential access to scarce resources shapes the relationship between groups. Thus, under the feudal estate system, most production was agricultural, and the nobility owned the land. Peasants had little choice but to work according to terms dictated by the landowners.

SOCthink

> > > What is the story of social mobility in your family? To what extent have there been shifts both across and within generations? What factors, such as family connections or historical events, contributed to the social mobility that occurred?

Did You Know?

Hot or Not?

Is a classless society possible?

Using this type of analysis, Marx examined social relations within **capitalism**—the economic system in which private individuals control the means of production and the accumulation of profit is the main incentive for economic activity (D. Rosenberg 1991). Marx focused on the two classes that began to emerge as the feudal estate system declined: the bourgeoisie and the proletariat. The **bourgeoisie,** or capitalist class, owns the means of production, such as factories and machinery; the **proletariat** is the working class, who sell their labour power to the bourgeoisie. In capitalist societies, the members of the bourgeoisie maximize profit in competition with other firms. In the process, they exploit workers, who must exchange their labour for subsistence wages. In Marx's view, members of each class share a distinctive culture. Marx was most interested in the culture of the proletariat, but he also examined the ideology of the bourgeoisie, through which that class justifies its dominance over workers.

According to Marx, exploitation of the proletariat would inevitably lead to the destruction of the capitalist system, because the workers would revolt. Two keys help us to understand why: the problem of scarcity and the capitalist system of social relations. Marx believed that humans had to produce in order to survive, but as we saw in Chapter 1, how we do so is not narrowly determined by our genes. Our natural creative capacity, Marx believed, would lead to technological innovation that made it possible for us to produce enough food, clothes, shelter, and other goods that

eventually everyone would have more than enough. Capitalism actually encourages such technological innovation in the context of the competitive marketplace.

Once this technological obstacle to providing for all our needs was solved, Marx felt that the only obstacle to an equitable society would be the capitalist system of social relations. Its emphasis on private property enabled the few at the top, the bourgeoisie, to own and control much more than they could ever hope to need or want while the majority at the bottom, the proletariat, struggled. Eventually, Marx argued, the proletariat would see that they had no real interest in the existing set of social relations. They would develop **class consciousness**—a subjective awareness of common vested interests and the need for collective political action to bring about social change. This would lead to the overthrow of capitalism in favour of a system of more equitable distribution in the form of socialism and then communism.

A question that often arises in response to Marx's work is this: Why hasn't that revolution happened? One answer is that Marx thought capitalists would work against the development of such class consciousness by shaping society's accepted values and norms. The term **dominant ideology** describes a set of cultural beliefs and practices that helps to maintain powerful social, economic, and political interests. Private property is a core principle of this ideology, but our failure to recognize the collective efforts that go into the production of any products and services contributes as well. For Marx, the bourgeoisie controlled not only material resources but also the means of producing beliefs about reality through religion, education, and the media (Abercrombie et al. 1980, 1990; Robertson 1988). As a result, workers had to overcome what Marx termed **false consciousness**—an attitude held by members of a class that does not accurately reflect their objective position. A worker with false consciousness may adopt an individualistic viewpoint toward capitalist exploitation ("*I* am being exploited by *my* boss"). In contrast, the class-conscious worker realizes that all workers are being exploited by the bourgeoisie and have a common stake in revolution.

Weber's Multidimensional Model
Unlike Marx, Max Weber insisted that class does not totally define a person's position within the stratification system. Instead, writing in 1916, he identified three distinct components of stratification: class,

capitalism An economic system in which the means of production are held largely in private hands and the main incentive for economic activity is the accumulation of profits.
bourgeoisie Karl Marx's term for the capitalist class, comprising the owners of the means of production.
proletariat Karl Marx's term for the working class in a capitalist society.
class consciousness In Karl Marx's view, a subjective awareness held by members of a class regarding their common vested interests and need for collective political action to bring about social change.
dominant ideology A set of cultural beliefs and practices that helps to maintain powerful social, economic, and political interests.
false consciousness A term used by Karl Marx to describe an attitude held by members of a class that does not accurately reflect their objective position.

Lower-class Ukrainian women wait in long lines to purchase staples, such as eggs, with the government-issued food stamps that supplement their limited economic resources.

status, and party (Weber [1916] 1958). These three point to the importance of material, social, and organizational resources in shaping how much power people have.

Weber used the term **class** to refer to a group of people who have a similar level of economic resources. He agreed with Marx that this includes ownership of the means of production, but he went further than Marx, adding income, wealth, and skill knowledge to the equation. Regarding such knowledge, Marx thought that mechanization and extreme division of labour would make skill less significant under capitalism. But Weber argued that skill would continue to be a valuable commodity in the labour market and that by developing our skill knowledge—for example, by going to college or university— we could enhance our class position. For Weber, people who shared similar economic positions, such as workers in minimum-wage jobs, were in the same class. Although Weber agreed with Marx on the importance of this economic dimension of stratification, he argued that the actions of individuals and groups cannot be understood solely in economic terms.

Weber used the term **status group** to refer to people who have the same prestige or lifestyle. While class is an economic resource, status represents a social resource. Status is, to some extent, in the eye of the beholder. A person has status because others recognize the position that she or he occupies as distinctive relative to other positions,

class A group of people who have a similar level of economic resources.

status group People who have the same prestige or lifestyle, independent of their class positions.

party The capacity to organize to accomplish some particular goal.

whether higher or lower. Association with a group, such as medical doctors or schoolteachers, conveys status. Being part of such groups can limit our social interactions with others whom the group sees as outsiders. Such memberships are also often associated with a particular lifestyle, including the kind of car you drive or vacations you take, but status is not the same as economic class standing. In our culture, a successful pickpocket may belong to the same income class as a tenured professor. Yet the thief is widely regarded as a member of a low-status group, whereas the professor holds high status.

SOCthink

> > > How might a group coordinate their class, status, and party resources to accomplish their goals? Pick a group on campus or in your community that is seeking to bring about social change, and imagine how you might advise them using Weber's principles.

For Weber, the third major component of stratification involved organizational resources. **Party** refers to the capacity to organize to accomplish some particular goal. This is what we mean when we talk of a political party, but such organization extends beyond politics to all spheres of life. As we have seen before with Weber, bureaucracies represent the ideal form of this resource because they are organized explicitly to maximize available resources and

Theory

A Matter of Perspective

THEORETICAL PERSPECTIVES ON SOCIAL STRATIFICATION

Functionalist:

- inequality is necessary to some extent
- facilitates filling of range of social positions

Conflict:

- dominant class exploits lower classes; inequality continues to grow
- cultural capital means we have different "life chances"

Feminist:

- class and gender are strongly related
- women are disadvantaged within capitalist, patriarchal systems

Interactionist:

- stratification influences people's lifestyles
- sense of identity and self-worth tied to social position

than this as it is rooted in our perception of reality itself. For Bourdieu, because culture is hierarchically valued, it is a form of power.

Bourdieu argued that people in different social class positions possess different types of cultural capital. From NASCAR to Mozart, for example, the tastes of the working class differ from those of the upper class. Symphonic concerts, operas, and foreign films for instance, are considered "high culture," while "pop culture," including popular movies, TV shows, and music CDs, are considered "middle-brow" or below. People draw distinctions, for example, between watching *Masterpiece Theatre* versus *Trailer Park Boys* and listening to Pavarotti versus Britney Spears. Such judgments are based on a certain level of cultural elitism in which those at the top are able to define their preferences as apparently superior to those of the masses. The cultural capital of people who are working class, often disparaged as redneck or ghetto, is often valued least of all—until it is claimed by others as their own, as was the case with jazz, blues, rock and roll, and rap (Gans 1971).

> **cultural capital** Our tastes, knowledge, attitudes, language, and ways of thinking that we exchange in interaction with others.

When we interact with others, we draw on the cultural capital resources we possess. Such interaction is fairly easy with others who share the same basic set of resources. When interaction occurs with others who possess a different stock of cultural capital, however, it becomes more complex. We see these kinds of difficulties when executives try to interact casually with workers on the factory floor or when we find ourselves dining in a place where we aren't quite sure what

to accomplish their goals in the most efficient manner possible. For Weber, party was a potential resource, available to any individuals or groups who would seize it.

While treating class, status, and party as analytically distinct, Weber acknowledged that in practice, these three resources often combine to shape individual and group power. Each factor influences the other two, and in fact the rankings on these three dimensions often tend to coincide. For example, Pierre Elliott Trudeau was born into a wealthy family, attended the prestigious Jesuit Collège Jean-de-Brébeuf, Harvard University, and the London School of Economics, and went on to become Prime Minister of Canada. Like Trudeau, many people from affluent backgrounds achieve high status and demonstrate impressive political organization.

Bourdieu and Cultural Capital While Marx emphasized material resources and Weber highlighted the significance of social resources in the form of both status and party, sociologist Pierre Bourdieu added to these the significance of cultural resources. Bourdieu introduced the concept of **cultural capital,** by which he meant our tastes, knowledge, attitudes, language, and ways of thinking that we exchange in interaction with others. Often associated with artistic or literary preferences, cultural capital goes much deeper

POPSOC

Whether it is the rags-to-riches dreams of *American* and *Canadian Idol,* the glitz and glamour of *Dancing with the Stars,* the upper-middle-class aspirations of *The Apprentice,* or the conspicuous consumption of *Pimp My Ride,* TV shows have found social class lifestyle differences a tempting topic. Perhaps no program uses the contrast between class preferences as effectively, however, as does *Wife Swap* on ABC. In this show, two wives/mothers switch families for two weeks, frequently pitting families from different social classes against each other. The tension between their cultural capital resources is on display, highlighting the contrast between the two family environments.

the rules are. If this were only a matter of social difference between various subcultures, it might not be a big deal. But the cultural capital of the elite is also tied to their control over economic and social resources. As a result, cultural capital can be used as a form of exclusion from jobs, organizations, and opportunities. For example, a qualified applicant may lose out on a job during the interview due to inappropriate syntax or inadequate familiarity with cultural references, such as current news events or the latest in the world of golf. Employers tend to hire people they feel comfortable with, and cultural capital plays a significant role in that process (Kanter 1993).

a part of. It turns out that the old saying "It's not what you know; it's who you know" has some truth to it. Position and connections make it possible for us to increase the likelihood of accomplishing our goals. Finally, cultural resources include our tastes, language, and way of looking at the world. They represent our knowledge of cognitive, normative, and material elements of culture that we can draw on when acting to accomplish our goals. A simple but classic example involves knowing which fork to use for the various courses of a formal dinner. But it also includes knowing how to respond when we are put on the spot, whether in a business meeting, at a rock

> ### Anyone who has ever struggled with poverty knows how extremely expensive it is to be poor.
>
> James A. Baldwin

Compounding this problem of cultural inequality is the fact that our preferences and perceptions often pass down from parent to child in the same way that material capital is inherited. Parents teach their children linguistic patterns and cultural tastes, from the use of double negatives to the appreciation of literature. Cultural capital is also reproduced in the next generation in the context of schools, where class distinctions within the community shape the curriculum and patterns of discipline. Jonathan Kozol (2005), for example, in his most recent study on how education perpetuates inequality, told the story of an inner-city high school student who wanted to take an advanced placement class in preparation for college but was placed in a sewing class instead. As a friend of hers put it, the factory owners need workers, and it won't be their kids: "You're ghetto—so you sew!" (2005:180). Such transmission increases the likelihood that social advantage will be passed from one generation to the next.

Social mobility from this perspective involves more than just acquiring more money and better social connections. Winning the lottery, for example, does not transform a person at the bottom of the hierarchy into one at the top, or, as Bourdieu put it, "having a million does not in itself make one able to live like a millionaire" (1984:374). Such movement requires a social and cultural transformation as well. For mobility to happen, the individual must earn and learn a different set of knowledge and skills, as well as a whole new lifestyle: new tastes, attitudes, language, and thoughts. The same goes for someone who would drop from a higher rank into a lower one.

Material, Social, and Cultural Resources We can point to three critical categories of resources that shape the positions we occupy and influence our likelihood for social mobility. Material resources refer to economic resources that we own or control, including money, property, and land. Social resources include prestige based on the position we occupy and connections based on the social networks we are

concert, or in class. Viewing social class in terms of material, social, and cultural resources makes social class a much more useful concept when trying to map our social lives or figure out why we think and act as we do.

All societies have some degree of stratification, and tracking these three resources helps us to better understand how stratification works. As we saw in Chapter 8 on education, Davis and Moore (1945) suggested that, especially in societies with a complex division of labour, some positions are more important or require more skill. Perhaps we need to hold out the promise of high pay and prestige as a reward so that those with the necessary skill and determination take the time and money required to develop their talents. Even if we accept the principle that a certain degree of inequality is inevitable, however, questions remain about the extent of inequality that is practised. In addition, if inequality is to be tied to ability and effort, we need to investigate the degree to which positions are earned versus inherited. We turn next to an analysis of the degree of inequality that exists in Canada.

>> Social Class in Canada

Social class dividing lines in Canada are not as clear-cut or firm as they were historically in, say, England. When we take a step back, however, we see that social class differences do impact our everyday lives. We may not label them as such, and we might want to dismiss their significance. Nevertheless, when we look through the lens of class as highlighted by these three resources, we bring to the surface differences that we already recognize as important.

CULTURAL CAPITAL

In some ways it is easiest to look first at cultural resources because, while we recognize that such differences exist, we may feel that they are not such a big deal. If one person likes Chopin while another likes Willie Nelson, what difference does that make? As indicated above, however, such tastes do not exist in isolation; rather, they are tied to social and material resources as well and can serve as a means of exclusion (Halle 1993). Looking at just a few examples, we can appreciate the degree to which we already see class, even if we don't usually recognize it as such.

We can recognize class in the clothes we wear, and even in the terms we use to describe them, such as "business casual" or "blue collar." Some people would not be caught dead wearing a suit and tie (or maybe that's the only way they will wear them), while others are incapable of being comfortable in blue jeans and a T-shirt. And brands can matter, whether it's Roots, Sean Jean, J. McLaughlin, Gap, Rocawear, Juicy Couture, Lululemon, Wrangler, Calypso, Abercrombie & Fitch, Coach, or Gucci. Even the fabrics clothes are made of suggest class differences, with higher classes more likely to wear clothes made out of organic materials (such as wool, silk, or cotton) and lower classes

SOCthink

> > > Paul Fussell, in his book *Class: A Guide Through the American Status System,* argued that the writing on our clothes says a lot about our social class. What story do the logos, brands, and writing on your clothes tell about you? How might your clothing choices have differed had you been in a different class position?

more likely to wear synthetic fabrics (including nylon, rayon, and orlon). This is likely driven not only by the initial cost differences for such materials but also by the long-term care costs for dry-cleaning.

We also see class differences when it comes to houses. Just driving through neighbourhoods we recognize class indicators of houses: the distance they are located from the street; the composition of a driveway, if there is one; the fastidiousness of lawn care; the existence of flamingos, gnomes, or gazing balls; and the presence of pillars or fountains. When it comes to where we live, expressions such as "the wrong side of the tracks," and "snob hill," point to our recognition that class matters.

Similarly, class makes a difference when it comes to vacations. Elites might head to one of their several residences, or they might "winter" in the Caribbean. Middle-class people are more likely to head to Disney World or perhaps go on a cruise, though either dream vacation may be possible only after having saved for some time or going into debt. Because money and vacation time are often limited, working-class families are more likely to go on a one-week trip, probably not too far from home, to which they are more likely to drive, and it might involve camping.

> **prestige** The respect and admiration that an occupation holds in a society.
> **esteem** The reputation that a specific person has earned within an occupation.

We could look at other areas too, including what we eat (fast food versus haute cuisine), what we drink (Labatt versus fine wine), and what sports we watch (NASCAR and professional wrestling versus tennis and America's Cup yachting). In all kinds of ways, our preferences are shaped by our social class positions. Yet we seldom take seriously the source of such preferences or their effect on the choices we make and the doors that these choices may open or close to us.

STATUS AND PRESTIGE

We have a sense of where people fit relative to each other. Some we see as higher, while others we see as lower. We have seen as much already with regard to cultural preferences, but when it comes to status, it is not just what people like that we rank, but who they are. Sociologists seek to describe those systems of ranking and the advantages and disadvantages they convey.

Occupational Prestige One way sociologists describe the relative social class positions people occupy is by focusing on their occupational prestige. The term **prestige** refers to the respect and admiration that an occupation holds in a society. Fairly or not, "my daughter, the physicist" connotes something very different from "my daughter, the waitress." Prestige is independent of the particular individual who occupies a job, a characteristic that distinguishes it from esteem. **Esteem** refers to the reputation that a specific person has earned within an occupation. Therefore, we can say that the position of Prime Minister of Canada has high prestige even though it has been occupied by people with varying degrees of esteem. A hairdresser may have the esteem of his or her clients, but lacks the prestige of a corporate executive.

Using the results from a series of national surveys, sociologists have identified prestige rankings

Did You Know?

...The most expensive hotel room—at the Burj Al Arab Hotel in Dubai—costs US$30,000 per night. According to the 2006 Census, the median annual income for individuals in Canada is just under $26,000.

Prestige Rankings of Occupations

Occupation	Score	Occupation	Score
Surgeon	87	Farmer	40
Physician	86	Correctional officer	40
Lawyer	75	Receptionist	39
Dentist	74	Carpenter	39
Professor	74	Barber	36
Architect	73	Child care worker	35
Psychiatrist	72	Hotel clerk	32
Clergy	69	Bus driver	32
Pharmacist	68	Auto body repairer	31
Registered nurse	66	Truck driver	30
High school teacher	66	Salesworker (shoes)	28
Accountant	65	Garbage collector	28
Optician	65	Waiter and waitress	28
Elementary school teacher	64	Cook in a pizza shop	27
Banker	63	Bartender	25
Veterinarian	62	Farm worker	23
Legislator	61	Janitor	22
Airline pilot	60	Newspaper vendor	19
Police officer or detective	60	Prostitute	14
Prekindergarten teacher	55	Panhandler	11
Librarian	54		
Firefighter	53		
Social worker	52		
Dental hygienist	52		
Electrician	51		
Funeral director	49		
Farm manager	48		
Mail carrier	47		
Secretary	46		
Insurance agent	45		
Bank teller	43		
Nurse's aide	42		

Note: 100 is the highest and 0 the lowest possible prestige score.

Source: J. Davis et al. 2007; see also Nakao and Treas 1994.

socioeconomic status (SES) A measure of class that is based on income, education, occupation, and related variables.

for about 500 occupations. They created a scale with 0 as the lowest possible score and 100 as the highest, and ranked the occupations based on the results of their surveys. Surgeon, physician, lawyer, dentist, and professor were among the most highly regarded occupations, while bartender, farmworker, janitor, newspaper vendor, prostitute, and panhandler were at the bottom. Sociologists have found a significant amount of stability in such rankings from 1925 to the present (Nakao and Treas 1994:11). This suggests that we do confer status to people based on the positions they occupy. Someone with a higher status is more likely to get the benefit of the doubt because of the position she or he occupies, regardless of her or his individual characteristics, while the reverse is true for someone from a lower position.

Socioeconomic Status As a single variable, occupation provides us with a sense of where people stand, but status involves more than just occupational prestige. In their research, sociologists add variables to the mix to gain a more complete picture of social class standing. These include such things as the value of homes, sources of income, assets, years in present occupations, neighbourhoods, and considerations regarding dual careers. Adding these variables will not necessarily paint an alternative picture of class differentiation in Canada, but it does allow sociologists to measure class in a more complex and multidimensional way. When researchers use multiple measures, they typically speak of **socioeconomic status (SES),** a measure of social class that is based on income, education, occupation, and related variables.

One of the lessons we learn from SES research is that society often undervalues, in terms of prestige and pay, work that is essential for our individual and collective survival. In an effort to make the value of women's contribution to the economy more visible, for example, the International Women Count Network, a global grassroots feminist organization, has sought to give a monetary value to women's unpaid work. Besides providing symbolic recognition of women's contributions to society, they propose that this value also be used to calculate pension and other benefits that are based on wages received. The United Nations has placed an $11-*trillion* price tag on unpaid labour by women, largely in child care, housework,

our society. When factors such as gender, marital status, ethnicity, age, and race are accounted for, income and wealth inequality becomes evident.

We gain additional insight into this inequality by looking at the relative placement of households from bottom to top. One of the most common ways to present income dispersion is to line up all income-earning households from low to high and then break them into fifths or quintiles, which are blocks of 20 percent. Doing so allows us to get a sense of what the average income is within each of these quintiles, along with the percentage of the total income pie that each quintile earns.

> **income** Wages and salaries measured over some period, such as per hour or year.
> **wealth** The total of all a person's material assets, including savings, land, stocks, and other types of property, minus his or her debt at a single point in time.

As we can see in the accompanying graphs, looking at the population in this way shows a significant degree of

and agriculture. Whatever the figure, the continued undercounting of many workers' contributions to both family and the economy means that focusing only on prestige when it comes to evaluating status is insufficient. We must also consider the significance of other factors, especially income (United Nations Development Programme 1995; Wages for Housework Campaign 1999).

INCOME AND WEALTH

While cultural capital and status provide a clearer picture of how we perceive social class, income and wealth serve as its material foundation. **Income** refers to wages and salaries measured over some period, such as per hour or year. **Wealth** encompasses all a person's material assets, including savings, land, stocks, and other types of property, minus his or her debts at a single point in time. If you were to sell everything you own and pay off all your debts, what you had left would be the value of your wealth. These material resources make our class-based lifestyles possible (Bourdieu 1986). As such, if we are to understand social class in Canada, we need a clear picture of their distribution.

Income Income inequality is a basic characteristic of a class system. In 2006, the median household income in Canada was $63,600. In other words, half of all households had higher incomes in that year, and half had lower incomes. But this fact does not fully convey the income disparities in

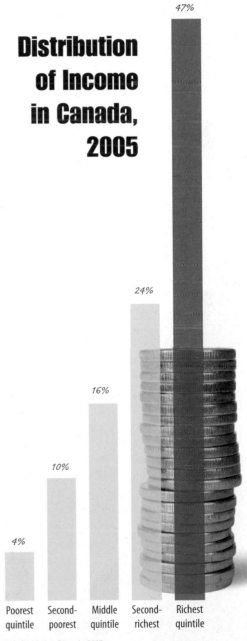

Distribution of Income in Canada, 2005

47%

24%

16%

10%

4%

| Poorest quintile | Second-poorest | Middle quintile | Second-richest | Richest quintile |

Source: Statistics Canada 2007c.

The Wealth Pie: Percent Share of
Total Wealth in Canada, 2005

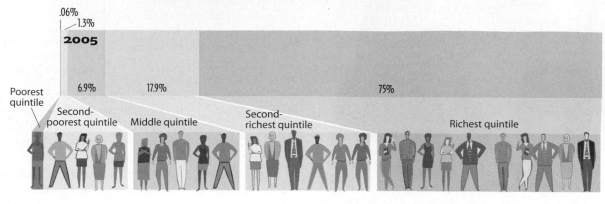

.06%
1.3%

2005

6.9%   17.9%   75%

Poorest
quintile

Second-
poorest quintile   Middle quintile   Second-
richest quintile   Richest quintile

Source: Statistics Canada 2007.

income inequality. In 2005, the average after-tax income in Canada for the poorest quintile was $12,200, compared to $114,300 for the highest quintile. The median net worth of Canadian families was $148,325; when broken down by gender, a significant disparity is evident: families headed by a man had a median net worth of just under $185,000, which is over $79,000 higher than families headed by a woman. Further differences can be seen when other factors are accounted for (Statistics Canada 2007c).

By all measures, income and wealth in Canada is distributed unevenly. Nobel Prize–winning economist Paul Samuelson has described the situation in the following way: "If we made an income pyramid out of building blocks, with each layer portraying $500 of income, the peak would be far higher than Mount Everest, but most people would be within a few feet of the ground" (P. Samuelson and Nordhaus 2005:383).

Canadians do not appear to be seriously concerned about income and wealth inequality in Canada. In a comparison of opinions about social inequality in 27 different countries, respondents in Canada were less likely to express concern about the extent of the income gap. Perhaps Canadians have embraced the ideology that this is a land of opportunity, and that income and wealth differentials simply reflect the degree of individual skill and effort put forth. Whatever the reason, Canadians seem to have largely accepted these disparities as a normal consequence of a free market economy (Osberg and Smeeding 2006).

Personal debt is also assumed to be a fairly normal result of our economy and lifestyle. In Canada, mortgages comprise the largest percentage of debt carried by Canadian families. Lines of credit are the fastest growing type of debt, due in large part to home equity arrangements, while personal savings are declining. Per capita debt in 2005 was $28,390, and approximately 69 percent of Canadian families had debt (Statistics Canada 2006d, 2007c). Economists expect this figure to rise as the economy continues to falter and more people experience job losses or less lucrative employment.

SOCthink

> > > Why do you think that most Canadians do not seem to be aware of or concerned about the degree of income inequality in the country? To what extent might it be due to the influence of the media, or the power of the dominant ideology?

The Shrinking Middle Class The cherished belief that the poor can rise to middle-class status has long been central to Canada's reputation as a land of opportunity. Indeed, the majority of Canadian adults identify themselves as

Percent of Total Debt of Canadian Families, 2005

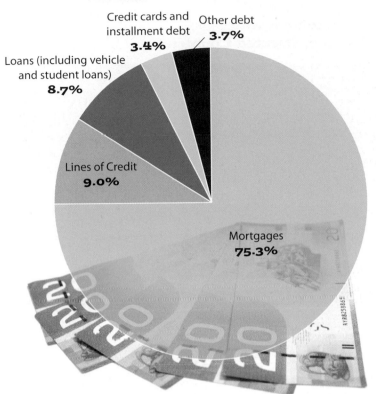

Credit cards and installment debt **3.4%**

Other debt **3.7%**

Loans (including vehicle and student loans) **8.7%**

Lines of Credit **9.0%**

Mortgages **75.3%**

Source: Statistics Canada 2006d.

belonging to the middle class, yet there is considerable popular and scholarly debate as to what constitutes "the middle class." Based on income, it is estimated that approximately 40 to 50 percent of the population would fall into this group, and economists and sociologists have noted that this group is shrinking. Instead, a broadly based middle class is slowly being replaced by two growing groups of rich and poor (Greenblatt 2005), much as Marx described in his "two great camps."

Sociologists and other scholars have identified several factors that have contributed to the shrinking size of the middle class:

- *Disappearing opportunities for those with little education.* Today, increasing numbers of jobs require formal schooling, yet only 59 percent of Canadians between the ages of 20 and 64 hold a post-secondary credential (Canadian Council on Learning 2009).

- *Global competition and rapid advances in technology.* These two trends, which began several decades ago, have rendered workers more replaceable than they once were. Increasingly, these trends are affecting the more complex jobs that were once the bread and butter of middle-class life. Experts disagree on whether they represent a permanent setback to the workforce or the foundation for new industries that will someday generate millions of new jobs. In the meantime, however, many Canadian households are struggling.

- *Growing dependence on the temporary workforce.* Some workers depend on temporary jobs for a second income, in order to maintain their middle-class lifestyle. For those workers who have no other job, these positions are tenuous at best, because they rarely offer health care coverage or retirement benefits.

- *The rise of new-growth industries and nonunion workplaces.* In the past, workers in heavy industry were able to achieve middle-class incomes through the efforts of strong labour unions. But today, the growth areas in the economy are fast-food restaurants and large retail outlets. Though these industries have added employment opportunities, they are at the lower end of the wage scale.

In response to these concerns, observers note that living standards in Canada are improving. Middle-class families want large homes, college or university degrees for their children, and

WILL PROGRAM FOR FOOD

WILL CONSULT FOR FOOD

access to multiple recsources—the cost of which has been rising faster than inflation. Accomplishing these goals, however, has often meant becoming a dual-income family, working longer hours, or taking multiple jobs (Leonhardt 2007; Massey 2007).

POVERTY

According to the World Bank, at least 80 percent of the people on Earth live on less than US$10 per day. UNICEF estimates that 25,000 children die each day due to poverty. But what is poverty? What standards do we use to measure poverty? The efforts of sociologists and other social scientists to better understand poverty are complicated by the difficulty in defining it.

low income cut-off (LICO) The Canadian equivalent of a poverty line. A family is poor if the amount spent on the basic necessities exceeds a certain proportion of income (this figure varies based on family size, community size, and economic conditions).

market basket measure (MBM) A measure that takes into account more than subsistence needs to determine the cost of living a life comparable to community standards.

Canada's official definition of poverty demonstrates the complexity of the task. Unlike most developed nations, Canada does not have an official "poverty line." The most common measurement (and most similar to a poverty line) is the **low income cut-off (LICO)**: any individual or family that by necessity spends 20 percent more of after-tax income on the basics (food, clothing, shelter) than the average family is considered poor. LICOs vary depending upon the size of family and the size of community. In 2001, Statistics Canada introduced the **market basket measure (MBM)**

Going GLOBAL

The Poverty Rate in Households with Children, Selected Countries

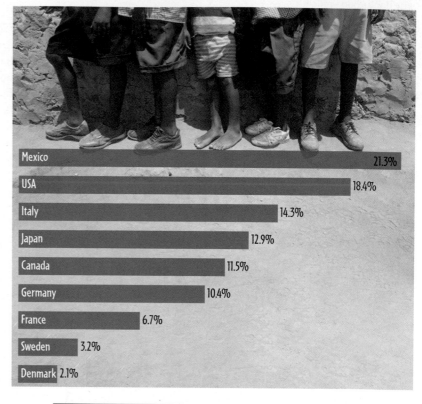

Mexico	21.3%
USA	18.4%
Italy	14.3%
Japan	12.9%
Canada	11.5%
Germany	10.4%
France	6.7%
Sweden	3.2%
Denmark	2.1%

Note: Data are for 2000 except for Germany (2001) and Mexico (2002). Poverty threshhold is 50 percent of nation's median income.

Source: Förster and d'Ercole 2005:36.

as a more comprehensive approach to determining the extent of poverty. The MBM considers more than whether subsistence needs are met, calculating the cost of living a life comparable to community standards. Using different measures may result in different estimates of poverty rates; however, both reveal poverty to be an issue in Canada.

to those above them. Someone who would be considered poor by Canadian standards would be well off by global standards of poverty; hunger and starvation are daily realities in many regions of the world.

There has been ongoing debate about the usefulness of an official measurement of poverty in Canada. Absolute

Civilization is unbearable, but it is less unbearable at the top.

Timothy Leary

The difficulty in defining poverty is evidenced by government programs that conceive of poverty in either absolute or relative terms.

Absolute poverty refers to a minimum level of subsistence below which no family should be expected to live. In most countries, this is the poverty line.

In contrast, **relative poverty** is a floating standard of deprivation by which people at the bottom of a society, whatever their lifestyles, are judged to be disadvantaged in comparison with the nation as a whole. Therefore, even if the poor today are better off in absolute terms than the poor of the 1930s or 1960s, they are still seen as poor relative

poverty statistics are used to argue that poverty is clearly not a significant problem. Taking a functionalist approach, many critics from the "right" in the political spectrum suggest that considering the country's social safety net, those who are living in absolute poverty are doing so by choice, refusing to avail themselves of social programs, or are poor as a result of personal failure. Those on the "left" side of the debate, who represent conflict and

absolute poverty A minimum level of subsistence that no family should be expected to live below.
relative poverty A floating standard of deprivation by which people at the bottom of a society, whatever their lifestyles, are judged to be disadvantaged in comparison with the nation as a whole.

who find it harder to secure the necessary financing. Although sons commonly follow in the footsteps of their fathers, women are less likely to move into their fathers' positions. Consequently, gender remains an important factor in shaping social mobility. Women in Canada (and in other parts of the world) are especially likely to be trapped in poverty, unable to rise out of their low-income status (Heilman 2001).

On the positive side, although today's women lag behind men in employment, their earnings have increased faster than their mothers' did at a comparable age, so that their incomes are substantially higher. The one glaring exception to this trend involves the daughters of low-income parents. Because these women typically care for children—many as single parents—and sometimes for other relatives as well, their mobility is severely restricted (Isaacs 2007b).

>> Life Chances

One of the lessons we learn from sociology is that class matters. Max Weber saw class as being closely related to people's **life chances**—that is, their opportunities to provide themselves with material goods, positive living conditions, and favourable life experiences (Gerth and Mills 1958). Life chances are reflected in measures such as housing, education, and health. Occupying a higher position in a society improves individuals' life chances and brings greater access to social rewards. In contrast, people in the lower social classes are forced to devote a larger proportion of their limited resources to the necessities of life.

life chances The opportunities people have to provide themselves with material goods, positive living conditions, and favourable life experiences.

In fact, our very survival can be at stake. When the supposedly unsinkable British ocean liner *Titanic* hit an iceberg in 1912, it was not carrying enough lifeboats to

Education Pays: Full-Time, Full-Year Workers, Ages 25–64, 2005

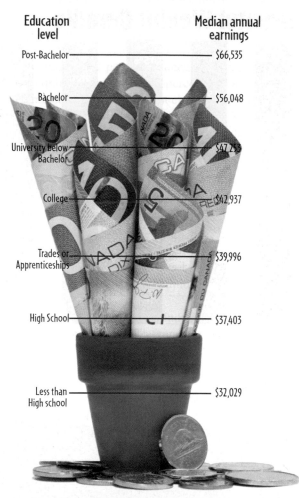

Education level	Median annual earnings
Post-Bachelor	$66,535
Bachelor	$56,048
University below Bachelor	$47,253
College	$42,937
Trades or Apprenticeships	$39,996
High School	$37,403
Less than High school	$32,029

Source: Statistics Canada, 2006 Census of Population.

SOCthink

> > > What factors have shaped your life chances? What kinds of resources have you inherited from others? What resources might you have lacked access to?

accommodate all passengers. Plans had been made to evacuate only first- and second-class passengers. About 62 percent of the first-class passengers survived the disaster. Despite a rule that women and children would go first, about a third of those passengers were male. In contrast, only 25 percent of the passengers in third class survived. The first attempt to alert them to the need to abandon ship came well after other passengers had been notified (D. A. Butler 1998; Crouse 1999; Riding 1998).

Class position also affects people's vulnerability to natural disasters. When Hurricane Katrina hit the Gulf Coast of the United States in 2005, affluent and poor people alike became its victims. However, poor people who did not own automobiles (100,000 of them in New Orleans alone) were less able than others to evacuate in advance of the storm. Those who survived its fury had no nest egg to draw on, and thus were more likely than others to accept relocation wherever social service agencies could place them—sometimes hundreds or even thousands of kilometres from home (Department of Homeland Security 2006).

Some people have hoped that the Internet revolution would help to level the playing field by making information and markets uniformly available. Unfortunately, however, not everyone can get onto the information superhighway, so yet another aspect of social inequality has emerged—the **digital divide.** The poor, minorities, and those who live in rural communities and inner cities are not getting connected at home or at work. A recent government study found that despite falling computer prices, the Internet gap between the haves and have-nots has not narrowed. For example, approximately 88 percent of adults with household incomes of $86,000 or more used the Internet in 2005, compared to 61 percent of those living in households with incomes below $86,000. As wealthier people switch to high-speed Internet connections, they

Did You Know?

. . . Warren Buffett, who in 2009 was the world's second richest man (Bill Gates was in first place), pays a far lower percentage of his income for U.S. payroll, Social Security, and Medicare taxes than do the secretaries and clerks who work for him. He used this information to argue that wealthy people such as him unfairly benefit from the current tax system.

will be able to take advantage of even more sophisticated interactive services, and the digital divide will grow even wider (Pew Internet Project 2007; Statistics Canada 2006b).

Wealth, status, and power may not ensure happiness, but they certainly provide additional ways of coping with problems and disappointments. For this reason, the opportunity for advancement—for social mobility—is of special significance to those at the bottom of society. These people want the rewards and privileges that are granted to high-ranking members of a culture.

If we are to better understand why we think and act the way we do, we must consider the impact of social class. The positions we occupy shape our access to material, social, and cultural resources, which in turn shapes our future positions. In Canada, we promote the idea that anyone who is willing to

> **digital divide** The relative lack of access to the latest technologies among low-income groups, racial and ethnic minorities, rural residents, and the citizens of developing countries.

work hard can get ahead. The principle of meritocracy—that we earn our positions—is at the heart of that faith which represents a rejection of aristocracy in which positions are inherited. Class patterns in Canada call into question the degree to which principle and practice meet.

>> Summary

Social class is one of the major bases of stratification in Canadian society. Economic position— your income and wealth—is the primary determinant of social class. Certain groups are disproportionately represented among the poorer classes in Canada—the elderly, women, Aboriginal peoples, and recent immigrants to the country. Those who are in the highest classes tend to have the greatest status and power. Great disparities in income and wealth distribution exist; the rich really are getting richer, and the poor are getting poorer.

get involved! Calculate! Figure out how to manage your budget in these tough economic times. Veterans Affairs considers a responsible budget to be an aspect of wellness. Check out their advice at: www.vac-acc.gc.ca.

For REVIEW

I. What is social class?
- Like slavery, caste, and estate, it is a stratification system in which people and groups are ranked, but it places them based primarily on economic position.

II. How does social class operate?
- Three categories of resources are key: material, including income and wealth; social, including social networks and prestige; and, cultural, including tastes, education, and knowledge. Power is based on access to and control over these resources.

III. What are the consequences of social class?
- While class-based systems are more open than the others, our life chances are shaped by our inherited class position and the material, social, and cultural resources that go with it. For most people, the social mobility that does occur, whether in terms of occupation, income, or wealth, is of a relatively short distance.

Thinking CRITICALLY...

1. Considering the difficulty in establishing measures of poverty, should there be a universal standard applied to all countries? Why or why not?
2. Think of examples where class and status, as articulated by Weber do not correspond—for example, someone who might have high status, yet belong to a low economic class, or someone wealthy who does not enjoy membership in a high-status group.
3. Review Bourdieu's concept of cultural capital. In what ways has your own cultural capital prepared you for higher education?

Pop Quiz

1. Social inequality refers to
   a. the structured ranking of entire groups of people that perpetuates unequal economic rewards and power in a society.
   b. social ranking based primarily on economic position.
   c. the positive or negative reputation an individual has in the eyes of others.
   d. a condition in which members of society have different amounts of wealth, prestige, or power.

2. The stratification system in which hereditary ranks are usually religiously dictated is the
   a. class system.
   b. estate system.
   c. caste system.
   d. slave system.

3. According to Daniel Rossides' model of the class system in capitalist societies, the class that includes the most people is the
   a. lower class.
   b. working class.
   c. upper-middle class.
   d. upper class.

4. A plumber whose father was a physician is an example of
   a. downward intergenerational mobility.
   b. upward intergenerational mobility.
   c. downward intragenerational mobility.
   d. upward intragenerational mobility.

5. According to Karl Marx, the class that owns the means of production is the
   a. nobility.
   b. proletariat.
   c. Brahman.
   d. bourgeoisie.

6. Which of the following were viewed by Max Weber as distinct components of stratification?
   a. conformity, deviance, and social control
   b. class, status, and party
   c. class, caste, and age
   d. class, prestige, and esteem

7. According to Pierre Bourdieu, our tastes, our education, the way we talk, and the things we like all represent forms of
   a. social capital.
   b. esteem.
   c. cultural capital.
   d. intelligence.

8. The respect or admiration that an occupation holds in a society is referred to as
   a. status.
   b. esteem.
   c. prestige.
   d. ranking.

9. Canada does not have an official poverty line. Instead, the most common measurement of poverty is
   a. social status.
   b. low income cut-off.
   c. poverty index.
   d. education level.

10. If people are considered to be disadvantaged in comparison with the overall population of the nation in which they live, they are seen to be living in
    a. absolute poverty
    b. abject poverty.
    c. relative poverty.
    d. detached poverty.

1. (d); 2. (c); 3. (b); 4. (a); 5. (d); 6. (b); 7. (c); 8. (c); 9. (b); 10. (c)

McGraw Hill connect™

McGraw-Hill Connect™ —Available 24/7 with instant feedback so you can study when you want, how you want, and where you want. Take advantage of the Study Plan—an innovative tool that helps you customize your learning experience. You can diagnose your knowledge with pre- and post-tests, identify the areas where you need help, search the entire learning package for content specific to the topic you're studying, and add these resources to your personalized study plan. Visit www.mcgrawhillconnect.ca to register—take practice quizzes, search the e-book, and much more.

11

GLOBAL INEQ

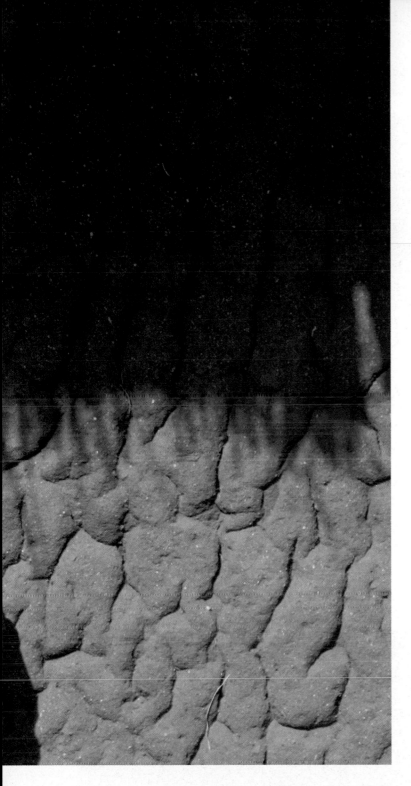

UALITY

WHAT'S TO COME

In this chapter you will...

- gain an understanding of the bases of global stratification

- identify the impact of modernization

- learn about what differentiates us, and what we share

STRUGGLING TO SURVIVE IN A WORLD OF PLENTY

In spring of 2008, riots broke out in countries around the world in response to a global food crisis. From sub-Saharan African nations to countries including Egypt, India, and Yemen, people took to the streets in response to skyrocketing prices and food shortages. Hit hardest by the effects of this crisis were people in the poorest countries, where the margin between survival and starvation is razor-thin.

In Haiti, where more than three-quarters of the population live on less than $2 a day, price increases have been devastating. Georges Jean Wesner gets up every day at 4:00 A.M. to walk two hours to get two small pails of rice and beans from a charity food kitchen—the only source of food he and his family have had for weeks. "I'm 52 years old, I have lots of energy and I want to work," he says, "but I can't work because there is no work" (Williams 2008). People are turning to patties made of mud, oil, and sugar, about which Olwich Louis Jeune, 24, says, "It's salty and it has butter, and you don't know you're eating dirt. . . . It makes your stomach quiet down" (Lacey 2008).

In the Darfur region of Sudan, Khamisa Tafaela worried because her 10-month-old son was vomiting and suffering from diarrhea. She had already lost one son who had the same symptoms. She, along with her husband and their five children, had been living in a camp in West Darfur for over four years with thousands of others forced from their homes in Sudan. For the second month in a row, she had been living on halved food rations, not because there was insufficient food, but because it was too dangerous to get the food from the warehouses to the camps (*Sudan Tribune* 2008).

We see in this Darfur story that the food crisis may be due not only to insufficient food but also to insufficient access to food. Dominique Strauss-Kahn, the Managing Director of the International Monetary Fund, says, "There is enough food to feed the world . . . the problem is that prices have risen and many people cannot afford food. So we need to get food—or the money to buy food—to those most in need" (IMF 2008). In other words, we produce enough globally so that everyone can have enough, but we do not allocate resources in such a way that people now facing starvation can gain access to the food they need to survive.

As You READ >>

- How did the global divide develop?
- How significant is global stratification?
- Why did the global movement for universal human rights develop?

>> The Global Divide

The modern world is characterized as a "global village" in which we're all interconnected, yet when it comes to resources, the global divide is immense. Millions of people struggle on the very edge of survival even as others around the world lead lives of relative comfort and leisure. A few centuries ago, most people were poor. There was a significant divide between the few who were extremely wealthy and the many who lacked significant resources, with little concept of a middle class between the nobility and the peasants. In much of Europe, life was as difficult as it was in Asia or South America. This was true until the Industrial Revolution and increased agricultural productivity resulted in explosive economic growth. However, the ensuing rise in living standards was not evenly distributed across the world.

We get a glimpse of the relative share of resources, and their consequences, by looking at splits between developing and industrial nations. For example, the likelihood of dealing with the death of a child or the burden of disease is much greater for those in developing nations. At the same time, the industrial nations of the world, with a much smaller share of the total population, have much higher incomes and many more exports than the developing nations. People in industrial nations also tend to receive better health care and have greater security due to the amount those nations spend on health care, infrastructure, and the military (Sachs 2005a; Sutcliffe 2002). When we think of these inequalities, we often highlight the divide *between* countries—that is, distinguishing the "poor" from the "wealthy" nations. But as we will see, the divide *within* countries in terms of income, wealth, poverty, and social mobility is also significant.

Average income varies significantly across the nations of the world along a continuum from those that are the richest in natural resources to those that are the poorest. The contrast between those at the top and those at the bottom is stark. For example, in 2006, per capita gross national product (the average value of goods and services produced per citizen) in the industrialized countries of Canada, Japan, Switzerland, Belgium, and Norway was more than $31,000. By comparison, at least 10 countries had a per capita gross national product of $900 or less.

>> Perspectives on Global Stratification

Theorists have taken a step back to look at this global system from a top-down, macro perspective. In so doing, they provide us with insights into how the world system developed and how the various parts fit together. We will focus on three areas of analysis: the rise of modernization, the legacy of colonialism, and the growth of multinational corporations.

Gross National Income per Capita, 2007

Gross National Income per Capita, 2007

Calcualted using pruchasing power parity in international dollars

- High income ($11,116 or more)
- Upper middle income ($3596–$11,115)
- Lower middle income ($906–$3595)
- Low income ($905 or less)
- Data not available

Going GLOBAL

Fundamental Global Inequality

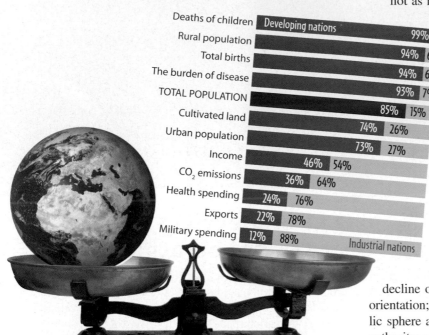

	Developing nations	Industrial nations
Deaths of children	99%	1%
Rural population	94%	6%
Total births	94%	6%
The burden of disease	93%	7%
TOTAL POPULATION	85%	15%
Cultivated land	74%	26%
Urban population	73%	27%
Income	46%	54%
CO₂ emissions	36%	64%
Health spending	24%	76%
Exports	22%	78%
Military spending	12%	88%

Note: In this comparison, industrial nations include the United States and Canada, Japan, western Europe, and Australasia. Developing nations include Africa, Asia (except for Japan), Latin America, eastern Europe, the Caribbean, and the Pacific.

Source: Adapted from Sutcliffe 2002:18.

from both Karl Marx and Émile Durkheim, who believed that societies would all inevitably evolve along a similar path, ending up in some shared version of the good society. For Durkheim this meant a natural balance between interdependence and individual freedom; for Marx it meant some form of socialism. For his part, though his vision was not as hopeful, Max Weber believed that all societies would move toward a rational-legal form of authority.

This notion that the present was superior to the past, with its petty tyrannies and irrational superstitions, and that the future would unite us all, shaped how people viewed the world throughout much of the 20th century. Many people supposed that, through **modernization,** nations would move from traditional forms of social organization toward forms characteristic of post–Industrial Revolution societies. Features of the latter include a complex division of labour in which work is specialized; the separation of institutions including family, economy, government, education, and religion into specialized spheres, each with their own experts; the decline of the local and the rise of a societal or global orientation; the rise of rational decision making in the public sphere and a corresponding decline in public religious authority; and the spread of both cultural diversity, as more peoples from different backgrounds come into contact with each other, and a corresponding growth in egalitarianism as a value that embraces such diversity (Bruce 2000).

modernization The far-reaching process by which nations pass from traditional forms of social organization toward those characteristic of post–Industrial Revolution societies.

THE RISE OF MODERNIZATION

Early sociologists often assumed that society was progressing toward some common positive future. We certainly get that sense

SOCthink

> > > Early sociologists were optimistic that positive social change was inevitable. To what extent do you think people today share this vision of the inevitable rise of the good society? How might cynicism about the possibility for change contribute to the maintenance of the status quo?

From this modernization perspective, countries such as China and India are in the process of becoming modern societies. Even if the transition from traditional to modern is difficult for many, the presupposition is that their people will benefit in the long term. According to these theorists, just as many people in Canada and Europe experienced displacement and poverty in the early years of the Industrial Revolution, only later to lead more comfortable lives, the same future awaits people in such developing nations.

Many sociologists today are quick to note that terms such as *modernization* and even *development* contain an ethnocentric bias. There is an implicit sense in this model that

THE PROGRESS OF THE CENTURY.

THE LIGHTNING STEAM PRESS.   THE ELECTRIC TELEGRAPH.   THE LOCOMOTIVE.   THE STEAMBOAT.

people in such nations are more "primitive" and that modern Western culture is more advanced, more "civilized." The unstated assumption is that what "they" (people living in developing countries) really want is to become more like "us" (people in modern industrialized nations). According to this vision, they want both our economic development and our cultural values including democracy, freedom, and

consumerism. Such modernization, then, represents a form of cultural imperialism. Many groups around the world reject this path, viewing such "development" as an attack on their way of life including their core values and norms.

THE LEGACY OF COLONIALISM

An alternative perspective to modernization focuses on colonialism as a model for better understanding the expansion of our interconnected world. **Colonialism** occurs when a foreign power maintains political, social, economic, and cultural domination over a people for an extended period. In simple terms, it is rule by outsiders. The long reign of the British Empire over much of North America, parts of Africa, and India is an example of colonial domination. The same can be said of French rule over Algeria, Tunisia, and other parts of North Africa. Relations between the colonial nation and the colonized people are similar to those between the dominant capitalist class and the proletariat, as described by Marx.

> colonialism The maintenance of political, social, economic, and cultural dominance over a people by a foreign power for an extended period.

By the 1980s, such global political empires had largely disappeared. Most of the nations that were colonies prior to World War I had achieved political independence and

When it comes to the portrayal of people from around the world in North American television shows and films, we often see negative stereotypes reinforced. An exception is Canadian series *Little Mosque on the Prairie*, which has been widely praised for its portrayal of members of a Muslim community living in a small prairie town. But in 2004, nearly half of all Middle Eastern characters shown on U.S. television were criminals, compared to only 5 percent of White characters. And in an analysis of about 1000 films over 20 years, communications professor Jack Shaheen found that only 5 percent of Arab and Muslim characters were presented in a positive light. The good news, he said, is that in recent years, this figure has grown to about 30 percent, pointing to *Babel* and *Syriana* as examples.

established their own governments. However, for many of these countries, the transition to genuine self-rule was not yet complete. Colonial domination had established patterns of economic exploitation that continued even after nationhood was achieved—in part because the former colonies were unable to develop their own industry and technology. Their dependence on more industrialized nations, including their former colonial masters, for managerial and technical expertise, investment capital, and manufactured goods kept the former colonies in a subservient position. Such continuing dependence and foreign domination are referred to as **neocolonialism**.

Sociologist Immanuel Wallerstein (1974, 1979a, 2000) views the global economic system as being divided between nations that control wealth and nations from which resources are taken. Through his **world systems analysis,** Wallerstein has described the unequal economic and political relationships in which certain industrialized nations (among them the United States, Japan, and Germany) and their global corporations dominate the core of this system. At the

neocolonialism Continuing dependence of former colonies on foreign countries.

world systems analysis A view of the global economic system as one divided between certain industrialized nations that control wealth and developing countries that are controlled and exploited.

dependency theory An approach contending that industrialized nations continue to exploit developing countries for their own gain.

semiperiphery of the system are countries with marginal economic status, such as Israel, Ireland, and South Korea. Canada is characterized as falling somewhere between the categories of core and semi-periphery. Our standard of living and level of development warrant Canada's inclusion in the former category, but our high dependence upon export to core nations suggests semi-peripheral status. Wallerstein suggests that the poor developing countries of Asia, Africa, and Latin America are on the periphery of the world economic system. The key to Wallerstein's analysis is the exploitative relationship of core nations toward noncore nations. Core nations and their corporations control and exploit noncore nations' economies. Unlike other nations, they are relatively independent of outside control (Chase-Dunn and Grimes 1995).

The division between core and periphery nations is both significant and remarkably stable. A study by the International Monetary Fund (2000) found little change over the past century for the 42 economies studied. The only changes were Japan's movement up into the group of core nations and China's movement down toward the margins of the semiperiphery nations. Yet Wallerstein (2000) speculates that the world system as we currently understand it may soon undergo unpredictable changes. The world is becoming increasingly urbanized, a trend that is gradually eliminating the large pools of low-cost workers in rural areas. In the future, core nations will have to find other ways to reduce their labour costs. The exhaustion of land and water resources through clear-cutting and pollution is also driving up the costs of production.

Wallerstein's world systems analysis is the most widely used version of **dependency theory.** According to this theory, even as developing countries make economic advances,

World Systems Analysis at the Beginning of the 21st Century

Core	Semiperiphery	Periphery
Canada	China	Afghanistan
France	India	Bolivia
Germany	Ireland	Chad
Japan	Mexico	Dominican Republic
United Kingdom	Pakistan	Egypt
United States	Panama	Haiti
		Philippines
		Vietnam

Note: Figure shows only a partial listing of countries.

SOCstudies

Did You Know?

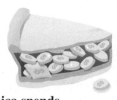

... Jamaica spends 27.9 percent of its government budget on debt relief and 16.1 percent on health and education. Such ratios are not uncommon in developing nations, although Lebanon spends 52.1 percent on debt service.

they remain weak and subservient to core nations and corporations in an increasingly intertwined global economy. This interdependency allows industrialized nations to continue to exploit developing countries for their own gain.

According to world systems analysis and dependency theory, a growing share of the human and natural resources of developing countries is being redistributed to the core industrialized nations. This redistribution happens in part because developing countries owe huge sums of money to industrialized nations as a result of foreign aid, loans, and trade deficits. The global debt crisis has intensified the Third World dependency rooted in colonialism, neocolonialism, and multinational investment. International financial institutions are pressuring indebted countries to take severe measures to meet their interest payments. As conflict theorists have noted, the result is that developing nations may be forced to devalue their currencies, freeze workers' wages, increase privatization of industry, and reduce government services and employment.

Closely related to these problems is **globalization**—the worldwide integration of government policies, cultures, social movements, and financial markets through trade and the exchange of ideas. Because the forces of world financial markets transcend governance by conventional nation-states, international organizations such as the World Bank and the International Monetary Fund have emerged as major players in the global economy. The function of these institutions, which are heavily funded and influenced by core nations, is to encourage trade and development and to ensure the smooth operation of international financial

SOCthink

> > > How has the rise of multinational corporations and the trend toward globalization affected you, your family, and your community, both positively and negatively?

markets. As such, they are seen as promoters of globalization and defenders primarily of the interests of core nations. Critics call attention to a variety of related issues, including violations of workers' rights, the destruction of the environment, the loss of cultural identity, and discrimination against minority groups in periphery nations.

> **globalization** The worldwide integration of government policies, cultures, social movements, and financial markets through trade and the exchange of ideas.
> **multinational corporation** A commercial organization that is headquartered in one country but does business throughout the world.

THE GROWTH OF MULTINATIONAL CORPORATIONS

Worldwide, corporate giants have played a key role in the rise of globalization. The term **multinational corporations** refers to commercial organizations that are headquartered in

Theory
A Matter of Perspective

THEORETICAL PERSPECTIVES ON GLOBAL INEQUALITY

Functionalist:
- associated with modernization theory
- global divide results from ability of industrial nations to produce technology and more wealth; other nations must move away from traditional cultures in order to keep pace

Conflict:
- associated with dependency theory
- industrial nations exploit developing countries, rendering them economically dependent and increasing their debt load

Feminist:
- associated with dependency theory
- highlights the dual disadvantage of women on the basis of economic status and gender

Interactionist:
- along with conflict and feminist perspectives, emphasizes the human cost of globalization
- microlevel examination of the effects of global stratification and the understanding of what constitutes human "rights"

one country but do business around the world. Such private trade and lending relationships are not new; merchants have conducted business abroad for hundreds of years, trading gems, spices, garments, and other goods. Today's multinational giants are not merely buying and selling overseas; they are also producing goods all over the world (I. Wallerstein 1974). Through deindustrialization, corporate executives also have relocated production jobs around the globe.

Increasingly, it is not just production jobs that are being relocated. Today's global factories may now have the "global office" alongside them. Multinationals based in core nations are beginning to establish reservation services and centres for processing data and insurance claims in the periphery nations. As service industries become a more important part of the international marketplace, many companies are concluding that the low costs of overseas operations more than offset the expense of transmitting information around the world.

These multinational corporations are huge, with total revenues on a par with the total value of goods and services exchanged in entire nations. Foreign sales represent an important source of profit for multinational corporations, encouraging them to expand into other countries (in many cases, the developing nations). The Canadian economy is heavily dependent on foreign commerce, much of which is conducted by American multinationals. Statistics Canada identifies the United States as Canada's largest foreign investor, with 59 percent of Canada's total foreign direct investment in 2007 (this amounts to $289 billion). Canada is the fifth largest investor in the United States.

Going GLOBAL

Multinational Corporations Compared to Nations

Rank	Corporate revenue / Gross domestic product	Millions of dollars
1	$351.1 Wal-Mart (USA)	
	369.1 Sweden	
2	$347.2 Exxon Mobil (USA)	
	342.0 Turkey	
3	$318.8 Royal Dutch Petroleum (Britain/Netherlands)	
	306.2 Austria	
4	$274.3 BP British Petroleum (Britain)	
	273.1 Poland	
5	$207.3 General Motors (USA)	
	206.1 Colombia and Hungary	
6	$204.7 Toyota Motor (Japan)	
	203.0 Pakistan and Chile	
7	$200.6 Chevron (USA)	
	196.9 Finland	
8	$190.2 Daimler Chrysler (Germany)	
	181.3 Portugal	
9	$172.4 Conoco Philips (USA)	
	173.1 Argentina	
10	$168.4 Total (France)	
	171.1 Ireland	

Note: Total is an oil, petroleum, and chemical company. Where two nations are listed, the country with the larger GDP is listed first.

Sources: For corporate data, *Fortune* 2007; for GDP data, World Bank 2007a14–16.

Modernization

Consistent with the modernization approach, some analysts believe that the relationship between the corporation and the developing country is mutually beneficial. Multinational corporations can help the developing nations of the world by bringing industries and jobs to areas where subsistence agriculture once served as the only means of survival. Multinationals also promote rapid development through the diffusion of inventions and innovations from industrial nations. The combination of skilled technology and management provided by multinationals and the relatively cheap labour available in developing nations benefits the corporation. Multinationals can take maximum advantage of technology while reducing costs and boosting profits. Through their international ties, multinationals also make the nations of the world

SOCthink

> > > Multinational corporations have become so big that they have more economic resources than do some nations. What consequences arise from the fact that they can relocate their headquarters, offices, and production facilities anywhere in the world? How might this affect a nation's political power?

more interdependent. These ties may prevent certain disputes from reaching the point of serious conflict. A country cannot afford to sever diplomatic relations or engage in warfare with a nation that is the headquarters for its main business suppliers or a key market for its exports.

Dependency Critics of multinational expansion challenge this favourable evaluation of the impact of corporations. They argue that multinationals exploit local workers to maximize profits. For example, Starbucks—the international coffee retailer based in Seattle—gets some of its coffee beans from farms in Guatemala. But to earn enough money to buy a pound of Starbucks coffee, a Guatemalan farm worker would have to pick 500 pounds of beans, representing five days of work (Entine and Nichols 1996).

The pool of cheap labour in the developing world prompts multinationals to move factories out of core countries. Workers in these developing countries do not have the same kinds of legal protections and also lack unions to fight on their behalf. In industrialized countries, organized labour insists on decent wages and humane working conditions, but governments seeking to attract or keep multinationals may develop a "climate for investment," including repressive anti-labour laws that restrict union activity and collective

bargaining. If labour's demands become too threatening, the multinational firm will simply move its plant elsewhere, leaving a trail of unemployment behind. Nike, for example, has moved its factories from the United States to Korea to Indonesia to Vietnam in search of the lowest labour costs.

Workers in Canada and other core countries are beginning to recognize that their own interests are served by helping to organize workers in developing nations. As long as multinationals can exploit cheap labour abroad, they will be in a strong position to reduce wages and benefits in industrialized countries. With this in mind, in the 1990s, labour unions, religious organizations, campus groups, and other activists began to mount public relations campaigns to pressure companies such as Nike, Starbucks, Reebok, Gap, and Wal-Mart to improve wages and working conditions in their overseas operations (Global Alliance for Workers and Communities 2003; Gonzalez 2003).

Sociologists studying the effects of foreign investment by multinationals have found that, although it initially may contribute to a host nation's wealth, such investment eventually increases economic inequality within developing nations. This finding holds for both income and ownership. The upper and middle classes benefit most from economic expansion; the lower classes are less likely to benefit. And because multinationals invest in limited economic sectors and restricted regions of a nation, only some sectors benefit. The expansion of such sectors of the host nation's economy, such as hotels and high-end restaurants, appears to retard growth in agriculture and other economic sectors. Moreover, multinational corporations often buy out or force out local entrepreneurs and companies, thereby increasing economic and cultural dependence (Chase-Dunn and Grimes 1995; Kerbo 2009; I. Wallerstein 1979b).

>> Stratification Around the World

As these economic investments by multinationals suggest, at the same time that the gap between rich and poor nations is widening, so too is the gap between rich and poor citizens within nations. As discussed earlier, stratification in developing nations is closely related to their relatively weak and dependent position in the global economy. Local elites work hand in hand with multinational corporations and prosper from such alliances. At the same time, the economic system creates and perpetuates the exploitation of industrial and agricultural workers. That's why foreign investment in developing countries tends to increase economic inequality (Bornschier et al. 1978; Kerbo 2009).

Percent Shares of Global Household Wealth

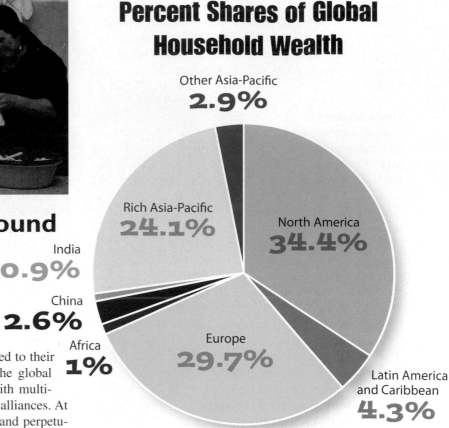

Other Asia-Pacific
2.9%

Rich Asia-Pacific **24.1%**

India **0.9%**

China **2.6%**

Africa **1%**

North America **34.4%**

Europe **29.7%**

Latin America and Caribbean **4.3%**

Source: Davies et al. 2007.

INCOME AND WEALTH

Global inequality is staggering, as the graphs on this page suggest. In at least 22 nations around the world, the most affluent 10 percent of the population receives at least 40 percent of all income. Among these countries are the African nation of Namibia (the leader, at 65 percent of all income) as well as Colombia, Mexico, Nigeria, and South Africa (Shorrocks et al. 2006).

When it comes to wealth, the top 10 percent of the world's population own 85 percent of global household wealth, and the top 1 percent own 40 percent. On the other end of the spectrum, the bottom 50 percent of the world's population combined own 1 percent of global wealth. Median household wealth globally is estimated to be US$2129 per adult. To make it into the top 1 percent takes US$510,000. Analyzing the distribution globally, the bulk of the wealth is held by countries in North America, Europe, and the rich Asia-Pacific nations (Davies et al. 2007).

Looking in more detail at the world's top 10 percent of wealth holders, 25 percent come from the United States, 21 percent come from Japan, and Germany, Italy, Britain, France, and Spain combine for 29 percent. Within nations, the amount of wealth held by the top 10 percent varies. Denmark demonstrates the most significant amount of wealth inequality, with the top 10 percent of wealth holders there owning 76.4 percent of household wealth—significantly more than Japan, where the top

Distribution of Income in Nine Nations

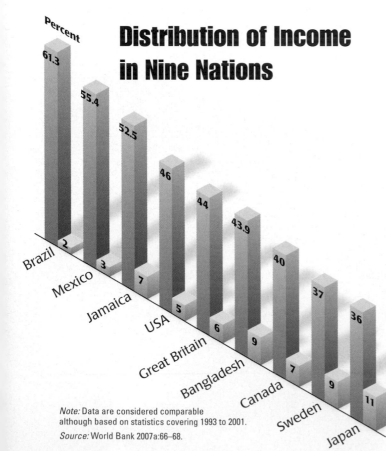

Percent

Brazil 61.3 / 2
Mexico 55.4 / 3
Jamaica 52.5 / 7
USA 46 / 5
Great Britain 44 / 6
Bangladesh 43.9 / 9
Canada 40 / 7
Sweden 37 / 9
Japan 36 / 11

Highest 20%

Lowest 20%

Note: Data are considered comparable although based on statistics covering 1993 to 2001.

Source: World Bank 2007a:66–68.

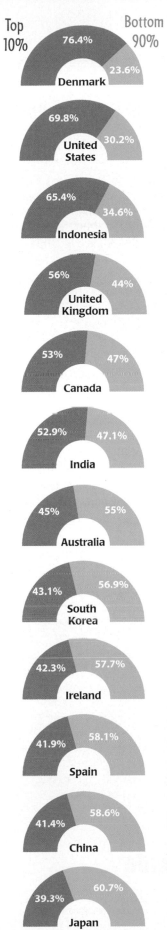

Top 10%   Bottom 90%

76.4%   23.6%
Denmark

69.8%   30.2%
United States

65.4%   34.6%
Indonesia

56%   44%
United Kingdom

53%   47%
Canada

52.9%   47.1%
India

45%   55%
Australia

43.1%   56.9%
South Korea

42.3%   57.7%
Ireland

41.9%   58.1%
Spain

41.4%   58.6%
China

39.3%   60.7%
Japan

Amount of Wealth Held by the Top 10 Percent

Source: Davies et al. 2007.

10 percent hold 39.3 percent of the wealth.

Women in developing countries often face significant obstacles, making it difficult for them to attain economic assets. Karuna Chanana Ahmed, an anthropologist from India who has studied women in developing nations, calls women the most exploited of oppressed people. Beginning at birth, women face sex discrimination. They are commonly fed less than male children, are denied educational opportunities, and often are hospitalized only when they are critically ill. Only one-third of Pakistan's sexually segregated schools are for women, and one-third of those schools have no buildings. Inside or outside the home, women's work is devalued. And when economies fail, as they did in 2009, women in many countries—including Canada—were the first to be laid off from work (J. Anderson and Moore 1993; Kristof 1998). In Kenya and Tanzania, it is illegal for a woman to own a house. In Saudi Arabia, women are prohibited from driving, walking alone in public, and socializing with men outside their families (C. Murphy 1993).

POVERTY

In developing countries, any deterioration in the economic well-being of the least well-off threatens their very survival. Poverty is a worldwide problem that blights the lives of billions of people, but it, too, is distributed unequally. If we drew a map in which the size of each country was based on the number of poor people there, Africa and Asia would appear huge compared to the relatively affluent areas of industrialized North America and Europe.

In 2000, the United Nations launched the Millennium Project, whose objective is to eliminate extreme poverty worldwide by the year 2015. This is an ambitious goal. Today, almost 3 billion people subsist on $2 a day or less. To accomplish the project's goal, planners estimate that industrial nations must set aside 0.7 percent of their **gross national product (GNP)**—the value of a nation's goods and services—for aid to developing nations.

At the time the Millennium Project was launched, only five countries were giving at that target rate: Denmark, Luxembourg, the Netherlands, Norway, and Sweden. To match their contribution proportionally, the United States would need to multiply its present aid level by 45. In 2006–2007, Canada's official development aid was roughly half of what is needed

> **gross national product (GNP)** The value of a nation's goods and services.

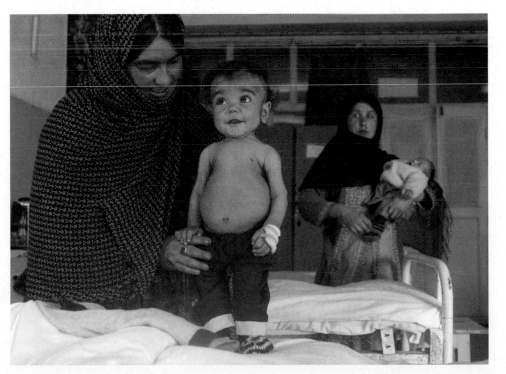

to meet the target of 0.7 percent. Although Canada is often characterized as a "leader" in international aid, and the U.S. delivers far more aid to foreign countries and multinational organizations than any other nation, both lag behind other advanced industrial nations in terms of per capita spending on foreign aid (Kerbo 2009; Sachs 2005a; World Bank 2007a). For instance, in 2004, Canada's per capita foreign aid was US$76; in contrast, France's was US$156, and Norway's US$439. Unfortunately, due to the global economic recession, it is reasonable to predict that international aid will decrease, rather than increase.

In February 2009, Canada's Conservative federal government refocused its aid programs, arguing that funding was not being effectively distributed. The government selected 20 countries where resources would be especially

SOCthink

> > > What are the major obstacles to accomplishing the Millennium Project's goals? To what extent are they economic, social, and/or cultural? Is it simply a matter of will?

charitable giving are much higher in the United States and Canada than in other industrial nations. Even more significant are remittances—the money that immigrants send home to relatives. According to a 2007 report, individual remittances in the United States in 2005 to-

> In a world of increasing inequality, the legitimacy of institutions that give precedence to the property rights of the Haves over the human rights of the Have Nots is inevitably called into serious question.
>
> **David Korten**

directed, adding a number of new countries to Canada's list of favoured recipients; among them: Afghanistan, Haiti, and the West Bank/Gaza regions.

Direct government-to-government foreign aid is only one way of alleviating poverty, however. While per capita aid from the government may not be high, private spending by North American residents is. Rates of individual

talled US$61 billion, far higher than the second-ranked country, the United Kingdom, with US$6.6 billion, and third-place Canada, with US$6.1 billion (*The Economist* 2007a; Hudson Institute 2007; World Bank 2006b).

When it comes to aid, even a small amount of capital can make a big difference. Microfinance programs, which involve relatively small grants or loans, have encouraged marginalized

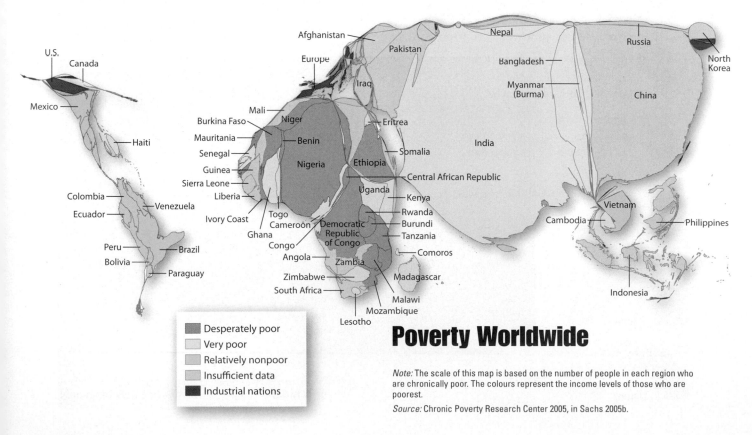

Legend:
- Desperately poor
- Very poor
- Relatively nonpoor
- Insufficient data
- Industrial nations

Poverty Worldwide

Note: The scale of this map is based on the number of people in each region who are chronically poor. The colours represent the income levels of those who are poorest.

Source: Chronic Poverty Research Center 2005, in Sachs 2005b.

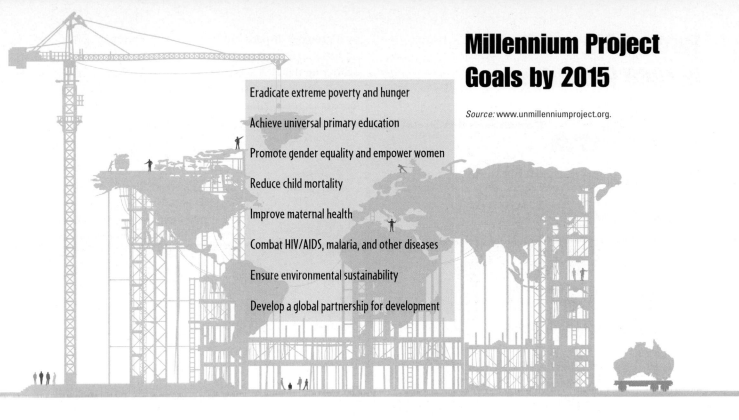

Millennium Project Goals by 2015

Source: www.unmillenniumproject.org.

Eradicate extreme poverty and hunger

Achieve universal primary education

Promote gender equality and empower women

Reduce child mortality

Improve maternal health

Combat HIV/AIDS, malaria, and other diseases

Ensure environmental sustainability

Develop a global partnership for development

people to invest not in livestock, which may die, or jewellery, which may be stolen, but in technological improvements such as small cooking stoves. In Indonesia, for example, some 60,000 microloans have enabled families who once cooked their food in a pit to purchase stoves. Improvements like these not only enable people to cook more food at a more consistent temperature but can become the basis of small-scale home businesses (*The Economist* 2005g).

SOCIAL MOBILITY

Although significant global inequality exists, perhaps sufficient social mobility exists to provide hope for those born without significant access to

5 Movies on GLOBAL INEQUALITY

Babel
Four stories on hardship from around the globe.

Born into Brothels
Children are forced into prostitution due to poverty.

Life and Debt
The IMF exploits Jamaica.

Maria Full of Grace
A factory worker is forced to transport heroin to the United States.

Invisible Children
Ugandan children go unnoticed.

resources. As we saw in the previous chapter, mobility can and does happen in Canada, though the majority of such movement is over only short distances. Here we will look at the possibility for mobility in both industrial nations and developing nations, as well as consider the impact gender has on mobility.

Intergenerational Mobility Across Nations To measure intergenerational mobility, sociologists and economists look at statistical correlation between the economic standings of parents and children: the higher the correlation (usually expressed as a percentage), the lower the level of social mobility. As demonstrated in the table on page 250, intergenerational mobility varies across countries. The United Kingdom and the United States have the lowest level of intergenerational mobility, while Canada and the Nordic countries have high rates of social mobility (Corak 2006).

In developing nations, macrolevel social and economic changes often overshadow microlevel movement from one occupation to another. For example, there is typically a substantial wage differential between rural and urban areas, which leads to high levels of migration to the cities. Yet the urban industrial sectors of developing countries generally cannot provide sufficient employment for all those seeking work.

In large developing nations, the most socially significant mobility is the movement out of poverty. This type of mobility is difficult to measure and confirm, however, because economic trends can differ from one area of a country to another. For instance, China's rapid income growth has been accompanied

Foreign Aid per Capita in Eight Countries

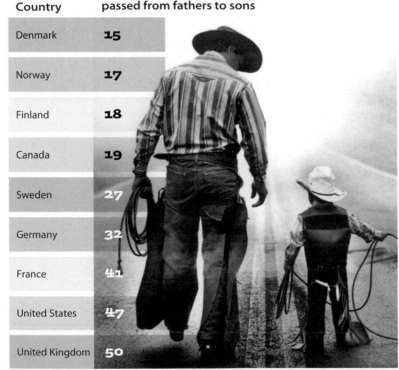

Country	Total aid in $ millions of dollars	Per capita aid in dollars
Australia	1.4	$72
USA	25.8	$87
Canada	2.8	$88
Germany	9.2	$113
Japan	17.3	$135
Great Britain	8.5	$142
France	8.9	$145
Norway	2.0	$407

Note: Data for bilateral aid in 2005 released by World Bank in 2007.

Source: World Bank 2007a:14–16, 346.

Intergenerational Earnings Mobility by Country

Country	Percentage of earning advantage passed from fathers to sons
Denmark	15
Norway	17
Finland	18
Canada	19
Sweden	27
Germany	32
France	41
United States	47
United Kingdom	50

Source: Corak 2006.

by a growing disparity in income between urban and rural areas and among different regions. Similarly, in India during the 1990s, poverty declined in urban areas but may have remained static at best in rural areas. Around the world, social mobility is also dramatically influenced by catastrophes such as crop failure and warfare (World Bank 2000).

Gender Differences and Mobility Only recently have researchers begun to investigate the impact of gender on the mobility patterns of developing nations. Many aspects of the development process—especially modernization in rural areas and the rural-to-urban migration just described—may result in the modification or abandonment of traditional cultural practices and even marital systems. The effects on women's social standing and mobility are not necessarily positive. As a country develops and modernizes, women's vital role in food production deteriorates, jeopardizing both their autonomy and their material well-being. Moreover, the movement of families to the cities weakens women's ties to relatives who can provide food, financial assistance, and social support.

In the Philippines, however, women have moved to the forefront of the indigenous peoples' struggle to protect their ancestral land from exploitation by outsiders. Having established their right to its rich minerals and forests, members of indigenous groups had begun to feud among themselves over the way in which the land's resources should be developed. Aided by the United Nations Partners in Development Programme, women volunteers established the Pan-Cordillera Women's Network for Peace and Development, a coalition of women's groups dedicated to resolving local disputes. The women mapped boundaries, prepared development plans, and negotiated more than 2000 peace pacts among community members. They have also run in elections, campaigned on issues related to social problems, and organized residents to work together for the common good (United Nations Development Programme 2000:87).

... Working 14 hours a day at 13 cents an hour, it would take seamstress Robin Akther of the Western Dresses factory in Dhaka, Bangladesh, 50 years to earn $16,200.

A CASE STUDY:
SOCIAL STRATIFICATION IN MEXICO

To get a more complete picture of these global stratification issues, it helps to look at a particular case. Here we will focus on the dynamics of stratification in Mexico, a country of 102 million people.

In May 2003, on a stretch of highway in southern Arizona, the open doors of an abandoned tractor trailer revealed the dead bodies of 19 Mexicans. The truck had been carrying a group of about 75 men, women, and children across the Sonoran Desert illegally into the United States when the people hidden inside began to suffer from the intense desert heat. Their story is not unusual. In recent years, as many as 500 people per year have died trying to cross the U.S.–Mexican border. From October 2007 through June 2008, according to border patrol officials in Arizona, 61 died in the Tucson sector alone.

Why do Mexicans risk their lives crossing the dangerous desert that lies between the two countries? The answer to this question can be found primarily in the income disparity between the two nations—one an industrial giant and the other a partially developed country still recovering from a history of colonialism and neocolonialism. Since the early 20th century, there has been a close cultural, economic, and political relationship between Mexico and the United States, one in which the United States is the dominant party. According to Immanuel Wallerstein's analysis, the United States is at the core while neighbouring Mexico is still on the semiperiphery of the world economic system.

Mexico's Economy If we compare Mexico's economy to that of the United States, differences in the standard of living and in life chances are quite dramatic, even though Mexico is considered a semiperiphery nation. Gross national income is a commonly used measure of an average resident's economic well-being. In 2007, the gross national income per person in the United States came to $44,260; in Mexico, it was a mere $11,330. About 87 percent of adults in the United States have a high school education, compared to only 13 percent of those in Mexico. And fewer than 7 of every 1000 infants in the United States die in the first year of life, compared to about 21 per 1000 in Mexico (Bureau of the Census 2007a:Table 1312; Haub 2005).

Not only is Mexico unquestionably a poor country, but the gap between its richest and poorest citizens is one of the widest in the world. The top quintile earns 55.4 percent of total income while the bottom earns just 3 percent. The World Bank reports that, in 2006, 20 percent of Mexico's population survived on just $2 per day. At the same time, the wealthiest 10 percent of Mexico's people accounted for 39 percent of the nation's income. According to a *Forbes* magazine portrait of the world's wealthiest individuals, that year Mexico ranked 11th in terms of the number of residents who were among the world's wealthiest people (Kroll and Fass 2006; World Bank 2007a:67).

Political scientist Jorge Castañeda (1995:71) calls Mexico a "polarized society with enormous gaps between rich and poor, town and country, north and south, white and brown (or *criollos* and *mestizos*)." He adds that the country is also divided along lines of class, race, religion, gender, and age. To better understand the nature of the stratification within Mexico, we will examine race relations and the plight of Mexican Indians, the status of Mexican women, and immigration to the United States and its impact on the U.S.–Mexican borderlands.

Did You Know?

... The "tomato capital" of Canada, Leamington, Ontario (population 16,000), is home to a Mexican consulate. Opened in 2005, it is an important resource for the large numbers of migrant farm workers who come to the area each year.

Race Relations in Mexico: The Colour Hierarchy

Mexico's indigenous Indians account for an estimated 14 percent of the nation's population. More than 90 percent of them live in houses without sewers, compared to 21 percent of the population as a whole. And whereas just 10 percent of Mexican adults are illiterate, the proportion for Mexican Indians is 44 percent (Boudreaux 2002; *The Economist* 2004b; G. Thompson 2001b).

The subordinate status of Mexico's Indians is but one reflection of the nation's colour hierarchy, which links social class status to the appearance of racial purity. At the top of this hierarchy are the *criollos,* the 10 percent of the population who are typically White, well-educated members of the business and intellectual elites, with familial roots in Spain. In the middle is the large, impoverished *mestizo* majority, most of whom have brown skin and a mixed racial lineage as a result of intermarriage. At the bottom of the colour hierarchy are the destitute, full-blooded Mexican Indian minority and a small number of Blacks, some descended from 200,000 African slaves brought to Mexico. This colour hierarchy is an important part of day-to-day life—enough so that some Mexicans in the cities use hair dyes, skin lighteners, and blue or green contact lenses to appear more White and European. Ironically, however, nearly all Mexicans are considered part Indian because of centuries of intermarriage (Castañeda 1995; DePalma 1995).

Many observers take note of widespread denial of prejudice and discrimination against people of colour in Mexico. Schoolchildren are taught that the election of Benito Juárez, a Zapotec Indian, as president of Mexico in the 19th century proves that all Mexicans are equal. Yet there has been a marked growth in the past decade of formal organizations and voluntary associations representing indigenous Indians (Escárcega 2008; Stavenhagen 1994; Utne 2003).

The Status of Women in Mexico In 1975, Mexico City hosted the first international conference on the status of women, convened by the United Nations. Much

SOCthink

> > > Over 20,000 migrant workers—many of them Mexican—come to Canada each year to work as farm labourers, earning roughly minimum wage. Some unionists argue that this is exploitation, and claim the workers are denied protections that Canadian workers enjoy. Yet anecdotal evidence suggests workers are earning as much as 10 times what they would earn in Mexico for the same work, and 95 percent of workers who enter Canada under the migrant workers program continue to return each season. Furthermore, farmers report that even in economically difficult times, they cannot find Canadians willing to do the work. Do you think migrant workers are being exploited? Why do you suppose Canadian workers are reluctant to do this work, even when jobs are scarce?

of the discussion concerned the situation of women in developing countries; in that regard, the news is mixed. Women now constitute 45 percent of the labour force—an increase from 31 percent in 1980, but still less than in industrial countries. Unfortunately, Mexican women are even more mired in the lowest-paying jobs than their counterparts in industrial nations. In the political arena, though they rarely occupy top decision-making positions, women have significantly increased their representation in the national legislature, to 23 percent. Mexico now ranks 39th among 189 nations in female representation—well ahead of Great Britain, France, and slightly ahead of Canada (Bureau of the Census 2007a:Table 133; Inter-Parliamentary Union 2007).

Even when Mexican women work outside the home, they often are not recognized as active and productive household members, whereas men are typically viewed as heads of the household. As one consequence, women find it difficult to obtain credit and technical assistance in many parts of the country and to inherit land in rural areas. Within the manufacturing and service industries, women generally receive little training and tend to work in the least-automated and least-skilled jobs. This occurs in large part because there is little expectation that women will pursue career advancement, organize for better working conditions, or become active in labour unions (Kopinak 1995; Martelo 1996; see also Young 1993).

In recent decades, Mexican women have begun to organize to address an array of economic, political, and health issues. Since women continue to serve as the household managers for their families, even when they work outside the home, they are well aware of the consequences of the inadequate public services in lower-income urban neighbourhoods. As far back as 1973, women in Monterrey—the nation's third-largest city—began protesting the continuing disruptions of the city's water supply. After individual complaints to city officials and the water authority proved fruitless, social networks of female activists began to emerge. These activists sent delegations to confront politicians, organized protest rallies, and blocked traffic as a means of gaining media attention. Though their efforts brought improvements in Monterrey's water service, the issue of reliable and safe water remains a concern in Mexico and many other developing countries (Bennett 1995).

The Borderlands Growing recognition of the borderlands reflects the increasingly close and complex relationship between Mexico and the United States. The term **borderlands** refers to the area of common culture along the border between Mexico and the United States. Legal and illegal emigration from Mexico to the United States, day labourers crossing the border regularly to go to work in the United States, the implementation of the North American Free Trade Agreement (NAFTA), the exchange of media across the border—all make the notion of separate Mexican and U.S. cultures obsolete in the borderlands.

The economic position of the borderlands is rather complicated, as demonstrated by the emergence of *maquiladoras*. These are foreign owned factories established just across the border in Mexico, where the companies that own them do not have to pay taxes or provide insurance and benefits to workers. As of 2006, *maquiladoras* employed 1.1 million people, paying entry-level workers between $4 and $5 per day. Since many of these firms come from the United States and sell their products to Mexico's vast domestic market, their operations deepen the impact of U.S. consumer culture on Mexico's urban and rural areas (Federal Reserve Bank of Dallas 2006; *Migration News* 2005c).

The *maquiladoras* have contributed to Mexico's economic development, but not without some cost. Their unregulated growth allows owners to exploit workers with jobs that lack security, possibilities for advancement, and decent wages. Moreover, many of the U.S.-owned factories require female job applicants to take a urine test to screen out those who are pregnant—a violation of Mexican law as well as of NAFTA, and the source of numerous cases of sex discrimination (Dillon 1998; Dougherty and Holthouse 1999).

> **borderlands** The area of common culture along the border between Mexico and the United States.

Ironically, the *maquiladoras* are now experiencing the same challenge from global trade as U.S. manufacturing plants did. Beginning in 2001, some companies began shifting their operations to China. Average Mexican labour costs (wages plus benefits) are just $2 to $2.50 an hour, but Chinese labor costs are even lower—50 cents to $1 an hour. Of the 700,000 new *maquiladora* jobs created in NAFTA's first seven years, 43 percent were eliminated between 2000 and 2003 (*Migration News* 2002c, 2004).

Immigration to the United States From the Mexican point of view, the United States too often regards Mexico simply as a reserve pool of cheap labour, encouraging Mexicans to cross the border when workers are needed but discouraging and cracking down on them when they are not. Some people, then, see immigration more as a labour market issue than a law enforcement issue. Viewed from the perspective of Wallerstein's world systems analysis and

The Borderlands

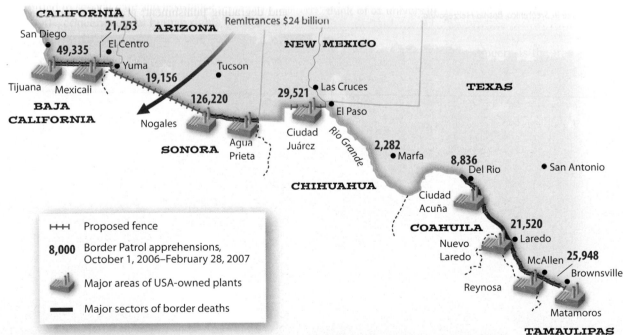

Source: Prepared by Schaefer 2009 based on Marosi 2007; Romano and Ramirez 2007; G. Thompson 2001a.

by carrying a purse if you are male. That was exactly the assignment given to sociology students when their professors asked them to behave in ways that they thought violated the norms of how a man or woman should act. The students had no trouble coming up with gender-norm transgressions, and they kept careful notes on others' reactions to their behaviour, ranging from amusement to disgust (Nielsen et al. 2000).

Women's Gender Roles

How does a girl come to develop a feminine self-image, while a boy develops one that is masculine? Socialization from parents, school, friends, and the mass media all contribute to a person's sense of what kind of thoughts, actions, and appearance are appropriate. We receive from these agents of socialization images of what society considers ideal, and we face positive and negative sanctions for deviating from such standards.

In 2004, Dove launched a series of ads in what they called the Campaign for Real Beauty (www.campaignforrealbeauty.com). In preparation for this campaign, they conducted a formal research project in which they hired academic researchers to conduct surveys

Hot or Not?

To what extent is homophobia driven by the desire to maintain clear and absolute differences between men and women?

Theory
A Matter of Perspective

THEORETICAL PERSPECTIVES ON GENDER

Functionalist:
- gender differentiation is important to the maintenance of social stability

Conflict:
- gender inequality is rooted in unequal distribution of power between women and men; also connected to social class and economic participation

Feminist:
- gender is an organizing principle; women's subjugation is integral to patriarchal social structures

Interactionist:
- gender distinctions are reflected in people's everyday lives; we perform gender

of women from 10 countries around the world. They found that only 2 percent of women around the world feel comfortable describing themselves as beautiful. This was in spite of the fact that these women distinguished between beauty (which they maintain involves happiness, confidence, dignity, and humour) and physical attractiveness (which involves how a person looks). Regarding their weight and body shape, overall, just 13 percent of women said they were very satisfied. In the survey, 68 percent strongly agreed that "the media and advertising set an unrealistic standard of beauty that most women can't ever achieve." Dove set out to address this through an advertising campaign that featured a wide range of body types and highlighted an expanded definition of beauty.

In spring 2009, Britain's Susan Boyle reignited debates about "true" beauty. As a contestant on a network talent show, Boyle's "frumpy" appearance prompted derision from the audience and judges, but her singing ability soon had the crowds cheering. Many people encouraged Boyle not to change; others insisted a makeover was crucial. Amongst the debate, she became a media sensation; over 1 million people have watched her inspiring performance online.

An Experiment in Gender Norm Violation by College and University Students

SOCstudies

Norm Violations by Men

Wear fingernail polish
Needlepoint in public
Throw Tupperware party
Cry in public
Have pedicure
Apply to baby-sit
Shave body hair

Norm Violations by Women

Send men flowers
Spit in public
Use men's bathroom
Buy jockstrap
Talk knowledgeably about cars
Buy/chew tobacco
Open doors for men

Source: Nielsen et al. 2000:287.

While television consistently portrays youth, thinness, and beauty as essential to this ideal, it is far from alone in stereotyping women. Studies of children's books published in North America in the 1940s, 1950s, and 1960s found that females were significantly underrepresented in central roles and in illustrations. The books portrayed virtually all female characters as helpless, passive, incompetent, and in need of a strong male caretaker. Studies of picture books published from the 1970s through the 1990s found some improvement, but males still dominated the central roles. While authors portrayed males as a variety of characters, they tended to show females primarily in traditional roles, such as mother, grandmother, or volunteer —even if they also held nontraditional roles, such as working professional (Etaugh 2003).

The pervasiveness of these traditional gender roles extends even to unpaid labour as volunteers. Sociologists Thomas Rotolo and John Wilson (2007), drawing on a representative national sample of over 90,000 adults, found that men and women are equally likely to volunteer, but male volunteers from high-prestige occupations are much more likely than women to serve on boards and committees. An exception to this was men who work in traditionally "feminine" fields such as education and the fine arts. Female volunteers, in contrast, are disproportionately involved in direct charitable service as caregivers, nurturers, and food preparers. A significant exception is involvement in political campaigns, where gender roles are not pronounced among volunteers. In all areas of life, the activities of women and men are shaped and restricted by gender roles and expectations.

Men's Gender Roles How about stay-at-home fathers? Until recent decades, such an idea was unthinkable. Yet, in a nationwide U.S. survey conducted in 2002, 69 percent of respondents said that if one parent stays home with the children, it makes no difference whether that parent is the mother or the father. Only 30 percent thought that the mother should be the one to stay home. Although people's conceptions of gender roles are obviously changing, the fact is that the phenomenon

Going GLOBAL

Satisfaction with Body Weight and Shape

	Very/ somewhat satisfied ■+■	Very satisfied	Somewhat satisfied	Neither	Very/somewhat dissatisfied	DK/Refused
USA	55%	16%	39%	8%	36%	1%
Canada	69%	20%	49%	8%	23%	
UK	50%	16%	34%	14%	36%	
Italy	63%	12%	51%	19%	18%	
France	57%	2%	55%	18%	24%	1%
Netherlands	64%	21%	43%	11%	25%	
Portugal	65%	7%	58%	17%	18%	
Brazil	63%	9%	54%		37%	
Argentina	69%	26%	43%	4%	27%	
Japan	20%	3%	17%	20%	59%	1%

0%   20%   40%   60%   80%   100%

Source: Etcoff et al. 2004.

of men staying home to care for their children is still unusual. For every stay-at-home dad, there are 38 stay-at-home moms (Fields 2004a:11–12; Robison 2002).

While attitudes toward parenting may be changing, studies show little change in the traditional male gender role. Men's roles are socially constructed in much the same way as women's. Family, peers, and the media all influence how a boy or man comes to view his appropriate role in society. The male gender role includes proving one's masculinity at work and in sports—often by using force in dealing with others—as well as initiating and controlling sexual relations. In a recent study of stay-at-home fathers in Canada and Belgium, sociologists Andrea Doucet and Laura Merla (2007) found that these men maintain connections to traditional sources of masculine identity.

Males who do not conform to the socially constructed gender role often face criticism and even humiliation. Boys who deviate from expected patterns of masculinity risk being called a "chicken," "sissy," or "fag" even by fathers or brothers (Katz 1999). And grown men who pursue nontraditional occupations, such as preschool teaching or nursing, must constantly deal with others' misgivings and strange looks. In one study, interviewers found that such men frequently had to alter their behaviour in order to minimize others' negative reactions. One 35-year-old nurse reported that he had to claim he was "a carpenter or something like that" when he "went clubbing," because women weren't interested in getting to know a male nurse. The subjects made similar accommodations in casual exchanges with other men (Cross and Bagilhole 2002:215).

multiple masculinities The idea that men learn and play a full range of gender roles.

There may be a price to pay for such narrow conceptions of manhood. Boys who successfully adapt to cultural standards of masculinity may grow up to be inexpressive men who cannot share their feelings with others. They remain forceful and tough, but they are also closed and isolated. In fact, a small but growing body of scholarship suggests that these traditional gender roles may be putting men at a disadvantage. Today girls outdo boys in high school, grabbing a disproportionate share of the leadership positions, from valedictorian to class president to yearbook editor—everything, in short, except captain of the boys' athletic teams. And their advantage continues after high school. In the 1980s, girls in Canada became more likely than boys to attend university. By 2006, women accounted for over 58 percent of university students nationwide. Men continue to outnumber women at the doctoral level, but the gap is closing (Statistics Canada 2008c).

In the last 40 years, inspired in part by the contemporary feminist movement, increasing numbers of men in Canada have criticized the restrictive aspects of the traditional male gender role. Australian sociologist R. W. Connell (1987, 2002, 2005) has written about **multiple masculinities,** meaning that men learn and play a range of gender roles. These may include a nurturing-caring role, an effeminate-gay role, or their more traditional role. Sociologist Michael Kimmel gave voice to this broader conception of what it means to be a man when he was sitting with his newborn son in the park. When a woman came up to him and said that he was expressing his "feminine side," he responded, "I'm not expressing anything of the sort, ma'am. I'm being tender and loving and nurturing toward my child. As far as I can tell, I'm expressing my *masculinity*" (Kimmel 2004:290–91).

Ideas about "proper" masculine and feminine behaviour may contribute to gendered violence. As addressed in Chapter 6, the majority of violent crime is perpetrated by men, which our society seems to take for granted. In contrast, there is public shock and outrage when women commit violent acts. Why is this? Certainly our cultural expectations of gender are in evidence: men are expected to be aggressive and dominant, but women are not. Feminist theorists have argued that historically such beliefs informed legal and social responses to violence against women. (See Chapter 7 for a discussion of family violence.)

GENDER ACROSS CULTURES

We have already seen that our conception of gender shifts over time. We turn next to ways that gender varies across

> **Did You Know?**
>
> . . . 1995 was the first time unpaid work was included in the Canadian Census. In 2005, men reported spending 2.5 hours per day on unpaid household work; women reported spending 4.3 hours.

cultures. If biology alone determined gender categories, we would expect to find universal agreement about the definitions of the sexes. What we find instead is that not all cultures divide people into female and male in the same way.

Some cultures assume the existence of three or four gender categories. Judith Lorber (1994) notes that "male women," biological males who live for the most part as women, and "female men," biological females who live for the most part as men, can be found in various societies. "Female men" can be found in some African and Native American societies, where they take on male work and family roles. "Male women" include the *berdaches* of the Native Americans of the Great Plains and *hijras* of India. Michael Kimmel (2004) describes the *xanith* of Oman in the Middle East:

> They work as skilled domestic servants, dress in men's tunics (but in pastel shades more associated with feminine colors), and sell themselves in passive homosexual relationships. They are permitted to speak with women on the street (other men are prohibited). At sex-segregated public events, they sit with the women. However, they can change their minds. (p. 65)

These gender categories are a well-accepted part of their social lives. Individuals who fill them are not simply tolerated or viewed as deviant. The *berdache*, for example, have high status because they are thought to have special powers (Kimmel, 2004).

Beginning with the path-breaking work of Margaret Mead ([1935] 2001) and continuing through contemporary fieldwork, these scholars have shown that gender roles can vary greatly from one physical environment, economy, and political system to the next. Peggy Reeves Sanday's (2002, 2008) work in West Sumatra, Indonesia, for example, describes the 4-million-member Minangkabau society as one in which men and women are not competitors but partners for the common good. This society is characterized by a nurturing approach to the environment, blended with Islamic religious ethics. Women control the land through inheritance; in the event of a divorce, the ex-husband leaves with only his clothes. The larger community may be governed by men, women, or both men and women working together. Sanday's findings, together with Mead's, confirm the influential role of culture and socialization in gender-role differentiation.

FEMINIST THEORY

As noted in Chapter 1, "the" feminist perspective encompasses a number of different theoretical and practical orientations. While feminists share common goals—to ensure women are valued, fairly represented, and included in society, and to eradicate gender inequality—there is considerable diversity in how they think these goals are best achieved. For instance, *liberal* feminism encourages individual women to work within the current social structure, to strive for equal rights through political, legal, and social reforms. This approach is critiqued by *socialist* feminism, which argues that the very structure of capitalist society is inherently exploitive, and so in keeping with the vision of Karl Marx and Friedrich Engels, advocates a collective movement (revolution) that will bring about a more just society. *Radical* feminism goes even further, arguing that the elimination of gender altogether is a necessary precondition for an egalitarian society.

These are only a few of the multiple feminist approaches; there are many others, including (but not limited to) postmodern feminism, ecofeminism, Black feminism, multiracial feminism, and cultural feminism, and furthermore, each approach may have a number of subtypes within it. The diversity of feminist theory speaks to its goal of inclusion: many voices are represented.

> **instrumental leader** The person in the family who bears responsibility for the completion of tasks, focuses on more distant goals, and manages the external relationship between one's family and other social institutions.
> **expressive leader** The person in the family who bears responsibility for the maintenance of harmony and internal emotional affairs.

>> Gender and Inequality

The work of early sociologists such as Harriet Martineau and Charlotte Perkins Gilman highlighted the significance of gender inequality, placing particular emphasis upon the family structure as a key contributor to women's subordinate position in society. Yet in the 1950s, sociologists Talcott Parsons and Robert Bales (1955) argued that families needed both an instrumental and an expressive leader. The **instrumental leader** is the person in the family who bears responsibility for completion of tasks, focuses on more distant goals, and manages the external relationship between the family and other social institutions. The **expressive leader** is the person in the family who bears responsibility for the maintenance of harmony and internal emotional affairs. According to this functionalist theory, women's interest in expressive goals frees men for instrumental tasks, and vice versa. Women become naturally anchored in the family as wives, mothers, and household managers; men become anchored in the occupational world outside the home. This functionalist argument has its roots in the treatment of gender within classical sociology, which, as Rosalind Sydie points out, takes the form of a "dichotomized social universe" in which men and women are presented as fundamentally, *naturally* different (1987:5–10).

As a result of insights from feminist theorists and findings from further research, sociologists now argue that such separate abilities are not innate but are instead social constructs. The key sociological task is to analyze how

SOCthink

> > > Given that our understandings of gender vary across time and place, why are we so committed to the notion that gender differences are narrowly determined by biology?

gender expectations are created and maintained—for example, through gender-role socialization—and then to investigate the consequences of such constructs. We turn next to how resources are distributed based on gender.

WOMEN IN CANADA

Women in Canada have been "persons" for less than 100 years. During that time, great strides have been made, and many "firsts" have occurred—first female Member of Parliament, first female Chief Justice of the Supreme Court—yet many women still confront barriers to full participation in public life.

Labour Force Participation The labour market has opened up significantly since Betty Friedan published *The Feminine Mystique* in 1963. Today, millions of women—married or single, with or without children, pregnant or recently having given birth—are in the labour force. Overall, 58 percent of women aged 15 and over were in the paid labour force in 2006, compared to 42 percent 30 years earlier. Employment rates of women with children have risen dramatically in Canada, with 73 percent of all women with children under the age of 16 at home participating in paid employment. In 1976, only 39 percent of this group were employed. The growth is even greater among women with very young children: Where in 1976, only 28 percent of women with children under the age of three worked outside the home, by 2006 this number had jumped to 64 percent (Statistics Canada 2008e).

glass ceiling An invisible barrier that blocks the promotion of a qualified individual in a work environment because of the individual's gender, race, or ethnicity.

Still, women entering the job market find their options restricted in important ways. Particularly damaging is occupational segregation, or confinement to sex-typed "women's jobs." For example, as illustrated in the table, women are overrepresented in fields such as nursing and clerical support. Entering such sex-typed occupations often places women in "service" roles that parallel the traditional gender-role standard.

Women are underrepresented in occupations historically defined as "men's jobs," which often offer much greater financial rewards and prestige than women's jobs. For example, in 2006, women comprised approximately 47 percent of the paid labour force of Canada, yet they constituted less than 25 percent of senior management and science positions, and less than 7 percent of those employed in trades, transport, and construction. However, some gains have been made in selected occupations (see the table to the right).

When it comes to getting promotions, women sometimes encounter attitudinal or

Canadian Women's Participation in the Paid Labour Force, 1995–2005

Source: Statistics Canada, "The Core Age Labour Force," Catalogue no. 75-001-XIE.

organizational bias that prevents them from reaching their full potential. The term **glass ceiling** refers to an invisible barrier that blocks the promotion of a qualified individual in a work environment because of the individual's gender, race, or ethnicity. A 2007 study showed that women held less than 15 percent of the seats on the boards of directors of the 500 largest corporations in the United States. Furthermore, only 11 of those corporations had a female CEO while 489 had a male in that post (Catalyst 2007; Guerrera and Ward 2007).

Canadian Women in Selected Occupations, 2006

Women as Percentage of Total Employed in Occupation	
Underrepresented	
Trades, transport, and construction	6.9%
Natural and applied sciences	21.8%
Senior management	23.8%
Overrepresented	
Nursing, therapy, other health-related	86.5%
Clerical and administrative	69.1%
Cashiers	85.2%
Retail sales	58.6%
Roughly equally represented	
Business and finance	49.7%
Professional health occupations	53.5%
Tour and travel occupations	51.4%

Source: Statistics Canada, "Industry—North American Industry Classification System 2002, Occupational—National Occupational Classification for Statistics 2006," Catalogue no. 97-559-XCB2006023.

Income He works. She works. Both are physicians—a high-status occupation with considerable financial rewards. He makes $85,043. She makes $58,587.

These median earnings for physicians in Canada were released by Statistics Canada in 2008. The discrepancy by gender is typical of the findings of the Census Division's detailed study of occupations and income. Food service managers? He makes $31,040; she makes $22,158. Financial accountants? He earns $62,944; she earns $48,661. Statisticians compared earnings for more than 700 occupations ranging from dishwasher to chief executive. After adjusting for workers' age, education, and work experience, they came to an unmistakable conclusion: across the board, there is a substantial gender gap in the median earnings of full-time workers.

Men do not always earn more than women for doing the same work, but among the occupational categories studied by Statistics Canada, exceptions to this pattern are extremely rare.

What accounts for these wage gaps between men and women in the same occupation? The U.S. Census Bureau studied the following characteristics of men and women in the same occupation:

- Age and degree of formal education
- Marital status and the presence of children at home
- Specialization within the occupation (for example, family practice versus surgical practice)
- Years of work experience
- Hours worked per year

Taking all these factors into consideration reduced the pay gap between men and women by only 3 cents. Even taking

Actual and Projected Wage Gaps Between Male and Female Earnings

	1994	2001	2011	2031
Percentage gap between men's and women's earnings				
All ages	27.5	29.2	26.5	21.9
Age 25–44	20.9	21.3	17.6	16.9
Age 45–64	42.9	43.6	38.8	29.0

Source: Kelly Rathie, "Male Versus Female Earnings—Is the Gender Gap Converging?" *Economist Ltd.*, Spring 2002, vol 7, no 1

such factors into account, women still earned 80 cents for every dollar earned by men. In sum, the disparity in pay between men and women cannot be explained by pointing to women's career choices (Government Accountability Office 2003; Weinberg 2004, 2007).

While women are at a disadvantage in male-dominated occupations, the same is not true for men in female-dominated occupations. Sociologist Michelle Budig (2002) examined a national database containing career information on more than 12,000 men, collected over the course of 15 years. She found that men were uniformly advantaged in female occupations. Although male nurses, elementary school teachers, and librarians may experience some scorn in the larger society, they get paid more than women in those jobs, and they are more likely to be encouraged to become administrators. Observers of the labour force have termed

Did You Know?

... **Married mothers spend about twice as much time per week on child care and housework as married fathers. Mothers spend about 13 hours per week on child care and 19 hours on housework compared to 7 and 10, respectively, for fathers.**

right to control one's body—in particular, reproductive rights. In 1988, after decades of debate among the public and within Parliament, the Supreme Court of Canada struck down Canada's abortion law. Canada is now one of a small number of countries without a law governing abortion; it is treated as a medical procedure in accordance with provincial and medical regulations.

As more and more women became aware of sexist attitudes and practices—including attitudes they themselves had accepted through socialization into traditional gender roles—they began to challenge male dominance. A sense of sisterhood, much like the class consciousness that Marx hoped would emerge in the proletariat, became evident. Individual women identified their interests with women as a whole, and they rejected the principle that their happiness depended upon their acceptance of submissive and subordinate roles.

FEMINISM TODAY

Current national surveys show that while women generally endorse feminist positions, they do not necessarily accept the label "feminist." In 1987, 57 percent of U.S. women considered themselves feminists; the proportion had dropped to about 25 percent by 2001. Both women and men prefer to express their views on complex issues such as abortion, sexual harassment, pornography, and welfare individually rather than under the banner of feminism. Still, feminism is very much alive in the growing acceptance of women in nontraditional roles and even the basic acknowledgment that a married mother not only can work outside the home but perhaps belongs in the labour force. A majority of women say that, given the choice, they would prefer to work outside the home rather than stay home and take care of a house and family, and about one-quarter of women prefer "Ms." to "Miss" or "Mrs." (Feminist Majority Foundation 2007; J. Robison 2002).

While women still face inequality, much has changed. In 2008, for example, U.S. Senator Hillary Clinton came extremely close to securing the Democratic nomination for president and Sarah Palin was selected as Republican John McCain's running mate. While there are still people who believe that women are not suited to such positions of power, they are in the minority. Our dominant cultural values now suggest that we believe women should not be denied opportunity based on their sex. The only way for these values to be realized in practice is if people continue to fight to make them a reality. Another group which has had to fight against stereotypes

Hot or Not?

Does the label "feminist" have positive or negative connotations in today's society?

waves, the third wave of feminism is sometimes characterized as more individualistic in approach, and as lacking cohesion. But those active in the third wave contend that the movement has broadened to allow for expanded areas of social concern, and to accommodate multiple voices and viewpoints. Their global perspective includes challenging universal definitions of femininity, fighting against racism and homophobia, and embracing diverse identities.

Of the many important fights feminists have fought on behalf of women, the most fundamental involves the

Did You Know?

... Despite facing criminal charges, death threats, and attacks on his medical clinics, Dr. Henry Morgentaler has remained a steadfast supporter of women's rights to abortion for over 40 years. In 2008 he was awarded the prestigious Order of Canada. An Ipsos Reid poll found that 65 percent of Canadians supported awarding him this honour.

and social expectations is the elderly. As we will examine in the rest of this chapter, aging presents unique challenges, but also opportunities.

>> Aging and Society

In addition to *The Feminine Mystique,* Betty Friedan (1993) wrote another book later in life in which she addressed many of the stereotypes about aging. In *The Fountain of Age,* she argued that, just as was the case with gender, cultural presuppositions related to aging were limiting people's opportunity. In so doing, she contributed to the movement to change our cultural perceptions about what it means to be elderly and opened up more opportunities for older citizens.

Like gender stratification, age stratification varies from culture to culture. One society may treat older people with reverence, while another sees them as unproductive and "difficult." The Sherpas—a Tibetan-speaking Buddhist people in Nepal—live in a culture that idealizes old age. Almost all elderly members of the Sherpa culture own their homes, and most are in relatively good physical condition. Typically, older Sherpas value their independence and

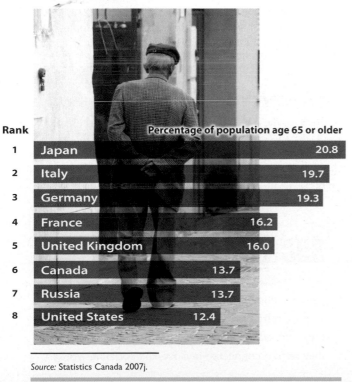

Going **GLOBAL**

World's "Oldest" G-8 Countries Versus Canada, 2006

Rank		Percentage of population age 65 or older
1	Japan	20.8
2	Italy	19.7
3	Germany	19.3
4	France	16.2
5	United Kingdom	16.0
6	Canada	13.7
7	Russia	13.7
8	United States	12.4

Source: Statistics Canada 2007j.

prefer not to live with their children. Among the Fulani of Africa, however, older men and women move to the edge of the family homestead. Since that is where people are buried, the elderly sleep over their own graves, for they are viewed socially as already dead (M. Goldstein and Beall 1981; Stenning 1958; Tonkinson 1978).

Understandably, all societies have some system of age stratification that associates certain social roles with distinct periods in life. Some of this age differentiation seems inevitable; it would make little sense to send young children off to war or to expect older citizens to handle physically demanding tasks, such as loading freight at shipyards. However, as is the case with stratification by gender, in Canada, age stratification goes far beyond the physical constraints on human beings at different ages.

"Being old" is a master status that commonly overshadows all others in this country. Once people have been labelled "old," the designation has a major impact on how others perceive them, and even on how they view themselves. Negative stereotypes of the elderly contribute to their position as a minority group subject to discrimination. There is one crucial difference between older people and other subordinate groups, such as racial and ethnic minorities or women: All of us who live long enough will eventually assume the ascribed status of older person.

Around the world, there are more than 453 million people age 65 and over, representing about 7 percent of the world's population. By 2050, one in three people will be over 65. In an important sense, the aging of the world's population represents a major success story that unfolded during the latter 20th century. Through the efforts of both national governments and international agencies, many societies have drastically reduced the incidence of disease and the rate of death. Consequently, these nations—especially the industrialized countries of Europe and North America—now have increasingly higher proportions of older members (Haub 2005; He et al. 2005; Kinsella and Phillips 2005; Vidal 2004).

>> Perspectives on Aging

Aging is one important aspect of socialization throughout the life course—the lifelong process through which an individual learns the cultural norms and values of a particular society. There are no clear-cut definitions for different

periods of the aging cycle in Canada. In the recent past, old age has been regarded as beginning at 65, which corresponds to the retirement age for many workers, but not everyone in Canada accepts that definition. With increases in life expectancy, writers are beginning to refer to people in their 60s as the "young old," to distinguish them from those in their 80s and beyond—the "old old."

The particular problems of the elderly have become the focus of a specialized field of research and inquiry known as **gerontology**—the study of the sociological and psychological aspects of aging and the problems of the aged. It originated in the 1930s, as an increasing number of social scientists became aware of the plight of the elderly.

Gerontologists rely heavily on sociological principles and theories to explain the impact of aging on the individual and society. They also draw on psychology, anthropology, physical education, counselling, and medicine in their study of the aging process. Three perspectives on aging—disengagement theory, activity theory, and age discrimination—arise out of these studies.

gerontology The study of the sociological and psychological aspects of aging and the problems of the aged.

disengagement theory A theory of aging that suggests that society and the aging individual mutually sever many of their relationships.

SOCthink

> > > What do you think about getting old? Can you picture yourself at age 65? What might your life look like?

DISENGAGEMENT THEORY

After studying elderly people in good health and relatively comfortable economic circumstances, Elaine Cumming and William Henry (1961) introduced their **disengagement theory,** which implicitly suggests that society and the aging individual mutually sever many of their relationships. Highlighting the significance of social order in society, disengagement theory emphasizes that passing social roles on from one generation to another ensures social stability.

According to this functionalist theory, the approach of death forces people to drop most of their social roles—including those of worker, volunteer, spouse, hobby enthusiast, and even reader. Younger members of society then take on these functions. The aging person, it is held, withdraws into an increasing state of inactivity while preparing for death. At the same time, society withdraws from the elderly by segregating them residentially (in retirement homes and communities), educationally (in programs designed solely for senior citizens), and recreationally (in senior citizens' centres). Implicit in disengagement theory is the view that society should help older people to withdraw from their accustomed social roles.

Since it was first outlined more than four decades ago, disengagement theory has generated considerable controversy. Some gerontologists have objected to the implication that older people want to be ignored and put away—and even more to the idea that they should be encouraged to withdraw from meaningful social roles. Critics of disengagement theory insist that society forces the elderly into an involuntary and painful withdrawal from the paid labour force and from meaningful social relationships. Rather than voluntarily seeking to disengage, older employees find themselves pushed out of their jobs—in many instances, even before they are entitled to maximum retirement benefits (Boaz 1987).

People who are elderly have been fighting that trend, and postretirement employment has been increasing in recent decades. By 2009, mandatory retirement had been eliminated in most provinces and territories of Canada (though some exceptions and provisions remain). Many people express both the desire and financial necessity to keep working. Increasing numbers are moving into "bridge jobs"—employment that spans the period between the end of their career and their retirement. Unfortunately, the elderly can easily be victimized in such bridge jobs. Psychologist Kathleen Christensen (1990), warning of "bridges over troubled water," emphasizes that older employees do not want to end their working days as minimum-wage jobholders engaged in activities unrelated to their careers (Doeringer 1990; Hayward et al. 1987).

ACTIVITY THEORY

In 2006, at the age of 85, Hazel McCallion was elected to her 11th consecutive term as mayor of Mississauga, Ontario. Her hard work and forthright attitude have earned her the affectionate nickname of "Hurricane Hazel." In office since 1978, McCallion shows no signs of slowing down.

SOCthink

> > > Consider people over the age of 65 that you have known well, such as grandparents or great-grandparents. How did their lifestyle change after they crossed that age barrier? To what extent did they remain connected in close-knit social networks?

How important is it for older people to stay actively involved, whether at a job or in other pursuits? A tragic disaster in Chicago in 1995 showed that it can be a matter of life and death. An intense heat wave lasting more than a week—with a heat index exceeding 46 degrees Celsius on

5 Movies on GENDER AND AGE

Thelma and Louise
Two women have had enough.

Transamerica
A male-to-female transsexual travels the country with her son.

Away From Her
A marriage is tested by Alzheimer's disease.

Cocoon
Florida retirees meet E.T.

Magnolia
A man holds motivational seminars on masculinity.

two consecutive days—resulted in 733 heat-related deaths. About three-fourths of the deceased were 65 or older. Subsequent analysis showed that older people who lived alone had the highest risk of dying, suggesting that social contacts and support networks for the elderly literally help to save lives (Klinenberg 2002; Schaefer 1998a).

Often seen as the opposite of disengagement theory, **activity theory** suggests that those elderly people who remain active and socially involved will be best adjusted. Proponents of this perspective acknowledge that a 70-year-old person may not have the ability or desire to perform various social roles that he or she had at age 40. Yet they contend that old people have essentially the same need for social interaction as any other group.

The improved health of older people—sometimes overlooked by social scientists—has strengthened the arguments

of activity theorists. Illness and chronic disease are no longer quite the scourge of the elderly that they once were. The recent emphasis on fitness, the availability of better medical care, greater control of infectious diseases, and the reduction in the number of fatal strokes and heart attacks have combined to reduce the traumas of growing old.

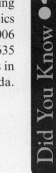

Accumulating medical research also points to the importance of remaining socially involved. Among those who decline in their mental capacities later in life, deterioration is most rapid in those who withdraw from social relationships and activities. Fortunately, the aged are finding new ways to remain socially engaged, as evidenced by their increasing use of the Internet, especially to keep in touch with family and friends (Korczyk 2002).

Admittedly, many activities open to the elderly involve unpaid labour, for which younger adults may receive salaries. Unpaid elderly workers include hospital volunteers (versus aides and orderlies), drivers for charities such as the Red Cross (versus chauffeurs), tutors (as opposed to teachers), and craftspeople for charity bazaars (as opposed to carpenters and dressmakers). However, some companies have recently begun programs to hire retirees for full- or part-time work.

Though disengagement theory suggests that older people find satisfaction in withdrawal from society, conveniently receding into the background and allowing the next generation to take over, proponents of activity theory view such withdrawal as harmful to both the elderly and society. Activity theorists focus on the potential contributions of older people to the maintenance of society. In their opinion, aging citizens will feel satisfied only when they can be useful and productive in society's terms—primarily by working for wages (Civic Ventures 1999; Crosnoe and Elder, Jr., 2002; Dowd 1980; Quadagno 2005).

activity theory A theory of aging that suggests that those elderly people who remain active and socially involved will be best adjusted.
ageism Prejudice and discrimination based on a person's age.

AGEISM AND DISCRIMINATION

Physician Robert Butler (1990) became concerned 30 years ago when he learned that a housing development near his home in metropolitan Washington, D.C., barred the elderly. Butler coined the term **ageism** to refer to prejudice and discrimination based on a person's age. For example, we may choose to assume that someone cannot handle a rigorous job because he is "too old," or we may refuse to give someone a job with authority because she is "too young."

In order to more fully understand issues regarding aging, it is important to also consider the impact of social structure

on patterns of aging. Critics argue that neither disengagement nor activity theory answers the question of *why* social interaction must change or decrease in old age. The low status of older people is seen in prejudice and discrimination against them, in age segregation, and in unfair job practices—none of which are directly addressed by either disengagement or activity theory. In addition, these theories often ignore the impact of social class on the lives of the elderly.

The privileged upper class generally enjoys better health and vigour and has less likelihood of dependency in old age. Affluence cannot forestall aging indefinitely, but it can soften the economic hardships people face in later years. Although pension plans, retirement packages, and insurance benefits may be developed to assist older people, those whose wealth allows them access to investment funds can generate the greatest income for their later years.

In contrast, the working class often faces greater health hazards and a greater risk of disability; aging is particularly difficult for those who suffer job-related injuries or illnesses. Working-class people also depend more heavily on Old Age and Canada Pension benefits. And during inflationary times, their relatively fixed incomes from these sources barely keep pace with the escalating costs of food, housing, utilities, and other necessities (Atchley and Barusch 2004).

POPSOC

In 2002, the U.S. Senate Special Committee on Aging convened a panel on the media's portrayal of older people and sharply criticized media and marketing executives for bombarding audiences with negative images of the aged. How many characters on top TV shows today can you think of who are over 65? How does that compare to the number of characters you can think of who are under 30?

>> Aging in Canada

Just as women face institutional discrimination because they are female, people who are elderly face discrimination because they are old. While these trends may change as the average age of the population increases, we still see a pattern of unequal treatment.

CANADA "GROWS OLDER"

Mary Arnott swims in the Etobicoke Olympium pool twice a week, enjoys parties, and follows the Blue Jays. It sounds like a fairly unremarkable life, but consider this: Mary is 99 years old. Still living independently, she is one of a growing number of Canadians who are changing the way we think about "old age" (Kopun 2009). At age 82, Lenore Schaefer decided to bring her dancing shoes out of retirement and enter the world of competitive ballroom dancing. Having been a successful dancer in her youth, she decided it was time. She competed for the rest of her life, winning over 200 awards. When she was 101, she won a dance competition, leading to her appearance on the *Tonight Show with Jay Leno*. Stories such as Mary's and Lenore's are becoming less uncommon in our society (Himes 2001; Rimer 1998).

While Canada's population is currently younger than those of most of the G8 countries (see "Going Global" on page 275), a trend of aging has already begun: one in seven Canadians is a senior citizen. In 2006, the number of seniors in Canada reached 4 million, with 13.7 percent of the population being 65 years or older. Of these, the "old" seniors—those 85 years of age and over—are the fastest growing category. Based on current figures, it is projected that population aging will accelerate in 2011, when the first baby boom cohort reaches the age of 65, and this rapid growth will continue for at least 20 years. By 2031, seniors would almost double their current proportion, comprising between 23 and 25 percent of the total population.

Why is Canada growing older? First, at approximately 1.5 children per woman, the fertility rate has been below replacement level (2.1) for several decades. Second, life expectancy

"Good news, honey—seventy is the new fifty."

has risen appreciably, with men now living on average 77.7 years, and women an average of 82.5 years. Accordingly, more than half of Canadian seniors (56 percent) are female.

This gender pattern is also seen among the Aboriginal population, with women living longer than men. However, the life expectancy of Aboriginal people is lower than that of members of the general population. This gap is most evident among the Inuit population: in 2001, compared against the rest of Canada, the life spans of Inuit women and men were shorter by 11 and 15 years respectively (CBC News 2008). Provincial and territorial differences in aging patterns are also evident.

The aging of Canada is a phenomenon that demands attention by social scientists, advocates for the elderly, and government policy makers. Instead of worrying about low voter turnout among young people, politicians would do well to court the votes of older people, since they are the most consistent and active voters.

On a local scale, one of the more recent residential patterns we find among senior citizens has been the tendency to congregate together. Many do not reside in nursing homes or planned retirement communities. Instead, they congregate in areas that gradually become informal centres for senior citizens. Social scientists have dubbed such areas "naturally occurring retirement communities" (NORCs). NORCs can be as small as a single apartment building or as large as a neighbourhood in a big city. The larger they are, the more likely they are to attract business establishments that cater to the elderly, such as pharmacies, medical supply outlets, and small restaurants, making them even more attractive to older citizens.

The largest known NORC in the United States is Co-op City, a high-rise apartment complex in the Bronx, north of Manhattan. Built in the 1960s, the huge community was meant to house low-income workers and their families in apartments that were relatively spacious by New York City's standards. More than three decades later, many of the buildings' first residents are still there, "aging in place," as the social workers say. Today, roughly 8000 of Co-op City's 50,000 residents are 65 or older (A. Feuer 2002; Lansprey 1995; Perry 2001). In contrast to the "natural" emergence of NORCs, some cities are recognizing the economic benefit of marketing themselves as retirement communities. A successful example of this is the town of Elliot Lake, in Northern Ontario, which reinvented itself as a retirement community when its main industry (uranium mining) shut down in the 1980s.

WEALTH AND INCOME

While there is variation in wealth among the nation's older population, as a group they are on average less well-off financially than most other groups. Yet the typical senior citizen enjoys a standard of living that is much higher now than at any point in the nation's past. Class differences among the elderly remain evident but tend to narrow somewhat. Those older people who enjoyed middle-class incomes while younger tend to remain better off after retirement, but less so than before (Denise Smith and Tillipman 2000).

To some extent, older people owe their overall improved standard of living to a greater accumulation of wealth—in the form of home ownership, private pensions, and other financial

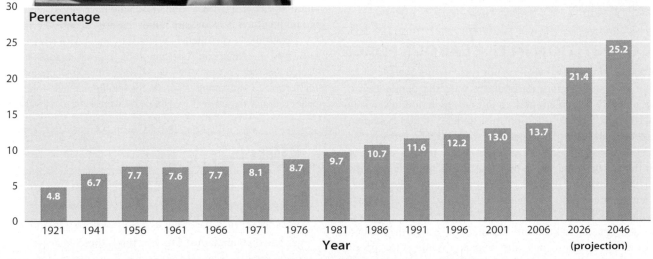

Actual and Projected Growth of the Elderly Population of Canada

Source: Statistics Canada, "Portrait of the Canadian Population in 2006, by Age and Sex, 2006 Census," Catalogue no. 97-551-XIE.

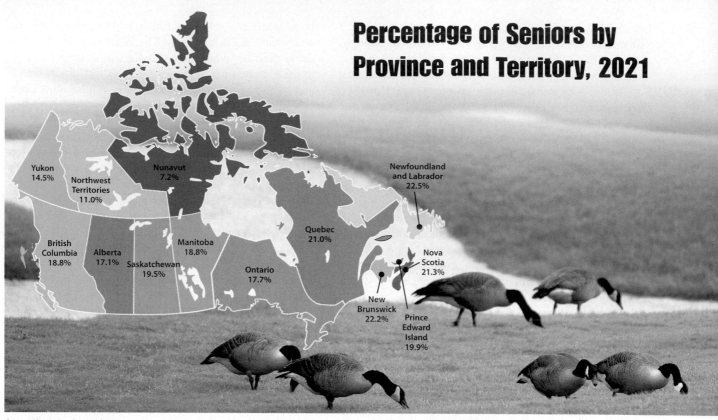

Percentage of Seniors by Province and Territory, 2021

- Yukon 14.5%
- Northwest Territories 11.0%
- Nunavut 7.2%
- Newfoundland and Labrador 22.5%
- British Columbia 18.8%
- Alberta 17.1%
- Saskatchewan 19.5%
- Manitoba 18.8%
- Ontario 17.7%
- Quebec 21.0%
- Nova Scotia 21.3%
- New Brunswick 22.2%
- Prince Edward Island 19.9%

Source: Statistics Canada 2007j.

assets. But the maturation of the public pension system has also been a significant factor. Indeed, pension plans (public and private) and individual registered retirement savings plans account for approximately 75 percent of income among the senior population (Health Canada 2002). As conflict and feminist theorists have noted, members of groups who face a greater likelihood of income inequality earlier in their lives—such as women, Aboriginal peoples, and members of visible minorities—continue to do so when they are older. For instance, women who are now elderly lived through eras in which working for pay outside the home was discouraged for women. As a result, many older women are now forced to rely on sources of government assistance, whereas older men are more likely to have employment-related income sources such as company pensions.

COMPETITION IN THE LABOUR FORCE

Participation in paid work is not typical after the age of 65, but that is changing, particularly with the elimination of mandatory retirement and an aging population that wishes to remain "useful." In 2005, just under 320,000 Canadians aged 65 and over participated in the paid labour force (Statistics Canada 2007m). Level of education has a significant influence on labour force participation among seniors: those with a university degree are eight times more likely to participate in the paid labour force than those with eight years or less of formal schooling. As the proportion of seniors with post-secondary education continues to grow, their labour force participation may also expand. While some people view these workers as experienced contributors to the labour

force, others see them as "job stealers," a biased judgment similar to that directed against illegal immigrants. This mistaken belief not only intensifies age conflict but leads to age discrimination (Gendell 2008).

Although firing people simply because they are old contravenes the Canadian Human Rights Act and provincial human rights codes, courts have upheld the right to lay off older workers for economic reasons. Critics contend that, later, the same firms hire young, cheaper workers to replace experienced older workers. When economic growth began to slow in 2001 and companies cut back on their workforces, the number of complaints of age bias rose sharply as older workers began to suspect they were bearing a disproportionate share of the layoffs. In the current recession, older workers are being pressured to accept "buyouts," and those who have already retired are finding their pensions are not necessarily secure.

A controlled experiment conducted by the AARP (formerly known as the American Association of Retired Persons) confirmed that older people often face discrimination when applying for jobs. Comparable résumés for two applicants—one 57 years old and the other 32 years old—were sent to 775 large

SOCthink

> > > The Hooters restaurant chain, known for hiring only physically attractive young women to work as servers, has been accused of both age and gender discrimination. Do you think these charges are justified?

firms and employment agencies around the United States. In situations for which positions were actually available, the younger applicant received a favourable response 43 percent of the time. By contrast, the older applicant received favourable responses only 17 percent of the time. One Fortune 500 corporation asked the younger applicant for more information while informing the older applicant that no appropriate positions were open (Bendick et al. 1993; Neumark 2008).

Perhaps in part due to the rising numbers of people who continue to work, some companies have come to realize that older workers can be an asset. One study found that older workers can be retrained in new technologies, have lower rates of absenteeism than younger employees, and are often more effective salespeople. The study focused on two corporations based in the United States (the hotel chain Days Inns of America and the holding company Travelers Corporation of Hartford) and a British retail chain—all of which have long-term experience in hiring workers age 50 or over. Indeed, more and more corporations are actively trying to recruit retired people, recognizing their comparatively lower turnover rates and often superior work performance (Freudenheim 2005; Telsch 1991).

DEATH AND DYING

In the film *The Bucket List*, Morgan Freeman and Jack Nicholson play the two main characters, who are diagnosed with terminal cancer and have less than one year to live. They make a list of all the things they would like to do before they

Gerontologist Richard Kalish (1985) laid out some of the issues people must face in order to have a "good death." These included completing unfinished business, such as settling insurance and inheritance matters; restoring harmony to social relationships and saying farewell to friends and family; dealing with medical needs; and making funeral plans and other arrangements for survivors. In accomplishing these tasks, the dying person actively contributes to smooth intergenerational transitions, role continuity, compliance with medical procedures, and minimal disruption of the social system, despite the loss of a loved one.

> First you are young; then you are middle-aged; then you are old; then you are wonderful.
>
> Lady Diana Cooper

"kick the bucket." On the list are things they had never dared to do, such as travelling the world and sky-diving, but it also includes reconciling broken relationships.

Until recently, death was a taboo topic in North America. Death represents a fundamental disruption that cannot be undone, so we often find it easier to live with a sense of denial about our mortality. In the words of sociologist Peter Berger, "Death presents society with a formidable problem . . . because it threatens the basic assumptions of order on which society rests" (1969:23). However, psychologist Elisabeth Kübler-Ross (1969), through her pioneering book *On Death and Dying,* greatly encouraged open discussion of the process of dying. Drawing on her work with 200 cancer patients, Kübler-Ross identified five stages of the experience: denial, anger, bargaining, depression, and finally acceptance.

While we may still be uncomfortable with the topic, *The Bucket List*'s portrayal of a "good death" represents one of the ways we have become more open about it.

We have also begun to create institutions to facilitate our wishes for a good death. The practice of **hospice care,** introduced in England in the 1960s, is devoted to easing this final transition. Hospice workers seek to improve the quality of a dying person's last days by offering comfort and by helping the person to remain at home, or in a homelike setting at a hospital or other special facility, until the end. Over the past 25 years, voluntary hospices have been established across Canada, particularly in British Columbia and Ontario, where there are more than 280 communities with hospices (www.pilgrimshospice.ca).

Recent studies in Canada suggest additional ways in which people have broken through the historical taboos about death. For example, bereavement practices—once highly structured—are becoming increasingly varied and

hospice care Treatment of the terminally ill in their own homes, or in special hospital units or other facilities, with the goal of helping them to die comfortably, without pain.

therapeutic. More and more people are actively addressing the inevitability of death by making wills, leaving "living wills" (health care proxies that explain their feelings about the use of life support equipment), donating organs, and providing instructions for family members about funerals, cremations, and burials. Given medical and technological advances and increasingly open discussion and negotiation regarding death and dying, it is possible that good deaths may become a social norm in Canada (La Ganga 1999; J. Riley 1992).

Sociology often confronts us with things that can make us uncomfortable. Whether that is gender inequality, age inequality, or even death, the point of doing so is a more complete understanding of what we do and why we do it. Such knowledge can lead us to new and better practices that provide greater understanding, fairness, equality, and opportunity. Through practising the sociological imagination, as Betty Friedan did in the case of gender and age, we can make the world a better place.

>> Summary

We can learn a lot about a society by looking at how it treats its members on the basis of gender and age. Who is valued and treated with respect? Who has better employment opportunities and is commensurately rewarded for their work? Who is most vulnerable to violence and abuse? Canadians must consider these questions honestly if we are to work toward a more just society.

get involved!

Resist! There are growing resources out there that encourage new ways to attain healthier body images for women and men. The website of the organization About-Face (www.about-face.org) brings public awareness to negative stereotypes of women in the media. Visit the site and explore the lists of "winners" and "offenders" in the media.

For REVIEW

I. How has opportunity for women in Canada changed over time?
  • In the 1950s, women's primary roles were wife and mother. Since that time, largely due to the efforts of the second wave of the women's movement, their labour force participation and income have risen significantly.

II. To what extent does gender still shape access to resources?
  • Women continue to be paid less than men for similar work, tend to be segregated into a narrower range of female-dominated occupations, bear greater responsibility for housework, and are underrepresented as elected officials.

III. How do sociologists approach the study of aging?
  • There is a debate about the degree to which old age represents a stage during which elderly people are expected to fade away, making way for the next generation, versus a stage when they are denied opportunities and face discrimination. Increased willingness to talk about death shows that we are becoming more open about discussing aging and its consequences.

Thinking CRITICALLY...

1. In what ways do you "do gender?"
2. What is beneficial and problematic about mandatory retirement? Have your employment opportunities been affected by its elimination?
3. Consider the portrayal of women and the elderly in popular culture. What similar messages or patterns do you detect?

Pop Quiz

1. Both males and females are physically capable of learning to cook and sew, yet most Western societies determine that women should perform these tasks. This illustrates the operation of
   a. gender roles.
   b. sociobiology.
   c. homophobia.
   d. comparable worth.

2. An important element shaping traditional views of proper "masculine" and "feminine" behaviour is fear of homosexuality. This fear, along with accompanying prejudice, is referred to as
   a. lesbianism.
   b. femme fatalism.
   c. homophobia.
   d. claustrophobia.

3. What is the expression used when claiming that gender for men is not narrowly limited to traditional conceptions of masculinity?
   a. disengagement
   b. gender modification
   c. sex
   d. multiple masculinities

4. Cross-cultural research by anthropologists Margaret Mead and Peggy Reeves Sanday has shown that
   a. biology is the most important factor in determining the social roles of males and females.
   b. cultural conditioning is the most important factor in defining the social roles of males and females.
   c. biology and cultural conditioning have an equal impact in determining the social roles of males and females.
   d. biology and cultural conditioning have a negligible impact in determining the social roles of males and females.

5. As of 2006, what percentage of adult women were in the labour force?
   a. 28 percent
   b. 41 percent
   c. 58 percent
   d. 76 percent

6. In Canada, abortion is currently
   a. legal under federal law.
   b. considered a medical procedure.
   c. illegal.
   d. a and b above.

7. The expression "second shift" refers to
   a. doing the emotional work of maintaining family relationships.
   b. maintaining the household including housework in addition to a job outside the home.
   c. having a work shift ranging approximately between 4:00 P.M. and midnight.
   d. doing paid labour at the workplace.

8. The primary accomplishment of the first wave of the women's movement was
   a. equal pay legislation.
   b. gaining the right to an abortion.
   c. earning the right to nondiscrimination in the workplace.
   d. winning the right to vote.

9. Which theory argues that elderly people have essentially the same need for social interaction as any other group and that those who remain active and socially involved will be best adjusted?
   a. disengagement theory
   b. institutional discrimination theory
   c. activity theory
   d. ageism theory

10. The two primary factors behind Canada's aging population are
    a. high immigration and lowered life expectancy.
    b. increased life expectancy and low fertility rate.
    c. low fertility rate and low immigration.
    d. paid labour force participation and increased life expectancy.

1. (a); 2. (c); 3. (d); 4. (b); 5. (c); 6. (b); 7. (b); 8. (d); 9. (c); 10. (b)

of a dominant group; distinct physical or cultural traits; ascribed status (also the case for a dominant group—see Chapter 5); a strong sense of group solidarity; and a tendency toward in-group marriage (see discussions of exogamy and endogamy in Chapter 7). The term "minority" can be misleading: it does not necessarily correspond to actual numbers within the population. That is, even if a group comprises a numeric majority, they may be a minority group due to their relative lack of power in the society.

Race and ethnicity historically have served as markers of minority group status. The term **racial group** describes a group that is set apart from others because of physical differences that have taken on social significance. Whites, African Canadians, and Asian Canadians are all considered racial groups in Canada. Although the construct of race emphasizes the significance of external physical differences, it is the culture of a particular society that identifies and attaches social significance to those differences. An **ethnic group** is one that is set apart from others primarily because of its national origin or distinctive cultural patterns. In Canada, examples of ethnic groups are Jews, Polish Canadians, and Portuguese Canadians, to name only a few. As a nation comprised primarily of immigrants and their descendants, Canada has a significant amount of racial and ethnic diversity.

racial group A group that is set apart from others because of physical differences that have taken on social significance.
ethnic group A group that is set apart from others primarily because of its national origin or distinctive cultural patterns.
racial formation A sociohistorical process in which racial categories are created, inhibited, transformed, and destroyed.

RACE

We tend to think of race as strictly a biological category, but researchers for the Human Genome Project (HGP), who mapped the entire genetic code, concluded that race as we understand it does not exist. Craig Venter (2000), one of the project's lead scientists, declared in his presentation of the HGP results that "the concept of race has no genetic or scientific basis," and in a later interview, he said, "Race is a social concept, not a scientific one" (Angier 2000). The researchers found that all humans share the same basic genetic material, and physical manifestations such as skin colour represent different combinations, in greater or lesser degrees, of the same shared genes.

When it comes to genetic variation, the biological differences within what we think of as racial groups are actually greater than the differences between those groups. Genetic researchers Luca Cavalli-Sforza, Paolo Menozzi,

and Alberto Piazza (1994), for example, point out that people from northeast China are genetically closer to Europeans, Inuit, and North American Indians than they are to people from south China (p. 78). In fact, the overall degree of human genetic variation is quite small when compared with genetic variation among other large mammals—due primarily to the fact that communities of human beings have always interacted, even across great distances (MacEachern 2003:20).

Social Construction of Race The racial categories that we typically take for granted grow out of sociocultural traditions and historical experiences that are specific to various groups. If we look cross-culturally, we see that different groups define racial categories in different ways at different times. Each society defines which differences are important while ignoring other characteristics that could serve as a basis for social differentiation. In Canada, we see differences in both skin colour and hair colour. Yet people learn informally that differences in skin colour have a dramatic social and political meaning while differences in hair colour do not.

When observing skin colour, many people in North America tend to lump others rather casually into the traditional categories of "Black," "White," and "Asian." More subtle differences in skin colour often go unnoticed. In many nations of Central America and South America, by contrast, people recognize colour gradients on a continuum from light to dark skin colour. Brazil has approximately 40 colour groupings, while in other countries people may be described as "Mestizo Honduran," "Mulatto Colombian," or "African Panamanian." What we see as "obvious" differences, then, are subject to each society's social definitions.

Racial definitions are crystallized through what Michael Omi and Howard Winant (1994) have called **racial formation**—a sociohistorical process in which racial categories are created, inhibited, transformed, and destroyed. In this process, those who have power define groups of people according to a racist social structure. The Canadian government's system of classification reduces the diverse and unique tribes of Aboriginal peoples into three groups: Indians, Métis, and Inuit. Through the Indian Act, Indians are

SOCthink

> > > To what extent does the race you belong to shape opportunities you face? How conscious are you of your race and its impact?

somehow "natural." This can happen through the use of **stereotypes,** for example, which are unreliable generalizations about all members of a group that do not recognize individual differences within the group. Anthropologist Ashley Montagu (1997), who was at the forefront of the movement to use scientific evidence to demonstrate the socially constructed nature of race, suggested that "the very word (*race*) is racist; that the idea of 'race,' implying the existence of significant biologically determined mental differences rendering some populations inferior to others, is wholly false" (p. 31).

Multiple Identities Determining the background of Canada's population is a complicated endeavour. In the 2006 Census, almost 13 million people in Canada (slightly more than 41 percent of the population) reported having more than one ethnic origin. Individuals' methods of self-identification may differ from official categories; hence the inclusion of "Other" as an option on many forms. Racial categories have themselves varied over time, providing additional support for the notion that our definition of race is not so much determined by biology as it is subject to historical and cultural forces.

The historical approach to racial classification of including only a handful of choices is part of a long history that dictates single-race identities. This move by the

> **stereotype** An unreliable generalization about all members of a group that does not recognize individual differences within the group.

further differentiated as Status and Non-Status. The categories are themselves indicative of earlier times: "Indian" is not generally used as a term today; "First Nations peoples" is more widely accepted. While First Nations peoples have their own methods of determining who is a band member, the governmental criteria—despite being elaborate—is not as inclusive. The extent to which and frequency with which peoples are subject to racial formation is such that no one escapes it.

An American example of racial formation from the 1800s involves what was known as the "one-drop rule." If a person had even a single drop of "Black blood"—that is, if any of his or her ancestors, no matter how remote, were Black—society defined and viewed that person as Black, even if he or she appeared to be White. Clearly, race had social significance, enough so that White legislators established official standards about who was "Black" and who was "White."

The one-drop rule was a vivid example of the social construction of race—the process by which people come to define a group as a race based in part on physical characteristics, but also on historical, cultural, and economic factors. For example, in the 1800s, immigrant groups such as Italian Americans and Irish Americans were seen not as "White" but as members of another race who were not necessarily trustworthy (Ignatiev 1995). The social construction of race is an ongoing process that is subject to debate, especially in a diverse society such as Canada, where each year increasing numbers of children are born to parents of different racial backgrounds.

Even though these differences are socially constructed, their consequences are no less real. Race is often used to justify unequal access to economic, social, and cultural resources based on the assumption that such inequality is

Racial Groups in Canada, 2006

Source: Statistics Canada, "Canada's Ethno Cultural Mosaic," Census 2006, Catalogue no. 97-563.

Census Division to expand choice points toward a growing awareness of population diversity. It also reflects the struggle by many individuals, especially young adults, against social pressure to choose a single identity, and instead openly embrace multiple heritages. The classic case is Tiger Woods, the world's best-known golfer. Woods created his own racial category, referring to himself as "Cablinasian," a combination of his Caucasian, Black, American Indian, and Asian (Chinese and Thai) ancestry.

ETHNICITY

An ethnic group is set apart from others explicitly because of its national origin or cultural patterns. Distinctive characteristics can include language, diet, sports, and religious beliefs, along with various traditions, norms, and values.

prejudice A negative attitude toward an entire category of people, often an ethnic or racial minority.

ethnocentrism The tendency to assume that one's own culture and way of life represent the norm or are superior to all others.

racism The belief that one race is supreme and all others are innately inferior.

The distinction between racial and ethnic minorities is not always clear-cut. As the socially constructed nature of race becomes clearer, factors such as the significance of national origin and cultural traditions become more important in our understanding of racial groups. Despite categorization problems, however, sociologists maintain that the distinction between racial groups and ethnic groups is socially significant. The fact that race is constructed makes it no less real in terms of how it shapes our identities, how we have defined it historically, how we have experienced it individually, and how it has been used politically and economically.

Although we will look at various ethnic and racial groups in more detail later in the chapter, it is important to understand the significance such categories have in society. As we have already seen, often they are used to justify exclusion from critical resources. This exclusion is rooted in both values and norms, that is, in how we think and how we act. When it comes to race and ethnicity, the terms that describe such practices are *prejudice* and *discrimination*.

>> Prejudice and Discrimination

In recent years, campuses across Canada and the United States have been the scene of bias-related incidents. Student-run newspapers and radio stations have ridiculed racial and ethnic minorities; threatening literature has been stuffed under the doors of minority students; tensions have escalated between groups with longstanding political and religious differences; and graffiti endorsing the views of White supremacist organizations such as the Ku Klux Klan have been scrawled on campass walls. In some cases, there have even been violent clashes (Bunzel 1992; Schaefer 2008a). Such acts grow out of attitudes people have about other groups.

PREJUDICE

Prejudice is a negative attitude toward an entire category of people, often an ethnic or racial minority. If you resent your roommate because he or she is sloppy, you are not necessarily guilty of prejudice. However, if you immediately stereotype your roommate on the basis of such characteristics as race, ethnicity, or religion, that is a form of prejudice. Prejudice tends to perpetuate false definitions of individuals and groups.

Sometimes prejudice results from **ethnocentrism**—the tendency to assume that one's own culture and way of life represent the norm or are superior to all others. Ethnocentric people judge other cultures by the standards of their own group. This leads quite easily to prejudice against cultures they view as inferior.

One important and widespread ideology that reinforces prejudice is **racism**—the belief that one race is supreme and all others are innately inferior. When racism prevails in a society, members of subordinate groups generally

Did You Know?

...The Right Honourable Lincoln M. Alexander is a prominent Canadian of West Indian descent. Since 1993, an award in his name has been given to youth who work to eliminate racial discrimination in Ontario.

Before passage of the Civil Rights Act in 1964, segregation of public accommodations was the norm throughout the Southern United States.

Categorization of Reported Hate Crimes in Canada, 2006

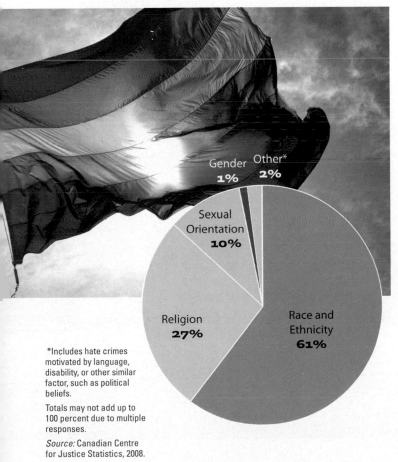

Gender 1%
Other* 2%
Sexual Orientation 10%
Religion 27%
Race and Ethnicity 61%

*Includes hate crimes motivated by language, disability, or other similar factor, such as political beliefs.

Totals may not add up to 100 percent due to multiple responses.

Source: Canadian Centre for Justice Statistics, 2008.

experience prejudice, discrimination, and exploitation. A **hate crime** is a criminal offence committed because of the offender's bias against an individual based on race, religion, ethnicity, national origin, or sexual orientation. In 2006, Canadian police services, covering 87 percent of the population, reported a total of 892 hate crimes. Yet the 2004 General Social Survey (GSS) counted over 260,000 incidents of hate-motivated crime in the 12 months preceding the survey, findings that are consistent with the 1999 GSS. These discrepancies are likely due in part to underreporting by victims; for example, only 40 percent of those mentioned in the 2004 GSS were reported to police. Subjective interpretation is another factor—while individuals may perceive an incident as motivated by hate, the police must assess on the basis of law. The official statistics, as compiled by police services, are presented in the graph on this page.

Over the past three generations, nationwide surveys have consistently shown growing support for integration, interracial dating, and the election of minority group members to public office—including even the presidency of the United States. Nevertheless, there are persistent patterns of unequal treatment. People claim not to be prejudiced, affirming principles such as equal opportunity, yet many fail to put these ideals into practice. In his classic work, *The Vertical Mosaic: An Analysis of Social Class and Power in Canada*, John Porter argues that the power elite in this country is comprised of primarily White, Anglo-Saxon men of wealth. While Canada's population may be

> **hate crime** A criminal offence committed because of the offender's bias against an individual based on race, religion, ethnicity, national origin, or sexual orientation.

Members of the Ku Klux Klan, masked in white robes and hoods, used night-time cross-burnings to instill terror.

a cultural mosaic, Porter's research suggests a vertical arrangement of ethnic groups is in place.

In their 1997 study revisiting Porter's work, Lian and Matthews found some movement in terms of social mobility, but Canadians demonstrated only conditional willingness to accept difference, with least acceptance of difference expressed as skin colour or social distance. A more recent investigation also found that among immigrants to Canada, skin colour is the biggest barrier to feeling a sense of belonging: the darker one's skin, the greater the alienation (Taylor 2009).

colour-blind racism The use of race-neutral principles to perpetuate a racially unequal status quo.
discrimination The denial of opportunities and equal rights to individuals and groups because of prejudice or other arbitrary reasons.

Some suggest that **colour-blind racism,** which uses the principle of race neutrality to perpetuate a racially unequal status quo, is at work. In such cases, commitment to the principle of equality actually serves to perpetuate inequality. In a system where inequality based on race and ethnicity is built into the structure of society, unwillingness to address these issues explicitly in those terms serves to perpetuate the status quo. Although it might seem counter to the principle of equality, some nations have established quotas in political representation and hiring to force the social structure to provide greater opportunity, a controversial practice that is expressly prohibited under Canadian employment equity legislation.

DISCRIMINATION

Prejudice often leads to **discrimination**—the denial of opportunities and equal rights to individuals and groups because of prejudice or other arbitrary reasons. While prejudice is a way of thinking, discrimination involves action. Imagine that a White corporate president with a prejudice against First Nations people has to fill an executive position, and the most qualified candidate for the job is an Inuit person. If the president refuses to hire this candidate and instead selects an inferior White candidate, he or she is engaging in an act of racial discrimination.

Discriminatory Behaviour Prejudiced attitudes should not be equated with discriminatory behaviour. Although the two are generally related, they are not identical; either condition can be present without the other. A prejudiced person does not always act on his or her biases. For example, the White president of a company might choose—despite his or her prejudices—to hire the Inuit individual because that person is the most qualified. That

Federal troops were needed to support the U.S. Supreme Court decision that led to the integration of schools in the 1950s.

Median Income by Racial Group and Gender

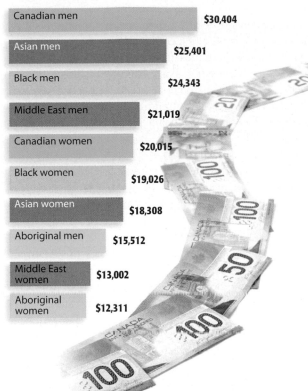

Canadian men	$30,404
Asian men	$25,401
Black men	$24,343
Middle East men	$21,019
Canadian women	$20,015
Black women	$19,026
Asian women	$18,308
Aboriginal men	$15,512
Middle East women	$13,002
Aboriginal women	$12,311

Source: Statistics Canada, "Employment Income Groups and Constant Dollars, Sex, Visible Minority Groups and Immigrant Status for Population 15 yrs and Over," Catalogue no. 97-F0019-XCB20011047.

would be prejudice without discrimination. On the other hand, a White corporate president with a completely respectful view of the Inuit might refuse to hire them for executive posts out of fear that biased clients would take their business elsewhere. In that case, the president's action would constitute discrimination without prejudice.

hiring, a White job applicant with a prison record received slightly more callbacks than a Black applicant with no criminal record. Over time, the cumulative impact of such differential behaviour contributes to significant differences in access to critical resources. For example, as illustrated in the table above, income varies significantly based on race and gender in Canada.

The Glass Ceiling Discrimination persists even for the most educated and qualified minority group members

> It is not that individuals in the designated groups are inherently unable to achieve equality on their own, it is that the obstacles in their way are so formidable and self-perpetuating that they cannot be overcome without intervention. It is both intolerable and insensitive if we simply wait and hope that the barriers will disappear with time. Equality in employment will not happen unless we make it happen.

Justice Rosalie Silberman Abella
Royal Commission on Equality
in Employment, 1985

Sometimes racial and ethnic discrimination is overt. Internet forums like Craigslist.org or Roommate.com feature classified ads that state "African Americans and Arabians tend to clash with me" or "Clean, Godly Christian men only." While antidiscrimination laws prevent such notices from being published in the newspapers, existing law has not caught up with online bigotry in hiring and renting (Liptak 2006).

As described in Chapter 2, in sociologist Devah Pager's 2003 experiment investigating racial discrimination in

from the best family backgrounds. Despite their talent and experience, they sometimes encounter attitudinal or organizational bias that prevents them from reaching their full potential. Recall that the term *glass ceiling* refers to an invisible barrier that blocks the promotion of a qualified individual in a work environment because of the individual's gender, race, or ethnicity (Schaefer 2006; Yamagata et al. 1997).

Did You Know?

... Blacks and Whites have significantly different perceptions of local law enforcement. In a 2007 survey, when asked how much confidence they had in local police, 42 percent of Whites and 14 percent of Blacks had a "great deal," while 31 percent of Blacks and 10 percent of Whites had "very little."

Racial Profiling Another form of discrimination involves **racial profiling,** which is any arbitrary action initiated by an authority based on race, ethnicity, or national origin rather than on a person's behaviour. Generally, racial profiling occurs when law enforcement officers, including customs officials, airport security, and police, assume that people who fit a certain description are likely to engage in illegal activities. This practice is often based on very explicit stereotypes. For example, a bar that refuses to serve Aboriginal customers because of a belief they will get drunk and rowdy is committing racial profiling. Black Canadians have reported being pulled over for DWB— "driving while Black"—particularly when travelling in expensive cars.

While racial profiling is most often associated with law enforcement, in recent years health scares have caused members of particular racial groups to be treated with suspicion. For example, during the SARS outbreak, many Asian Canadians came under scrutiny. In 2009, as the H1N1 flu spread around the world, Canada considered restricting Mexican labourers from entering the country.

Research on the ineffectiveness of racial profiling, coupled with complaints about the stigmatization it fosters, has led to growing demands to end the practice. However, in the years following the 2001 terrorist attacks on the United States, federal authorities in both the U.S. and Canada have subjected foreign students from Arab countries to special questioning, and they scrutinize legal immigrants identified as Arab or Muslim for possible illegal activity. Arab and Muslim detainees in the U.S. have also been prosecuted for violations that were routinely ignored among immigrants of other ethnicities and faiths (Withrow 2006).

The existence of the glass ceiling often results from the fears and prejudices of many middle- and upper-level White male managers, who believe that the inclusion of women and minority group men in management circles will threaten their own prospects for advancement. Employment equity in Canada has gone through a number of articulations, from broad statements of equal opportunity

THE PRIVILEGES OF THE DOMINANT

One often-overlooked aspect of discrimination is the privileges that dominant groups enjoy at the expense of

> Whites of course have the privilege of not caring, of being colorblind. Nobody else does.
>
> Ursula K. LeGuin

racial profiling Any police-initiated action based on race, ethnicity, or national origin rather than on a person's behaviour.

in the 1950s and 1960s to voluntary Affirmative Action programs in the 1970s to the passing of Employment Equity Acts in 1986 and 1995. It has been met with some resistance, and characterized by some as "reverse discrimination," but it in fact supports equal employment opportunities for all, not just select groups.

others. For instance, we tend to focus more on the difficulty women have balancing career and family than on the ease with which men avoid household chores and advance in the workplace. Similarly, we concentrate more on discrimination against racial and ethnic minorities than on the advantages members of the White majority enjoy. Indeed, most White people rarely think about their "Whiteness," taking their status for granted. However, sociologists and other social scientists are becoming increasingly interested in what it means to be "White," for White privilege is the other side of the proverbial coin of racial discrimination.

The feminist scholar Peggy McIntosh (1988) became interested in White privilege after noticing that most men would not acknowledge the privileges attached to being male—even if they would agree that being female had its disadvantages. She wondered whether White people suffer from a similar blind spot regarding their own racial privilege. Intrigued, McIntosh began to list all the ways in which she benefitted from her Whiteness. She soon realized that the list of unspoken advantages was long and significant.

McIntosh found that as a White person, she rarely needed to step out of her comfort zone, no matter where she went. If she wished to, she could spend most of her time with people of her own race. She could find a good place to live in a pleasant neighbourhood, buy the foods she liked to eat from almost any grocery store, and get her hair styled in almost any salon. She could attend a public meeting without feeling that she did not belong, that she was different from everyone else.

McIntosh discovered, too, that her skin colour opened doors for her. She could cash cheques and use credit cards without suspicion, and she could browse through stores without being shadowed by security guards. She could be seated without difficulty in a restaurant. If she asked to see the manager, she could assume he or she would be of her own race. If she needed help from a doctor or a lawyer, she could get it.

McIntosh also realized that her Whiteness made the job of parenting easier. She did not need to worry about protecting her children from people who didn't like them. She could be sure that their books would show pictures of people who looked like them and that their history texts would describe White people's achievements. She knew that the television programs they watched would include White characters.

Finally, McIntosh had to admit that others did not constantly evaluate her in racial terms. When she appeared in public, she didn't need to worry that her clothing or behaviour might reflect poorly on White people. If she was recognized for an achievement, it was seen as her own accomplishment, not that of an entire race. And no one ever assumed that the personal opinions she voiced should be those of all White people. Because McIntosh blended in with the people around her, she wasn't always onstage.

These are not all the privileges White people take for granted as a result of their membership in the dominant racial group in Canada. As Devah Pager's study showed, White job seekers enjoy a tremendous advantage over equally well-qualified—even better-qualified—Blacks. Whiteness *does* carry privileges—to a much greater extent than most White people realize.

Myths and Realities about Employment Equity

Myth: Employment Equity means treating everyone the same.

Reality: Employment Equity means treating everyone with fairness, taking into account people's differences.

Myth: Employment Equity results in "reverse discrimination."

Reality: Employment Equity means everyone has equal employment opportunities—not just a select group.

Myth: Employment Equity is all about quotas.

Reality: Quotas are explicitly prohibited by the Employment Equity Act.

Myth: Employment Equity means hiring unqualified people.

Reality: Employment Equity means providing all qualified and qualifiable individuals with equal employment opportunities—not just a select few.

Myth: Employment Equity threatens the seniority principle.

Reality: Employment Equity and seniority share a common goal: to make sure that employment opportunities are fair, without favouritism or discrimination.

Myth: Employment Equity means lowering job standards.

Reality: Employment Equity examines job standards to ensure that job criteria are realistic and job related.

Myth: It is too difficult and expensive to accommodate persons with disabilities.

Reality: It generally costs less than $500 to adapt a workstation to accommodate a person with a disability.

Source: Human Resources and Skills Development Canada, www.hrsdc.gc.ca.

SOCthink

> > > McIntosh recommends that we all step back and consider unearned advantages we inherit due to the positions we may occupy. What would be on your list? What disadvantages might you inherit?

SOCthink

> > > Why might institutional discrimination be an even greater concern than interpersonal discrimination?

INSTITUTIONAL DISCRIMINATION

Such persistent patterns of inequality suggest that discrimination is practised not only by individuals in one-to-one encounters but also by institutions in their daily operations. Social scientists are particularly concerned with the ways in which structural factors such as employment, housing, health care, and government operations main-

institutional discrimination
A pattern of treatment that systematically denies access to resources and opportunities to individuals and groups as part of the normal operations of a society.

tain the social significance of race and ethnicity. **Institutional discrimination** refers to a pattern of treatment that denies access to resources and opportunities to individuals and groups as part of the normal operations of a society. This kind of discrimination consistently affects certain racial and ethnic groups more than others.

Prior to the establishment of the Charter of Rights and Freedoms, many Canadian policies were overtly discriminatory (see, for example, the discussion of immigration policy later in this chapter). But has the Charter succeeded in eradicating institutional discrimination? This is certainly open to debate. In Canada, we often point to the actions of other countries, including the United States, as evidence that by comparison, our country treats its citizens fairly and equally.

Perhaps the most blatant act of institutional discrimination in Canadian history is the treatment of Aboriginal peoples, most notably the enforced residential schooling of First Nations children (as discussed in Chapter 8). A recent American example of institutional discrimination occurred in the wake of the September 11, 2001 terrorist attacks on the United States. Under pressure to prevent terrorist takeovers of commercial airplanes, the U.S. Congress passed the Aviation and Transportation Security Act, which was intended to strengthen airport screening procedures. The law stipulated that all airport screeners must be U.S. citizens. Nationally, 28 percent of all airport screeners were legal residents but not citizens of the United States; as a group, they were disproportionately Latino, Black, and Asian. Many observers noted that other airport and airline workers, including pilots, cabin attendants, and even armed National Guardsmen stationed at airports, need not be citizens. Currently, the constitutionality of the act is being challenged. Even well-meant legal measures can have disastrous consequences for racial and ethnic minorities (H. Weinstein 2002).

In some cases, even ostensibly neutral institutional standards can have discriminatory effects. An example of this is found in the leasing of institutional space to student groups that segregate women in worship. The University of Toronto agreed to do so, noting that the lessee has autonomy in the way they use the space. McGill University argued it was inappropriate for a public institution to allow its space to be used for religious purposes, and thus refused. Interestingly, neither institution actually addressed the issue of women's rights, but the standards applied could be understood to be discriminatory with respect to gender (Stein 2007).

Attempts have been made to eradicate or compensate for discrimination, such as the review of land claims by First Nations peoples, as well as financial compensation for the abusive treatment they endured in residential schools. The Charter of Rights and Freedoms has led to the enactment of laws against institutional discrimination. Yet discriminatory practices continue to pervade nearly all areas of life

Perceptions of Discrimination

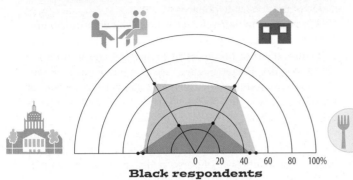

Black respondents

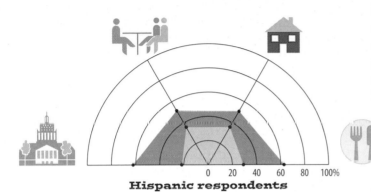

Hispanic respondents

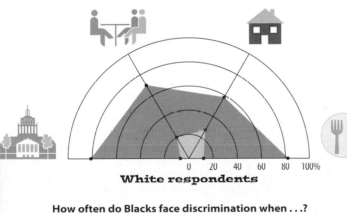

White respondents

How often do Blacks face discrimination when . . . ?

🏛	Applying to a college or university	🏠	Renting an apartment or buying a house
🧑‍🤝‍🧑	Applying for a job	🍴	Eating at a restaurant or shopping in a retail store
▨	Almost always/frequently	▨	Not often/hardly ever

Source: Pew Research Center 2007:30.

in Canada. In part, that is because various individuals and groups actually benefit from racial and ethnic discrimination in terms of money, status, and influence. Discrimination permits members of the majority to enhance their wealth, power, and prestige at the expense of others. Less qualified people get jobs and promotions simply because they are members of the dominant group. Such individuals and groups will not surrender these advantages easily.

>> Sociological Perspectives on Race and Ethnicity

Sociologists seek to understand and explain why prejudice and discrimination develop and persist and what might be done to address them. As we have seen, often such negative characteristics exist because they serve certain interests. Here we will look at how prejudice and discrimination contribute to the maintenance of the existing social order by reinforcing the dominant culture.

SOCIAL ORDER AND INEQUALITY

One of the ways we see such beliefs and practices perpetuated is through acceptance of the dominant ideology that supports them. Prejudice and discrimination are rooted in fundamental beliefs about the natural order of the world. Such values provide a moral justification for maintaining an unequal society that routinely deprives minority groups of their rights and privileges. Whites, for example, justified slavery by asserting that Africans were physically and spiritually subhuman and devoid of souls. It is easy in retrospect to find such beliefs appalling, but they became part of what people assumed was natural and were therefore difficult to challenge.

This does not mean, however, that certain groups do not intentionally promote such beliefs at the expense of others. Prejudice and discrimination help to preserve the existing system of inequality. **Exploitation theory,** for example, argues that such practices are a basic part of the capitalist economic system (Blauner 1972; Cox 1948; Hunter 2000). Racism keeps minorities in low-paying jobs, thereby supplying the capitalist ruling class with a pool of cheap labour. Moreover, by forcing racial minorities to accept low wages, capitalists can restrict the wages of all members of the proletariat. Business owners can always replace workers from the dominant group who demand higher wages with minorities who have no choice but to accept low-paying jobs. This increases the likelihood that working-class members of the majority group will develop racist attitudes toward working-class members of minority groups, whom they view as threats to their jobs. As a result they direct their hostilities not toward the capitalists, but

> **exploitation theory** A belief that views racial subordination as a manifestation of the class system inherent in capitalism.

Hot or Not?

Should companies establish hiring targets based on race, ethnicity, or gender to ensure greater opportunity?

SOCstudies

toward other workers, thereby not challenging the structure of the existing system.

Maintaining these practices, however, comes at significant cost to society. For example, a society that practises discrimination fails to use the resources of all individuals. Discrimination limits the search for talent and leadership to the dominant group. Discrimination also aggravates social problems such as poverty, delinquency, and crime. Such effects require the investment of a good deal of time and money in which the primary goal is to maintain barriers to the full participation of all members (Rose 1951).

Challenging prejudice and discrimination, however, involves questioning taken-for-granted views of the world in which people have invested their faith and trust. Women in the 1950s in Canada had to do just that. They challenged the idea that it was "natural" for women to stay at home and have babies rather than get an education and enter the paid labour force. At the same time, workers in the civil rights movement faced a similar challenge in confronting social attitudes that represented barriers to the full participation of visible minorities in society.

> **contact hypothesis** The theory that in cooperative circumstances interracial contact between people of equal status will reduce prejudice.
> **genocide** The deliberate, systematic killing of an entire people or nation.

THE CONTACT HYPOTHESIS

At its heart, racism is about division, separating the human population into "us versus them." As society becomes more global and pluralistic, more people from diverse cultural backgrounds have increased opportunities to interact with others unlike themselves on a daily basis. When people interact with others as people, rather than as stereotypes or distant others, the possibility arises for prejudice and discrimination to decrease.

Take, for example, a South Asian woman who is transferred from a job on one part of an assembly line to a similar position working next to a White man. At first, the White man is patronizing, assuming that she must be incompetent. For her part, the woman is cold and resentful; even when she needs assistance, she refuses to admit it. After a week, the growing tension between the two leads to a bitter quarrel. Yet over time, each slowly comes to appreciate the other's strengths

Civil rights activist Rosa Parks being fingerprinted upon her arrest in 1955 for her act of civil disobedience in refusing to give up her seat on a bus to a White man.

and talents. A year after they begin working together, these two workers become respectful friends. This story is an example of the contact hypothesis in action.

The **contact hypothesis** states that in cooperative circumstances, interracial contact between people of equal status will cause them to become less prejudiced and to abandon old stereotypes. People begin to see one another as individuals and to discard the broad generalizations characteristic of stereotyping. Note the phrases "equal status" and "cooperative circumstances." In our assembly line example, if the two workers had been competing for one vacancy as a supervisor, the racial hostility between them might have worsened, highlighting the significance of power and position when it comes to the issue of racism (Allport 1979; Fine 2008).

As visible minorities slowly gain access to better-paying and higher-responsibility jobs, the contact hypothesis may take on even greater significance. The trend in our society is toward increasing contact between individuals from dominant and subordinate groups. That may be one way of eliminating—or at least reducing—racial and ethnic stereotyping and prejudice. Another may be the establishment of interracial coalitions, an idea suggested by sociologist William Julius Wilson (1999). To work, such coalitions would obviously need to provide an equal role for all members.

PATTERNS OF INTERGROUP RELATIONS

The possibility of equal status, however, is shaped by how societies handle racial and ethnic differences. Some are more open to diverse groups maintaining their cultural traditions. Others pressure groups to abandon their beliefs and practices in favour of those of the dominant society. We will focus on six characteristic patterns of intergroup relations: genocide, expulsion, amalgamation, assimilation, segregation, and pluralism. Each pattern defines the dominant group's actions and the minority group's responses. The first two are relatively rare, though their consequences are extreme; the final four are more common.

Genocide The most devastating pattern of intergroup relations is **genocide**—the deliberate, systematic killing of an entire people or nation. This is precisely what happened when Turkish authorities killed 1 million Armenians beginning in 1915. The term is most commonly associated with Nazi Germany's extermination of 6 million European Jews, along with gays, lesbians, and the Romani people ("Gypsies"), during World War II. The term also describes the United States' policies toward Native Americans in the 19th century. In 1800, the Native American (or American Indian) population of the United States was about 600,000; by 1850, warfare with the U.S. cavalry, disease, and forced relocation had reduced it to 250,000. A contemporary example of genocide occurred in Rwanda in 1994, where 800,000 people were slaughtered in a campaign sponsored by the government.

In a survey about media portrayals of African Americans, the majority of Whites and Hispanics felt that the way Blacks are portrayed in television and films is better today than it was 10 years ago. Among African Americans, however, 43 percent agreed. Blacks were also more likely than the other groups to say that negative portrayals have a negative impact on society's views of Blacks. Both Blacks and Whites agreed, at almost identical levels, that hip hop and rap have a bad influence on society today.

Expulsion Another extreme response is **expulsion**—the systematic removal of a group of people from society. Between 1755 and 1763, as many as 11,000 Acadians were expelled from what is now known as the Annapolis Valley in Nova Scotia. In 1979, Vietnam expelled nearly 1 million ethnic Chinese, partly as a result of centuries of hostility between Vietnam and neighbouring China. Similarly, Serbian forces began a program of "ethnic cleansing" in 1991, in the newly independent states of Bosnia and

Herzegovina. Throughout the former Yugoslavia, the Serbs drove more than 1 million Croats and Muslims from their homes. Some they tortured and killed; others they abused and terrorized, in an attempt to "purify" the land (Cigar 1995; Petrovic 1994). More recently, the government of Sudan has pushed people off their land and out of the country in Darfur.

Amalgamation When a majority group and a minority group combine to form a new group, **amalgamation** results. This often occurs through intermarriage over several generations. This pattern can be expressed as $A + B + C \rightarrow D$, where A, B, and C represent different groups in a society, and D signifies the end result, a unique cultural-racial group unlike any of the initial groups (Newman 1973). In Canada, the Métis are an example of amalgamation, as European traders and Western Cree peoples established close relations and ultimately intermarriage in the 1700s.

> **expulsion** The systematic removal of a group of people from society.
> **amalgamation** The process through which a majority group and a minority group combine to form a new group.
> **assimilation** The process through which a person forsakes his or her own cultural tradition to become part of a different culture.

Assimilation In India, many Hindus complain about Indian citizens who emulate the traditions and customs of the British. In France, people of Arab and African origin, many of them Muslim, complain they are treated as second-class citizens—a charge that provoked riots in 2005. In Australia, Aborigines who have become part of the dominant society refuse to acknowledge their darker-skinned grandparents on the street. All of these cases are examples of the effects of **assimilation**—the process through which a person forsakes his or her own cultural tradition to become part of a different culture. Generally, it is practised by minority group members who want to conform to the standards of the dominant group. Assimilation can be described as a pattern in which $A + B + C \rightarrow A$. The majority, A, dominates in such a way that members of minorities B and C imitate it and attempt to become indistinguishable from it (Newman 1973).

Assimilation can strike at the very roots of a person's identity. In North America, some immigrants have changed their ethnic-sounding family names to names that better fit into the dominant White Protestant culture. Jennifer Anastassakis, for example, changed her name to Jennifer Aniston, Ralph Lipschitz became Ralph Lauren, Natalie Portman switched from Natalie Hershlag, and the Academy Award–winning British actress Helen Mirren gave up her birth name of Ilyena Vasilievna Mironova. Name changes, switches in religious affiliation, and the dropping of native languages can obscure one's roots and heritage. Especially across generations, assimilation can lead to the virtual death of a culture in that family's history. It is not uncommon for grandchildren of immigrants who have not

5 Movies on RACE AND ETHNICITY

Bend It Like Beckham
A British Indian girl plays soccer against her parents' wishes.

Mississippi Burning
Two detectives search for missing civil rights activists.

Do the Right Thing
Racial tension in Brooklyn.

Real Women Have Curves
Spanish American women in the United States.

The Namesake
A man comes to appreciate his origins.

learned the language or the cultural traditions of their ancestors to regret this loss.

Segregation Separate schools, separate seating on buses and in restaurants, separate washrooms, even separate drinking fountains—these were all part of the lives of African Americans in the Southern U.S. when segregation ruled early in the 20th century. **Segregation** refers to the physical separation of two groups of people in terms of residence, workplace, and social events. Generally, a dominant group imposes this pattern on a minority group; for example, the Government of Canada (representing the dominant White population) forced First Nations peoples onto reserves. Segregation is rarely complete, however. Intergroup contact inevitably occurs, even in the most segregated societies.

> **segregation** The physical separation of two groups of people in terms of residence, workplace, and social events; often imposed on a minority group by a dominant group.
> **apartheid** A former policy of the South African government, designed to maintain the separation of Blacks and other non-Whites from the dominant Whites.
> **pluralism** Mutual respect for one another's cultures among the various groups in a society, which allows minorities to express their own cultures without experiencing prejudice.

From 1948 (when it received its independence) to 1990, the Republic of South Africa severely restricted the movement of Blacks and other non-Whites by means of a wide-ranging system of segregation known as **apartheid.** Apartheid even included the creation of separate homelands where Blacks were expected to live. However, decades of local resistance to apartheid, combined with international pressure, led to marked political changes in the 1990s. In 1994, a prominent Black activist, Nelson Mandela, became South Africa's president in the first election in which Blacks (the majority of the nation's population) were allowed to vote. Mandela had spent almost 28 years in South African prisons for his anti-apartheid activities. His elec-

Former South African President Nelson Mandela oversaw that country's transition from a segregated society.

SOCthink

> > > In 1990, Baltej Singh Dhillon was accepted into the RCMP, but was told he would not be permitted to wear his turban. As a practising Sikh, wearing of a turban is considered a religious duty, and so Dhillon sought an exception to the policy. When this was denied, he claimed violation of his religious rights, a claim that was supported by the Charter of Rights and Freedoms. Dhillon remained an RCMP officer, and continued to wear his turban. This legal ruling set a powerful precedent.

Can you think of any occupations in which religious and ethnic rituals and traditions (such as clothing, facial hair, rules about the body) could not legitimately be observed? If so, as an employer, what reasons would you give in order to justify contravening the Charter?

tion was widely viewed as the final blow to South Africa's oppressive policy of segregation.

Long-entrenched social patterns are difficult to change, however. A recent analysis of living patterns in U.S. metropolitan areas shows that, despite federal laws that forbid housing discrimination, residential segregation is still the norm. Across the nation, neighbourhoods remain divided along both racial and ethnic lines. The average White person lives in an area that is at least 83 percent White, while the average African American lives in a neighbourhood that is mostly Black. The typical Latino lives in an area that is 42 percent Hispanic. Overall, segregation flourishes at the community and neighbourhood levels, despite the increasing diversity of the nation as a whole (Lewis Mumford Center 2001).

Whatever the country, residential segregation directly limits people's economic opportunity. Sociologists Douglas Massey and Nancy Denton (1993), in a book aptly titled *American Apartheid,* noted that segregation separates poor members of visible minorities from job opportunities and isolates them from successful role models. This pattern repeats itself the world over, from Toronto to Oldham, England, and Soweto, South Africa.

Pluralism In a pluralistic society, a subordinate group does not have to forsake its lifestyle and traditions. **Pluralism** is based on mutual respect for one another's cultures among the various groups in a society. This pattern allows a minority group to express its own culture and still participate without prejudice in the larger society. Earlier, we described amalgamation as A + B + C → D, and assimilation as A + B + C → A. Using this same approach, we can conceive of pluralism as A + B + C → A + B + C; that is, all the groups coexist in the same society (Newman 1973).

Switzerland exemplifies the modern pluralistic state. There the absence of both a national language and a dominant religious faith leads to a tolerance for cultural diversity. In addition, various political devices safeguard the interests of ethnic groups. By contrast, Great Britain has had difficulty achieving cultural pluralism in a multiracial society. East Indians, Pakistanis, and Blacks from the Caribbean and Africa experience prejudice and discrimination within the dominant White society there. Some British citizens advocate cutting off all Asian and Black immigration, and a few even call for expulsion of those non-Whites currently living in Britain.

In Canada, the ideal of pluralism is entrenched in law with the Multiculturalism Act, which not only protects minorities who engage in cultural expression, but encourages them to do so. Canada's Official Languages Act is another important piece of legislation intended to recognize distinct cultures within the country.

Few societies have a more diverse population than Canada; the nation is truly a multi-racial, multi-ethnic society. Of course, this has not always been the case. Until the arrival of the first French settlers in the 1600s, Canada had been the exclusive domain of the First Nations peoples. The effects of colonialism, territorial battles within this nation, and the steady flow of immigration to Canada have all influenced the racial and ethnic composition of our present-day society.

The racial and ethnic groups perhaps most traditionally associated with Canada are French Canadians, White ethnics, and First Nations peoples.

Theory
A Matter of Perspective

THEORETICAL PERSPECTIVES ON RACE AND ETHNICITY

Functionalist:

- dominant majority group benefits from the subordination of minority groups
- linked to: amalgamation, assimilation, segregation

Conflict:

- dominant majority group has vested interest in maintaining position of power; perpetuates inequality through economic exploitation
- linked to: exploitation, expulsion

Feminist:

- gender, race, and class intersect; multiple bases of inequality
- linked to: segregation, exploitation

Interactionist:

- labelling occurs through stereotypes and profiling; however, diverse contacts may foster understanding
- linked to assimilation, expulsion, segregation, pluralism, contact hypothesis

>> Race and Ethnicity in Canada

FRENCH CANADIANS

From the earliest days of settlement, the status of the French in Canada (who today comprise roughly one-quarter of the country's population) has been unequal to that of the dominant English population. Although legislation such as the Quebec Act of 1774, the Constitution Act of 1791, and the Confederation Act of 1867 recognized the special status of francophones, they continued to be marginalized. The 1969 Official Languages Act brought visibility to the French minority, and today, after over 200 years of marginalization, French nationalism is strong, including political representation through the Parti Québécois and the Bloc Québécois. As they continue to define their unique identity—including some support for sovereignty—French Canadians are both an important social and political group in Canada and the greatest threat to Canadian unity.

WHITE ETHNICS

Although Canada is becoming increasingly diverse, a significant segment of the population is made up of White ethnics whose ancestors arrived from Europe within the last century. According to the 2006 Census, 67 percent of Canadians claimed European origins, but it is important to remember that like other groups, White ethnics are not homogeneous in ancestry or experiences. Some members continue to live in close-knit ethnic neighbourhoods—such as the long-established Italian Canadian communities—while others have largely assimilated into the larger society.

Many White ethnics today identify only sporadically with their heritage. **Symbolic ethnicity** refers to an emphasis on concerns such as ethnic food or political issues rather than on deeper ties to one's ethnic heritage. It is reflected in the occasional family trip to an ethnic bakery, the celebration of a ceremonial event such as St. Joseph's Day among Italian Canadians, or concerns about the future of Northern Ireland among Irish Canadians. Except in cases in which new immigration reinforces old traditions, symbolic ethnicity tends to decline with each passing generation (Alba 1990; Winter 2008).

FIRST NATIONS PEOPLES

The history of the First Nations peoples in Canada is one of resilience. By the mid-1800s, the British-based authorities had abandoned any recognition of the autonomy of the First Nations peoples; the Gradual Civilization Act of 1857 was essentially a policy of assimilation. Among the devastating results of this act was the forced residential schooling of children, in which horrific abuse occurred. The 1876 Indian Act brought First Nations peoples under the formal protection (or control) of the federal government. In the mid-20th century, the First Nations peoples became a more active political presence, fighting for and securing the right to vote in all Canadian provinces between 1949 and 1969, and the federal franchise in 1960. They have continued to pursue treaty rights and the right to self-government, and bring national and international attention to the discrimination they continue to face.

As discussed in chapters throughout this text, the effects of their unequal treatment are evident, with the Aboriginal population being overrepresented in penal institutions, poor households, and certain health conditions, and underrepresented in higher education and the paid labour force. Yet after enduring more than a century and a half of degradation, Canada's First Nations peoples maintain a sense of pride and identity.

symbolic ethnicity An ethnic identity that emphasizes concerns such as ethnic food or political issues rather than deeper ties to one's ethnic heritage.

model or **ideal minority** A subordinate group whose members have succeeded economically, socially, and educationally despite past prejudice and discrimination.

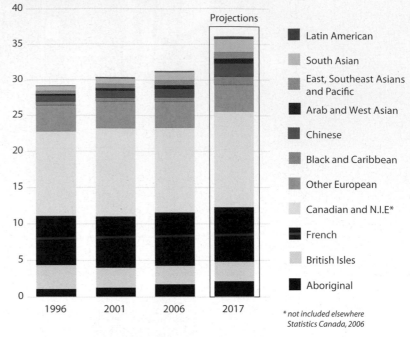

Diversity in Canada 1996–2006, and 2017 projections

Projections

- Latin American
- South Asian
- East, Southeast Asians and Pacific
- Arab and West Asian
- Chinese
- Black and Caribbean
- Other European
- Canadian and N.I.E*
- French
- British Isles
- Aboriginal

1996   2001   2006   2017

*not included elsewhere
Statistics Canada, 2006

Source: Annual Report on the Operation of the Canadian Multiculturalism Act 2007–2008.

CANADA'S MOSAIC

The 2006 Census reported more than 200 different ethnic origins (ancestry), with many people reporting more than one. To collect data on race, the census specified 10 categories of visible minorities, with an additional option of "Other." These are broad racial categories, such as South Asian (which includes East Indian, Pakistani, Punjabi, and Sri Lankan) and Black (which includes African, Haitian, Jamaican, and Somali). All persons who are non-Caucasian and non-Aboriginal are to be counted among these 11 categories. The table above illustrates Canada's recent patterns of diversity, as well as projected demographics.

Asian Canadians comprise a significant proportion of Canada's population. At 1.25 million, South Asians were the largest visible minority group in Canada in 2006, replacing the Chinese for the first time, who are now the second largest visible minority group, with 1.2 million people. Asian Canadians, particularly the Chinese, have endured considerable discrimination in this country, including head taxes to discourage immigration to Canada, disenfranchisement, and the Chinese Immigration Act of 1923 (also known as the Chinese Exclusion Act), which barred them from entering the country.

Asian Canadians are often held up as a **model** or **ideal minority** group, because they have succeeded economically, socially, and educationally despite past prejudice and discrimination. Taken from a functionalist perspective, groups who succeed against the odds are tangible evidence that with perseverance, anyone can get ahead. However, as conflict theorists rightly note, the success of model

minority groups is conveniently highlighted to mask systemic discrimination; failure to attain such success is attributed to personal failings.

White ethnics and racial minorities have often been antagonistic to one another because of economic competition. As Blacks, Asians, and First Nations peoples emerge from the lower class, they must compete with working-class Whites for jobs, housing, and educational opportunities. In these current times of rising unemployment, any such competition can generate intense intergroup conflict.

While different ethnic and racial groups deal with their own unique issues, they share a common concern: How ethnic can people be—how much can they deviate from an essentially White, Anglo-Saxon, Protestant norm—before society punishes them for their desire to be different? Despite our official commitment to, and pride in, our nation's multicultural policies, Canadian society does seem to reward people for assimilating. Yet as we have seen, assimilation is not an easy process, nor does it guarantee freedom from discrimination. In the years to come,

more and more people will face the challenge of fitting in, not only in Canada but around the world, as the flow of immigrants from one country to another continues to increase.

>> Immigration

Worldwide, immigration is at an all-time high. Each year, about 2.3 percent of the world's population, or 146 million people, move from one country to another. According to Statistics Canada, between 2001 and 2006, approximately 240,000 immigrants entered Canada each year, boosting Canada's population growth rate to 5.4 percent, the fastest growth rate of all G8 countries. In fact, two-thirds of Canada's population growth now comes from immigration, and projections suggest that by 2030, it could account for *all* growth (Kwan 2007). Additionally, in 2007, Canada admitted more than 429,000 permanent residents, temporary foreign workers, and foreign students. Foreign-born people account for 19.8 percent of the total population of Canada (Citizenship and Immigration Canada 2008). Globally, these mass migrations have had a tremendous social impact. The constantly increasing numbers of immigrants and the pressure they put on employment opportunities and welfare capabilities in the countries they enter raise troubling questions for many of the world's economic

Going **GLOBAL**

World Immigration Since 1500

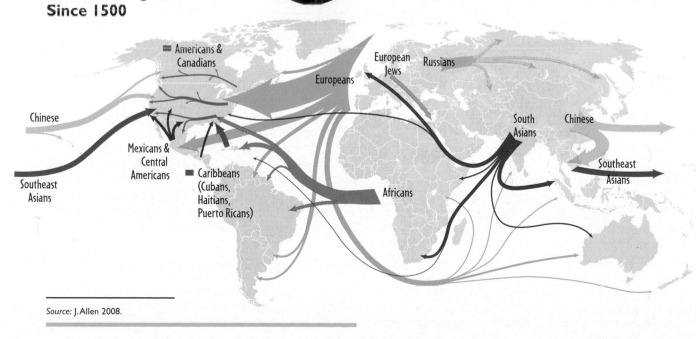

Source: J. Allen 2008.

powers. Who should be allowed in? At what point should immigration be curtailed (Schmidley and Robinson 2003; Stalker 2000)?

IMMIGRATION TRENDS

The migration of people is not uniform across time or space. At certain times, war or famine may precipitate large movements of people, either temporarily or permanently. Temporary dislocations occur when people wait until it is safe to return to their home areas. However, more and more migrants who cannot eke out an adequate living in their home nations are making permanent moves to developed nations. The major migration streams flow into North America, the oil-rich areas of the Middle East, and the industrial economies of western Europe and Asia. Currently, seven of the world's wealthiest nations (including Canada, Germany, France, the United Kingdom, and the United States) shelter about one-third of the world's migrant population but less than one-fifth of the world's total population. As long as disparities in job opportunities exist among countries, there is little reason to expect this international trend to reverse.

Even though the sending nation loses a significant source of labour and talent due to emigration, the process does contribute to its economy. For example, it reduces the size of the population that an economy with limited resources has a difficult time supporting, and it leads to

Taking Part in the Community

Proportion of immigrants participating in selected groups and organizations, by generation in Canada, 2002

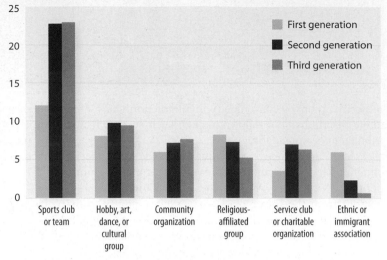

Note: Refers to Canada's non-Aboriginal population aged 15 and older. Because more than one type of organization could be reported, the total of all organizations is greater than 100 percent.
Source: Statistics Canada, Ethnic Diversity Survey, 2002.

reluctant to seek outside help. Finally, because many new immigrants view their new home country as a dangerous place to raise a family, women must be especially watchful over their children's lives (Hondagneu-Sotelo 2003).

One consequence of global immigration has been the emergence of transnationals—people or families who move across borders multiple times in search of better jobs and

> **One day our descendants will think it incredible that we paid so much attention to things like the amount of melanin in our skin or the shape of our eyes or our gender instead of the unique identities of each of us as complex human beings.**
>
> Franklin Thomas

an economic infusion in the form of remittances—monies that immigrants send back to their home nations. Worldwide, immigrants send more than $300 billion a year back home to their relatives—an amount that represents a major source of income for developing nations (DeParle 2007; Leys 2008).

Immigrants continue to face obstacles due to their relative lack of resources. Immigrant women, for example, face all the challenges that immigrant men do, plus some additional ones. Typically, they bear the responsibility for obtaining services for their families, particularly their children. Women are often left to navigate the bureaucratic tangle of schools, city services, and health care, as well as the unfamiliar stores and markets they must shop at to feed their families. Women who require special medical services or are victims of domestic violence are often

education. The industrial tycoons of the early 20th century, whose power outmatched that of many nation-states, were among the world's first transnationals. Today, however, millions of people, many of very modest means, move back and forth between countries much as commuters do between city and suburbs. More and more of these people have dual citizenship. Rather than being shaped by allegiance to one country, their identity is rooted in their struggle to survive—and in some instances prosper—by transcending international borders (Croucher 2004; Sassen 2005).

IMMIGRATION POLICIES

Countries that have long been a destination for immigrants, such as Canada, usually have policies to determine who has preference to enter. Often, clear racial and ethnic

Going GLOBAL

Top 10 Country of Birth of Recent Immigrants, 1981 to 2006

Rank	2006 Census	2001 Census	1996 Census	1991 Census	1981 Census
1	People's Republic of China	People's Republic of China	Hong Kong	Hong Kong	United Kingdom
2	India	India	People's Republic of China	Poland	Viet Nam
3	Philippines	Philippines	India	People's Republic of China	United States
4	Pakistan	Pakistan	Philippines	India	India
5	United States	Hong Kong	Sri Lanka	Philippines	Philippines
6	South Korea	Iran	Poland	United Kingdom	Jamaica
7	Romania	Taiwan	Taiwan	Viet Nam	Hong Kong
8	Iran	United States	Viet Nam	United States	Portugal
9	United Kingdom	South Korea	United States	Lebanon	Taiwan
10	Columbia	Sri Lanka	United Kingdom	Portugal	People's Republic of China

Note: "Recent immigrants" refers to landed immigrants who arrived in Canada within five years prior to a given census.

Source: Statistics Canada, Census of Population, 2006.

Act and emphasis on education, occupation, and language skills has significantly altered the pattern of sending nations. Where previously Europeans dominated, over the last 40 years immigrants have come primarily from Asia. To a large degree, fear and resentment of racial and ethnic diversity is a key factor in opposition to immigration. In many nations, people are concerned that the new arrivals do not reflect and will not embrace their own cultural and racial heritage.

In the wake of the September 11, 2001 attacks in the United States, immigration procedures have been complicated by the need to detect potential terrorists. Illegal immigrants especially, but even legal immigrants, have faced increased scrutiny by government officials around the world. For would-be immigrants to many nations, the wait to receive the right to enter a country—even to join relatives—has increased substantially, as immigration officials scrutinize what were once routine applications more closely.

The intense debate over immigration reflects deep value conflicts in the cultures of many nations. One strand of our culture, for example, has traditionally emphasized egalitarian principles and a desire to help people in time of need. At the same time, hostility to potential immigrants and refugees—whether the Chinese in the early 1900s, European Jews in the 1930s and 1940s, or selected groups today—reflects not only racial, ethnic, and religious prejudice but a desire to maintain the dominant culture of the in-group by excluding those viewed as outsiders.

biases are built into these policies. The history of Canada's immigration policy and the response from citizens to immigrants includes some revealing (and disturbing) incidences in this regard.

For example, in the early 1900s, Black Americans were actively discouraged from immigrating to Canada on the grounds that they were ill-suited to the climate. The head tax on Chinese immigrants was set at $50 in 1885, increased to $100 in 1900, and in 1903, increased once more to $500. Between 1901 and 1918, $18 million was collected from Chinese immigrants; several years later, they would be completely barred from entering Canada. Doukhobors, Mennonites, and Hutterites were prohibited from entry in 1919 because of their "peculiar habits and modes of life." In 1939, the SS *St. Louis*, with more than 900 Jewish refugees on board, was denied permission to land by Canada and the United States. The ship was forced to sail back to Europe, where three-quarters of the refugees died at the hands of the Nazis (Canadian Council for Refugees).

Since the 1960s, Canada has encouraged the immigration of people who already have relatives here, as well as people who have needed skills. The elimination of the "nation of origin" eligibility condition in the Immigration

SOCthink

> > > Birthrates in Canada, as in many industrialized nations, are low. Populations in many countries face natural decrease and will shrink without immigration to compensate for those low birthrates. Given this, why does immigration still cause such tension among many communities in Canada? Might this change as people realize they need those immigrants?

>> Summary

Racial and ethnic differences are to a large degree constructed, but that does not make them any less real in their effects. People experience prejudice and discrimination on the basis of both perceived and real differences. Hate crimes and the practice of racial profiling target certain members of society. At an institutional level, groups and individuals are denied equal rights and opportunities. Despite all this, all kinds of people are embracing their heritage, celebrating traditions and valuing their respective (and sometimes multiple) identities. As a nation, Canada officially promotes and supports multiculturalism; perhaps in time, all its citizens will do so as well.

get involved!

Investigate! Most immigrant groups have museums dedicated to preserving their heritage. Find one in your area and learn the local immigrant story. If a local museum is not available, take advantage of online museums that preserve that history.

For REVIEW

I. How do sociologists define race and ethnicity?
- Race is shaped by biological differences but is defined by the social significance that groups attach to external physical characteristics. Ethnicity is rooted in cultural and national traditions that define a population. Sociologists emphasize the significance of culture and its consequences for both.

II. What are prejudice and discrimination, and how do they operate?
- Prejudice involves attitudes and beliefs while discrimination involves actions. In both cases, they represent a negative response to a group of people that denies them full equality as persons. Institutional discrimination is built in to the structure of society itself, systematically denying some groups access to key resources.

III. What are the consequences of race and ethnicity for opportunity?
- Racial and ethnic groups in Canada face differing levels of opportunity based on their relative position in society. Despite an official commitment to multiculturalism, many groups continue to face significant structural inequality.

Thinking CRITICALLY...

1. How do you identify yourself? By nationality, or by racial or ethnic identity? Which is most relevant to your everyday life and your sense of "who you are"?

2. Under what circumstances might assimilation benefit an individual? What are some of the disadvantages of assimilation? If you were transported to a country with a very different culture than that to which you are accustomed, what would you need to know in order to successfully assimilate?

3. Canada is often characterized as a "mosaic" where ethnic groups can maintain their cultural beliefs and traditions, while the United States is considered "a melting pot" where people are expected to assimilate. Based on your knowledge of living in Canada, do you feel this is an accurate description of this country?

Pop Quiz

1. A group that is set apart because of its national origin or distinctive cultural patterns is a(n)
   a. assimilated group.
   b. ethnic group.
   c. minority group.
   d. racial group.

2. According to the findings of the Human Genome Project, race
   a. determines intellectual ability.
   b. is a biological, not a social, concept.
   c. explains significant social outcomes.
   d. has no genetic or scientific basis.

3. The piece of Canadian legislation that is responsible for the encouragement and protection of those who engage in cultural expression is the
   a. Immigration Act.
   b. Employment Equity Act.
   c. Official Languages Act.
   d. Multiculturalism Act.

4. Suppose that a White employer refuses to hire an Inuit person and selects an inferior White applicant. This decision is an act of
   a. prejudice.
   b. ethnocentrism.
   c. discrimination.
   d. stigmatization.

5. The term that Peggy McIntosh uses to describe the unearned advantages that those in the majority take for granted is
   a. privilege.
   b. discrimination.
   c. racism.
   d. institutional discrimination.

6. Working together as computer programmers for an electronics firm, a South Asian woman and a Jewish man overcome their initial prejudices and come to appreciate each other's strengths and talents. This scenario is an example of
   a. the contact hypothesis.
   b. a self-fulfilling prophecy.
   c. amalgamation.
   d. reverse discrimination.

7. Intermarriage over several generations, resulting in various groups combining to form a new group, would be an example of
   a. pluralism.
   b. assimilation.
   c. segregation.
   d. amalgamation.

8. Jennifer Anastassakis changed her name to Jennifer Aniston. Her action was an example of
   a. expulsion.
   b. assimilation.
   c. segregation.
   d. pluralism.

9. The largest visible minority group in Canada is
   a. Chinese.
   b. South Asians.
   c. White ethnics.
   d. First Nations peoples.

10. A group that endured prejudice and discrimination, but has succeeded economically, socially, and educationally is referred to as a
    a. symbolic ethnicity.
    b. assimilated group.
    c. model or ideal minority.
    d. dominant class.

1. (b); 2. (d); 3. (d); 4. (c); 5. (a); 6. (a); 7. (d); 8. (b); 9. (b); 10. (c)

14

HEALTH, MEI
ENV

ICINE & RONMENT

LIVING ON MOTHER EARTH

Earth is alive. At least it functions as if it is. So claims scientist James Lovelock, the originator of Gaia theory, which analyzes the planet and its interdependent parts as if it were a single, living organism. Today, Lovelock claims, humans are in danger of pushing this living system out of balance.

Gaia (pronounced "GUY-uh") is the ancient Greek earth goddess. Lovelock chose this name for his theory to emphasize that all living things represent a single interdependent system. He believes that we must develop an integrated vision of life to better understand the environment and our relationship with it.

Lovelock argues that Gaia maintains conditions on earth suitable for life through feedback loops. The oxygen cycle, in which humans and other animals breathe in oxygen and exhale carbon dioxide while plants do the reverse, is one simple example. Lovelock and his colleagues demonstrate that temperature, the salinity of oceans, and oxygen and methane levels are regulated by similar systems. Balance is maintained through natural evolution in which life responds to environmental conditions in ways that perpetuate its survival. If things get out of balance, organisms respond in ways that seek a return to balance.

Like all living things, however, Gaia can become sick and potentially even die. Lovelock has already played a significant role in averting an environmental crisis. In 1957, Lovelock invented the electron capture detector (ECD), which measures minute traces of particles. The ECD provided marine biologist Rachel Carson with data she used in her book *Silent Spring* (1962), which helped give birth to the modern environmental movement. Carson found that cancer-causing pesticides, such as DDT, were distributed around the world far from their sources of origin. She argued that our local actions have global consequences.

Gaia theory tells us we are globally interconnected. By looking at the planet as if it were a single organism, we can recognize how the various parts affect each other. Such a perspective is akin to that of the sociologist who looks at society and the way its various parts work together. We ignore such interdependent processes, and any cues that they may be out of balance, at our peril.

- What does sociology contribute to something as seemingly biological as health?
- What is social epidemiology?
- What environmental lessons do we learn from sociology?

>> Culture, Society, and Health

In the same way, when it comes to health and illness, we must take seriously the interdependent connections that shape our likely outcomes. To understand health, we cannot focus on biology alone. We must consider relationships, contexts, and the significance and impact of culture and society. The communities in which we live shape how we think about health and the body, as do our access to health care and our exposure to health risks.

health As defined by the World Health Organization, a state of complete physical, mental, and social well-being, and not merely the absence of disease and infirmity.

culture-bound syndrome A disease or illness that cannot be understood apart from some specific social context.

We can begin, however, with a general definition of health from the preamble to the 1946 constitution of the World Health Organization. The WHO defines **health** as a "state of complete physical, mental, and social well-being, and not merely the absence of disease and infirmity" (Leavell and Clark 1965:14). This absolute standard provides an ideal type of what constitutes health, although in practice most people fall somewhere along a continuum between this ideal on one extreme and death on the other.

Our culture influences where we place ourselves along that continuum. Different places present us with differing levels of health risk. The type of health care available and our access to it also influences what we come to count as essential care, as do the risks we face. In rural areas, for example, residents must travel many kilometres to see a doctor. On the other hand, people who live in the country may escape many of the stresses and strains, along with environmental risks, that plague people who live in cities. Cultural preferences also influence which procedures and treatments we seek. For instance, organ transplants are rare in Japan, as the Japanese do not generally favour harvesting organs from brain-dead donors.

Researchers have shown that diseases, too, are rooted in the shared meanings of particular cultures. The term **culture-bound syndrome** refers to a disease or illness that cannot be understood apart from some specific social context. This means that there is something particular about the culture—how it is organized, what it believes, what is expected of members—that contributes to that malady (Shepherd 2003; U.S. Surgeon General 1999b).

Did You Know?

. . . The average Canadian woman is 5 feet 3 inches tall, weighs 153 pounds, and wears a size 14 dress, while the average model is 5 feet 9 inches tall, weighs 110 pounds, and wears a size 0 or 2.

In North America, a culture-bound syndrome known as anorexia nervosa has received increasing attention in recent decades. First described in England in the 1860s, this condition is characterized by an intense fear of becoming obese and a distorted image of one's body. Those who suffer from anorexia nervosa (primarily young women in their teens or 20s) lose weight drastically through self-induced semistarvation. Anorexia nervosa is best understood in the context of Western culture, which typically views the slim, youthful individual as healthy and beautiful, and the fat person as ugly and lacking in self-discipline.

Until recently, researchers dealt with the concept of culture-bound syndromes only in cross-cultural studies. However, recent increases in immigration, along with efforts by the medical establishment to reach out to immigrant communities, have led to a belated recognition that not everyone views medicine in the same way. Medical practitioners are now being trained to recognize cultural beliefs that are related to medicine. For example, people from Central America may consider pain a consequence of the imbalance of nature, and Muslim women are particularly concerned about personal modesty. Health care professionals are increasingly incorporating such knowledge into their practices.

Culture can also influence the relative incidence of a disease or disorder. In her book *The Scalpel and the Silver Bear*, Dr. Lori Arviso Alvord, the first Navajo woman to become a surgeon, writes of the depression and alcoholism that attend life on the reservation. These diseases, she says, are born from "historical grief": "Navajo children are told of the capture and murder of their forefathers and mothers, and then they too must share in the legacy." Alcoholism is a significant problem in Aboriginal communities, and rates of FASD (Fetal Alcohol Spectrum Disorder) in First Nations and Inuit communities are much higher than the national average. Aboriginal people have also been found to have higher rates of heart disease and Type 2 diabetes than the general population (Health Canada 2009).

>> Sociological Perspectives on Health and Illness

Whether we are considered "healthy" or "ill" is not our decision alone to make. Family, friends, co-workers, physicians, and others all shape how we perceive the state of our own and others' health. To fully understand the scope of health and illness in society, we have to consider how society defines illness, what the consequences of such definitions are, and how social position and access to resources shape health outcomes.

ILLNESS AND SOCIAL ORDER

From the functionalist perspective, illness represents a threat to the social order. If too many people are sick at the same time, it not only presents a problem for those who are ill but also undercuts our collective ability to perform tasks necessary for the continued operation of society. This can result in debates over what constitutes being "sick enough" to be considered truly ill. At what point, for example, do we stay home from school or work due to illness, and who gets to decide? All of us have likely faced this dilemma, sometimes dragging ourselves out of bed and going anyway because we felt we needed to be there, whether for the sake of ourselves or for others.

Anorexia is not a new disease, though it is discussed much more openly today. Canadian singer Alanis Morissette has acknowledged struggling with anorexia and bulimia during her teenage years.

When people cross the line into illness, they take on what sociologists call the **sick role,** a term that refers to societal expectations about the attitudes and behaviour of a person labelled as ill (Parsons 1951, 1975). Fit members of society exempt the sick from normal, day-to-day responsibilities and generally do not blame them for their condition. Yet the sick are obligated to attempt recovery, which includes seeking competent professional care. This obligation arises from the sense of responsibility we have to perform our normal roles in society, whether as student, worker, parent, or more. It also is motivated by the reality that we may well face sanctions from others for failing to return to those normal roles quickly. In fact, especially in the context of competitive work environments, we often look down on those who seem to get sick too easily or frequently, suspecting that they are either lazy or weak. Such attitudes present significant difficulties for those facing chronic health problems.

sick role Societal expectations about the attitudes and behaviour of a person viewed as being ill.

SOCthink

> > > What factors shape your likelihood of doing all you can to avoid "being sick"? How might the power others have over you influence your actions? What positions do they occupy relative to you?

Physicians and nurses have the power to label people as healthy or sick and, thus, to function as gatekeepers for the sick role. For example, instructors often require students to get a note from a health care professional to verify a claim of illness as a legitimate excuse for missing a paper or an exam. The ill person becomes dependent on the doctor or nurse, because the latter control the resources the patient needs, whether it be a note for a professor or a prescription for medication. We look to such professionals to solve our health care needs, trusting that they have sufficient expertise and experience to diagnose and treat our problems.

Factors such as gender, age, social class, and ethnic group all influence patients' judgments regarding their own state of health. Younger people may fail to detect the warning signs of a dangerous illness, while the elderly may focus too much on the slightest physical malady. Whether one is employed also seems to affect one's willingness to assume the sick role—as does the impact of socialization into a particular occupation or activity. For example, from an early age, athletes learn to define certain ailments as "sports injuries" and so do not regard themselves as "sick" when suffering from such maladies.

POWER, RESOURCES, AND HEALTH

The faith we place in physicians to heal what ails us has helped them attain significant levels of prestige and power.

Theory
A Matter of Perspective

THEORETICAL PERSPECTIVES ON HEALTH

Functionalist:
- health is important if society is to function smoothly; people must be able to perform their roles
- the sick role excuses people from responsibilities, but only temporarily

Conflict:
- health is linked to social inequality; those with greatest power and resources have better access to required elements for health
- differences in education, income, living conditions, and diet are linked to varying levels of health

Feminist:
- women are especially subjected to processes of medicalization
- patriarchal assumptions and practices in health care system negatively affect women's health

Interactionist:
- individuals and societies define "health"
- process of labelling has social consequences

Sociologist Eliot Freidson (1970:5) has likened the status of medicine today to that of state religions in the past—it has an officially approved monopoly on the right to define health and to treat illness. Theorists use the phrase "medicalization of society" to refer to the growing role of medicine as a major institution of social control (Conrad 2007; McKinlay and McKinlay 1977; Zola 1972, 1983).

The Medicalization of Society Social control involves techniques and strategies for regulating behaviour in order to enforce the distinctive norms and values of a culture. How does medicine manifest its social control? First, medicine has greatly expanded its domain of expertise in recent decades. Physicians now examine a wide range of issues in addition to basic health, among them sexuality, old age, anxiety, obesity, child development, alcoholism, and drug addiction. We tolerate this expansion of the boundaries of medicine because we hope that these experts can provide factual and effective cures to complex human problems, as they have to various infectious diseases.

The social significance of this expanding medicalization is that once a problem is viewed from a medical model framework—once medical experts become influential in proposing and assessing relevant public policies—it becomes more difficult for common people to join the discussion and exert influence on decision making. It also becomes more difficult to view these issues as being shaped by social, cultural, or psychological factors, rather than simply by physical or medical factors (Caplan 1989; Conrad 2007; Starr 1982).

A second way that medicine serves as an agent of social control is by retaining absolute jurisdiction over many health care procedures. It has even attempted to guard its jurisdiction by placing health care professionals such as chiropractors and nurse-midwives outside the realm of acceptable medicine. Despite the fact that midwives first brought professionalism to child delivery, they have been portrayed as having invaded the "legitimate" field of obstetrics. Midwives struggled for many years to gain the legitimacy they have today. The legalization and availability of midwifery in most Canadian provinces today is a testament to their determination and to the efforts of women's health advocates.

Inequities in Health Care Another serious concern regarding power and resources in the context of contemporary medicine involves the glaring inequities that exist in health care. As conflict theorists highlight, around the world poor areas tend to be underserved because medical services concentrate where the wealth is. The United States has approximately 27 physicians per 10,000 people. In Canada, where physician incomes are lower, the rate is 9.8 family physicians per 10,000 people, thus prompting concerns about the "doctor shortage." However, compared

alongside African nations, which have fewer than 1 doctor per 10,000 people, Canada's shortage is clearly relative.

The supply of health care in poorer countries is further reduced by what is referred to as **brain drain**—the immigration to Canada and other industrialized nations of skilled workers, professionals, and technicians who are desperately needed in their home countries. As part of this brain drain, physicians, nurses, and other health care professionals have come to Western nations from developing countries such as India, Pakistan, and various African states. Their emigration out of the Third World represents yet another way in which the world's core industrialized nations enhance their quality of life at the expense of developing countries (Bureau of the Census 2007a:Table154; CIHI 2008; World Bank 2007a:92–94). Adding insult to injury, many health care professionals who come to Canada are not allowed to practise unless they earn recertification here. Thus two nations are being denied their much-needed services.

Such inequities in health care have clear life-and-death consequences. For example, there are dramatic differences in infant mortality rates between developing countries such as Afghanistan, Sierra Leone, and Pakistan and industrial nations like Iceland, Japan, and Australia. The **infant mortality rate** is the number of deaths of infants under one year old per 1000 live births in a given year. This measure is an important indicator of a society's level of health care; it reflects prenatal nutrition, delivery procedures, and infant screening measures. Such differences in infant mortality reflect unequal distribution of health care resources based on the wealth or poverty of various nations. Surprisingly, despite the national wealth of the United States, at least 42 nations have lower infant mortality rates, including Canada. An additional way that developing

> **brain drain** The immigration to Canada and other industrialized nations of skilled workers, professionals, and technicians who are desperately needed in their home countries.
> **infant mortality rate** The number of deaths of infants under one year old per 1000 live births in a given year.

5 Movies on HEALTH AND MEDICINE

The Doctor
A doctor has an eye-opening experience when he becomes a patient.

I Am Legend
A virus destroys humankind while one man looks for a cure.

Philadelphia
One man's battle with AIDS and the society that shuns him.

Sicko
A documentary criticizing the U.S. health care system.

Pride of the Yankees
The story of Lou Gehrig and his disease.

Going GLOBAL

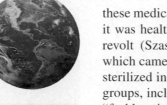

Infant Mortality Rates in Selected Countries

Infant deaths per 1000 live births

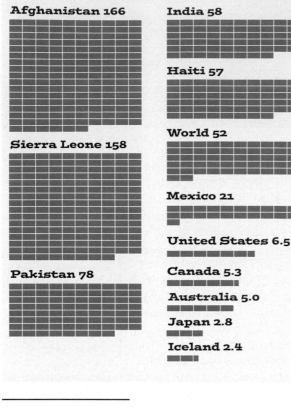

Afghanistan 166

Sierra Leone 158

Pakistan 78

India 58

Haiti 57

World 52

Mexico 21

United States 6.5

Canada 5.3

Australia 5.0

Japan 2.8

Iceland 2.4

Source: Haub 2007.

countries suffer the consequences of health care inequality is in reduced life expectancy. In Africa and much of Latin America and Asia, life expectancy is far lower than in the industrialized nations.

Labelling and Power As interactionist theorists have demonstrated, sometimes the power to label and the power to oppress go hand in hand. A historical example illustrates perhaps the ultimate extreme in labelling social behaviour as a sickness. As enslavement of Africans in the United States came under increasing attack in the 19th century, medical authorities provided new rationalizations for the oppressive practice. Noted physicians published articles stating that the skin colour of Africans deviated from "healthy" white skin colouring because Africans suffered from congenital leprosy. Moreover, physicians classified the continuing efforts of enslaved Africans to escape from their White masters as an example of the "disease" of drapetomania (or "crazy runaways"). The prestigious *New Orleans Medical and Surgical Journal* suggested that the remedy for this "disease" was to treat slaves kindly, as one might treat children. Apparently,

these medical authorities would not entertain the view that it was healthy and sane to flee slavery or join in a slave revolt (Szasz 1971). Under Alberta's Sterilization Act, which came into effect in 1928, thousands of people were sterilized in an effort to limit reproduction among certain groups, including visible minorities and those considered "feeble-minded." After being acknowledged to be a violation of citizens' constitutional rights, the act was finally repealed in 1972.

By the late 1980s, the power of one particular label—"person with AIDS"—had become quite evident. This label often functions as a master status that overshadows all other aspects of a person's life. Once someone is told that he or she has tested positive for HIV, the virus associated with AIDS, that person is forced to confront immediate and difficult questions: Should I tell my family members? My sex partners? My friends? My co-workers? My employer? How will these people respond? People's intense fear of the disease has led to prejudice and discrimination—even social ostracism—against those who have (or are suspected of having) AIDS. A person who has AIDS must deal not only with the serious medical consequences of the disease but also with the distressing social consequences associated with the label.

AIDS caught major social institutions—particularly the government, the health care system, and the economy—by surprise when it was first noticed by medical practitioners in the 1970s. It has since spread around the world, with the first North American cases of AIDS reported at the beginning of the 1980s. Rather than being a distinct disease, AIDS is actually a predisposition to various diseases that is caused by a virus, the human immunodeficiency virus (HIV). The virus gradually destroys the body's immune system, leaving the carrier vulnerable to infections such as pneumonia that those with healthy immune systems generally can resist.

As of 2007, more than 63,000 Canadians were living with HIV/AIDS. While there has been a decline in incidence within the general population, Aboriginal people are disproportionately represented in rates of new infections and those living with the disease. Globally, an estimated 33.2 million people are now infected; however, the disease is not evenly distributed. Those areas least equipped to deal with it—the developing nations of sub-Saharan Africa—face the greatest challenge (Centers for Disease Control and Prevention 2007c).

Because those in high-risk groups—gay men and IV drug users—were stigmatized in society and comparatively powerless, policy makers in Western nations were slow to respond to the AIDS crisis. Over time, however, the response has improved, and today

Hot or Not?

Considering the current doctor shortage, should Canada relax its rules requiring physicians trained in other nations to become recertified?

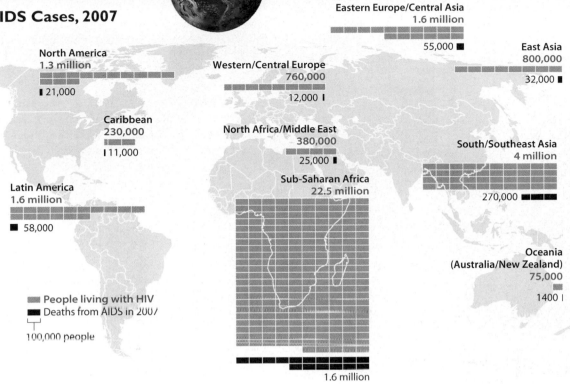

Going GLOBAL

HIV/AIDS Cases, 2007

North America
1.3 million
■ 21,000

Caribbean
230,000
■ 11,000

Latin America
1.6 million
■ 58,000

Western/Central Europe
760,000
12,000 ▮

North Africa/Middle East
380,000
25,000 ■

Sub-Saharan Africa
22.5 million
1.6 million

Eastern Europe/Central Asia
1.6 million
55,000 ■

East Asia
800,000
32,000 ■

South/Southeast Asia
4 million
270,000 ■■■

Oceania (Australia/New Zealand)
75,000
1400 ▮

■ People living with HIV
■ Deaths from AIDS in 2007
100,000 people

Note: Midpoint estimates for December 2007. Total number of adults and children living with HIV, 33.2 million; total number of estimated adult and child deaths during 2007, 2.1 million.

Sources: Centers for Disease Control and Prevention 2007a; UNAIDS 2007.

people with HIV or AIDS who receive appropriate medical treatment are living longer than they did in the past. The high cost of drug treatment programs has generated intensive worldwide pressure on the major pharmaceutical companies to lower the prices to patients in developing nations, especially in sub-Saharan Africa. Bowing to this pressure, several of the companies have agreed to make the combination therapies available at cost. As a result, the accessibility of HIV treatment has increased steadily, though inequalities remain. By the beginning of 2008, only 11 percent of mothers who need therapy to prevent transmission of the virus to their babies were receiving it (R. Wolf 2008).

According to labelling theorists, we can view a variety of life experiences as illnesses or not. Recently, the medical community has recognized premenstrual syndrome, posttraumatic disorders, and hyperactivity as medical disorders. Probably the most noteworthy medical example of labelling is the case of homosexuality. For years, psychiatrists classified being gay or lesbian as a mental disorder subject to treatment. This official sanction by the psychiatry profession became an early target of the growing gay and lesbian rights movement in the United States and Canada. In 1974, homosexuality was removed from the *Diagnostic and Statistical Manual of Mental Disorders* (Conrad 2007).

NEGOTIATING CURES

In practice, we seek to strike a balance between the authority of the physician and the agency of the patient. Physicians use cues to reinforce their prestige and power. According to medical sociologist Brenda Beagan (2001), the technical language students learn in medical school becomes the basis for the script they follow as novice physicians. The familiar white coat and stethoscope is their costume—one that helps them to appear confident and professional at the same time that it identifies them as doctors to patients and other staff members. Beagan found that many medical students struggle to project the appearance of competence they think their role demands, but over time most become accustomed to expecting respect and deference.

Patients, on the other hand, are not passive. Sometimes patients play an active role in health care by failing to follow a physician's advice. For example, some patients stop taking medications long before they should. Some take an incorrect dosage on purpose, and others never even fill their prescriptions. Such noncompliance results in part from the prevalence of self-medication in our society; many people are accustomed to self-diagnosis and self-treatment.

Patients' active involvement in their health care can have very positive consequences. Some patients consult books, magazines, and websites about preventive health care techniques, attempt to maintain a healthful and nutritious diet, carefully monitor any side effects of medication, and adjust the dosage based on perceived side effects.

Did You Know?

... In research looking at how social class operates, sociologist Annette Lareau found that middle-class parents and children were more likely to engage with physicians, asking questions and questioning diagnoses. Working-class patients were more deferential to the doctor's authority.

social epidemiology The study of the distribution of disease, impairment, and general health status across a population.

Recognizing this change, pharmaceutical firms are advertising their prescription drugs directly to potential customers. For their part, medical professionals are understandably suspicious of these new sources of information. A study published in the *Journal of the American Medical Association* in 2001 found that health information on the Internet is often incomplete and inaccurate, even on the best sites. Nevertheless, there is little doubt that Internet research is transforming patient–physician encounters (Berland 2001; Gerencher 2007).

>> Social Epidemiology

By looking at patterns of health and illness throughout society, we can better understand which factors are at work in shaping health outcomes. **Social epidemiology** is the study of disease distribution, impairment, and general health status across a population. Initially, epidemiology concentrated on the scientific study of epidemics, focusing on how they started and spread. Contemporary social epidemiology is much broader in scope, concerned not only with epidemics but also with nonepidemic diseases, injuries, drug addiction and alcoholism, suicide, and mental illness. Recently, epidemiologists took on the new role of tracking bioterrorism. In 2001, they mobilized to trace an anthrax outbreak and prepare for any terrorist use of smallpox or other lethal microbes. Epidemiologists draw on the work of a wide variety of scientists and researchers, among them physicians, sociologists, public health officials, biologists, veterinarians, demographers, anthropologists, psychologists, and meteorologists.

Researchers in social epidemiology commonly use two concepts: incidence and prevalence. **Incidence** refers to the number of new cases of a specific disorder that occur within a given population during a stated period, usually a year. For example, the incidence of AIDS in Canada in 2007 was 1243 cases. In contrast, **prevalence** refers to the total number of cases of a specific disorder that exist at a given time. The prevalence of AIDS in Canada through 2007 was 63,604 cases (Public Health Agency of Canada 2007).

When disease incidence figures are presented as rates—for example, the number of reports per 100,000 people—they are called **morbidity rates.** This is distinct from the **mortality rate,** which refers to the incidence of death in a given population. Sociologists find morbidity rates useful because they can reveal whether a specific disease occurs more frequently among one segment of a population than another. As we shall see, social class, race, ethnicity, gender, and age can all affect a population's morbidity rates.

Did You Know?

...In recent years, the popularity of hand sanitizers has exploded. From 2002 to 2003, Canadian sales grew by 187 percent, and In 2008, sales of hand sanitizers in the United States exceeded US$117 million.

SOCIAL CLASS

Social class is clearly associated with differences in morbidity and mortality rates. Studies in Canada and other countries have consistently shown that people in the lower classes have higher rates of mortality and disability than others. One study concluded that North Americans whose family income was less than $10,000 could expect to die seven years sooner than those with an income of at least $25,000 (Pamuk et al. 1998).

A number of factors appear to influence the effect class has on health. Crowded living conditions, substandard

and difficult to treat illness becomes (Prus 2007).

Karl Marx would have argued, and some contemporary sociologists agree, that many capitalist societies care more about maximizing profits than they do about the health and safety of industrial workers. As a result, government agencies may not take forceful

incidence The number of new cases of a specific disorder that occur within a given population during a stated period.
prevalence The total number of cases of a specific disorder that exist at a given time.
morbidity rate The incidence of disease in a given population.
mortality rate The incidence of death in a given population.

> It is a lot harder to keep people well than it is to just get them over a sickness.
>
> DeForest Clinton Jarvis

housing, poor diet, and stress all contribute to the ill health of many low-income people in Canada. In certain instances, poor education and low levels of literacy may lead to a lack of awareness of measures necessary to maintain good health. Financial strains are certainly a major factor in the health problems of less affluent people.

What is particularly troubling about social class differences is that they appear to be cumulative. Little or no health care in childhood or young adulthood is likely to mean more illness later in life. The longer that low income presents a barrier to adequate health care, the more chronic

action to regulate conditions in the workplace, and workers suffer many preventable job-related injuries and illnesses. As we will see later in this chapter, research also shows that the lower classes are more vulnerable to environmental pollution, another consequence of capitalist production, than are the affluent, not only where they work but where they live.

RACE AND ETHNICITY

The health profiles of many racial and ethnic minorities reflect the social inequality evident in Canada. The poor economic and environmental conditions of the First Nations communities are manifested in high morbidity and mortality rates for Aboriginal persons. It is true that some afflictions, such as sickle-cell anemia among Blacks, are influenced by genetics, but in most instances, environmental factors contribute to the differential rates of disease and death.

Social epidemiologists have demonstrated that morbidity rates are primarily influenced by social class and wealth, not race and ethnicity per se, but visible minorities and Aboriginal persons are disproportionately represented among the poor. First Nations communities in particular have limited access to many of the social determinants of health, such as fresh and nutritious food, clean water, education, literacy, income, and employment. As mentioned earlier, the Aboriginal population in Canada has higher incidence of HIV/AIDS, heart disease, and Type 2 diabetes. Tuberculosis infection rates are eight to 10 times higher than among the general population. And, largely in response to widespread poverty, alcohol and marijuana use among Aboriginal youth is higher than it is for their Caucasian counterparts (Health Canada 2006; Lemstra et al. 2009).

As noted earlier in this chapter, infant mortality is regarded as a primary indicator of health care. A recent study found that the mortality rate among Aboriginal newborns is as much as four times that of non-native

newborns in Canada, the United States, Australia, and New Zealand. In Canada, the infant mortality rate for children on reserves is twice that of non-natives, and among Inuit babies, that rate rises to four times higher (Smylie and Adomako 2009). Aboriginal children also suffer more ear infections, respiratory illness, and dental problems. Rates of obesity of children living on reserves are more than four times higher than the national average. All these conditions contribute to childhood morbidity, and potentially, mortality. Disturbing as these figures are, social epidemiologists note that the lack of reliable statistics for non-status First Nations people, Métis, and Aboriginal persons living off-reserve mean there could be even more serious health problems among the native population than currently documented.

The medical establishment is not exempt from institutional discrimination. Despite Canada's commitment to "universal" accessibility, there is evidence that minorities receive inferior care due to cultural bias on the part of practitioners, language barriers, and cultural differences and expectations. In the United States, national clinical studies have shown that even allowing for differences in income and insurance coverage, racial and ethnic minorities are less likely than other groups to receive standard health care and life-saving treatment (Dressler et al. 2005; A. Green et al. 2007).

Numerous examples in the history of African American health care demonstrate that such institutional discrimination has been around for a long time. For example, in the notorious Tuskegee syphilis study, begun by the U.S. federal government in the 1930s, doctors knowingly withheld treatment from Black men infected with syphilis in order to observe the progression of the disease. Another study, conducted from 1992 to 1997, was designed to determine whether there is a biological or genetic basis for violent behaviour. Researchers misled the parents of young subjects, all of whom were Black males, by telling them that the children would undergo a series of tests and questions. In fact, the boys were given potentially risky doses of the same drug found in the now-banned Fen-phen weight-loss pill, which causes heart irregularities.

Having to deal with the effects of racism may itself contribute to the medical problems of Blacks (Waitzkin 1986). The stress that results from racial prejudice and discrimination helps to explain the higher rates of hypertension found among African Americans (and Hispanics) compared to

Did You Know?

... In 1979, the measured obesity rate in Canada was 13.8 percent. Twenty-five years later, in 2004, that number had risen to 23.1 percent, and experts argue it continues to rise.

However, in 2007, a self-reporting study found that only 16 percent of Canadians identify as obese.

Source: Statistics Canada 2008g.

Whites. Hypertension—twice as common in Blacks as in Whites—is believed to be a critical factor in Blacks' high mortality rates from heart disease, kidney disease, and stroke (Morehouse Medical Treatment and Effectiveness Center 1999).

Some First Nations peoples adhere to cultural beliefs that make them less likely to use the public health care system. While specific approaches may vary among different Aboriginal groups or bands, all embrace a more holistic understanding of wellness than is offered within mainstream Western medicine. For instance, prescribed by an elder, plant material may be worn in a **medicine pouch** by persons seeking the mercy and protection of the spirits. Sweat lodges are used for spiritual healing and purification. These are but two examples of a belief system that emphasizes care for body, mind, and spirit, and the promotion of health through harmony with one's environment. Holistic medicine is further discussed later in this chapter.

As immigration expands Canada's racial and ethnic mosaic, health care professionals must become more culturally sensitive in providing care. For example, Muslim women may not display their body, so examinations must be conducted in an alternate fashion. English may not be the first language of those seeking care, and so family members or independent interpreters may need to be consulted and included in decisions. Some doctors have faced dilemmas in being asked to perform procedures that are important within particular cultures, but violate their own ethics or federal laws, such as female "circumcision," otherwise known as female genital mutilation—a distinction that clearly demonstrates differing views.

GENDER AND SEXUALITY

A large body of research indicates that compared with men, women experience a higher prevalence of many illnesses, although they do have a longer life expectancy. There are some variations—for example, men are more likely to have parasitic diseases, whereas women are more likely to become diabetic—but as a group, women appear to be in poorer health than men.

The apparent inconsistency between the ill health of women and their greater longevity appears to be tied to lifestyle differences between men and women that grow out of gendered norms. Women's lower rate of cigarette smoking (reducing their risk of heart disease, lung cancer, and emphysema), lower consumption of alcohol (reducing the risk of auto accidents and cirrhosis of the liver), and lower rate of employment in dangerous occupations explain about one-third of their greater longevity than men. Researchers argue that women are much more likely than men to seek treatment, to be diagnosed as having a disease, and thus to have their illnesses reflected in the data examined by epidemiologists.

Feminists have noted that with everything from birth to beauty being treated in an increasingly medical context, women have been particularly vulnerable to the medicalization of society. Ironically, even given the increased power of the medical establishment in women's lives, medical researchers have often excluded them from clinical studies. Female physicians and researchers charge that sexism lies at the heart of such research practices and insist there is a desperate need for studies of female subjects (Rieker and Bird 2000).

medicine pouch Indigenous healing method; pouch containing plant material is worn by Aboriginal peoples seeking the mercy and protection of the spirits.

Further research is also required into the health care needs and experiences of homosexuals and transgendered persons. Lesbians are particularly underrepresented in health studies, as they face the combined effects of gender and heterosexual bias. Medical professionals must be better educated to address the physical, emotional, and *social* complexities of sexuality. (Tjepkema 2008)

MENTAL HEALTH

Mental and emotional health is an important component of well-being, and one in which gender differences are evident. While women are diagnosed more often with mental illnesses, they tend to be relatively less serious conditions, whereas when men are diagnosed as being mentally ill, the severity is

Did You Know?

. . . Emily Howard Jennings Stowe (1831–1903) was the first Canadian woman to practise medicine in Canada. Refused entry to medical school in this country, she received her training in the United States and established a practice in Toronto in 1867. Ontario would not grant her a medical licence until 1880.

usually greater. Men's cultural reluctance to seek medical help may contribute to these patterns—that is, diagnosis comes only when the condition has become significantly worse. Due to the stigma associated with mental illness, many people—both men and women—may refuse to seek treatment. According to the Canadian Mental Health Association, approximately 20 percent of Canadians will experience a mental illness in their lifetime, and at least 1 percent of the population is affected by a persistent and disabling form of mental illness.

AGE

Health is the overriding concern of the elderly. Most older people in Canada report having at least one chronic illness, but only some of those conditions are potentially life threatening or require medical care. The quality of life among older people is of particular concern in the face of potentially escalating health problems and a steadily aging population. Arthritis is common among older Canadians, and many have visual or hearing impairments that can interfere with the performance of everyday tasks.

Due to isolation, ill health, or as a result of aging, older people are especially vulnerable to decline of brain function. Rates of dementia, Alzheimer's, and Parkinson's disease are on the rise in Canada.

Increased health risks and chronic conditions mean older Canadians are more likely to visit doctors. Nearly nine out of 10 seniors report having seen a general practitioner in the past year, and 44 percent had four or more contacts with the doctor. More than one-third of seniors have seen a specialist in the past year, compared with one-quarter of adults aged 18 to 64 (Statistics Canada 2007i). As Canada's population continues to age, the disproportionate use of the health care system by older adults is a critical factor in all discussions about the cost of health care and possible reforms of the health care system.

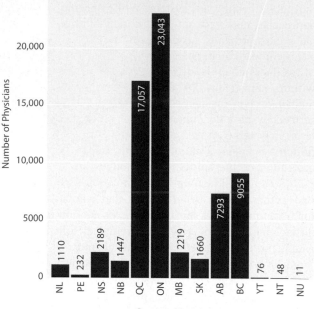

Number of Physicians by Province/Territory, Canada, 2008

Notes: Includes active physicians, which are defined as physicians that have an MD degree and a valid address (mail sent to the physician by Scott's Directories is not returned). Includes physicians in clinical practice and those not working in a clinical practice. Data exclude residents, physicians in the military, as well as semi-retired and retired physicians. Data exclude non-licensed physicians who requested that their information not be published as of December 31 of the reference year. Data as of December 31 of the reference year.

Source: Scott's Medical Database, Canadian Institute for Health Information.

A person's odds of good health are shaped by her or his class, race and ethnicity, gender, and age. Even geography matters, as there are differences in the number of

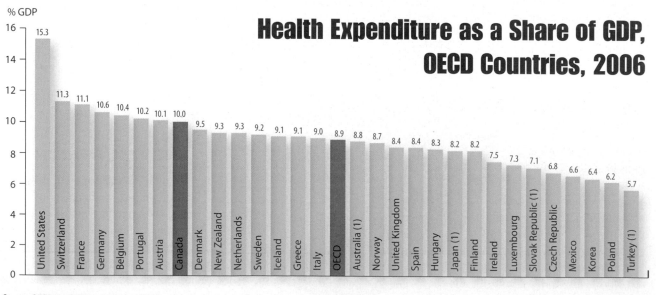

Health Expenditure as a Share of GDP, OECD Countries, 2006

Source: OECD Health Data 2008, June 2008.

physicians from one province to the next. Health care professionals and program advisors need to take such differential effects into account when considering what constitutes equitable health care coverage. Any attempts to do so, however, are constrained by the cost of health care.

>> Health Care in Canada

The costs of health care have skyrocketed in recent decades, from $23 billion in 1980 to over $142 billion in 2005. Projected estimates anticipate Canada will be spending $243 billion by the year 2020.

Canada currently spends 10 percent of its GDP on health care, with an average expenditure of US$3678 per capita (OECD 2008).

Thus the health care system of Canada has clearly moved beyond the day when general practitioners living in a neighbourhood or community typically made house calls and charged modest fees for their services. Health care has become a big business, changing the nature of relationships between doctors, nurses, and patients.

A HISTORICAL VIEW

Canada's system of universal health care had its origins in Saskatchewan, the first province to establish a public hospital insurance program. Under the guidance of Premier Tommy Douglas, it began in 1947 with a pilot

Hot or Not?

Do private medical clinics represent a threat to Canada's public health care system?

project in the town of Swift Current, with full provincial coverage by the following year. In 1958, the federal government followed suit with the Hospital Insurance and Diagnostic Services Act, the first national hospital insurance plan in North America. In 1968, the Medical Care Act was passed, providing universal health insurance to all Canadians.

Canadians highly value their health care system. In an Ipsos Reid poll conducted in 2008, universal health care ranked ninth on the list of 101 things Canadians value about their country, and the "father of Canadian health care," Tommy Douglas, came in at number 36. Surveys gauging public response to the current system indicate most would welcome improvements in such aspects as wait times and the option of complementary private insurance, but there is little support for disbanding our publicly funded system.

However, Douglas' ideas have not been without their detractors. In response to the 1962 introduction of a full public medicare program in Saskatchewan (through which all doctors' fees would be paid, not just those working in hospitals), the province's doctors staged a high-profile strike. Charges of communism and socialism were levied against the government, but the public administration of medical care nonetheless became national policy.

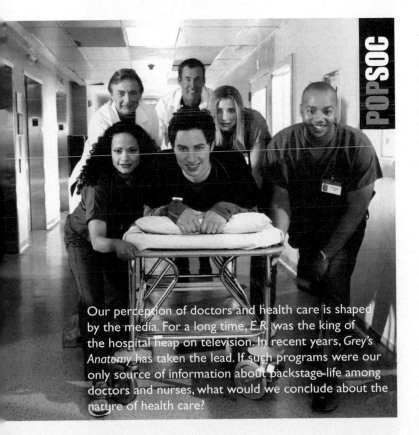

Our perception of doctors and health care is shaped by the media. For a long time, *E.R.* was the king of the hospital heap on television. In recent years, *Grey's Anatomy* has taken the lead. If such programs were our only source of information about backstage life among doctors and nurses, what would we conclude about the nature of health care?

POPSOC

THE ROLE OF GOVERNMENT

Since 1984, health care in Canada has been structured according to the principles of the Canada Health Act. In keeping with Douglas' ideals, this federal statute ensures that all Canadians have access to medical services on the basis of need, rather than the ability to pay. Provinces and territories receive transfer payments from the federal government to administer and deliver their own programs in accordance with the act. Canada's health care system is publicly funded—that is, financed through taxation revenue at the federal, provincial, and territorial levels. Some provinces charge additional health care premiums, calculated according to income, but non-payment of a premium does not result in restriction of access to care. The respective responsibilities of the various levels of government are outlined in the Canada Health Act, with the federal government being responsible for the majority of duties.

In addition to its role as overseer, the federal government directly delivers health services to select groups: the military, federal inmates, the RCMP, veterans, and Aboriginal peoples, though members of the latter three groups often use the general public system. All health needs of these groups are to be met by the federal government.

The principles of the Canada Health Act are:

1. *Public administration*
The provincial and territorial plans must be carried out by public institutions on a non-profit basis.

2. *Comprehensiveness*
All medically necessary services provided by hospitals and doctors must be insured.

3. *Universality*
All residents of a province or territory are entitled to uniform health coverage.

4. *Accessibility*
All Canadians must have reasonable access to medically necessary services.

5. *Portability*
Health coverage must be provided when an insured person moves or travels within the country or travels outside Canada.

Of course, principles do not always correspond with practice. Most Canadians have experienced or are aware of occasions where at least one of the above principles was not met. Doctor shortages, lack of beds, wait times, limited access to specialists and specialized tests and treatments, closing of emergency rooms, overworked nurses, differential care for rural and urban populations, and differential care for different groups of people in our society all speak to the disjuncture between the principles and the reality. Following Weber, perhaps it is more useful to think of these principles as "ideal types," abstract benchmarks against which we compare our actual health care system.

PHYSICIANS, NURSES, AND PATIENTS

The power of medicine and the prestige of doctors have risen together. As the occupation became more professional and training became more standardized, some of the depersonalizing effects of working in bureaucratic organizations came to influence role performance. This was true in regard to doctors' relationships with both nurses and patients.

Considering doctors' relationships with patients, and reflecting on the training she received, Dr. Lori Arviso Alvord writes, "I had been trained by a group of physicians who placed much more emphasis on their technical abilities and clinical skills than on their abilities to be caring and sensitive" (Alvord and Van Pelt 1999:13). Despite many efforts to formally introduce a humanistic approach to patient care into the medical school curriculum, patient overload and cost cutting by hospitals have tended to undercut positive relations. Moreover, widespread publicity about wait times, malpractice suits, and high medical costs have further strained the physician–patient relationship.

Just as physicians have maintained dominance in their interactions with patients, they have controlled interactions with nurses. Despite having extensive training, nurses commonly take orders from physicians. Traditionally, the relationship between doctors and nurses has paralleled the male dominance of Canada: Most physicians have been male, while virtually all nurses have been female.

Like other women in subordinate roles, nurses have been expected to perform their duties without challenging the authority of men. Psychiatrist Leonard Stein (1967) referred to this process as the "doctor–nurse game." According to the rules of this game, the nurse must never openly disagree with the physician. When she has recommendations concerning a patient's care, she must communicate them indirectly, in a deferential tone. For example, if asked

SOCthink

> > > Have you noticed a gendered difference in the way doctors interact with their patients? If so, what might be some of the reasons this occurs?

by a hospital's medical resident, "What sleeping medication has been helpful to Mrs. Brown in the past?" (an indirect request for a recommendation), the nurse will respond with a disguised recommendation, such as "Pentobarbital 100 mg was quite effective night before last." Her careful response allows the physician to authoritatively restate the same prescription as if it were his idea.

In an occupation that was once predominantly male, increasing numbers of women are becoming physicians. More than half of students entering medical school in Canada are women. An equivalent pattern in nursing has not occurred, however. While there are more male nurses now than in the past, the overwhelming majority of registered nurses—in Canada, 94 percent—are female (CIHI 2008). Women also tend to be concentrated in certain fields of medicine, including family practice and paediatrics. Surgical specialties are heavily populated by men.

A study of male and female medical residents suggests that the increasing number of women physicians may alter the traditional doctor–patient relationship. The study found male residents to be more focused on the intellectual challenges of medicine and the prestige associated with certain medical specialties. In contrast, female residents were more likely to express a commitment to caring for patients and devoting time to them. As women continue to enter and move higher in the hierarchies of the medical profession, sociological studies will surely be done to see whether these apparent gender differences persist.

ALTERNATIVES TO TRADITIONAL HEALTH CARE

In traditional forms of health care, people rely on physicians and hospitals for the treatment of illness. Yet a significant proportion of adults in Canada attempt to maintain good health or respond to illness through the use of alternative health care techniques. For example, in recent decades, interest has been growing in holistic (sometimes spelled

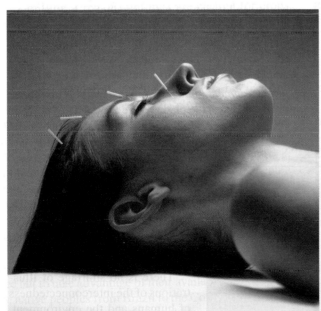

wholistic) medical principles, first developed in China. **Holistic medicine** refers to therapies in which the health care practitioner considers the person's physical, mental, emotional, and spiritual characteristics. The individual is regarded as a totality rather than a collection of interre-

SOCthink

> > > What do you think about alternative medicine? Would you be willing to get assistance from a holistic healer? What background factors, such as age, race and ethnicity, or gender, might play a role in your willingness or unwillingness to do so?

lated organ systems. Treatment methods include massage, chiropractic medicine, acupuncture (which involves the insertion of fine needles into surface points), respiratory exercises, and the use of herbs as remedies. Nutrition, exercise, and visualization may also be used to treat ailments that traditionally are addressed through medication or hospitalization (Sharma and Bodeker 1998).

> **holistic medicine** Therapies in which the health care practitioner considers the person's physical, mental, emotional, and spiritual characteristics.

Practitioners of holistic medicine do not necessarily function totally outside the traditional health care system. Some have medical degrees and rely on X-rays and EKG machines for diagnostic assistance. Others who staff holistic clinics, often referred to as wellness clinics, reject the use of medical technology. The recent resurgence of holistic medicine comes amid widespread recognition of the value of nutrition and the dangers of overreliance on prescription drugs (especially those used to reduce stress, such as Valium).

Although a number of post-secondary institutions in Canada now offer credit programs in complementary and alternative therapies such as massage or holistic nutrition, the mainstream medical community based upon the Western model of medicine continues to have dominance. Furthermore, many of these treatments are not covered under publicly funded plans; thus they are cost-prohibitive for many Canadians.

On the international level, the World Health Organization (WHO) has begun to monitor the use of alternative medicine around the world. According to the WHO, 80 percent of people who live in the poorest countries in the world use alternative medicine, from herbal treatments to the services of a faith healer. In most countries, these

> **Did You Know?**
>
> . . . More than 70 percent of Canadians regularly use complementary and alternative therapies such as vitamins and minerals, herbal products, and other natural health products.
>
> *Source*: Public Health Agency Canada 2008.

ENVIRONMENTAL JUSTICE

In Canada, longstanding land disputes exist between Aboriginal communities and the federal and provincial governments. Many of these are in regards to issues of ownership and rights, but there have also been a number of incidences of disruption to their communities and lives, as well as contamination of the land and drinking water by outside industry. Construction of gas pipelines, mercury contamination, and logging and destruction of forests are just some of the situations that

> environmental justice A legal strategy based on claims that racial minorities are subjected disproportionately to environmental hazards.

disparities that break along racial and social class lines. In general, poor people and people of colour are much more likely than others to be victimized by the everyday consequences of economic development, including air pollution from expressways and incinerators.

In Sydney Harbour, Nova Scotia, years of industrial waste from coke-ovens has resulted in extensive contamination of the surrounding land and water. It is believed the wastes contain as many as 15 varieties of cancer-related chemicals, and indeed, cancer rates among those living near the area are significantly higher than in other parts of the province. Birth defects and miscarriages have also been documented. Environmental activists Maude Barlow, of the Council of Canadians, and Elizabeth May, lawyer and leader of the Green Party, describe the extent of the hazard and the glaring lack of effective governmental response in their book *Frederick Street: Life and Death on Canada's Love Canal* (2000).

Aboriginal communities are among the most frequently affected by environmental hazards. Mercury contamination of ground and surface water, such as occurred in the Grassy Narrows village in British Columbia, has caused serious health problems. As well, natural habitats have been destroyed by logging and gas pipelines, threatening the traditional existence of the First Nations peoples.

Sociologists Paul Mohai and Robin Saha (2007) examined over 600 hazardous waste treatment, storage, and disposal facilities in the United States. They found that non-Whites and Latinos make up 43 percent of the people who live within a mile from these dangerous sites. There are two possible explanations for this finding. One is that racial and ethnic minorities possess less power than others, so that they cannot prevent toxic sites from being located in their backyards. The other is that they end up settling near the sites after they are constructed, because economics and the forces of discrimination push them into the least desirable living areas.

> **Suburbia is where the developer bulldozes out the trees, then names the streets after them.**
>
> Bill Vaughn

have arisen, and in some cases, the effects have been felt for decades and over several generations.

Environmental justice is a legal strategy based on claims that racial minorities are subjected disproportionately to environmental hazards. Some observers have heralded environmental justice as the "new civil rights of the 21st century" (Kokmen 2008:42). Since the advent of the environmental justice movement, activists and scholars have identified other environmental

SOCthink

> > > Disputes around natural resources have been going on for years in Canada. What factors make it so difficult to come to a resolution? How might access to resources shape the duration of such struggles?

Canada does have legislation intended to protect people from exposure to environmental dangers, such as the Canadian Environmental Protection Act, but in Canada and around the world, the poor and oppressed continue to bear the brunt of environmental degradation. In the 1990s, the United States federal government,

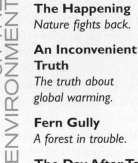

5 Movies on THE ENVIRONMENT

The Happening
Nature fights back.

An Inconvenient Truth
The truth about global warming.

Fern Gully
A forest in trouble.

The Day After Tomorrow
Man against nature.

WALL-E
A robot in the year 2700 discovers his destiny.

unable to find a disposal site for spent nuclear fuel, turned to tribal reservations. Agents eventually persuaded a tiny band of Goshute Indians in Skull Valley, Utah, to accept more than 44,000 barrels of the highly radioactive substance, which will remain dangerous for an estimated 10,000 years. The government dropped the plan only after opposition from surrounding towns and cities, whose residents objected to the movement of the material through their communities. This was not the first time the U.S. government had attempted to persuade the impoverished tribe to accept environmentally objectionable installations. The

Scientist David Suzuki has become Canada's best-known environmental advocate and indeed, his television appearances have earned him celebrity status.

military's nerve gas storage facility resides on or near the reservation, along with the Intermountain Power Project, which generates coal-fired electrical power for consumers in California (Eureka County 2006; Foy 2006). In recent years, municipalities in Ontario, unable to find cities willing to create landfill space, have been sending their garbage to the United States. While the receiving towns are paid for this service, there are environmental consequences from this practice, including the air pollution from trucks hauling refuse across the border.

In considering environmental issues, sociologists have emphasized the interconnectedness of humans and the environment, as well as the divisiveness of race and social class. Scientific findings can also play a role in our understanding of the nature and scope of environmental concerns. Of course, when such findings affect government policy and economic regulations, they become highly politicized. Such struggles are inevitable when core values and differential access to resources are at stake.

>> Environmental Problems

Unfortunately, as we have already seen, the environmental problems caused by development have effects far beyond the places where they are created. Witness Muhammad Ali, a Bangladeshi man who has had to flee floodwaters five times in the last decade. Scientists believe that global warming is to blame both for worsening monsoons and for the raging waters of the Jamuna River, swollen by abnormally high glacier melt from the Himalayas. Every time the river floods, Ali tears down his house, made of tin and bamboo, and moves to higher ground. But he is running out of land to move to. "Where we are standing, in five days it will be gone," he says. "Our future thinking is that if this problem is not taken care of, we will be swept away" (Goering 2007).

Increasingly, people are recognizing the need to address such challenges to the environment. In a 2008 survey, 63 percent agreed that the effects of global warming are already manifest or will occur within five years. Of those surveyed, 49 percent of adults said that protection of the environment should be given priority. This contrasted with 42 percent who said that the government should pursue economic growth even if the environment suffers (Gallup 2008c; Jacobe 2008). Three environmental areas are of particular concern: air pollution, water pollution, and global warming.

AIR POLLUTION

Worldwide, more than 1 billion people are exposed to potentially health-damaging levels of air pollution.

rivers, and lakes. Consequently, many bodies of water have become unsafe for fishing and swimming, let alone drinking. Around the world, pollution of the oceans is an issue of growing concern. Such pollution results regularly from waste dumping and is made worse by fuel leaks from shipping and occasional oil spills. When the oil tanker *Exxon Valdez* ran aground in Prince William Sound, Alaska, in 1989, its cargo of 11 million gallons of crude oil spilled into the sound and washed onto the shore, contaminating 2068 kilometres (1285 miles) of shoreline. Altogether, about 11,000 people joined in a massive cleanup effort that cost over US$2 billion, yet the effects of the disaster continue to be felt today. Globally, oil spills occur regularly. In 2002, the oil tanker *Prestige* spilled twice as much fuel as the *Valdez,* greatly damaging coastal areas in Spain and France (ITOPF 2006).

Less dramatic than large-scale accidents or disasters, but more common in many parts of the world, are problems with the basic water supply. Worldwide, over 1.1 billion people lack safe and adequate drinking water, and 2.6 billion have no acceptable means of sanitation—a

Unfortunately, in cities around the world, residents have come to accept smog and polluted air as normal. Urban air pollution is caused primarily by emissions from automobiles and secondarily by emissions from electric power plants and heavy industries. Smog not only limits visibility but can lead to health problems as uncomfortable as eye irritation and as deadly as lung cancer. Such problems are especially severe in developing countries. The WHO estimates that up to 700,000 premature deaths per year could be prevented if pollutants were brought down to safer levels (Carty 1999; World Resources Institute 1998).

People are capable of changing their behaviour, but they are also often unwilling to make such changes permanent. During the 1984 Olympics in Los Angeles, authorities asked residents to carpool and stagger their work hours to relieve traffic congestion and improve the quality of the air athletes would breathe. These changes resulted in a remarkable 12-percent drop in ozone levels. After the Olympics ended, however, people reverted to their normal behaviour, and the ozone levels climbed once again. Similarly, China took drastic action to ensure that Beijing's high levels of air pollution did not mar the 2008 Olympic Games. Construction work in the city ceased, polluting factories and power plants closed down, and workers swept roads and sprayed them with water several times a day. This temporary solution, however, has not solved China's ongoing pollution problem (*The Economist* 2008b). The 2010 Winter Olympics in Vancouver claimed to be more environmentally responsible than previous events, yet tens of thousands of trees were cut down to make way for Olympic venues.

WATER POLLUTION

Throughout North America, waste materials dumped by industries and local governments have polluted streams,

problem that further threatens the quality of water supplies. As noted earlier in this chapter, many of Canada's Aboriginal communities have unsafe water supplies. In 2005, the drinking water on the Kashechewan reserve in northern Ontario was found to be contaminated with E. coli bacteria. Many members of the community were evacuated, and millions of dollars spent to upgrade the water treatment plant. Subsequent investigation revealed the inadequacy of water treatment facilities on many First Nations reserves. The health costs of unsafe water are enormous (United Nations Development Programme 2006).

Going GLOBAL

Projected Emissions of Greenhouse Gases, 2025

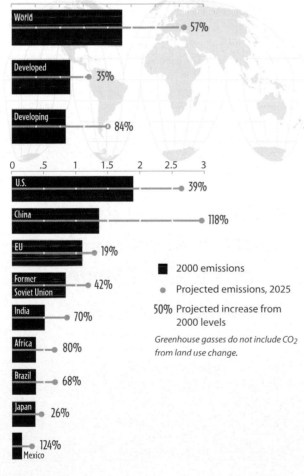

Trillions of tonnes of carbon equivalent

World		57%
Developed		35%
Developing		84%

U.S.		39%
China		118%
EU		19%
Former Soviet Union		42%
India		70%
Africa		80%
Brazil		68%
Japan		26%
Mexico		124%

■ 2000 emissions

● Projected emissions, 2025

50% Projected increase from 2000 levels

Greenhouse gasses do not include CO_2 from land use change.

In 2000, the United States was the largest emitter of CO_2 from fossil fuels. China is expected to take the lead by 2025.

Source: Baumert 2005.

GLOBAL WARMING

The scientific evidence for global warming is clear, consistent, and compelling, yet we continue to struggle with how seriously we should take it. "Global warming" refers to the significant rise in the earth's surface temperatures that occurs when industrial gases like carbon dioxide turn the planet's atmosphere into a virtual greenhouse. Even one additional degree of warmth in the globe's average surface temperature can increase the likelihood of wildfires, shrinkage of rivers and lakes, expansion of deserts, and torrential downpours, including typhoons and hurricanes. Scientists now track carbon dioxide emissions around the world and can map the current and projected CO_2 contribution each country makes. (See "Going Global" to the left.)

Although scientific concern over global warming has heated up, climate change remains low on policy makers' list of concerns. For some politicians, the problem seems too abstract and distant. Others recognize that effective solutions demand a difficult-to-manage multinational

We can again draw on world systems analysis when it comes to seeing who pays the highest price for global warming. Historically, core nations have been the major emitters of greenhouse gases. Today, much manufacturing has moved to semiperiphery and periphery nations, where greenhouse gas emissions are escalating. Ironically, many of those who are now calling for a reduction in the human activity that contributes to global warming are located in core nations, which have contributed disproportionately to the problem. We want our hamburgers, but we decry the destruction of the rainforests to create grazing land for cattle. We want inexpensive clothes and toys, but we condemn developing countries for depending on coal-fired power plants, the number of which are expected to increase 46 percent by 2030. The challenge of global warming, then, is closely tied to global inequality (M. Jenkins 2008; J. Roberts et al. 2003).

One of the primary factors causing this global environmental crisis is the rise in global population (Ehrlich and Ehrlich 1990). As of July 2008, there were 6.7 billion people on the planet, an increase of 1.7 billion since 1987. To put this in terms of the human ecology model, the more people there are on the planet, the more resources we need to use to sustain them, the more waste they produce that we must process, and the more strain we place on our capacity to house us all (Ehrlich 1968; Ehrlich and Ehrlich 1990; Ehrlich and Ellison 2002).

response, and they fear that their nation may bear too much of the cost. The Kyoto Protocol was intended to provide a unified response in which the nations of the world would take collective responsibility to reduce global emissions of greenhouse gases. To date, 169 countries have signed the accord, but the United States, which produces 24 percent of the world's carbon dioxide, has failed to ratify it, and while Canada was one of the first countries to sign, concrete measures to address global warming have not been implemented. Opponents of the protocol argue that doing so would place the nation at a disadvantage in the global marketplace (Landler 2005; United Nations Development Programme 2007:59).

Estimated Time for Each Successive Increase of 1 Billion People in World Population

Population Level	Time taken to reach new population level	Year of Attainment
First billion	Human history before 1800	1804
Second billion	123 years	1927
Third billion	32 years	1959
Fourth billion	15 years	1974
Fifth billion	13 years	1987
Sixth billion	12 years	1999
Seventh billion	13 years	2012
Eighth billion	14 years	2026
Ninth billion	17 years	2043

Source: Bureau of the Census 2008b.

Percentage of People Citing Pollution and Environmental Problems as a Top Global Threat

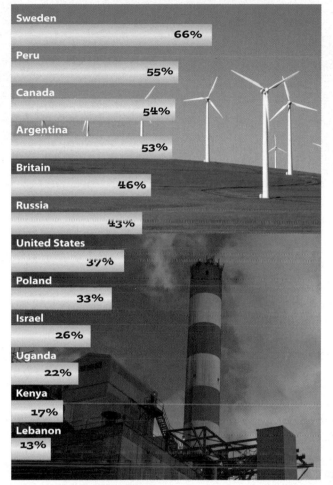

Country	Percentage
Sweden	66%
Peru	55%
Canada	54%
Argentina	53%
Britain	46%
Russia	43%
United States	37%
Poland	33%
Israel	26%
Uganda	22%
Kenya	17%
Lebanon	13%

Source: Pew Research Center 2007b.

Technological advances also contribute to increased environmental concerns. At least since the Industrial Revolution and the invention of the steam engine, the automobile, coal-burning power plants, and more, the environmental effects of technological innovation have been extreme. Biologist Barry Commoner argues that additional contributors to the probem include plastics, detergents, synthetic fibers, pesticides, herbicides, and chemical fertilizers. We appreciate the lifestyles that such innovations allow us to experience, but we pay a significant price for their benefits (Commoner 1971, 1990).

THE GLOBAL RESPONSE

Globalization can be both good and bad for the environment. On the negative side, it can create a race to the bottom, as polluting companies relocate to countries with less stringent environmental standards. Also of concern is that globalization allows multinationals to exploit the resources of developing countries for short-term profit. From Mexico to China, the industrialization that often accompanies globalization has increased pollution of all types.

Yet globalization can have a positive impact as well. As barriers to the international movement of goods, services, and people fall, multinational corporations have an incentive to carefully consider the cost of natural resources. Overusing or wasting resources makes little sense, especially when they are in danger of depletion (Kwong 2005). Perhaps, as Émile Durkheim might have argued long ago, by recognizing the negative effects of our global expansion, along with our mutual interdependence, we will take the steps necessary to bring about positive social change.

There are signs that individuals, countries, and corporations are beginning to understand and appreciate our interdependence. Recent polls indicate that Canadians are aware of the effects of environmental degradation, and are pledging to be more conscious of their consumption of products and energy use. The 100-mile diet and other local eating initiatives are gaining in popularity as individuals strive to reduce their carbon footprint. Individuals are taking greater responsibility for their global impact by recycling and switching to fluorescent light bulbs. Increasing numbers of corporations are "going green" and even finding profits in doing so. Sociology helps us to better see the ways we are interconnected by highlighting the significance of the system as a whole, as well as raising awareness about the inequalities that are a consequence of the global system we have constructed. Such analysis can prepare us to more effectively respond to the global challenges we face.

>> Summary

Health is not merely the absence of disease. As the World Health Organization explains, health incorporates our physical, mental, and social well-being. Through social epidemiology, we can observe patterns of health and illness, and take steps to address those social factors that negatively influence our well-being. Functionalists argue that healthy bodies are necessary for the smooth operation of society, thus the sick role is intended to be a temporary state. Interactionists note the effects of labelling and the stigma associated with particular conditions. Conflict theorists critique the inequities of access to the necessary basics for health and proper care. Environmental destruction poses further threats to our health, and we must recognize our respective roles in protecting the earth and ourselves.

get involved!

Investigate! Research the air and water quality in your community. Talk with local environmental officials about the extent to which current quality levels have improved or deteriorated in the past few years. How adequate are the indicators of quality they utilize? What evidence do leaders cite regarding the extent to which federal, provincial, or municipal policies have affected water and air quality? What changes in policy may be necessary to meet desired quality goals?

For REVIEW

I. What does sociology contribute to something as seemingly biological as health?

    • Our understanding of what counts as health and illness is shaped by the society to which we belong. Similarly, control over resources shapes our likelihood of exposure to illness and our access to health care.

II. What is social epidemiology?

    • Social epidemiology involves the study of factors that shape the health status of various groups within a population. In Canada and elsewhere, social class, race and ethnicity, gender, and age all have an impact.

III. What environmental lessons do we learn from sociology?

    • The natural environment represents our human home, within which all social interaction occurs, and the way we organize our social relations shapes the impact we have on the environment. Countries that control a larger amount of resources have a bigger impact and therefore bear a greater responsibility for those effects.

Thinking CRITICALLY...

1. How inclusive is your definition of health? Does it refer only to physical condition, or do you take into account your emotional and spiritual well-being? When you say you are healthy, what do you mean?

2. Should "alternative" therapies be covered under Canada's health care system? What criteria would you use to assess whether a treatment would be eligible for coverage?

3. The importance of "being green" is a heavily promoted message today. Do you think people are more environmentally aware than they were a decade ago? If so, is this awareness translating into action? In what ways are you "green"?

Pop Quiz

1. A disease that cannot be understood apart from its specific social context is an example of
   a. human ecology.
   b. culture-bound syndrome.
   c. the sick role.
   d. social epidemiology.

2. The expansion of medicine's domain of expertise and its assertion of absolute jurisdiction over many health care procedures are examples of
   a. labelling and power.
   b. social epidemiology.
   c. the medicalization of society.
   d. human ecology.

3. Which one of the following nations has the lowest infant mortality rate?
   a. the United States
   b. Sierra Leone
   c. Canada
   d. Japan

4. Compared against the general population, Aboriginal persons have higher rates of
   a. tuberculosis.
   b. HIV/AIDS.
   c. Type 2 diabetes.
   d. all of the above.

5. The principles of the Canada Health Act resemble what sociological concept?
   a. brain drain
   b. medicalization
   c. alternative therapies
   d. ideal types

6. Tommy Douglas' vision for a publicly funded health care system had its origins in
   a. Ontario.
   b. Manitoba.
   c. Saskatchewan.
   d. Alberta.

7. When products such as vitamins and minerals, herbal products, and other natural health products are included, the percentage of Canadians who report using alternative or complementary therapies is
   a. 50 percent.
   b. 70 percent.
   c. 10 percent.
   d. 25 percent.

8. The sociological perspective that emphasizes the interrelationships between people and their environment is known as
   a. human ecology.
   b. resource allocation.
   c. environmental justice.
   d. labelling theory.

9. The industrialized nations of North America and Europe account for 12 percent of the world's population. What percentage of worldwide consumption are they responsible for?
   a. 15 percent
   b. 30 percent
   c. 45 percent
   d. 60 percent

10. What is the international treaty that sought to reduce global emissions of greenhouse gases?
    a. the Valdez Treaty
    b. the Kyoto Protocol
    c. the Port Huron Statement
    d. the Gore Accord

1. (b); 2. (c); 3. (d); 4. (d); 5. (d); 6. (c); 7. (b); 8. (a); 9. (d); 10. (b)

As You READ >>

- How and why does social change happen?
- What factors shape the success of a social movement?
- What does it mean to practise sociology?

>> Global Social Change

We are at a truly dramatic era in history in terms of global social change. Within the past two decades, we have witnessed the computer revolution and the explosion of Internet connectivity; the collapse of communism; major regime changes and severe economic disruptions in Africa, the Middle East, and Eastern Europe; the spread of AIDS; the first verification of the cloning of a complex animal, Dolly the sheep; and the first major terrorist attack on North American soil. Today we continue to face global challenges including international terrorism, skyrocketing energy costs, and global warming along with other environmental threats.

The transformation of society has been a fundamental concern of sociologists from the very beginning. At the time of sociology's birth, social life was undergoing dramatic change. The taken-for-granted norms and values that made sense in a traditional agricultural society no longer fit with the lived experience of most people. The Industrial Revolution, the rise of capitalism, and the transformation from aristocratic to democratic rule all challenged traditional practices and beliefs. Sociological theory and research provide us with tools that allow us to make sense of where we are now and where we are headed.

The collapse of communist regimes in the former Soviet Union and the nations of Eastern Europe in the late 1980s and early 1990s, for example, took many people by surprise. Yet prior to the collapse, sociologist Randall Collins (1986, 1995) had observed a crucial sequence of events that most observers missed. Long before it happened, Collins had argued that Soviet expansionism had resulted in an overextension of resources, including disproportionate spending on the military. Such overextension strains a regime's stability. Moreover, geopolitical theory suggests that nations in the middle of a geographic region, such as the Soviet Union, tend to fragment into smaller units over time. Collins predicted that the confluence of social crises on several frontiers would precipitate the collapse of the Soviet Union.

History ultimately followed the path Collins predicted it might. In 1979, the success of the Iranian revolution spurred an upsurge of Islamic fundamentalism in nearby Afghanistan, as well as in Soviet republics with substantial Muslim populations. At the same time, resistance to communist rule was growing both throughout Eastern Europe and within the Soviet Union itself. In addition, as Collins predicted, a dissident form of communism arose within the Soviet Union, facilitating the breakdown of the regime. Beginning in the late 1980s, Soviet leader Mikhail Gorbachev chose not to use military power and other types of repression to crush dissidents in Eastern Europe. Instead, he offered plans for democratization and social reform of Soviet society, and he seemed willing to reshape the Soviet Union into a loose federation of somewhat autonomous states. In 1991, six republics on the western periphery declared their independence, and within months, the entire Soviet Union had formally disintegrated into Russia and a number of other independent nations.

Did You Know?

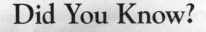

...Of NATO's 26 member countries, Canada has the greatest land area, yet is sixth in total military spending, with 1.3 percent of its GDP going toward defence expenditures. In contrast, the United States spends more on national defence than the rest of the world, allocating 4 percent of its GDP.

Sociology helps us to understand such shifts by paying attention both to large-scale, or macro, shifts that alter the basic landscape of society and the relationships among groups, and to the small-scale, or micro, changes in social

of people finishing high school and attending college or university has skyrocketed, women have entered the paid labour force in significant numbers, life expectancy has risen, technological innovation has exploded, men and

All change is not growth, as all movement is not forward.

Ellen Glasgow

interaction within which decisions are made that can alter the course of history. We construct society through our everyday actions. As such, we have the power to change society by altering the choices we make. Of course, some people, due to their control over valued resources, have more power than do others. Sociology can better focus our attention so that we might understand which direction change might follow.

>> Sociological Perspectives on Social Change

As humans, we are creative beings. We continually innovate and experiment, developing new technologies, ideas, and ways of doing things. Each of these represents an example of **social change,** which involves significant alteration over time in behaviour patterns and culture. Social change can occur so slowly as to be almost undetectable to those it affects, but it can also happen with breathtaking rapidity. In the past century or so, for example, the Canadian population has more than doubled, the percentage

women have been marrying later, and family size has shrunk. In our global, interdependent world, there is no reason to suspect that such changes will cease, and many future changes will be difficult to predict.

Explaining social change is clearly a challenge in the diverse and complex world we inhabit. Nevertheless, theorists from several disciplines have sought to analyze social change. In some instances, they have examined historical events to arrive at a better understanding of contemporary changes. We will look at change from three perspectives so that we might better identify issues we should include when considering how and why change happens.

THE EVOLUTION OF SOCIETIES

One approach to understanding how societies change draws upon the principle of evolution. It was inspired, in part, by Charles Darwin's (1809–1882) work on the biological evolution of species. Darwin's approach stresses a continuing progression of successive generations of life forms as they adapt to their environment. For example, human beings came at a later stage of evolution than reptiles and represent a more complex form of life. Social theorists seeking an analogy to this biological model

> **social change** Significant alteration over time in behaviour patterns and culture, including norms and values.

SOCstudies

Global Demographics: Patterns and Predictions

By 2020, the world's population is projected to be 8 billion.

Most of that growth will take place in today's developing countries.

Over half of the world's population will be from Asia, including China and India.

By 2015, a majority of the world's population will live in cities—the first time in human history.

The Changing Face of Canada

Fifty years ago, most immigrants to Canada came from Europe; today, most are from Asia.

By 2017, members of visible minorities are expected to comprise between 19 and 23 percent of Canada's population.

By 2025, Canada's population is expected to be around 35 million (an increase of approximately 2 million from today's population). Much of this growth will stem from international migration.

By 2026, one in five Canadians will be 65 or older.

Source: National Research Council Canada 2005.

proposed **evolutionary theory,** in which society is viewed as moving in a definite direction. Early evolutionary theorists generally agreed that society was progressing from the simple to the complex, which they assumed was superior.

Early sociologists and anthropologists believed it was possible to study what they referred to at that time as simple or "primitive" societies for clues about the essential building blocks that serve as the foundation for all societies. August Comte (1798–1857), who coined the term "sociology," was an evolutionary theorist of change. He saw human societies as moving forward in their thinking, from mythology to the scientific method. Similarly, Émile Durkheim ([1893]1933) maintained that society progressed from simple to more complex forms of social organization. Both believed that by gaining an understanding of the principles of order and change in such societies, we would be able to more effectively shape the direction our modern, more complex societies would take.

> **evolutionary theory** A theory of social change that holds that society is moving in a definite direction.
>
> **equilibrium model** The view that society tends toward a state of stability or balance.

SOCthink

> > > Why would early theorists have thought of traditional societies as "primitive"? How is this a reflection of the evolutionary theoretical paradigm they adopted?

Since that time, we have learned that the idea that societies will follow a singular path from simple to complex, from primitive to modern, is flawed. The notion that traditional societies are simple or primitive has proven to be both incorrect and ethnocentric. Such societies demonstrate significant levels of sophistication and innovation, in terms of both social relations and technological adaptation to their environments. In addition, there is no single path of social evolution that all societies must pass through. Social change can impact one area of social life, such as politics, while leaving other areas of life relatively unchanged, such as work and the economy. For example, a society might move toward a democratic form of government, but the traditional nature of work, primarily small-scale and agricultural, might stay the same.

Though there are limits to the evolutionary model of social change, it does provide a helpful metaphor when thinking about how change happens. For example, we can look to past practices to better understand where new ways of thinking and acting come from. In addition, it highlights the role that context or environment plays in shaping change. In biology, when the environment changes, mutations in species can occur, making them more fit to survive in that new context than were past generations. For Darwin, however, this did not mean that the new was superior to the old; it was simply more likely that the new would survive given changed environmental circumstances. The

danger when applying this analogy to society is to assume that those who adapt to changed circumstances are superior. The truth is that all societies must adapt to change. Sometimes it comes fast and is thus easier to recognize, and other times it is gradual. Sometimes that change comes from within, and other times it is a product of environmental forces, whether social or natural.

EQUILIBRIUM AND SOCIAL ORDER

Another approach to understanding social change is rooted in the principle that societies naturally seek to attain stability or balance. The functionalist perspective maintains that any social change that occurs represents necessary adjustments as society seeks to return to that state of equilibrium. For example, sociologist Talcott Parsons (1902–1979), an advocate of this approach, viewed even prolonged labour strikes or civilian riots as temporary disruptions in the status quo rather than as significant alterations in the social structure. According to his **equilibrium model,** as changes occur in one part of society, adjustments must be made in other parts. If not, society's equilibrium will be threatened, and strains will occur.

Parsons (1966) maintained that four processes of social change are inevitable. The first, differentiation, refers to the increasing complexity of social organization. We see this in the form of job specialization as is evident in more bureaucratic systems. The transition from a healer—a single person who handles all your health care needs—to a

Theory
A Matter of Perspective

THEORETICAL PERSPECTIVES ON SOCIAL CHANGE

Functionalist:
- social change and social stability must be kept in balance

Conflict:
- social change can correct social inequalities, provided power and resources are appropriately used

Feminist:
- social change can bring justice to those disadvantaged by social location (who often are the instigators of change)

Interactionist:
- social change requires new understandings of the social world

series of positions, including physician, anesthetist, nurse, and pharmacist, is an illustration of differentiation in the field of medicine. This process is accompanied by adaptive upgrading, in which social institutions become more specialized in their purposes. The division of physicians into obstetricians, internists, surgeons, and so forth is an example of adaptive upgrading.

The third process Parsons identified is the inclusion of groups that were previously excluded because of their gender, race, ethnicity, and social class. Recently, medical schools have practised inclusion by admitting increasing numbers of women and visible minorities. Finally, Parsons contended that societies experience value generalization—the development of new values that legitimate a broader range of activities. The acceptance of preventive and alternative medicine is an example of value generalization: Society has broadened its view of health care. All four processes identified by Parsons stress consensus—societal agreement on the nature of social organization and values (B. Johnson 1975; Wallace and Wolf 1980).

SOCthink

> > > Why might the equilibrium model have a difficult time addressing issues such as inequality and poverty as social problems to be solved?

One of the sources of potential strain that can lead to such social adaptation involves technological innovation. For example, sociologist William F. Ogburn (1922) distinguished between material and nonmaterial aspects of culture. Material culture includes inventions, artifacts, and technology; nonmaterial culture encompasses ideas, norms, communications, and social organization. Ogburn pointed out that technology often changes faster than do the ideas and values with which we make sense of such change. Thus, the nonmaterial culture typically must respond to changes in the material culture. Ogburn introduced the term **culture lag** to refer to the period of adjustment when the nonmaterial culture is still struggling to adapt to new material conditions. One example is the Internet. Its rapid uncontrolled growth raises questions about whether to regulate it, and if so, how much.

In certain cases, the changes in the material culture can strain the relationships between social institutions. For example, new means of birth control have been developed in recent decades. Large families are no longer economically necessary, nor are they commonly endorsed by social norms. But certain religious faiths, among them Roman Catholicism, continue to extol large families and to disapprove methods of limiting family size, such as contraception and abortion. This issue represents a lag between aspects of the material culture (technology) and nonmaterial culture (religious beliefs). Conflicts may also emerge between religion and other social institutions, such as

government and the educational system, over the dissemination of birth control and family-planning information (M. Riley et al. 1994a, 1994b).

From Parsons' point of view, such tensions represent little more than normal adjustments needed to maintain the inevitable balance that is the natural state of all societies. Though his approach explicitly incorporates the evolutionary notion of continuing progress, the dominant theme in this model is stability. Society may change, but it remains stable through new forms of integration. For example, in place of the kinship ties that provided social cohesion in the past, people develop laws, judicial processes, and new values and belief systems. Parsons and other functionalist theorists would argue that those parts of society that persist, even including crime, terrorism, and poverty, do so because they contribute to social stability. Critics note, however, that his approach virtually disregards the use of coercion by the powerful to maintain the illusion of a stable, well-integrated society (Gouldner 1960).

RESOURCES, POWER, AND CHANGE

Such theories are helpful, but it is not enough to look at change as part of the natural evolution or equilibrium of societies. As conflict theorists point out, some groups in society, because they control valued resources, are able either to inhibit or to facilitate social change more effectively than are others. Although Karl Marx, for example, accepted the evolutionary argument that societies develop along a particular path, he did not view each successive stage as an inevitable improvement over the previous one. History, according to Marx, proceeds through a series of stages, and within each stage, those who control the means of production in turn control and exploit an entire class of people. Thus, ancient society exploited slaves, the estate system of feudalism exploited serfs, and modern capitalist society exploits the working class. Ultimately, through a socialist revolution led by the proletariat, human society would move toward the final stage of development: a classless communist society, or "community of free individuals," as Marx described it in 1867 in *Das Kapital* (see Bottomore and Rubel 1956:250).

> **culture lag** A period of adjustment when the nonmaterial culture is still struggling to adapt to new material conditions.
> **vested interests** Those people or groups who will suffer in the event of social change and who have a stake in maintaining the status quo.

Marx argued that conflict is a normal and desirable aspect of social change. In fact, change must be encouraged if we are to challenge and one day eliminate social inequality. In his view, people are not restricted to a passive role in responding to inevitable cycles or changes in the material culture. Rather, Marxist theory offers a tool for those who wish to seize control of the historical process and gain their freedom from injustice (Lauer 1982). Efforts to promote social change are, however, likely to meet with resistance.

Certain individuals and groups have a stake in maintaining the existing state of affairs. Social economist Thorstein Veblen (1857–1929) coined the term **vested interests** to

Internet access. Another sign of the global nature of this expansion has been the increase in languages used on the Internet. While English continues to lead, Chinese usage increased 470 percent between 2000 and 2008 compared to only 167 percent for English (Internet World Stats 2008).

Unfortunately, a digital divide persists, and not everyone can get onto the information highway, especially not the less affluent. Moreover, this pattern of inequality is global. In Africa, for example, only 3.6 percent of the population has access to the Internet. The core nations that Immanuel Wallerstein described in his world systems analysis have a virtual monopoly on information technology; the peripheral nations of Asia, Africa, and Latin America depend on the core nations both for technology and for the information it provides. For example, North America, Europe, and a few industrialized nations in other regions possess almost all the world's Internet hosts—computers that are connected directly to the worldwide network.

One way to address this divide is to provide computing technology to those people who do not have it. The "One Laptop per Child" (OLPC) campaign seeks to do just that (http://laptop.org). In January 2005, Nicholas Negroponte of the Massachusetts Institute of Technology announced his revolutionary idea for just such a give-away. For several years, he had been trying to develop a low-cost computer, called the XO, for the 1.2 billion children of the developing world. Negroponte's goal was to sell the laptop for $100, complete with a wireless hookup and a battery with a five-year life span. His intention was to persuade foundations and the governments of industrial countries to fund the distribution, so that the laptop would be available to the children for free. As of June 2008, OLPC had distributed almost 700,000 computers around the world to children in Peru, Haiti, Cambodia, Mexico, Rwanda, Iraq, and more.

SOCthink

> > > From a purely business point of view, what would be the pros and cons of giving a free XO to every needy child in the developing world? Would the social benefits of doing so outweigh the business costs and benefits?

Internet Use and Penetration by World Region

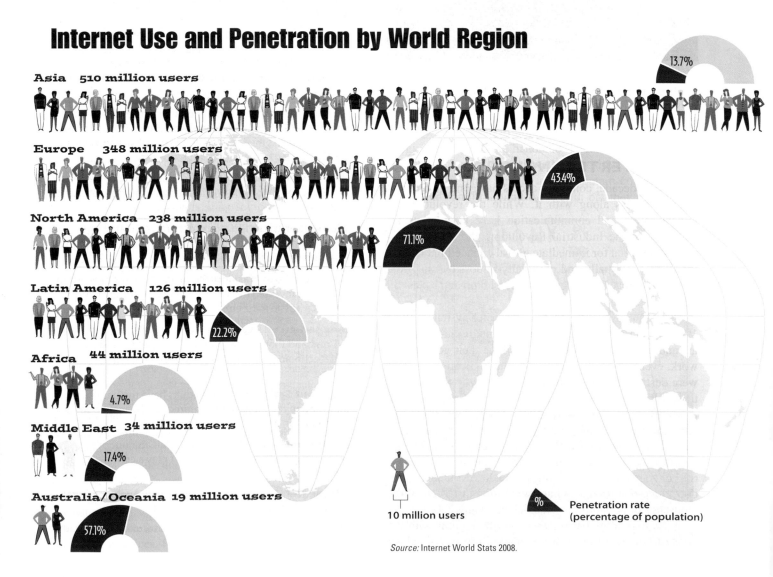

Asia   510 million users   13.7%

Europe   348 million users   43.4%

North America   238 million users   71.1%

Latin America   126 million users   22.2%

Africa   44 million users   4.7%

Middle East   34 million users   17.4%

Australia/Oceania   19 million users   57.1%

10 million users

% Penetration rate (percentage of population)

Source: Internet World Stats 2008.

PRIVACY AND CENSORSHIP IN A GLOBAL VILLAGE

In addition to the digital divide, sociologists have also raised concerns about threats to privacy and the possibility of censorship. Recent advances have made it increasingly easy for business firms, government agencies, and even criminals to retrieve and store information about everything from our buying habits to our Web-surfing patterns. In public places, at work, and on the Internet, surveillance devices now track our every move, be it a keystroke or an ATM withdrawal. As technology spreads, so does the exposure to risk. In January 2007, Canadians learned of the electronic theft of customer information from TJX Companies Inc., the U.S.-based owner of Winners and HomeSense stores. Between mid-2005 and December 2006, the security breach allowed hackers to steal credit and debit card information stored in the company's database, prompting many financial institutions to issue new accounts to cardholders.

At the same time that these innovations have increased others' power to monitor our behaviour, they have raised fears that they might be misused for undemocratic purposes. In short, new technologies threaten not just our privacy but our freedom from surveillance and censorship (O'Harrow, Jr. 2005). There is, for example, the danger that the most powerful groups in a society will use technology to violate the privacy of the less powerful. Indeed, officials in the People's Republic of China have attempted to censor online discussion groups and Web postings that criticize the government. Civil liberties advocates remind us that the same abuses can occur in even the most democratic of nations if citizens are not vigilant in protecting their right to privacy (Magnier 2004).

In the United States, legislation regulating the surveillance of electronic communications has not always upheld citizens' right to privacy. In 1986, the federal government passed the Electronic Communications Privacy Act, which outlawed the surveillance of telephone calls except with the permission of both the U.S. attorney general and a federal judge. Telegrams, faxes, and email did not receive the same

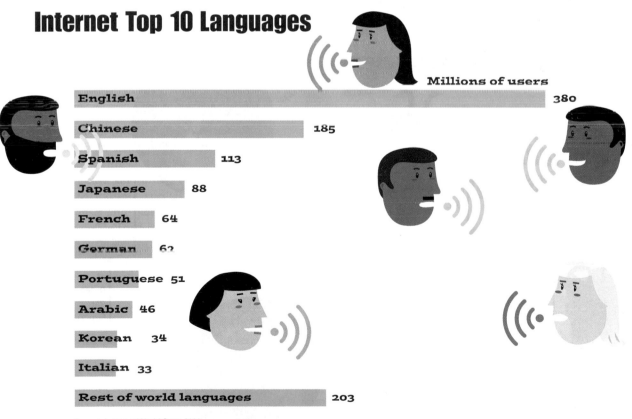

Internet Top 10 Languages

Millions of users

English	380
Chinese	185
Spanish	113
Japanese	88
French	64
German	62
Portuguese	51
Arabic	46
Korean	34
Italian	33
Rest of world languages	203

Source: Internet World Stats 2008.

Abbreviations

ALB.	ALBANIA
AZERB.	AZERBAIJAN
BELG.	BELGIUM
BOS.	BOSNIA-HERZEGOVINA
BULG.	BULGARIA
CRO.	CROATIA
CZECH.	CZECH REPUBLIC
EST.	ESTONIA
HUNG.	HUNGARY
LITH.	LITHUANIA
LUX.	LUXEMBOURG
MACE.	MACEDONIA
MONT.	MONTENEGRO
NETH.	NETHERLANDS
ROM.	ROMANIA
RUSS.	RUSSIA
SERB.	SERBIA
SLOVAK.	SLOVAKIA
SLOVN.	SLOVENIA
SWITZ.	SWITZERLAND
U.A.E.	UNITED ARAB EMIRATES

Absolute poverty A minimum level of subsistence that no family should be expected to live below.

Achieved status A social position that a person attains largely through his or her own efforts.

Activity theory A theory of aging that suggests that those elderly people who remain active and socially involved will be best adjusted.

Adoption In a legal sense, a process that allows for the transfer of the legal rights, responsibilities, and privileges of parenthood to a new legal parent or parents.

Ageism Prejudice and discrimination based on a person's age.

Agency The freedom individuals have to choose and to act.

Agrarian society The most technologically advanced form of pre-industrial society. Members are engaged primarily in the production of food, but they increase their crop yields through technological innovations such as the plough.

Alienation Loss of control over our creative human capacity to produce, separation from the products we make, and isolation from our fellow producers.

Amalgamation The process through which a majority group and a minority group combine to form a new group.

Anomie Durkheim's term for the loss of direction felt in a society when social control of individual behaviour has become ineffective.

Anomie theory of deviance Robert Merton's theory of deviance as an adaptation of socially prescribed goals or of the means governing their attainment, or both.

Anticipatory socialization Processes of socialization in which a person "rehearses" for future positions, occupations, and social relationships.

Apartheid A former policy of the South African government, designed to maintain the separation of Blacks and other non-Whites from the dominant Whites.

Applied sociology The use of the discipline of sociology with the specific intent of yielding practical applications for human behaviour and organizations.

Argot Specialized language used by members of a group or subculture.

Ascribed status A social position assigned to a person by society without regard for the person's unique talents or characteristics.

Assimilation The process through which a person forsakes his or her own cultural tradition to become part of a different culture.

Authority Institutionalized power that is recognized by the people over whom it is exercised.

Bilateral descent A kinship system in which both sides of a person's family are regarded as equally important.

Borderlands The area of common culture along the border between Mexico and the United States.

Bourgeoisie Karl Marx's term for the capitalist class, comprising the owners of the means of production.

Brain drain The immigration to Canada and other industrialized nations of skilled workers, professionals, and technicians who are desperately needed in their home countries.

Bureaucracy A component of formal organization that uses rules and hierarchical ranking to achieve efficiency.

Bureaucratization The process by which a group, organization, or social movement increasingly relies on technical-rational decision making in the pursuit of efficiency.

Capitalism An economic system in which the means of production are held largely in private hands and the main incentive for economic activity is the accumulation of profits.

Caste A hereditary rank, usually religiously dictated, that tends to be fixed and immobile.

Causal logic The relationship between a condition or variable and a particular consequence, with one event leading to the other.

Census family A married or common-law couple, with or without children, or a lone parent living with at least one child, in the same dwelling.

Charismatic authority Power made legitimate by a leader's exceptional personal or emotional appeal to his or her followers.

Class A group of people who have a similar level of economic resources.

Class consciousness In Karl Marx's view, a subjective awareness held by members of a class regarding their common vested interests and need for collective political action to bring about social change.

Class system A social ranking based primarily on economic position in which achieved characteristics can influence social mobility.

Closed system A social system in which there is little or no possibility of individual social mobility.

Coalition A temporary or permanent alliance geared toward a common goal.

Code of ethics The standards of acceptable behaviour developed by and for members of a profession.

Cognitive theory of development The theory that children's thought progresses through four stages of development.

Cohabitation The practice of living together as a couple without marrying.

Colonialism The maintenance of political, social, economic, and cultural dominance over a people by a foreign power for an extended period.

Colour-blind racism The use of race-neutral principles to perpetuate a racially unequal status quo.

Communism As an ideal type, an economic system under which all property is communally owned and no social distinctions are made on the basis of people's ability to produce.

Conflict perspective A sociological approach that assumes that social behaviour is best understood in terms of tension between groups over power or the allocation of resources, including housing, money, access to services, and political representation.

Conformity The act of going along with peers—individuals of our own status who have no special right to direct our behaviour.

Contact hypothesis The theory that in cooperative circumstances interracial contact between people of equal status will reduce prejudice.

Content analysis The systematic coding and objective recording of data, guided by some rationale.

Control group The subjects in an experiment who are not introduced to the independent variable by the researcher.

Control theory A view of conformity and deviance that suggests that our connection to members of society leads us to systematically conform to society's norms.

Control variable A factor that is held constant to test the relative impact of an independent variable.

Correlation A relationship between two variables in which a change in one coincides with a change in the other.

Correspondence principle The tendency of schools to promote the values expected of individuals in each social class and to prepare students for the types of jobs typically held by members of their class.

Counterculture A subculture that deliberately opposes certain aspects of the larger culture.

Credentialism An increase in the lowest level of education required to enter a field.

Crime A violation of criminal law for which some governmental authority applies formal penalties.

Cultural capital Our tastes, knowledge, attitudes, language, and ways of thinking that we exchange in interaction with others.

Cultural relativism The viewing of people's behaviour from the perspective of their own culture.

Cultural transmission A school of criminology that argues that criminal behaviour is learned through social interactions.

Cultural universal A common practice or belief shared by all societies.

Culture The totality of our shared language, knowledge, material objects, and behaviour.

Culture-bound syndrome A disease or illness that cannot be understood apart from some specific social context.

Culture lag A period of adjustment when the nonmaterial culture is still struggling to adapt to new material conditions.

Culture shock The feelings of disorientation, uncertainty, and even fear that people experience when they encounter unfamiliar cultural practices.

Degradation ceremony An aspect of the socialization process within some total institutions, in which people are subjected to humiliating rituals.

Deindustrialization The systematic, widespread withdrawal of investment in basic aspects of productivity, such as factories and plants.

Democracy In a literal sense, government by the people.

Denomination A large, organized religion that is not officially linked to the state or government.

Dependency theory An approach that contends that industrialized nations continue to exploit developing countries for their own gain.

Dependent variable The variable in a causal relationship that is subject to the influence of another variable.

Deviance Behaviour that violates the standards of conduct or expectations of a group or society.

Dictatorship A government in which one person has nearly total power to make and enforce laws.

Differential association A theory of deviance that holds that violation of rules results from exposure to attitudes favourable to criminal acts.

Differential justice Differences in the way social control is exercised over different groups.

Diffusion The process by which a cultural item spreads from group to group or society to society.

Digital divide The relative lack of access to the latest technologies among low-income groups, racial and ethnic minorities, rural residents, and the citizens of developing countries.

Discovery The process of making known or sharing the existence of an aspect of reality.

Discrimination The denial of opportunities and equal rights to individuals and groups because of prejudice or other arbitrary reasons.

Disengagement theory A theory of aging that suggests that society and the aging individual mutually sever many of their relationships.

Dominant ideology A set of cultural beliefs and practices that helps to maintain powerful social, economic, and political interests.

Downsizing Reductions in a company's workforce as part of deindustrialization.

Dramaturgical approach A view of social interaction in which people are seen as theatrical performers.

Ecclesia A religious organization that claims to include most or all members of a society and is recognized as the national or official religion.

Economic system The social institution through which goods and services are produced, distributed, and consumed.

Education A formal process of learning in which some people consciously teach while others adopt the social role of learner.

Egalitarian family An authority pattern in which spouses are regarded as equals.

Elite model A view of society as being ruled by a small group of individuals who share a common set of political and economic interests.

Endogamy   The restriction of mate selection to people within the same group.

Environmental justice   A legal strategy based on claims that racial minorities are subjected disproportionately to environmental hazards.

Equilibrium model   The view that society tends toward a state of stability or balance.

Established sect   A religious group that is the outgrowth of a sect, yet remains isolated from society.

Estate system   A system of stratification under which peasants were required to work land leased to them by nobles in exchange for military protection and other services. Also known as feudalism.

Esteem   The reputation that a specific person has earned within an occupation.

Ethnic group   A group that is set apart from others primarily because of its national origin or distinctive cultural patterns.

Ethnocentrism   The tendency to assume that one's own culture and way of life represent the norm or are superior to all others.

Ethnography   The study of an entire social setting through extended systematic observation.

Evolutionary theory   A theory of social change that holds that society is moving in a definite direction.

Exogamy   The requirement that people select a mate outside certain groups.

Experiment   An artificially created situation that allows a researcher to manipulate variables.

Experimental group   The subjects in an experiment who are exposed to an independent variable introduced by a researcher.

Exploitation theory   A belief that views racial subordination as a manifestation of the class system inherent in capitalism.

Expressive leader   The person in the family who bears responsibility for the maintenance of harmony and internal emotional affairs.

Expulsion   The systematic removal of a group of people from society.

Extended family   A family in which relatives—such as grandparents, aunts, or uncles—live in the same household as parents and their children.

Face-work   The efforts people make to maintain a proper image and avoid public embarrassment.

False consciousness   A term used by Karl Marx to describe an attitude held by members of a class that does not accurately reflect their objective position.

Familism   Pride in the extended family, expressed through the maintenance of close ties and strong obligations to kinfolk outside the immediate family.

Feminism   The belief in social, economic, and political equality for women.

Feminist perspective   Actually comprised of many perspectives, this approach focuses upon the differential treatment of women and men, alongside other forms of inequality.

Folkway   Norms governing everyday behaviour, whose violation raises comparatively little concern.

Force   The actual or threatened use of coercion to impose one's will on others.

Formal norm   A norm that generally has been written down and that specifies strict punishments for violators.

Formal social control   Social control that is carried out by authorized agents, such as police officers, judges, school administrators, and employers.

Functionalist definition of families   A definition of families that focuses on what families do for society and for their members.

Functionalist definition of religion   The idea that religion unifies believers into a community through shared practices and a common set of beliefs relative to sacred things.

Functionalist perspective   A sociological approach that emphasizes the way in which the parts of a society are structured to maintain its stability.

Fundamentalism   Rigid adherence to core religious doctrines, often accompanied by a literal application of scripture or historical beliefs to today's world.

Gemeinschaft   A close-knit community, often found in rural areas, in which strong personal bonds unite members.

Gender   The social and cultural significance that we attach to the biological differences of sex.

Gender role   Expectations regarding the proper behaviour, attitudes, and activities of males or females.

Generalized other   The attitudes, viewpoints, and expectations of society as a whole that we take into account in our behaviour.

Genocide   The deliberate, systematic killing of an entire people or nation.

Gerontology   The study of the sociological and psychological aspects of aging and the problems of the aged.

Gesellschaft   A community, often urban, that is large and impersonal, with little commitment to the group or consensus on values.

Glass ceiling   An invisible barrier that blocks the promotion of a qualified individual in a work environment because of the individual's gender, race, or ethnicity.

Globalization   The worldwide integration of government policies, cultures, social movements, and financial markets through trade and the exchange of ideas.

Goal displacement   Overzealous conformity to official regulations of a bureaucracy.

Gross national product (GNP)   The value of a nation's goods and services.

Group   Any number of people with similar norms, values, and expectations who interact with one another on a regular basis.

Hate crime   A criminal offence committed because of the offender's bias against an individual based on race, religion, ethnicity, national origin, or sexual orientation.

Hawthorne effect   The unintended influence that observers of experiments can have on their subjects.

Health   As defined by the World Health Organization, a state of complete physical, mental, and social well-being, and not merely the absence of disease and infirmity.

Heterosexism   The structural and institutional organization of society that privileges heterosexuality over other forms of sexuality.

Hidden curriculum   Standards of behaviour that are deemed proper by society and are taught subtly in schools.

Holistic medicine   Therapies in which the health care practitioner considers the person's physical, mental, emotional, and spiritual characteristics.

Homogamy   The conscious or unconscious tendency to select a mate with personal characteristics similar to one's own.

Homophobia   Fear of and prejudice against homosexuality.

Horizontal mobility   The movement of an individual from one social position to another of the same rank.

Horticultural society   A pre-industrial society in which people plant seeds and crops rather than merely subsist on available foods.

Hospice care   Treatment of the terminally ill in their own homes, or in special hospital units or other facilities, with the goal of helping them to die comfortably, without pain.

Human ecology   The area of study concerned with the interrelationships between people and their environment.

Human relations approach   An approach to the study of formal organizations that emphasizes the role of people, communication, and participation in a bureaucracy and tends to focus on the informal structure of the organization.

Human rights   Universal moral rights possessed by all people because they are human.

Hunting-and-gathering society   A pre-industrial society in which people rely on whatever foods and fibres are readily available in order to survive.

Hypothesis   A testable statement about the relationship between two or more variables.

I   The acting self that exists in relation to the Me.

Ideal type   A construct or model for evaluating specific cases.

Impression management   The altering of the presentation of the self in order to create distinctive appearances and satisfy particular audiences.

Incest taboo   The prohibition of sexual relationships between certain culturally specified relatives.

Incidence   The number of new cases of a specific disorder that occur within a given population during a stated period.

Income   Wages and salaries measured over some period of time, such as per hour or year.

Independent variable   The variable in a causal relationship that causes or influences a change in a second variable.

Industrial society   A society that depends on mechanization to produce its goods and services.

Infant mortality rate   The number of deaths of infants under one year old per 1000 live births in a given year.

Influence   The exercise of power through a process of persuasion.

Informal economy   Transfers of money, goods, or services that are not reported to the government.

Informal norm   A norm that is generally understood but not precisely recorded.

Informal social control   Social control that is carried out casually by ordinary people through such means as laughter, smiles, and ridicule.

In-group   Any group or category to which people feel they belong.

Innovation   The process of introducing a new idea or object to a culture through discovery or invention.

Institutional discrimination   A pattern of treatment that systematically denies access to resources and opportunities to individuals and groups as part of the normal operations of a society.

Instrumental leader   The person in the family who bears responsibility for the completion of tasks, focuses on more distant goals, and manages the external relationship between one's family and other social institutions.

Interactionist perspective   A sociological approach that generalizes about everyday forms of social interaction in order to explain society as a whole.

Intergenerational mobility   Changes in the social position of children relative to their parents.

Interview   A face-to-face or telephone questioning of a respondent to obtain desired information.

Intragenerational mobility   Changes in social position within a person's adult life.

Invention   The combination of existing cultural items into a form that did not exist before.

Iron law of oligarchy   A principle of organizational life under which even a democratic organization will eventually develop into a bureaucracy ruled by a few individuals.

Kinship   The state of being related to others.

Labelling theory   An approach to deviance that attempts to explain why certain people are viewed as deviants while others engaged in the same behaviour are not.

Laissez-faire A form of capitalism under which people compete freely, with minimal government intervention in the economy.

Language A system of shared symbols; it includes speech, written characters, numerals, symbols, and nonverbal gestures and expressions.

Law Formal norms enforced by the state.

Liberation theology Use of a church, primarily Roman Catholicism, in a political effort to eliminate poverty, discrimination, and other forms of injustice from a secular society.

Life chances The opportunities people have to provide themselves with material goods, positive living conditions, and favourable life experiences.

Life course approach A research orientation in which sociologists and other social scientists look closely at the social factors that influence people throughout their lives, from birth to death.

Looking-glass self A concept that emphasizes the self as the product of our social interactions.

Low income cut-off (LICO) The Canadian equivalent of a poverty line. A family is poor if the amount spent on the basic necessities exceeds a certain proportion of income (this figure varies based on family size, community size, and economic conditions).

Luddites Rebellious craft workers in 19th-century England who destroyed new factory machinery as part of their resistance to the Industrial Revolution.

Machismo A sense of virility, personal worth, and pride in one's maleness.

Macrosociology Sociological investigation that concentrates on large-scale phenomena or entire civilizations.

Market basket measure (MBM) A measure that takes into account more than subsistence needs to determine the cost of living a life comparable to community standards.

Master status A status that dominates others and thereby determines a person's general position in society.

Material culture The physical or technological aspects of our daily lives.

Matriarchy A society in which women dominate in family decision making.

Matrilineal descent A kinship system in which only the mother's relatives are significant.

McDonaldization The process by which the principles of efficiency, calculability, predictability, and control shape organization and decision making.

Me The socialized self that plans actions and judges performances based on the standards we have learned from others.

Mean A number calculated by adding a series of values and then dividing by the number of values.

Mechanical solidarity Social cohesion based on shared experiences, knowledge, and skills in which things function more or less the way they always have, with minimal change.

Median The midpoint, or number that divides a series of values into two groups of equal numbers of values.

Medicine pouch Indigenous healing method; pouch containing plant material is worn by Aboriginal peoples seeking the mercy and protection of the spirits.

Microsociology Sociological investigation that stresses the study of small groups and the analysis of our everyday experiences and interactions.

Midlife crisis A stressful period of self-evaluation that begins at about age 40.

Minority group A subordinate group whose members, even if they represent a numeric majority, have significantly less control or power over their own lives than the members of a dominant or majority group have over theirs.

Mixed economy An economic system that combines elements of both capitalism and socialism.

Mode The single most common value in a series of scores.

Model or ideal minority A subordinate group whose members have succeeded economically, socially, and educationally despite past prejudice and discrimination.

Modernization The far-reaching process by which nations pass from traditional forms of social organization toward those characteristic of post–Industrial Revolution societies.

Monarchy A form of government headed by a single member of a royal family, usually a king, queen, or some other hereditary ruler.

Monogamy A form of marriage in which two people are married only to each other.

Monopoly Control of a market by a single business firm.

Morbidity rate The incidence of disease in a given population.

Mores Norms deemed highly necessary to the welfare of a society.

Mortality rate The incidence of death in a given population.

Multinational corporation A commercial organization that is headquartered in one country but does business throughout the world.

Multiple masculinities The idea that men learn and play a full range of gender roles.

Natural science The study of the physical features of nature and the ways in which they interact and change.

Neocolonialism Continuing dependence of former colonies on foreign countries.

New religious movement (NRM) or cult A small, alternative faith community that represents either a new religion or a major innovation in an existing faith.

New social movement An organized collective activity that addresses values and social identities, as well as improvements in the quality of life.

Nonmaterial culture Ways of using material objects, as well as customs, ideas, expressions, beliefs, knowledge, philosophies, governments, and patterns of communication.

Nonverbal communication The use of gestures, facial expressions, and other visual images to communicate.

Norm An established standard of behaviour maintained by a society.

Nuclear family A married couple and their unmarried children living together.

Obedience Compliance with higher authorities in a hierarchical structure.

Objective method A technique for measuring social class that assigns individuals to classes on the basis of criteria such as occupation, education, income, and place of residence.

Observation A research technique in which an investigator collects information through direct participation and/or by closely watching a group or community.

Offshoring The transfer of work to foreign contractors.

Oligarchy A form of government in which a few individuals rule.

Open system A social system in which the position of each individual is influenced by his or her achieved status.

Operational definition Transformation of an abstract concept into indicators that are observable and measurable.

Organic solidarity A collective consciousness that rests on mutual interdependence, characteristic of societies with a complex division of labour.

Organized crime The work of a group that regulates relations among criminal enterprises involved in illegal activities, including prostitution, gambling, and the smuggling and sale of illegal drugs.

Out-group A group or category to which people feel they do not belong.

Party The capacity to organize to accomplish some particular goal.

Patriarchy A society in which men dominate in family decision making.

Patrilineal descent A kinship system in which only the father's relatives are significant.

Peace The absence of war, or more broadly, a proactive effort to develop cooperative relations among nations.

Personality A person's typical patterns of attitudes, needs, characteristics, and behaviour.

Peter principle A principle of organizational life according to which every employee within a hierarchy tends to rise to his or her level of incompetence.

Pluralism Mutual respect for one another's cultures among the various groups in a society, which allows minorities to express their own cultures without experiencing prejudice.

Pluralist model A view of society in which many competing groups within the community have access to government, so that no single group is dominant.

Political system The social institution that is founded on a recognized set of procedures for implementing and achieving society's goals.

Politics In Harold Lasswell's words, "who gets what, when, and how."

Polyandry A form of polygamy in which a woman may have more than one husband at the same time.

Polygamy A form of marriage in which an individual may have several husbands or wives simultaneously.

Polygyny A form of polygamy in which a man may have more than one wife at the same time.

Post-industrial society A society whose economic system is engaged primarily in the processing and control of information.

Postmodern society A technologically sophisticated, pluralistic, interconnected, globalized society.

Power The ability to exercise one's will over others even if they resist.

Power elite A small group of military, industrial, and government leaders who control the fate of the United States.

Prejudice A negative attitude toward an entire category of people, often an ethnic or racial minority.

Prestige The respect and admiration that an occupation holds in a society.

Prevalence The total number of cases of a specific disorder that exist at a given time.

Primary group A small group characterized by intimate, face-to-face association and cooperation.

Private troubles Obstacles that individuals face as individuals rather than as a consequence of their social position.

Profane The ordinary and commonplace elements of life, as distinguished from the sacred.

Proletariat Karl Marx's term for the working class in a capitalist society.

Protestant ethic Max Weber's term for the disciplined commitment to worldly labour driven by a desire to bring glory to God, shared by followers of Martin Luther and John Calvin.

Public issues Obstacles that individuals in similar positions face; also referred to by sociologists as "social problems."

Qualitative research Research that relies on what is seen in field or naturalistic settings more than on statistical data.

Quantitative research Research that collects and reports data primarily in numerical form.

Questionnaire A printed or written form used to obtain information from a respondent.

Racial formation A sociohistorical process in which racial categories are created, inhibited, transformed, and destroyed.

Racial group A group that is set apart from others because of physical differences that have taken on social significance.

Racial profiling Any police-initiated action based on race, ethnicity, or national origin rather than on a person's behaviour.

Racism The belief that one race is supreme and all others are innately inferior.

Random sample A sample for which every member of an entire population has the same chance of being selected.

Rational-legal authority Authority based on formally agreed upon and accepted rules, principles, and procedures of conduct that are established in order to accomplish goals in the most efficient manner possible.

Reference group Any group that individuals use as a standard for evaluating themselves and their own behaviour.

Relative deprivation The conscious feeling of a negative discrepancy between legitimate expectations and present actualities.

Relative poverty A floating standard of deprivation by which people at the bottom of a society, whatever their lifestyles, are judged to be disadvantaged in comparison with the nation as a whole.

Reliability The extent to which a measure produces consistent results.

Religious belief A statement to which members of a particular religion adhere.

Religious experience The feeling or perception of being in direct contact with the ultimate reality, such as a divine being, or of being overcome with religious emotion.

Religious ritual A practice required or expected of members of a faith.

Remittances The monies that immigrants return to their families of origin; also called *migradollars*.

Representative democracy A form of government in which certain individuals are selected to speak for the people.

Research design A detailed plan or method for obtaining data scientifically.

Resocialization The process of discarding former behaviour patterns and accepting new ones as part of a transition in one's life.

Resource mobilization The ways in which a social movement utilizes such resources as money, political influence, access to the media, and personnel.

Rite of passage A ritual marking the symbolic transition from one social position to another.

Role conflict The situation that occurs when incompatible expectations arise from two or more social positions held by the same person.

Role exit The process of disengagement from a role that is central to one's self-identity in order to establish a new role and identity.

Role strain The difficulty that arises when the same social position imposes conflicting demands and expectations.

Role taking The process of mentally assuming the perspective of another and responding from that imagined viewpoint.

Sacred Elements beyond everyday life that inspire respect, awe, and even fear.

Sample A selection from a larger population that is statistically representative of that population.

Sanction A penalty or reward for conduct concerning a social norm.

Sandwich generation The generation of adults who simultaneously try to meet the competing needs of their parents and their children.

Sapir-Whorf hypothesis The idea that the language a person uses shapes his or her perception of reality and therefore his or her thoughts and actions.

Science The body of knowledge obtained by methods based on systematic observation.

Scientific management approach An approach to the study of formal organizations that emphasizes maximum work efficiency and productivity through scientific planning of the labour process.

Scientific method A systematic, organized series of steps that ensures maximum objectivity and consistency in researching a problem.

Second shift The double burden—work outside the home followed by child care and housework—that many women face and few men share equitably.

Secondary analysis A variety of research techniques that make use of previously collected and publicly accessible information and data.

Secondary group A formal, impersonal group in which there is little social intimacy or mutual understanding.

Sect A relatively small religious group that has broken away from some other religious organization to renew what it considers the original vision of the faith.

Secularization Religion's diminishing influence in the public sphere, especially in politics and the economy.

Segregation The physical separation of two groups of people in terms of residence, workplace, and social events; often imposed on a minority group by a dominant group.

Self A distinct identity that sets us apart from others.

Serial monogamy A form of marriage in which a person may have several spouses in his or her lifetime, but only one spouse at a time.

Sex The biological differences between males and females.

Sexism The ideology that one sex is superior to the other.

Sick role Societal expectations about the attitudes and behaviour of a person viewed as being ill.

Significant other An individual who is most important in the development of the self, such as a parent, friend, or teacher.

Single-parent family A family in which only one parent is present to care for the children.

Slavery A system of enforced servitude in which some people are owned by others as property.

Social change Significant alteration over time in behaviour patterns and culture, including norms and values.

Social control   The techniques and strategies for preventing deviant human behaviour in any society.

Social disorganization theory   The theory that attributes increases in crime and deviance to the absence or breakdown of communal relationships and social institutions, such as the family, school, church, and local government.

Social epidemiology   The study of the distribution of disease, impairment, and general health status across a population.

Social inequality   A condition in which members of society have different amounts of wealth, prestige, or power.

Social institution   An organized pattern of beliefs and behaviour centred on basic social needs.

Social interaction   The ways in which people respond to one another.

Social mobility   Movement of individuals or groups from one position in a society's stratification system to another.

Social movement   An organized collective activity to bring about or resist fundamental change in an existing group or society.

Social network   A series of social relationships that links individuals directly to others, and through them indirectly to still more people.

Social role   A set of expectations for people who occupy a given social position or status.

Social science   The study of the social features of humans and the ways in which they interact and change.

Social structure   The way in which a society is organized into predictable relationships.

Socialism   An economic system under which the means of production and distribution are collectively owned.

Socialization   The lifelong process through which people learn the attitudes, values, and behaviours appropriate for members of a particular culture.

Societal-reaction approach   Another name for *labelling theory.*

Society   The structure of relationships within which culture is created and shared through regularized patterns of social interaction.

Sociobiology   The systematic study of how biology affects human social behaviour.

Socioeconomic status (SES)   A measure of class that is based on income, education, occupation, and related variables.

Sociological imagination   An awareness of the relationship between an individual and the wider society.

Sociology   The systematic study of the relationship between the individual and society and of the consequences of difference.

Status   A term used by sociologists to refer to any of the full range of socially defined positions within a large group or society.

Status group   People who have the same prestige or lifestyle, independent of their class positions.

Stereotype   An unreliable generalization about all members of a group that does not recognize individual differences within the group.

Stigma   A label used to devalue members of certain social groups.

Stratification   A structured ranking of entire groups of people that perpetuates unequal economic rewards and power in a society.

Subculture   A segment of society that shares a distinctive pattern of mores, folkways, and values that differs from the pattern of the larger society.

Substantive definition of religion   The idea that religion has a unique content or substance relating to the sacred that separates it from other forms of knowledge and belief.

Substantive definition of the family   A definition of the family based on blood, meaning shared genetic heritage; and law, meaning formal social recognition and affirmation of a shared bond among members.

Survey   A study, generally in the form of an interview or questionnaire, that provides researchers with information about how people think and act.

Symbol   A gesture, object, or word that forms the basis of human communication.

Symbolic ethnicity   An ethnic identity that emphasizes concerns such as ethnic food or political issues rather than deeper ties to one's ethnic heritage.

Teacher-expectancy effect   The impact that a teacher's expectations about a student's performance may have on the student's actual achievements.

Technology   "Cultural information about how to use the material resources of the environment to satisfy human needs and desires."

Terrorism   The use or threat of violence against random or symbolic targets in pursuit of political aims.

Theory   In sociology a set of statements that seeks to explain problems, actions, or behaviour.

Total institution   An institution that regulates all aspects of a person's life under a single authority, such as a prison, the military, a mental hospital, or a convent.

Totalitarianism   Virtually complete government control and surveillance over all aspects of a society's social and political life.

Tracking   The practice of placing students in specific curriculum groups on the basis of their test scores and other criteria.

Traditional authority   Legitimate power conferred by custom and accepted practice.

Trained incapacity   The tendency of workers in a bureaucracy to become so specialized that they develop blind spots and fail to notice potential problems.

Transnational crime   Crime that occurs across multiple national borders.

Underclass   The long-term poor who lack training and skills.

Validity   The degree to which a measure or scale truly reflects the phenomenon under study.

Value   A collective conception of what is considered good, desirable, and proper—or bad, undesirable, and improper—in a culture.

Value neutrality   Max Weber's term for objectivity of sociologists in the interpretation of data.

Variable   A measurable trait or characteristic that is subject to change under different conditions.

Vertical mobility   The movement of an individual from one social position to another of a different rank.

Vested interests   Those people or groups who will suffer in the event of social change and who have a stake in maintaining the status quo.

Victimization survey   A questionnaire or interview given to a sample of the population to determine whether people have been victims of crime.

Victimless crime   A term used by sociologists to describe the willing exchange among adults of widely desired, but illegal, goods and services.

War   Conflict between organizations that possess trained combat forces equipped with deadly weapons.

Wealth   The total of all a person's material assets, including savings, land, stocks, and other types of property, minus their debt at a single point in time.

White-collar crime   Illegal acts committed by affluent, "respectable" individuals in the course of business activities.

World systems analysis   A view of the global economic system as one divided between certain industrialized nations that control wealth and developing countries that are controlled and exploited.

A

Aaronson, Daniel, and Bhashkar Mazumder. 2007. "Intergenerational Economic Mobility in the U.S., 1940 to 2000." FRB Chicago Working Paper No. WP 2005-12, revised February, 2007. Federal Reserve Bank of Chicago. Accessed June 21, 2008 (http://ssrn.com/abstract=869435).

AARP. 1999. "New AARP Study Finds Boomers Vary in Their Views of the Future and Their Retirement Years." AARP news release, June 1. Washington, DC.

——— 2004. "Baby Boomers Envision Retirement II: Survey of Baby Boomers' Expectations for Retirement." Prepared for AARP Environmental Analysis by Roper ASW. Washington, DC: AARP. Accessed May 13, 2008 (http://assets.aarp.org/rgcenter/econ/boomers_envision.pdf).

Abada, Teresa, Feng Hou, and Bali Ram. 2008. "Group Differences in Educational Attainment Among the Children of Immigrants." Analytical Studies Branch Research Paper Series, Statistics Canada. Ottawa: Minister of Industry. Catalogue no. 11F0019M–No. 308.

ABC News. 2007. "Iraq: Where Things Stand: March 19, 2007." Accessed March 30 (http://abc.go.com/).

ABC Radio Australia. 2006. "China: Crackdown in Air Pollution ahead of 2008 Beijing Olympics." Accessed May 2 (www.abc.net.au).

Abercrombie, Nicholas, Bryan S. Turner, and Stephen Hill, eds. 1990. *Dominant Ideologies.* Cambridge, MA: Unwin Hyman.

Abercrombie, Nicholas, Stephen Hill, and Bryan S. Turner. 1980. *The Dominant Ideology Thesis.* London: George Allen and Unwin.

——— 2000. *The Penguin Dictionary of Sociology,* 4th ed. New York: Penguin Books.

Aberle, David E., A. K. Cohen, A. K. Davis, M. J. Leng, Jr., and F. N. Sutton. 1950. "The Functional Prerequisites of a Society." *Ethics* 60 (January): 100–111.

Acosta, R. Vivian, and Linda Jean Carpenter. 2001. "Women in Intercollegiate Sport: A Longitudinal Study: 1977–1998." Pp. 302–308 in *Sport in Contemporary Society: An Anthology,* 6th ed., ed. D. Stanley Eitzen. New York: Worth.

Addams, Jane. 1910. *Twenty Years at Hull-House.* New York: Macmillan.

———. 1930. *The Second Twenty Years at Hull-House.* New York: Macmillan.

Adler, Freda. 1975. *Sisters in Crime: The Rise of the New Female Criminal.* New York: McGraw-Hill.

Adler, Freda, Gerhard O. W. Mueller, and William S. Laufer. 2004. *Criminology and the Criminal Justice System,* 5th ed. New York: McGraw-Hill.

Adler, Patricia A. 1993. *Wheeling and Dealing: An Ethnography of an Upper-Level Drug Dealing and Smuggling Community,* 2d ed. New York: Columbia University Press.

Adler, Patricia A., and Peter Adler. 1985. "From Idealism to Pragmatic Detachment: The Academic Performance of College Athletes." *Sociology of Education* 58 (October): 241–250.

——— 1988. "Intense Loyalty in Organizations: A Case Study of College Athletics." *Administrative Science Quarterly* 33: 401–417.

——— 1991. *Backboards and Blackboards.* New York: Columbia University Press.

——— 1995. "Dynamics of Inclusion and Exclusion in Preadolescent Cliques." *Social Psychology Quarterly* 58 (3): 145–162.

——— 1996. "Preadolescent Clique Stratification and the Hierarchy of Identity." *Sociological Inquiry* 66 (2): 111–142.

——— 1998. *Peer Power: Preadolescent Culture and Identity.* New Brunswick, NJ: Rutgers University Press.

——— 2003. "The Promise and Pitfalls of Going into the Field." *Contexts* (Spring): 41–47.

——— 2004. *Paradise Laborers: Hotel Work in the Global Economy.* Ithaca, NY: Cornell University Press.

——— 2005. "Self-Injurers as Loners: The Social Organization of Solitary Deviance." *Deviant Behavior.*

——— 2007. "The Demedicalization of Self-Injury: From Psychopathology to Sociological Deviance." *Journal of Contemporary Ethnography* 36 (October): 537–570.

——— 2008. "The Cyber Worlds of Self-Injurers: Deviant Communities, Relationships, and Selves." *Symbolic Interaction* 31 (1): 33–56.

Adler, Patricia A., Peter Adler, and John M. Johnson. 1992. "Street Corner Society Revisited." *Journal of Contemporary Ethnography* 21 (April): 3–10.

Adler, Patricia A., Steve J. Kless, and Peter Adler. 1992. "Socialization to Gender Roles: Popularity Among Elementary School Boys and Girls." *Sociology of Education* 65 (July): 169–187.

Alain, Michel. 1985. "An Empirical Validation of Relative Deprivation." *Human Relations* 38 (8): 739–749.

Allen, John L. 2008. *Student Atlas of World Politics.* 8th ed. New York: McGraw-Hill.

Allport, Gordon W. 1979. *The Nature of Prejudice,* 25th anniversary ed. Reading, MA: Addison-Wesley.

Alter, Alexandria. 2007. "Is This Man Cheating on His Wife?" *The Wall Street Journal,* August 10, p. W1. Accessed June 3, 2008 (http://online.wsj.com/article/SB118670164592393622.html).

Amato, Paul R. 2001. "What Children Learn from Divorce." *Population Today,* January, pp. 1, 4.

American Lung Association. 2003. "Scenesmoking." Accessed December 19 (www.scenesmoking.org).

American Sociological Association. 1997. *Code of Ethics.* Washington, DC: American Sociological Association (www.asanet.org/members/ecoderev.html).

———. 2001. *Data Brief: Profile of ASA Membership.* Washington, DC: American Sociological Association.

———. 2005a. "Need Today's Data Yesterday." Accessed December 17 (www.asanet.org).

———. 2005b. "Careers and Jobs Home." Accessed December 17 (www.asanet.org/page.ww? section=careers+and+Jobs&name=Careers+and+ Jobs+Home).

———. 2006. "Current Sections." Accessed May 18 (www.asanet.org/page.ww?section=Sections& name=Overview).

———. 2006a. *Careers in Sociology with an Undergraduate Degree in Sociology,* 7th ed. Washington, DC: ASA.

———. 2006b. "What Can I Do with a Bachelor's Degree in Sociology." *A National Survey of Seniors Majoring in Sociology: First Glances: What Do They Know and Where are They Going?* Washington DC: American Sociological Association. Accessed August 2, 2008 (http://www.asanet.org/galleries/default-file/b&b_first_report_final.pdf).

———. 2007. *2006 Guide to Graduate Departments of Sociology.* Washington, DC: ASA.

Amnesty International. 1994. *Breaking the Silence: Human Rights Violations Based on Sexual Orientation.* New York: Amnesty International.

———. 2006. "Amnesty International: Facts and Figures on the Death Penalty." Accessed February 19 (www.amnesty.org).

———. 2007. "Amnesty International: Facts and Figures on the Death Penalty." Accessed February 17 (www.amnesty.org).

Anderson, Elijah. 1990. *Streetwise: Race, Class, and Change in an Urban Community.* Chicago: University of Chicago Press.

Anderson, John Ward, and Molly Moore. 1993. "The Burden of Womanhood." *Washington Post National Weekly Edition* 10 (March 22–28): 6–7.

Angier, Natalie. 2000. "Do Races Differ? Not Really, Genes Show." *New York Times,* August 22, p. F6. Accessed June 30, 2008 (http://query.nytimes.com/gst/fullpage.html?res=9E07E7DF1E3EF931A1575BC0A9669C8B63&scp=2&sq=natalie+angier&st=nyt).

Arias, Elizabeth. 2004. "United States Life Tables, 2002." *National Vital Statistics Report,* November 10.

Associated Press. 2007. "Exxon Mobil Appealing $2.5 Billion Compensation for *Valdez* Spill." *Anchorage Daily News,* January 17.

Association of American Medical Colleges. 2007. *Facts Applicants, Matriculates and Graduates.* Accessed March 31, 2008 (www.aamc.org/data/facts/start.htm).

———. 2008. *U.S. Medical School Faculty, 2006.* Accessed March 31 (www.aamc.org/data/facultyroster/usmsfø6/start.htm).

Atchley, Robert C. 1976. *The Sociology of Retirement.* New York: Wiley.

Atchley, Robert C., and Amanda S. Barusch. 2004. *Social Forces and Agency: An Introduction to Social Gerontology,* 10th ed. Belmont, CA: Thompson.

Austin, April. 2002. "Cellphones and Strife in Congo." *Christian Science Monitor,* December 5, p. 11.

B

Babad, Elisha Y., and P. J. Taylor. 1992. "Transparency of Teacher Expectancies Across Language, Cultural Boundaries." *Journal of Educational Research* 86: 120–125.

Baby Name Wizard. 2008. "NameVoyager." Accessed August 2, 2008 (www.babynamewizard.com).

Bailey, Sue. 2009. "Native Infant Mortality Rate Four Times Non Natives': Report." *Toronto Star*, March 30, 2009.

Bainbridge, William Sims. 2007. "The Scientific Research Potential of Virtual Worlds." *Science* 317 (July 27): 472–476.

Baker, Maureen. 2001. "The Future of Family Life." In Maureen Baker, ed. *Families: Changing Trends in Canada*, 4th ed. Toronto: McGraw-Hill Ryerson: 285–302.

Baker, Therese L. 1999. *Doing Social Research.* 3d ed. New York: McGraw-Hill.

Baldwin, James. [1965] 1985. "White Man's Guilt." Pp. 409–414 in *The Price of the Ticket: Collected Non-Fiction, 1948–1985.* New York: St. Martin's Press.

Baldwin, John R., and Wulong Gu. 2008. "Outsourcing and Offshoring in Canada." Economic Analysis Research Paper Series, Statistics Canada. Catalogue no. 11F0027M–No. 055.

Barboza, David. 2006. "Citing Public Sentiment, China Cancels Release of 'Geisha.'" *New York Times,* February 1, p. B6.

Barlow, Maude, and Elizabeth May. 2000. *Frederick Street: Life and Death on Canada's Love Canal.* Toronto: HarperCollins.

Barrett, David B., Todd M. Johnson, and Peter F. Crossing. 2005. "Worldwide Adherents of All Religions, Mid-2004" and "Religions Adherents in the United States of America 1900–2005." P. 282 in *Encyclopedia Britannica, Yearbook 2005.* Chicago: Encyclopedia Britannica.

———. 2006. "The 2005 Annual Megacensus of Religions." Pp. 282–283 in 2006 *Book of the Year.* Chicago: Encyclopedia Britannica.

Barrionuevo, Alexei. 2008. "Amazon's 'Forest Peoples' Seek a Role in Striking Global Climate Agreements." *New York Times,* April 6, p. 6.

Basso, Keith H. 1972. "Ice and Travel Among the Fort Norman Slave: Folk Taxonomies and Cultural Rules." *Language in Society* 1 (March): 31–49.

Baudrillard, Jean. [1981] 1994. *Simulacra and Simulation.* Ann Arbor: The University of Michigan Press.

Bauerlein,Monika. 1996. "The Luddites Are Back." *Utne Reader* (March/April): 24, 26.

Baum, Katrina. 2006. "Identity Theft, 2004." *Bureau of Justice Statistics Bulletin* (April).

BBC. 2006. "Madrid Bans Waifs from Catwalks." September 13. Accessed June 7, 2008 (http://news.bbc.co.uk/2/hi/europe/5341202.stm).

Beagan, Brenda L. 2001. " 'Even If I Don't Know What I'm Doing I Can Make It Look Like I Know What I'm Doing': Becoming a Doctor in the 1990s." *Canadian Review of Sociology and Anthropology* 38: 275–292.

Bearman, Peter S., James Moody, and Katherine Stovel. 2004. "Chains of Affection: The Structure of Adolescent Romantic and Sexual Networks." *American Journal of Sociology* 110 (July): 44–91.

Becker, Howard S. 1952. "Social Class Variations in the Teacher–Pupil Relationship." *Journal of Educational Sociology* 25 (April): 451–465.

———. 1963. *The Outsiders: Studies in the Sociology of Deviance.* New York: Free Press.

———, ed. 1964. *The Other Side: Perspectives on Deviance.* New York: Free Press.

———. 1973. *The Outsiders: Studies in the Sociology of Deviance,* rev. ed. New York: Free Press.

Beeghley, Leonard. 1978. *Social Stratification in America: A Critical Analysis of Theory and Research.* Santa Monica, CA: Goodyear.

Bell, Daniel. 1953. "Crime as an American Way of Life." *Antioch Review* 13 (Summer): 131–154.

———. 1999. *The Coming of Post-Industrial Society: A Venture in Social Forecasting.* With new foreword. New York: Basic Books.

Bendick, Marc, Jr., Charles W. Jackson, and J. Horacio Romero. 1993. *Employment Discrimination Against Older Workers: An Experimental Study of Hiring Practices.* Washington, DC: Fair Employment Council of Greater Washington.

Benford, Robert D. 1992. "Social Movements." Pp. 1880–1887 in *Encyclopedia of Sociology,* vol. 4, ed. Edgar F. Borgatta and Marie Borgatta. New York: Macmillan.

Bennett, Vivienne. 1995. "Gender, Class, and Water: Women and the Politics of Water Service in Monterrey, Mexico." *Latin American Perspectives* 22 (September): 76–99.

Berger, Peter. 1969. *The Sacred Canopy: Elements of a Sociological Theory of Religion.* Garden City, NY: Anchor Books.

Berger, Peter L., and Thomas Luckmann. 1966. *The Social Construction of Reality: A Treatise in the Sociology of Knowledge.* New York: Doubleday.

Berkeley Wellness Letter. 1990. "The Nest Refilled" (February): 1–2.

Berland, Gretchen K. 2001. "Health Information on the Internet: Accessibility, Quality, and Readability in English and Spanish." *Journal of the American Medical Association* 285 (March 23): 2612–2621.

Berlin, Brent, and Paul Kay. 1991. *Basic Color Terms: Their Universality and Evolution.* Berkeley: University of California Press.

Bernstein, Basil. 1962. "Social Class, Linguistic Codes and Grammatical Elements." *Language and Speech* 5: 221–240.

Bianchi, Suzanne M., and Daphne Spain. 1996. "Women,Work, and Family in America." *Population Bulletin* 51 (December).

Bianchi, Suzanne M., John P. Robinson, and Melissa A. Milkie. 2006. *Changing Rhythms of American Family Life.* New York: Russell Sage Foundation.

Bibby, Reginald W. 2002. *Restless Gods: The Renaissance of Religion in Canada.* Toronto: Stoddart Publishing.

———. 2004. *The Future Families Project: A Survey of Canadian Hopes and Dreams.* Ottawa: Vanier Institute of the Family.

Biddlecom, Ann, and Steven Martin. 2006. "Childless in America." *Contexts* 5 (Fall): 54.

Black, Donald. 1995. "The Epistemology of Pure Sociology." *Law and Social Inquiry* 20 (Summer): 829–870.

Blau, Peter M., and Otis Dudley Duncan. 1967. *The American Occupational Structure.* New York: Wiley.

Blau, Peter M., and Marshall W. Meyer. 1987. *Bureaucracy in Modern Society,* 3d ed. New York: Random House.

Blauner, Robert. 1972. *Racial Oppression in America.* New York: Harper and Row.

Blinder, Alan S. 2006. "Offshoring: The Next Industrial Revolution." *Foreign Affairs* (March/April).

Blow, Charles M. 2008. "All Atmospherics, No Climate." New York Times, April 19. Accessed July 4, 2008 (http://www.nytimes. com/2008/04/19/opinion/19blow.html).

Blumer, Herbert. 1955. "Collective Behavior." Pp. 165–198 in *Principles of Sociology,* 2d ed., ed. Alfred McClung Lee. New York: Barnes and Noble.

———. 1969. *Symbolic Interactionism: Perspective and Method.* Englewood Cliffs, NJ: Prentice Hall.

Boaz, Rachel Floersheim. 1987. "Early Withdrawal from the Labor Force." *Research on Aging* 9 (December): 530–547.

Bornschier, Volker, Christopher Chase-Dunn, and Richard Rubinson. 1978. "Cross-National Evidence of the Effects of Foreign Investment and Aid on Economic Growth and Inequality: A Survey of Findings and a Reanalysis." *American Journal of Sociology* 84 (November): 651–683.

Bottomore, Tom, and Maximilien Rubel, eds. 1956. *Karl Marx: Selected Writings in Sociology and Social Philosophy.* New York: McGraw-Hill.

Boudreaux, Richard. 2002. "Indian Rights Law Is Upheld in Mexico." *Los Angeles Times,* September 7, p. A3.

Bourdieu, Pierre. 1962. *The Algerians.* Preface by Raymond Aron. Boston: Beacon Press.

———. 1984. *Distinction: A Social Critique of the Judgment of Taste.* Cambridge, MA: Harvard University Press.

———. 1986. "The Forms of Capital." Pp. 241–258 in *Handbook of Theory and Research for the Sociology of Education,* ed. J. G. Richardson. New York: Greenwood Press.

———. 1998a. *Acts of Resistance: Against the Tyranny of the Market.* New York: New Press.

———. 1998b. *On Television.* New York: New Press.

Bowles, Samuel, and Herbert Gintis. 1976. *Schooling in Capitalistic America: Educational Reforms and the Contradictions of Economic Life.* New York: Basic Books.

Brady, Jeff. 2009. "Flu Worries Pump Up Sales of Hand Sanitizer." October 19, 2009. National Public Radio. Accessed November 2, 2009 (http://npr.org/templates/story.php?storyId=113700183&ft= 1&f=1006).

Brazeau, Robyn, and Jodi-Anne Brzozowski. 2008. "Violent Victimization in Canada." *Matter of Fact.* November 2008. Statistics Canada. Catalogue no. 89-630-X.

Brazao, Dale. 2009. "Ruby Dhalla's Nanny Trouble." *Toronto Star,* May 5, 2009.

Brazao, Dale, and Robert Cribb. 2009. "Nannies Trapped in Bogus Jobs." *Toronto Star,* March 14, 2009.

Brewer, Rose M., and Nancy A. Heitzeg. 2008. "The Racialization of Criminal Punishment." *American Behavioral Scientist* 51 (January): 625–644.

Brown, David K. 2001. "The Social Sources of Educational Credentialism: Status Cultures, Labor Markets, and Organizations." *Sociology of Education* 74 (Extra Issue): 19–34.

Brown, Robert McAfee. 1980. *Gustavo Gutierrez.* Atlanta: John Knox.

Brown Women, Blond Babies. 1992. A film by Marie Boti and Florchita Bautista. Diffusion Multi-Monde.

Bruce, Steve. 2000. *Choice and Religion: A Critique of Rational Choice Theory.* New York: Oxford University Press.

Budig, Michelle J. 2002. "Male Advantage and the Gender Composition of Jobs: Who Rides the Glass Escalator?" *Social Problems* 49 (2): 258–277.

Bulle, Wolfgang F. 1987. *Crossing Cultures? Southeast Asian Mainland.* Atlanta: Centers for Disease Control and Prevention.

Bunzel, John H. 1992. *Race Relations on Campus: Stanford Students Speak.* Stanford, CA: Portable Stanford.

Bureau of Labor Statistics. 2006. "Number of Jobs Held, Labor Market Activity, and Earnings Growth Among the Youngest Baby Boomers: Results from a Longitudinal Survey." *News,* August 25. Washington, DC: BLS.

———. 2007. "Labor Force (Demographic) Data." February 13. Accessed February 28 (www.bls.gov).

Bureau of the Census. 1975. *Historical Statistics of the United States, Colonial Times to 1970.* Washington, DC: U.S. Government Printing Office.

———. 1994. *Statistical Abstract of the United States, 1994.* Washington, DC: U.S. Government Printing Office.

———. 1998. "Race of Wife by Race of Husband." Internet release of June 10.

———. 2003a. *Statistical Abstract of the United States, 2003.* Washington, DC: U.S. Government Printing Office.

———. 2003b. *Characteristics of American Indians and Alaska Natives, by Tribe and Language: 2000.* Washington, DC: U.S. Government Printing Office.

———. 2004. *Statistical Abstract of the United States, 2004–2005.* Washington, DC: U.S. Government Printing Office.

———. 2005a. *Statistical Abstract of the United States, 2006.* Washington, DC: U.S. Government Printing Office.

———. 2005b. "Total Midyear Population for the World: 1950–2050." Updated April 26. Accessed June 1 (www.census.gov/ipc/www/ worldpop. html).

———. 2005c. *Florida, California and Texas Future Population Growth.* Census Bureau Reports, CB05-52. Washington, DC: U.S. Government Printing Office.

———. 2005d. "International Data Base." Accessed April 26 (www .census.gov/ipc/www/idbnew. html).

———. 2005e. "World Population: 1950–2050." April 2005 version. Accessed May 3, 2006 (www. census.gov/ipc/www/img/worldpop. gif).

———. 2005f. "American Fact Finder: Places with United States." Accessed December 12 (http:// factfinder.census.gov).

———. 2005g. "Hurricane Katrina Disaster Area." Accessed December 15 (www.census.gov).

———. 2006a. *Statistical Abstract of the United States, 2007.* Washington, DC: U.S. Government Printing Office.

———. 2006b. "American Community Survey 2006: Table R1601. Percent of People 5 Years and Over Who Speak a Language Other Than English at Home." Accessed October 14, 2007 (http:// Factfinder.census.gov).

———. 2007a. *Statistical Abstract of the United States, 2008.* Washington, DC: U.S. Government Printing Office.

———. 2007b. "American Community Survey 2006" (www.census .gov).

———. 2007c. "Current Population Survey, 2005 to 2007. Annual Social and Economic Supplements." Accessed December 29 (www .census.gov/hhes/www/income/income06/statemhi3.html).

———. 2007d. "America's Families and Living Arrangements: 2006." Current Population Survey (www.census.gov).

———. 2008a. *Statistical Abstract of the United States.* Washington, DC: U.S. Government Printing Office.

———. 2008b. "Total Midyear Population for the World: 1900–2050." Data updated March 27, 2008. Accessed April 9 (www.census .gov).

————. 2008c. "Nearly Half of Preschoolers Receive Child Care from Relatives." Press Release, February 28 (www.census.gov).

Burkeman, Oliver. 2007. "Virtual World Wakes Up to Violent Protest." *Manchester Guardian,* February 16, p. 6.

Burns, John R. 1998. "Once Widowed in India, Twice Scorned." *New York Times,* March 29, p. A1.

Butler, Daniel Allen. 1998. *"Unsinkable: The Full Story."* Mechanicsburg, PA: Stackpole Books.

Butler, Robert N. 1990. "A Disease Called Ageism." *Journal of American Geriatrics Society* 38 (February): 178–180.

C

Calhoun, Craig. 1998. "Community Without Propinquity Revisited." *Sociological Inquiry* 68 (Summer): 373–397.

Call, V. R., and J. D. Teachman. 1991. "Military Service and Stability in the Family Life Course." *Military Psychology* 3: 233–250.

Calliste, Agnes. 2001. "Black Families in Canada: Exploring the Interconnections of Race, Class, and Gender." Pp. 401–419 in *Family Patterns, Gender Relations.* Bonnie J. Fox, ed. Toronto: Oxford University Press.

Campaign 2000. 2006. "Oh Canada! Too Many Children in Poverty for Too Long: 2006 Report Card on Child and Family Poverty in Canada" (www.campaign2000.ca/rc/rc06/06_C2000National ReportCard.pdf).

Canadian Centre for Justice Statistics. 2002. *Cyber-Crime: Issues, Data Sources, and Feasibility of Collecting Police-Reported Statistics.* Ottawa: Minister of Industry. Catalogue no. 85-558-XIE. Prepared by Melanie Kowalski.

————. 2008. "Crime Statistics in Canada, 2007." *Juristat* 28 (7). Statistics Canada—Catalogue no. 85-002-X. Ottawa: Minister of Industry.

————. 2008. *Profile Series: Hate Crime in Canada.* "Findings: Incidence of Police-reported and Victim-reported Hate Crime." (www.statcan.gc.ca/pub/85f0033m/2008017/5200141-eng.htm). Last modified June 9, 2008.

Canadian Chamber of Commerce. 2009. *Immigration: The Changing Face of Canada.* Policy Brief, Economic Policy Series, February 2009.

Canadian Council for Refugees. "A Hundred Years of Immigration to Canada, 1900–1999." Accessed May 18, 2009 (www.ccrweb.ca/history.html).

Canadian Council on Learning. 2009. "Post-Secondary Education in Canada: Who is Missing Out?" *Lessons in Learning.* April 1, 2009 (www.cclcca.ca/CCL/Reports?LessonsInLearning/Lin-L200900401PSEUnderrepresented.htm).

Canadian Institute for Health Information. 2008. "Spending on Health Care to Reach $5,170 per Canadian in 2008." November 13, 2008 release. Accessed April 27, 2009 (http://secure.cihi.ca/cihiweb/dispPage.jsp?cw_page=media_13nov2008_e).

————. 2008. "Table: Percentage Distribution of Registered Nurses by Sex and Province/Territory, Canada, 2006." Health Human Resources–Registered Nurses–Demographic Trends. Accessed October 30, 2009 (http://secure.cihi.ca/cihiweb/en/images/hpdb/hpdb_registered_nurses_figure1_e.jpg).

Canadian Mental Health Association. "Fast Facts: Mental Health/Mental Illness." Accessed October 30, 2009 (www.cmha.ca/bins/content_page.asp?cid=6-20-23-43).

Canadian Press. 2007. "Nuclear Family Still Thrives in Some Parts of Canada." September 12, 2007. Accessed March 30, 2009 (www.ctv.ca).

————. 2008. "Accused of Cheating, Facebook Student Optimistic." *Toronto Star,* March 11.

————. 2009. "Canada Limits Foreign Aid Recipients." February 23, 2009. Accessed April 22, 2009 (www.ctv.ca).

————. 2009. "High Mortality Rate Among Native Infants Called a Tragedy." March 31, 2009. Accessed June 3, 2009 (www.cbc.ca/health/story/2009/03/31/native-infant-health.html).

Canadian Sociology and Anthropology Association. 1994. *Statement of Professional Ethics of the Canadian Sociology and Anthropology Association* (www.csaa.ca/structure/Code.htm#Preamble).

Caplan, Ronald L. 1989. "The Commodification of American Health Care." *Social Science and Medicine* 28 (11): 1139–1148.

Caplow, Theodore, and Louis Hicks. 2002. *Systems of War and Peace,* 2d ed. Lanham, MD: University Press of America.

Carey, Anne R., and Elys A. McLean. 1997. "Heard It Through the Grapevine?" *USA Today,* September 15, p. B1.

Carr, Deborah. 2007. "Baby Blues." *Contexts* (Spring): 62.

Carroll, Joseph. 2005. "Who Supports Marijuana Legalization?" November 1. Accessed January 19, 2007 (www.galluppoll.com).

Carson, Rachel. 1962. *Silent Spring.* Boston: Houghton Mifflin.

Carty, Win. 1999. "Greater Dependence on Cars Leads to More Pollution in World's Cities." *Population Today* 27 (December): 1–2.

Castañeda, Jorge G. 1995. "Ferocious Differences." *Atlantic Monthly* 276 (July): pp. 68–69, 71–76.

Castells, Manuel. 1983. *The City and the Grass Roots.* Berkeley: University of California Press.

————. 1997. *The Power of Identity.* Vol. 1 of *The Information Age: Economy, Society and Culture.* London: Blackwell.

————. 1998. *End of Millennium.* Vol. 3 of *The Information Age: Economy, Society and Culture.* London: Blackwell.

————. 2000. *The Information Age: Economy, Society and Culture* (3 vols.), 2d ed. Oxford and Malden, MA: Blackwell.

————. 2001. *The Internet Galaxy: Reflections on the Internet, Business, and Society.* New York: Oxford University Press.

Catalyst. 2007. *2007 Catalyst Census of Women Board Directors, Corporate Officers, and Top Earners.* New York: Catalyst.

————. 2008. "Women and Minorities on Fortune 100 Boards." The Prout Group, the Executive Leadership Council, and the Hispanic Association on Corporate Responsibility. Accessed June 30 (http://www.catalyst.org/file/86/1-17-08%20abd%20study.pdf).

Cavalli-Sforza, L. Luca, Paolo Menozzi, and Alberto Piazza. 1994. *The History and Geography of Human Genes.* Princeton, NJ: Princeton University Press.

CBC News. 2004. "In Depth: Inside Walkerton." December 20, 2004. Accessed May 19, 2009.

————. 2005. "In Depth: Romeo Dallaire." Updated March 9, 2005. Accessed May 30, 2009.

————. 2005. "In Depth: Racial Profiling" May 26, 2005. Accessed May 19, 2009.

————. 2005. "In Depth: Wal-Mart—Timeline of World's Largest Retailer." June 30, 2005. Accessed April 19, 2009.

————. 2006. "In Depth: Canada's Military—Women in the Canadian Military." May 30, 2006. Accessed April 19, 2009.

————. 2007. "Features: Faith-based Schools." Jennifer Wilson. September 17, 2007. Accessed June 2, 2009.

————. 2007. "Poverty Fuelling Rise in Aboriginal Gang Activity: Expert." September 21, 2007. Accessed April 22, 2009.

————. 2008. "Higher Obesity Rates Found in Off-Reserve Aboriginal People: Study." January 23, 2008. Accessed June 3, 2009.

————. 2008. "Health Care Often Inaccessible to Inuit: Report–Inuit Life Expectancy 15 Years Less Than Canadian Average." December 4, 2008. Accessed June 3, 2009.

————. 2008. "In Depth: Canada's Military—Canadian Forces in the 21st Century." April 21, 2008. Accessed May 9, 2009.

————. 2008. "Voter Turnout Drops to Record Low." October 12, 2008. Accessed April 19, 2009.

———. 2009. "Applicants Scarce for Toronto's Africentric School Experiment." January 9, 2009. Accessed January 23, 2009.

———. 2009. "In Depth: Abortion Rights: Significant Moments in Canadian History." January 13, 2009. Accessed April 27, 2009.

———. 2009. "Justice Minister Reiterates Need for Bail Changes." June 25, 2009. Accessed June 30, 2009.

———. 2009. "Polygamy Charges in Bountiful, B.C., Thrown Out." September 23, 2009. Accessed October 8, 2009.

CBS News. 1979. Transcript of *Sixty Minutes* segment, "I Was Only Following Orders." March 31, pp. 2–8.

Center for Corporate Diversity. 2008. "Nordic 500, 2006–2008." Accessed March 17 (www.managementwomen.no).

Centers for Disease Control and Prevention. 2007a. *HIV/AIDS Surveillance Report.* Revised June 2007. Atlanta, GA: CDC.

———. 2007b. "U.S. Public Health Service Syphilis Study at Tuskegee." Accessed April 25 (www.cdc.gov).

———. 2007c. "HIV/AIDS Among Women." Revised June 2007. Accessed March 21 (www.cdc.gov.hiv.topics/women/resources/factsheets/women.htm).

Centre for Addiction and Mental Health. 2005. "Heavy Drinking, Levels of Stress High Among University Students—Canadian Campus Survey." Accessed March 31, 2009 (http://camh.net/News_events/News_releases_and_media_advisories_and_backgrounders/os-dus2005_highlights.html).

Chambliss, William. 1973. "The Saints and the Roughnecks." *Society* 11 (November/December): 24–31.

Charter, David, and Jill Sherman. 1996. "Schools Must Teach New Code of Values." *London Times,* January 15, p. 1.

Chase-Dunn, Christopher, and Peter Grimes. 1995. "World-Systems Analysis." Pp. 387–417 in *Annual Review of Sociology, 1995,* ed. John Hagan. Palo Alto, CA: Annual Reviews.

Cheng, Shu-Ju Ada. 2003. "Rethinking the Globalization of Domestic Service." *Gender and Society* 17 (2): 166–186.

Cherlin, Andrew. 2004. "The Deinstitutionalization of American Marriage." *Journal of Marriage and the Family* 66: 848–861.

———. 2006. "On Single Mothers 'Doing' Family." *Journal of Marriage and Family* 68 (November): 800–803.

———. 2008. *Public and Private Families: An Introduction,* 5th ed. New York: McGraw-Hill.

———. 2008. "Can the Left Learn the Lessons of Welfare Reform?" *Contemporary Sociology* 37 (March): 101–104.

Chesney-Lind, Meda. 1989. "Girls' Crime and Women's Place: Toward a Feminist Model of Female Delinquency." *Crime and Delinquency* 35: 5–29.

Childfree News. 2007. "Canadian Birthrate Falls Far Below U.S." March 15, 2007. Accessed March 30, 2009 (http://childfreenews.blogspot.com/2007/03/canadian-birthrate-falls-far-below-us.html).

China Daily. 2004. "Starbucks Takes Aim at China Chain." Accessed July 21 (www2.chinadaily.com.cn).

Christensen, Kathleen. 1990. "Bridges over Troubled Water: How Older Workers View the Labor Market." Pp. 175–207 in *Bridges to Retirement,* ed. Peter B. Doeringer. Ithaca, NY: IRL Press.

Christensen-Hughes, Julia, and Donald McCabe. 2006. "Academic Misconduct within Higher Education in Canada." *Canadian Journal of Higher Education* 36 (2): 1–21.

Cigar, Norman. 1995. *Genocide in Bosnia: The Policy of "Ethnic Cleansing."* College Station: Texas A&M University Press.

Citizens' Forum on Canada's Future. 1991. *Report to the People and Government of Canada.* Ottawa: Privy Council Office.

Citizenship and Immigration Canada. 2008. "Facts and Figures 2008—Immigration Overview: Permanent and Temporary Residents." Accessed May 10, 2009 (www.cic.gc.ca/english/resources/statistics/facts2008/figures.asp).

———. 2009. *Annual Report on the Operation of the Canadian Multiculturalism Act 2007–2008.* Ottawa. © Her Majesty the Queen in Right of Canada, 2009 Catalogue no. CH31-1/2008.

Civic Ventures. 1999. *The New Face of Retirement: Older Americans, Civic Engagement, and the Longevity Revolution.* Washington, DC: Peter D. Hart Research Associates.

Clark, Burton, and Martin Trow. 1966. "The Organizational Context." Pp. 17–70 in *The Study of College Peer Groups,* ed. Theodore M. Newcomb and Everett K. Wilson. Chicago: Aldine.

Clark, Warren. 2006. "Interreligious Unions in Canada." *Canadian Social Trends.* Statistics Canada. Catalogue no. 11-008.

Clark, Warren, and Grant Schellenberg. 2006. "Who's Religious?" *Canadian Social Trends.* Statistics Canada Catalogue no. 11-008.

Clarke, Adele E., Janet K. Shim, Laura Maro, Jennifer Ruth Fusket, and Jennifer R. Fishman. 2003. "Bio Medicalization: Technoscientific Transformations of Health, Illness, and U.S. Biomedicine." *American Sociological Review* 68 (April): 161–194.

Clarke, Edward H. 1874. *Sex in Education; or, A Fair Chance for Girls.* Boston: James R. Osgood.

Clausen, Christopher. 2002. "To Have . . . or Not to Have." *Utne Reader* (July–August): 66–70.

Clinard, Marshall B., and Robert F. Miller. 1998. *Sociology of Deviant Behavior,* 10th ed. Fort Worth, TX: Harcourt Brace.

CNN. 2006. "Skinny Models Banned from Catwalk." September 13. Accessed June 7, 2008 (http://www.cnn.com/2006/WORLD/europe/09/13/spain.models/index.html)

Colby, David C. 1986. "The Voting Rights Act and Black Registration in Mississippi." *Publius* 16 (Fall): 123–137.

Cole, Elizabeth S. 1985. "Adoption, History, Policy, and Program." Pp. 638–666 in *A Handbook of Child Welfare,* ed. John Laird and Ann Hartman. New York: Free Press.

Cole, Mike. 1988. *Bowles and Gintis Revisited: Correspondence and Contradiction in Educational Theory.* Philadelphia: Falmer.

Coleman, Isobel. 2004. "The Payoff from Women's Rights." *Foreign Affairs* 83 (May/June): 80–95.

Coleman, James William. 2006. *The Criminal Elite: Understanding White-Collar Crime,* 6th ed. New York: Worth.

Collins, Gail. 2003. *America's Women.* New York: HarperCollins.

Collins, Randall. 1975. *Conflict Sociology: Toward an Explanatory Sociology.* New York: Academic Press.

———. 1980. "Weber's Last Theory of Capitalism: A Systematization." *American Sociological Review* 45 (December): 925–942.

———. 1986. *Weberian Sociological Theory.* New York: Cambridge University Press.

———. 1995. "Prediction in Macrosociology: The Case of the Soviet Collapse." *American Journal of Sociology* 100 (May): 1552–1593.

Collura, Heather. 2007. "Roommate Concerns Fed by Facebook." *USA Today,* August 8, p. D6.

Commission on Civil Rights. 1976. *A Guide to Federal Laws and Regulations Prohibiting Sex Discrimination.* Washington, DC: U.S. Government Printing Office.

———. 1981. *Affirmative Action in the 1980s: Dismantling the Process of Discrimination.* Washington, DC: U.S. Government Printing Office.

Commoner, Barry. 1971. *The Closing Circle.* New York: Knopf.

———. 1990. *Making Peace with the Planet.* New York: Pantheon Books.

Connell, R. W. 1987. *Gendered Power: Society, the Person, and Sexual Politics.* Stanford, CA: Stanford University Press.

———. 2002. *Gender.* Cambridge, UK: Polity Press.

———. 2005. *Masculinities,* 2d ed. Berkeley: University of California Press.

References

Cool, Julie. 2008. *Women in Parliament*. Revised October 9, 2008. Ottawa: Parliamentary Information and Research Service, Library of Parliament. PRB 05-62E. Accessed at www.parl.gc.ca/information/library/PRBpubs/prb0562-e.htm#awomen.

Cooley, Charles. H. 1902. *Human Nature and the Social Order*. New York: Scribner.

Coontz, Stephanie. 1992. *The Way We Never Were: American Families and the Nostalgia Trap*. New York: Basic Books.

———. 2005. *Marriage, a History: From Obedience to Intimacy or How Love Conquered Marriage*. New York: Viking.

———. 2006. "A Pop Quiz on Marriage." *New York Times*, February 19, p. 12.

———. 2008. "The Future of Marriage." *Cato Unbound*, January 14. Accessed June 9 (http://www.cato-unbound.org/2008/01/14/stephanie-coontz/the-future-of-marriage/).

Corak, Miles. 2006. "Do Poor Children Become Poor Adults? Lessons from a Cross Country Comparison of Generational Earnings Mobility." Institute for the Study of Labor (IZA) Discussion Paper No. 1993, March. Accessed June 24, 2008 (http://papers.ssrn.com/sol3/papers.cfm?abstract_id=889034).

Conrad, Peter, ed. 2005. *The Sociology of Health and Illness: Cultural Perspectives*, 7th ed. New York: Worth.

———. 2007. *The Medicalization of Society: On the Transformation of Human Conditions into Treatable Disorders*. Baltimore, MD: Johns Hopkins University Press.

Cooper, K., S. Day, A. Green, and H. Ward. 2007. "Maids, Migrants and Occupational Health in the London Sex Industry. *Anthropology and Medicine* 14 (April) 41–53.

Côte, Francois, and Tim Williams. 2008. *The Arctic: Environmental Issues*. Ottawa: Library of Parliament. PRB 08-04E.

Côté, James E. 2000. *Arrested Adulthood: The Changing Nature of Identity and Maturity in the Late World*. New York: New York University.

Couch, Carl J. 1996. *Information Technologies and Social Orders*. Edited with an introduction by David R. Maines and Shing-Ling Chien. New York: Aldine de Gruyter.

Cox, Oliver C. 1948. *Caste, Class, and Race: A Study in Social Dynamics*. Detroit: Wayne State University Press.

Cranswick, Kelly, and Donna Dosman. 2008. "Eldercare: What We Know Today." *Canadian Social Trends*. Statistics Canada Catalogue no. 11-008.

Criminal Intelligence Service Canada. 2008. *CISC Report on Organized Crime* (www.cisc.gc.ca/media/media_2008/highlights_2008_e.html).

Crosnoe, Robert, and Glen H. Elder, Jr. 2002. "Successful Adaptation in the Later Years: A Life Course Approach to Aging." *Social Psychology Quarterly* (4): 309–328.

Cross, Simon, and Barbara Bagilhole. 2002. "Girls' Jobs for the Boys? Men, Masculinity and Non-traditional Occupations." *Gender, Work, and Organization* 9 (April):204–226.

Croucher, Sheila L. 2004. *Globalization and Belonging: The Politics of Identity in a Changing World*. Lanham, MD: Rowman and Littlefield.

Crouse, Kelly. 1999. "Sociology of the Titanic." *Teaching Sociology Listserv*, May 24.

CTV News. 2004. "Walkerton Chronology." December 20, 2004. Accessed February 3, 2009.

———. 2005. "Mexican Consulate Opens in Tiny Farm Community." August 30, 3005. Accessed April 22, 2009.

Cullen, Francis T., Jr., and John B. Cullen. 1978. *Toward a Paradigm of Labeling Theory*, Ser. 58. Lincoln: University of Nebraska Studies.

Cullen, Lisa Takevchi. 2007. "Till Work Do Us Part." *Time*, October 8, pp. 63–64.

Cumming, Elaine, and William E. Henry. 1961. *Growing Old: The Process of Disengagement*. New York: Basic Books.

Currie, Elliot. 1985. *Confronting Crime: An American Challenge*. New York: Pantheon Books.

———. 1998. *Crime and Punishment in America*. New York: Metropolitan Books.

Curtiss, Susan. 1977. *Genie: A Psycholinguistic Study of a Modern Day "Wild Child."* New York: Academic Press.

———. 1985. "The Development of Human Cerebral Lateralization." Pp. 97–116 in *The Dual Brain*, ed. D. Frank Benson and Eran Zaidel. New York: Guilford Press.

D

Dahl, Robert A. 1961. *Who Governs?* New Haven, CT: Yale University Press.

Daisey, Mike. 2002. *21 Dog Years: Doing Time @ Amazon.com*. New York: Free Press.

Daley, Suzanne. 1999. "Doctors' Group of Volunteers Awarded Nobel." *New York Times*, October 16, pp. A1, A6.

Dalla, Rochelle L., and Wendy C. Gamble. 2001. "Teenage Mothering and the Navajo Reservation: An Examination of Intergovernmental Perceptions and Beliefs." *American Indian Culture and Research Journal* 25 (1): 1–19.

Dallaire, Roméo. 2003. *Shake Hands with the Devil: The Failure of Humanity in Rwanda*. Toronto: Random House Canada.

Daniszewski, John. 2003. "Al-Jazeera TV Draws Flak Outside—and Inside—the Arab World." *Los Angeles Times*, January 5, pp. A1, A5.

Darwin, Charles. 1859. *On the Origin of Species*. London: John Murray.

Davies, Christie. 1989. "Goffman's Concept of the Total Institution: Criticisms and Revisions." *Human Studies* 12 (June): 77–95.

Davis, James A., Tom W. Smith, and Peter V. Marsden. 2007. *General Social Surveys, 1972–2006: Cumulative Codebook*. Chicago: National Opinion Research Center.

Davies, James B., Anthony Shorrocks, Susanna Sandstrom, and Edward N. Wolff. 2007. "The World Distribution of Household Wealth." Center for Global, International and Regional Studies. Mapping Global Inequalities—conference papers. Paper mgi-5, presented November 28. Accessed June 23, 2008 (http://repositories.cdlib.org/cgirs/mgi/mgi-5).

Davis, Gerald. 2003. *America's Corporate Banks Are Separated by Just Four Handshakes*. Accessed March 7 (www.bus.umich.edu/research/ davis.html).

———. 2004. "American Cronyism: How Executive Networks Inflated the Corporate Bubble." *Contexts* (Summer): 34–40.

Davis, Kingsley. 1940. "Extreme Social Isolation of a Child." *American Journal of Sociology* 45 (January): 554–565.

———. 1947. "A Final Note on a Case of Extreme Isolation." *American Journal of Sociology* 52 (March): 432–437.

———. [1949] 1995. *Human Society*, New York: Macmillan.

———, and Wilbert E. Moore. 1945. "Some Principles of Stratification." *American Sociological Review* 10 (April): 242–249.

Davis, Nanette J. 1975. *Sociological Constructions of Deviance: Perspectives and Issues in the Field*. Dubuque, IA: Wm. C Brown.

Death Penalty Information Center. 2006. "Number of Executions by State and Region Since 1976." Accessed February 19 (www.deathpenalty info.org).

———. 2008. "Facts About the Death Penalty." Accessed January 12 (www.deathpenaltyinfo.org).

Deegan, Mary Jo, ed. 1991. *Women in Sociology: A Bio-Biographical Sourcebook*. Westport, CT: Greenwood.

Delawala, Imtyaz. 2002. "What Is Coltran?" January 21 (www.abcnews.com).

DeMott, Benjamin. 1990. *The Imperial Middle: Why Americans Can't Think Straight About Class.* New York: William Morrow.

DeNavas-Walt, Carmen, Bernadette D. Proctor, and Cheryl Miller. 2005. "Income, Poverty and Health Insurance Coverage in the United States: 2004." *Current Population Reports,* Ser. P-60, No. 229. Washington, DC: U.S. Government Printing Office.

DeNavas-Walt, Carmen, Bernadette D. Proctor, and Jessica Smith. 2007. "Income, Poverty, and Health Insurance Coverage in the United States: 2006." *Current Population Reports,* Ser. P-60, No. 233. Washington, DC: U.S. Government Printing Office.

DePalma, Anthony. 1995. "Racism? Mexico's in Denial." *New York Times,* June 11, p. E4.

DeParle, Jason. 2005. "Hispanic Group Thrives on Federal Aid." *New York Times,* May 3, pp. A1, A16.

———. 2007. "In a World on the Move, a Tiny Land Strains to Cope." *New York Times,* June, p. A1.

———. 2007. "Migrant Money Flow: A $300 Billion Current." *New York Times,* November 18, work section p. 3.

Department of Homeland Security. 2006. *The Federal Response to Hurricane Katrina: Lessons Learned.* Washington, DC: U.S. Government Printing Office.

Department of Justice. 2000. *The Civil Liberties Act of 1988: Redress for Japanese Americans.* Accessed June 29 (http://www.usdoj.gov/crt/ora/main. html).

———. 2005. *Crime in the United States, 2004.* Washington, DC: U.S. Government Printing Office.

———. 2007. "Hate Crime Statistics, 2006" (www.fbi.gov/ucr/ucr.htm).

———. 2007a. *Crime in the United States, 2006.* Washington, DC: U.S. Government Printing Office.

Department of Justice Canada. 2003. "Minority Views on the Canadian Anti-Terrorism Act." Accessed July 1, 2009 (http://canada.justice.gc.ca/eng/pi/rs/rep-rap/2003/rr03_4/p2_4.html).

Department of National Defence. 2009. "Canadian Forces Recruiting: Aboriginal Peoples in the CF" (www.forces.ca).

Devitt, James. 1999. *Framing Gender on the Campaign Trail: Women's Executive Leadership and the Press.* New York: Women's Leadership Conference.

Dickens, Charles. 1843. *A Christmas Carol.* London: Chapman and Hall. Accessed July 7, 2008 (www.gutenberg.org/dirs/4/46/46-h/46 h.htm).

Diebel, Linda. 2008. "Ex-Olympian Forced to Choose Between Marriage and Mohawk Status in Kahnewake." *Toronto Star,* June 1, 2008.

Dillon, Sam. 1998. "Sex Bias at Border Plants in Mexico Reported by U.S." *New York Times,* January 13, p. A6.

———. 2004. "Education Can Be Long, Hard Haul for Nation's Rural Kids." *Chicago Tribune,* May 28, p. 13.

Doeringer, Peter B., ed. 1990. *Bridges to Retirement: Older Workers in a Changing Labor Market.* Ithaca, NY: ILR Press.

Domhoff, G. William. 1978. *Who Really Rules? New Haven and Community Power Reexamined.* New Brunswick, NJ: Transaction.

———. 2006. *Who Rules America?* 5th ed. New York: McGraw-Hill.

Dominion Institute of Canada. 2008. *2008 Youth Election Study.* Prepared by Innovative Research Group. October 1, 2008.

———. 2008. "Youth Voter Turnout Expected to Drop." October 1, 2008. (www.dominion.ca/release01102008.pdf).

Doress, Irwin, and Jack Nusan Porter. 1977. *Kids in Cults: Why They Join, Why They Stay, Why They Leave.* Brookline, MA: Reconciliation Associates.

Doucet, A., and L. Merla. 2007. "Stay-at Home-Fathering: A Strategy for Balancing Work and Home in Canadian and Belgian Families." *Community, Work and Family* 10 (4): 453–471.

Dougherty, John, and David Holthouse. 1999. "Bordering on Exploitation." Accessed March 5 (www.phoenixnewtime.com/issies/1998-07-09/ feature.html).

Dougherty, Kevin, and Floyd M. Hammack. 1992. "Education Organization." Pp. 535–541 in *Encyclopedia of Sociology,* vol. 2, ed. Edgar F. Borgatta and Marie L. Borgatta. New York: Macmillan.

Dowd, James J. 1980. *Stratification Among the Aged.* Monterey, CA: Brooks/Cole.

Dowden, C. 2001. *Quality of Life in the Canadian Forces: Results from the National Survey.* Ottawa: Director Human Resources Research and Evaluation, National Defence Headquarters.

———. 2002. *Quality of Life in the Canadian Forces: Results from the National Survey—CF Spouses.* Ottawa: Director Human Resources Research and Evaluation, National Defence Headquarters.

Dressler, William W., Kathryn S. Oths, and Clarence C. Gravlee. 2005. "Racial and Ethnicity in Public Health Research: Models to Explain Health Disparities." Pp. 231–252 in *Annual Review of Anthropology 2005,* ed. William H. Durham. Palo Alto, CA: Annual Reviews.

Dubner, Stephen J. 2007. "Everything You Always Wanted to Know About Street Gangs (But Didn't Know Whom to Ask)." Freakanomics blog, *New York Times,* August 6. Accessed June 10, 2008 (http://freakonomics.blogs.nytimes.com/2007/08/06/everything-you-always-wanted-to-know-about-street-gangs-but-didnt-know-whom-to-ask/).

Du Bois, W.E.B. [1903] 1994. *The Souls of Black Folk.* New York: Dover.

———. [1909] 1970. *The Negro American Family.* Cambridge, MA: M.I.T. Press.

———. [1940] 1968. *Dusk of Dawn.* New York: Schocken Books.

Dugger, Celia. 2006. "Peace Prize to Pioneer of Loans for Those Too Poor to Borrow." *New York Times,* October 14, pp. A1, A6.

Dukes, Richard L., Tara M. Bisel, Karoline N. Burega, Eligio A. Lobato, and Matthew D. Owens. 2003. "Expression of Love, Sex, and Hurt in Popular Songs: A Content Analysis of All-Time Greatest Hits." *Social Science Journal*: 643–650.

Duneier, Mitchell. 1994a. "On the Job, but Behind the Scenes." *Chicago Tribune,* December 26, pp. 1, 24.

———. 1994b. "Battling for Control." *Chicago Tribune,* December 28, pp. 1, 8.

———. 1999. *Sidewalk.* New York: Farrar, Straus and Giroux.

Dunn, J. 2004. *A State of Crisis? An Exploratory Examination of Family Breakdown in the CF.* Ottawa: Department of National Defence.

Durkheim, Émile. [1887] 1972. "Religion and Ritual." Pp. 219-238 in *Émile Durkheim: Selected Writings,* ed. A. Giddens. Cambridge: Cambridge University Press.

———. [1893] 1933. *Division of Labor in Society,* trans. George Simpson. New York: Free Press.

———. [1897] 1951. *Suicide,* trans. John A. Spaulding and George Simpson. New York: Free Press.

———. [1895] 1964. *The Rules of Sociological Method,* trans. Sarah A. Solovay and John H. Mueller. New York: Free Press.

———. [1912] 2001. *The Elementary Forms of Religious Life,* trans. Carol Cosman. New York: Oxford University Press.

Duxbury, L.E., S. Lyons, and C.A. Higgins. 2007. "Dual-Income Families in the New Millennium: Reconceptualizing Family Type." *Advances in Developing Human Resources* 9 (4): 472–486.

Dykman, Jason. 2006. "America by the Numbers." *Time,* vol. 168, October, pp. 41–54.

E

Ebaugh, Helen Rose Fuchs. 1988. *Becoming an Ex: The Process of Role Exit.* Chicago: University of Chicago Press.

Eckenwiler, Mark. 1995. "In the Eyes of the Law." *Internet World* (August): 74, 76–77.

Economic Mobility Project. 2007. *Economic Mobility of Immigrants in the United States.* Washington, DC: Pew Charitable Trust.

References

The Economist. 2004a. "Veil of Tears." (January 15).
———. 2004b. "Battle on the Home Front." (February 21): 8–10.
———. 2005a. "Back to the Beach?" (January 8): 54–55.
———. 2005b. "We Are Tous Québécois." (January 8): 39.
———. 2005c. "Behind the Digital Divide." (March 2): 22–25.
———. 2005d. "Chasing the Dream." (August 6): 53–55.
———. 2005e. "The Mountain Man and the Surgeon." (December 24): 24–26.
———. 2005f. "The Hidden Wealth of the Poor." (November 5): 1–14.
———. 2005g. "Not Here, Surely?" (December 10): 31–32.
———. 2006. "The World's Largest Economies." (April 1): 84.
———. 2006a. "The World's Largest Economies." (April 1): 84.
———. 2007a. "Giving to Charity: Bring Back the Victorians." (February 17): 56–57.
———. 2007b. "Africa and the Internet: The Digital Gap." (October 12): 64.
———. 2008a. "Maharishi Mahesh Yogi." (February 16): 95.
———. 2008b. "A Ravenous Dragon: A Special Report on China's Quest for Resources." (March 15): 1–22.

Edwards, Harry. 1973. *Sociology of Sport.* Homewood, IL: Dorsey Press.

Ehrenreich, Barbara. 2001. *Nickel and Dimed: On (Not) Getting By in America.* New York: Metropolitan.

Ehrenreich, Barbara, and Arlie Russell Hochschild. 2003. *Global Woman: Nannies, Maids, and Sex Workers in the New Economy.* New York: Metropolitan Books.

Ehrlich, Paul R. 1968. *The Population Bomb.* New York: Ballantine Books.

Ehrlich, Paul R., and Anne H. Ehrlich. 1990. *The Population Explosion.* New York: Simon and Schuster.

Ehrlich, Paul R., and Katherine Ellison. 2002. "A Looming Threat We Won't Face." *Los Angeles Times,* January 20, p. M6.

Eitzen, D. Stanley. 2003. *Fair and Foul: Beyond the Myths and Paradoxes of Sport,* 2d ed. Lanham, MD: Rowman and Littlefield.

Elections Canada. 2007. "Explaining the Turnout Decline in Canadian Federal Elections: A New Survey of Non-Voters" (www.elections.ca/content.asp?section=loi&document=youth&dir=tur/tud&lang=e&textonly=false).

Elliott, Michael. 2005. "Hopelessly Divided: Being a Fan Is Like Having Your Own Personal Time Machine." *Time Magazine,* June 20, p. 76.

Ellison, Brandy. 2008. "Tracking." Pp. 301–304 in *Encyclopedia of Race, Ethnicity, and Society,* vol. 2, ed. Richard T. Schaefer. Thousand Oaks, CA: Sage.

Ellison, Ralph. 1952. *Invisible Man.* New York: Random House.

Ellul, Jacques. 1964. *The Technological Society.* New York: Knopf.

Eltman, Frank. 2007. "Wealthy Couple Charged with Slavery." Associated Press, May 24.

Ely, Robin J. 1995. "The Power of Demography: Women's Social Construction of Gender Identity at Work." *Academy of Management Journal* 38 (3): 589–634.

Engels, Friedrich [1884] 1959. "The Origin of the Family, Private Property, and the State." Pp. 392–394 in *Marx and Engels: Basic Writings on Politics and Philosophy,* ed. Lewis Feuer. Garden City, NY: Anchor Books.

Entine, Jon, and Martha Nichols. 1996. "Blowing the Whistle on Meaningless 'Good Intentions.'" *Chicago Tribune,* June 20, p. A21.

Erksine, William, and Roberta Spatter-Roth. 2006. *ASA Research Brief: Profile of 2005 ASA Membership.* Washington, DC: American Sociological Association.

Escárcega, Sylvia. 2008. "Mexico." Pp. 898–902 in *Encyclopedia of Race, Ethnicity, and Society,* vol. 2, ed. Richard T. Schaefer. Thousand Oaks, CA: Sage.

Etaugh, Claire. 2003. "Witches, Mothers and Others: Females in Children's Books." *Hilltopics* (Winter): 10–13.

Etcoff, Nancy, Susie Orbach, Jennifer Scott, and Heidi D'Agostino. 2004. "The Real Truth About Beauty: A Global Report—Findings of the Global Study on Women, Beauty and Well-Being." Commissioned by Dove, a Unilever Beauty Brand. Accessed June 28, 2008 (http://www.campaignforrealbeauty.com/uploadedfiles/DOVE_white_paper_final.pdf).

Etzioni, Amitai. 1964. *Modern Organization.* Englewood Cliffs, NJ: Prentice Hall.

———. 1965. *Political Unification.* New York: Holt, Rinehart and Winston.

Eureka County. 2006. "EPA Hears Testimony on Proposed Radiation Rule." *Nuclear Waste Office Newsletter* (Eureka County Yucca Mountain Information Office) 11 (Winter).

F

Farr, Grant M. 1999. *Modern Iran.* New York: McGraw-Hill.

Fausto-Sterling, A. 2000. "The Five Sexes, Revisited." *The Sciences* (July/August): 18–23.

Feagin, Joe R. 1983. *The Urban Real Estate Game: Playing Monopoly with Real Money.* Englewood Cliffs, NJ: Prentice Hall.

———. 1989. *Minority Group Issues in Higher Education: Learning from Qualitative Research.* Norman: Center for Research on Minority Education, University of Oklahoma.

———. 2001. "Social Justice and Sociology: Agenda for the Twenty-First Century." *American Sociological Review* 66 (February): 1–20.

———, Harnán Vera, and Nikitah Imani. 1996. *The Agony of Education: Black Students at White Colleges and Universities.* New York: Routledge.

Featherman, David L., and Robert M. Hauser. 1978. *Opportunity and Change.* New York: Aeodus.

Feminist Majority Foundation. 2007. "Feminists Are the Majority." Accessed February 25 (www.feminist.org).

Ferree, Myra Marx. 2005. "It's Time to Mainstream Research on Gender." *Chronicle of Higher Education* 51 (August 21): B10.

Ferree, Myra Marx, and David A. Merrill. 2000. "Hot Movements, Cold Cognition: Thinking about Social Movements in Gendered Frames." *Contemporary Society* 29 (May): 454–462.

Feuer, Alan. 2002. "Haven for Workers in Bronx Evolves for Their Retirement." *New York Times,* August 5. Accessed June 27, 2008 (http://query.nytimes.com/gst/fullpage.html?res=9D07E7D9133BF936A3575BC0A9649C8B63).

Feuer, Lewis S. 1989. *Marx and Engels: Basic Writings on Politics and Philosophy.* New York: Anchor Books.

Fields, Jason. 2001. "America's Families and Living Arrangements." *Current Population Reports,* Ser. P-20, No. 537. Washington, DC: U.S. Government Printing Office.

———. 2003. "Children's Living Arrangements and Characteristics: March 2002." *Current Population Reports,* Ser. P-20, No. 547. Washington, DC: U.S. Government Printing Office.

Fine, Gary Alan. 1987. *With the Boys: Little League Baseball and Preadolescent Culture.* Chicago: University of Chicago Press.

Fine, Gary C. 2008. "Robbers Cave." Pp. 1163–1164 in *Encyclopedia of Race, Ethnicity, and Society,* vol. 3, ed. Richard T. Schaefer. Thousand Oaks, CA: Sage.

Finkel, Steven E., and James B. Rule. 1987. "Relative Deprivation and Related Psychological Theories of Civil Violence: A Critical Review." *Research in Social Movements* 9: 47–69.

First Nations Health Council, British Columbia. 2008. "Traditional Medicine." Accessed May 26, 2009 (www.fnhc.ca/index.php/initiatives/community_health/traditional_medicine/).

Fishman, Charles. 2006. *The Wal-Mart Effect: How the World's Most Powerful Company Really Works—and How It's Transforming the American Economy.* New York: Penguin Books.

Fitzgerald, Kathleen J., and Diane M. Rodgers. 2000. "Radical Social Movement Organization: A Theoretical Model." *The Sociological Quarterly* 41 (4): 573–592.

Flacks, Richard. 1971. *Youth and Social Change.* Chicago: Markham.

Fletcher, Connie. 1995. "On the Line: Women Cops Speak Out." *Chicago Tribune Magazine,* February 19, pp. 14–19.

Flynn, Patrice. 2007. "Microfinance: The Newest Finance Technology of the Washington Consensus." *Challenge* 50 (March/April): 110–121.

Förster, Michael, and Marco Mira d'Ercole. 2005. *Income Distribution and Poverty in OECD Countries in the Second Half of the 1990s.* Paris: OECD.

Fortune. 2007. "Global 500." July 14.

Fouchè, Gladys. 2008. "Norway's Gender Deadline Passes."*The Guardian Weekly,* April 1, p.15.

Foy, Paul. 2006. "Interior Rejects Goshute Nuclear Waste Stockpile." *Indian Country Today* 20 (September 18): 1.

Freidson, Eliot. 1970. *Profession of Medicine.* New York: Dodd, Mead.

French, Howard W. 2000. "The Pretenders." *New York Times Magazine,* December 3, pp. 86–88.

———. 2004b. "China's Textbooks Twist and Omit History." *New York Times* (December 6), p. A10.

———. 2008. "Lines of Grinding Poverty, Untouched by China's Boom." *New York Times,* January 13, p. 4.

Freudenburg, William R. 2005. "Seeing Science, Courting Conclusions: Reexamining the Intersection of Science, Corporate Cash, and the Law." *Sociological Forum* 20 (March): 3–33.

Freudenheim, Milt. 2005. "Help Wanted: Oldest Workers Please Apply." *New York Times,* March 23, pp. A1, C3.

Fridlund, Alan. J., Paul Erkman, and Harriet Oster. 1987. "Facial Expressions of Emotion; Review of Literature 1970–1983." Pp. 143–224 in *Nonverbal Behavior and Communication,* 2d ed., ed. Aron W. Seigman and Stanley Feldstein. Hillsdale, NJ: Lawrence Erlbaum.

Friedan, Betty. 1963. *The Feminine Mystique.* New York: Dell.

———. 1993. *The Fountain of Age.* New York: Simon and Schuster.

Friedman, Thomas L. 2005. *The World Is Flat: A Brief History of the Twenty-first Century.* New York: Farrar, Straus and Giroux.

Furstenberg, Sheela Kennedy, Jr., Vonnie C. McCloyd, Rubén G. Rumbaut, and Richard A. Setterstein, Jr. 2004. "Growing Up Is Harder to Do." *Contexts* 3: 33–41.

Fuwa, Makiko. 2004. "Macro-Level Gender Inequality and the Division of Household Labor in 22 Countries." *American Sociological Review* 69 (December): 751–767.

G

Gallup. 2007a. "Death Penalty." Accessed February 17 (www.gallup.com).

———. 2008a. "Abortion." Accessed March 6 (www.gallup.com).

———. 2008b. "Homosexual Relations." Accessed March 6 (www.gallup.com).

———. 2008c. "Religion." Accessed March 14 (www.gallup.com).

———. 2008d. "Environment." Accessed March 18 (www.gallup.com).

Gallup Opinion Index. 1978. "Religion in America, 1977–1978." (January).

Gamson, Joshua. 1989. "Silence, Death, and the Invisible Enemy: AIDS Activism and Social Movement 'Newness.'" *Social Problems* 36 (October): 351–367.

Gannon, Marie. 2005. *General Social Survey on Victimization, Cycle 18: An Overview of Findings.* Minister of Industry, Statistics Canada, Social and Aboriginal Statistics Division. Catalogue no. 85-565-XIE.

Gans, Herbert. 1971. "The Uses of Poverty: The Poor Pay All." *Social Policy* (July/August): 20–24.

Garcia-Moreno, Claudia, Henrica A. F. M. Jansen, Mary Ellsberg, Lori Heise, and Charlotte Watts. 2005. *WHO Multi-Country Study on Women's Health and Domestic Violence Against Women.* Geneva, Switzerland: WHO.

Gardner, Gary, Erik Assadourian, and Radhika Sarin. 2004. "The State of Consumption Today." Pp. 3–21 in *State of the World 2004,* ed. Brian Halweil and Lisa Mastny. New York: Norton.

Garfinkel, Harold. 1956. "Conditions of Successful Degradation Ceremonies." *American Journal of Sociology* 61 (March): 420–424.

———. 1967. *Studies in Ethnomethodology.* New Jersey: Prentice-Hall.

Garner, Roberta. 1996. *Contemporary Movements and Ideologies.* New York: McGraw-Hill.

———. 1999. "Virtual Social Movements." Paper presented at Zaldfest: A Conference in Honor of Mayer Zald, September 17, Ann Arbor, MI.

Gay, Lesbian and Straight Education Network. 2008. "About GLSEN." Accessed March 14 (www.glsen.org).

Gecas, Viktor. 1992. "Socialization." Pp. 1863–1872 in *Encyclopedia of Sociology,* vol. 4, ed. Edgar F. Borgatta and Marie L. Borgatta. New York: Macmillan.

Geist, Eric L., Vasily V. Titov, and Costas E. Synolakis. 2006. "Tsunami: Wave of Change." *Scientific American* 294 (January): 56–63.

Gentleman, Amelia. 2007. "Police Ignore Serial Killings in Delhi Slum, Exposing Unequal Justice for India's Poor." *New York Times,* January 7, p. 8.

Gerencher, Kristen. 2007. "New Online Consumer Health Site Aims Big." Accessed May 20 (www.marketwatch.com).

Gerth, H. H., and C. Wright Mills. 1958. *From Max Weber: Essays in Sociology.* New York: Galaxy.

Giddens, Anthony. 1991. *Modernity and Self- Identity: Self and Society in the Late Modern Age.* Cambridge, UK: Polity.

Giordano, Peggy C. 2003. "Relationships in Adolescence." Pp. 257–281 in *Annual Review of Sociology, 2003,* ed. Karen S. Cook and John Hagan. Palo Alto, CA: Annual Reviews.

Giroux, Henry A. 1988. *Schooling and the Struggle for Public Life: Critical Pedagogy in the Modern Age.* Minneapolis: University of Minnesota Press.

Glenn, David. 2007. "Anthropologists in a War Zone: Scholars Debate Their Role." *Chronicle of Higher Education* 54 (September 30): A1, A10–A12.

Glionna, John M. 2004. "Finding a Voice in Politics." *Los Angeles Times,* May 22, pp. A1, A22.

Global Alliance for Workers and Communities. 2003. *About Us.* Accessed April 28 (www.theglobalalliance.org).

Goering, Laurie. 2007. "The First Refugees of Global Warming." *Chicago Tribune,* May 2, pp. 1, 25.

———. 2008. "Women Urge Larger Role in Easing World's Ills." *Chicago Tribune,* March 11, p. 11.

Goffman, Erving. 1959. *The Presentation of Self in Everyday Life.* New York: Doubleday.

———. 1961. *Asylums: Essays on the Social Situation of Mental Patients and Other Inmates.* Garden City, NY: Doubleday.

———. 1963. *Stigma: Notes on Management of Spoiled Identity.* Englewood Cliffs, NJ: Prentice Hall.

———. 1979. *Gender Advertisements.* Cambridge, MA: Harvard University Press.

———. 1997. [1978]. "Response Cries." As cited in Charles Lemert and Ann Branaman, eds., *The Goffman Reader.* Oxford: Blackwell Publishing.

Golden, Frederic. 1999. "Who's Afraid of Frankenfood?" *Time,* November 29, pp. 49–50.

References

Goldstein, Melvyn C., and Cynthia M. Beall. 1981. "Modernization and Aging in the Third and Fourth World: Views from the Rural Hinterland in Nepal." *Human Organization* 40 (Spring): 48–55.

Gole, Nilofer. 1997. "Lifting the Veil—Reform vs. Tradition in Turkey—An Interview."*Manushi,* May 1.

Gonnut, Jean Pierre. 2001. Interview. June 18, 2001.

Gonzalez, David. 2003. "Latin Sweatshops Pressed by U.S. Campus Power." *New York Times,* April 4, p. A3.

Gottfredson, Michael, and Travis Hirschi. 1990. *A General Theory of Crime.* Palo Alto, CA: Stanford University Press.

Gottlieb, Lori. 2006. "How Do I Love Thee?" *Atlantic Monthly,* March, pp. 58, 60, 62–68, 70.

Gould, Larry A. 2002. "Indigenous People Policing Indigenous People: The Potential Psychological and Cultural Costs." *Social Science Journal* 39: 171–188.

Gouldner, Alvin. 1960. "The Norm of Reciprocity." *American Sociological Review* 25 (April): 161–177.

———. 1970. *The Coming Crisis of Western Sociology.* New York: Basic Books.

Government Accountability Office. 2003. *Women's Earnings: Work Patterns Partially Explain Difference Between Men's and Women's Earnings.* Washington, DC: U.S. Government Printing Office.

Green, Alexander R., Dana R. Carney, Daniel J. Pallin, Long H. Ng´o, Kristal L. Raymond, Lisa I. Iezzoni, and Mahzarin R. Ban´aji. 2007. "Implicit Bias Among Physicians and Its Prediction of Thrombolysis Decisions for Black and White Patients." *Journal of General Internal Medicine* 9 (September): 1231–1238.

Greenhouse, Steven. 2007. "Low Pay and Broken Promises Greet Guest Workers in U.S." *New York Times,* February 28, pp. A, A14.

Gross, Jane. 2005. "Forget the Career. My Parents Need Me at Home." *New York Times,* November 24, pp. A1, A20.

———. 2007. "U.S. Joins Overseas Adoption Overhaul Plan." *New York Times,* December 11, p. A25.

Groza, Victor, Daniela F. Ileana, and Ivor Irwin. 1999. *A Peacock or a Crow: Stories, Interviews, and Commentaries on Romanian Adoptions.* Euclid, OH: Williams Custom Publishing.

Guerrera, Francesco, and Andrew Ward. 2007. "Women on March to Top of U.S. Companies." *Financial Times,* March 28, p.17.

Gutiérrez, Gustavo. 1990. "Theology and the Social Sciences," Pp. 214–225 in *Liberation Theology at the Crossroads: Democracy or Revolution?* ed. Paul E. Sigmund. New York: Oxford University Press.

H

Hacker, Andrew. 1964. "Power to Do What?" Pp. 134–146 in *The New Sociology,* ed. Irving Louis Horowitz. New York: Oxford University Press.

Halle, David. 1993. *Inside Culture: Art and Class in the American Home.* Chicago: University of Chicago Press.

Hamilton, Anita. 2007. "Is Facebook Overrated?" *Time* 170 (December 3), pp. 46–48.

Harlow, Harry F. 1971. *Learning to Love.* New York: Ballantine Books.

Harrington, Michael. 1962. *The Other America: Poverty in the United States.* Baltimore: Penguin Books.

———. 1980. "The New Class and the Left." Pp. 123–138 in *The New Class,* ed. B. Bruce Briggs. Brunswick, NJ: Transaction.

Harris, Judith Rich. 1998. *The Nurture Assumption: Why Children Turn Out the Way They Do.* New York: Free Press.

Haskins, Ron. 2008. "Wealth and Economic Mobility." Chap. 4 in *Getting Ahead or Losing Ground: Economic Mobility in America.* Washington, DC: Pew Charitable Trusts. Accessed June 20 (http://economicmobility.org/assets/pdfs/EMP_WealthandEconomic Mobility_ChapterIV.pdf).

Haub, Carl. 2004.*World Population Data Sheet, 2004.* Washington, DC: Population Reference Bureau.

———. 2005. *2005 World Population Data Sheet.* Washington, DC: Population Reference Bureau.

———. 2007. *2007 World Population Data Sheet.* Washington, DC: Population Reference Bureau.

Haviland, William A. 2002. *Cultural Anthropology,* 10th ed. Belmont, CA: Wadsworth.

Harland, William A., Harald E. L. Prins, Dana Walrath, and Bunny McBride. 2005. *Cultural Anthropology: The Human Challenge,* 11th ed. Belmont, CA: Wadsworth.

Hayden, H. Thomas. 2004. "What Happened at Abu Ghraib." Accessed August 7 (www.military.com).

Hayward, Mark D., William R. Grady, and Steven D. McLaughlin. 1987. "Changes in the Retirement Process." *Demography* 25 (August): 371–386.

Health Canada. 2002. *Canada's Aging Population.* Ottawa: Minister of Public Works and Government Services; Health Canada Division of Aging and Seniors.

———. 2006. *Canadian Public Opinion, Attitudes, and Knowledge—A National Survey of Canadians' Use of Alcohol and Other Drugs— Canadian Addiction Survey.* Catalogue no. H128-1/06-491E.

———. 2009. "First Nations, Inuit, and Aboriginal Health." Accessed April 27, 2009 (www.hc-sc.gc.ca/fniah-spnia/index-eng.php).

Heckert, Druann, and Amy Best. 1997. "Ugly Duckling to Swan: Labeling Theory and the Stigmatization of Red Hair." *Symbolic Interaction* 20 (4): 365–384.

Heilman, Madeline E. 2001. "Description and Prescription: How Gender Stereotypes Prevent Women's Ascent up the Organizational Ladder." *Journal of Social Issues* 57 (4): 657–674.

Henly, Julia R. 1999. "Challenges to Finding and Keeping Jobs in the Low-Skilled Labor Market." *Poverty Research News* 3 (1): 3–5.

Herring, Hubert B. 2006. "A Teacher's Year, a C.E.O.'s Day: The Pay's Similar." *New York Times,* September 5, p. 2.

Hertz, Rosanna. 2006. *Single by Chance. Mothers by Choice.* New York: Oxford University Press.

Hewlett, Sylvia Ann, and Carolyn Buck Luce. 2005. "Off-Ramps and On-Ramps: Keeping Talented Women on the Road to Success." *Harvard Business Review* (March): 43–53.

Higher Education Research Institute. 2004. *Trends in Political Attitudes and Voting Behavior Among College Freshmen and Early Career College Graduates: What Issues Could Drive This Election?* Los Angeles: HERI, University of California, Los Angeles.

———. 2005. *The Spiritual Life of College Students.* Los Angeles: HERI.

Himes, Vristine L. 2001. "Elderly Americans." *Population Bulletin* 56 (December).

Hirschi, Travis. 1969. *Causes of Delinquency.* Berkeley: University of California Press.

Hitlin, Steven, and Jane Allyn Piliavin. 2004. "Values: Reviving a Dormant Concept." Pp. 359–393 in *Annual Review of Sociology, 2004,* ed. Karen S. Cook and John Hagan. Palo Alto, CA: Annual Review of Sociology.

Hochschild, Arlie Russell. 1989. *The Second Shift: Working Parents and the Revolution at Home.* New York: Viking Press.

———. 1990. "The Second Shift: Employed Women Are Putting in Another Day of Work at Home." *Utne Reader* 38 (March/April): 66–73.

———. 2000. "The Nanny Chain." *The American Prospect,* January 3, pp. 32–36. Accessed December 13, 2005 (www.prospect.org/print/v11/4/hochschild-a.html).

———. 2005. *The Commercialization of Intimate Life: Notes from Home and Work.* Berkeley: University of California Press.

———, with Anne Machung. 1989. *The Second Shift: Working Parents and the Revolution at Home.* New York: Viking Penguin.

Hodge, Jarrah. 2006. "'Unskilled Labour': Canada's Live-in Caregiver Program." *Undercurrent* 3, 2: 60–66.

Hodge, Robert W., and Peter H. Rossi. 1964. "Occupational Prestige in the United States, 1925–1963." *American Journal of Sociology* 70 (November): 286–302.

Holden, Constance. 1980. "Identical Twins Reared Apart." *Science* 207 (March 21): 1323–1328.

———. 1987. "The Genetics of Personality." *Science* 257 (August 7): 598–601.

Holder, Kelly. 2006. "Voting and Registration in the Election of November 2004." *Current Population Reports,* Ser. P-20, No. 556. Washington, DC: U.S. Government Printing Office.

Hollingshead, August B. 1975. *Elmtown's Youth and Elmtown Revisited.* New York: Wiley.

Holmes, Mary. 2006. "Love Lives at a Distance: Distance Relationships over the Lifecourse." *Sociological Research Online* 11 (3).

Homans, George C. 1979. "Nature Versus Nurture: A False Dichotomy." *Contemporary Sociology* 8 (May): 345–348.

Home School Legal Defense Association. 2005. "State Laws" and "Academic Statistics on Homeschooling." Accessed May 12 (www.hslda.org).

Hondagneu-Sotelo, Pierrette, ed. 2003. *Gender and U.S. Immigration: Contemporary Trends.* Berkeley: University of California Press.

Horowitz, Helen Lefkowitz. 1987. *Campus Life.* Chicago: University of Chicago Press.

Horrigan, John B. 2007. *A Typology of Information and Communication Technology Users.* Washington, DC: Pew Internet and American Life Project.

Howard, Michael C. 1989. *Contemporary Cultural Anthropology,* 3d ed. Glenview, IL: Scott, Foresman.

Howard, Russell D., and Reid L. Sawyer. 2003. *Terrorism and Counterterrorism: Understanding the New Security Environment.* Guilford, CT: McGraw-Hill/Dushkin.

Huang, Gary. 1988. "Daily Addressing Ritual: A Cross-Cultural Study." Paper presented at the annual meeting of the American Sociological Association, Atlanta.

Hudson Institute. 2007. *Index of Global Philanthropy 2007.* Hudson Institute's Center for Global Prosperity (http://gpr.hudson.org).

Hughes, Everett. 1945. "Dilemmas and Contradictions of Status." *American Journal of Sociology* 50 (March): 353–359.

Human Resources and Skills Development Canada. 2004. "Employment Equity: Myths and Realities" (www.hrsdc.gc.ca/eng/lp/lo/lswe/we/publications/mr/myths_realities.shtml).

———. 2007. "Indicators of Well-Being—Special Report: What Difference Does Learning Make to Financial Security?" January 9, 2007.

———. 2009. "Indicators of Well-Being in Canada. Financial Security—Low Income Incidence." Accessed May 2, 2009 (www4.hrsdc.gc.ca/.3ndic.1t.4r@-eng.jsp?iid=23).

Hunter, Herbert M., ed. 2000. *The Sociology of Oliver C. Cox: New Perspectives: Research in Race and Ethnic Relations,* vol. 2. Stamford, CT: JAI Press.

Hurn, Christopher J. 1985. *The Limits and Possibilities of Schooling,* 2d ed. Boston: Allyn and Bacon.

I

Ignatiev, Noel. 1995. *How the Irish Became White.* New York: Routledge.

Igo, Sarah E. 2007. *The Average American: Surveys, Citizens, and the Making of a Mass Public.* Cambridge, MA: Harvard University Press.

Innocence Project. 2008. "Facts on Post-Conviction DNA Exonerations." Accessed January 12 (www.innocenceproject.org).

———. 2008. "Innocence Project Case Profiles." Accessed January 12 (www.innocenceproject.org/know/).

International Crime Victim Survey. 2004. *Nationwide Surveys in the Industrialized Countries.* Accessed February 20 (www.ruljis.leidenuniv.nl/ group/jfcr/www/icvs).

International Institute for Democracy and Electoral Assistance. 2005. "Turnout in the World–Country by Country Performance." Modified March 7, 2005. Accessed March 15, 2008 (www.idea.int).

International Monetary Fund. 2000. *World Economic Outlook: Asset Prices and the Business Cycle.* Washington, DC: IMF.

———. 2008. "IMF Helping Countries Respond to Food Price Crisis." *IMF Survey Magazine: In the News,* June 3. Washington, DC: IMF. Accessed August 12 (www.imf.org/external/pubs/ft/survey/so/2008/NEW060308A.htm).

Internet World Stats. 2008. "Usage and Population Statistics." Accessed March 20 (www.internetworldstats.com).

Inter-Parliamentary Union. 2007. *Women in National Parliaments.* February 29. Accessed April 1 (www.ipu.org).

Ipsos Reid. 2008. "Canadians Choose the People, Places, Events, Accomplishments, and Symbols that Define Canada." Poll conducted on behalf of The Dominion Institute and the Department of Citizenship and Immigration Canada, March 31–April 22, 2008.

———. 2008. "In Wake of Constitutional Crisis, New Survey Demonstrates that Canadians Lack Basic Understanding of Our Country's Parliamentary System." Released December 15, 2008.

Iraq Analysis Group. 2007. "About Iraq Analysis Group." Accessed January 19 (Iraqanalysis.org).

IRIN. 2008. "Burkina Faso: Food Riots Shut Down Main Towns." UN Office for the Coordination of Humanitarian Affairs. Accessed August 12 (www.irinnews.org/report.aspx?ReportID=76905).

Isaacs, Julia B. 2007a. *Economic Mobility of Families Across Generations.* Washington, DC: Economic Mobility Project, Pew Charitable Trusts.

———. 2007b. *Economic Mobility of Men and Women.* Washington, DC: Economic Mobility Project.

ITOPF. 2006. "Statistics: International Tanker Owners Pollution Federation Limited." Accessed May 2 (www.itopf.com/stats.html).

J

Jackson, Elton F., Charles R. Tittle, and Mary Jean Burke. 1986. "Offense-Specific Models of the Differential Association Process." 33 (April) :335–356.

Jackson, Philip W. 1968. *Life in Classrooms.* New York: Holt.

Jacobe, Dennis. 2008. "Half of Public Favors the Environment over Growth." Accessed April 9 (www.gallup.com).

Jacobs, David, Zhenchao Qian, Jason T. Carmichael, and Stephanie L. Kent. 2007. "Who Survives on Death Row? An Individual and Contextual Analysis." *American Sociological Review* 72 (August): 610–632.

Jacobs, Jerry. 2003. "Detours on the Road to Equality: Women, Work and Higher Education." *Contexts* (Winter): 32-41.

Jacobson, Jodi. 1993. "Closing the Gender Gap in Development." Pp. 61–79 in *State of the World,* ed. Lester R. Brown. New York: Norton.

Jasper, James M. 1997. *The Art of Moral Protest: Culture, Biography, and Creativity in Social Movements.* Chicago: University of Chicago Press.

Jenkins, J. Craig. 2004. "Social Movements: Resource Mobilization Theory." Pp. 14368–14371 in *International Encyclopedia of the Social and Behavioral Sciences,* ed. Neil J. Smelser and Paul B. Baltes. New York: Elsevier.

Jenkins, Matt. 2008. "A Really Inconvenient Truth." *Miller-McCure* 1 (March–April): 38–41.

Jewison, Norman. 1971. *The Fiddler on the Roof.* Videorecording. Directed by Norman Jewison. 179 minutes. Santa Monica, CA: Metro-Goldwyn-Mayer.

Johne, Marjo. 2008. "Good-Faith Efforts." September 22, 2008. Accessed July 24, 2009 (www.globecampus.ca).

Johnson, Allan G. 1997. *The Forest and the Trees: Sociology as Life, Practice, and Promise.* Philadelphia: Temple University Press.

Johnson, Benton. 1975. *Functionalism in Modern Sociology: Understanding Talcott Parsons.* Morristown, NJ: General Learning.

Johnston, David Cay. 1994. "Ruling Backs Homosexuals on Asylum." *New York Times,* June 12, pp. D1, D6.

Jones, Stephen R. G. 1992. "Was There a Hawthorne Effect?" *American Journal of Sociology* 98 (November): 451–568.

Joseph, Jay. 2004. *The Gene Illusion: Genetic Research in Psychiatry and Psychology Under the Microscope.* New York: Algora Books.

Josephson Institute of Ethics. 2006. "2006 Report Card on the Ethics of American Youth." Los Angeles: Josephson Institute. Accessed August 12, 2008 (http://charactercounts.org/pdf/reportcard/reportcard-all.pdf).

Jost, Kenneth. 2008. "Women in Politics."*CQ Researcher* 18 (March 21).

———. 2006b. "Where's Mao? Chinese Revise History Books." *New York Times,* September 1, pp. A1, A6.

Juergensmeyer, Mark. 2003. *Terror in the Mind of God: The Global Rise of Religious Violence,* 3d ed. Berkeley: University of California Press.

K

Kaiser Family Foundation. 2001. *Few Parents Use V-Chip to Block TV Sex and Violence.* Menlo Park, CA: Kaiser Family Foundation.

———. 2005. *Sex on TV: 2005.* Santa Barbara, CA: Kaiser Family Foundation.

———. 2007. "Parents Say They're Getting Control of Their Children's Exposure to Sex and Violence in the Media—Even Online." Accessed January 2, 2008 (www.kff.org/entmedia/entmedia061907nr.cfm).

Kalish, Richard A. 1985. *Death, Grief, and Caring Relationships.* 2d ed. Monterey, CA: Brooks/Cole.

Kalita, S. Mitra. 2006. "On the Other End of the Line."*Washington Post National Week Edition,* January 9, pp. 20–21.

Kanter, Rosabeth Moss. 1993. *Men and Women of the Corporation.* New York: Basic Books.

Kapos, Shia. 2005. "Bloom Falls off the Rose for Internet Matchups." *Chicago Tribune,* February 14, sect. 4, pp. 1, 7.

Kapstein, Ethan B. 2006. "The New Global Slave Trade." *Foreign Affairs* 85 (November/December): 103–115.

Karney, Benjamin R., and John S. Crown. 2007. "Families Under Stress: An Assessment of Data, Theory, and Research on Marriage and Divorce in the Military." Santa Monica, CA: RAND Corporation.

Kasavin, Greg. 2003. "Real Life: The Full Review." GameSpot, July 11. Accessed June 3, 2008 (http://www.gamespot.com/gamespot/features/all/gamespotting/071103minusworld/1.html).

Katovich, Michael A. 1987. Correspondence, June 1.

Katz, Jason. 1999. *Tough Guise: Violence, Media, and the Crisis in Masculinity.* Videorecording. Directed by Sut Jhally. Northampton, MA : Media Education Foundation.

Katz, Michael. 1971. *Class, Bureaucracy, and the Schools: The Illusion of Educational Change in America.* New York: Praeger.

Kaufman, Gayle and Frances Goldscheider. 2007. "Do Men 'Need' a Spouse More than Women?: Perceptions of the Importance of Marriage for Men and Women." *Sociological Quarterly* 48: 29–46.

Kavada, Anastasia 2005. "Exploring the Role of the Interest in the 'Movement for Alternative Globalization': The Case of the Paris 2003 European Social Forum." *Westminster Papers in Communication and Culture* 2 (1): 72–95.

Kempadoo, Kamala, and Jo Doezema, eds. 1998. *Global Sex Workers: Rights, Resistance, and Redefinition.* New York: Routledge.

Kentor, Jeffrey, and Yong Suk Jang. 2004. "Yes, There Is a (Growing) Transnational Business Community:" *International Sociology* 19 (September): 355–368.

Keown, Leslie-Anne. 2007. "Canadians and Their Non-Voting Political Activity." *Canadian Social Trends.* Statistics Canada. Catalogue no. 11-008.

Kerbo, Harold R. 2009. *Social Stratification and Inequality: Class Conflict in Historical, Comparative, and Global Perspective,* 7th ed. New York: McGraw-Hill.

Kimmel, Michael. 2004. *The Gendered Society,* 2d ed. New York: Oxford University Press.

———. 2006. "A War Against Boys?" *Dissent* (Fall): 65–70.

Kinsella, Kevin, and David R. Phillips. 2005. "Global Aging: The Challenge of Success." *Population Bulletin* 60 (March).

Kiper, Dmitry. 2008. "GodTube.com Puts Christian Worship Online." *Christian Science Monitor,* February 6.

Kirby, Jason, and Nancy MacDonald. 2008. "How B.C. Became a World Crime Superpower." *Maclean's* May 7, 2008 (www.macleans.ca/canada/national/article.jsp?content=20080507_2603 2_26032).

Kiser, Edgar. 1992. "War." Pp. 2243–2247 in *Encyclopedia of Sociology,* ed. Edgar F. Borgatta and Marie L. Borgatta. New York: Macmillan.

Kitchener, Richard F. 1991. "Jean Piaget: The Unknown Sociologist." *British Journal of Sociology* 42 (September): 421–442.

Klein, Stefan. 2006. *The Science of Happiness: How Our Brains Make Us Happy—And What We Can Do to Get Happier.* New York: Marlowe.

Klinenberg, Eric. 2002. *Heat Wave: A Social Autopsy of Disaster in Chicago.* Chicago: University of Chicago Press.

Kohut, Andrew. 2007a. "How Young People View Their Lives, Futures, and Politics: A Portrait of 'Generation Next.'" Survey conducted in association with the Generation Next Initiative and documentary produced by MacNeil/Lehrer Productions. Washington, DC: Pew Research Center for the People & the Press. Accessed June 1, 2008 (http://people-press.org/reports/pdf/300.pdf).

———. 2007b. "Rising Environmental Concern in 47-Nation Survey: Global Unease with Major World Powers." The Pew Global Attitudes Project. Washington, DC: Pew Research Center. Accessed June 3, 2008 (http://pewglobal.org/reports/pdf/256.pdf).

Kokmen, Leyla. 2008. "Environmental Justice for All." *Utne Reader* (March–April): 42–46.

Kolata, Gina. 1999. *Clone: The Road to Dolly and the Path Beyond.* New York: William Morrow.

Kopinak, Kathryn. 1995. "Gender as a Vehicle for the Subordination of Women *Maquiladora* Workers in Mexico." *Latin American Perspectives* 22 (Winter): 30–48.

Kopun, Francine. 2009. "Still Swimming: On Eve of Her 100th Birthday, Mary Arnott Reflects on Her Life." *Toronto Star*, May 2, 2009.

Korczyk, Sophie M. 2002. *Back to Which Future: The U.S. Aging Crisis Revisited.* Washington, DC: AARP.

Kottak, Conrad. 2004. *Anthropology: The Explanation of Human Diversity.* New York: McGraw-Hill.

Kozol, Jonathan. 2005. *The Shame of the Nation: The Restoration of Apartheid Schooling in America.* New York: Crown.

Kreider, Rose M. 2005. "Number, Timing, and Duration of Marriages and Divorces: 2001." *Current Population Reports,* 70–97. Washington, DC: U.S. Government Printing Office.

———. 2008. "Living Arrangements of Children: 2004." *Current Population Reports,* No. 114. Washington, DC: U.S. Government. Printing Office.

Kriesberg, Louis. 1992. "Peace." Pp. 1432–1436 in *Encyclopedia of Sociology,* ed. Edgar F. Borgatta and Marie L. Borgatta. New York: Macmillan.

Kristof, Nicholas D. 1998. "As Asian Economies Shrink, Women Are Squeezed Out." *New York Times,* June 11, pp. A1, A12.

Kroll, Luisa, and Allison Fass. 2006. "The World's Billionaires." *Forbes* (March 9).

Kronstadt, Jessica, and Melissa Favreault. 2008. "Families and Economic Mobility." Washington, DC: Economic Mobility Project. Accessed August 13 (www.economicmobility.org/reports_and_research/literature_reviews?id=0004).

Kübler-Ross, Elisabeth. 1969. *On Death and Dying.* New York: Macmillan.

Kwan, Jennifer. 2007. "Update 1—Canada Has Highest Population Growth Among G8." March 13, 2007. Accessed May 12, 2009 (www.reuters.com).

Kwong, Jo. 2005. "Globalization's Effects on the Environment." *Society* 42 (January/February): 21–28.

L

Labaton, Stephan. 2003. "10 Wall St. Firms Settle with U.S. in Analyst Inquiry." *New York Times,* April 29, pp. A1, C4.

Lacey, Marc. 2008. "Hunger in Haiti Increasing Rapidly." *International Herald Tribune,* April 17. Accessed August 12 (http://www.iht.com/articles/2008/04/17/news/Haiti.php).

Ladner, Joyce. 1973. *The Death of White Sociology.* New York: Random Books.

La Ganga, Maria L. 1999. "Trying to Figure the Beginning of the End." *Los Angeles Times,* October 15, pp. A1, A28, A29.

Landler, Mark. 2005. "Mixed Feelings as Kyoto Pact Takes Effect." *New York Times,* February 16, pp. C1, C3.

Lang, Eric. 1992. "Hawthorne Effect." Pp. 793–794 in *Encyclopedia of Sociology,* vol. 2, ed. Edgar F. Borgatta and Marie L. Borgatta. New York: Macmillan.

Lansprey, Susan. 1995. "AAAs and 'Naturally Occurring Retirement Communities' (NORCs)." Accessed August 4, 2003 (www.aoa.gov/housing/norcs.html).

Lareau, Annette. 2003. *Unequal Childhoods: Class, Race, and Family Life.* Berkeley: University of California Press.

Lasch, Christopher. 1977. *Haven in a Heartless World: The Family Besieged.* New York: Basic Books.

Lasswell, Harold D. 1936. *Politics: Who Gets What, When, How.* New York: McGraw-Hill.

Lauer, Robert H. 1982. *Perspectives on Social Change,* 3d ed. Boston: Allyn and Bacon.

Laumann, Edward O., John H. Gagnon, and Robert T. Michael. 1994a. "A Political History of the National Sex Survey of Adults." *Family Planning Perspectives* 26 (February): 34–38.

Leavell, Hugh R., and E. Gurney Clark. 1965. *Preventive Medicine for the Doctor in His Community: An Epidemiologic Approach,* 3d ed. New York: McGraw-Hill.

Le Bon, Gustav. 1895. *The Crowd: A Study of the Popular Mind.* New York: Macmillan.

Lee, Alfred McClung. 1983. *Terrorism in Northern Ireland.* Bayside, NY: General Hall.

Lehne, Gregory K. 1995. "Homophobia Among Men: Supporting and Defining the Male Role." Pp. 325–336 in *Men's Lives,* ed. Michael S. Kimmel and Michael S. Messner. Boston: Allyn and Bacon.

Lemert, Edwin M. 1951. *Social Pathology.* New York: McGraw-Hill.

Lemstra M., et al. 2009. "The Role of Economic and Cultural Status as Risk Indicators for Alcohol and Marijuana Use Among Adolescents." *Paediatrics and Child Health* 14, 4: 225–230.

Lengermann, Patricia Madoo, and Jill Niebrugge-Brantley. 1998. *The Women Founders: Sociology and Social Theory, 1830–1930.* Boston: McGraw-Hill.

Lenski, Gerhard. 1966. *Power and Privilege: A Theory of Social Stratification.* New York: McGraw-Hill.

Leonhardt, David. 2007. "Middle-Class Squeeze Comes with Nuances." *New York Times,* April 25, pp. C1, C12.

Levinson, Daniel J., with Charlotte N. Darrow et al. 1978. *The Seasons of a Man's Life.* New York: Knopf.

Levinson, Daniel J., with Judy D. Levinson. 1996. *The Season of a Woman's Life.* New York: Knopf.

Levitt, Steven D., and Stephen J. Dubner. 2005. *Freakonomics: A Rogue Economist Explores the Hidden Side of Everything.* New York: William Morrow.

Lewis Mumford Center. 2001. *Ethnic Diversity Grows, Neighborhood Integration Is at a Standstill.* Albany, NY: Lewis Mumford Center.

Lian, Jason Z., and David Ralph Matthews. 1998. "Does the Vertical Mosaic Still Exist? Ethnicity and Income in Canada, 1991." *Canadian Review of Sociology and Anthropology* 35, 4: 461–481.

Library and Archives Canada. 2005. "Women in Canadian Sport: Waneek Horn-Miller." Accessed July 20, 2009 (http://collectionscanada.ca/women/002026-234-e.html).

Lieberson, Stanley. 2000. *A Matter of Taste: How Names, Fashions, and Culture Change.* New Haven, CT: Yale University Press.

Lindsay, Colin. 2008. "Canadians Attend Weekly Religious Services Less Than 20 Years Ago." *Matter of Fact,* June 2008. Statistics Canada. Catalogue no. 89-630-X.

Lino, Mark. 2005. *Expenditures on Children by Families, 2004.* Washington, DC: U.S. Department of Agriculture, Center for Nutrition Policy and Promotion.

Liptak, Adam. 2006. "The Ads Discriminate, but Does the Web?" *New York Times,* March 5, p. 16.

Livernash, Robert, and Eric Rodenburg. 1998. "Population Change, Resources, and the Environment." *Population Bulletin* 53 (March).

Lofland, Lyn H. 1975. "The 'Thereness' of Women: A Selective Review of Urban Sociology." Pp. 144–170 in *Another Voice,* ed. M. Millman and R. M. Kanter. New York: Anchor/Doubleday.

Lopata, Helena Znaniecki. 1971. *Occupation: Housewife.* New York: Oxford University Press.

Lorber, Judith. 1994. *Paradoxes of Gender.* New Haven, CT: Yale University Press.

Luffman, Jacqueline. 2006. "The Core-Age Labour Force." *Perspectives.* September. Statistics Canada, Catalogue no. 75-001-XIE.

Lumpe, Lora. 2003. "Taking Aim at the Global Gun Trade." *Amnesty Now* (Winter): 10–13.

Lundquist, Jennifer Hickes. 2006. "Choosing Single Motherhood." *Contexts* 5 (Fall): 64–67.

Luster, Tom, Kelly Rhoades, and Bruce Haas. 1989. "The Relation Between Parental Values and Parenting Behavior: A Test of the Kohn Hypothesis." *Journal of Marriage and the Family* 51 (February): 139–147.

Lyall, Sarah. 2002. "For Europeans, Love, Yes; Marriage, Maybe." *New York Times,* March 24, pp. 1–8.

Lynn, Barry C. 2003. "Trading with a Low-Wage Tiger." *The American Prospect* 14 (February): 10–12.

M

MacDonald, Brian. 2007. "Afghanistan and the Polls: Change the Question—Change the Numbers." *The Conference of Defence Associations,* CDA Commentary 9—2007, September 10, 2007.

MacEachern, Scott. 2003. "The Concept of Race in Anthropology." Pp. 10–35 in *Race and Ethnicity: An Anthropological Focus on the United States and the World,* ed. R. Scupin. Upper Saddle River, NJ: Prentice Hall.

Mack, Raymond W., and Calvin P. Bradford. 1979. *Transforming America: Patterns of Social Change,* 2d ed. New York: Random House.

Mackenzie, Hugh. 2007. "The Great CEO Pay Race: Over Before It Begins." *Canadian Centre for Policy Alternatives.* Toronto: December 2007.

Maclean's (online). 2007. "Polygamy: Legal in Canada." Ken McQueen, June 25, 2007. Accessed on March 30, 2009 (www.macleans.ca/article.jsp?content=20070625_106285_106285).

————. 2009. "B.C. Polygamy Case Dismissed." September 23, 2009. Accessed on October 8, 2009 (www2.macleans.ca/2009/09/23/b-c-polygamy-case-dismissed/).

Magnier, Mark. 2004. "China Clamps Down on Web News Discussion." *Los Angeles Times,* February 26, p. A4.

Mangan, Katherine. 2006. "Survey Finds Widespread Cheating in M.B.A. Programs." *The Chronicle of Higher Education* (September 19). Accessed June 6 (http://chronicle.com/daily/2006/09/2006091902n.htm).

Mann, Horace. [1848] 1957. "Report No. 12 of the Massachusetts School Board." Pp. 79–97 in *The Republic and the School: Horace Mann on the Education of Free Men,* ed. L. A. Cremin. New York: Teachers College.

Marijuana Policy Project. 2007. *State-By-State Medical Marijuana Laws 2007.* Washington, DC: Marijuana Policy Project (www.mpp.org/legislation/stateby-state-medical-marijauna-laws.html).

Marketwire. 2007. "Belinda Stronach and Rick Mercer Launch National Spread the Net Campus Challenge: Winning Campus to be Featured in the Rick Mercer Report." September 13, 2007. Accessed April 22, 2009 (www.marketwire.com/press-release/Spread-The_net-769677.html).

Marosi, Richard. 2007. "The Nation: A Once-Porous Border is a Turning-Back Point." *Los Angeles Times,* March 21, pp. A1, A20.

Martelo, Emma Zapata. 1996. "Modernization, Adjustment, and Peasant Production." *Latin American Perspectives* 23 (Winter): 118–130.

Martin J.A., B. E. Hamilton, P. D. Sutton, S. J. Ventura, F. Menacker, S. Kirmeyer, and M. L. Munson. 2007. *Births: Final Data for 2005.* National Vital Statistics Reports vol. 56, no 6. Hyattsville, MD: National Center for Health Statistics.

Martin, Marvin. 1996. "Sociology Adapting to Changes." *Chicago Tribune,* July 21, sec. 18, p. 20.

Martin, Susan E. 1994. "Outsider Within the Station House: The Impact of Race and Gender on Black Women Politics." *Social Problems* 41 (August): 383–400.

Martineau, Harriet. [1837] 1962. *Society in America.* Edited, abridged, with an introductory essay by Seymour Martin Lipset. Garden City, NY: Doubleday.

————. [1838] 1989. *How to Observe Morals and Manners.* Philadelphia: Leal and Blanchard. Sesquentennial edition, ed. M. R. Hill. New York: Transaction.

Marx, Karl, and Friedrich Engels. [1847] 1955. *Selected Work in Two Volumes.* Moscow: Foreign Languages Publishing House.

Massey, Douglas S. 1998. "March of Folly: U.S. Immigration Policy After NAFTA." *The American Prospect* (March/April): 22–23.

————. 2007. *Categorically Unequal: The American Stratification System.* New York: Russell Sage Foundation.

Massey, Douglas S., and Nancy A. Denton. 1993. *American Apartheid: Segregation and the Making of the Underclass.* Cambridge, MA: Harvard University Press.

Mathieu, Emily, and Tanya Talaga. 2008. "Grandparents Fear Loss of Funding." *Toronto Star,* November 21, 2008.

Mayeda, Andrew. 2009. "Ottawa Girds for Polygamy Challenge." *National Post,* March 25, 2009.

McAdam, Doug. 1988. *Freedom Summer.* New York: Oxford University Press.

McGue, Matt, and Thomas J. Bouchard, Jr. 1998. "Genetic and Environmental Influence on Human Behavioral Differences." Pp. 1–24 in *Annual Review of Neurosciences.* Palo Alto, CA: Annual Reviews.

McIntosh, Peggy. 1988. "White Privilege and Male Privilege: A Personal Account of Coming to See Correspondence Through Work and Women's Studies." Working Paper No. 189, Wellesley College Center for Research on Women, Wellesley, MA.

McKinlay, John B., and Sonja M.McKinlay. 1977. "The Questionable Contribution of Medical Measures to the Decline of Mortality in the United States in the Twentieth Century." *Milbank Memorial Fund Quarterly* 55 (Summer): 405–428.

McLaughlin, Emma, and Nicola Kraus. 2002. *The Nanny Diaries: A Novel.* New York: St. Martin's Press.

McNeil, Donald G., Jr. 2002. "W.H.O. Moves to Make AIDS Drugs More Accessible to Poor Worldwide." *New York Times,* August 23, p. D7.

Mead, George H. 1934. *Mind, Self and Society,* ed. Charles W. Morris. Chicago: University of Chicago Press.

————. 1964a. *On Social Psychology,* ed. Anselm Strauss. Chicago: University of Chicago Press.

————. 1964b. "The Genesis of the Self and Social Control." Pp. 267–293 in *Selected Writings: George Herbert Mead,* ed. Andrew J. Reck. Indianapolis, IN: Bobbs-Merrill.

Mead, Margaret. 1973. "Does the World Belong to Men—Or to Women?" *Redbook* 141 (October): pp. 46–52.

————. [1935] 2001. *Sex and Temperament in Three Primitive Societies.* New York: Perennial, Harper-Collins.

Meier, Robert F., and Gilbert Geis. 1997. *Victimless Crime? Prostitution, Drugs, Homosexuality, Abortion.* Los Angeles: Roxbury Books.

Melby, Todd. 2007. "Exploring Why We Have Sex." *Contemporary Sexuality* 41 (October): 1, 4–6.

Melia, Marilyn Kennedy. 2000. "Changing Times." *Chicago Tribune,* January 2, sec. 17, pp. 12–15.

Mendez, Jennifer Bickman. 1998. "Of Mops and Maids: Contradictions and Continuities in Bureaucratized Domestic Work." *Social Problems* 45 (February): 114–135.

Merton, Robert. 1948. "The Bearing of Empirical Research upon the Development of Social Theory." *American Sociological Review* 13 (October): 505–515.

————. 1968. *Social Theory and Social Structure.* New York: Free Press.

————, and Alice S. Kitt. 1950. "Contributions to the Theory of Reference Group Behavior." Pp. 40–105 in *Continuities in Social Research: Studies in the Scope and Methods of the American Soldier,* ed. Robert K. Merton and Paul L. Lazarsfeld. New York: Free Press.

Meston, Cindy M., and David M. Buss. 2007. "Why Humans Have Sex." *Archives of Sexual Behavior* 36: 477–507.

Michels, Robert. [1915] 1949. *Political Parties.* Glencoe, IL: Free Press.

Migration News. 2002. "Mexico: Bush, IDs, Remittances." (December). (http:// migration.ucdavis.edu).

————. 2004. "NAFTA at 10." (January). (http://migration. ucdavis.edu).

————. 2005a. "Mexico: Migrants, Mexicans in U.S. Economy." (April). (http://migration. ucdavis.edu).

————. 2005b. "Offshoring." (January). (http://migration.ucdavis.edu).

————. 2005c. "Maquiladoras" (July). (http://migration.ucdavis.edu).

————. 2008a. "Mexico: Remittances, NAFTA, Taxes." (January). (http://migration.ucdavis.edu.mn).

————. 2008b. "Japan, Korea." (January). (http://migration.ucdavis.edu.mn).

Milan, Anne. 2000. "One Hundred Years of Families." *Canadian Social Trends.* Statistics Canada–Catalogue no. 11-008.

Milgram, Stanley. 1963. "Behavioral Study of Obedience." *Journal of Abnormal and Social Psychology* 67 (October): 371–378.

———. 1975. *Obedience to Authority: An Experimental View.* New York: Harper and Row.

Miller, David L. 2000. *Introduction to Collective Behavior and Collective Action,* 2d ed. Prospect Heights, IL: Waveland Press.

Miller, David L., and JoAnne DeRoven Darlington. 2002. *Fearing for the Safety of Others: Disasters and the Small World Problem.* Paper presented at the annual meeting of the Midwest Sociological Society, Milwaukee, WI.

Miller, Reuben. 1988. "The Literature of Terrorism." *Terrorism* 11 (1): 63–87.

Mills, C.Wright. 1959. *The Sociological Imagination.* New York: Oxford University Press.

———. [1956] 2000. *The Power Elite.* New edition with afterword by Alan Wolfe. New York: Oxford University Press.

Milner, Jr., Murray. 2006. *Freaks, Geeks, and Cool Kids: American Teenagers, Schools, and the Culture of Consumption.* New York: Routledge.

Minnesota Center for Twin and Family Research. 2008. "Minnesota Center for Twins and Family Research." Accessed January 7 (http:mctfr.psych.umn.edu/research).

Mirapaul, Matthew. 2001. "How the Net Is Documenting a Watershed Moment." *New York Times,* October 15, p. E2.

Mishel, Lawrence, Jared Bernstein, and Sylvia Allegretto. 2007. *The State of Working America, 2006/2007.* Ithaca, NY: Cornell University Press.

Mizruchi, Mark S. 1996. "What Do Interlocks Do? An Analysis, Critique, and Assessment of Research on Interlocking Directorates." Pp. 271–298 in *Annual Review of Sociology,* 1996, ed. John Hagan and Karen Cook. Palo Alto, CA: Annual Reviews.

Moaddel, Mansoor. 2007. "What the Iraqi Study Group Missed: The Iraqi People." *Footnotes* 35 (January): 1, 4.

Moen, Phyllis, and Patricia Roehling. 2005. *The Career Mystique: Cracks in the American Dream.* Lanham, MD: Rowman and Littlefield.

Mogelonsky, Marcia. 1996. "The Rocky Road to Adulthood." *American Demographics* 18 (May): 26–29, 32–35, 56.

Mohai, Paul, and Robin Saha. 2007. "Racial Inequality in the Distribution of Hazardous Waste: A National-Level Reassessment." *Social Problems* 54 (3): 343–370.

Monahan, Mary T. 2007. *2007 Identity Fraud Survey Report: Identity Fraud Is Dropping, Continued Vigilance Necessary.* Pleasanton, CA: Javelin Strategy and Research.

Montagu, Ashley. 1997. *Man's Most Dangerous Myth: The Fallacy of Race,* 6th ed. abridged student ed. Walnut Creek, CA: AltaMira Press.

Moore, David W. 2002. "Americans' View of Influence of Religion Settling Back to Pre-September 11 Levels." *Gallup Poll Tuesday Briefing* (December 31).

Moore, Molly. 2006. "Romance, but not Marriage." *Washington Post National Weekly Edition,* November 27, p. 18.

Moore, Wilbert E. 1967. *Order and Change: Essays in Comparative Sociology.* New York: Wiley.

———. 1968. "Occupational Socialization." Pp. 861–883 in *Handbook of Socialization Theory and Research,* ed. David A. Goslin. Chicago: Rand McNally.

Morehouse Medical Treatment and Effectiveness Center. 1999. *A Synthesis of the Literature: Racial and Ethnic Differences in Access to Medical Care.* Menlo Park, CA: Henry J. Kaiser Family Foundation.

Morris, Aldon. 2000. "Reflections on Social Movement Theory: Criticisms and Proposals." *Contemporary Sociology* 29 (May): 445–454.

Morris, Bonnie Rothman. 1999. "You've Got Romance! Seeking Love on Line." *New York Times,* August 26, p. D1.

Morrison, Denton E. 1971. "Some Notes Toward a Theory on Relative Deprivation, Social Movements, and Social Change." *American Behavioral Scientist* 14 (May/June): 675–690.

Morselli, Carlo, Pierre Tremblay, and Bill McCarthy. 2006. "Mentors and Criminal Achievement." *Criminology* 44 (1): 17–43.

Murdock, George P. 1945. "The Common Denominator of Cultures." Pp. 123–142 in *The Science of Man in the World Crisis,* ed. Ralph Linton. New York: Columbia University Press.

———. 1949. *Social Structure.* New York: Macmillan.

———. 1957. "World Ethnographic Sample." *American Anthropologist* 59 (August): 664–687.

Murphy, Caryle. 1993. "Putting Aside the Veil." *Washington Post National Weekly Edition,* April 12–18, pp. 10–11.

N

NAACP Legal Defense and Educational Fund. 2007. *Death Row U.S.A. Winter 2007.* Washington, DC: NAACP Legal Defense and Educational Fund.

Nakao, Keiko, and Judith Treas. 1994. "Updating Occupational Prestige and Socioeconomic Scores: How the New Measures Measure Up." *Sociological Methodology* 24 (1994): 1–72.

National Advisory Commission on Criminal Justice. 1976. *Organized Crime.* Washington, DC: U.S. Government Printing Office.

National Geographic. 2002. "A World Transformed." (September).

———. 2005. *Atlas of the World,* 8th ed. Washington, DC: Author.

National Post. 2005. "The Canadian Values Study: A Joint Project of Innovative Research Group, the Dominion Institute, and the National Post." Survey conducted between September 22 and 23, 2005.

———. 2009. "Religious Groups Mount Transit Ad Campaign to Refute God is Dead Claim." March 19, 2009.

National Research Council of Canada. 2005. "Looking Forward: S&T for the 21st Century." September 16, 2005. Accessed April 23, 2009 (www.nrc-cnrc.gc.ca/aboutUS/ren/nrc-foresight_10_e.html).

Neuman, W. Lawrence. 2000. *Social Research Methods: Qualitative and Quantitative Approaches.* Boston: Allyn and Bacon.

Newman, William M. 1973. *American Pluralism: A Study of Minority Groups and Social Theory.* New York: Harper and Row.

Neumark, David. 2008. "Reassessing the Age Discrimination in Employment Act." Washington DC: AARP Public Policy Institute. Accessed June 27 (www.aarp.org/research/work/agediscrim/2008_09_adea.html).

Nielsen, Joyce McCarl, Glenda Walden, and Charlotte A. Kunkel. 2000. "Gendered Heteronormativity: Empirical Illustrations in Everyday Life." *Sociological Quarterly* 41 (2): 283–296.

Niezen, Ronald. 2005. "Digital Identity: The Construction of Virtual Selfhood in the Indigenous Peoples' Movement." *Comparative Studies in Society and History* 47 (3): 532–551.

Nolan, Patrick, and Gerhard Lenski. 2006. *Human Societies: An Introduction to Macrosociology,* 10th ed. Boulder, CO: Paradigm.

Norris, Poppa, and Ronald Inglehart. 2004. *Sacred and Secular: Religion and Politics Worldwide.* Cambridge: Cambridge University Press.

O

Oberschall, Anthony. 1973. *Social Conflict and Social Movements.* Englewood Cliffs, NJ: Prentice Hall.

O'Donnell, Jayne, and Richard Willing. 2003. "Prison Time Gets Harder for White-Collar Crooks." *USA Today,* May 12, pp. A1, A2.

Office of the Correctional Investigator of Canada. 2006. "Report Finds Evidence of Systemic Discrimination Against Aboriginal Inmates in Canada's Prisons." News release October 16, 2006 based on *Annual Report of the Office of the Correctional Investigator of Canada 2005–2006.* Accessed at www.oci-bec.gc.ca/comm/press/press20061016-eng.aspx.

———. 2009. "Backgrounder: Aboriginal Inmates—The Numbers Reveal a Critical Situation." January 9, 2009. Accessed at www.oci-bec.gc.ca/rpt/annrpt/annrpt20052006info-eng.aspx.

Office of Justice Programs. 1999. "Transnational Organized Crime." *NCJRS Catalog* 49 (November/ December): 21.

Ogburn, William F. 1922. *Social Change with Respect to Culture and Original Nature.* New York: Huebsch (reprinted 1966, New York: Dell).

Ogburn, William F., and Clark Tibbits. 1934. "The Family and Its Functions." Pp. 661–708 in *Recent Social Trends in the United States,* ed. Research Committee on Social Trends. New York: McGraw-Hill.

Omi, Michael, and Howard Winant. 1994. *Racial Formation in the United States: From the 1960s to the 1990s,* 2d ed. New York: Routledge.

Onishi, Norimitso. 2003. "Divorce in South Korea: Striking a New Attitude." *New York Times,* September 21, p. 19.

Orfield, Gary, and Chungmei Lee. 2007. *Historic Reversals, Accelerating Resegregation, and the Need for New Integration Strategies.* Los Angeles: Civil Rights Project, UCLA.

Organisation for Economic Co-operation and Development. 2006. "Starting Strong II: Early Childhood Education and Care–Country Summary: Canada." Accessed February 5, 2009 (www.oecd.org/dataoecd/16/44/37423348.pdf).

———. 2007. "Education Indicators." *Education at a Glance 2007* (www.oecd.org/edu/eag2007).

———. 2007. "Statistics on Average Effective Age and Official Age of Retirement in OECD Countries" (www.oecd.org/document/47/0,3343,en_2649_34747_39371887_1_1_1_37419,00.html).

———. 2008. *OECD Health Data 2008* (www.oecd.org/health/healthdata).

———. 2008. *OECD Employment Outlook 2008* (www.oecd.org/document/25/0,3343,en_2649_33927_40762969_1_1_1_1,00.html).

Orum, Anthony M. 1989. *Introduction to Political Sociology: The Social Anatomy of the Body Politic,* 3d ed. Englewood Cliffs, NJ: Prentice Hall.

———. 2001. *Introduction to Political Sociology,* 4th ed. Upper Saddle River, NJ: Prentice Hall.

Osberg, Lars. 2008. *A Quarter Century of Economic Inequality in Canada, 1981–2006.* Toronto: Canadian Centre for Policy Alternatives.

Osberg, Lars, and Timothy Smeeding. 2006. "'Fair' Inequality? Attitudes To Pay Differentials: The United States in Comparative Perspective." *American Sociological Review* 71: 450–473.

P

Pager, Devah. 2003. "The Mark of a Criminal Record." *American Journal of Sociology* 108 (March): 937–975.

Pager, Devah, and Lincoln Quillian. 2005. "Walking the Talk? What Employers Say Versus What They Do." *American Sociological Review* 70 (June): 355–380.

Pamuk, E., D. Makui, K. Heck, C. Reuban, and K. Lochren. 1998. *Health, United States 1998 with Socioeconomic Status and Health Chartbook.* Hyattsville, MD: National Center for Health Statistics.

Park, Hwa-Ok. 2005. "Grandmothers Raising Grandchildren: Family Well-Being and Economic Assistance." *Focus* 24 (Fall): 19–27.

Park, Kristin. 2005. "Choosing Childlessness Weher's Typology of Action and Motives of the Voluntarily Childless." *Sociological Inquiry* (August): 372–402.

Park, Robert E. 1922. *The Immigrant Press and Its Control.* New York: Harper.

Parker, Alison. 2004. "Inalienable Rights: Can Human-Rights Law Help to End U.S. Mistreatment of Noncitizens?" *American Prospect* (October): A11–A13.

Parsons, Talcott. 1951. *The Social System.* New York: Free Press.

———. 1966. *Societies: Evolutionary and Comparative Perspectives.* Englewood Cliffs, NJ: Prentice Hall.

———. 1975. "The Sick Role and the Role of the Physician Reconsidered." *Milbank Medical Fund Quarterly Health and Society* 53 (Summer): 257–278.

Parsons, Talcott, and Robert Bales. 1955. *Family: Socialization, and Interaction Process.* Glencoe, IL: Free Press.

Passero, Kathy. 2002. "Global Travel Expert Roger Axtell Explains Why." *Biography,* July, pp. 70–73, 97–98.

Patterson, Thomas E. 2003. *We the People,* 5th ed. New York: McGraw-Hill.

———. 2005. "Young Voters and the 2004 Election." Cambridge, MA: Vanishing Voter Project, Harvard University.

Paxton, Pamela, Sheri Kunovich, and Melanie M. Hughes. 2007. "Gender in Politics." Pp. 263–285 in *Annual Review of Sociology 2007.* Palo Alto, CA: Annual Reviews.

Pelton, Tom. 1994. "Hawthorne Works' Glory Now Just So Much Rubble." *Chicago Tribune,* April 18, pp. 1, 6.

Perrow, Charles. 1986. *Complex Organizations,* 3d ed. New York: Random House.

Perry, Joellen. 2001. "For Most, There's No Place like Home." *U.S. News & World Report* 130 (June 4): 66.

Peter, Laurence J., and Raymond Hull. 1969. *The Peter Principle.* New York: William Morrow.

Petersen, William. 1979. *Malthus.* Cambridge, MA: Harvard University Press.

Petrásová, Alexandra. 2006. *Social Protection in the European Union.* Brussels: European Union.

Petrovic, Drazen. 1994. "Ethnic Cleansing—An Attempt at Methodology." *EJIL* 5: 1–19.

Pew Internet Project. 2007. "Demographics of Internet Users." Accessed January 11 (www.pewinternet.org/trends/User_Demo_6.15.07.htm).

———. 2008. "Demographics of Internet Users." Accessed April 18 (www.pewinternet.org/trends/User_Demo_2.15.08.htm).

Pew Research Center. 2007. "Optimism about Black Progress Declines: Blacks See Growing Values Gap Between Poor and Middle Class." Washington, DC: Pew Research Center. Accessed July 1, 2008 (http://pewsocialtrends.org/assets/pdf/Race.pdf).

———. 2007b. "Global Unease with Major World Powers: Rising Environmental Concern in 47-Nation Survey." Pew Global Attitudes Project. Washington, DC: Pew Research Center. Accessed July 4, 2008 (http://pewglobal.org/reports/display.php?ReportID=256).

———. 2008. "U.S. Religious Landscape Survey." Pew Forum on Religion in Public Life. Washington, DC: Pew Research Center. Accessed June 14, 2008 (http://religions.pewforum.org/pdf/report-religious-landscape-study-full.pdf).

Piaget, Jean. 1954. *The Construction of Reality in the Child,* trans. Margaret Cook. New York: Basic Books.

Pinkerton, James P. 2003. "Education: A Grand Compromise." *Atlantic Monthly* 291, January/ February, pp. 115–116.

Polletta, Francesca, and James M. Jasper. 2001. "Collective Identity and Social Movements." Pp. 283–305 in *Annual Review of Sociology, 2001,* ed. Karen S. Cook and Leslie Hogan. Palo Alto, CA: Annual Review of Sociology.

Population Reference Bureau. 1996. "Speaking Graphically." *Population Today* 24 (June/July): b.

———. 2004. "Transitions in World Population." *Population Bulletin* 59 (March).

Postman, Neil. 1988. "Questioning the Media." Videorecording. The January Series, January 12. Grand Rapids, MI: Calvin College.

Prus, Steven G. 2007. "Age, SES, and Health: A Population Level Analysis of Health Irregularities over the Lifecourse." *Sociology of Health and Illness* 29 (March): 275–296.

Pryor, John H., Sylvia Hurtado, Victor B. Saenz, José Luis Santos, and William Korn. 2007a. *The American Freshman: Forty Year Trends.* Los Angeles: Higher Education Research Institute, UCLA.

Public Health Agency of Canada. 2007. *HIV and AIDS in Canada. Selected Surveillance Tables to June 30, 2007.* Surveillance and Risk Assessment Division, Centre for Infectious Disease Prevention and Control, Public Health Agency of Canada. (www.phac-aspc.gc.ca/aids-sida/publication/index.html#surveillance).

———. 2008. "Complementary and Alternative Health." April 1, 2008. Accessed on April 20, 2009 (www.phac-aspc.gc.ca/chn-rcs/cah-acps-eng.php).

Public Safety Canada. 2007. *Youth Gangs in Canada: What Do We Know?*

Q

Quart, Alissa. 2003. *Branded: The Buying and Selling of Teenagers.* New York: Perseus.

Quinney, Richard. 1970. *The Social Reality of Crime.* Boston: Little, Brown.

———. 1974. *Criminal Justice in America.* Boston: Little, Brown.

———. 1979. *Criminology,* 2d ed. Boston: Little, Brown.

———. 1980. *Class, State and Crime,* 2d ed. New York: Longman.

R

Rainie, Lee. 2001. *The Commons of the Tragedy.* Washington, DC: Pew Internet and American Life Project.

Ramet, Sabrina. 1991. *Social Currents in Eastern Europe: The Source and Meaning of the Great Transformation.* Durham, NC: Duke University Press.

Raymond, Mélanie. 2008. "High School Dropouts Returning to School." Culture, Tourism and the Centre for Education Statistics, Minister of Industry and Statistics Canada. Catalogue No. 81-595-M–No. 055.

Reid, Luc. 2006. *Talk the Talk: The Slang of 65 American Subcultures.* Cincinnati, OH: Writer's Digest Books.

Reinharz, Shulamit. 1992. *Feminist Methods in Social Research.* New York: Oxford University Press.

Religious Tolerance. 2008. "Female Genital Mutilation (FGM): Informational Materials." Accessed March 1 (www.religioustolerance.org).

Ribando, Clare M. 2008. *CRS Report for Congress: Trafficking in Persons.* Washington, DC: Congressional Research Service.

Riding, Alan. 1998. "Why 'Titanic' Conquered the World." *New York Times,* April 26, sec. 2, pp. 1, 28, 29.

Rieker, Patricia R., and Chloe E. Bird. 2000. "Sociological Explanations of Gender Differences in Mental and Physical Health." Pp. 98–113 in *Handbook of Medical Sociology,* ed. Chloe Bird, Peter Conrad, and Allan Fremont. New York: Prentice Hall.

Rifkin, Jeremy. 1995. "Afterwork." *Utne Reader* (May/June): 52–62.

Riley, John W., Jr. 1992. "Death and Dying." Pp. 413–418 in *Encyclopedia of Sociology,* vol. 1, ed. Edgar F. Borgatta and Marie L. Borgatta. New York: Macmillan.

Riley, Matilda White, Robert L. Kahn, and Anne Foner. 1994a. *Age and Structural Lag.* New York: Wiley InterScience.

Riley, Matilda White, Robert L. Kahn, and Anne Foner, in association with Karin A. Mock. 1994b. "Introduction: The Mismatch between People and Structures." Pp. 1–36 in *Age and Structural Lag,* ed. Matilda White Riley, Robert L. Kahn, and Anne Foner. New York: Wiley InterScience.

Rimer, Sara. 1998. "As Centenarians Thrive, 'Old' Is Redefined." *New York Times,* June 22, pp. A1, A14.

Ritzer, George. 2002. *McDonaldization: The Reader.* Thousand Oaks, CA: Pine Forge Press.

———. 2004a. *The McDonaldization of Society,* rev. new century ed. Thousand Oaks, CA: Pine Forge Press.

———. 2004b. *The Globalization of Nothing.* Thousand Oaks, CA: Pine Forge Press.

———. 2008. *The McDonaldization of Society 5.* Thousand Oaks, CA: Sage.

Robelon, Erik W. 2007. "Moment-of-Silence' Generates Loud Debate in Illinois." *Education Week* (October 24).

Roberson, Debi, Ian Davies, and Jules Davidoff. 2000. "Color Categories Are Not Universal: Replications and New Evidence from Stone Age Culture." *Journal of Experimental Psychology* 129 (3): 369–398.

Roberts, J. Timmons, Peter E. Grimes, and Jodie L. Ma'nale. 2003. "Social Roots of Global Environmental Change: A World-Systems Analysis of Carbon Dioxide Emissions." *Journal of World-Systems Research* 9 (Summer): 277–315.

Robison, Jennifer. 2002. "Feminism—What's in a Name?" Accessed February 25, 2007 (www.galluppoll.com).

Rodriguez, Richard. 2002. *Brown: The Last Discovery of America.* New York: Penguin Books.

Romano, Andrew, and Jessica Ramirez. 2007. "The Immigration Mess." *Newsweek,* June 18, p. 37.

Rose, Arnold. 1951. *The Roots of Prejudice.* Paris: UNESCO.

Rose, Peter I., Myron Glazer, and Penina Migdal Glazer. 1979. "In Controlled Environments: Four Cases of Intense Resocialization." Pp. 320–338 in *Socialization and the Life Cycle,* ed. Peter I. Rose. New York: St. Martin's Press.

Rosenberg, Douglas H. 1991. "Capitalism." Pp. 33–34 in *Encyclopedic Dictionary of Sociology,* 4th ed., ed. Dushkin Publishing Group. Guilford, CT: Dushkin.

Rosenthal, Robert, and Lenore Jacobson. 1968. *Pygmalion in the Classroom.* New York: Holt.

Rosin, Hanna. 2007. *God's Harvard: A Christian College on a Mission to Save America.* New York: Harcourt.

Rossi, Alice S. 1968. "Transition to Parenthood." *Journal of Marriage and the Family* 30 (February): 26–39.

———. 1984. "Gender and Parenthood." *American Sociological Review* 49 (February): 1–19.

Rossides, Daniel W. 1997. *Social Stratification: The Interplay of Class, Race, and Gender.* 2d ed. Upper Saddle River, NJ: Prentice Hall.

Roszak, Theodore. 1969. *The Making of a Counterculture.* Garden City, NY: Doubleday.

Rotolo, Thomas, and John Wilson. 2007. "Sex Segregation in Volunteer Work." *The Sociological Quarterly* 48: 559–585.

Royal Canadian Mounted Police. 2006. "Canada / US Organized Crime Threat Assessment" (www.rcmp-grc.gc.ca/oc-co/octa-mlco-eng.htm).

———. 2006. *Feature Focus: Youth Gangs and Guns.*

———. 2006. *Native Spirituality Guide* (www.rcmp-grc.gc.ca/pubs/abo-aut/spirit-spiritualite-eng.htm).

Rubin, Alissa J. 2003. "Pat-Down on the Way to Prayer." *Los Angeles Times,* November 25, pp. A1, A5.

Ryan,William. 1976. *Blaming the Victim,* rev. ed. New York: Random House.

Rymer, Russ. 1993. *Genie: An Abused Child's Flight from Science.* New York: HarperCollins.

S

Saad, Lydia. 2003. "What Form of Government for Iraq?" Accessed September 26 (www.gallup.com).

———. 2004. "Divorce Doesn't Last." *Gallup Poll Tuesday Briefing,* March 30 (www.gallup.com).

———. 2005. "Gay Rights Attitudes a Mixed Bag." Accessed May 20 (www.gallup.com).

Sachs, Jeffrey D. 2005a. *The End of Poverty: Economic Possibilities for Our Time.* New York: Penguin Books.

———. 2005b. "Can Extreme Poverty Be Eliminated?" *Scientific American* 293 (September): 56–65.

Sacks, Peter. 2007. *Tearing Down the Gates: Confronting the Class Divide in American Education.* Berkeley: University of California Press.

Safire, William. 2006. "Netroots." *New York Times,* November 19. Accessed July 7, 2008 (www.nytimes.com/2006/11/19/magazine/19wwln_safire.html).

Sale, Kirkpatrick. 1996. *Rebels Against the Future: The Luddites and Their War on the Industrial Revolution* (with new preface by author). Reading, MA: Addison-Wesley.

Salem, Richard, and Stanislaus Grabarek. 1986. "Sociology B.A.s in a Corporate Setting: How Can They Get There and of What Value Are They?" *Teaching Sociology* 14 (October): 273–275.

Samuelson, Paul A., and William D. Nordhaus. 2005. *Economics,* 18th ed. New York: McGraw-Hill.

Sanday, Peggy Reeves. 2002. *Women at the Center: Life in a Modern Matriarchy.* Ithaca, NY: Cornell University Press.

———. 2008. Homepage. Accessed March 15 (www.sas.upenn.edu/~psanday/).

Sassen, Saskia. 2005. "New Global Classes: Implications for Politics." Pp. 143–170 in *The New Egalitarianism,* ed. Anthony Giddens and Patrick Diamond. Cambridge: Policy.

Sayer, Liana C., Suzanne M. Bianchi, and John P. Robinson. 2004. "Are Parents Investing Less in Children? Trends in Mothers' and Fathers' Time with Children." *American Journal of Sociology* 110 (July): 1–43.

Scanlan, Stephen J, and Seth L. Feinberg. 2000. "The Cartoon Society: Using *The Simpsons* to Teach and Learn Sociology." *Teaching Sociology* 28: 127–139.

Schaefer, Richard T. 1998a. "Differential Racial Mortality and the 1995 Chicago Heat Wave." Paper presented at the annual meeting of the American Sociological Association, August, San Francisco.

———. 1998b. *Alumni Survey.* Chicago, IL: Department of Sociology, DePaul University.

———. 2006. *Racial and Ethnic Relations,* 10th ed. Upper Saddle River, NJ: Prentice-Hall.

———. 2008a. *Race and Ethnicity in the United States,* 11th ed. Upper Saddle River, NJ: Prentice Hall.

———. 2008b. "'Power' and 'Power Elite.'" In *Encyclopedia of Social Problems,* ed. Vincent Parrillo. Thousand Oaks, CA: Sage.

———. 2009. *Sociology: A Brief Introduction,* 8th edition. New York: McGraw-Hill.

Schaefer, Richard T., Edith Smith, and Jana Grekul. 2009 *Sociology,* Second Canadian Edition. Toronto: McGraw-Hill Ryerson.

Schaffer, Scott. 2004. *Resisting Ethics.* New York: Palgrave Macmillan.

Scharnberg, Kirsten. 2002. "Tattoo Unites WTC's Laborers." *Chicago Tribune,* July 22, pp. 1, 18.

Schellenberg, Grant, and Yuri Ostrovsky. 2007. "2007 General Social Survey Report: The Retirement Plans and Expectations of Older Workers." *Canadian Social Trends.* Statistics Canada 11-008-X No. 86 2008002.

Schmidley, A. Dianne, and J. Gregory Robinson. 2003. *Measuring the Foreign-Born Population in the United States with the Current Population Survey: 1994–2002.* Washington, DC: Population Division, U. S. Bureau of the Census.

Schnaiberg, Allan. 1994. *Environment and Society: The Enduring Conflict.* New York: St. Martin's Press.

Schur, Edwin M. 1965. *Crimes Without Victims: Deviant Behavior and Public Policy.* Englewood Cliffs, NJ: Prentice Hall.

———. 1968. *Law and Society: A Sociological View.* New York: Random House.

———. 1985. "'Crimes Without Victims: A 20 Year Reassessment." Paper presented at the annual meeting of the Society for the Study of Social Problems.

Schurman, Rachel. 2004. "Fighting 'Frankenfoods': Industry Opportunity Structures and the Efficacy of the Anti-Biotech Movement in Western Europe." *Social Problems* 51 (2): 243–268.

Schwartz, Shalom H., and Anat Bardi. 2001. "Value Hierarchies Across Cultures: Taking a Similarities Perspective." *Journal of Cross-Cultural Perspective* 32 (May): 268–290.

Scott, Alan. 1990. *Ideology and the New Social Movements.* London: Unwin Hyman.

Scott, Greg. 2005. "Public Symposium: HIV/AIDS, Injection Drug Use and Men Who Have Sex with Men." Pp. 38–39 in *Scholarship with a Mission,* ed. Susanna Pagliaro. Chicago: DePaul University.

Second Life. 2008. "Economic Statistics." Accessed January 8 (http://secondlife.com/whatis/economy_stats.php).

Seidman, Steven. 1994. "Heterosexism in America: Prejudice against Gay Men and Lesbians." Pp. 578–593 in *Introduction to Social Problems,* ed. Craig Calhoun and George Ritzer. New York: McGraw-Hill.

Sharma, Hari M., and Gerard C. Bodeker. 1998. "Alternative Medicine." Pp. 228–229 in *Britannica Book of the Year 1998.* Chicago: Encyclopedia Britannica.

Shepherd, Jean. 2003. *Japan Performs First Transplants from Brain-Dead Donor.* Accessed June 14 (www.pntb.org/ff-rndwrld.html).

Shirky, Clay. 2008. Here Comes Everybody: The Power of Organizing Without Organizations. New York: Penguin Books.

Shorrocks, Anthony, James Davies, Susanna Sandström, and Edward Wolff. 2006. *The World Distribution of Household Wealth.* Helsinki, Finland: United Nations University and World Institute for Development Economics Research.

Shostak, Arthur B. 2002. "Clinical Sociology and the Art of Peace Promotion: Earning a World Without War." Pp. 325–345 in *Using Sociology: An Introduction from the Applied and Clinical Perspectives,* ed. Roger A. Straus. Lanham, MD: Rowman and Littlefield.

Shupe, Anson D., and David G. Bromley. 1980. "Walking a Tightrope." *Qualitative Sociology* 2: 8–21.

Silicon Valley Cultures Project. 2004. The Silicon Valley Cultures Project website. Accessed February 3, 2005 (www2.sjsu.edu/depts/anthropology/svcp).

Silver, Ira. 1996. "Role Transitions, Objects, and Identity." *Symbolic Interaction* 10 (1): 1–20.

Silver, Warren. 2007. "Crime Statistics in Canada, 2006." *Juristat* 27 (5). Statistics Canada Catalogue no. 85-002. Ottawa.

Simon, Stephanie. 2007. "It's Easter; Shall We Gather at the Desktops?" *Los Angeles Times,* April 8, p. A13.

Smelser, Neil. 1963. *The Sociology of Economic Life.* Englewood Cliffs, NJ: Prentice Hall.

————. 1981. *Sociology.* New Jersey: Prentice-Hall.

Smith, Christian. 1991. *The Emergence of Liberation Theology: Radical Religion and Social Movement Theory.* Chicago: University of Chicago Press.

Smith, Dan. 1999. *The State of the World Atlas,* 6th ed. London: Penguin Books.

Smith, Denise, and Hava Tillipman. 2000. "The Older Population in the United States." *Current Population Reports,* Ser. P-20, No. 532. Washington, DC: U.S. Government Printing Office.

Smith, Tom W. 2001. *Estimating the Muslim Population in the United States.* New York: American Jewish Committee.

————. 2003. *Coming of Age in 21st Century America: Public Attitudes Toward the Importance and Timing of Transition to Adulthood.* Chicago: National Opinion Research Center.

Smylie, Janet, and Paul Adomako (eds.). 2009. *Indigenous Children's Health Report: Health Assessment in Action.* Toronto: Keenan Research Centre–Research Programs, Centre for Research on Inner City Health, St. Michael's Hospital.

Snyder, Thomas D. 1996. *Digest of Education Statistics, 1996.* Washington, DC: U.S. Government Printing Office.

Sorokin, Pitirim A. [1927] 1959. *Social and Cultural Mobility.* New York: Free Press.

Spielmann, Peter James. 1992. "11 Population Groups on 'Endangered' List." *Chicago Sun-Times,* November 23, p. 12.

Sprague, Joey. 2005. *Feminist Methodologies for Critical Research: Bridging Differences.* Lanham, MD: AltaMira Press.

Squire, Peverill. 1988. "Why the 1937 *Literary Digest* Poll Failed." *Public Opinion Quarterly* 52: 125–133.

Stalker, Peter. 2000. *Workers Without Frontiers.* Boulder, CO: Lynne Reinner.

Stark, Rodney, and William Sims Bainbridge. 1979. "Of Churches, Sects, and Cults: Preliminary Concepts for a Theory of Religious Movements." *Journal for the Scientific Study of Religion* 18 (June): 117–131.

————. 1985. *The Future of Religion.* Berkeley: University of California Press.

Starr, Paul. 1982. *The Social Transformation of American Medicine.* New York: Basic Books.

Statistics Canada. 2002. *Ethnic Diversity Survey: Portrait of a Multicultural Society.* Catalogue no. 89-593-XIE.

————. 2003a. Detailed Tables: "Wage and Salary Groups (22) in Constant (2000) Dollars, Sex (3), Immigrant Status and Period of Immigration (10D) and Historical Highest Level of Schooling (6) for Paid Workers 15 years and Over, for Canada, Provinces and Territories, 1995 and 2000—20% Sample Data." From 2001 Census of Canada.

————. 2003b. "Religion in Canada." 2001 Census Analysis Series. Catalogue no. 96F0030X1E2001015.

————. 2005. "Population Projections." *The Daily,* December 15. Accessed March 31, 2009 (www.statcan.gc.ca/daily-quotidien/051215/dq051215b-eng.htm).

————. 2006a. "Television Viewing." *The Daily,* March 31, 2006. Accessed January 15, 2009 (www.statcan.gc.ca/daily-quotidien/060331/dq060331b-eng.htm).

————. 2006b. "Canadian Internet Use Survey." *The Daily,* August 15, 2006. Accessed January 15, 2009 (www.statcan.gc.ca/daily-quotidien/060815/dq060815b eng.htm).

————. 2006c. "Concept: Census Family." Statistics Canada. Last modified July 3, 2006 (www.statcan.gc.ca/concepts/definitions/cfamily-rfamille-eng.htm).

————. 2006d. *The Wealth of Canadians: An Overview of the Results of the Survey of Financial Security 2005.* Pension and Wealth Research Paper Series. Ottawa: Statistics Canada. Catalogue no. 13F0026MIE-No. 001.

————. 2006e. "Health Reports: Seniors' Use of Health Care." *The Daily,* February 7, 2006. Accessed June 12, 2009 (www.statcan.gc.ca/daily-quotidien/060207/dq060207a-eng.htm).

————. 2006f. "Study: Balancing Career and Care." *The Daily,* November 22, 2006. Accessed April 2, 2009 (www.statcan.gc.ca/daily-quotidien/061122/dq061122c-eng.htm).

————. 2006g. "Child care: An Eight-Year Profile." *The Daily,* April 5, 2006. Accessed April 2, 2009 (www.statcan.gc.ca/daily-quotidien/060405/dq060405a-eng.htm).

————. 2007a. "Study: Using the Internet for Education Purposes." *The Daily,* October 30, 2007. Accessed January 15, 2009 (www.statcan.gc.ca/daily-quotidien/071030/dq071030b-eng.htm).

————. 2007b. "Study: A Comparison of Urban and Rural Crime Rates." *The Daily,* June 28, 2007. Accessed March 30, 2009 (www.statcan.gc.ca/daily-quotidien/070628/dq070628b-eng.htm).

————. 2007c. *Income in Canada 2005.* Catalogue no. 75-202-77-XIE.

————. 2007d. Employment Income Groups (22) in Constant (2000) Dollars, Sex (3), Visible Minority Groups (14) and Immigrant Status (3) for Population 15 Years and Over, for Canada, Provinces and Territories, 1995 and 2000. Topic-based Tabulations. Catalogue no. 97F0019XCB2001047.

————. 2007e. "2006 Census: Immigration, Citizenship, Language, Mobility and Migration." *The Daily,* December 4, 2007. Accessed May 14, 2009 (www.statcan.gc.ca/daily-quotidien/071204/dq071204a-eng.htm).

————. 2007f. "Place of Birth for the Immigrant Population by Period of Immigration, 2006 Counts and Percentage Distribution, for Canada, Provinces and Territories—20% Sample Data" (www12.statcan.ca/census-recensement/2006/dp-pd/hlt/97-557/T404-eng.cfm?Lang=E&T=404&GH=4&GF=1&SC=1&S=1&O=D).

————. 2007g. Unpaid Work (20), Age Groups (7) and Sex (3) for Population 15 Years and Over, for Canada, Provinces, Territories, 2001 Census—20% Sample Data. Topic-based Tabulations. Catalogue no. 95F0390XCB2001003.

————. 2007h. "2006 Census: Families, Marital Status, Households and Dwelling Characteristics." *The Daily,* September 12, 2007. Accessed April 2, 2009 (www.statcan.gc.ca/daily-quotidien/070912/dq070912a-eng.htm).

————. 2007i. "Study: Going to the Doctor." *The Daily,* February 21, 2007. Accessed March 11, 2009 (www.statcan.gc.ca/daily-quotidien/070221/dq070221b-eng.htm).

————. 2007j. *Portrait of the Canadian Population in 2006, by Age and Sex, 2006 Census.* Catalogue no. 97 551 XIE.

————. 2007k. "Age Groups (13) and Sex (3) for the Population of Canada, Provinces and Territories, 1921 to 2006 Censuses—100% Data (table). Topic-based tabulation. 2006 Census of Population. Catalogue no. 97-551-XCB2006005.

————. 2007l. *Immigration in Canada: A Portrait of the Foreign-born Population, 2006 Census.* Catalogue no. 97-557-XIE.

————. 2007m. "A Portrait of Seniors." *The Daily,* February 27, 2007. Accessed April 24, 2009 (www.statcan.gc.ca/daily-quotidien/070227/dq070227b-eng.htm).

————. 2007n. "2006 Census: Age and Sex." *The Daily,* July 17, 2007. Accessed April 24, 2009 (www.statcan.gc.ca/daily-quotidien/070717/dq070717a-eng.htm).

————. 2007o. "Study: Delayed Transitions of Young Adults." *The Daily,* September 18, 2007. Accessed March 11, 2009 (www.statcan.gc.ca/daily-quotidien/070918/dq070918b-eng.htm).

————. 2007p. "Study: The Busy Life of Teens." *The Daily,* May 23, 2007. Accessed March 11, 2009 (www.statcan.gc.ca/daily-quotidien/070523/dq070523b-eng.htm).

————. 2008a. "Suicides and Suicide Rate, by Sex and by Age Group." CANSIM table. Catalogue no. 84F0209X.

————. 2008b. Detailed Tables: "Family Income Groups (22) in Constant (2005) Dollars and Economic Family Structure (14) for the Economic Families in Households of Canada, Provinces, Territories, Census Metropolitan Areas and Census Agglomerations, 2000 and 2005—20% Sample Data (table). Topic-based tabulation. 2006 Census of Population. Catalogue no. 97-563-XCB2006023. Ottawa. Released May 1, 2008.

————. 2008c. *Educational Portrait of Canada, 2006 Census.* Catalogue no. 97-560-XIE2006001.

————. 2008d. *Aboriginal Peoples in Canada in 2006: Inuit, Métis, and First Nations, 2006 Census.* Catalogue no. 97-558-XIE.

————. 2008e. *Canada's Changing Labour Force, 2006 Census.* Catalogue no. 97-559-X.

————. 2008f. "Median (1) 2005 Earnings for Full-Year, Full-Time Earners by Education, Both Sexes, Total–Age Group 25 to 64, for Canada, Provinces and Territories, and Census Divisions—20% Sample Data (Table)." *Income and Earnings Highlight Tables, 2006 Census.* Catalogue no. 97-563-XWE2006002. Ottawa. Released May 1, 2008.

————. 2008g. "Study: Estimates and Effects of Obesity Based on Self-Reported Data Versus Direct Measures." *The Daily*, May 14, 2008. Accessed May 15, 2009 (www.statcan.gc.ca/daily-quotidien/080514/dq080514c-eng.htm).

————. 2008h. "Industry–North American Industry Classification System 2002 (23), Occupation–National Occupational Classification for Statistics 2006 (60), Class of Worker (6) and Sex (3) for the Labour Force 15 Years and Over of Canada, 2006 Census—20% Sample Data (table). Topic-based tabulation." 2006 Census. Catalogue no. 97-559-XCB2006023.

————. 2008i. "Back to School–September 2008." Accessed April 2, 2009 (www.statcan.gc.ca/pub/81-004-x/2008003/article/5203237-eng.htm).

————. 2008j. "Crime Statistics." *The Daily*, July 17, 2008. Accessed March 1, 2009 (www.statcan.gc.ca/daily-quotidien/080717/dq080717b-eng.htm).

————. 2008k. *Income in Canada 2006.* Catalogue no. 75-202-X.

————. 2008l. *Canada's Ethnocultural Mosaic, 2006 Census.* Catalogue no. 97-562-X.

————. 2009. "Family Portrait: Continuity and Change in Canadian Families and Households in 2006: National Portrait: Census Families." February 2, 2009. Accessed February 26, 2009 (www12.statcan.ca/census-recensement/2006/as-sa/97-553/p4-eng.cfm).

Stavenhagen, Rodolfo. 1994. "The Indian Resurgence in Mexico." *Cultural Survival Quarterly* (Summer/Fall): 77–80.

Steele, Jonathan. 2005. "Annan Attacks Britain and U.S. over Erosion of Human Rights." *Guardian Weekly,* March 16, p. 1.

Stein, Janice. 2007. "Reflections on Rights and Religion." *Toronto Star*, June 2, 2007.

Stenning, Derrick J. 1958. "Household Viability Among the Pastoral Fulani." Pp. 92–119 in *The Developmental Cycle in Domestic Groups,* ed. John R. Goody. Cambridge, UK: Cambridge University Press.

"Steve Nash in His Own Words." 2006. *Santa Clara Magazine* Winter 2006. (www.scu.edu/scm/winter2006/ownwords.cfm).

Steward, Samuel M. 1990. *Bad Boys and Tough Tattoos: A Social History of the Tattoo with Gangs, Sailors, and Street-Corner Punks.* Binghamton, NY: Harrington Park Press.

Sudan Tribune. 2008. "Darfur's Poorest Squeezed by Ration Cuts." (June 22). Accessed August 12 (www.sudantribune.com/spip.php?article27608).

Suitor, J. Jill, Staci A. Minyard, and Rebecca S. Carter. 2001. "'Did You See What I Saw?' Gender Differences in Perceptions of Avenues to Prestige Among Adolescents." *Sociological Inquiry* 71 (Fall): 437–454.

Sullivan, Harry Stack. [1953] 1968. *The Interpersonal Theory of Psychiatry.* ed. Helen Swick Perry and Mary Ladd Gawel. New York: Norton.

Sullivan, Kevin. 2006. "Bridging the Digital Divide." *Washington Post National Weekly Edition,* July 17, pp. 11–12.

Sumner, William G. 1906. *Folkways.* New York: Ginn.

Sutcliffe, Bob. 2002. *100 Ways of Seeing an Unequal World.* London: Zed Books.

Sutherland, Edwin H. 1937. *The Professional Thief.* Chicago: University of Chicago Press.

————. 1940. "White-Collar Criminality." *American Sociological Review* 5 (February): 1–11.

————. 1949. *White Collar Crime.* New York: Dryden.

————. 1983. *White Collar Crime: The Uncut Version.* New Haven, CT: Yale University Press.

Sutherland, Edwin H., Donald R. Cressey, and David F. Luckenbill. 1992. *Principles of Criminology,* 11th ed. New York: Rowman and Littlefield.

Swatos, William H., Jr., ed. 1998. *Encyclopedia of Religion and Society.* Lanham, MD: AltaMira.

Swidler, Ann. 1986. "Culture in Action: Symbols and Strategies." *American Sociological Review* 51 (April): 273–286.

Sydie, R.A. 1987. *Natural Women, Cultured Men: A Feminist Perspective on Sociological Theory.* Toronto: Methuen.

Szasz, Thomas S. 1971. "The Same Slave: An Historical Note on the Use of Medical Diagnosis as Justificatory Rhetoric." *American Journal of Psychotherapy* 25 (April): 228–239.

————. 1974. *The Myth of Mental Illness,* rev. ed. New York: Harper and Row.

T

Tannen, Deborah. 1990. *You Just Don't Understand: Women and Men in Conversation.* New York: Ballantine Books.

————. 1994a. *Talking from 9 to 5.* New York: William Morris.

————. 1994b. *Gender and Discourse.* New York: Oxford University Press.

Taylor, Lesley Ciarula. 2009. "Darker the Skin, Less You Fit." *Toronto Star*, May 14, 2009.

Taylor, Verta. 1995. "Watching for Vibes: Bringing Emotions into the Study of Feminist Organizations." Pp. 223–233 in *Feminist Organizations: Harvest of the New Women's Movement,* ed. Myra Marx Ferree and Patricia Yancy Martin. Philadelphia: Temple University Press.

————. 1999. "Gender and Social Movements: Gender Processes in Women's Self-Help Movements." *Gender and Society* 13: 8–33.

————. 2004. "Social Movements and Gender." Pp. 14348–14352 in *International Encyclopedia of the Social and Behavioral Sciences,* ed. Neil J. Smelser and Paul B. Baltes. New York: Elsevier.

Telsch, Kathleen. 1991. "New Study of Older Workers Finds They Can Become Good Investments." *New York Times,* May 21, p. A16.

Terkel, Studs. 2003. *Hope Dies Last: Keeping the Faith in Difficult Times.* New York: New Press.

Terry, Sara. 2000. "Whose Family? The Revolt of the Child-Free." *Christian Science Monitor,* August 29, pp. 1, 4.

Thomas, William I. 1923. *The Unadjusted Girl.* Boston: Little, Brown.

Thomas, William I., and Dorothy Swain. 1928. *The Child in America: Behavior Problems and Programs.* New York: Knopf.

Thompson, Ginger. 2001a. "Chasing Mexico's Dream into Squalor." *New York Times,* February 11, pp. 1, 6.

————. 2001b. "Why Peace Eludes Mexico's Indians." *New York Times,* March 11, sec. WK, p. 16.

Tierney, John. 1990. "Betting the Planet." *New York Times Magazine,* December 2, pp. 52–53, 71, 74, 76, 78, 80–81.

———. 2003. "Iraqi Family Ties Complicate American Efforts for Change." *New York Times,* September 28, pp. A1, A22.

Tierney, William G., and Karri A. Holley. 2008. "Intelligent Design and the Attack on Scientific Inquiry." *Cultural Studies Critical Methodologies* 8 (February): 39–49.

Tilly, Charles. 1993. *Popular Contention in Great Britain 1758–1834.* Cambridge, MA: Harvard University Press.

———. 2004. *Social Movements, 1768–2004.* Boulder, CO: Paradigm.

Tjepkema, Michael. 2008. *Health Care Use Among Gay, Lesbian, and Bisexual Canadians.* Statistics Canada Catalogue no. 82-003-X Health Reports.

Tolbert, Kathryn. 2000. "In Japan, Traveling Alone Begins at Age 6." *Washington Post National Weekly Edition* 17, May 15, p. 17.

Tonkinson, Robert. 1978. *The Mardudjara Aborigines.* New York: Holt.

Tönnies, Ferdinand. [1887] 1988. *Community and Society.* Rutgers, NJ: Transaction.

Toosi, Mitra. 2005. "Labor Force Projections to 2014: Returning Boomers." *Monthly Labor Review* (November): 25–44.

———. 2007. "Labor Force Projections to 2016: More Workers in their Golden Years." *Monthly Labor Review* (November): 33–52.

Touraine, Alain. 1974. *The Academic System in American Society.* New York: McGraw-Hill.

Tran, Kelly. 2004. "Visible Minorities in the Labour Force: 20 Years of Change." *Canadian Social Trends,* Statistics Canada. Catalogue no. 11-008.

Treasury Board of Canada Secretariat. 2005. "Aboriginal Peoples." *Canada's Performance Report 2005: Annex 3–Indicators and Additional Information* (www.tbs-sct.gc.ca/report/govrev/05/ann304-eng.asp).

Turcotte, André. 2007. *What Do You Mean I Can't Have a Say? Young Canadians and Their Government.* Canadian Policy Research Networks. Document number: 48799.

Turkle, Sherry. 2004. "How Computers Change the Way We Think." *Chronicle of Higher Education* 50 (January 30): B26–B28.

Turner, Bryan S., ed. 1990. *Theories of Modernity and Postmodernity.* Newbury Park, CA: Sage.

Twitchell, James B. 2000. "The Stone Age." Pp. 44–48 in *Do Americans Shop Too Much?* ed. Juliet Schor. Boston: Beacon Press.

U

United Nations Development Programme. 1995. *Human Development Report 1995.* New York: Oxford University Press.

———. 2000. *Poverty Report 2000: Overcoming Human Poverty.* Washington, DC: UNDP.

———. 2006. *Human Development Report 2006. Beyond Scarcity: Power, Poverty and the Global Water Crisis.* New York: UNDP.

———. 2007. *Fighting Climate Change: Human Solidarity in a Divided World. Human Development Report 2007/2008.* New York: UNDP.

United Nations Human Development Reports, 2008 (http://hdr.undp.org/en/statistics/).

United Nations Population Division. 2005. *World Fertility Report 2003.* New York: UNPD.

Urbina, Ian. 2002. "Al Jazeera: Hits, Misses and Ricochets." *Asia Times,* December 25.

———. 2004. "Disco Rice, and Other Trash Talk." *New York Times,* July 31, p. A11.

U.S. Census Bureau. 2004. *Current Population Survey (CPS)—Definitions and Explanations.* Washington, DC: U.S. Census Bureau. Accessed June 8, 2008 (www.census.gov/population/www/cps/cpsdef.html).

———. 2007. "Valentine's Day 2008: Feb. 14." Facts for Features, CB08-FF.02. Accessed June 9, 2008 (www.census.gov/Press-Release/www/releases/archives/facts_for_features_special_editions/010968.html).

———. 2007b. "Table 6—Median Duration of Marriages for People 15 Years and Over by Sex, Race, and Hispanic Origin: 2004." Accessed June 9, 2008 (www.census.gov/population/www/socdemo/marr-div/2004detailed_tables.html).

———. 2007c. "Table H-2: Share of Aggregate Income Received by Each Fifth and Top 5 Percent. All Races: 1967 to 2006." Accessed June 20, 2008 (www.census.gov/hhes/www/income/histinc/inchhtoc.html).

———. 2007d. "Table H-3: Mean Household Income Received by Each Fifth and Top 5 Percent. All Races: 1967 to 2006." Accessed June 20, 2008 (www.census.gov/hhes/www/income/histinc/inchhtoc.html).

———. 2007e. "Table H-6: Regions—All Races by Median and Mean Income: 1975 to 2006." Accessed June 20, 2008 (www.census.gov/hhes/www/income/histinc/inchhtoc.html).

———. 2007f. "PINC-03. Educational Attainment–People 25 Years Old and Over, by Total Money Earnings in 2006, Work Experience in 2006, Age, Race, Hispanic Origin, and Sex." Accessed June 21, 2008 (http://pubdb3.census.gov/macro/032007/perinc/new03_028.htm).

———.2007g. "Age and Sex of All People, Family Members and Unrelated Individuals Iterated by Income-to-Poverty Ratio and Race." Table POV01. Accessed June 27, 2008 (http://pubdb3.census.gov/macro/032007/pov/new01_100_01.htm).

———.2007h. "Table 2: Percent Reaching Stated Anniversary, by Marriage Cohort and Sex, for First and Second Marriages: 2007." Accessed August 12, 2008 (www.census.gov/population/socdemo/marital-hist/2004/Table2.2004.xls)

U.S. Department of Education, National Center for Education Statistics. 2007. *The Condition of Education 2007.* NCES 2007-064. Washington, DC: U.S. Government Printing Office. Accessed August 12, 2008 (http://eric.ed.gov/ERICWebPortal/contentdelivery/servlet/ERICServlet?accno=ED497043).

U.S. Patent and Trademark Office. 2008. "All Technologies (Utility Patents) Report." Accessed August 12 (www.uspto.gov/go/taf/all_tech.htm).

U.S. Surgeon General. 1999b. "Overview of Cultural Diversity and Mental Health Services." In Chap. 2, *Surgeon General's Report on Mental Health.* Washington, DC: U.S. Government Printing Office.

Utne, Leif. 2003. "We Are All Zapatistas." *Utne Reader* (November–December): 36–37.

V

Vasagar, Jeeran. 2005. "'At Last Rwanda Is Known for Something Positive.'" *Guardian Weekly,* July 22, p. 18.

Veblen, Thorstein. [1899] 1964. *Theory of the Leisure Class.* New York: Macmillan.

———. 1919. *The Vested Interests and the State of the Industrial Arts.* New York: Huebsch.

Veenhoven, R. 2006. *Average Happiness in 95 Nations 1995–2005.* World Database of Happiness, Rank Report 2006-1d. Accessed August 12, 2008 (worlddatabaseofhappiness.eur.nl).

Venkatesh, Sudhir. 2008. *Gang Leader for a Day: A Rogue Sociologist Takes to the Street.* New York: Penguin Books.

Venter, Craig. 2000. "Remarks at the Human Genome Announcement, at the Whitehouse." Accessed June 30, 2008 (www.celera.com/celera/pr_1056647999).

Vidal, John. 2004. "One in Three People Will Be Elderly by 2050." *Guardian Weekly,* April 1, p. 5.

Villarreal, Andrés. 2004. "The Social Ecology of Rural Violence: Land Scarcity, the Organization of Agricultural Production, and the Presence of the State." *American Journal of Sociology* 110 (September): 313–348.

W

Wages for Housework Campaign. 1999. "Wages for Housework Campaign." Circular. Los Angeles: Author.

Wagley, Charles, and Marvin Harris. 1958. *Minorities in the New World: Six Case Studies.* New York: Columbia University Press.

Waldman, Amy. 2004a. "India Takes Economic Spotlight, and Critics Are Unkind." *New York Times,* March 7, p. 3.

———. 2004b. "Low-Tech or High, Jobs Are Scarce in India's Boon." *New York Times,* May 6, p. A3.

———. 2004c. "What India's Upset Vote Reveals: The High Tech Is Skin Deep." *New York Times,* May 15, p. A5.

Wallace, Ruth A., and Alison Wolf. 1980. *Contemporary Sociological Theory.* Englewood Cliffs, NJ: Prentice Hall.

Wallerstein, Immanuel. 1974. *The Modern World System.* New York: Academic Press.

———. 1979a. *Capitalist World Economy.* Cambridge, UK: Cambridge University Press.

———. 1979b. *The End of the World as We Know It: Social Science for the Twenty-First Century.* Minneapolis: University of Minnesota Press.

———. 2000. *The Essential Wallerstein.* New York: New Press.

Wal-Mart. 2009. *Canada Fact Sheet,* September 2009 (www.walmartstores.com).

Wang, Meiyan, and Fand Cai. 2006. *Gender Wage Differentials in China's Urban Labor Market.* Research Paper No. 2006/141. United Nations University World Institute for Development Economics Research.

Watts, Duncan J. 2004. "The 'New' Science of Networks." Pp. 243–270 in *Annual Review of Sociology 2004,* ed. Karen S. Cook and John Hagan. Palo Alto, CA: Annual Reviews.

Weber, Max. [1913–1922] 1947. *The Theory of Social and Economic Organization,* trans. A. Henderson and T. Parsons. New York: Free Press.

———. [1904] 1949. *Methodology of the Social Sciences,* trans. Edward A. Shils and Henry A. Finch. Glencoe, IL: Free Press.

———. [1904] 2009. *The Protestant Ethic and the Spirit of Capitalism,* trans. Talcott Parsons. New York: Scribner.

———. [1916] 1958a. "Class, Status, Party," Pp. 180–195 in *From Max Weber: Essays in Sociology,* ed. H. H. Gerth and C. Wright Mills. New York: Oxford University Press.

———. [1916] 1958b. *The Religion of India: The Sociology of Hinduism and Buddhism.* New York: Free Press.

Wechsler, Henry, J. E. Lee, M. Kuo, M. Seibring, T. F. Nelson, and H. Lee. 2002. "Trends in College Binge Drinking During a Period of Increased Prevention Efforts: Findings from Four Harvard School of Public Health College Alcohol Surveys: 1993–2001." *Journal of American College Health* 50 (5): 203–217.

Weinberg, Daniel H. 2004. "Evidence from Census 2000 About Earnings by Detailed Occupation for Men and Women." Census 2000 Special Reports, CENSR-15. Washington, DC: U.S. Census Bureau. Accessed June 26, 2008 (www.census.gov/prod/2004pubs/censr-15.pdf).

———. 2007. "Earnings by Gender: Evidence from Census 2000." *Monthly Labor Review* (July/August): 26–34.

Weinstein, Deena, and Michael A. Weinstein. 1999. "McDonaldization Enframed." Pp. 57–69 in *Resisting McDonaldization,* ed. Barry Smart. London: Sage.

Weinstein, Henry. 2002. "Airport Screener Curb Is Regretful." *Los Angeles Times,* November 16, pp. B1, B14.

West, Candace, and Don H. Zimmerman. 1983. "Small Insults: A Study of Interruptions in Cross Sex Conversations Between Unacquainted Persons." Pp. 86–111 in *Language, Gender, and Society,* ed. Barrie Thorne, Chris Kramarae, and Nancy Henley. Rowley, MA: Newbury House.

———. 1987. "Doing Gender." *Gender and Society* 1 (June): 125–151.

Western Interstate Commission for Higher Education. 2003. *Knocking at the College Door–2003.* Boulder, CO: WICHE.

———. 2008. "Knocking at the College Door 2008." Accessed July 24 (http://wiche.edu/agendabook/May_08/presentations/MizePrescott.pdf).

White, Adrian. 2007. A Global Projection of Subjective Well-being: A Challenge to Positive Psychology? *Psychtalk* 56: 17–20.

Whyte, William Foote. 1981. *Street Corner Society: Social Structure of an Italian Slum,* 3d ed. Chicago: University of Chicago Press.

Wickman, Peter M. 1991. "Deviance." Pp. 85–87 in *Encyclopedic Dictionary of Sociology,* 4th ed., ed. Dushkin Publishing Group. Guilford, CT: Dushkin.

Wiggins, Steve, and Stephanie Levy. 2008. "Rising Food Prices: A Global Crisis." Briefing Paper, April. London: Overseas Development Institute. Accessed August 12 (www.odi.org.uk/publications/briefing/bp37-april08-rising-food-prices.pdf).

Wilford, John Noble. 1997. "New Clues Show Where People Made the Great Leap to Agriculture." *New York Times,* November 18, pp. B9, B12.

Williams, Carol J. 1995. "Taking an Eager Step Back." *Los Angeles Times,* June 3, pp. A1, A14.

Williams, Christine L. 1992. "The Glass Escalator: Hidden Advantages for Men in the 'Female' Professions." *Social Problems* 39 (3): 253–267.

———. 1995. *Still a Man's World: Men Who Do Women's Work.* Berkeley: University of California Press.

Williams, Mike. 2008. "Rising Cost of Food Devastates Haiti." *Atlanta Journal Constitution,* June 17. Accessed August 12 (www.ajc.com/news/content/news/stories/2008/06/16/haiti_food_crisis.html).

Williams, Wendy M. 1998. "Do Parents Matter? Scholars Need to Explain What Research Really Shows." *Chronicle of Higher Education* 45 (December 11): B6–B7.

Wills, Jeremiah B., and Barbara J. Risman. 2006. "The Visibility of Feminist Thought in Family Studies." *Journal of Marriage and Family* 68 (August): 690–700.

Wilson, John. 1973. *Introduction to Social Movements.* New York: Basic Books.

Wilson, Robin. 2007. "The New Gender Divide." *Chronicle of Higher Education* 53 (January 26): A36–A39.

Wilson, William Julius. 1980. *The Declining Significance of Race: Blacks and Changing American Institutions,* 2d ed. Chicago: University of Chicago Press.

———. 1987. *The Truly Disadvantaged: The Inner City, the Underclass and Public Policy.* Chicago: University of Chicago Press.

———, ed. 1989. *The Ghetto Underclass: Social Science Perspectives.* Newbury Park, CA: Sage.

———. 1996. *When Work Disappears: The World of the New Urban Poor.* New York: Knopf.

———. 1999. *The Bridge over the Racial Divide: Rising Inequality and Coalition Politics.* Berkeley: University of California Press.

Wilson, William Julius, J. M. Quane, and B. H. Rankin. 2004. "Underclass." *International Encyclopedia of Social and Behavioral Sciences.* New York: Elsevier.

References

Wirth, Louis. 1928. *The Ghetto.* Chicago: University of Chicago Press.

———. 1931. "Clinical Sociology." *American Journal of Sociology* 37 (July): 49–60.

———. 1938. "Urbanism as a Way of Life." *American Journal of Sociology* 44 (July): 1–24.

Withrow, Brian L. 2006. *Racial Profiling: From Rhetoric to Reason.* Upper Saddle River, NJ: Prentice Hall.

Wolf, Naomi. 1992. *The Beauty Myth: How Images of Beauty Are Used Against Women.* New York: Anchor.

Wolf, Richard. 2006. "How Welfare Reform Changed America." *USA Today,* July 18, pp. 1A, 6A.

Word, David L., Charles D. Coleman, Robert Nunziator, and Robert Kominski. 2007. "Demographic Aspects of Surnames from Census 2000." Accessed January 2, 2008 (www.census.gov/genealogy/www/surnames.pdf).

World Bank. 2000. *World Development Report 2000/2001.* Washington, DC: World Bank.

———. 2001.*World Development Report 2002. Building Instructions for Markets.* New York: Oxford University Press.

———. 2003a.*World Development Report 2003: Sustainable Development in a Dynamic World.* Washington, DC: World Bank.

———. 2003b. *Development Indicators 2003.* Washington, DC: World Bank.

———. 2004. *World Development Report 2005. A Better Investment Climate for Everyone.* Washington, DC: World Bank.

———. 2005. *World Development Indicators 2005.* Washington, DC. World Bank.

———. 2006. *Repositioning Nutrition as Central to Development: A Strategy for Large-Scale Action.* Washington, DC: World Bank.

———. 2006a. *World Development Indicators 2006.* New York: World Bank.

———. 2006b. *Global Economic Prospects 2006.* Washington, DC: World Bank.

———. 2006c. "Microfinance Comes of Age." December 7. Accessed April 24, 2007 (www.worldbank.org).

———. 2007a. *World Development Indicators 2007.* New York: World Bank.

———. 2008. "Total GNI 2006 (Atlas Method)." Quick Reference Tables. Accessed June 16 (http://siteresources.worldbank.org/DATASTATISTICS/Resources/GNI.pdf).

World Development Forum. 1990. "The Danger of Television." (July 15): 4.

World Resources Institute. 1998. *1998–1999 World Resources: A Guide to the Global Environment.* New York: Oxford University Press.

Wright, Erik Olin, David Hachen, Cynthia Costello, and Joy Sprague. 1982. "The American Class Structure." *American Sociological Review* 47 (December): 709–726.

Y

Yinger, J. Milton. 1970. *The Scientific Study of Religion.* New York: Macmillan.

Young, Gay. 1993. "Gender Inequality and Industrial Development: The Household Connection." *Journal of Comparative Family Studies* 124 (Spring): 3–20.

Z

Zarembo, Alan. 2003. "Funding Studies to Suit Need." December 7, pp. A1, A20.

———. 2004. "A Theater of Inquiry and Evil." *Los Angeles Times,* July 15, pp. A1, A24, A25.

Zellner, William M. 1995. *Counter Cultures: A Sociological Analysis.* New York: St. Martin's Press.

Zimbardo, Philip G. 1972. "Pathology of Imprisonment." *Society* 9 (April). 4, 6, 8.

———. 2004. "Power Turns Good Soldiers into 'Bad Apples.'" *Boston Globe,* May 9 (www.prisonexp.org).

———. 2007. *The Lucifer Effect: Understanding How Good People Turn Evil.* New York: Random House.

Zola, Irving K. 1972. "Medicine as an Institution of Social Control." *Sociological Review* 20 (November): 487–504.

———. 1983. *Socio-Medical Inquiries.* Philadelphia: Temple University Press.

Zweigenhaft, Richard L., and G. William Domhoff. 2006. *Diversity in the Power Elite: How It Happened, Why It Matters,* 2d ed. New York: Rowman and Littlefield.

Photos

Credits